WARE'S
VICTORIAN '
OF SLANG AND PHRASE

Ware's Victorian Dictionary of Slang and Phrase

J. REDDING WARE

Introduction by
John Simpson

Bodleian Library
UNIVERSITY OF OXFORD

Paperback edition published in 2015
This edition first published in 2013 by the Bodleian Library
Broad Street, Oxford OX1 3BG
Reprinted in 2018

www.bodleianshop.co.uk

First published in 1909 by George Routledge & Sons Limited, London, as *Passing English of the Victorian Era: a Dictionary of Heterodox English, Slang, and Phrase*, by J. Redding Ware, as a supplement to *Dictionary of Slang and Colloquial English*, J. S. Farmer and W. E. Henley.

ISBN: 978 1 85124 448 5

Introduction © John Simpson, 2013
This edition © Bodleian Library, University of Oxford, 2013

All rights reserved

No part of this book may be reproduced, stored in a retrieval system, or transmitted in any form or by any means, electronic, mechanical, photocopying, recording, or otherwise, without the written permission of the Bodleian Library, except for the purpose of research or private study, or criticism or review.

Cover design by Dot Little at the Bodleian Library
Designed and typeset by JCS Publishing Services Ltd
in 9.75 on 11.7 Caslon Pro
Printed and bound in Great Britain by TJ International Ltd, Padstow, Cornwall, on 80gsm Munken Cream

British Library Catalogue in Publishing Data
A CIP record of this publication is available from the British Library

INTRODUCTION

I ought to disapprove of James Redding Ware. For a dictionary writer he takes enormous liberties with his reader, and the opening lines of his Preface did not endear him to more high-minded reviewers. He wrote: 'Here is a numerically weak collection of instances of "Passing English". It may be hoped that there are errors on every page, and also that no entry is 'quite too dull.' And yet his dictionary (originally entitled *Passing English of the Victorian Era: A Dictionary of Heterodox English, Slang, and Phrase* and published in 1909) is one of the most engaging and enjoyable English dictionaries you are likely to find.

Every page is full of examples of the characteristically rambling but compelling style with which he treats expressions that might never find their way into more straitlaced dictionaries:

Blood Ball (*London Tr.*). The butchers' annual hopser, a very lusty and fierce-eyed function. The female contingent never wear crimson – as being too trady.

Champion Slump of 1897 (*London*, 1897). Motor car. On and after Lord Mayor's Day of 1896 the motor car claimed English highways for their own. On the 10th there was a procession from Westminster to Brighton, with such a lamentable result that the 'slump' or catastrophe prefaced 1897 . . . By the end of November they were called the 'Margarine Messes', which grew out of their first satiric name – 'The Butter Beauties' – from their colour . . .

Willie – Willie – wicked, wicked! (*Street*). Satiric street reproach addressed to a middle-aged woman talking to a youth. From a country court case in which a middle-aged landlady sued for a week's rent from a young man lodger whose defence was that he left the house because the plaintiff would not only come into his room, but would proceed to sit on his bed.

INTRODUCTION

The mysterious life of James Redding Ware

Until recently, relatively little was known about Ware's life, but gradually the facts are beginning to emerge. Those that we know throw some light on the contents and style of his dictionary.

James was born on 17 October 1832 to James and Elizabeth Ware of Union Street in Southwark, and he was baptized six weeks later at St Saviour's Church, Southwark. Union Street runs east–west between the Marshalsea Road and Blackfriars Road, just south of the Thames at Bankside. His father James was a grocer, and young James had two younger brothers, Charles and Robert Gilbert. According to the 1841 census all but James were living at home on census night.

But there were problems in the household of the Southwark grocer. The *Standard* for 1 December explains graphically:

> Southwark. – Yesterday James Redding Ware, a lad of 16, the son of a grocer and cheesemonger in Union-street, was brought up charged with threatening the life of his father.
>
> The Complainant stated, that hearing a noise in one of his upper rooms, he went upstairs, and found that the defendant had been beating one of his brothers. He (the father) corrected the defendant by striking him with a cane, and afterwards went down into his shop, and had not been long there when the defendant also entered the shop, and seized a long and sharp bacon-knife off the counter, approached him in a menacing attitude, and exclaimed that he would have his life for striking him.

We learn from the newspaper report that James was an aggressive child, and that there were serious conflicts in the family: it was evident that the mother 'encouraged the boy, and was proceeding to abuse her husband' in the courtroom. James's father asserts that his son had been well educated and had a place 'in a mercantile house in the City'.

James threatened that his father would not live three months if he were sent to gaol. He was indeed sent to gaol for a short spell, and his father was dead within five weeks, on 4 January 1849 – but from 'Delirium Tremens . . . Typhus', according to his death certificate.

The family continued at 102 Union Street, with James's mother running the grocer's with her son James as her assistant (plus two shopmen, according to the 1851 census entry). By the time of the

1861 census the family was no longer there. James's brother Charles had started his career as an engineer in the Royal Navy, at anchor with the *Procris* in Plymouth Sound, and it is likely that James's younger brother (and perhaps even James too) went to sea, although James is back as a mercantile clerk lodging in nearby Camberwell by 1861.

Just before this, we see the earliest evidence that James intended to embark on a literary career, from an advertisement in the *Athenaeum* of 21 August 1858: 'To Littérateurs and Publishers. – WANTED, by an experienced, well-educated Young Man, the place of AMANUENSIS or READER. Salary moderate. – Address J. R. Ware, Tomlin's, Walton, Aylesbury, Bucks.'

The year 1860 marked the beginning of James Redding Ware's prolific career as a writer, with the publication of *The Fortunes of the House of Pennyl: A Romance of England in the Last Century*. He turned his hand to journalistic fiction in the 1860s, publishing over the years in many of the popular and often sensational magazines of the period: the *National Magazine, Sharpe's London Magazine of Entertainment and Instruction for General Reading, Belgravia, Bow Bells* and others. He wrote plays, composed lyrics for songs, made translations and generally lived the life of a bohemian Grub Street writer. By 1871 he was lodging as an author of 'Newspaper Fiction &c' at No 494 Old Kent Road, according to the census, and was a junior warden of the Urban (Freemason's) Lodge, meeting with theatrical types and writers in the Urban Club associated with the Lodge.

By now he was a much more respected member of society than his earlier life had promised. In the mid-1870s he moved to rooms at No 50a Lincoln's Inn Fields, where he stayed for many years. He had been living something of a double life, as – drawing presumably partly on his early experiences – he became a writer of 'casebook' stories documenting sensational police cases, this time under the pseudonym of 'Andrew Forrester Jr'. Forrester's *Revelations of a Private Detective* was published by Ward & Lock in 1863, and his most well-known 'Forrester' work, *The Female Detective*, followed in 1864. Ware is credited with producing here one of the earliest female detectives in English fiction. The story of his pamphlet *The Road Murder*, describing another celebrated case of the period, has recently received a modern retelling as *The Suspicions of Mr Whicher* by Kate Summerscale. A small selection of his other popular works includes a guide to the Isle of Wight (1869), an edition of *The Modern Hoyle* (1870?) and *The Life and Times of Colonel Fred Burnaby* (1885), as he turned his hand to anything in the fiction or non-fiction line that might help to pay the rent.

Ware remained unmarried. Much of his later life was spent compiling his dictionary. *The Times* of 25 March 1909 records his death 'on 23rd inst., at his residence, 37, Hanover-street, Peckham, . . . aged 76 years', very shortly after the dictionary was published.

Ware's Passing English of the Victorian Era

Nowadays Ware's best-known work is his *Passing English*, reproduced in facsimile here. This was published in 1909, but he had started work on it many years earlier. Formally his publishers, Routledge, introduced it as a supplement to John Farmer and William Henley's one-volume *Dictionary of Slang and Colloquial English* (1905), itself an abridgement of their extensive seven-volume *Slang and its Analogues*, but in fact the tone of *Passing English* places it in something of a class of its own.

Ware intended his book to amuse as well as inform. His notion of *Passing English* was loose: it represented not just informal language that was passing out of use at the end of the nineteenth century, but also any expression that was part of contemporary changing English. Although he published it in 1909, the bulk of the material on which the book was based derives from the last two decades of the nineteenth century, so he is able to review this with some element of hindsight. He includes voguish late-Victorian expressions ('Cads on castors' = bicyclists; 'Whoa, Emma!') that had indeed drifted into obsolescence by the time the dictionary was published, but also new idioms, sometimes from America, many of which were taken on by British English speakers and are still with us today (for example: 'axe to grind', 'bone idle', 'let her rip', 'silly moo!').

His lexicographical method is arguably modern, as he based his selection largely on printed evidence that he (and, one imagines, other interested parties) had collected principally from newspaper and other ephemeral sources. He cites many of these quotations (normally giving title and date) within his 4,000-plus entries, so we can follow his preferred reading in the papers of the day: the *Daily Chronicle*, the *Daily Mail*, the *Daily Telegraph*, the *Illustrated London News* and so on.

The latest quotations date from 1902, though the majority date from the 1880s and 1890s.

He includes both words and phrases, and the core of his work covers vocabulary and expressions that he encountered during his life in and around the music halls, theatres and streets of London:

Bone (*London*, 1882). A thin man. Hence – 'The bone has made a remark.' (Surrey Pantomime, London, 1882.)

For us, this results in a remarkable picture of how English was changing in the late nineteenth century, viewed through the eyes of an engaging, apparently clubbable and very readable observer. The life of London spills out over his pages in ways that would be impossible in a more sober dictionary, and his 'voice' attests to the excitement and frustrations of the city.

The types of English that he addresses can be seen from the idiosyncratic labelling system that he adopts. Rather than referring stiffly to 'colloquial' or 'informal' or 'slang' English, he luxuriates in a labelling style that is (to our eyes) far too precise, and yet demonstrates the sort of precision and tone that the author aspires to: '*London Apprentices*', '*Slums*', '*Passionate Pilgrims*', '*Dangerous Classes*', '*Italian Organ-Grinders*', '*Music Hall*', '*Wilful American*', '*Doubtful Soc.*', '*Colloquial Imbecile*' and so forth.

There are some areas of life in which he seems particularly interested. His knowledge of the music hall and the theatre is prodigious and is demonstrated in fascinating detail as he lingers over the celebrated artists of the day who are nowadays no more than names or sometimes entirely forgotten:

Canary (*Music Hall*, 1870). Chorus-singer amongst the public – generally in gallery. Invented by Leybourne, a comic singer, probably to give him rest between the verses, he being pulmonary. 'Go it, canaries', he flatteringly would say, meaning that they sang like canaries.

Ware would have been happier if the march of technology had stopped sometime around 1850, and he includes numerous expressions (often rather slighting) for the new-fangled bicycles and motor cars; he was painfully aware of changes in hairstyles and fashion generally over the decades, and can with the help of his printed evidence place the introduction of a new 'look' to a precise year. Later research indicates that here, as elsewhere, he is sometimes over-precise, but his witness is a significant pointer to how his contemporaries would have viewed these new fashions. He is familiar with tavern talk, and regales us with numerous ways in which one could order beer in the public houses of turn-of-the-century London. He includes rhyming slang ('elephant's trunk' = drunk), backslang ('Zeb taoc' = best coat), and transpositions ('Eenque' = queen). He knows his own area south of the Thames very well, and sometimes includes terms that he locates geographically to the roads around where he lived (such as 'Copper captain' *Queen's Bench Prison*, Southwark, and 'Magdalen marm' *Southwark*). The curious additions labelled 'Devonshire' seem to arise from discussions with his brother, whose naval life took him there ('Any birds may roost in my bonnet', 'Another summer'), as do the occasional entries labelled '*Engineers*' ('Keep the boiler clear'). There is perhaps a wry allusion to his 'Forrester' stories at 'Confidence-queen . . . A female detective – outcome of American state of society'. In general, Ware is a jackdaw plucking transient or emerging expressions from wherever he can, for the information and amusement of his readers.

There is one particular area where he is on rather shaky ground from today's perspective, and that is etymology. If Ware is uncertain of the origin of a word, he prefers to have a stab at this rather than to leave it unglossed. He has a tendency to source expressions from French if he can (sometimes perverting the facts but at other times hitting the nail on the head): see, for example, 'Full as a goat' and 'Not the cheese'. He also likes to derive words from proper names, again sometimes without a shred of evidence, and in so doing producing nonsensical gibberish (for example: 'Dog-cheap', 'Doping', and 'Flabbergast'). It is not unusual for him to call on royalty for the introduction of a word: 'Comfy' (probable origin – a royal nursery), 'Cruel classes', and 'German gospel'. But this all attests to the popular feeling at the time that everything ought to be open to explanation. His historical notes are sometimes wayward, but often offer us a peek into late Victorian life that we would otherwise have to search far and wide to find (see 'Balaclava', 'Cow with the iron tail', 'Essex lion').

He defines in the vocabulary of his day, and this occasionally results in expressions that would be unacceptable and sometimes even offensive in a more modern dictionary. But his dictionary would be a different animal without them: their inclusion informs us about the prevailing contemporary culture and slang's proximity to the language of insult and stereotype. Once or twice he favours terms that are unfamiliar to the general reader today: an *onomatope* is a word formed by onomatopoeia (the sound fitting the sense); 'to be on all fours with' = 'to present an exact comparison or analogy with'; an 'evasion of' is a 'euphemism for'. But otherwise his defining terminology is perfectly understandable today – if rather discursive:

Munching house (*City*, 1850). Onomatope for Mansion House – from the lusty-feeding going on there.

Cinder-shifter (*Fashion*, 1878). A hat with open-work brim, the edge of which was turned up perpendicularly. On all fours with the poke bonnet, called 'coal-scuttle'.

Several of Ware's entries indicate his views on language. We have already seen that he is modern in terms of regarding language as being in a state of constant flux. He alludes from time to time to the fact of a word or expression being 'accepted', identifying a gap between occasional usage and general acceptance. He distinguishes (sometimes spuriously, in modern terms) between registers of usage and date of introduction: see, for example, 'Muffin-wallopers' (*Middle Class London*, 1880) or 'Hunder-hand' (*Street Boys*, 1880). He likes to trace the emergence of words:

Casket (*Amer.*). Evasion of 'coffin'. First mentioned in Webster, in edition of 1879. Coming to England slowly.

In this case his comment is supported by the evidence in the *Oxford English Dictionary* (first edition 1884–1928), which some reviewers wished hopelessly that he had taken more notice of. But commentators were dismissive of Ware's attempts to understand American English. Edmund Lester Pearson, *Books in Black or Red* (1923, p. 75), notes:

Mr. J. Redding Ware . . . essayed the definition of much American slang. His success may be explained by supposing that he had attended a college said to exist in Great Britain for the purpose of teaching ignorance about things American . . . How else . . . could he have defined 'stuck-up' as meaning 'moneyless' – very figurative expression derived from being 'stuck-up' by highwaymen, after which, this etymologist profoundly remarks, 'You have no money left in your pocket'.

From time to time Ware makes a telling observation on language change:

Cocoa (*Nautical*). Comic shape of Toko . . . When a word has become time-weary, it is often newly editioned by being exchanged for a well-known word which rhymes with it.

But Ware's dictionary was popular with some reviewers and with the general public. It is cited directly over 150 times in the *Oxford English Dictionary*, almost fifty times for the first recorded evidence for a word or meaning. We know that James Joyce used it for background colour when assembling his novel *Ulysses*, and it is used as a source book by Ware's successor Eric Partridge and by any serious lexicographer of the language of the period. Whereas Ware's journalism has faded into obscurity, and his fiction and police casebook work is only gradually finding a new audience, his dictionary has remained an entertaining guide to informal English ever since it was first published in 1909.

PREFACE

HERE is a numerically weak collection of instances of 'Passing English'. It may be hoped that there are errors on every page, and also that no entry is 'quite too dull'. Thousands of words and phrases in existence in 1870 have drifted away, or changed their forms, or been absorbed, while as many have been added or are being added. 'Passing English' ripples from countless sources, forming a river of new language which has its tide and its ebb, while its current brings down new ideas and carries away those that have dribbled out of fashion. Not only is 'Passing English' general; it is local; often very seasonably local. Careless etymologists might hold that there are only four divisions of fugitive language in London—west, east, north and south. But the variations are countless. Holborn knows little of Petty Italia behind Hatton Garden, and both these ignore Clerkenwell, which is equally foreign to Islington proper; in the South, Lambeth generally ignores the New Cut, and both look upon Southwark as linguistically out of bounds; while in Central London, Clare Market (disappearing with the nineteenth century) had, if it no longer has, a distinct fashion in words from its great and partially surviving rival through the centuries—the world of Seven Dials, which is in St Giles's—St James's being practically in the next parish. In the East the confusion of languages is a world of 'variants'—there must be half-a-dozen of Anglo-Yiddish alone— all, however, outgrown from the Hebrew stem. 'Passing English' belongs to all the classes, from the peerage class who have always adopted an imperfection in speech or frequency of phrase associated with the court, to the court of the lowest costermonger, who gives the fashion to his immediate *entourage*. Much passing English becomes obscure almost immediately upon its appearance—such as 'Whoa, Emma!' or 'How's your poor feet?' the first from an inquest in a back street, the second from a question by Lord Palmerston addressed to the then Prince of Wales upon the return of the latter from India. 'Everything is nice in my garden' came from Osborne. 'O.K.' for 'orl kerrect' (All Correct) was started by Vance, a comic singer, while in the East district, 'to Wainwright' a woman (*i.e.* to kill her) comes from the name of a murderer of that name. So boys in these later days have substituted 'He's a reglar Charlie' for 'He's a reglar Jack' meaning Jack Sheppard, while Charley is a loving diminutive of Charles Peace, a champion scoundrel of our generation. The Police Courts yield daily phrases to 'Passing English', while the life of the day sets its mark upon every hour. Between the autumn of 1899, and the middle of 1900, a Chadband became a Kruger, while a plucky, cheerful man was described as a 'B.P.' (Baden Powell). Li Hung Chang remained in London not a week, but he was called 'Lion Chang' before he had gone twice to bed in the Metropolis. Indeed, proper names are a great source of trouble in analysing Passing English. 'Dead as a door nail' is probably—as O'Donnel. The phrase comes from Ireland, where another fragment—'I'll smash you into Smithereens'—means into Smither's ruins—though no one seems to know who Smithers was. Again, a famous etymologist has assumed 'Right as a trivet' to refer to a kitchen-stove, whereas the 'trivet' is the last century pronunciation of Truefit, the supreme Bond Street wig-maker, whose wigs were perfect—hence the phrase. Proper names are truly pitfalls in the study of colloquial language. What is a 'Bath Oliver,' a biscuit invented by a Dr Oliver of Bath; again there is the bun named after Sally Lunn, while the Scarborough Simnel is a cake accidentally discovered by baking two varying superposed cakes in one tin. In Scarborough, some natives now say the cake comes down from the pretender Simnel, who became cook or scullion to Henry VII. Turning in another direction, it may be suggested that most exclamations are survivals of Catholicism in England, such as 'Ad's Bud'—'God's Bud' (Christ); 'Cot's So'—'God's oath'; 'S'elp me greens'—meaning groans; more blue (still heard in Devonshire) — *morbleu* (probably from Bath and the Court of Charles II.)—the 'blue death' or the 'blue-blood death'—the crucifixion. 'Please the pigs' is evidently pyx; while the dramatic 'sdeath is clearly 'His Death'; even the still common 'Bloody Hell' is 'By our lady, hail', the lady being the Virgin. There are hundreds of these exclamations, many wholly local.

Preface

Amongst authors perhaps no writer has given so many words to the language as Dickens — from his first work, 'Pickwick', to almost his last, when he popularised Dr Bowdler; anglicization is, however, the chief agent in obscuring meanings, as, for instance, gooseberry fool is just gooseberry fouille, moved about—of course through the sieve. Antithesis again has much to answer for. 'Dude' having noted itself, 'fade' was discovered as its opposite; 'Mascotte' a luck-bringer having been brought to England, the clever ones very soon found an antithesis in Jonah, who, it will be recalled, was considered an unlucky neighbour. Be it repeated—not an hour passes without the discovery of a new word or phrase—as the hours have always been—as the hours will always be. Nor is it too ambitious to suggest that passing language has something to do with the daily history of the nation. Be this all as it may be—here is a phrase book offered to, it may be hoped, many readers, the chief hope of the author, in relation with this work, being that he may be found amusing, if neither erudite nor useful. *Plaudite.*

J. R. W.

ABBREVIATIONS USED

ab.	about
abbrev.	abbreviation
Amer.	American
art.	artistic
Austral.	Australia
Bk.	Book
Ca.	Canto
c. Eng.	common English
cent.	century
cf.	compare
ch.	chapter
C. L.	common life
com., comm.	common
commerc.	commercial
corr.	corruption
crit.	criticism
D. C.	*Daily Chronicle*
D. cls.	Dangerous Classes
D. M.	*Daily Mail*
D. N.	*Daily News*
D. T.	*Daily Telegraph*
E.	East
e.g.	for example
E. N.	*Evening News*
Eng., Engl.	England, English
Hist.	historical
i.e.	that is
I. L. N.	*Illustrated London News*
Ind.	Indian
L.	Low Class
L. C. and D.	London, Chatham Dover
L. C.	Lower Class
Lit.	literary
Lond., Lon.	London
M. Class	Middle Class
Metrop.	Metropolitan
Mid.	Middle
Milit.	Military
M. P.	*Morning Post*
Mus. Hall	Music Hall
N.	North
Newsp. Cutting	Newspaper cutting
N. Y.	New York
O. Eng.	Old English
on	onwards, as 1890 on = 1890 and years following
O. S.	old style
P. House	Public House
Peo.	*The People*
Peop.	Peoples'
polit.	political
Pub. Sch.	Public School
q. v.	which see
qq. v.	which (plural) see
R.	Railway, Royal
Ref.	*Referee*
S.	South
Sat. Rev.	*Saturday Review*
Soc.	Society
Span., Sp.	Spanish
st.	stanza
St.	*Standard*
S. Exch.	Stock Exchange
Theat., Theatr.	Theatrical
Tr.	Trade
Univ.	University
U.S.A.	United States of America
v.	against
W.	West

PASSING ENGLISH

A. D. (*Ball-room programme*). A Drink, disguised, thus:

PROGRAMME OF DANCES.

1. Polka................	Polly J.
2. Valse................	A. D.
3. Valse................	Miss F.
4. Lancers.............	Polly J.
5. Valse................	A. D.
6. Valse................	Miss M. A. T.
7. Quadrille..........	Polly J.
8. Valse................	A. D.
Etc., etc.	

The ingeniousness of this arrangement is that young ladies see 'A. D.', and assume the youth engaged.

Abernethy (*Peoples'*). A biscuit, so named after its inventor, Dr Abernethy (*see* Bath Oliver).

Abisselfa (*Suffolk*). Alone. From 'A by itself, A'; an old English way of stating the alphabet.

Abney Park (*East London*). About 1860. An abbreviation of Abney Park cemetery, a burial ground for a large proportion of those who die in the East End of London. Cemetery is a difficult word which the ignorant always avoid. Now used figuratively, *e.g.*, 'Poor bloke, he's gone to Abney Park'—meaning that he is dead.

We had a friendly lead in our court t'other night. Billy Johnson's kid snuffed it, and so all the coves about got up a 'friendly' to pay for the funeral to plant it decent in Abney.—*Cutting.*

About and About (*Soc.*, 1890 on). Mere chatter, the conversation of fools who talk for sheer talking's sake, *e.g.*, 'A more about and about man never suggested or prompted sudden murder.'

In an age of windy and pretentious gabble—when the number of persons who can, and will, chatter 'about and about the various arts is in quite unprecedented disproportion to the number of those who are content to study these various arts in patience, and, above all, in silence—there was something eminently salutary in Millais' bluff contempt for the more presumptuous theories of the amateurs. —*D. T.*, 14th August 1896.

Above - board (*Peoples'*). Frank, open. From sailors' lingo. Not between decks or in the hold, but above all the boards in the ship.

Abraham's Willing (*Rhyming*). Shilling. Generally reduced to willing, *e.g.*, 'Lend us a willing.'

He don't care an Abraham's willing for anybody.—*Newsp. Cutting.*

Absolutely True (*Soc.*, ab. 1880). Absolutely false, from the title of a book, the statements in which, of a ghostly character, were difficult of acceptation.

Abyssinian Medal (*Military*). A button gone astray from its buttonhole, one in the region of the abdomen. Introduced after the Abyssinian War. (*See* Star in the East.)

Academy (*London*). A billiard-room. Imported from Paris, 1885.

An edict has been promulgated (Paris) forbidding the playing of games of chance on public thoroughfares or in cafés for money, and it is chiefly directed against the billiard rooms, or academies as they are called here.—*D. T.*, 26th July 1894.

Academy Headache. When art became fashionable to a severe degree this malady appeared; now applied generically to headaches acquired at any art galleries.

Art critics complain of 'Academy headache' and of the fatigue produced by leagues of coloured canvases.—*D. N.*, 15th April 1885.

There has yet to arise the philosopher who can explain to us the precise cause of the 'Academy headache'. . . . It is an experience familiar to many who 'do' the great collection at Burlington House. Most persons who go to the Academy know the malady well.—*D. N.*, 4th June 1885.

Academic Nudity (*Oxford*). Appearance in public without cap or gown.

After a tranquil pipe in a friend's room we set out again. Shall we take cap and gown, or shall we venture forth in a state of 'Academic nudity'? Perish the slavish thought! We go without them.—*Cutting*.

Accident. A child born out of wedlock.

Accidented (*Lit.*, 1884). Liable to surprise.

An operatic season thus accidented can hardly prove prosperous, but may be pregnant of good if it teach intending managers of Italian opera to rely on general excellence of *ensemble*, rather than on stars that may at any moment be eclipsed.—*Globe*, 1st July 1885.

According to Cocker (*Peoples'*). Quite correct, according to rule. Cocker flourished in 1694, when the first edition of his *Arithmetic* appeared at the sign of the Black Boy on London Bridge. In the beginning there was no sense of the preposterous in declaring a thing was 'according to Cocker'. Probably the quaintness of the name brought down the dignity of the phrase.

According to Gunter (*Peoples'*). Used precisely as 'according to Cocker'. Gunter was a distinguished arithmetician, and the inventor of a chain and scale for measuring. 'Gunter's chain' is dragged over the land to this day. 'Give me the Gunter' is as common a phrase amongst surveyors as 'Give me the chain'.

Acknowledge the Corn (*Amer. English*). Adroit confession of minor offence to intensify the denial of the major offence: *e.g.*, 'Sir, I believe you are after my wife—and you certainly pocketed my meerschaum last Sunday evening at 10.30.' To which the answer might be: 'Well, I acknowledge the corn—I took the pipe by incident, so to speak; but as to Mrs H., I'm as innocent as the skipping lamb.' Said to arise from an ordinary horse-lifting case in the West of U.S.A. The victim was accused of stealing four horses from one point and four feeds of corn from another for the said four horses. 'I acknowledge the corn,' said the sufferer — but legend says he was lynched in spite of the admission.

Acting Ladies (*Theatrical*, 1883). Indifferent *artistes*. Mrs Langtry, moving in society, having (1882) appeared as an actress in London, and in the same year gone to America, where she made vast sums of money, many ladies of more education than dramatic ability turned their attention to the stage. Eleven out of a dozen totally failed, and few 'twelfths' kept before the public: hence an 'acting lady' soon came, amongst theatrical people, to represent an incapable actress: *e.g.*, 'She isn't a comedian, you know, she's an acting lady.'

Acting ladies, in my opinion, should be severely left alone. There is no pleasing them or their friends. — *Entr'acte*, February 1883.

Actor's Bible (*Theatrical*). The *Era*. This phrase was one of the first directed against sacred matters, about the time when *Essays and Reviews* was much discussed (1860-70).

Mr Sydney Grundy, whose sensitiveness sometimes outruns his discretion, issued a challenge to Mr Clement Scott in 'the Actor's Bible'.—*Ref.* 1883.

There was a motion in the Court of Chancery on Friday, before Mr Justice Chitty, to commit the proprietor of the 'Actor's Bible' for contempt of Court for allowing certain remarks about 'unprincipled imitators' of Miss Geneviève Ward to appear in print.—*Cutting*.

Adam and Eve's togs (*Peoples'*). Nakedness. (*See* Birth-day suit.)

Adam's Ale (*Peoples'*). Water—probably from the time of the Stuart Puritans. If so, it forms a good example of national history in a word or phrase.

Ad's my Life (*Peoples'*; 18 *cent.*). An 18 cent. form of 'God's my life'. (*See* Odd's life.)

Ad's Bud (18 *cent.*). God's Bud, *i.e.*, Christ. Common in H. Fielding.

Advertisement Conveyancers (*Soc.*, 1883). Street Advertisement Board Carriers. (*See* Sandwich Men.) Brought in by W. E. Gladstone (2nd May 1883), during his speech at the inauguration dinner of the National Liberal Club in these words:

These fellow-citizens of ours have it for their lot that the manly and interesting proportions of the human form are in their case disguised both before and after by certain oblong formations which appear to have no higher purpose than what is called conveying an advertisement.—*Newsp. Cutting.*

Society accepted the phrase and the Premier's enemies shot many a shaft anent it.

Ægis (*Latin*). A shield, hence protection, patronage, from Minerva's habit of putting her invisible shield in front of her favourites when in battle.

Madam Adelina Patti appeared yesterday afternoon under the ægis of Messrs Harrison, and once more gathered a great audience round her.—*D. T.*, 4th June 1897.

Æstheticism (*Soc.*, 1865 - 1890). Ideal social ethics, represented outwardly by emblems, chiefly floral, the more significant flowers being the white lily and the sunflower.

The women wore their dresses chiefly in neutral tints, and especially in three series, viz.:—greens, dead leaf (the yellows, or yellowish, of the series); olive (the middle path of colour); and sage (the blues of the series). In each of these series there were scores of tints. The pomegranate was also a fetish. (*See* Grego.)

The joke of æstheticism and sunflowers had been smiled at and had died once or twice between 1865 and 1878 before it was familiar enough to the public for dramatic purposes.—*D. N.*, 27th January 1887.

Affigraphy (*Coster*). To a T, exactly. A corruption of autograph—the vulgar regarding a signature as of world-wide importance and gravity. (*See* Sivvy.)

Afters (*Devon*). Sweets—pies and puddings. 'Bring in the afters' is a common satirical remark in poor Devonshire houses, especially when there are no 'afters' to follow. Also used in Scotland, *e.g.*, 'Hey mon, a dinner, an' nae afters!'

Afternoon Calls (*Soc.*, 19 *cent.*). Referring to exclusive society, who have never accepted the afternoon 'drums' and five o'clock teas, but adhered to the more formal 15-minute afternoon visit.

You had not observed that sort of thing before marriage? Never. What I saw of her was at afternoon calls.—Lord Gerard's evidence in Lord Durham's Nullity of Marriage suit, March 1885.

Afternoonified (*Soc.*). Smart.

What may prove a popular new adjective made its first appearance last week. A lady entered a fashionable drapery store. The lady found nothing to please her. The shopwalker then was called. This individual, with a plausible tale or compliment, will invariably effect a sale after all other means have failed. In reply to his question whether the goods were not suitable, the fastidious customer answered: 'No, thank you; they are not "afternoonified" enough for me.' In the case of a lady armed with an argument of such calibre what was the shopwalker to say or do? Like a wise man, he expressed his regret and beat a dignified retreat. The lady did the same, but the adjective remained. — *D. T.*, July 1897.

'**After you with the push**' (*Peoples'*). Said, with satirical mock politeness, in the streets to any one who has roughly made his way past the speaker, and 'smudged' him.

Aggeravators, Hagrerwaiters (*Costermongers*). Side-curls still worn by a few conservative costermongers. Of two kinds—the ring, or ringlet (the more ancient), and the twist, dubbed, doubtless in the first place by satirists, 'Newgate Knockers'. Indeed the model of this embellishment might have been the knocker of the door of the house of the governor of that gaol. The aggravation may mean that these adornments excite envy in those who cannot grow these splendours, or that they aggravate or increase the admiration of the fair sex. The younger costers wear rival forehead tufts—such as the Quiff, the Guiver, or the Flop. There is, however, one golden rule for these fashions—the hair must stop short of the eyelids.

Agony in Red (*Soc.*). Vermilion costume. When the æsthetic craze was desperately 'on' (1879-81), terms used in music were applied to painting, as a 'nocturne in silver-grey,' a 'symphony in amber,' a 'fugue in purple,' an 'andante in shaded violet'. Hence it was an easy transition to apply terms of human emotions to costumes.

There are many terrible tints even now to be found among the repertory of the

Agreeable Rattle (*Soc.*, ab. 1840). A chattering young man. The genus has long since disappeared. The A. R. went out with the great Exhibition of 1857.

Roderick Doo appeared to be what the ladies call an agreeable rattle.—Albert Smith, *Mr Ledbury* (1842).

Ah, dear me! (*Soc.*, 18 *and* 19 *cents.*). An ejaculation of sorrow, perhaps from 'Ah, Dieu mais!' which in its turn came from *Ay de mi* (*q.v.*). Probably introduced by Catherine of Braganza or one of her French contemporaries at Whitehall ('Ah, dear me, but it's a wicked world').

Ah, que je can be bete! (*Half-Soc.*, 1899). A new macaronic saying— French and English. Amongst the lower classes another ran 'Twiggy-vous the chose?'

'Aipenny Bumper (*London Streets*). A two-farthing omnibus ride, descriptive of the vehicles in question which were not generally great works in carriage-building, until the London County Council started (1899) a line of ½d. 'busses between Waterloo Station and Westminster along the Strand. The L.C.C. 'busses were as good as any others, and better than most.

Air-hole (*Soc.*, 1885-95). A small public garden, generally a dismally converted graveyard, with the ancient gravestones set up at 'attention' against the boundary walls.

For some years past the churchyard has been disused, and the Metropolitan Public Gardens Association, with a keen eye for what it not inaptly terms 'air-holes,' has been making strenuous efforts to secure it as an ornamental space.— *D. T.*, 1st June 1895.

Air-man-chair (*Music-hall* transposition). Chairman — effected by taking the 'ch' from the beginning and adding it, with 'air', to the termination. Very confusing and once equally popular, *e.g.*, 'The air-man-chair is got up no end to-night,' *i.e.*, is well dressed. The chairman has now been abolished in music-halls. He was supposed to keep order and lead choruses. The modern public now do these things for themselves.

Albany Beef (*Amer.*). Unattractive viands.

The *New York Herald* concludes by observing that 'ioukkà', which it calls 'really the national soup of Russia', to 'one of simple tastes, must resemble Hudson River sturgeon, otherwise known as Albany beef, struck by Jersey lightning'.—G. A. Sala, in *D. T.*, 30th June 1883.

Albertine (*Soc.*, 1860-80). An adroit, calculating, business-like mistress; from the character of that name in *Le Père Prodigue* (A. Dumas *fils*). She is in his play an economical housewife, but looks to her own ledger with remorseless accuracy. The word is used and understood in England only by persons of high rank. In France it is used by all classes as a term of reproach, addressed even to a wife for any display of niggardliness. (*See* Nana, *Cheri*.)

Alderman hung in Chains (*City*). A fat turkey decked with garlands of sausages. From the appearance of the City fathers, generally portly— becoming more so when carrying their chains of office over their powerful busts.

Alderman (*Peoples'*). Half a dollar = half a crown, which by the way is fivepence more than the American 'half'. Its origin beyond the reach of discovery; it is probably derived from some remote alderman who when on the bench habitually ladled out this coin to applicants for relief.

Alexandra Limp (*Soc.*, ab. 1872). An affected manner of walking seen for several years amongst women. Said to have been imitated from the temporary mode in which the then Princess of Wales walked after some trouble with a knee. (*See* Buxton Limp, Grecian Bend, Roman Fall.)

Alhambra War Whoop (*Theatrico-political*, 1870). The 'historical' defiance cast at each other by the Germans and French in London during the Franco-German war. Speaking of the destruction of the theatre by fire (Dec. 1882) G. A. Sala wrote at the time in *The Illus. London News*:

Do you remember the 'War Whoop at the Alhambra'? That was during the Franco-German war in 1870—in the late Mr Sawyer's time, and just after the refusal of the dancing licence to the place. The enterprising lessee, not to be baffled by the unkind action of the Areopagus of Clerkenwell Green, determined to 'take it out' in international noise; so every evening towards the close of the performance he organised one band which played the 'Marseillaise', the strains of which were immediately followed by the enlivening notes of the German 'Wacht am Rhein'. Then ensued the Alhambresque 'War Whoop'. The Frenchmen in the house cheered their own melody to the echo, and groaned, whistled, and yelled at the Teutonic air. The Germans, on their side, received the 'Wacht am Rhein' with clamorous exultation, and hooted and bellowed at the 'Marseillaise'. The English portion of the audience impartially screamed and howled. The appalling *charivari* nightly drew crowds to the Alhambra; but the excitement did not last long.

All (*L. Peoples'*). Perfect, extreme, complete, absolute—the sum of street gentlemen's admiration, *e.g.*, 'She's all there,' 'All a lark,' 'All on,' 'All a neat bit.'

'It's all bosh.' All is a big word. Does he refer to the meeting, the Royal Exchange, the speeches, the speakers, or the existence of unemployed thousands? His favourite word comes in again in the supplementary remark: 'It's all a game.' My friend says he is a French polisher, and he smells like one. He further informs me that he belongs to some mysterious commonwealth, that he is a teetotaler, a vegetarian, a non-smoker. When I hint to him—emphasizing his own term—that he is all too good for me, he cheerily comforts me with 'Not a bit of it; it's all right'. This is as it should be—all bosh, all a game, all right.— *D. N.*, 5th February 1885. (*See* Neat.)

All his buttons on (*C. L.*, 1880 on). Sharp, alive, active, not to be deceived.

He is eighty-three years of age, but as we say hereabouts, has all his buttons on (laughter), and he says, 'I never heard of greater nonsense in all my life. Here I am, W. G. of the "Blue Boar", who, if the Duke of So-and-So gives me notice in September to quit next Lady Day, have to leave my licence behind me without any compensation.'—Sir W. Harcourt, *Speech in Bermondsey*, 20th May 1890.

All a-cock (*Peoples'*). Overthrown, vanquished. It may be a version of knocked into a cocked hat, (*q.v.*), or, more probably it is derived from cockfighting; *e.g.*, 'He's all a kick,' meaning a dying bird, from the motion of the legs during the agony of death. This would pass into 'cock' readily, seeing that the conquering bird was always called 'a game' one; or 'he just only tripped me, an' I was all a-cock in a one-two'.

All a treat (*Street*). Perfection of enjoyment, sometimes used satirically to depict mild catastrophe.

All-fired (*Amer.*). A euphemism for hell-fired, used as a general intensive, *e.g.*, 'I was in an all-fired rage.'

All it is worth (*Amer.*). To the fullest extent, as fully as possible.

Scalchi, to use a side-walk phrase, played Siebel for all the character was worth, and was evidently the favourite. —*N. Y. Mercury*, 1883.

All my eye and Betty Martin (*Peoples'*). An expression of disbelief, evasive declaration that the person addressed is a liar. Perhaps the finest example extant of colloquial exclamations reaching to-day from pre-Reformation times. St Martin was, and is, the patron saint of beggars. The prayer to St Martin opens, 'O, mihi, beate Martine.'

This phrase was used by English mendicants (and is still used by South-Italian beggars) when asking for alms. When indiscriminate charity 'went out' in England at the date of the Reformation, this phrase fell into bad repute as representing a lazy and lying class. It is still used by the commoner classes as an expression of doubt, though it has been very widely superseded by 'humbug' (*q.v.*).

All my own (*London Apprentices*, 19 *cent.*). Freedom, mastership. Its use is disappearing with the tendency to abolish apprenticeship.

I'm quite in the world alone
And I'll marry you
If you'll be true,
The day I'm all my own.—(1896).

All my eye and my elbow (*London*, 1882). Fictional: appears to be a flight of genius starting from 'all my eye and Betty Martin', got into form, not because Betty Martin had become vulgar, but possibly because her vague identity led to conventional divergencies. There is a smart aspect about this term, for, while eye and elbow offered a weak alliteration, there is some sort of association and agreement in the action of these personal belongings, for one can wink with the eye and nudge with the elbow at once.

All of a piece (*Peoples'*). Awkward, without proper distribution or relation of parts, *e.g.*, 'He lounged in—all of a piece.' 'Have you seen his new Venus? Awful—all of a piece.'

All over grumble (*Peoples'*). Obvious.

In some of the things that have been seen here it has been a case of *all over grumble*, but Thursday's show was all over approval.—*Ref.*, 28th March 1886.

All over red (*Railway, to public*, 1840 on). Dangerous, to be avoided. From red being the colour signal of danger throughout the railway world. The phrase has been accepted by the public at large. (*See* Be Green, White Light, Paint the Town Red.)

All poppy cock (*Amer.*). Mere brag, nonsense. Perhaps a figure of speech drawn from the natural history of the field-poppy, which looks very braw, military, cockish, and flaunting, but which tumbles to pieces if touched, or droops and faints almost directly it is gathered.

All right up to now (*Street*). Smiling, serene. Derived from *enceinte* women making the remark as to their condition. Used by Herbert Campbell as a catch-phrase in Covent Garden Theatre Pantomime, 1878.

All-round muddle (*Stock Exchange*, 1870). Complete entanglement.

Her 'bondage' is not of lengthened duration, inasmuch as the husband, finding himself in an all-round muddle, shoots himself dead.—*Cutting*.

When reporters get hold of a new phrase they are liable to work it to death. At present they are grinding away at 'all-round'. They tell about the all-round fighter, the all-round baseball player, the all-round reporter, the all-round thief, and the all-round actor. One reporter said the other day that whisky was the best all-round mischief-maker there was in the world, and he probably hasn't been all-round either.—*Cutting*, 1888.

All very fine and large (*Lond.*, 1886). Satirical applause; from the refrain of a song sung by Mr Herbert Campbell.

How many people passed the turnstiles at the Alexandra Palace I am not in a position to say, but that the attendance was all very fine and large is beyond dispute.—*Ref.*, 7th August 1887.

Alley (*Peoples'*). A go-between. Evidently from 'aller', to go.

Mrs Cox was an alley for her.—Bravo Coroner's Inquest.

Allee samee (*Pidgeon English*). All the same. Used by Chinese cheap abourers when detected in trying to cheat. 'Washy money allee samee,' applied by Anglo-Asiatics in a satirical spirit where things are not quite satisfactory. 'It appeared that they were not quite married, but that they lived together allee samee.'—*N. Y. Mercury*, February 1883.

Alligators (*Amer.*). People of Florida, so named from the alligators there; used also because the Floridans are supposed to be as greedy as these reptiles. Of course, an invention of some other State or States.

'Will you kindly tell me which way the wind blows?' asked a Northern invalid of the landlord of a Florida hotel. 'Certainly, sir,' replied the landlord, stepping to the door; 'the wind now blows due north, sir.' 'Thank you.' A little later the landlord said to the bookkeeper: 'Have you made out Mr Smith's bill yet?' 'No, sir.' 'Well, just charge one dollar to his account for information about the direction of the wind.'

Alls (*Public-House*). Waste pot at public-houses. On all public-house pewter counters may be seen holes, down which go spillings of everything. Popular mistrust runs to the belief that these collections are used up—hence the comment upon bad beer. 'This must be alls.' As a fact, the brewer allows a barrel of good beer for every barrel of alls forwarded to the brewery. What does the brewer do with it? This is indeed wanting to know, at the end of the book, what became of the executioner? Probability is in favour of the sewer-grating.

Allsopp (*Peoples'*). Short for Allsopp's Pale Ale.

Ally Luja lass (*Lond. Street*, 1886 on). Hallelujah lass was the name given to the girl contingent of the Salvation Army, when the movement rose into importance in London, and General Booth made an effort to purchase all the theatres, succeeding, however, only in one case, that of the Grecian Theatre, City Road.

She sed thay wur Ally Luja's lasses. 'Ally Luja's asses,' I sed; 'thay wants kikkin.'—*Comic Report of a Salvation Meeting* (1870).

Ally Sloper (*Street*, 1870 on). A dissipated-looking old man with a red and swollen nose. Invented by Mr Charles Ross, who ran him in print for a score of years.

Almighty dollar (*Amer.*). This expression, a derisive synonym for money or Mammon, originated with Washington Irving. It is found in his *Creole Village*, and reads thus:

'The Almighty Dollar, that great object of universal devotion throughout our land, seems to have no genuine devotees in these peculiar villages.'

Alphonse (*Soc.*, 1870 on). A man of position who accepts money from a married woman or women richer, and probably older, than himself, as recompense for remaining her or their lover. Quite understood in Paris—not known out of society in London. From the play *Monsieur Alphonse* (Alexandre Dumas, *fils*).

There was yesterday evening and up to the small hours of the morning a serious riot in the Latin Quarter, caused by the students who continue from time to time to make violent demonstrations against those professional allies of certain women—men who bear the name of 'Alphonse'—a sobriquet invented by Alexandre Dumas, one which has passed into the language.—*Newsp. Cutting*.

Altogether (*Soc.*, 1894). The nude in art. From Du Maurier's *Trilby*, who is an artist's model. 'I sit for the altogether.'

The *New York Mercury*, 27th September 1895, has this heading: Will the next fad be photographs of modern woman taken in the 'altogether'? Society women now have their busts done in marble, their hands and arms in bronze, and their legs photographed.

In *The Demagogue and Lady Phayre*, the labour leader appears as a figure of rude nobility. The proportions are not heroic; they are simply life-size. In the altogether they make up an individuality rich, massive, and imposing. —*Weekly Sun*, 29th December 1895.

They wore little underclothing—scarcely
  anything—or no—thing—
And their dress of Coan silk was quite
  transparent in design—
Well, in fact, in summer weather, something like the 'altogether',
And it's there I rather fancy, I shall
  have to draw the line!
  —Mr W. S. Gilbert's 'The Grand
     Duke', March 1896.

There was no earthly necessity why the *Hôtel du Libre Échange* should be an improper play, except that the modern French audience revels in impropriety. They like it, they wallow in it, and they destroy their native ingenuity in construction and invention with what we may call 'the cult of the altogether'.—*D. T.*, 30th April 1896.

Altogethery (*Soc.*). Drunk—from the tendency of a drunken man to lounge himself. Byron uses the term in a letter of 1816.

Amen Corner (*Californian*). A church.

Sunday found them, judge and lawyers, seated in the 'amen corner'.— *All the Year Round*, 31st October 1868.

A'mighty (*Amer.*). One of the first evasions of an oath - like word. It is, of course, a corruption of 'almighty'.

As you know, young fellur, them goats is a'mighty kewrous anymal—as kewrous as weemen is.

Ammedown Shop (*Poor*). Corruption of Hand-me-down Shop. A good example of a phrase getting bastardized into one meaningless word. 'George, my dear, ammedown my gal's Turkey-red frock.'

Amok. *See* Run a-muck.

Anatomy (*Peoples'*, formerly *Literary*). A thin needy boy, or old withered soul. In common English, it has been reduced to natermy, *e.g.*, 'He were a perfick 'nattermy.'

A boy of twelve stood leaning against a fence on Duffield Street, hat pulled down, feet crossed, and his right hand going up occasionally to wipe his nose, when along came another anatomy about his size.—*Detroit Free Press*.

Ancient Mariners (*Cambridge Univ.*). Graduates still associated with the University who continue to row.

At Cambridge Fawcett rowed stroke (the necessary position of a blind man) in the crew of 'Ancient Mariners', as the older members of the University who still ply the oar are called.—*D. N.*, 7th November 1884.

Androgynaikal (*Art.*). Appertaining to the nude figure, and to the anatomy of both sexes.

Simeon Solomon's notion of the classic ideal in his picture called 'Sacramentum amoris', a small figure, as nude as may be, girt with a skin of a panther and a light blue sash, and background of yellow drapery, but of that peculiar type of form to which the term 'androgunaikal' is applied in art, and holding a long thyrsus.—*Newsp. Cutting*.

Angel (*N. London Street*). A woman of the town fringing the Angel at Islington, *e.g.*, 'What are you doing here? *you* ain't a Angel—you're only a Sluker' (*i.e.*, St Luker, from the Parish of St Luke, in the City Road, which is considered at the Angel as socially below Islington, as it is comparatively depressed in its physical want of elevation in comparison with the Angel, which is quite at the top of the hill).

Angel-makers (*Peop.*, 1889 on). Baby-farmers; because so many of the farmed babies die. Probably from the French 'Faiseuses des anges'.

'ANGEL - MAKING'.—Another case of baby-farming, or 'angel-making', as it is called in Austria, has just been discovered by the Lemberg police, who have arrested three women on the charge of systematically starving to death infants committed to their care.—*Newsp. Cutting*, December 1892.

They are not only under a cloud owing to the deaths of Miss Thompson and Mademoiselle Madet, but every day a fresh charge is laid at their doors, and some people have even gone so far as to describe them as members of a band of what Parisians call 'angel-makers'.—*D. T.*, 7th December 1896.

Angels on Horseback (*Virginia*). Fricasseed oysters—meaning exquisite. Origin not known.

Anglican Inch (*Church*, 1870 on). Description given by the ritualistic clergy of the short square whisker which is so much affected by the Broad Church party. The Rits (*q.v.*) call themselves the 'Church of England', the generally accepted Broad Church, or Taits as they were called in Archbishop Tait's time, are 'Anglicans'—hence the 'inch'. (*See* St Alban's Clean Sweep.)

Anguagela (*Transposed*) Language. A good example of the confusion produced by transposing and repeating a syllable or letter; *e.g.*,

How the Lord Chamberlain's people pass this stuff goodness only knows. Perhaps they don't understand the French anguagela.

Animal (*L. C. and D. Railway Passengers*, 1860). Synonym for the 'Elephant and Castle' station. 'Third-class Animal' is, or was, quite understood by the railway booking-clerks of the district.

Animal (*Tavern*). A disguised, or flippant, reference amongst boon companions to the tavern, used in common when the sign is zoological, such as the Bull, Bear, Lion, Dragon—but more especially referring to the Elephant and Castle (S. London); until (1882) this place was exceptionally dubbed 'Jumbo' (*q.v.*).

Anno Domini, B.C. (*Soc.*, 1890 on). Relating to unknown longevity.

'He must be very anno domini, mustn't he?' 'A.D.? my dear fellow, say B.C.'

Anonyma (*Soc.*, 1862). A name given to women of gallantry in an article in the *Times* commenting on a well-known Phryne of that day. The word lasted many years and came to be synonymous with a gay woman.

She could kick higher in the can-can than any anonyma there.—*N. Y. Mercury*, 1882.

Anti-queer-uns (*Soc.*, 18 *cent.*). A perversion of 'antiquarians', due to Foote.

So many interesting associations cluster around the remains of the old nunnery at Godstow, a mile or two out of Oxford, that it is rather surprising so little attention has been bestowed on the ruin. Perhaps it may be difficult even for 'Anti-queer-uns', as Foote calls them, to get up much enthusiasm over nameless graves.—*D. N.*, 3rd February 1885.

Anti-Tox (*Amer.*, reaching England 1885). A drug to sober a drunken person. Tox is, of course, the abbreviation of intoxication.

A reporter noticed the singular fact that nearly every one who went into a leading saloon was under the influence of some powerful stimulant, and nearly every one who came out was painfully sober. Then he determined to go in and see about it. 'Have a dose of Anti-Tox?' asked the barkeeper, recognising the reporter. 'It's the greatest thing on earth; you come to me rocking from one side of the saloon to the other and reeking with the fumes of the vilest whisky, and I will make a new man of you while you are getting out a twenty-cent piece.'—*Minneapolis Gaz.*, 1885.

'Apenny-lot day (*Costers'*). A bad time for business—really, when everything has to be sold cheap.

Apostle of culture (*Soc.*, 1880). An individual who sets up as a perfect judge of taste. Probably started by Sir Francis Burnand in *Punch*.

Our self-elected apostle of culture has told us that it is as ridiculous to say that such and such a colour is the fashion as it would be to assert that B flat was the fashionable key.—*D. N.*, 13th January 1885.

Apostles of murder (*Polit.*, 1867 on). A name given generally to political agitators who included assassination in their programme.

To say nothing of dynamite, and of that horrible compound found at Liverpool which presents the innocent appearance of sawdust but of which every grain is an explosive agency, the apostles of murder are reported to have employed methods of offence even more diabolical.—*D. N.*, 6th April 1883.

Apple-jack (*Amer.*). Spirit distilled from cider or from the pulp of apples already pressed for cider. (*See* Sweet Waters.) 'Jack' is a common term for spirits in U.S.A. In Normandy this liquor is calvados.

'A grindstun can,' remarked a weazened farmer, who had just called for some apple-jack.—*Newsp. Cutting*, 1883.

Apples (*Corruption of Rhyming Slang*). Stairs, as thus: 'Apples and pears—stairs.' 'Bill an' Jack's gone up apples.'

'Apples and pears in no birdlime—time.'—(*Rhyming Street*, 1882).

An obscure mode of describing sudden ejection from a house; *e.g.*,

The flunkeys had me down stairs (apples and pears) in no time (birdlime).

'Appy dosser (*Low Life*, 19 cent.). A satirical description of a homeless creature, so wretched as not to have the few halfpence necessary to pay for a 'doss', or bed in a common lodging-house.

Elizabeth, poor storm-tossed bit of one of the myriad wrecks that strew the ocean of life, homeless and starving, dying of an agonizing ailment, was, having neither money nor friends, what is professionally known as a ''appy dosser'. That is to say, she would crawl at night into the open passages of a low lodging-house, and fall down where she could—in the yard or the passage—and sleep.—*Ref.*, February 1882.

Archer up (*London*, 1881). Safe to win. Formerly a popular phrase of congratulation. A man was seen running for and catching a 'bus: 'Archer up,' shouted the on-lookers. A man appeared in new clothes: 'Archer up!' Another threatened to knock another down: 'Archer up!' here used probably satirically. The phrase took its rise from a celebrated jockey who suddenly sprang to the front in 1881, and carried everything before him. It is short for 'Archer is up in the saddle'. He rode with an absolute recklessness which may account for his end, for he shot himself. At once the phrase passed away utterly, and was heard no more.

Arctics (*Amer.*). Winter clothing, which in the earlier settled States is decidedly built on a vast scale.

I hate a hotel where you have to get up at 4.15 A.M., dress in a cold room, and walk down to the station because the 'bus doesn't go to that train, and about half-way down you discover that you left your arctics in the office.—*Newsp. Cutting.*

Ardent (*Soc.*, 1870). A shortened form of 'ardent spirits'. From the Mexican *aqua ardente*, through America.

After this we all felt in such good humour that the bottle passed freely, and I fear that more than one of our number swallowed a little too much of the ardent.—*Newsp. Cutting*, 1878.

Arer (*Peoples'*). More so. From 'are', emphatically used. 'We *are*, and what's more, we can't be any arer.'

'Arf-a-mo' (*Peoples'*, 1890 on). Abbreviation of 'half a moment', *cf.*, 'half a sec.' and 'half a tick' (of a watch).

I'll bet you never noticed all the things
    that you can do
In half a mo'—half a mo',
So cock your ears and listen and I'll
    mention one or two,
In half a mo'—half a mo'.
Tho' you're as sane as Satan you can go
    clean off your dot,
And then start backing gee-gees on a
    system very hot;
Have five-and-twenty thousand quids and
    lose the blessed lot
In half a mo'—half a mo'.
Chorus: In half a mo'—half a mo'
    Your pluck and perseverance
        you can show,
    You can go with other people
    Down a sewer, climb a steeple,
    Fall an' break your blooming
        neck in half a mo'.
                —1896.

Arf-an-arf (*London Public-house*, 19 cent.). Half-and-half. A mixture half of black beer (porter) and half ale. (*See* Cooper.)

Arf'arf'an'arf (*Peoples'*). A figure of speech, meaning 'drunk', the substitution of cause for effect, the intoxication being the latter, 'arfarfanarf' the former. It may be thus explained, arf'=half pint of; arfanarf =half and half=half ale and half beer=half and half. This liquor is fourpence the quart, therefore, the mystic refreshment is called for as 'arf o' four d arfanarf', the 'd' being used to express pence=*denarii*. Is used to describe drunken men, *e.g.*, "'E's very arfarfanarf'—really meaning that he has had many 'arfs'.

Argol-bargol. To have a row. May be argue turned into argol, from the old term 'argil' (*see* the Grave-digger in *Hamlet*), corrupted from 'ergo'. The 'bargol' is a rhymed invention following a common habit. The whole term, however, is pervaded apparently by depreciation:—' Well —well—d'yer want ter argol-bargol?'

Aristocratic veins (*Theatrical*). Blue lines of colour usually frescoed on the temples, and sometimes on the backs of the hands and wrists. Supposed to be a mark of high and noble birth. Sometimes adopted by women in society. 'Pass me the smalt, girl— I want to put in my veins.' (*See* Mind the Paint.)

Arkansas tooth-pick (*Amer.*). A bowie-knife. Arkansas is notorious for sudden blood-letting.

And he jabbed an eighteen Arkansas tooth-pick into—whoever it happened to be.—*Mark Twain*.

He had a seductive way of drawing his 18-inch Arkansas tooth-pick, and examining it critically with a sinister smile, while humbly requesting the temporary loan of five dollars.—*Texas Siftings*.

'Arrydom (*Soc.*, 1885). The kingdom and rule of 'Arry, the typical London cad.

It seems a pity that the *Whitehall Review* did not confine itself to saying, in the speech of 'Arrydom, 'You're another,' instead of appealing to a special jury.—*Sat. Rev.*, 26th March 1885.

'Arry's Worrier (*Peoples'*, 1885 on). The deadly and bronchitical concertina common to 'Arry's hand, and as deadly as his fist or his ' Hinglish '.

If our readers are inclined to be curious, they may, on further investigation, discover the player of 'Arry's' favourite 'worrier' in the form of a patient-looking little lady, who sits on the stonework of the railings which guard the select piece of grass and trees. —*People*, 19th February 1897.

'Arrico Veins (*Common people*, 19 *cent.*). Varicose veins.

'Bless yer, 'arrico veins don't kill. I know an old lady o' ninety-one, an' she's 'ad 'em these forty years. Ill-conwenient, but they ain't dangerous—on'y a leak.'

Artful Fox (*Music-hall*, 1882). A nonsense rhyme for 'box'.

You capture the first liker at him in a snug artful *fox* at some chantin ken where there's a bona varderin serio comic, and Isle of Francer engaged.—From *Biography of the Staff Bundle Courier*, the gentleman who accompanies 'serio-comics' from music-hall to music-hall when 'doing turns'.

Artistic Merit (*Society*, 1882). A satirical criticism of a flattering portrait. A celebrated sculptors' case (Belt *v.* Lawes, 1882) brought this term into a general use. Belt complained that Lawes had said of him that he (Belt) had no 'artistic merit,' and that all his many busts were artistically finished by competent men, commonly called 'studio ghosts'. Belt and his friends maintained that he possessed not only good modelling power, which was also denied, but finishing power also. For Lawes, the then President of the Royal Academy (Sir F. Leighton) and many other eminent art followers gave evidence that Belt had no artistic merit. Gradually, during a long trial of over forty days, the public grew to comprehend that in sculpture 'artistic merit' might mean the use of flattering refinement in finish. Hence arose the use of the phrase as an euphemism for flattery.

Sincerity may raise a costume ball from the mere pastime of an evening to an undertaking involving culture, patience, and self-denial, and bring about a result not perhaps without 'artistic merit'.—*Newsp. Cutting*, February 1885.

Fancy asking a policeman to decide upon the morality or immorality of a ballet! You might as well ask a policeman to pass judgment on the decency of a statue of Venus, and at the same time to criticise its 'artistic merits'.—*Ref.*, 11th February 1883.

Ashkenazic. German and Polish Jews.

Ash-plant (*Military*, 1870). Light, unvarnished, unpeeled, rough-cut ash swish, for carrying in the hand. Subalterns at Dover first carried these swishes, value about 1d., the head formed by a knot got at a branching. They became very fashionable, and soon, owing to their valuelessness, very common. Therefore, after a time, they were mounted in gold or silver, the swish remaining unpeeled, and in no way polished or varnished.

Bringing his ash-plant down on the counter with ten Slade force, he said, 'If that's the sort of man you are, I'm off to take tea with Miss Murnford.' And he offed.—*Bird o' Freedom*, 7th March 1883.

Ask another (*Street*, 1896 on). A protest against a reiterated or worn-out joke, an expression of boredom; directed at a 'chestnut', *e.g.*, 'I say, Joe, when's a door not a door?' to which Joe disgustedly replies, 'Oh, ask another.'

Aspect (*Lond., chiefly Hatton Garden district*). A look of eager love. Used chiefly in the Italian quarter, but spreading. Where there is a foreign colony in London, as French in Soho, Italian in Clerkenwell Road, German in Clerkenwell, the English amongst them, to some extent fraternizing, adopt any forcible word or phrase used by them, as, for instance, in the Whitechapel district the Jewish 'selah' (God be with you, or good-bye) has become 'so long', a phrase which has spread all over England. Amongst Italians 'aspetto' is a very common word. Used alone no doubt it may be translated, 'Hold on a bit!' but it retains its meaning 'look', 'aspect', and it is this translation which has been accepted by the observant English lower-middle-class in the Italian district. A fiery youth looking too fiercely into the eyes of a gutter donzella, she observes, 'aspetto —aspetto!' Her English sister has accepted the word, and under similar circumstances cries, 'Not too much aspect, Tom!' Applied also in other ways, *e.g.*, 'Well, Jack, not too much aspect, or you might run agin one o' my fists!'

Aspinall (*Peoples'*). Enamel. Also as a verb. From Aspinall, the inventor and manufacturer of an oxidized enamel paint.

Astarrakan (*Street*, 1890). A jocular mispronunciation of the astrachan fur. Used satirically, after Mr Gus Elen's (1898) song, the first line of the chorus running:

Astarrakan at the bottom of my coat.

Atavism (*Society*, c. 1890-5). The antithesis of decadent. The difference between these newly meaninged words is very marked. The decadent may show ability, genius even, but his life demonstrates that he is in a general way mentally, morally, and physically inferior to his forebears; and, as a rule, he dies childless, or his children have no families. The atavist, on the other hand, is a human being who is relegated by some hidden natural force to a condition assimilating to an early form of mankind. He is therefore, as a rule, a physical improvement upon his immediate or modern forebears, and even possibly a mental superior—but morality from the modern standpoint has little or no existence for him. He tends to the animal life—he takes what he wants; society calls him a kleptomaniac; plain people dub him a thief, while as a dipsomaniac he again imitates the mammal, which, once indulged in liquor, becomes a hopeless drunkard. An atavist may become a decadent; a decadent never becomes an atavist.

Athletic Drolls (*Music-hall*, 1860 on). Comic performers whose songs were interspersed with gymnastic feats. (*See* Knockabout Drolls, Singing Drolls.)

Atlantic Greyhounds (*Soc.*). Quick Atlantic steamers.

The booking of passengers desirous of securing berths on board one or other of the 'Atlantic greyhounds' now plying between the Old and New Worlds far exceeds the accommodation available for their reception.—*D. T.*, 20th May 1895.

Attorney-General's Devil (*Legal*).

He was chosen by Sir John Holker, whose practical shrewdness was seldom at fault, to succeed the present Lord Justice Bowen as junior counsel to the Treasury, commonly called 'Attorney-General's Devil'.—*Newsp. Cutting*, 1883.

The working barrister who does the heavy work of a K.C. or other legal big-wig is generally called a 'devil'. But the term is dying out owing to increased legal amenities.

Auctioneer (*Peoples'*). The fist—because it 'knocks down'.

Milo, the boxer, was an accomplished man. He did not, however, use the sculptor's hammer, but rather the 'auctioneer' of the late Mr Thomas Sayers.—*D. N.*

Auditorium (*Press*, 1870). The portion of a theatre occupied by the audience—called the theatre until Dion Boucicault took 'Astley's', spoilt the ceiling by cutting ventilating holes in it, and then wrote a long letter to the *Times* in which he spoke of the improvements he had made in 'the auditorium'. The word was at once accepted with much laughter. Now used seriously.

Some time before the curtain rose large crowds of seat-seekers might have been observed surging down the tunnels that lead to the auditorium of this house (Opera Comique, now swept away).—*Ref.*, 14th June 1885.

Aunt Sally (*Low London*). A black-faced doll. Early in the century the sign of a rag-shop; afterwards adopted as an entrancing cock-shy, a pipe either forming the nose or being placed between the teeth. From Black Sall and Dusty Bob, characters in the elder Pierce Egan's *Life in London*, and probably adopted owing to the popularity of that work, precisely as in a later generation many of Dickens's characters were associated with trade advertisements. Aunt Sally is vanishing, even at race-courses. Soon, but for a portrait, she will be only a memory. Very significant of Pierce Egan's popularity, which from 1820 to 1840 was as great as that of Dickens, whose fame threw Egan into obscurity.

Aunt's sisters (*London Middle-class*). A foolish perversion of 'ancestors'.

Corrie Roy was once more restored to the home of his aunt's sisters.—*Comic Romance.*

Away (*London Thieves' Etiquette*). A man is never spoken of as 'in prison', though he is there for many a 'stretch'. It would evince great want of etiquette to mention the detaining locality, *e.g.*, 'Mine's away, bless 'is 'art,' the grass-widow of lower life will say, as indicative that her husband is in jail. The answer should be, 'A 'appy return 'ome to 'im, mum.'

'Awkins (*Lower Classes*, 1880 on). A severe man, one not to be trifled with. Name-word from the Judge, then Sir Frederic Hawkins, who about this time impressed the lower and criminal classes as a 'hanging' judge, *e.g.*, 'Joe, don't you play around Tom Barr—'e's a 'Awkins, and no mistake.'

'Awkins (*Mid-London*, 1905). A princely costermonger. From a music-hall song sung by Albert Chevalier, with the catch line, 'And 'Enery 'Awkins is a first-class name'.

And, indeed, if not in Walworth, where should Mr Hawkins be supreme? It is the epical home, so to speak, of his race—a district traversed by that Old Kent-road in which their lyric hero 'knocked' the passers-by with the unexpected splendours of his attire and turn-out. Disestablishment is not understood to trouble his repose, and the downfall of the Welsh Church would probably leave him as unmoved as the just man in Horace, so long as the 'Harp' of the same nationality continues to open its hospitable doors to himself and Mrs Hawkins on their 'Sundays out'.—*D. T.*, 14th May 1895.

Axe to grind (*Amer.-Engl.*). *I.e.*, a personal end to serve, originally a favour to ask; from men in backwoods pretending to want to grind their axes when in reality they required a drink. Mr Ebbs, an American etymologist, says that the origin of this phrase has been attributed to Benjamin Franklin. It is true, many of his sayings in *Poor Richard* bear a striking similarity to the saying; still, not one of them can be tortured into the above phrase.

Every one seems to have had what the Americans call 'an axe to grind'.—Yates, *Recollections* (1884).

Finally, Mr Irving stepped forward, and in a voice trembling with emotion, bade farewell to his American friends. He said among other things: 'Now that I can speak without fear or favour, and without the suspicion that I have an axe to grind, I can say for the first time how deeply grateful we are for the innumerable acts of kindness received from the American people.'—*Newsp. Cutting*, April 1885.

Conservatives with axes to grind will soon make the word Beaconsfield as wearisome by mere iteration as the word Jubilee.—*D. N.*, 7th April 1887.

Axe-grinders (*American*). Men who grumble, especially politically.

Willard's Hotel was closed, and, even if it had not been, with its *clientèle* of bar-loafers, swaggerers, drunkards, and axe-grinders (a class of politicians peculiar to Washington hotels), it would not have been the place for Mr Dickens in his state of health.—Dolby, *Dickens as I knew him.*

Ay de mi, sometimes **Ay de my** (*Hist.*). It pervades all Western European literature. It is found in

Tom Cringle's Log, also in *Gil Blas*, bk. xi. 5.

> Ay de my ! un anno felice
> Parece un soplo ligero ;
> Perô fin dicha un instante
> Es un siglo de tormento.

Smollett translates the phrase 'alas'. It was Carlyle's favourite protest, and is found frequently in Froude's biography of him :

> The dinners, routs, callers, confusions inevitable to a certain length. *Ay de mi* —I wish I was far from it.

It was probably brought to England by Catherine of Braganza. (*See* ' Oh dear me ! ')

B

B's. (*Fenian*, 1883). Patriotic Brotherhood. In questionable taste. The members of the Patriotic Brotherhood, or Irish Invincibles, thus styled themselves. It may have had some absurd association with the 'busy bee'.

> Patrick Duffy was sworn, and deposed —Finnegan and Devlin were at a meeting of the society held in the spring of 1881. I knew James Hauratty and Patrick Geogeghan, who were both 'B's'.—*Report of the Patriotic Brotherhood Conspiracy* (Trial at Belfast, 26th March 1883).

B.C. play (*Theatrical*, 1885). Classical drama ; *Before Christ*. Invented *apropos* to Claudian (Princess's Theatre).

> The authors are wise to eschew low comedy. There wasn't much of it in the time of Pericles. George cannot come in and talk about milking his hay and mowing his cows as he did in ' Claudian '. One of our best low comedians, he is not at home in a B.C. period.—*Ref.*, 28th March 1886.

B.H. (*Peoples'*, 1880). Bank holiday.

B.K.'s (*Military*). Barracks. Used by officers, non-coms., and privates, down to the drummer-boy. (*See* H. Q.)

B.P. (*Theatrical*). British Public. (*See* Pub.)

> 'Have you read Leader's manifesto on taking possession of Her Majesty's Theatre ?' 'We have, and feel sure there's a good time coming for the B.P.'—*Bird o' Freedom*, 1883.

> Harvey writes and arranges, not to please me, who don't pay, but the great B.P., who do.—*Ref.*, 9th August 1885.

> 'My dear Wilfred,—They tell me you are in a wax about the exceptions I took to your article. I am extremely sorry to touch any line of yours, but B.P. must be considered, you know !'—Ouida, *An Altruist*, 1896.

B. and P. (*Lond.*). Initials of two young men whose public proceedings resulted, about 1870, in a long police-court inquiry and trial. (*See* Beanpea.)

B Flat (*Peoples'*). Proof of advance of education, being a sort of pun lying between *si bémol* or B flat, and an intimate insect (now rapidly being evicted by a survival of the fittest), which has been too fatally associated with the family of Norfolk Howard (*q.v.*).

Baby (*Tavern*, 1875). The conviction amongst men given to creature-comforts that the cheapest soda and spirits refresher rose to sixpence at least, led the ærated water manufacturers to invent the half-bottle (2d.), which from its small size was dubbed ' baby ' by all men. ' Give me a baby lemonade ' was understood by all barmaids, who never blushed. The term has lapsed.

Baby and Nurse (*Tavern*, 1876). A small bottle of soda-water and two-penny-worth of spirit in it. This is the nurse. Accepted terms even by queens of the taps and handles. Where more than 'two' of spirits is required numerals come by their own again. The phrase has lapsed.

Baby's public-house (*Peoples'*). Nature's fount.

> Among them is a six-year-old baby that is suckled at the breast when it asks for baby's public-house, and that fills up the intervals between refreshment by smoking cigarettes. Fact !—*Ref.*, 5th October 1884.

Bab'sky (*Liverpool*). Corruption of Bay o' Biscay.

> The place where the arch was erected is about the most exposed part of the town when the wind is high, and in consequence is generally styled the ' Bab'sky '.—*Newsp. Cutting*, May 1886.

Back answers (*C. Eng.*, 19 *cent.*). Sharp retorts, quick-tongued replies, dorsal eructations, without any concession to the laws of etiquette.

> He went to the station and gave no 'cheek' or 'back-answers' to any one.—*Cutting.*

Back down (*American*). To yield.

If we may—we indicate an apologetic foreign policy by remarking that the Government 'backs down'.

That is to say, 'makes a back', as boys at leap-frog, to enable the other players to get over.

Back-hairing (*Street*). Feminine fighting, in which the occipital locks suffer severely.

His Honour said no doubt there had been a great deal of provocation, but the rule was when a woman had her back hair pulled down and her face scratched, she back-haired and scratched in return. *Newsp. Cutting.*

Back-hair parts (*Theatrical*). Rôles in which the agony of the performance at one point in the drama admits of the feminine tresses in question floating over the shoulders.

Like the famous lady who never would undertake any but 'back-hair' parts, the Parisian *comédienne* could only with difficulty be prevailed upon to become a stage heroine whose garments have to express the depths of an unpicturesque poverty.—*D. N.*, November 1884.

Back o' the green (*Theatre and Music-hall*). This is a sort of *rebus*, the 'green' being an imperfect rhyme for 'scenes', also referring to that historical 'green' curtain which has now almost passed away. It represents 'behind the scenes'.

Back row hopper (*Theatrical*). Chiefly used in taverns affected by the commoner members of 'the profession'. 'He's a back row hopper' is said of an impecunious man who enters one of these houses on the pretence of looking for somebody, and the certain hope of finding somebody ready and willing to pay for a drink.

Back slang it (*Thieves'*). To go out the back way.

Back-scene (*Devonshire*). Literal. The second word direct from the French '*seant*', and an interesting example of evasive French-English— found only in Devon.

Backs, The (*Cambridge*). Literally the backs of several of the greater colleges, notably Trinity and John's— seen from the opposite side of the Cam.

St Andrews boasts her links, Oban is proud of her bay, Cambridge has her 'backs', and whoever visited Liverpool without hearing of her docks?—*D. N.*

Backsheesh (*Anglo-Arabic*). Bribe. The origin of this word is historical. When Mohamed Ali endeavoured, after his lights, to bring Egypt within the pale of civilization, he sought to abate the endless begging exercised by most of his subjects. To this end he assured his people that if they did not beg, foreigners would always make them a *backsheesh*, or 'present'. The natives accepted the theory, but only to apply it to their old practice. They begged, as they beg to this day, as much as ever; but they made their entreaties elegant by asking for a backsheesh— the one word of Arabic that every Englishman in Egypt learns, even if he acquire no other.

The people who talk of bribery and 'backsheesh' in such circumstances are imperfectly informed as to desert customs and slang. To give a Sheikh who gets for you a hundred camels, say £60, is not an act of bribery. It is merely paying him a commission.— *D. N.*, 16th March 1883.

Bad cess to ye! (*Irish*). Cess—board and lodging. An amiable Celtic benediction. An Act of Parliament was passed during Strafford's viceroyalty 'for the better regulating of Ireland', wherein we find these words: 'Whereas there are many young gentlemen of this kingdom (Ireland), that have little or nothing to live on of their own, and will not apply themselves to labour, but live coshering on the country, cessing themselves and their followers, their horses and their greyhounds, upon the poorer inhabitants,' etc., etc. This phrase is in common use in England—where the two words are supposed to mean ill-luck, as indeed they do, *e.g.*, 'Bad cess to you, Joe—wherever you go!'

Bad crowd (*Californian*). A man of indifferent character.

She then went out to tell the feminine convention on the back stoop what a bad crowd Jabez used to be when he kept a chicken-ranch on the Stanislaus in '51.— *San Francisco Mail.*

Bad egg (*Peoples'*). A person hopelessly beyond cure, perfectly disreputable. Originally American, though no longer used in the U.S. Colloquial in England.

A man out West, by the name of Thomas Egg, having committed some crime, his neighbours gave him the appellation of a 'bad Egg', which, in its application to vice, with man, woman, or child, they are invariably called bad eggs. It is also used to denote a good man, by calling him a good egg. And this is used either to denote his moral or pecuniary standing.—*American Paper*.

Bad form (*Soc.*, 1860 on). The opposite of Correct Fashion. Derived from the racing stable.

The very low bodices of some seasons ago are now considered 'bad form' (a quite untranslatable phrase).—*D. N.*, 'Dresses for dances', 15th December 1885.

This ingenious piece of tactics in taking cover was looked upon as 'bad form', even by the other hill men, who appreciated the scruples of British humanity.—*Newsp. Cutting*.

(*See* No class.)

Bad hat (*Middle-class*, 19 *cent.*). A queer chum, dissatisfactory mess-mate, disreputable person. Probably Irish, from the worst Hiberian characters always wearing bad high hats (caps are not recognised in kingly Ireland).

What a shocking bad hat! is the next cry, with something of an historical flavour about it, that I can recollect. The observation is not yet wholly extinct, I should say, although its meaning has entirely vanished from the public ken; but, according to Sir William Fraser, in his *Words on Wellington*, the origin of this derisive criticism on a gentleman's head-gear was as follows: 'When the first Reform Parliament met, the Duke went into the Peers' Gallery of the House of Commons—Sir William Fraser says that it was the Bar, but this part of his statement is due, I should say, to a slip of the pen—to survey the members. Expecting, of course to be questioned, and knowing that his words would be repeated, the Duke, prompt as usual, was ready for the inquisition; and when asked, on walking back to the House of Lords, what he thought of the new Parliament, he evaded responsibility by saying, "I never saw so many shocking bad hats in my life." The catchword soon lost its political associations, and after a few years, was merged in the purely imbecile query, "Who's your hatter?"'—G. A. Sala, in *D. T.*, 28th July 1894.

Bad Shilling (*Common*). The last, *e.g.*, 'That's a bad shillin', that is, for there ain't another beyinde it, you know.'

Bad young man (*L. Peoples*', 1881). Antithesis to Good Young Man (*q.v.*).

That the fatted calf, who had never been a prodigal, should suffer death in honour of the bad young man has never seemed to me strict dramatic justice.—*Ref.*, 18th January 1885.

Badger, to (*Peoples*'). To worry. From worrying a badger in his hole until he comes out to show fight. (*See* Draw.) It forms a remarkable example of complete inversion of the original meaning, for it was the badger which was worried—he was never the worrier. Nowadays he is the aggressor.

Immediately after the explosion at the House of Commons on Saturday I went to see 'the scene'. Thanks to the courtesy of the officials in charge—sorely badgered by M.P.'s, peers, and public persons, who had come out of idle curiosity—I was able to make a thorough inspection both of the House and of Westminster Hall.—*Ref.*, 1st February 1885. (*See* also G.O.M.)

Badges and Bulls' eyes (*Army*, 1899). In the Boer Revolt (October 1899), the officers' medals and badges offered fatal bulls' eyes for the Bore rifles.

The question has been much discussed whether, in view of the terrible gaps made in the roll of officers, they were not even yet too much marked out as Boer targets by what General Gatacre called badges and bulls' eyes.—*D. T.*, 21st December 1899.

Bag o' Beer. (*Lowest people's*). Bacchanalian brevity—for it means, and nothing else than a quart—half of fourpenny porter and half of fourpenny ale. This once stood 'pot o' four 'arf an' 'arf', reduced to 'four 'arf', and thence to 'bag o' beer'.

Bags o' Mystery. (*Peoples*'). A satirical term for sausages, because no man but the maker knows what is in them.

'If they're going to keep running-in polony fencers for putting rotten geegee into the bags of mystery, I hope they won't leave fried-fish-pushers alone.'

This term took its rise about 1850, long before the present system of market-inspection was organised. But this term remained long after sausages were fairly wholesome. The 'bag' refers to the gut which contained the chopped meat.

Bag and Baggage. Thoroughly, completely. It once more became popular from a phrase in a speech by Gladstone in reference to the Turk in

Europe, whom he recommended should be turned out of Europe 'bag and baggage'.

The truth of the matter is that all the petty States which won over the sympathies of sentimental politicians by their eternal whinings against that 'big bully, the Turk', have proved themselves past masters in the art of oppressing minorities, now that the tables have turned. They would like to carry into effect the 'bag and baggage' theory, and make a clean sweep of foreigners, to whatever race or religion these latter may belong.—*D. T.*, 13th August 1885.

Bagger, Bag-thief. (*Thieves'*). A stealer of rings by seizing the hand. Possibly from the French 'bague', a ring.

Baiard (*Peoples'*). A good fellow. Still now and again heard in the provinces; of course from Bayard, the chevalier '*sans peur et sans reproche*'.

'Thou'rt a real baiard—thou art. How now, mates, what baiards have we here?'—Garrick, *Abel Drugger*.

Bailiff of Marsham (*Fens*, 17 cent.). Ague.

There was so much water constantly lying about Ely, that in olden times the Bishop of Ely was accustomed to go in his boat to Cambridge. When the outfalls of the Ouse became choked, the surrounding districts were subject to severe inundations; and after a heavy fall of rain, or after a thaw in winter, when the river swelled suddenly, the alarm spread abroad—'The Bailiff of Bedford is coming'—the Ouse passing through that town. But there was even a more terrible bailiff than he of Bedford, for when a man was stricken down by the ague, it was said of him, he is arrested by the Bailiff of Marsham, this disease extensively prevailing all over the district when the poisoned air of the marshes began to work.—Smiles, *Lives of the Engineers.*

A fine example of passing English being helped by old phrases, for when the draining of the fens had been practically accomplished, ague ceased as an endemic disease. The term, however, is still heard now and again at any point between Boston in the north and Chelmsford in the south. It is metaphorically used to suggest approaching death.

Baked dinner (*Jocose, Prison*, 19 cent.). Bread—which is baked. The phrase was habitually used at Bridewell, this prison having been utilized until quite recently as a place of detention rather than as a prison for the punishment of troublesome city apprentices bound to freed men of the City of London. They were taken before the City Chamberlain, who in extreme cases sent the youngsters to Bridewell, in Bridge Street, Blackfriars, where a painting or two of Hogarth's are still to be found. Here the offenders were kept in honourable durance for a fortnight or more without labour, their only punishment being the absence of liberty. It was upon these neophytes that the trick was played of telling them that they were to have 'Baked Dinner'. Their disappointment, and the explanation of the term afforded huge merriment, reiterated on every possible occasion.

Baker's Dozen. Thirteen—grimly used for a family of twelve and another.

The 'baker's dozen', meaning thirteen, dates back to the time of Edward I., when very rigid laws were enacted regarding the sale of bread by bakers. The punishment for falling short in the sale of loaves by the dozen was so severe that, in order to run no risk, the bakers were accustomed to give thirteen or fourteen loaves to the dozen, and thus arose this peculiar expression.—*Newsp. Cutting.*

Balaclava (1856-60). A full beard, first seen upon the faces of the English army upon their return to England from Crimea. The new departure was instantly dubbed with the name of the most popular of the three great battles (Alma, Balaclava, Inkermann), the name probably being chosen by reason of the brilliancy of the charge of the Light Brigade. French writers who had visited the Great Exhibition of 1851, and who had been struck by the absolute absence of the moustache (except in the case of some military men), and the utter absence of the beard, without exception, were astonished upon return visits half-a-dozen years afterwards, to find Englishmen were bearded like the pard. Britons upon the principle of reaction always going the whole hog, grew all the hair they could, and the mere moustache of Frenchmen was nowhere in the fight. Interestingly enough, exactly as the wild, unkempt beard of 'The Terror' dwindled into the moustache for the young, and the côtelette (mutton-chop) for the elderly, so the Balaclava (which abated the razor, as a daily protesting sacrifice to anti-gallicanism) toned down by '70, into the various beards of to-day—the Peaked, the Spade, the Square, and other varieties of Tudor beards. These remained until the Flange, or Dundreary (*see* 1872-73),came in and cleared the chin, to be followed by the Scraper. To-day the 'York' prevails—the short, pointed beard still worn by the Prince of Wales.

Bald-head (*American*). An old man.

The house-fly flies an average of three miles per day. He can't be biting babies and bald heads all the time, you know.—*Texas Siftings.*

Byron used this term contemptuously in *The Two Foscari*, Act iii., sc. 1. MARINA.—'Held in the bondage of ten bald heads,'—referring to the Council of Ten.

Bald-headed Butter (*Com. London*). Butter free from hairs. First publicly heard in a police-court case, where the satire had led an indignant cheesemonger to take law in his own hands.

'Waiter, I'll take a bit of bald-headed butter, if you please.'

Balley, To (*Com. Lond.*). To be off, *e.g.*, 'I thought it was time to be off, so I balleyed.' (*See* Skip, Valse, Polka.)

Balloon (*Tailors'*). A week's enforced idleness from want of work. French, *bilan*, officially a balance-sheet book, figuratively a sentence, condemnation.

Balloon-juice (*Public-house*, 1883). Soda-water; presumably suggested by its gassy nature.

It's as good as a bottle of balloon-juice after a night's hard boozing.—*Newsp. Cutting.*

Balloon-juice Lowerer. A total abstainer, the 'lowerer' from the use of 'to lower' for 'to swallow'.

To be a booze fencer now, is to be a mark for every balloon-juice lowerer who can't take a drop of beer or spirits without making a beast of himself.—*Newsp. Cutting.*

Bally (*Sporting*, 1884 on). Excessive, great. Perhaps an evasion of 'bloody'.

'Too bad, too bad! after getting fourteen days or forty bob, the bally rag don't even mention it. I shall turn teetotal'. . . . 'Has that bally Ptolemy won, d'ye know? What price did he start at?' . . . 'If you had been born an elephant instead of a bally jackass, you would have had your trunk on the end of your nose, when you could have seen to it yourself.'—*Sporting Times*, 11th April 1885.

Balmedest Balm (*Low London*). Balm in the extreme.

'It is just a little the balmedest balm you ever plastered on your love-stricken heart. Try it, Annetta; and don't be afraid of it; spread it on thick.'—*Newsp. Cutting.*

Balsam (*Sporting*). Money. From both medicaments being of such an agreeable character. Originally confined to dispensing chemists.

Ban (*Com. Irish*, 18 *cent.* on). Lord-Lieutenant. There is a supposed association between 'ban', curse or edict, and 'banshee', the precursor of sorrow. Still in use, *e.g.*, 'Bedad, one ban or anoder, 'tis the same man.'

Banbury (*London*, 1894). One of the more recent shapes of 'jam', 'biscuit', 'cake', 'confectionery', 'tart' (*qq.v.*) —a loose woman.

Witness took several names and addresses, and some of the females described themselves as 'Banburys', and said they got their living as best they could.—Raid on the Gardenia Club, *The People*, 4th February 1894.

Baned (*Prov.*). Poisoned, *e.g.*, 'I'll have 'ee baned like a rat.' Abbreviation of henbane.

What if my house is troubled with a rat,
And I be pleased to give ten thousand ducats
To have it baned?
—*Merchant of Venice*, Act iv.

Banded (*Low London*). Hungry. May be Romany, or literal, hunger pressing like a band on the stomach, *e.g.*, 'I've been fair banded all the blooming week.'

Bang (*S. Exchange*). To loudly and plentifully offer a certain stock with the intention of lowering its price.

When any adventurers — call them bears or bulls, or any other animals— start to bang the shares, do not lend yourself to the game they are playing; sit close on your shares.—*D. T.*, 2nd June 1898.

Bang (To) (*Fashion*, 1870-95). Mode of dressing the hair in a line of fixed curls over the forehead. Chiefly used by women in England. Introduced by the then Princess of Wales. Commonly called to 'fringe' the hair.

An American lady has written: 'If for

a few brief hours of triumphant bang you are willing to undergo a long night of anguish, roll three rows of these wooden fire-crackers in your perfumed tresses.'—*D. N.*, 21st October 1886.

The man who bangs his hair hasn't enough sense to blow out his brains, even if he possessed any.—*N. Y. Commerc. Advertiser.*

This fashion at last gave way (1895) to 'undulated bands' covering the forehead, and, more fashionably, also the ears.

Bang Mary (*Kitchen*). The English cook's translation of 'bain Marie', the small saucepans within another saucepan of boiling water, an apparatus devised by a French cook named Marie. This obvious simplification of French is a good example of the vulgar habit of fitting foreign words to well-known English ones of something like similar sound ('folk-etymology').

Bang through the Elephant (*Low London*). A finished course of dissipation, as thus: drunk rhymed into elephant's trunk, abbrev. to elephant.

'You're no fool, don't you know, you're up to slum; been right bang through the elephant.'

Bang Up (*Low London*). First-class, superior. 'Bang' probably from the commanding cry of a cannon or gun, while 'up' is always an aspiring adverb, or even verb. However, 'bang' may be a vivid translation of 'bien', an exclamation certainly used at the court of Charles II.

Bang up to the Elephant (*London*, 1882). Perfect, complete, unapproachable. The 'Elephant' ('Elephant and Castle Tavern,' South London), had for years been the centre of South London tavern-life when (1882) Jumbo, an exceptionally large elephant at the Zoological Gardens, became popular through certain articles in the *D. T.* The public were pleased to think Jumbo refused to leave England and the gardens for America. He, however, did ultimately, with no emotion, leave behind him this bit of passing English.

'The fly flat thinks himself so blooming sharp, so right bang up to the elephant, that he's got an idea that no sharper would ever try to take him on.'

Banian Day. *See* Banyan Day.

Banjoeys (*Soc.*, 90's). Banjoists. A happy application of the comic joey —comic since the time of Grimaldi. An evasion of the 'ist' and invention of a friendly term at the same time. Said to be a trouvaille by the Prince of Wales, who brought banjo orchestras into fashion, being a banjoey himself.

Bank Up, To (*N. Country coal districts*). To complete, to more than complete—referring to building up a huge fire, *e.g.*, 'Us sooped yell till niight, an' then us poot away room! Then we banked up with a jolly dance— and the tykes did go it.'

The Helston Flora Day—or 'Furry Day'—was a go-as-you-please sort of festivity, where people danced in the streets, waltzed in and out each other's doors, and hilariously 'banked up' these entertainments by holding a bird show and running foot races.—*D. T.*, 20th August 1896.

Banker Chapel Ho (*E. London*). Whitechapel, and, in another shape, vulgar language. The word got in this way. In the first place, it is a ludicrous Italian translation—*Bianca*, white; *cappella*, chapel = White Chapel. Then Anglicization entering in, the first word got into 'Banker' and the second back into Chapel, with the addition of the rousing and cheery 'Oh!' 'Ah, Mrs Dicks, but you know the force of the sweet Italian quotation "Giotto Cimabue di Fra Angelico in Sistine"!' To which Mrs D——, originally from the district, might reply: 'Now, Ned, there's a good feller, none o' your Banker Chapel Ho!'

Bant, To (*Soc.*, 1860 on). To reduce stoutness. From the name 'Banting', that of a very fashionable funeral undertaker, who reduced himself many stones by the use of non-fat-producing food. He had a whale-bone frame made to fit his once large waistcoats and coats, and wore the whole over his reduced size—removing this armour to produce a full effect.

The Globe Dime under Meehan and Wilson has not been behind its neighbours in furnishing attractive novelties, leading off with John Craig, a champion of obesity, who has 'banted' down to a net weight of 758 pounds avoirdupois.— *N. Y. Mercury*, 13th January 1885.

Banyan Day (*Middle-class*). No meat; only 'bread and cheese and kisses' through twenty-four hours. Of course from India and the Army, the cooling banyan suggesting that all the rupees went yesterday.

If the actor has been taking the M.P. unawares on banyan day, when there wasn't enough cold meat to go round, I certainly think he owes him an apology.—*Ref.*, 25th February 1882.

In Devonshire the word is even applied to scrappy, tawdry dressing, *e.g.*, 'What a banyan sight to be sure!' (The word must be pronounced as a spondee).

Those were the halcyon days of British industries. The banyan days have been with the miners since then, and seem likely to stay.—*Ref.*, 2nd May 1886.

They told me that on Mondays, Wednesdays, and Fridays, the ship's company had no allowance for meat, and that these meagre days were called banyan days, the reason of which they did not know; but I have since learned they take their denomination from a sect of devotees in some parts of the East Indies, who never taste flesh.—Smollett, *Roderick Random*, ch. xxv.

'Banyan' is sometimes used for the skin.

The first hour found him beastly drunk; the second, robbed and stripped to his banyan. — *Rattlin the Reefer*, ch. xliii.

Barbecue (*Old English*). Any animal, bird, or large fish cooked whole, without cutting, from beard (*barbe*) to tail (*queue*).

The triumphal procession of a band of music, to welcome Mrs Langtry, was a comparatively ancient device smacking somewhat of both the circus and the institution known in America as a '*barbecue*' (a festival where a bullock or sheep is roasted entire, set to music).—*Newsp. Cutting*.

In the United States the word now represents a noisy political meeting.

I see they announce a big, old-fashioned barbecue to be given next week by the Brooklyn Democrats, at which Cleveland and Hendricks, Presidential candidates, are to participate. This barbecue holdin' used to be a very popular form of political excitement in the olden time.—*Newsp. Cutting*.

The barbecue was announced as a 'Monster Democratic Rally', and 'A Grand Political Carnival and Ox-Roast'.—*Newsp. Cutting*.

Barber's Cat (*Peoples'*). A skinny man. Perhaps a corruption of 'bare brisket', also used for a thin fellow—the brisket being the thinnest part of beef.

Barclay Perkins (*Peoples'*). Stout From the brewing firm Barclay, Perkins & Co.

Barges (*Peoples'*, c. 1884). Imitation breasts, which arrived from France, and prevailed for about four years. Named probably from their likeness to the wide prow of canal-barges.

Bark up a wrong Tree (*American*, *e.g.*, 19 *cent.*). Mr Rees, an American etymologist, says:

This is a very common expression at the West. It originated, as many of these vulgarisms do, from very simple causes. In hunting, a dog drives a racoon, as he imagines, up a certain tree, at the foot of which he keeps up a constant barking, by which he attracts the attention of his master, who vainly looks on the tree indicated. While endeavouring to find the animal he discovers it on another tree, from which it escapes and gets beyond his reach. Hence the phrase 'To bark up the wrong tree'. It has become general in its application, denoting that a person has mistaken his object, or pursuing the wrong cause to obtain it, etc.

Barkis is Willin' (*Peoples'*, 1850). Form of proposal of marriage, still very popular in lower-middle classes. From Dickens' *David Copperfield*, ch. v.

'Ah,' he said, slowly turning his eyes towards me. 'Well, if you was writin' to her p'raps you'd recollect to say that Barkis was willin': would you?'

Characters hardly less distinguishable for truth as well as oddity are the kind old nurse and her husband, the carrier, whose vicissitudes alike of love and mortality are condensed into three words since become part of universal speech, *Barkis is willin'*. Foster, *Life of Dickens*, vol. iii., p. 18.

In cross-examination she said that the drinking fits usually occurred when Mr Dunn was from home. She did not think that the Walls were fit company for Mrs Dunn. Mr Wall did not pay the witness any attention. Mrs Wall wanted to force her son on the witness, but she resented it. — Sir C. Russell: 'Was "Barkis willing"?'—The witness: 'No.' (Laughter.)—*Dunn v. Dunn & Wall*, 30th January 1888.

Barmy (*Peoples'*). Generally 'a bit barmy', rather mad, 'cracked'. From St Bartholomew, the patron saint of mad people. The pronunciation of the saint's name was Barthelemy—passing into Bartlemy (*cf.* Bartlemy Fair), and Barmy became the final form, *e.g.*, 'The family has always been a bit barmy in the crumpet.' (Why crumpet should stand for head is, so far, beyond discovery.)

Barn. A public ball-room; probably because one of the last of the London garden ball-rooms was Highbury Barn, North London. (*See* Barner.)

Barn-stormers (*Theatrical*, 18 *cent.* on). Inferior actors who play in barns. Used, of course, in scorn by those comedians who have reached permanent footlights. The term has now almost passed away in consequence of the enormous increase in the number of theatres which now exist, even in the smallest towns. The 'barnstormers' hire a barn near a village, and there give their performance—frequently of Shakespeare.

Miss Helen Bancroft, who recently played in this city, was announced as with a barn-storming company. *N. Y. Mercury*, 1883.

Barner (*North London*, 1860-80). A 'roaring' blade, a fast man of North London; from Highbury Barn, one of those rustic London gardens which became common casinos. The term remained until the Barn was swept away for building purposes.

Barneries (*Strand*, 1887). Last outcome of S. Kensington exhibitions ending in '-ries'.

Considerable commotion ensued at the Adelphi Stores, Strand, on account of the new proprietress, Miss Barnes, being presented with a testimonial. Miss B. has already won favour in her new venture, and it is thought the 'Barneries' will be much affected by *the* profession.—*Ref.*, 20th February 1887.

Barney (*L. Eng.*). A quarrel, row, generally of an innocuous character.

Then Selby runs out, and goes into the lodging-house to get another knife, but I stops him, and the barney was all over, but as we was agoing along to the hospital up comes a copper. — *People*, 6th January 1895.

Baron George (*S. London*, 1882). A portly man. This term was derived from the Christian name of a Mr George Parkes, a portly theatrical lessee in S. London, who came to be called Baron George; *e.g.*, 'He's quite the Baron George!'

Barrel of Salt, To take with a (*American*). To accept under reserve, with incredulity. From the Latin phrase *cum grano salis*.

He is therefore to be taken with a barrel of salt.—*Newsp. Cutting.*

Barrel of Treacle (*Low London*). The condition of love, suggested by the sweetness of this cloying synonym.

'Pon our sivey, we don't want to poke fun at chaps who've fallen into that barrel of treacle called love, and make up to their little lumps of soap in the operpro sort of way, and no blooming kid.—*Newsp. Cutting*, 1883.

Barrered (*Low Life*). A corruption of barrowed, from to barrow or put in a barrow, not that of the gardener but of the coster. Distinct from 'shettered' (*q.v.*), intimating that the drunken gentleman was removed by his friends and not by the police; *e.g.*, 'Which mum, we 'ad to barrer 'im 'ome. He were too that 'eavy to carry.' In St Giles the highest shapes of involuntary locomotion is 'wheeled' (in a cab)—then follows barrered—then the declension is reached in 'shettered' (shuttered). This term is passing away with the shutters themselves.

Barrikin (*Com. London*). Barking, chatter.

Let 'em say what they like, and howl themselves dotty. Their barrikin only makes 'em thirsty, and when they've got hot coppers through chucking the barrikin out too blooming strong they go in for a little quiet booze themselves, make no error.—*Newsp. Cutting.*

Barrister's (*Thieves'*). A thieves' coffee-house, derived from a celebrated host of this name.

The witness remarked that he could not waste his time; and Richards said he could not make out where he was, and he would go to the 'barrister's' and look for him. (The witness explained, amid a roar of laughter, that a 'barrister's' was a slang term for a coffee-house frequented by thieves.)—*Cutting.*

Baseball (*American*, 1880 on). Small, insignificant. Sometimes heard in Liverpool. Suggested by the small size of the ball in question.

Yesterday a *Mercury* reporter saw Heer within the prison walls. As he stepped into the corridor from his cell he evinced some nervousness, and stroked a 'baseball' moustache faintly perceptible on his upper lip, with his cigarette-stained fingers.—*N. Y. Mercury*, 1880.

Bash (*Thieves'*, 1870). To beat heavily with the fist only. Probably the most modern onomatope — the word doubtless being an attempt to vocalize the sound made by a fist striking full in the face.

This real lady said, 'I ain't any the wuss for being able to take my own part, and I should think myself very small beer, and no kid, if I couldn't bash any dona in our court.'—*Newsp. Cutting.*

Women of susceptible and nervous temperaments are asked to come to theatres and see for themselves how they hocuss and 'bash' people at low riverside houses.—*Cutting.*

Mr Chaplin: 'Bless me, yes! Didn't you know that he had offered Greenwood, of *The Telegraph*, a Civil List pension if he would get Lord Randolph "bashed" and dropped into the Thames?'—*Ref.*, 1882.

Basher (*Mod. Low. Lond.*). A name applied to low fighting rowdies paid to bruise and damage.

The villain of the piece and the 'bashers', or hireling assassins, are supposed to carry on their trade unchecked in Ratcliffe Highway and Wapping.

Basket of Oranges (*Australian, passing to England*). Pretty woman. A metaphor founded on another metaphor—the basket of oranges being a phrase for a discovery of nuggets of gold in the gold fields. One of the few flashes of new language from Australasia; *e.g.*, 'She's a basket of oranges fit for any man's table.'

Bastile (*Street*, 18 *cent.* on). Any place of detention, but generally a prison or a workhouse. More commonly 'Steel'. The horror of the Bastile felt by all Frenchmen in the 18th century spread to England, and the name was associated with oppression. The word was particularly applied to Cold Bath Fields prison, Clerkenwell, which was called 'The Steel' until its final fall about 1890. The last new application of this word was (1870) to the Peabody Buildings for working men, erected in the Black Friars Road, London. It was the first of these buildings, which have long since been accepted and even battled for by working people. But at first the prejudice was very marked. The term has not been applied since 1880.

Bath Oliver (*W. Eng.*, 18 *cent.* on). A biscuit with a historical character.

'Bobs' fights on 'Bath Olivers'. Shortly before leaving for the Cape he paid a visit to his sister, Mrs Sherston, of Bath, and took away with him to the front a bountiful supply of Bath Olivers. He sent home for a further supply, which Lady Roberts took with her when she went to join him. It is not every one who has heard of the Oliver. It is a biscuit, and owes its name to the celebrated Dr Oliver, a Bath physician, and the friend of Pope, Warburton, and other eighteenth century notabilities. When on his death-bed, the doctor called for his coachman, and gave him the recipe for the biscuits, ten sacks of flour, and a hundred sovereigns. The lucky fellow started making and selling the biscuits in a small shop in Green Street, Bath. And there they are made and sold to this day.—*M. A. P.*, 19th May 1900.

Batter through (*Peoples'*). To struggle, beat thro', from French *battre*, to beat, probably used in the time of Charles II.; *e.g.*, 'He battered through the part somehow!'

Batty-fang (*Low London*). To thrash thoroughly. Evidently *battre à fin*. But how it passed into English, or whence it came, unless from the heated court of Charles II., it would be difficult to say.

Baub (*Cockney*, 19 *cent.*). One of the commonest modes of evasively referring to the Deity—modes in which some idea of the original word, either in length, syllable, or letters, or even rhyme, is to be traced; *e.g.*, 'S'elp me Baub, I didn't go for to do it.' However, the word really comes from Catholic England, and is 'babe'— meaning the infant Saviour.

Baudinguet (*Parisian*). A nickname given to Prince Napoleon in 1848, from the name of the mason who aided the Prince to escape from Ham, where he was imprisoned. It stuck to Napoleon III. even to 1870, when a war correspondent at Sarbrück (July 1870) asked a soldier if he knew whether the emperor had arrived. The reply was: 'Oui; Baudinguet est arrivé.'

Bayreuth Hush (*Soc.*, 1890). Intense silence. From the noiselessness of the opera house at Bayreuth (Bavaria) when a Wagner festival is about to commence.

If it cannot be said that the peculiar order of stillness known as the 'Bayreuth hush' made itself felt in the Covent Garden opera house last evening, yet there is no denying the spirit of expectation and attention in which a full audience brought itself to the opening performance of the long-expected *Ring* cycle.—*D. T.*, 7th June 1898.

Bazaar Rumour (*Army*, 1882 on). Doubtful news. Equivalent to 'Hamburg'. The result of the Egyptian occupation, referring to native news spread through the bazaars of Cairo.

I am able to contradict on official authority the statement published in London that there was a bazaar rumour that the Mahdi and his followers were marching on Dongola. — *D. N.*, 10th November 1884.

Bazaar'd (*Soc.*, 1882). Robbed. From the extortion exercised by remorseless, smiling English ladies at bazaars. Applied everywhere. Replaced, 'rooked' in society; *e.g.*, 'I was awfully bazaar'd at Sandown.'

A gentleman coming home from a bazaar met a highwayman, who accosted him with the professional formula of 'Your money or your life.' 'My dear sir,' said the gentleman, 'I should be most happy to give you my money if I had any, but I have just been to a bazaar.' The highwayman at once acknowledged the force of this argument, and further was so touched by the circumstances that he offered the victim a small contribution. — *Newsp. Cutting*.

Beach-comber (*Nautical*). A pirate, a beach-loafer, or a yachting tourist. In its earlier shape it referred to the pirate who made a landing and swept up all he could—that is, he 'combed the beach'. The pirate being quite dead in the Western Seas, this sense of the term is now only applied in the East, and generally to the Chinese *marin d'industrie*. The use of the word in its earlier meaning is sometimes figurative, especially on the American coast, *e.g.*, 'I was beach-combed out of every red cent.' In its later sense the word means a globe-trotter, or rather a beach-trotter, who travels only on land within easy distance of his wandering yacht.

It would be better to enter the army from the ranks, or to go gold-mining in Chiapas, or try ivory and Central Africa, or even to be a beach-comber in some insular paradise of the Southern Seas, which, as Mr Stevenson is showing, is the best kind of lotus-eating life left to mankind. — *D. N.*, 11th February 1891.

Probably Mr Stevenson would not be displeased at the title of a literary beach-comber. — *D. N.*, 27th December 1890.

Beadles (*American*). People of Virginia; probably from their high, old-fashioned behaviour, which the Northerner associates with that expiring church functionary.

Beak (*Low London*, 18 and 19 *cent.*). A magistrate. Probably from lawyers, as Thackeray has somewhere remarked, being celebrated for a vast expanse of aquiline nose. Mr G. A. Sala (*D. T.*, 28th July 1896), urges a different origin:

A contributor to *Notes and Queries* states that Hookey Walker was a magistrate of much-dreaded acuteness and incredulity, whose Roman nose gave the title of 'beak' to all his successors. The term is derived from the Anglo-Saxon 'beag', a necklace or collar worn as an emblem of authority. Sir John Fielding, half-brother of the novelist, was known as the 'blind beak', and he died in 1780, sixty years before the cry of 'Hookey Walker' became popular.

Beak-hunter (*Thieves'*). Annexer of poultry.

Bean-eater (*New York*). A term of scorn for a citizen of Boston, referring to the former Sunday custom observed by some Bostonians of accepting for dinner on that day cold belly of pork, and colder beans. (*See* Stars and Stripes.)

Circus tricks! circus tricks! you bean-eaters! Can't you tell when a feller's a-dying. — *Cutting*.

Beanfeast (*Peoples'*). A treat. Used generally in reference to enjoyments, and derived from the yearly feast of employees in factories and shops, of which much of the expense is borne by the employer. Originally the treat consisted of broad beans and boiled bacon, which must have been a great delight when few green vegetables were obtainable throughout winter.

Oh, it was quite a beanfeast—only one mouse [=black-eye]. — *Cutting*.

Sometimes it is used satirically to denote a riot, *e.g.*, 'What a beanfeast!' parallel with the American 'picnic'.

Beano (*Peoples'*). Great rejoicing. From bean-feast, reduced to bean, with the ever rejoicing *o* added. (*See* Boyno.) It may be a connected coalition with 'bueno'—common in London Docks—being Lingua Franca.

One day last week I said 'Good-bye!'
To my kids, my wife, and home,
I met some pals, and away we went
For a 'beano' by the foam.
— *Cutting*, 1897.

Beaner (*Peoples'*). Chastisement. 'To give beans' is to inflict punishment, a phrase derived from boys beating each other with a collection of horse-beans in the foot of a sock. The word 'beaner' is sometimes used ironically, calling something agreeable which is quite otherwise, e.g., 'That's a beaner—that is!'

Beanpea (*London Streets*). A coalescing of B and P (*q.v.*) into one word, the *d* being dropped. Doubtless the outcome of time, and the droll idea of combining the two vegetables which come in almost at the same time. Still hastily, too hastily, applied to effeminate youths. The case was thrown out of Court when it came before Lord Chief-Justice Cockburn.

Beans. Sovereigns. Possibly a corruption of *bien* (a sovereign being certainly a 'bien'). But it may be a market-gardeners' trade phrase. But if so, why beans? Why not strawberries, or asparagus, or some other of the more valuable products?

Be-argered (*Peoples'*). Drunk. The 'argered' is 'argumentative', a drunken man being commonly full, not only of beer, but also of argument.

Beast (*Youths'*, 1870). A bicycle—the first endearing metaphor bestowed upon this locomotive. Used in no way derogatively, but as though a horse—a hunter. (*See* Bone-shaker, Craft, Crock.) But, as time went on and the 'byke' became a power, it ceased to be associated with a mere animal; by 1897 no term could be too distinguished by which to designate the all-conquering machine.

Beat-up (*Soc.*, 19 *cent.*). To call upon unceremoniously; from beating-up game, which is certainly not treated with politeness when wanted, e.g., 'I'll beat you up on Monday, or when I can.' (*See* Stir up, Have out.)

Beau (*Peoples'*). A man of fashion—early 18 century, of course direct from the French, and evidently from 'est il beau?' for before 'homme' it changes its formation: 'un bel homme!' Johnson says, 'A man whose great care is to deck his person.' Still used in country places. 'What a beau ye be, Tummis!' Earliest classic use by Dryden, 'What will not beaux attempt to please the fair?' Swift says, 'You will become the delight of nine ladies in ten, and the envy of ninety-nine beaux in a hundred.' Never now heard in towns. (*See* Spark.)

Beau-catcher (*Peoples'*, 1854-60). A flat hook-shaped curl, after the Spanish manner, gummed on each temple, and made of the short temple hair, spelt sometimes *bow-catcher*. It is synonymous with 'Kiss curl'. Now obsolete on this side of the Pyrenees.

Beaver-tail (*Mid.-class*, 1860). A feminine mode of wearing the back-hair, turned up loose in a fine thread net (called 'invisible') which fell well on to the shoulders. When the net is now worn, generally by lazy girls of the people, it is fixed above the neck. Obviously from the shape of the netted hair to a beaver's flat and comparatively shapeless tail. The well-marked fashion in hair for the people's women folk which followed was the 'Piccadilly Fringe' (*q.v.*).

Bedder (*Oxford-'er'*). Bedroom.

Bedford Go (*Tavern*, 1835-60). A peculiar oily chuckle usually accompanied by the words, 'I b'lieve yer my bu-o-oy.' From the style of Paul Bedford, an actor for many years with Wright, at the old Adelphi. Bedford always was famous for his chuckle, but he raised it to fame in connection with the above credo, uttered in the celebrated melodrama, *The Green Bushes*. (*See* Joey, O. Smith.)

Bee (*American*). An industrious meeting—as quilting, or apple-gathering.

One day the boys over in the Bend had a hanging bee and invited us to come down and see a chap swing for his crimes.—*Detroit Free Press*, January 1883.

Beef (*Theatrical*, 1880). A bawl or yell. Probably the career of this word is—'bull—bellow—beef,' the last word elegantly suggesting the declaration of a noisy bull.

At the back was the musical box, and an obliging hammer-wholloper beefed the names of the different squallers and bawlers as they slung on the boards.—*Cutting*.

Beef (*Clare Market*—extinct). Cat's meat, e.g., 'Give me my mouser's one d. of beef.'

Beef a Bravo (*Music-hall*). To bellow, bravo like a bull, in order to lead the applause for a friend who has just left the stage.

Beef-à-la-Mode (*Com. London*). Stewed beef called *à-la-mode* on the *lucus a non lucendo* principle—for it is not a fashionable dish. It came from Paris, where, in the days of sign-boards, a restaurant where this dish was sold showed the sign of a bullock seated in clothes of fashion.

You can swill yourselves out with *beef-à-la-mode*, as toffs call it, for two d., or you can indulge in the aristocratic sausage and mashed and half-a-pint of pongelow all for four d.—*Cutting.*

Beef-heads or Cow-boys (*American*). People of Texas and the West of U.S.A.—from the general employment of the inhabitants being the harrying of cattle.

Beef-headed. Stupid. Cattle being heavy, stolid, and torpid.

Beef-tugging (*City*). Eating cookshop meat, not too tender, at lunchtime. Dinner is not clerkly known in the E.C. district as occurring between 1 and 2 P.M.

Been and gone and done it (*Peoples'*). Very general mode of saying that the speaker has got married, *N.B.*—gone is in this relation generally pronounced 'gorne'.

Marius and Florence St John have 'been and gorne and done it' at last. The registrar of hatches, matches, and dispatches has tied what for them is the 'dissoluble' knot.—*Newsp. Cutting.*

Been there (*Amer.-Eng.*, 1870). Had experience; *e.g.*, 'Thank 'ee—no betting; I've been there.'

Some reasons why I left off drinking whiskey, by one who has been there.—Paper in *Philadelphia, Sat. Ev. Post*, 1877.

He wants a man who understands his case, who sympathises with him, who has been there himself, and who will give him a vent for his emotions at a reasonable rate per line.—*N. York Puck,* 14th September 1883.

Beer and Skittles (*Peoples'*). A synonym for pleasure; *e.g.*, 'Ah, Joe, if a bloke's life was all beer and skittles *we* shouldn't be doing time.'

But life on a yacht is not all beer and skittles, nor is it always afternoon. There is the dreadful morning time, when the crew begin to stir on deck, and earthquake and chaos seem to have come.—*D. N.*, 22nd August 1885.

Beerage (*Soc.*, 19 *cent.*). A satirical rendering of peerage, referring to the brewery lords, chiefly of the great houses of Allsopp and of Guinness.

Dr Edwards as a temperance worker had some very strong things to say a few months ago on the subject of the ennoblement of rich brewers. Of course he opposed it on moral grounds, but some of the old nobility would be inclined to agree with his denunciation of the 'beerage' for other reasons—*Newsp. Cutting.*

Beer-bottle (*Street*). A stout, red-faced man.

Beer-eaters (19 *cent.*). A great consumer of beer, one who more than drinks it—who lives on it.

The Norwegians are a fine and a sturdy race, but not at all like I had imagined them, after all I had read about Sigurd and Sintram and Sea-egg-fried, and the Beerseekers, who must not be confounded with a race peculiar to London, found mainly upon licensed premises, and distinguished among their kind as the Beer-eaters.—*Ref.*, 21st August 1887.

Beer-juggers (*Amer. Miner's*). Bar-women.

The only busy people in the place were the wife of the pianist, who sat by him industriously sewing, and the women who sold drink. These latter are called beer-juggers, and fill a large place in the evening life of the miner. *Journey Round the World*: 'of LEADVILLE.'—*D. N.*, October 1883.

Beer O! (*Trades*). The cry when an artisan does a something, or omits to do a something, the result of which in either case being a fine to be paid in pongelow. The exclamation is taken up by the whole shop, or rather was, as the custom is now obsolete.

Beetroot Mug (*Street*). A red face—passed for many years into Ally Sloper, a character in comic fiction since 1870, invented by Charles Ross, a humorist of the more popular kind.

Before the War (*Soc.*, 1880). From America. A new shape of 'the good old times'. Whenever a ganache in the U.S.A. wants to condemn the present he compares it with the time 'before the War (1860-65)'.

'How beautiful the moon is to-night!' remarked an American belle to her lover, as they spooned in the open. 'Yes,' was the reply; 'but you should have seen it before the war!'—*Newsp. Cutting.*

Begorra, also **By Jabers** (*Irish*). Solemn Irish oaths. Both words have been adopted by common English folk.

Spoken—Yes, by jabers; he's the best boy that ever was. Sure he's shown such powers of discernment ever since the first day he was born, that begorra he knows more now than ever I've forgotten. —*Newsp. Cutting.*

Behind Yourself (*Peoples'*, 1896 on). Too far behind, quite in the rear, far from absolutely up to date. Antithesis of Too previous; *e.g.*, 'What—you thought to-day was Thursday? Why, it's Saturday afternoon. You're behind yourself, man, and a deal at that.'

Behindativeness (*Soc.*, 1888). Referring to the dress pannier—one of the shapes with which fashion is for ever varying the natural outline of the feminine frame; *e.g.*, 'That lady has got a deal of behindativeness.'

Belcher (*Sporting*, 19 *cent.*). A handkerchief pattern, round spots, light or dark upon a dark or light ground. From a prize-fighter, Jim Belcher, who always carried into the ring a wiping handkerchief of this kind. After Belcher's time, the 'belcher' split up into colours, every prize-fighter having his own tints. Belcher's original was white spots on dark blue ground. Until quite recent years, a spotted neck-tie was called a Belcher: now called a 'moon-tie'.

At one time 'belchers' were made of that pattern which is affected in that spotty coat which Mr H. B. Conway sports in *The Widow Hunt.*—*Entr'acte*, June 1885.

Belittle, To. To make little of. An old word not found in most dictionaries, but brought into fresh use in 1898 by Mr Joseph Chamberlain, who about this time frequently used it.

Our whole policy has been belittled and ridiculed by the men who, when they were in office, kept our Colonies at arms' length.—*Mr J. Chamberlain*, 8th December 1898.

The hard-won victories he gained in the old times are belittled and made nothing of.—*Sun*, 6th December 1899.

Bell the Cat (*Peoples'*). To risk the lead. Still used without any real knowledge of its origin, but with thorough comprehension of its application, *e.g.*, 'Yes, but who'll tell him she's no good—who'll bell the cat? Some of us know he's got a bunch of fives.'

The proverb is of Scottish origin, and was thus occasioned: The Scottish nobility entered into a combination against a person of the name of Spence, the favourite of King James III. It was proposed to go in a body to Stirling to seize Spence and hang him; then to offer their services to the king, as his natural counsellors; upon which the Lord Gray observed, 'It is well said, but who will bell the cat?' alluding to the fable of the mice, who proposed to put a bell round the cat's neck, that they might be apprized of her coming. The Earl of Angus replied that he would bell the cat: which he accordingly did, and was ever after called Archibald Bell-Cat.

Belle à croquer (*Soc.*, 1860). Beautiful enough to command desire. Dating second French Empire, it lasted into 1883, in English Society, becoming in lower circles 'beller-croaker'.

It possesses the further advantage of being blue enough to make a blonde *belle à croquer*, and yet not too blue to make her darker sister look as delightful as Nature meant her.—*Newsp. Cutting*, 1883.

Bellering Cake (*School*). Cake in which the plums are so far apart that they have to beller (bellow) when they wish to converse.

Belly-washer (*Amer. Saloon*). Lemonade or aerated water. (*See* Rattle-belly-pop.)

Bellywengins (*E. Anglian, chiefly Suffolk*). A violent corruption of 'belly-vengeance', a cruel comment upon the sour village beer of those regions.

Belt (*Anglo-American*). To assault. From the army, where the belt was often used for aggressive purposes.

Mrs Tice, who saw her approaching, said: 'There comes that old maid; belt her.'—*Newsp. Cutting*.

Belt Case, The (*Soc.*). A symbol for years of wearisome tardiness. From a celebrated libel case, Belt *v.* Lawes (1882), which lasted on and off for weeks.

It is more interminable than the Belt case.—*D. N.*, 25th October 1883.

Ben (*Theatrical*, 19 *cent.*). Short for 'benefit'—'benefit' never being used under any consideration by any self-respecting actor when speaking in the profession. 'Benefit' succeeded 'bespeak', which was in use when Dickens wrote *Nicholas Nickleby*.

Ben (*Soc.*, 1880). A fib, a tarradiddle. The history of this word is fortunately preserved. A well-known Italian proverb was converted into *Se non e vero—e Benjamin trovato*. The 'Ben' was too evident to be resisted. Hence a fib was described as a Benjamin Trovato, passing into Ben Trovato, then Ben Tro, and finally Ben, whence it has got fatally confounded with 'ben', the abbrev. of 'benefit'.

The papers were rampant as to the

Czar's forty thousand dollar diamonds, and Modjeska's jewellery was one of the attractions of the season. Perhaps this story isn't true. Anyway, it will do to go into the Benjamin Trovato series.—*Ref.*, 29th March 1885.

Here is a little story which, if not true, ought to be, for it is at least of the Benjamin order.—*Newsp. Cutting.*

Ben-cull (*Thieves'*). A friend. Ben is from the Hatton Garden Italian *bene.*

Bench Winner (*Soc.*). A dog which has won many prizes at dog-shows—from the exhibits being placed upon benches.

The result is a series of paintings very aptly termed 'A dog show on canvas and paper', for not only are all the Royal favourites represented, but there is scarcely a bench winner of note not included.—*D. T.*, 11th February 1897.

The hounds are the property of Mr Edwin Brough, who has devoted himself to bloodhound breeding. It has been Mr Brough's practice not only to breed for bench points, but to train his animals to exercise those peculiar faculties with which they have been endowed by nature.—*D. N.*, 10th October 1888.

Bench Points (*London*). Ascertained and classified physical advantages. From show animals, especially dogs, being exhibited on benches. Applied also to women, *e.g.*, 'Her bench points were perfect, but I shouldn't like a wife of her build.'

Bend o' the Filbert (*Low*, 18 *cent.*). A bow or nod, filbert being elegantly substituted for the 'nob' or 'nut', both signifying head.

She gives him a bend o' the filbert as much as to crack 'ight-ri, its oper-pro for your nibs, you can take on '.—*Cutting.*

The above describes a serio-comic lady accepting by a nod, while acting or singing, the attentions of an admirer.

Bender (*London*). A sixpenny piece; so called from the rapidity with which this coin wears thin, and thereupon easily bends. This was especially the case thirty years since.

Bender (*Anglo-Amer.*). *E.g.*, 'Three sailors on a bender,' *i.e.*, 'on a drunken spree.' Possibly a conception of a 'Bon Dieu' used exclamatorily = 'My eye!' or 'Good heavens!' or it may be from some Spanish word adopted by Texas cow-boys after that State was wrested from Mexico (1845), creeping up north. It is common to sailors 'over the ditch'.

There was a distant rumbling and groaning, as if old Vesuvius was on a bender.—*Newsp. Cutting.*

In England the Bender is the elbow. (*See* Over the Bender.)

Bengal Blanket (*Anglo-Ind.*, 19 *cent.*). Used by soldiers who have been in India to describe the sun; *e.g.*, 'Yere's a London May—fifteen days, and I ain't seen a corner o' Bengal Blanket—what a climate!' (*See* Blue Blanket.)

Benjamin (*Maritime*, 19 *cent.*). A sailor's blue jacket, larger than the 'monkey' jacket which barely passes the hip-bones. It was the merciful invention of a Hebrew sailors'-tailor on Portsmouth Hard. The grateful tars appear to have given the name of this watcher of their winter comforts to the garment he invented. The word is now in general use for a jacket of dark-blue or black cloth made long and fitting to the figure. Generally called an 'Upper Benjamin'. Sailors also call the rare nautical waistcoat a 'Benjy'. Probably this was another invention, used in the diminutive form of the beneficent Benjamin.

Benjo (*Sailors'*, 19 *cent.*). A riotous holiday, a noisy day in the streets, probably from 'ben', or *buen giorno*; *e.g.*, 'Jim's out on a benjo.'

Beong (*Thieves'*). A shilling—probably a form of the French 'bien'; for indeed a shilling is very well when coppers only are, as a rule, ours.

Bermondsey Banger (*London*). A society-leader among the South London tanneries. He must frequent 'The Star', be prepared to hold his own, and fight at all times for his social belt.

Bespeak (*Theatrical*, 1830 - 50). A performance for the benefit of an actor or actress. The name took its rise from the patrons called upon by the beneficiare at the country theatre, giving a comparative consensus of opinion as to the piece in which the applicant should appear. It was superseded by 'benefit', which yielded to 'ben'. A good deal concerning bespeaks may be found in Dickens' *Nicholas Nickleby.*

Best Eye Peeled (*Amer.*). A figure of speech for extreme alacrity.

I tell you a driver on one of those vans has got to keep his best eye peeled every minute.—*Newsp. Cutting.*

Bet yer sweet life (*Amer.-Engl.*). Perfect assurance, complete conviction. 'Oh, no, certainly not,' said Mr Jones, smiling blandly. 'There are ups and downs in theatrical life; can't always make money—unless you have the right kind of a show. We've got a daisy, haven't we, Lunk?' 'Bechersweetlife,' said Mr Lunk emphatically.—1884.

Bet you a million to a bit of dirt (*Sporting*, 19 *cent.*). The thing is so sure that there can be no uncertainty. The betting man's Ultima Thule of confidence.

Bet your boots (*W. Amer*). Absolutely safe betting—the boots being the most serious item of expense in the Wild West uniform.

'You bet', or 'you bet yer life', or 'you bet yer bones', while to 'bet yer boots' is confirmation strong as holy writ —in the mines, at least.—*All the Year Round*, October 1868.

Betty Martin : *v*. All my eye and Betty Martin.

Between the Devil and the Deep Blue Sea. Scylla on the one side, Charybdis on the other—between two equal menaces. The phrase has no meaning as it reads—the devil and the deep blue sea have no relation. May this not be one of the frequent perversions of proper names to words well understood of the people? For instance, may it not refer to a couple of French admirals or generals 'Deville' and 'Duplessy'—'Between Deville and Duplessy'—inferring disaster for the middle party. The phrase is quite historical.

'I had to pay up—there was Hook on one side, and Crook on the other— I was between the Devil and the Deep Blue Sea.'

He may indeed be said to be between the devil and the deep sea—victims alike of Kurd and Turk.—*Joseph Hatton*, 6th February 1898.

Bever (*E. Anglian*). A four o'clock halt on the road for a drink. An interesting word, evidently from the Norman conjugation of *boire*. (*See* Levenses.)

Bexandebs (*E. London*, 18 *cent*. on). A young easy-go Jewess in the Wentworth Street district. A combination of Becks (Rebeccas) and Debs (Deborahs), used satirically, *e.g.*, 'The bexandebs are in full feather—it's Pentecost Shobboth!'

Beyond, The (*Amer*. 1878). Heaven. To this, one venerable old gentleman in the circle responded that he could now see around him daily his friends who had gone to the beyond, and that if he is riding in a street car and it is not crowded, they enter and sit beside and opposite him.—*N. Y. Mercury*, April 1885.

Beweep (1898). A new form of 'weep' brought in by the Tzar of Russia (20th May 1898) in a telegram referring to the death of W. E. Gladstone. It took the fashion at once.

The whole of the civilised world will beweep the loss of the great statesman whose political views were so widely humane and peaceful.—(Signed) Nicholas.

Bianca Capellas (*E. London*). An elegant evasion in describing White Chapellers—cigars understood; a very bad brand.

There was adjoining this a smoking-room or *salle d'attente*, in which were some stale English papers and the odour of equally stale cigars, also English— veritable Bianca Capellas—but of the sort of thing that we wanted there was no sign whatever.—*Ref.*, 6th June 1886.

Bible Mill (*Com. London*, 19 *cent.*). A public-house. An attack upon Bible classes; said of noisy talking in a tavern.

Bible Class, Been to a (*Printers' Satire*). A gentleman with two black eyes, got in a fight.

Bi-cameral (*Polit.*, 1885). Two chambers, Lords and Commons. First heard in 1885—used satirically by the opponents of a second chamber.

Mr Labouchere complained that of the sixteen members of the Cabinet— thirteen are peers, or the near kinsmen of peers. This fact is an evil resulting from several causes. The first is the bi-cameral system, to adopt the convenient pedantry of Continental writers. —*D. N.*, 9th September 1885.

Bi-cennoctury (*Theatrical*, 1870). The two hundredth night of a run, with which explanation we leave this marvellous bit of etymology to the mercy of a critical world.

Big Beck (*Kent*). A local oath, *e.g.*, 'By the big beck'—heard only in remote places. Probably refers to Thos. à Becket, and has come down from his canonized bones. Sometimes (still in Kent) 'By the Blessed Beck'. (*See* More blue).

Big Bird *Billy-ho*

Big Bird (*Theatrical*). A hissing figurative reference to the goose (*q.v.*) —a figure in itself for hissing; *e.g.*, 'Tom had the big bird last night, and he is in bed this morning.' However, this phrase sometimes has another meaning. At the Britannia Theatre the audiences began (about 1860) to compliment the accomplished villainy of the stage-villain by politely hissing him at the end of one act, to prove how well he had played the scoundrel. This thoroughly indigenous E. London fashion came West about 1878 where it was heard, perhaps at the Princess' for the first time. It has since spread, notoriously to the Adelphi (when still a dramatic house) and Drury Lane; but it has never become a W. London institution. In the E., if the villain did not get the 'big bird', he would consider that he was not on a par with Titus, and that he had lost his day, or rather evening, and he might fear for the renewal of his engagement.

Big end of a month (*Anglo-American*).

'The "big end of a month" is three weeks. I heard a market man speak of the "big end of a dozen" chickens.'

Big Heap (*Amer.* — old mining districts). A large sum of money—now current also in England.

Sam Adams had a ben. at the Pav. on Thursday night, and I hope he's made a big heap out of it.—*Newsp. Cutting.*

Big Numbers (*Anglo-French; old*). Bagnios. From the huge size of the number on the swinging door, never shut, never more than two or three inches open. The English grooms, stable-men, and their like in France often use this phrase: 'Joe's fond o' the big numbers.' 'Tom Four can't run over to the old home for Christmas —he's left too many of Nap's likenesses in the big numbers.' So extensively known throughout Europe was the association of big numbers and shady houses that, when about 1880, people began to place the numbers of their houses on their fanlights, for night observation, their neighbours were often quite unhappy (for a time); while even now many people shrink from the convenient custom.

Big Pot (*Music-hall*, 1878-82). A leader, supreme personage, the 'don'.

This phrase is probably one of the few that filter down in the world from Oxford, where, in the 50's it was the abbreviation of potentate. It referred to a college don, or a social magnate. It has remained permanently a peoples' phrase—the pot being associated with the noblest pewter in a public-house.

'Some of the failures you meet at the "York" will try to impress you with the fact that the comic singers in receipt of big salaries have made their reputation by means of "smut", and that if they (the unsuccessful ones) were to resort to a similar method of gaining the applause of audiences, the "big pots would not be in it".'—*Newsp. Cutting.*

The 'York' is an hotel in the Waterloo Road, S. London, where music-hall people still meet.

Billy born drunk (*L. London*). A drunkard beyond the memory of his neighbours.

He did not have 30 or 40 pots of beer that day. He could do a good many, but he was not going by the name of 'Billy born drunk'.—*People*, 6th January 1895.

Billy-cock (*Provincial*). A brimmed low, felt hat; a modern amelioration of bully-cock, a term now having little or no meaning, *e.g.*, 'Do you cock your hat at me, sir?' was the reply to this challenge—the cocking of the hat. Other authorities hold the word to refer to William III., and his mode of wearing the hat.

Billygoat in Stays (*Navy*, 1870-85). A term of contempt: probably the outcome of the astonishing use, by young naval officers, of waist-stays, during or about these years. Introduced by a young naval officer of the highest, who afterwards, on shore, came to be called 'cuffs'.

Billy-ho (*Peoples*', *Hist.*). In excelsis; suggests extreme vigour. May be from a proper name, 'Hough' for instance, confounded with the big 'O' so commonly used as a suffix to words of congratulation — as 'What cheer ho!' 'What ho!' etc.

The Marquis of Salisbury and Mr Biggar were having a cigar together. Said the Marquis: 'Weather keeps very dry; we want rain badly. I think Canterbury ought to issue a prayer for it.' 'Arrah! be asy wid yer Canterbury,' exclaimed Mr Biggar; 'it's just a new hat I'll be afther buying, and it's my umbrella I'll be lavin' at home, and shure it'll rain like billy-ho!'—*Ref.*, 9th August 1885.

Billy Turniptop (1890 *sqq*). An agricultural labourer. Probably an outgrowth of Tommy Atkins.

'Billy Turniptop' does not seem a very respectful description of the agricultural labourer, especially during election times, and the Unionist candidate for Doncaster has been sharply pulled up for using that cognomen. His explanation was that he was only quoting the speech of a representative of the opposite party.—*D. T.*, 10th July 1895.

Bin (*Harrogate*). A mineral spring. Satire based upon the wine-cellar.

It is considered high treason at Harrogate to drink from the Old Sulphur, or any other 'bin', as a Scottish robust invalid calls it, without first consulting medical authority.—*D. N.* (Harrogate), 31st August 1883.

Binder (*Lower Class*). An egg. Pint o' wash, two steps, an' a binder' —'a pint of tea, two slices of bread-and-butter, and an egg.' Alludes to its constipating action.

Bindery (*Amer.-Eng.*, 1879). A bookbinder's workshop.

The word 'bindery', a new-comer in England, though in common use in Canada and the United States, has recently been welcomed with something like a bonneting by correspondents of *Notes and Queries.—Newsp. Cutting*, 1879.

Binned (*Lond.*, 1883). Hanged; a ghastly word, referring to Bartholomew Binns, a hangman appointed in 1883.

Bird (*Theatrical*). Hissing — the bird being the goose (*q.v.*), whose general statements are of a depreciatory character.

Professor Grant, Q.C., had both 'the bird' and 'the needle' at the Royal on Monday.—*Age*, January 1884.

Pantomimes and Blackmailers. Threats of 'the bird'. Already three or four of the most prominent artistes engaged at one house have been molested after leaving the theatre at night, and threatened with 'the bird'—that is, hissing — unless their tormentors are well paid to remain quiet.—*People*, 6th January 1895.

Bird (*Theatrical*, 1840). A figurative name of The Eagle, which was the title of the tavern and pleasure-grounds out of which grew the Grecian Theatre, an elegant name never accepted by its patrons, except a few who called it the Greek. 'Bird' it remained until General Booth of the Salvation Army bought it up (1882). To this day an effigy of the 'bird' surmounts the main building. (*See* Brit., Vic., Eff., Delphy, Lane.)

Birdlime (*Low Class*, 19 *cent.*). Nonsense-rhyme for 'time'.

We have been awfully stoney in our birdlime, and didn't know where to turn for a yannep, so we've had to fill up our insides on something less than two quid a week.

Birdofreedomsaurin (*Amer.*). Bird-of-freedom soaring. A jocular mode of describing the altitude of the American eagle. Used mildly in England to deprecate any chance American extreme expression of patriotism.

I think that Prince Louis Napoleon was over-dressed. I know that in his green or purple stock (I forget which) he wore an immense breastpin representing an eagle in diamonds—not the eagle with displayed wings, that is, the American 'birdofreedomsaurin'—but an aquiline presentment with the wings closed—the eagle of Imperial sway.—G. A. Sala, in *D. T.*, 16th June 1894.

Birds may roost in my bonnet, Any (*Devonshire*). Self - praise. Speaker so little given to slander that the most Aristophanic birds could carry no disparagement of hers between heaven and earth; *e.g.*, 'Don't 'ee b'lieve it, Mrs Mog—any bird may a-roost in *my* bonnet.' 'A little bird told me' is in close relation with this phrase. The origin is to be found in Ecclesiastes, x. 20. 'For a bird of the air shall carry thee voice, and that which hath wings shall tell the matter.' The belief that birds carry messages between earth and heaven is common to all countries and times. In Europe the dove and the robin are the birds most associated with this charming superstition.

Birmingham School (*Soc.*). A polite evasion of radical; *e.g.*, 'We do not like his politics at the Duke's—he belongs too thoroughly to the Birmingham School'—about 1885. Since then Birmingham has climbed down or up; and the centre of radicalism is supposed to be Newcastle. 'The Newcastle Programme should be backed by the Marquis de Carabas!' (*See* Newcastle Programme.)

Biscuit and Beer Bet (*Street*, 19 cent.). A swindle—because the biscuit backer invariably loses, it being intended that he should lose—to the extent of glasses round, for instance. The bet is as follows: that one youth (the victim) shall not eat a penny biscuit before his antagonist has swallowed a glass of beer by the aid of a teaspoon without spilling any of the beer. The biscuit is so dry, and the anxious bettor so fills his mouth in the desire to win that he generally loses; *e.g.*, 'Yere's a mug—let's biscuit an' beer 'un.'

Bismarck (*Political; South German and French*, 1866). A term of contempt.

A good story is told of a Bavarian who, quarrelling the other day with one of his fellow-countrymen, abused him in the most violent language, and, after exhausting a very extensive vocabulary of invectives, at last called him 'Bismarck!' The phlegmatic German had borne all previous insults with praiseworthy patience; but, on hearing himself thus apostrophised, he flew into a tremendous passion, and cited his enemy before the courts. He was nonsuited on the plea that 'Bismarck' is a name, and does not necessarily imply an insult—at least, no such interpretation was to be found in any of the Bavarian law precedents. This is not the first time that the name of a Prime Minister has thus been popularly applied as a term of contempt. Under the Restoration it was a common incident to hear a cabby apostrophising a sulky or restive horse, 'Va donc, hé, Polignac!' and during the early part of the reign of the Grand Monarque, 'Mazarin' was equivalent to the refined exclamation, 'You pig!' which an attentive listener may be edified by hearing exchanged by the *gamins* of Paris in the present year of grace.—*Morning Star*, 1867.

After 1870, Bismarck was 'accepted' by Bavaria.

Bit-faker (*Thieves*). Counterfeit money-maker — from 'bit', money, and 'fake', to make, or rather cunningly to imitate.

Bit o' Beef (*Vulg.* 19 cent.). A quid of tobacco; less than a pipeful. A playful, or possibly a grim, reference to tobacco-chewing staying hunger. (*See* City sherry; Pound o' bacca.)

Bit o' blink (*Tavern*). Drink—rhyming slang.

Bit o' crumb (*C. L.*, 1882). A pretty plump girl—one of the series of words designating woman immediately following the introduction of 'jam' as the fashionable term (in unfashionable quarters) for lovely woman.

Then Joe fell in love with a dona—oh, what a bit of crumb.—*Newsp. Cutting.*

Bit of fat from the eye, Have a (*L. Class*). Suggestive of compliment —this phrase being seriously used at a spread, or dinner of sheep's head, the orbits of the eyes being lined with a fat supposed by the accustomed consumer to be exceptionally delicate.

Bit o' grease (*Anglo-Ind. Army*). A Hindoo stout woman of a smiling character, *e.g.*, 'She's a nice bit o' grease —*she* is.'

Bit of haw-haw (*London Tavern*, 1860 on). A fop. Possibly suggested by the hesitating commencing syllable used by many well-bred men—more frequently from modesty or caution than from any sense of impressing the idea of superiority.

When these young bits of haw-haw borrow a swallow tail coat and a crook stick, and a bit of window to shove into their weak peepers, and then go into the Gaiety with an order, strike us purple if they're not at their best then. They know all the actresses of course, and the way they talk about some of 'em would make a red stinker turn blue.—*Newsp. Cutting.*

Bit o' jam (1879). A pretty girl—good or bad.

He kisses me, he hugs me, and calls me his bit o' jam, and then chucks me down stairs just to show me there's no ill feeling; yet I love him like anything.—*Newsp. Cutting.*

Everything you see you just feel you would like to buy and take it home to the bit of jam.—*Newsp. Cutting.*

Bit o' pooh (*Workmen's*). Flattery —generally said of courtship—obtained very oddly. The exclamation 'pooh' generally expressing nonsense, the phrase suggests flattering courtship or blarny.

Bit o' prairie (*Strand*, 1850 on). A momentary lull in the traffic at any point in the Strand, so that the traveller can cross the road. From the bareness of the road for a mere moment, *e.g.*, 'A bit o' prairie—go.'

Bit o' raspberry (*Street*, 1883). An attractive girl. When 'jam' came to be used to describe a girl, the original *double intendre* suggested by a comic

song having become known—raspberry, as the most flavoursome of conserves, was used to describe a very pretty creature. Then the jam was dropped, and the 'bit o' affixed, and this phrase became classic.
'So,' said Bill, 'you're the bloke who's spliced my bit o' raspberry'.—*Cutting.*

Bit o' red (*Historical*, 18 *and* 19 *cent.*). A soldier, *e.g.*, 'A bit of red so lights up the landscape.'

Bit o' stuff (*Street*, 19 *cent.*). A lovely woman — not perhaps of a Penelope-like nature—rarely at home.
He waited for a bit of stuff near the stage door of the Comedy Theatre. He was an elderly cove and he had great patience.—*Cutting.*

Bit o' tripe (*L. Class*). One of the endearing names given to the wife —probably a weak rhyme.
This paper always comes useful, if it's only to wrap a Billingsgate pheasant in to take home to the bit of tripe. — *Cutting.*

Bit on, To have a (*Sporting*). To have a bet on—a 'bit' of money on—a race.
I hear that all the shining lights of the music hall who are accustomed to have a little 'bit on' were on the right side.—*Newsp. Cutting.*

Bit to go with (*Amer.-Eng.*). Generosity — as the result of self-satisfied superiority.
An American railway train can give most things in this world a bit to go with in the way of noise.—*Ref.*, 20th February 1887.

Bitch the pot (*University*, down to 1850). Amongst a tea-drinking party of men it was asked, 'Who'll bitch the pot?'—meaning who will pour out the tea.

Bitched (*Printers'*). Spoilt, ruined, in reference to type.

Bite the tooth. To (*Thieves'*). To be successful. Origin unknown.

Bite-etite, perhaps **Bitytite** (*Peoples', E. London*). Grotesque substitution of bite for the first four letters of 'appetite'. (*See* Drinkitite.)

Bite off more than one can chew (*American - English*). Referring to plug tobacco, and meaning that the person spoken of has undertaken more than he can accomplish.

Bits of Grey (*Soc.*, 1880). Elderly victims of both sexes present at balls and marriages, especially the latter, to give an air of staid dignity to the chief performers. 'Don't tell me—we had a small and early, all young—most miserable, growling, towering failure I ever endured. No stir-up for me without my bits of grey. They give tone to the whole thing.'—*Society Novel*, 1883.

Bits o' soap (*Com. Lond.*, 1883). Charming girls—of a kind.
I can imagine General Booth jumping in his boots when he piped that article in his paper. I wonder what all the converted bits o' soap thought about it.—*Cutting*, 1883.
(Booth became the self-appointed general of the Salvation Army, 1882-83.)

Bitter oath (*Peoples'*, 19 *cent.*). Emphatic intensification of oath ; *e.g.*, 'I'll take my bitter oath.' Oaths may be divided into two classes— those which appeal to heaven, as 'By God', and those which relate to an antithesis, as 'By hell', the former being the better oath. The masses, incapable of discriminating one kind from the other, simplified 'better oath' into 'bitter oath', as possessing more emphasis.

Bitties (*Thieves'*). Evasive term for skeleton-keys.

Bivvy (*London*). Beer; evidently from the French 'buvez' (Italian 'bevere') — the imperative mood of the verb being applied to the beer itself. The difficulty is to find the descent. It may have come from French prisoners very early in the nineteenth century, or from the French colonies in Soho, or (more likely) from the Italian organ-grinding regiment in the neighbourhood of Hatton Garden.

Black and white (*Thieves' rhyming*). Night. It would mean, when used, 'to-night'.

Black-bagging (1884). Dynamitarding—from the fact that where dynamite proceedings had failed at certain railway-terminuses the explosive charges were found in black bags.
Five thousand pounds reward for the discovery of the perpetrators of the outrage at London Bridge is too much. It is an encouragement to others to go black-bagging.—*Ref.*, 4th January 1885.

Black-ball (*Club*, 19 *cent.*). To reject by ballot. The word is now absolutely inappropriate, though still used by 'correct' clubmen. It had meaning when club elections were effected by each elector being given one white and one black ball, so that upon opening the ballot-box the colours decided, black naturally being a negative. So far as the declaration of the election was concerned, nothing could be better than this mode; but unfortunately every elector was troubled by the possession of the second ball, which he might drop and thereby betray his vote. This ball the voter certainly would have some inconvenience in depositing, apart from the watchfulness of neighbouring eyes. Hence the new mode of club-balloting with a box, having a hole in front large enough for the entrance of the hand, the bottom of the box being divided by a high partition, while the outside is marked 'Yes' (or 'Ay') and 'No'— referring to the two boxes formed by the partition. Only one ball is given to each voter, and thus he gets rid of his responsibility by depositing the ball either on one side or the other. Unfortunately nervous voters are frequently fogged the moment they lose sight of the right hand, while the ballot-box-carrier (where it is carried, instead of being placed on a table for the approach of the voter) has a frequent habit of tilting up the 'No' side of the box, so that if the ball is not firmly manipulated when inside the palladium, it may have a better chance of favouring the 'Ay'. Even this word itself is a difficulty, for its complication between 'ay' and 'ayes', together with its infrequency except as an interjection, helps to confuse timid voters. More recently the ballot boxes have been bearing the legends 'yes', 'no' — the affirmative always preceding the negative.

Black-bottle Scene (*Dublin*, 1822 on). Black beer-bottle throwing at obnoxious persons.

On the 14th of December 1822, on the occasion of the Marquis Wellesley, visiting the Theatre Royal, Dublin, an organized disturbance on the part of the Orangemen took place, in resentment of his Excellency's sympathy with Catholic Emancipation. The affray is always referred to as the 'black-bottle' riot; a black bottle having been flung at the Viceroy by an Orangeman in the top gallery. — *Newsp. Cutting.*

On any other occasion the incident might have passed unnoticed, but now the rumour of a 'black bottle' scene was in every one's mind. — *A. M. Sullivan*, 1877.

Black Eye (*American, political and social*). A reverse, especially political.

A black eye for Platt. — An Albany jury has decided that Governor Hill was right, and Quarantine Commissioner Platt wrong, and that the latter has all along been a resident of Owega, while holding office in New York. — *N. Y. Mercury*, 15th January 1888.

Often used to designate theatrical failure.

This inheritance proved a black eye to all concerned, because the new company lacked all the vocal and comedy requisites for a successful interpretation of this very popular work.

Black Ivory (*Slave - dealers*). A disguised way of referring to negro slaves.

Mr Steyn, a former Landdrost of Potchefstroom, in both letters and speeches, complained that 'loads of "black ivory" were being constantly hawked about the country'. — F. W. Chesson, in *D. N.*, 5th November 1883.

Black Jack (19 *cent.*). A black portmanteau of peculiar make.

William Wall deposed that he repaired the portmanteau produced, and recognised Burton as the man who brought it. Burton also brought another second-hand portmanteau called in the trade 'Black Jack'. — *Dynamite Case Report*, 4th March 1885.

Blackleg (*Labour*, 1889-90). A non-striker in industry. Blackleg had long been used for a swindler, but at this date it was first applied to non-Union men or non-strikers. Directly used in relation to the dock-strikes. Common to the labouring classes by June 1890.

It will be seen from the full report of the situation, which we print elsewhere, that the present stage of the conflict turns on the presence of the 'blackleg', to use the designation which the Dock labourers first popularised. — *Chaos in the Post Office*, in *D. N.*, 10th July 1890.

Black Maria (*Thieves'*, 19 *cent.*). The prison van, probably Anglicizing 'Black V.R.', this public conveyance being ink-coloured, and bearing V.R. on each side of it. To the ignorant V.R. would have no meaning; while Maria would; or it may be a rhyming effort. The New York prison van, though of course very different from the English carriage, bears the same name.

He 'protested' against entering the Black Maria, and on the way up 'would not admit' that he was going to the Workhouse, but by this time he probably feels at home up there.—*N. Y. Police Report*, 1883.

Upon the death of Queen Victoria, necessarily the initials on the prison van were changed to E.R.—the term for the vehicle, however, still remaining. A phrase was immediately found for E.R.—Energy Rewarded—a term accepted by even the nation, with applause. (*See* V.R., Virtue Rewarded, Vagabonds Removed, Sardine Box.)

Black-silk Barges (*Ball - room*). Stout women who ought to avoid dances. They dress in black silk to moderate in appearance their amplitude.

'It's time I sounded a retreat from dancing — I've had to dance with seventeen black-silk barges this blessed evening. Never again—never again.'

Black Strap (*Peoples', Old English*). Port wine. A corruption of 'black stirrup' cup. Sherry or sack (the first a corruption of Xeres, the second, an abbreviation, was always white wine; clarets and burgundies red; port black). The stirrup cup was always potent. The passage from black stirrup to black strap is too evident when port came amongst the people — more accustomed to strap than the stirrup. To this day strap is used for port.

Blank pleasure (*American*). A negative euphemism for the unending 'damned' — with a polite request added.

. . . that matter - of - fact business manager of ours says that, although we may put what we blank please in the editorial columns, he won't put a six-inch display in the advertising end of the paper for less than several hundred dollars cash, quarterly in advance.—*Texas Siftings*.

Blarney (*Irish*). Flattery. The *Blarney stone* is a protruding one, standing out from below a ruined window of ruined Blarney Castle (near Cork). Whoever kisses this stone, a very difficult feat, and one which requires help and strong holding hands while the aspirant leans over and down into space, is supposed to possess for ever after the gift of successful flattery.

The traditions respecting the kissing of the Blarney stone, to impart to the devotee a peculiar suavity of speech, is about three hundred years old. — *Newsp. Cutting*.

Blasé (*Fr.*, 1840). Wearied, bored. Brought to England with a farce called *L'Homme Blasé*, subsequently produced for Wright (Princess Theatre), in which version this actor was called Blasé. Succeeded by 'bored' about 1860.

Bleed (*Peoples'*). A perversion of the word 'blood', as 'She'll have his bleed'—usually said of a woman who is rating her husband.

Blenheim Cloud (*Polit.*). The influence of the Dukes of Marlborough over Woodstock, which lies in the shadow of Blenheim.

Against this the more sanguine point to the advantage of being free from what they call 'the Blenheim cloud', the Duke having formally declared that he takes no part in this election, and that all his people are free to vote as they choose.—*D. N., 1st July* 1885.

Blenheim Pippin, The (*Polit.*, 1883). An application of the name of a known variety of pippins, always a small apple, to describe Lord Randolph Churchill, a diminutive man, who, as a son of a Duke of Marlborough, was associated with Blenheim, the family seat in Oxfordshire.

. . . the Tories are, as a rule, followers of the strongest; and after the Blenheim Pippin's latest manifesto they will hardly know whether to throw in their lot with Tweedledum or Tweedledee.—*Entr'acte*, 7th April 1883.

Bless me soul (*Peoples'*). Bless me —Saul. Probably one of the few Puritanic exclamations—all of which were Biblical, ' Bless me, or my, soul' is nonsense, as it stands—for who blesses? Hence probably arose 'God bless my soul'. But this phrase is also meaningless, for the soul needs no blessing. 'God bless me' is reasonable. But here, 'soul' is the important word. In this conversation it should be remembered that Saul was held in high Puritanic esteem—as a patriarch of much power.

Blessing (*Irish*). Gratuity. Poetic way of putting it; will contrast with 'backsheesh' (*q.v.*) 'Sure, he's a man gives me a blessing every time he passes without pretending not to see me, he does.' In Devonshire a 'blessing' is a handful thrown in, *e.g.*, 'Plase to give' us a half-peck o' pays, and give us a blessing.'

Blew, To (*Com. Lond.*). To dissipate. This word is by no means to 'blow', but is suggested by 'blue'. 'I blewed' (or 'blew') means 'I spent', and probably is suggested by the dismal blue appearance of a man, penniless and recovering from a drunken fit. The word was turned to very droll account by a comic-singer, Herbert Campbell, in 1881. A medicinal pad to be worn over the liver was very much advertised; and a half life-size cut of a masculine and healthy patient with the 'liver pad' *in situ* created a great deal of comment. The singer put both together and came out with a ballad. 'Herbert Campbell's favourite song now is called "Clara blued her Liver Pad"', meaning that she had sold her specimen and spent the proceeds in drink— for you only 'blew' money when you do spend it in drink.

In about an hour he reached the Strand, and in less than another hour he had blewed his half-a-dollar, so he sat on a doorstep and wept as only boys who have run away from home and have got the stomach-ache can weep.— *Cutting.*

Blewed his red 'un (*Peoples'*). 'Red 'un' is an anglicization of 'redding' (a thieves') word for a watch, probably the name of a watch-receiver. The phrase therefore means 'Spent in drink the money raised on his watch.' Here brevity is indeed triumphant.

Blighter (*Theat.*, 1898). An actor of evil omen: it took the place of Jonah (*q.v.*).

'I never care about acting in a play which is likely to fail. Look at Jones. Splendid actor, but he has been connected with so many failures that he has got to be known as a blighter, and no one will engage him.'—*Cutting.*

Blind Hookey (*Peoples'*). A leap in the dark; *e.g.*, 'Oh, it's Blind Hookey to attempt it.' From a card game. The centre card is the banker's —the players put money against either of the four other cards. If the dealer's centre card is the highest of the five he takes all the bets. If his card is the lowest, he pays all four.

Blink. *See* Bit o' blink.

Blister, To (*Peoples'*, 1890 on). To punish with moderation: a modification of 'to pound'; *e.g.*, 'I'll blister 'im when I ketch 'im'—a promise of fisting. Used chiefly by cabmen in relation to magisterial fines, *e.g.*, 'I was blistered at Bow Street to-day for twenty hog.'

Blizzard Collar (*Soc.*, 1897). A high stand-up collar to women's jackets, coats. Suggestive of cold weather.

I must mention the very pretty Russian vests of fur that our élégantes have now adopted. They are tightly fitting, and fasten on the side; they have a short basque all round, a blizzard collar, and a fancy belting of jewelled enamelled plaques.—*D. T.*, 16th January 1897.

Bloater (*Peoples'*). An abbreviation of Yarmouth bloater: a fat person. From the fact that the first smoking process applied to the herring results in a remarkable swelling, which afterwards abates.

If intended for immediate eating, the herring is taken down after one firing, when it is swelled and puffed out like a roasted apple. It is then known to the true East Anglian as a blowen-herring— the word bloater is rejected by philologists as a foreign corruption—and here you probably have the true etymology of the familiar word. — *Yarmouth*, by W. Norman (Yarmouth, 1883).

Blob (*Cricket*, 1898). No runs. 'Blob' has taken the place of 'duck', or 'duck's egg'.

Block (*Scotch Thieves'*, 1868). A policeman in one syllable.

I think it would be a good idea for my mother to get the block privately and make an appeal to him; he would have a little feeling for her, I think.— Dundee garotter's letter, 1868.

Block (*Linen Drapers'*). A name applied curiously to the young lady of fine shape who in the mantle department tries on for the judgment of the lady customer.

Block a quiet pub. (*Peoples'*). To stop a long time in a tavern; *e.g.*, 'I don't care for theayters or sing-songs; but I like to block a quiet pub.', said the commercial; *i.e.*, to remain quietly drinking in an out-of-the-way public house. Generally said of a sot.

Bloke (*Lower Classes*, 19 *cent*). A friendly soul, inclined to be charitable.

This word has not the objectionable meaning it is often supposed to possess. On the contrary, it is mighty affectionate; e.g., 'Got a bit o' bacca, bloke?' if asked you in the streets is by no means offensively said. It is less than 'gentleman', more than 'mate'. 'He's a proper bloke' is simply a pæan.

Bloke is also a lover, or even an acquaintance.

Master Edward Graham, aged eight, and Miss Sarah King, aged nine, appeared at Bow Street as inseparable and incorrigible beggars in the Strand. 'Sally and her bloke' is said to be the unpoetical designation of the pair in the Strand.—*D. N.*, 1882.

In universities, an outsider, a mere book-grubber, *e.g.*, 'Balliol mere blokes. But they carry off everything.' (*See* Old Put, Muff.)

Blood (*Old*). By our Lord—one of the old Catholic exclamations.

Blood—it is almost enough to make my daughter undervalue my sense. — Fielding, *Tom Jones*, bk. vii., ch. 4.

The extended form is 'bloody'— by our lady—an asseveration referring to the Virgin, which becomes an apostrophe in the shape 'What the bloody hell'—'By our lady, hail.' 'What' thus appears to be a Protestant addition. About 1875, when the London School Board had influenced the metropolis for some half dozen years —this word and phrase were superseded by 'blooming', a sheer evasion which has survived the nineteenth century, and has quite passed into the lower layers of the language. In 18th century literature may be found the form 'blady hell', which suggests the origin very forcibly.

Some actors have been known to mutilate the speech in *Macbeth*, 'Be bloody, bold, and resolute', lest it should suggest the inconceivably wicked thought, 'Be bloody-bold, and resolute'. Now this extremely shocking word is nothing more nor less than a corruption of 'By'r lady'. How little do the dregs of our population, who, when they hurl out the word, imagine that it contains some frightful explosive, dream that they are appealing to the Virgin.—*D. T.*

Blood and 'ounds (*Irish*). Blood and *wounds* (Christ's)—an old pronunciation rhyming with 'pounds'; *e.g.*, 'Blood an' 'ounds — how the blood runs out uv 'un thin.' This phrase is a good example of the anglicization of words whose original meanings are from various causes lost. Probably most of the Catholic adjurations have been applied in the same such manner as this.

Blood Ball (*London Tr.*). The butchers' annual hopser, a very lusty and fierce-eyed function. The female contingent never wear crimson — as being too trady. (*See* Bung Ball.)

Blood Hole (*E. London*, 1880). A theatre in Poplar.

The irreverent ones of the district, whenever they mentioned the place, called it 'The Blood Hole'—in allusion, I presume, to the style of drama presented.—*Newsp. Cutting*.

Blood or Beer (*Street*). A challenge to fight or stand, *i.e.*, 'pay for' malt refreshment. A jocular phrase bordering on bullying. Real fighting is inducted by the phrase 'Take off your coat'! This is serious. 'Come on, ruffian. It's blood or beer'—is simply friendly suggestion.

Bloods (*Lowest Classes*) Wallflowers, from a not too clear association of colours. A higher figure of speech than Bugs (*q.v.*), but still painfully disgusting in association with this fresh-breathed blossom. 'Bloods, bloods—penny a bunch, bloods.'

Bloods (*Navy*). Sailor boys' title for 'Penny Dreadfuls'.

They expect lots of blood, wonderful adventures, gruesome illustrations, and a good deal of cheap sentiment', and they get it. As they get older, their tastes change. — Rev. G. Goodenough, Navy Chaplain.

Blood-worms (*London*, 19 *cent.*). Sausages in general, but a black-pudding of boiled hog's blood in particular. 'S'elp me sivvy, I've come down to blood-worms.' (*See* Sharp's Alley.)

Bloody carpet rags (*Amer.*, imported to Liverpool). A mutilated man.

All of a sudden the burly coloured man drew a razor from his pocket and started for the light-weight with the remark that he'd make bloody carpet rags of him.—*Newsp. Cutting*.

It should be added that the razor is the American negro's favourite weapon, carried as a rule in a high boot — something after the manner of a Scotch dirk in a Scotch sark.

Blooming Emag (*Street*, 1870). Back spelling: 'Emag' is 'game'. Selfishness in its perfect degree.

There nothing like cheek, yobs, whatever you're blooming emag may be. But be honest, even if you have to go out nailing to be honest.—*Cutting*.

Bloomeration (*London*, 1891). Illumination. First heard 9th November at Prince of Wales' illuminations.

Blooming little holiday (*Lowest Peoples'*). Saturnalia — liberty to be free, to be perfectly tyrannical.

An English defeat and panic, on English soil, would seem to the English rough the very beginning of the millennium, or, in his own language, 'a blooming little holiday.'—*Newsp. Cutting*, 1879.

Blouser (*obscure*). To cover up, to hide, to render nugatory, *e.g.*, 'Joe— you won't blouser me!" From the French, evidently. Probably used in an anti-Gallican spirit, when the blouse first appeared to cover over an honest Englishman's waistcoat; or it may be from the court of Charles II.

The Army is warned that the clergy will try to 'blouser' or mislead them, and to persuade people to refuse the use of halls, while all the time professing interest in the Army's holy labours.— *Newsp. Cutting* (about 1881).

Blow (*Peoples'*). To boast—from the noise made when a whale blows water through and up from the nostrils, with much noise. Introduced by sailors in the whale trade, common to England and America, and still surviving amongst the lower classes. A good example of a word arising from a new industry and passing away with it.

About the veracity of big game shooters, one is sometimes obliged to feel now and then a lingering doubt. They might remind an Australian reader of 'him who tried to blow', in a well-known line of a modern poet. 'Blow', it may be necessary to explain, is the Australian equivalent for 'brag' or 'boast'. Thus Othello 'blew' in the account of his adventures with which he obliged Desdemona.— *D. N.*, 25th February 1885.

'Blow' and 'blow upon' are sometimes still used in their old form, in the sense of to expose or betray.

All he asks is to pass him along his plate with whatever happens to be handy round the pantry, and he won't go away and blow how poor the steak is. He just eats whatever is set before him, and asks no questions.—*Cutting*.

Blow me tight (*Peoples'*). Below me with a firm hand—that is, sent to Hades. Used generally as a protest on the part of the speaker, and an assurance of truth. Generally followed by 'if', and sometimes 'but'. He means that he is willing to be damned if he lies.

It was reckoned out we'd get to Brighton at six o'clock last Saturday, blow me tight.—*Cutting*.

Blow-out (*Peoples'*). Dissipation— literally stretching the digestive apparatus.

At the end of a month a miner finds himself in possession of from £25 to £30, and, as a corollary, has what he calls 'a blow-out'.—*Newsp. Cutting*, 1883.

Blowing (*Thieves'*). 'A pickpocket's trull', quotes Byron in a note to the line 'Who on a lark with black-eyed Sal (his blowing)' (*Don Juan*, ca. xi. st. 19). Sometimes 'blowen'.

Blowsa-bella (*Theat.* 18 *cent.*). A vulgar, self-assertive woman, generally stout. Blowsa is probably from the French 'blouser', a verb got from 'blouse', meaning to attract by gutter arguments. Bella is of course an abbreviation of Isabella, and the whole phrase probably would mean a vulgar woman of the people giving herself false airs of grandeur. *The Daily News* (22nd Feb. 1883) throws perhaps some light on the word in reference to the Salvation Army.

Bluchers (*Mid. Class*; 1815 on). Plural of blucher, referring to the commonest of boots. From General von Blücher, the Prussian general-in-chief at the battle of Waterloo. When some clever *bootmaker* invented the now extinct Wellington boots, a humble imitator followed with the handy Blucher, and made quite a large fortune out of this idea—and the boots — the most frequent name for workmen's boots known to Britons, who have found this manufacture a handy weapon. (*See* Wellingtons.)

Blue (*Old English*). Dismal — evidently from the appearance of the countenance when showing anxiety or mistrust—as distinct from red anger. In this sense it is used in U.S.A. to

Blue Blanket   *Blue Moon*

this day; *e.g.*, 'This news will make our return to Yonkers rather blue', *i.e.*, melancholy. It will be found temp. George III. in a ballad, published in Dublin by Trojanus Laocoon, called *The All - devouring Monster*; *or New Five per C—t*, a satirical work which attacked a project, dating from England, of course, to put a duty of 5 per cent. upon all imports. Here is a triplet from the ballad in question:

The effects of the Tax will soon make us look Blue,
Its nature, its drift being known but to few;
Reverse of the Glass Act—this all men saw through.

In England, 19th century, 'blue' has been abandoned as describing melancholy, owing to its new meaning — one of vulgar, coarse, *double entendre*; *e.g.*, 'Have you got any new blue?' may be asked by one who is athirst for erotic entertainment. Perhaps comes in some obscure way from the French, where a bluette certainly means a short song, which skirts the wind of impropriety. The earlier meaning of blue is however still sometimes applied.

And yet, though things are all so blue, it's funny,
My missus never lets me *blue* the money.
—*Elephant and Castle pantomime*, 1882.

Blue Blanket (*Peoples'*, 19 *cent.*). The sky. 'I slept under the blue blanket last night. (*See* Bengal Blanket.)

Blue Caps (*Indian Mutiny*, 1857). Dublin Fusiliers.

The Dublin Fusiliers are 'The Blue Caps'. A despatch of Nana Sahib was intercepted, in which he referred to 'those blue-capped English soldiers who fight like devils'. The name stuck. At the Siege of Lucknow the bridge of Char Bagh was raked by four guns and defended on the flanks by four others. 'Who is to carry it?' asked Outram. 'My Blue Caps', replied Havelock; and they did.—Rev. E. J. Hardy.

Blue Damn. Evasive swearing. Celestial curse—the blue referring to the sacred purple blood of the Crucified.

Blue Funk (*Pub. Sch.*). Absolute panic—from the leaden colour of the skin when the owner is beyond question afraid.

Of Mr Weedon Grossmith's assumption it may be further said that it is calculated to develop his most approved strain of humour, which in schoolboy parlance is known as blue funk.—*People*, 28th February 1897.

He will, no doubt, tell people at home that he left the Soudan because he was invalided. That is not the case. He left us because he was in a blue funk.— *D. T.*, 6th July 1897.

Blue Grass (*Amer.*). People of Kentucky—from the peculiar tint of the grass.

The Kentucky correspondent of the *Cincinnati News - Journal* is evidently hard hit. This is what he writes: When the Bona Dea, out of her bounteousness, makes a Bluegrass woman, she takes care never to spoil the job. A soft, white, warm body, translucent with divine light, and curving to lines of beauty as naturally as the tendrils of a vine, is the groundwork upon which nature limits the human angel. . . . The brow of Juno and the bust of Hebe; the sea-nymph's pearly ear, the wood-nymph's springy step—these are a few of the charms nature gives the maiden of the Bluegrass.—*Newsp. Cutting.*

Even accepted as the title of a paper.

Blasphemous Libel.—Louisville (Ky.), 21st April.—Mr C. E. Moore, Editor of a newspaper, published here, known as *The Blue Grass Blade*, and who has been in prison for the last fortnight.—*Newsp. Cutting.*

Blue Grass Belle. A Kentuckian beauty.

While down in Kentucky last Fall, buying horses, he tipped a wink at a blue grass belle.—*Newsp. Cutting.*

Blue-handled Rake. The railing and steps leading to the platform of a fair-booth stage.

Blue Hen's Chick (*Devonshire*). A clever soul, *e.g.*, 'You're a blue hen's chick hatched behind the door'—said satirically.

Blue Jack (*Nautical*). Cholera morbus—from the colour of the skin in this disease. (*See* Yellow Jack.)

Blue-jacket (*Peoples'*, 19 *cent.*). A sailor—given from the colour of jacket. (*See* Lobster, Robin Redbreast.)

Blue Moon (*General, in all classes*). Absolutely lost in mystery, but probably an Anglicism of a word or words with which neither 'blue' nor 'moon' has anything to do. It imports indefinite futurity. Possibly meaning 'never', because a blue moon is never seen.

'I ain't a going to make a speech', said he, in a voice husky with emotion, 'because if I was to jaw till a blue moon I couldn't tell you more about her we've been and buried than you know already.' —'Cadgers in Mourning', *D. T.*, 8th February 1883.

Blue Noses (*American*). Canadians —obviously from the force of sharp weather on the Canadian nose. Probably contemptuous.

In Nova Scotia, has died a centenarian who had fought under Nelson and under Wellington. Did a grateful people follow the hero to the grave with proud tears? Not much. John Aberton was buried in a rough box on the day he died. There were no prayers, no funeral procession, no formalities, but the old patriot received the burial of a dog. This ought to make recruiting brisk in Canada and incite the blue noses to volunteer in a mass to defend Queen Victoria's codfish.—*N. Y. Mercury*, 1st January 1895.

Blue o'clock in the morning (*Street*). Pre-dawn, when black sky gives way to purple. Rhyming fancy, suggested by two o'clock in the morn. Suggestive of rollicking late hours.

The birdcatcher has often to be up 'at blue o'clock in the morning'. The rime is on the grass when he lays his nets. It is bitterly cold standing about in the fields.—*D. N.*, 12th October 1886.

Blue Pencil (To) (*Theat.*, 1885 on). Cutting down literature—first applied to dramatic pieces. From the colour of the pencil used. 'More blue pencil', said Mr Tree—it is the only way of writing a successful piece.

The actor will have a better chance after the blue pencil has eliminated the unnecessary verbiage in the dialogue.— *D. N.*, 17th February 1899.

Blue Pig (*Maine*, U.S.A.). Whisky. Maine is a temperance state, therefore liquor has to be asked for under various strange names, which have generally been satirically distinguished by a strange contradiction in their component parts, as in this instance. The phrase common in Liverpool.

There have been remarkable animals discovered in Maine before now—to wit, striped and blue pigs and Japanese dogs of scarlet hue. These creatures, however, have usually been found to be of the genus stalking-horse — that is, they merely served as screens for the sale of prohibited intoxicating fluids.—*D. N.*

Blue Ribbonite (*M. Class*, 1880). A sort of pun between 'nite' and 'knight', and one which gave the phrase rapid popularity. Outcome of the custom of wearing a blue ribbon on left breast of coat to demonstrate that the wearer was an abstainer.

With respect to the inconsistencies in the man who married Miss Dash drinking champagne and port, it should be remembered that he had not taken the pledge, and that he was concealing his identity. Besides, he said before the wedding breakfast that he was almost a blue-ribbonite—Brighton Bigamy Case, 20th and 24th October 1885.

Blue Ribbon Fakers (*London*, 1882). The progress of abstinence principles, practically started by Father Mathews (1815-71), is very interesting. The original abstainers made no daily public parade of their principles, and were not forbidden to associate with men who drank fermented liquors, or to have 'drinks' in the house, or to pay for drinks. Then followed the Good Templars (1860), who prohibited their followers from paying for others' alcoholic drinks, from having liquor in the house, or entering a tavern, even to buy a biscuit, but they showed no visible signs of their temperance. Then came the Blue Ribbon Army who (1882) instituted the daily assertion of their principles by wearing a scrap of bright blue ribbon in the left breast buttonhole of the coat. Street satirists dubbed them Blue Ribbon fakers.

The Blue Ribbon fakers may say what they fair like, but there are times when good brandy is new life—ask the squirts. About 1896 these blue ribbons became in some degree unpopular with abstainers, and were discarded. But so far no abstinence supporters had tabooed tobacco. It remained for the Salvation Army to add to all the abstinence principles hitherto adopted that of the rejection of tobacco in all its forms. As they operated chiefly amongst youths, their success as anti-tobacconalians was considerable. So far moderation or abstinence in relation to animal food has not yet been advanced—but it must follow in due course.

Blue Roses (*Literary*). Unattainable — sometimes blue dahlias, or tortoise-shell Tom cat, equal to squaring the circle. Blue roses is the most poetical of these phrases.

The blue cloud of a fame beyond Doré's reach floated ever before him; he was eternally allured by the blue roses of an impossible success.—*D. N.*, 25th June 1885.

Blue 'un (*Sporting*). A journal named *Winning Post*—so named from its tint, no doubt given to enter the ranks with the 'Pink 'un' and 'Brown 'un' (*see*)—all three fine examples of language produced by the habitually obvious, and of the tendency to shorten frequent phrases. Technically, blue 'un is a learned woman.

The application of the term to women, originated with Miss Hannah Moore's admirable description of a 'Blue Stocking Club' in her 'Bas Bleu'.—*Mill.*

Bluchers (*London*). Outsider cabs, not allowed, except upon emergency, to enter railway termini — probably in contradistinction to Wellingtons, just as the Wellington boot was the aristocratic foot-covering—the Blucher that of the general. The Blucher boot survives; the Wellington is a fossil.

It appears that when there is a deficiency of cabs at any station, outside or non-registered vehicles are called in on payment of a penny for the right of taking stand in the yard. With a nice regard for history, the drivers of these 'understudy' cabs are, in the vernacular of the fraternity, dubbed 'Bluchers'.—*D. T.*, 'Cab Strike', 23rd May 1894.

Bluff (*Californian*, 1849 on). To humbug, hector, bully, from an American card-game wherein the player sheerly seeks to domineer over his opponent, and gain by sheer audacity, without absolute reference to the cards he (the bluffer) holds. Probably from 'bluff', Californian for cliff; the word suggesting tall boasting.

'I bluffed 'im for a hour, but 'e wouldn't 'ave it at not no price. Mr Newton, the magistrate at Marlborough Street observed: This is a case of bluff. —Sir George Lewis: If you have made up your mind, I will retire from the case. —Mr Newton: Can you contradict the constables?—*People*, 3rd October 1895.

Tom Gossage afforded in his own character and habits an amusing example of how a man could get imbued with the peculiar vice of the time—and that was the game of brag—brag and the hard old vices of its kindred — bluff and poker. — *Newsp. Cutting.*

Bluffer (*Californian*, 1849 on). The noun followed the verb very rapidly.

The stranger went away and returned with the bluffer.—*Newsp. Cutting.*

Bobby (*Scottish*). A faithful person —abbreviation of Greyfriars Bobby, who has become a household word in the Canongate, Edinburgh. He was a devoted little terrier who kept watch and ward for a dozen years over the grave of his unknown master, buried in the strangers' corner of Greyfriars Cemetery, Edinburgh. Lady, then Miss Burdett Coutts, was so touched by this fidelity that she erected a little monument to his memory. 'Hey, mon, nae mair thanks, or maybe ye'll be getting the name o' Bobbie.'

Bobby Atkins. See Tommy Atkins.

Bobby's Labourers (*Volunteers*, 1868). Name given to special constables, chiefly volunteers, during this year—one of Fenian alarm—upon the principle that the s.c's did the work of the policemen—that is 'bobby'.

Bob, Harry and Dick (*Rhyming*, 1868). Sick — disguised way of admitting a crushed condition, the morn following a heavy drink. (*See* Micky.)

Bobolink (*American*). A talkative person, from being like a bird of this name. Abbreviation of Bob o' Lincoln.

This is the way somebody translates the bobolink's libretto: 'Chink a link, chink a link, tink tink, tinkle tootle, Tom Denny, Tom Denny, come pay me, with your chink a link, tinkle linkle, toodle loodle, popsidoodle, see, see, see!' making not the slightest pause from beginning to end.

Bobs (*Soc., passing to People*, 1900). Plural of Bob, exactly as Roberts is the plural of Robert — hence the genesis of the familiar name for General Roberts. Bobs was much applied in this year, especially to smart Irish terriers. B.P. (passing to Bups), was also in great vogue—of course the initials of General Baden Powell. This pluralising of nicknames had been growing for years.

Mr Ernest Wells, one of the founders and managers of the Pelican Club, and familiarly known in sporting, dramatic, and literary circles by his journalistic pseudonym of 'Swears', has, etc.—*D. T.*, 25th July 1900.

Tales, old Chestnuts, Hairs, Pots,

Pumps, were some of the plural nicknames in use about this period.

If a limber's slipped a trace,
  'Ook on Bobs;
If a marker's lost 'is place,
  Dress by Bobs;
For 'e's eyes all up 'is coat,
An' a bugle in 'is throat,
An' you will not play the goat,
  Under Bobs.
  —*Rudyard Kipling.*

Bobtail (*Peoples'*). Name given early in the 19th century to the dandies who wore the pointed tailcoats which followed the wide skirts of the 18th century, tails which must have been very striking. Name still given to a waiter by common classes. (*See* Claw-hammer.)

Bobtail (*Irish*). Appealing to the masses, to the passing penny. Irish, and probably dating from the introduction of the swallow-tail coat from England—doubtless despised at first, but still retained by the peasantry.

Boucicault said 'I introduced *The Poor of Liverpool*—a bobtail piece—with local scenery and Mr Cowper in the principal part (Badger). I share after £30 a night, and I am making £100 a week on the damned thing. I localise it for each town, and hit the public between the eyes; so they see nothing but fire. I can spin out these rough-and-tumble dramas as easily as a hen lays eggs. It's a degrading occupation, but more money has been made out of guano than out of poetry.'

Body Lining (*Drapers'*). Bread—very opposite, lining in this trade being what goes inside the bodice (or body) of a dress. 'Pass me half a yard of body-lining.' Body-lining itself is a strong twill.

Body Snatcher (*Street, London,* 1840-1860). A cabman—from the habit, before higher civilization amongst cabmen prevailed, of snatching their victim-patrons. Suggested by that other body-snatcher—the resurrection-man, who was but a memory in 1840.

Bohemian Bungery (*Strand District*). Public-house patronized by struggling authors. Bohemian having been introduced by Murger for a fighting author, artist, or musician, and the tea-pot brigade having dubbed a licensed victualler a bung, from that adjunct to the beer barrel—this phrase became one of the results of time. The Nell Gwynne was once a Bohemian Bungery.

Bohemian down to his boots (*Art and Lit.*). Bohemian in excelsis. 'He is a . . .—such as they are'—that is 'the boots'.

At that time a young man, Nelson Kneass, a scion of an old and proud family, was horrifying 'society' by going round blacking his face as a negro minstrel. He was a brother of District Attorney Kneass, of this city, was highly educated, but was a 'Bohemian down to his boots'. — *N. Y. Mercury,* 15th January 1888.

Boiled Owl (*People's*). Drunk—as a boiled owl. Here there is no common sense whatever, nor fun, wit, nor anything but absurdity. Probably another instance of a proper name being changed to a common or even uncommon word. May be drunk as Abel Doyle—which would suggest an Irish origin like many incomprehensible proverbs too completely Anglicised.

It is a well-known fact in natural history that a parrot is the only bird which can sing after partaking of wines, spirits, or beer; for it is now universally agreed by all scientific men who have investigated the subject that the expression, 'Drunk as a boiled owl' is a gross libel upon a highly respectable teetotal bird, which, even in its unboiled state, drinks nothing stronger than rain-water. —*D. T.,* 12th December 1892.

Also whitish, washed-out countenance, with staring sleepy eyes.

Both were admirably made up, and Twiss had just the boiled-owlish appearance that is gained by working all night in a printing-office. — *Ref.,* 31st May 1885.

(*See* Dead as O'Donnel, Smithereens.)

Boiled Shirt (*Middle Class*). Clean, white—from the fact that if the shirt is not boiled it remains dull grey. W. America, but common in England.

'Waal now, say, you with the boiled shirt. What did Miss Maslam reply when you put the question?'—*Newsp. Cutting,* 1897.

Boko (*Common*). A huge nose. Corruption of 'beaucoup', the 'o' being national and preferred to the French 'ou'. Said to be descended from the time of Grimaldi, who would observe while 'joey-ing' (*q.v.*) 'C'est beaucoup', and tapping his nose. The phrase still remains, Anglicised, for a rough observing to another rough of a third gentleman's nose, will make the statement, 'I say—boko!' When one Espinosa, a French dancer, came to London (1858), the size of his wonderful nose drew so much gallery observation of 'boko' that Mr J. Oxenford, in the *Times*, especially referred to the organ and assumed it was art. Thereupon, Espinosa wrote explaining that the nose in question was *un don de la nature*.

He was as thin and pale as a coffee palace bit of roast beef, and his boko was as high and red as the sun on a foggy morning.
If he thought he had a black spot on his boko he'd go into convulsions.

Boko-smasher (*Street*). For elucidation of this elegant occupation *see* Boko.

Bolt-upright (*Peoples'*). A good example of graphic application. From the rigidity of a bolt, *e.g.*, 'he was bolt-upright, mum—and were so all the time, as 'is dear father was a-thrashin' of him.'

Bolted to the Bran (*Polit.*). Thoroughly sifted — one of the few puns or jocular phrases of which Gladstone could ever be accused.

Now the great questions are initiated, discussed, sifted, 'bolted to the bran', to use an expression more than once adopted by Mr Gladstone, before they come formally under the notice of the House of Commons.—*D.N.*, 12th August 1885.

Bombast (*Hist.*). Windy words— from Bumbast—the word, with a *double entendre* used for the material for stuffing out trunk hose, 16th and 17th centuries.

When I came to unrip and unbumbast this Gargantuan bag-pudding, I found nothing in it but dog's tripes.—*Gabriel Harvey*.

I. Disraeli says '*Bombast* was the tailors' term in the Elizabethan era for the stuffing of horse-hair or wool used for the large breeches then in fashion—hence the term was applied to high-sounding phrases "all sound and fury, signifying nothing".'

Bone (*London*, 1882). A thin man. Hence—'The bone has made a remark.' (Surrey Pantomime, London, 1882.)

Bone-clother (*Medical*). Port wine —which is popularly supposed to induce muscle.

Bone Idle (*Scottish*). Could not be more so. Probably the one atom of slang, if this can be called slang, which Carlyle exercised; may be found in a letter to his mother (15th Feb. 1847). 'I have gone *bone idle* these four weeks and more, and have been well done to every way.'

Bone-shaker (*Youths*, 1870 on). The earliest bicycle — which tried to break bones incessantly.

Bone-shop (*Lower Classes*). Workhouse—another of the more figurative and satirical names for this establishment. Here it refers presumably and untruly to the nature of the nourishment as producing nothing visible over the pauper bones.

'Two of 'em lives in the blooming bone-shop and the other little devil is in the small-pox hospital.'

Boner Nochy (*Clerkenwell*; Italian quarter). Good-night — imitated by the Clerkenwellians, from the *bona notte* of the Italians in Eyre Street Hill, Little Bath Street, and Hatton Garden; or it may be from the Spanish 'noche'—through the U.S.A.

'In any case', said Don Miguel, rising and preparing to retire for the night, 'in any case, can you wonder that I hate the Argentine, and everything connected with it? Buenas noches, senor!'—*Ev. News*, 9th December 1898.

Bonner (*Oxford* '*er*'). Bonfire. This specimen of 'er' shows a spice of satirical wit, for it is suggestive of Bishop Bonner, who certainly lit up many bonfires—Smithfield way.

Bonnet (*Lower Class*). To smash another's hat over the eyes. From French (*bonnet - a - cap*), and time Charles II. Bonnet passed into hat, but 'to bonnet' went sliding down until now it is in the gutter. (*See* Cloak, In his sleeve, Shawl.)

Bonny Robby (*Provincial*). Pretty but frail girl, probably from 'buona roba'—common in the time and court of Charles II.

DRUG: There visits me a rich young widow? FACE: A bona roba?— Garrick's *Abel Drugger*.

Bono Johnny (*Pigeon Chinese*). A good fellow. A Chinese invention; used by English sailors as warrant of good intentions.

Bonse (*School*). Head. 'Look out, or I'll fetch you a whack across the bonse'.

Boo ; Boo-ers (*Theatrical*, 1900). First-night gallery critics who replaced the goose (hissing) by 'booing' — probably because it was easier and more secretive.

Who would have thought, when an ill-mannered gallery 'booed' Mr Kerker's sparkling entertainment more than twelve months ago that it would achieve an unparalleled success at the Shaftesbury?—*D. T.*, 9th May 1899.

(*See* Wreckers.)

Boobies' Hutch (*Military*, 19 cent.). A drinking point in barracks, which, under certain circumstances, is open after canteen is closed. Satire probably upon the fools who have never had enough.

Boodle (*Liverpool*). One of the New York terms for money. Probably from the Dutch.

Hangman ain't such a bad fellow. He always treats the boys after he receives 'the boodle' from the Sheriff for sending an unfortunate to the other side ; although some folks are really afraid to go near him, and wouldn't even pass his house, I'd just as leave drink with him as I would with you.—*N. Y. Mercury*, 3rd May 1885.

In vain did one of the American comic journals some time ago depict, with becoming scorn, a hoard of needy European nobles struggling for the possession of a demure American beauty who bears a bag of what is locally known as 'boodle', and in polite society as lucre, in her shapely arms. — *D. N.*, 15th September 1890.

Book-maker (*Racing*, 19 cent.). A professional betting man who makes a betting book upon every race, or about every race in a season. He lays against all horses. A bookmaker of position must make immense profits, under the two conditions of betting with men who can pay and with men who will accept all the conditions offered by the bookmaker. In fact, under these 'circs', he rarely loses, while the money he may make is almost limitless. Sometimes, however, when a favourite wins, the 'ring' (that is the mass of betting men), is hit heavily.

Bookie (*Sporting*, 1881). The endearing 'ie', common in Johnnie and chappie, adapted to bookmaker. The 'maker' dropped — the suffix added.

Booking (*Public School*). Anything but—for it is casting volumes from you as missiles at the enemy for the time being, *e.g.*, 'Jannery split—book him together ! '

It would be a pity to deprive them of the chance of such 'glorious fun' as the 'mobbing' and 'booking' (that is pelting with books) of the model school tyrant. —*Newsp. Cutting.*

Boomerang (*American*, 1882). A vain folly, the consequence of which returns upon the perpetrator. This phrase is of course based upon the peculiar trajectory of the Australian boomerang, which, properly thrown, returns to the feet of the missile-thrower. In 1883 a play was produced by Mr Daly in New York, with the title '728 — or Casting the Boomerang'. A New York dramatic critic in the course of an article upon this play, wrote :—'the various follies or boomerangs of the principal characters return in the course of the play to plague them'.

Boomlet (*City*, 1896). A small 'boom'. Satirical invention used to attack the prosperous enemy.

Without troubling you with details, I may mention that during the recent West Australian boom—or, as some of my Stock Exchange friends prefer to call it, 'boomlet'—we succeeded in realising, etc.—Mr H. Bottomley, 10th December 1897.

Boomster (*City*, 1898). One who booms.

Boost (*Liverpool - American*). A hoist, toss, elevation—from the mode of raising one in the world hurriedly, exercised by an angry bull or even cow.

The cowcumber kin be made an ornament, will stand in any climate, and the placques and chromos will encourage art and give a fresh boost to decoration.

Boot (*Tailors' and Bootmakers'*, 19 cent.). Money — one of the trade applications to describe money — just exactly as the grocer calls coin 'sugar' or the milkman 'cream'. 'We've had the boot for that job.' Probably an abbreviation of 'beautiful', this being an obviously likely, vulgar, poetical name for money. (*See*

Needful.) Sometimes only a shilling. 'Can I have the boot?'—asked for at the end of a day's work. Indeed 'boot' in its most ordinary form is an advance on the weekly wages—but one never under a shilling. The lower advance, sixpence, is called a slipper. Also used in the tailoring trade. A worker will say at closing time, 'Please, sir, could you oblige me with the boot', while a more retiring soul would ask—'Could I have a slipper, sir!'

Booth Star (*Minor Stage*). Leading actor or actress in a 'booth'. 'Let me tell you a booth star is a good thing. You often get four parts a night. It is great experience—and it is the first step to Drury Lane.'

Booze (*Low London*). Intoxicants of all kinds, but particularly beer. May be from a name, but probably is an onomatope of quite modern date, from the boozing noise made by drunkards when falling off to sleep. Booze is drink in general—boozy, the result of drinking slowly and tandem, also to sleep.

At the hearing of the Southampton election petition, witness describing a procession of costermongers said : 'I heard some men shout that they wanted some more booze'. Mr Justice Wright: 'What?' Mr Willis: 'Booze, my lord, drink'. Mr Justice Wright: 'Ah!'

Booze plausibly claims a sort of corrupt descent from the genuine, if low, English word to 'bouse,' which occurs in our literature as early as 1567.—*D. T.*, 2nd December 1895.

Mr O'Donovan, the Eastern traveller, said to a press-interviewer (*World*, 31st January 1885), 'this word is Persian for "beer"'. Was he indulging in one of his ordinary jokes? If not, then the coalescing of these words and meanings is a very remarkable etymological fact.

Boozer (*Street*, 19 *cent.*). The public-house, as well as the public-house frequenter.

Big Tim goes with him, while I pops around the boozer.—*People*, 6th January 1895.

Booze-fencers (*Com. Lon.*, 1880). Licensed victuallers — from 'booze' drink, and fencers sellers — probably a wilful corruption of 'dispensers'.

You may run down booze fencers as much as you like, but you take my tip that there are more real gentlemen among them than among any other class, upper ten included.—*Newsp. Cutting.*

Booze-pushers (*Low London*, 19 *cent.*). Variant of booze-fencer.

When a bloke is flatch kennurd the booze pushers will give him any rot in the house, and that's very hard lines.— *Newsp. Cutting.*

Booze-shunters (*P. House*, 1870). Beer-drinkers.

They have never robbed a man of a hard day's work, and are the best booze shunters in the world without ever getting slewed.

To 'shunt' in railway life is to move from place to place. The booze-shunter moves the beer, or 'booze,' from the pot into his visceral arrangements. The term was started by the S.W.R. porters and guards, who use the larger public-houses in the neighbourhood of the terminus in the Waterloo Road (London).

Bo-peep (*Nursery*). Exclamation of fun. Johnson does not comprehensively elucidate this word when he gravely says it is from 'bo' and 'peep'. 'The art', he says, 'of looking out, and drawing back, as if frighted, or with the purpose to fright one another.' SHAKESPEARE, who has everything, has this phrase once—

'Then they for sudden joy did weep
And I for sorrow sung,
That such a king should play bo-peep
And go the fools among.'

DRYDEN has : 'There devil plays at bo-peep, puts out his horns, etc.'

Bor (*E. Anglian*). May be a shortening of neighbour, but is probably a corruption of boy—politely applied even to the oldest male inhabitant.

Bore (*Soc.*, 19 *cent.*). Weary. From tunnelling operations — steady, deadly, incisive 'jaw'. One of the trade metaphors which has passed into society and still stops there. Never has come down in the social scale. 'Lord Tom bores one to death with Tel-el-Kebir.'

To bore in the hills, is it? Well—don't bore me about it. — Miss M. EDGEWORTH, *The Absentee* (1809).

Born Days (*Peoples'*). Intensifier. Days that are born in an individual life. 'In all my born days I was never so insulted.' Other authorities maintain it should be 'borne,' or burdened, days — while still more recondite etymologists maintain it is 'bourn' — from our progress daily to that bourn whence no traveller returns. Fine example of three different words with the same sound offering as many meanings. Almost as good or as bad as 'mala'.

Born a bit tired (*Soc.*, 1870 on). Sarcastic excuse for a chronically lazy man. 'You can't reasonably expect him to work a couple of hours per day—he was born a bit tired'.

According to Mr Alderman Taylor, of the London County Council, there exists the man who is 'born a bit tired'.—*D. T.*, 13th February 1897.

Born with a sneer (*Literary*, 1850 on). Said of an implacable critic, attributed to Douglas Jerrold, who was good at sneering himself.

'Lord X would laugh at the Holy Sepulchre—he was, etc.'.

Light opera has familiarised the public with the man who was 'born with a sneer'.—*D. T.*, 13th February 1897.

Bosh (*Lower Official English*). A term applied by market inspectors to butterine, oleomargarine and other preparations practically too long - windedly named to please the official mind. Now extended to all adulterants or adulterated food. Mr O'Donovan declared this word to be Persian, and that it means 'empty'. Certainly the word used as an exclamation is replete with the idea of emptiness. (See *World*, 31st January 1883.)

Boss Time (*Anglo-Amer.*). Great pleasure, a supreme holiday; *e.g.*, 'Eve had a boss time last winter hunting deer up in Michigan.'

Now used in England.

Botany Beer Party (*Soc.*, 1882). A meeting where no intoxicants are drunk. In this year temperance, which had been growing in society for years, became drunk on affectation.

Botany Beer, it has recently been decided on judicial authority, is not beer at all.—G. A. Sala, in *Ill. Lond. News*, 10th March 1883.

Botherums (*Agricultural*). Yellow marigolds.

Among the turnips the yellow marigolds flourish mightily, so mightily that they are called locally 'botherums' by the farmers, for they are most difficult to get rid of.—*Newsp. Cutting.*

Bottle Nose (*Amer. Boys*). Scornful designation of the aged nose—an organ which so frequently derogates from the promise of youth. Applied without mercy to those no longer young. Heard in Liverpool. (*See* Bald-head, Scare-crow.)

Bottle up (*People's*). To refrain, restrain oneself; in another sense, to hem in the enemy, literally or figuratively.

The old story of Spanish lack of preparation was repeated; vessels were foul from long absence from dock, coal was deficient, ammunition ran short, and instead of commanding a fleet 'in being', Admiral Cervara was glad to bottle himself up in the harbour of Santiago.—*D. T.*, 17th June 1898.

Bottled (*People's*, 1898). Arrested, stopped, glued in one place—re-introduced during the American-Spanish war, immediately after the U.S.A. squadron had bottled the Spanish fleet in Santiago by closing the narrow opening to the harbour of that city; *e.g.*, 'My wife's come to town—I'm bottled. Next week, Jane.'

Bottle o' Spruce (*Peoples'*, 18 *cent.*). Zero, nothing, abbreviation of Bottle of Spruce Beer, which was cheap, commonplace, almost valueless; *e.g.*, 'Of course, you say I don't care a bottle of spruce.'

It also implies twopence; this sum, early in the 19th century being the price of a bottle of spruce beer. A man now seeking twopence asks for the price of a pint. His grandfather would have asked for a bottle of spruce.

Boughten or Bought (*Provincial*). Adjective of disparagement. Bought as distinct from superior home-made goods. No longer heard. Very pleasant, as illustrating a time when every country-house, large and small, had its spinsters, weavers, stocking-knitters, and straw-plaiters. This word is the more interesting from a modern instance in Ireland, where vanned bread that is carted from the baker's is a term of disparagement as compared with home-made bread.

Bouguereau quality (*Art*, 1884). Riskily effeminate. From the name of the great French painter, whose style is almost unwholesomely refined. The word has become cruelly perverted by its translation into common-place art chat. Now very extensively used. The Bouguereau quality is not only applied to figure painting and to sculpture, but reaches landscape and portrait painting, decoration, and even literature. The Bouguereau quality in letters is now very marked, and refers to work by both sexes. It is also applied to manners, speech, and even dress—remarkable example of rapid growth of a word.

The exhibition includes several notable works by famous painters. M. Bouguereau's group called 'Spring' is alone worth seeing, being a very refined example of his exquisite painting of the nude.—*D. N.*, 19th July 1886.

Boulevard-journalist (*Fr.*, 1856). Immediately after Louis Napoleon seized upon the throne of France, a number of contentious little journals appeared, mostly of a personal and scandalous character, for politics had been practically slain. The serious journals styled these new issues 'journaux des boulevards', their writers 'Les journalistes boulevardiers'. These literary gnats especially attacked England, as a rule, hence the English press willingly Anglicised the term to describe an unscrupulous writer until 'Society journalist' was discovered and accepted.

Boulevardier (*Franco-Eng.*, 1854-70). Paris man about town of third-rate position; accepted in England; *e.g.*, 'He is only a boulevardier.'

Bounced (*Amer.*, 1880). Ignominiously ejected. Derivation speaks fatally for itself.

While he did not feel greatly injured by being bounced from a club which numbered only seven lame old men and two dogs, he wanted to feel that justice was on his side, and he therefore appealed to the Lime-Kiln Club for its decision.— *Newsp. Cutting*.

Quite accepted in England.

Bounced muchly (*Amer. Tavern*). To be expelled with exceeding vigour. Bounced is a modern discovery, but the adverb 'muchly' is due to the wild philology of the mirth-provoking Artemus Ward.

Bouncer (*P. House*, '80's). Expeller of noisy or even mildly drunken customers. (*See* 'Chucker out'.)

The 'bouncer' of the House of Commons, going into the gallery, tried to find the guilty individual.—*Newsp. Cutting*.

Every one who mixes much in society in Whitechapel will understand the functions of the bouncer. When tavern liberty verges on licence, and gaiety on wanton delirium, the bouncer selects the gayest of the gay and — bounces him. To 'bounce' is simply to prevail on persons whose mirth interferes with the general enjoyment to withdraw from society which they embarrass rather than adorn. The bouncer almost invariably uses gentle means and moral persuasion. He bounces the erring 'as if he loved them'. His reputation for strength and science are so great that no one cares to resist the bouncer, and the boldest hold their breath and let themselves be bounced without a murmur. (*See* 'Chucker out'.) —*D. N.*, 26th July 1883.

Bouncing (*Peoples'*). Big, rotund —probably from bonse—a huge round marble.

Moreover, he has females in his employ who have been with him ten years, and many of them are the healthy mothers of bouncing boys and girls. I'm not quite sure under what circumstances children bounce, but I believe the expression is applied to strapping infants; though, again, I do not know under what circumstances children strap.— G. R. Sims, *Ref.*, 28th December 1884.

Bound to Shine (*Amer.*). Praise. The antithesis of 'clouded over' (*q.v.*).

Bournemouth (*Theatri.*, 1882-83). The deported Gaiety Theatre (London) —said satirically. The house was very icy that winter, and produced colds, while Bournemouth is the sanatorium for weak-chested invalids.

We don't care about Bournemouth— our pleasant name for the Gaiety, as everybody there is dying of coughs and colds. — *Sporting Times*, 3rd February 1883.

Bowl for Timber (*Cricketers'*). To send the ball at the martyr-player's legs—the timber. Discountenanced in later years—rather as waste of time than with any view of repression of personal injury. 'Try for timber— he's quivery'—that is to say, nervous.

Bowl (*Thieves'*, 19 *cent.*). Discovery —from 'bowl out'—a cricketing term. Good as illustrating how a national pastime always provides new language.

Grizard went with them, and said he wanted them to look sharp and get to Covent Garden before the market was open, in case it came to a 'bowl'. This was at four in the morning. The Alderman: What is a 'bowl'? Witness: I understand it to be a find-out.

Bowler (*Middle Class*). Hard, dome-shaped, man's felt hat. This hat ('80) took the place of the deer-stalker, which was the first modern felt hat produced in London. The bowler was a make of a smaller kind altogether. Origin not known—but probably from the name of the manufacturer. Has quite passed into the language.

All the description that the railway officials can give of the man is that he appeared well dressed, and wore a dark overcoat, closely buttoned, and a bowler hat.—*D. T.*, 15th February 1897.

Bow-wow-mutton (*Naval*). So bad that it might be dog-flesh.

Boxing out (*Austral. from Amer.*). Boxing outing—or bout.

Boy (*Bolton*). Man. There are no men in Bolton—all are boys, even at ninety. This quality they share alone, throughout England, with post-boys—who never grow up.

Boy Jones, The (about 1840). Secret informant. A chimney boy-sweep of this name tumbled out of a chimney at Buckingham Palace, or was found there under a bed, and was supposed to have heard State secrets as between the Queen and the then Prince Albert. Event supposed to have accelerated chimney-sweeping by machinery. For years 'the boy Jones' was suggestive of secrecy. 'The person who told me, my son, was the boy Jones.' (*See* 'Jinks the Barber', 'Postman's Sister'.)

Boyno! (*Nautical*—from Lingua Franca, or S. American). Friendly valediction; sometimes been used at meeting as 'Hullo!' 'Boyno—how is it?'

At parting, 'Well—so long! Boyno!' From the Spanish 'bueno', equivalent of 'God speed you.'

'Bueno, senoretta!' said the dwarf, and walked away with the superintendent.

Brace up (*Thieves'*). Pawn stolen property. Corruption perhaps from Fr. 'Braser', to fabricate—at length; 'braser des faffes'—to fabricate false papers. May have been introduced by French criminals.

Bracelets (*Thieves'*). Humorous title for hand-cuffs; in itself a satirical description.

Brads (*North Country*). One of the trade names for money—in this case halfpence. The word comes from the boot-making trade, and is still in use in the north. Brads are small nails.

'Hey, lass, thee shalt hev' thy tay-tray when t' brads coom along.'

Bradshaw (*Middle Class*). Precise person, great at figures. From 'Bradshaw's Railway Guide'; *e.g.*, 'Quite a Bradshaw—my dear.'

Brag (*Soc.*, 1800-30). A game of cards in which the players tried to give the idea that they held better cards than they did. Hence the phrase, 'Don't brag by the card.'

Speculation does not greatly surprise me, I believe, because I feel the same myself; but it mortifies me deeply because speculation was under my patronage; and, after all, what is there so delightful in a pair royal of Braggers? It is but three nines or three knaves, or a mixture of them.—*Jane Austen's Letters*, 1809.

Bran New (*Peoples'*). A corruption of brand new, that which is branded with the name of the maker. Probably from Sheffield.

Brandy and Fashoda (*Soc.*, October 1898). Brandy and soda, of course. Good example of droll pleonasm. From the discovery of the French captain, Marchand, at Fashoda, almost immediately after the conquest of the dervishes at Omdurman (1898). (*See* S. and B.)

Brandy-shunter (*L. Class*). He that swalloweth frequent eau-de-vie.

Thomas Spencer Carlton, the eminent brandy-shunter, was born about thirty-five years ago of wealthy yet honest parents.—*Newsp. Cutting.*

Brass (*Metallic England*). Money. The commonest term for cash all over England, and almost the only one used in the copper and iron industries.

The prisoner and another man stopped the prosecutor, and explained that it was 'money to buy beer' that they wanted. 'Haven't any' said he. 'Yes, you have' shouted Quain; 'and we've got to have some of it. Now, then, brass up, or we'll shove you through it.'—*Newsp. Cutting.*

Brass-knocker (*Cadgers'*). Broken victuals. This may be a corruption from the Romany, but it is now suggestive of a house whose superior respectability warrants the absence of complete economy and the presence of pieces.

Brayvo Hicks (*Theat.*, 1830). A peculiar form of applause only used in approbation of muscular demonstration on the lower stage — especially broadsword exercise. Derived from Hicks, a celebrated favourite actor for many years, more especially 'upon the Surrey side'. After him he passed away the applausive phrase first applied to him was inherited for many years by his natural successors. It may still be heard in out-of-the-way little theatres. Applied in S. London widely ; *e.g.*, 'Brayvo Hicks—into 'er again. Mary — give 'er the gravil rash.'

Brayvo Rouse (*E. London*). Applause—approval. From the name of an enterprising proprietor of 'The Eagle', afterwards 'The Royal Grecian', a theatre situated in the City Road, now the Central London headquarters of the Salvation Army. This clever man was one of the first managers to give a long series of well-presented French light operas in English. All the best of Auber's work was dressed in English by Rouse — who, it is to be feared, annexed without 'authorial' complications. Whenever he appeared it was always 'Brayvo Rouse'. Old players still show his house in the City Road. 'Buck up — to it again — brayvo Rouse!'

Bread and Meat Man (*Military*). An officer of the Army Service Corps.

Bread-basket (*London Trade*, 19 *cent.*). Obvious invention of genius for stomach. Hence never extended to Ireland, where the equivalent is tatersack, the mouth being tatur-trap.

Miss Selina Slops was invited before his Worship, on the charge of smearing the face of B.O. 44 with a flatiron, while hot, and also with jumping upon his bread-basket, while in the execution of his duty.—*Cutting*.

Break (*L. Class*). Ruin, overcome, expose, injure — justly or unjustly. Expression of victory—'I broke 'im —I broke 'im through and through!' In middle classes 'to break a man' is an abbreviation of break away from him—to cease to know him—to cut him. This word obtains ever-increasing significations.

Breakdown (*Negro-plantation*). A particular kind of dance, for one generally, where the steps are varied, but the performer does not move far from his place; coming from the old French settlements of America, probably a corruption of 'Rigodon' — Anglicised or rather Americanised.

I have heard of burlesque actors dancing a 'breakdown', but the other day the *Echo*, on its broadsheet, announced, 'breakdown of an excursion train!'—*Entr'acte*, January 1883.

Breakers Ahead (*Nautical*). Necessarily, warning of coming danger.

'Melita' enjoyed a very short and inglorious career. It started with 'breakers ahead' and ended with brokers on the spot, I believe.—*Ref.*, 14th January 1883.

Breaking Camp (*American backwoods*). To change one's camping place; figuratively, to leave it by way of death.

I could have braced up under it if my poor Mary had got sick and died at home with me holdin' of her hand and consolin' her as she was breakin' camp for the other world.—*Newsp. Cutting*.

Breast the Tape (*Sporting*). Conquer, lead, overcome—from touching the tape with breast in running matches.

Leeds at the best of times does not rejoice in a very clear atmosphere; but when she wraps herself in a fog, she can give London a good start in the race for objectionableness and breast the tape an easy winner at the finish. — *Ref.*, 27th November 1887.

Breath strong enough to carry coal (*Anglo.-Amer.*). Drunk.

. . . comes home at three o'clock in the morning with a breath strong enough to carry the coal.—*Newsp. Cutting*.

Brekker (*Oxford 'er'*). Breakfast —a great find in the 'er' dialect, but probably in origin dating from the nursery.

Bremerhaven Miscreant (*Amer. polit.*, 1883). At this place were made the clock-work dynamite torpedoes which ('80 - '83) alarmed European society.

'Bremerhaven miscreant'. These toys, in which a charge of dynamite is exploded by clockwork, are manufactured, it is commonly believed, by Mr Crowe, of Peoria. In a free country, of course, where there is a large Irish vote, a clever mechanic may make what he pleases, and we are far from expressing the futile hope that the Government of the United States will interfere with the industry of Mr Crowe and his followers. But our nation, though averse to a policy of

Protection, might not unreasonably lay a heavy prohibitive duty on 'infernal machines'.—*D. N.*, March 1883.

Briar (*Peoples'*, 1870). A briar-root pipe. A modern invention, supposed to be of god-like comfort. 'Briar-root is sometimes used to describe a corrugated, badly-shaped nose.'

Brickfielder (*Australian*). Hot north wind, bringing with it a red impalpable dust from the interior. It penetrates even locks, and stains fabrics in drawers of a dull brick red —hence the graphic name. Generally comes after great heat in January, and portends a grateful change in the weather. 'What a brickfielder you are!'—meaning nuisance.

Bricky (*Peoples'*). Brave, fearless, adroit—after the manner of a brick; said even of the other sex, 'What a bricky girl she is.' (*See* 'Plucky', 'Cheeky'.)

Bridges-bridges (*Printers'*). A cry to arrest a long-winded story. Probably corruption of 'abregeons-abregeons'—in a deal Anglicized. (*See* 'Grasses', 'Chestnuts'.)

Bridges and no Grasses (*Printers'*). Secret. A bridge is an absentee without leave, who has not sent a substitute, or grass. When a combination is made to prevent a master from getting out his paper by the printers absenting themselves, this would be called Breaking the Bridge. The whole system belongs to a system of rattening, a system which is being swept away by the strides of education.

Bridgeting (*Amer.-Eng.*, 1866 on). Obtaining money under false pretences, or even by criminal process, from servant girls. This word has taken astounding journeys. It dates from Ireland, where so many female children are named after Saint Bridget that the name became as typical of the Irish serving-girl in New York as Pat (from St Patrick) is typical of the Irish working-man. From the fifties onward Bridget became synonymous in New York with domestic servant. In the sixties the Fenian leaders in New York discovered a new way of getting money by issuing notes of the Bank of the Republic of Ireland at 50 per cent. discount. Large sums were obtained through many years, and money is obtained even now from sentimental Irish servant women in New York—much of which has, it has been declared, aided the Irish Nationalist movement in the House of Commons. Term now applied in many directions.

Brief (*Peoples'*). Letter, or piece of paper with writing. Probably ancient. May be from the use by the First or Second George of this term for letter.

Brief (19 *cent.*). False reference. The system of false references has so increased that many masters do not ask for references, but accept the servant or clerk, discovering him to be honest or dishonest, as the peculiar disposition of the employer lies.

Brenner said, 'I've given the Jew boy another brief. I hope he'll pay me this time.' Alleged conspiracy to defraud Licensed Victuallers.—*Morning Advertiser*, 25th February 1892.

Brief (*Lawyers' Clerks'*). Pawnbroker's ticket, suggested perhaps by the shape. The synonyms for this signal of woe are countless, and the list is always growing.

'Ah, Sam, how are yer? 'ere, will you buy the brief of a good red 'un, in for a fifth its value?'—*Newsp. Cutting.*

This mystic enquiry refers to the duplicate (this paste-board being a simulacrum of a card firmly pinned to the pledge) of a pawned watch—a red 'un, a term which is probably the corruption of a proper name — say Redding. (*See* Tombstone.)

Brighton Bitter (*Public House*). Mild and bitter beer mixed—satirical reference to some Brighton ale-house keepers, who, knowing Sunday and Monday excursionists are only chance customers, never give these customers bitter beer, though they pay its price.

Brim (*Thieves'*). A fearless woman of the town. Origin evidently foreign —probably the French army, where a 'brimade' is equal to English military 'making hay', and introduced to London by way of Soho.

Bristols (*Soc.*, 1830 on). Visiting cards, from the date when these articles were printed upon Bristol—*i.e.*, cardboard; a superior Bristol make.

Inside Madame Bernhardt's house there is a register open for the signatures of callers, and the card basket shows a large collection of 'Bristols'. — *D. T.*, 17th February 1898.

Brit (*Theatr.*). An endearing diminutive conferred by its denizens on the Britannia Theatre; as, 'How do you get to the Brit?' 'Take a train east—one station this side of Jericho.' (*See* Bird, Vic, Eff, 'Delphi, and Lane.)

British Roarer (*Peoples'*). Our heraldic and symbolical lion.

The tribunes are dressed in red cloth, and are guarded by four comic Byzantine lions, which act as symbols of our British roarer.—*D. N.*, May 1883.

Broad Faker (*Thieves'*). Card-player, probably not wholly dissociated from cheating. Broad may simply refer to the width of the card; but it probably refers to the name of an early maker of cards—probably marked for cheating.

Broad-gauge Lady (*Railway Officials', passing to Peoples'*). One who makes rather a tight fit for five on a side. 'I know I'm a broad-gauge lady—but I can't help it, can I?' Herbert Campbell's 'gag', Drury Lane Panto. 1884-85. Passed away with the broad-gauge in the '90's.

Brogue (*Irish*). Local lingual accent—from the name of the foot-covering worn by the peasants. 'From the brogue to the boot' (gentleman) 'all speak the same of him, and can say no other'. Maria Edgeworth, *The Absentee*, ch. 9.

Broken Brigade (*Soc.*, 1880 on). Poor, younger sons living on their wits. 'Broken'—another form of 'stone-broke'.

The younger son has been brought up in almost precisely the same fashion as his elder brother. . . . When, therefore, he finds himself without the legitimate means to live and enjoy life, as he has been trained to do, he must either find illegitimate means or else join that party which has earned for itself the un-enviable name of the broken brigade. —*D. N.*, 26th September 1887.

Brokered (*L. C.*, 1897). A specimen of the daily making of language—here upon the pre-historic basis of the noun creating the verb. How much more concise than 'got the brokers in', and so much nearer the literal, for one broker who brokers, as a rule, suffices.

Defendant complained that she had been 'brokered' by mistake, and that she had to go out to wash to help pay this debt for another man, as her husband was only surety.—*D. T.*, 20th November 1897.

Brolly (*Public School*, 1875 on). Umbrella. This is evidently a corruption of umbrella. How did it come about? It descends from good society. Let us suppose the then Prince of Wales hears one of his children when very young make an effort to say umbrella, with 'brolly' for result, that he therefore applies the word very naturally to his umbrella; that he is heard at the Marlborough, where the word is adopted, and so passed on to the sons of the members of the club, who carry it down into their schools—whence it spreads. In King's College the word is quite naturalised. (*See* 'Gamp,' 'Gingham,' 'Sangster'.)

Brompton Boilers (*Art*, 1870 on). A three-roofed iron-built museum at S. Kensington. It got this name from the aspect of the building, and retained it nearly fifty years. They were only demolished in 1898.

As little is there room or reason for carting them (the pictures left to the nation by Sir Richard Wallace), off to South Kensington, especially so long as the administrative powers leave the 'Brompton boilers' in their present absolutely disgraceful condition.—*D. T.*, 2nd April 1899.

Brooks of Sheffield (*M. Cl.*, 1853 on). *Nemo*—warning to be careful as to names. 'Who was he?' oh—Brooks of Sheffield. From the first three numbers of David Copperfield—where David is referred to by Mr Murdstone in this name. Now passing away—but still used in the '80's. On all fours with Binks the Barber.

Never mind; I hear that Smith, the champion pugilist of the universe and all England, is going to find out who that there Brooks of Sheffield is who boasts that he knocked Smith out in a private glove fight.—*Ref.*, 31st July 1887.

Broom (*Soc.*, 1860 on). A would-be swell—a total pretence. Corruption of Brum, with the 'u' long, it being an abbreviation of Brummagem, which is a contemptuous pronunciation of Birmingham—for many years, until the '80s, a synonym for pinchbeck manufactures. Good example of substituting a known word for another less known — on this occasion the process taking place in Society itself.

Broomstick (*Canadian*). A gun or rifle. No word could more perfectly outline the peaceful character of the Canadian as distinct from his American brother, when it is borne in mind that the latter calls his gun, shooting iron. The domesticity of 'broomstick' yields history in itself.

Brother Bung (*London Tavern*). A fellow-publican; as, 'Oh, they're brother bungs', said contemptuously. However, after the usual smart English manner of taking even Mr John Bull by the horns, the less dignified publicans have accepted the situation amongst themselves, and will frequently say when meeting, 'How goes it, brother bung?'

Brougham (*Soc.*, 1820 [?]). A small, close carriage, named after Lord Brougham—it is even said invented by him. The name has lasted to this day as 'broom' amongst high-class people — though less well-informed souls will give the two syllables. Recently a smaller brougham with rounded front has come to be called, by leading people, 'cask', and even 'tub'.

Brown (*Mooney's, Strand*). Two pennyworth of whisky. Evasive, delicate mode of getting a 2d. drink, the usual whisky-gargle being half sixpence. Good example of a singularly local passing word. Mooney's is the Irish whisky-house of the whole Strand.

Brown George (*Oxford fin*, 1890 on). Large jug holding bath-water, from its colour, and the name of the earthenwarer.

Brown Polish (*Anglo-Amer.*). A mulatto. Outcome of the use of tan-coloured boots. Grotesquely graphic — on the lines of Day and Martin (1840) describing a negro, because D. & M.'s blacking was *so* black.

Brown Stone Fronts (*Amer. political*). Aristocrats.

The dream of the rich New Yorker, realised in the case of Mr Vanderbilt, is to live in a brown stone house.

In New York politics, efforts are sometimes made to bring about what are called the primary elections in July, because in that month, as it is said, 'the brown stone fronts are out of town'.—*D. N.*, 10th October 1883.

The height of respectability is to live in a brown stone-fronted house—that is to say, to show a bold veneer of brown stone to the world that passes along the main street, putting off your neighbours at the back with ordinary brick.—*Newsp. Cutting*.

Brown Study (*Soc.*) Deep study. But why brown? Blue, or black and white would be more appropriate. Possibly from a celebrated 'varsity man given to being lost in thought.

Brown to (*Com. Classes*). To understand. Origin very obscure—probably from a keen man of this name. 'He didn't brown to what she was saying'—not a little bit.' Possibly from meat proving its goodness by handsomely browning while on the roast.

Brown 'un, The (*Sporting*, 1870). *The Sporting Times*—from the then tone of its paper. (*See* Pink 'un.)

Brownies (*Lower London*, 1896). Common cigarettes—three for one halfpenny. From proper name, Brown. Outcome of cigarette-smoking.

To meet humbler feminine wants there are now halfpenny packets of cigarettes containing three, known as ' Brownies.'— *D. T.*, 3rd March 1898.

Bruffam (*Soc.*, 1860 on). A droll variation of Brougham, the small carriage known by that name—Brough itself being pronounced Bruff. Another illustration of the 'gh' eccentricities.

A story runs that Brougham, on being rallied by the Iron Duke as a man whose name would go down to posterity as a great lawyer, statesman, etc., but who would be best known by the name of the carriage which had been christened after him, retorted that the Duke's name would no doubt go down to posterity as that of a great general and the hero of a hundred fights, but that he would be best remembered by having a particular kind of boot named after him.—*Newsp. Cutting*.

Brulée (chiefly Naval, 1863). A very obscure word. Term is used at Vingt et un, and consists of the dealer helping himself to two cards, one from the top of the pack, the other from the bottom. This is permissible before the new dealer commences his deal. He has the option of making the brulée or not. If the two cards are not a natural (one ace and one court card or ten), he pays the unit to each player of the money played for—if it is a natural, he takes from each player from four to six times the stake, according to agreement. Sheer gambling. Not good form. 'N.B. Nap' (Napoleon) has completely swept away Vingt et un— and 'brulée avec' — as the French golden youth might say. Probably from the name of the inventor.

Brums (*R. S. Exchange*). N.W. Railway stock. All railway stocks have names of convenient brevity.

The nicknames of stocks at the Exchange are, on the whole, disrespectful. Thus, the ordinary stock of the London and North-Western Railway is known as 'Brums', although 'Brummagem' is anything but a proper description of so solid a property. 'Mids' will readily be recognized as Midland Railway stock ; and an equal facility of identification may be claimed for 'Chats' (Chatham and Dover), 'Mets' (Metropolitan), 'Districts' (Metropolitan District), and some others. 'Dovers', however, would scarcely sugggest at first sight the South - Eastern Railway, nor 'Souths' the London and South-Western ; while the North Staffordshire shares are irreverently spoken of as 'Pots,' after the Potteries.

The pet names are in every way preferable. Who would not cheerfully lose money on 'Berthas' (Brighton Ordinary), on 'Doras' (South-Eastern Deferred), on 'Noras' (Great Northern Deferred), on 'Saras' (Manchester, Sheffield, and Lincoln Deferred), or even on 'Dinahs' (Edinburgh and Glasgow Ordinary)? On the other hand, there is an added exasperation in the thought of having rashly 'put one's pile' on 'Caleys' (Caledonian Ordinary) or 'Haddocks' (Great Northern of Scotland Ordinary.) —*Newsp. Cutting*.

Brush (*Public House*). Odd name for a small glass, which is an inverted cone fixed on a thick stem of glass ; used for dram-drinking in London— and thus fancifully named from its outline to a house-painter's brush.

That little bloke, with no more flesh on him than on a one and ninepenny fowl, put away six pots of four-half, three kervoortens of cold satin in a two-out brush, a 'arf kervoorten of rum, and a bottle of whisky.—*Newsp. Cutting*.

Brush Power (*Artists'*, 1882). Simply—painting, e.g. 'Never was Mr Millais' brush power so manly and assured.'—*Crit. of R. Academy*, 1883, John Forbes-Robertson.

Bryant & May's 'Chuckaways' (*E. London*, 1876). Girls employed in B. & M.'s lucifer match factory. Here one reading is droll, the other perhaps very cruel—a combination too frequent in peoples' wit. Chuckaways is one of the graphic names given to lucifer matches, simply because after striking and using, the remainder of the lucifer is thrown or 'chucked' away. Here, in effect, the lucifer is applied to the cause, the maker. The rhyming too should be remarked. This same cruel meaning of chuckaway may be left to the imagination. Of course girl lucifer match-makers, following a miserable and unhealthy industry, are not the equals of Belgravian match-making mothers.

Bub (*Old Eng.*—now American). In *The Country Girl* the author often calls her husband 'bub.' In the States it is a friendly term addressed to a boy.

'Your husband ought to be arrested for working on Sunday!' 'Working on Sunday—come here, bub! Now, bub, if you'll prove that my husband ever worked on Sunday, or any other day in the week, I'll give you a dollar! I've lived with him for twenty years, and have always had to buy even his whiskey and tobacco, and now if he's gone to work I want to know it!' The boy backed off without another word.—1882.

Bubble (*Soc.*, 17 *cent.*). To cheat. 'To bubble you out of a sum of money.' Decker's *Horn-book*, 1609.

The well-meaning ladies of England, when they subscribed for that monument, had not the faintest notion of what they were doing. They were indeed 'bubbled', to use a phrase of Queen Anne's time.—*D. N.*, 1882.

POLLY. I'm bubbled.
LUCY. I'm bubbled.
POLLY. Oh, how I'm troubled.
—*Beggars' Opera*.

Still used by the lowest. 'I bubbled 'im to rights.' Equal to 'bilk'—a more modern word.

Bubble around (*Amer. - Eng.*). Rather a strong verbal attack, generally by way of the press. 'I will back a first-class British subject for bubbling around against all humanity.'—Besant & Rice, *The Golden Butterfly*, ch. 18.

Buck (*Soc.*, 18 *cent.*). Young man of fashion, derived not from the male deer, but a diminutive of 'buckram', a stiffening fabric used in setting out the full-skirted coats of the eighteenth century. The word lasted fashionably to about 1820. It is now only used by thoroughly vulgar people. Its fashionable equivalent in the middle of the nineteenth century was 'swell', which is rapidly being vulgarized. 'Toff' is an invention of the envious enemy. Buck obtained another meaning during the '70's—a sham cab fare. During the evening the Strand being gorged with crawler cabs, it was determined to keep empty cabs out of that thoroughfare from 10 to 11 P.M. Cabmen desirous of getting through on the chance of obtaining a fare from a Strand theatre or restaurant would ask passing young men—fairly dressed, if poor, to pretend to be a fare in order to get past the line of police. This fraudulent passenger came to be called by cabmen, and afterwards by the police, 'a buck', used no doubt satirically.

When a cabman wants to drive past the police to get access to theatre exits out of his own turn he puts a man into his cab and drives rapidly on, as if taking a fare away. This sham fare in street parlance, we learn, is 'only a buck'.—*D. N.*, 26th September 1887.

Mr Bridge said in this case it had not been shown that the man was 'a buck' in the ordinary acceptance of the term. Defendant had evidently allowed his friend to ride on the spring. This was an offence against the regulations, in addition to entailing extra labour on the horse. He hoped it would be understood that in future in such cases, and where 'bucks' were employed, the full penalty would be imposed. — *Newsp. Cutting*, October 1887.

Buck against (*Anglo-Amer.*). To oppose violently. From the stubborn bucking habit of stag and goat.

Buck up and take a chilly (*Navy*). Advice to a man to pull himself together after a hard drink. The 'chilly' may be literal, since cayenne is supposed to be a signal help in restoring the collapsed patient to sense and sobriety.

Buck or a doe (*Anglo-Amer.*). A man or woman, obviously from the habit and mode of thinking by backwoods' men.

The startled girl gave him a glance, but no other demonstration of recognition. 'It's kinder rough to rattle 'em along like freight in this way (coffined, dead), but where you ain't got no plantin' facilities of yer own it's got to be done. Was the lamented a buck or a doe?'—1883.

Buck Parties (*Soc.*). Bachelor meets. From Australia.

The one drawback to our pleasure has been the delicate state of Mrs Pen's health. This sent me out to what are called here 'buck parties', *i.e.*, parties of men only, when otherwise I should have gone with her to (what she calls) more civilised gatherings.—*Ref.*, 19th September 1888.

Bucket-shop (*City*, 1870 on). Stockjobber's, or outside broker's office. From U.S.A.

RUINED BY BUCKET SHOPS — A once prosperous merchant's defalcation and suicide. Montreal. Samuel Johnson . . . absconded. . . . Two detectives started with him for this city. . . . This morning he jumped from the train at the Tanneries, and was found dead with two bullets through his brain. Johnson is another victim of bucket-shop speculation. It is known that he has lost thousands of dollars in these places. The community is indignant at the manner in which so many citizens are being ruined by bucket shops, and steps will certainly be taken to close them.—*N. Y. Mercury*, 2nd October 1887.

Bucking match (*Negro*). Fight with heads. Fine example of throwback to savage life. Sheer atavism.

Stacey appeared to be the more belligerent of the two, insisted on having the quarrel out, and challenged Kline to fight him without fists or weapons. This is the usual manner among Philadelphia negroes to denominate a 'bucking match', which is not an infrequent method of settling disputes. — *Newsp. Cutting.*

Bucking the Tiger (*Anglo-Amer.*). Gambling heavily.

Entering by a green baize door, the visitors found themselves in a large and well-lighted room—the lair of the tiger. Gamblers usually speak of faro playing as 'bucking the tiger', but if any one imagines that the animal is other than a fat, sleek, attractive-looking feline they make a great mistake. Only the furry coat is exposed ; one must join in the play in order to get a glimpse of the fangs and claws.—*Newsp. Cutting.*

An oil region correspondent of a Philadelphia journal, who evidently 'has been there'—at both places—says that 'boring for oil is like "bucking the tiger"', or eating mushrooms ; if you live it is a mushroom ; if you die it is a toadstool. If you strike oil you have bored in the right place; if you don't you haven't.—*Newsp. Cutting.*

In the United States the operation of staking all one's money in a gaming hell is called 'bucking the tiger'.—G. A. SALA.

Bud (*Amer.-Eng.*). A young girl. Real original American discovery.

The American novelist is in rather a tight place. When he is in a tight place —or, indeed, whether he is or not—he usually takes the world into his confidence. His grievance at present is the censorship of the 'bud', or young girl, of his native land.—*D. N.*, 31st May 1889.

Buff to the Stuff (*Thieves'*, 19 *cent.*). Accomplices who swear to stolen property as theirs.

They might as well have the twenty quid as not, for they were sure to get out of it, as they were going to send some people to 'buff to the stuff', a slang term for claiming the property supposed to have been stolen, and stating that they had sold it.—*Newsp. Cutting.*

Buffalo Boys (*Music Hall*). Comic negroes, affecting stupidity, probably from one of the earliest nigger melodies.

Buffer (*Peoples'*). A catspaw, intermediator, illustrator of the couplet

'Those who in quarrels interpose
Often get a bloody nose.'

Comes in one line from the railway buffer, which breaks the impingement of railway carriages, and in another line from buffo, who in comic Italian opera is always ill-used. 'Poor old buffer,' said by Robson to the ghost of Lablache, the buffo, in *The Camp at the Olympic*, by J. R. Planché.

Buffer (*Navy*). A boatswain's mate —probably because he is the buffer state, so to speak, between boatswain and able seaman.

Buffer State (*Political*). A small territory dividing the countries or colonies of two greater states—as Belgium, which is a buffer state between France and Germany. Holland is another buffer state. So also is 'Andorre'. So also were Monaco and Mentone the 'buffer' once between France and Italy.

Buffs, Buffaloes (*Secret Society*) A jovial, so-called, secret society—'Ancient Order of Buffaloes.' Probably in the commencement from 'beau fellows'—as Hullo! my beau fellows!— beau being a word much used in the last century. The process of being made a buffalo fifty years ago was very simple, the victim being sworn on the sacred ibis. Before him and everyone of the elect a cork was placed, when the president told the acolyte that upon a given word every man was to seize his cork, the last to touch his cork having to pay 2s. 6d. The word was given, the victim seized his cork, and as no one budged or moved a hand, evidently he was the last to touch his cork. So he paid his half-crown. The Buffaloes (A.S.O.B.) have been for a long time a well-ordered society—possibly too jovial, but certainly in some degree charitable. They have proper officers, give annual jewels of gold, not perhaps of a very high carat, to their officers, and have ceremonials, in some degree choral, as the astonished outsider may learn for himself as, on passing a lodge, he hears the brethren proclaiming their intention to 'Chase the Buffalo', though where they would find the buffalo it would be difficult to say. Sisters, *i.e.*, brethren's wives, come without to hear these things, and go home trembling and minatory. The Buffs are strictly non-political.

Buffy (*Com. Lond.*). Drunk—probably Anglicized from bevvy. 'He always goes to bed buffy.' Or it may be swelled with drink, from French *bouffi—temp.* Charles II.

He, the driver, must get up earlier and go to bed without getting buffy, which he hadn't done for a week of Sundays, before he found that little game would draw in the dibs.—*Newsp. Cutting.*

Bug (*Amer.*). Abbreviation of bugbear—a nuisance.

The phraseology of Edison, to judge from his day-book records, is synthetic, strongly descriptive, and quaint. . . . A 'bug' is a difficulty which appears insurmountable to the staff. To the master it is 'an ugly insect that lives on the lazy, and can and must be killed.'— *Newsp. Cutting.*

Bugaboo (*Amer.*). A panic—of an absurd and unreasoning character. 'The recent Fenian bugaboo.'—1867.

Bug-eaters (*Amer.*). People of Nebraska. This word must be read 'beetle' in English. Refers to the enormous amount of insect life in this territory.

Bug-shooter (*Schools and Univs.*). A volunteer — volunteers not being popular with gown—the system being left to town.

If you join the Volunteers you are discourteously spoken of as a 'bug-shooter'.—*D. T.*, 14th August 1899.

Bugs (*Lowest Classes*). Wall-flowers. From their colour, signal example of lower class tendency to horribly vulgar association of ideas, even in relation to such pleasant visitors as these blooms—the first of the year—frequently seen in penny bunches in poorest neighbourhoods early in February. Who'll 'av a pennorth o' bugs? (*See* Bloods.)

Build up (*Thieves'*). To array in good clothes, for trade purposes.

Jennings agreed to 'build up' Archer with clothes, and at another meeting brought him a coat in order that he might appear respectable when he visited his old fellow-servants at the Lodge.—*Newsp. Cutting.*

Bulge, To get the (*Anglo-Amer.*). To gain an advantage; from the approaching conqueror in wrestling or fighting overcoming the opponent, so that the conqueror's chest-muscles are forward, or bulging.

Mr Dodsley has, to use the new phrase of American slang, 'the bulge' on Messrs Longmans.—*D. N.*, 19th June 1891.

'You wanted to get the bulge on it, didn't you?' 'Wanted to do what?' 'Wanted to get the bulge on it.' 'What do you mean by bulge?'—*N. Y. Mercury,* 1892.

Bull (*Common Lodging - House*). A second brew of tea.

The lodgers divide their food frequently, and a man seeing a neighbour without anything will hand him his teapot, and say, 'Here you are, mate; here's a bull for you.' A 'bull' is a teapot with the leaves left in for a second brew.—G. R. Sims, *Horrible London.*

Bull and Cow (*Rhyming*). A row.

Bull-doze, To bull-doze (*Amer.-Eng.*, 19 *cent.*). Political bullying. The origin of this phrase is absolutely lost, always supposing that it was ever found. Mr Rees, an American authority on obscure words, says (1887):

'A bull-doze is a term used in inflicting punishment upon an unruly animal; the weapon a strap made out of the hide of a bull. During the existence of slavery the term "bull-doze" was used when a negro was to be whipped; the overseer was instructed to give him as many lashes as was applied to an animal, hence the term 'bull-doze'." Maybe 'doze' has reference to dozen.

This word is also used in private life to describe pestering conduct:

Serves you just right for bull-dozing me a whole month to make this infernal excursion.—*Newsp. Cutting.*

The following quotation will show that even in the U.S.A. themselves this term is not fully understood:

'What do they mean by bull-dozing?' asked an inquisitive wife the other evening. 'I suppose they mean a bull that is half asleep.' And the injured one kept on with her sewing, but said nothing.

Bulley (*Westminster School*). The lappet of a King's scholar's gown—probably rather meant to describe the wearer than the gown.

Bullfinches (*Hunting*). High hedges—probably from the name of some owner or farmer opposed to hunting.

To the stag, we imagine, it is a matter of small concern whether his enemies are counter-jumpers or leapers of bullfinches.—*Newsp. Cutting,* March 1833.

A bullfinch in Ireland is a stone hedge.—*Athenæum,* 17th Feb. 1887, p. 221.

Bullock's horn (*Artizans' rhyming*). Pawn.

Put your kicksies in the bullock's horn.—*Cutting.*

Bully (*O. Eng.*). From bullocking and bull-tossing.

Yes, you villain, you have defiled my own bed, you have, and then you have charged me with bullocking you into owning the truth. It is very likely, an't please your worship, that I should bullock him.—Fielding, *Tom Jones,* bk. ii. ch. 6. (*See* Bully-rag.)

Bully (*Amer.*). Capital, good, excellent — perhaps from French Colonial times in the south, and from 'bouilli'—the stewed beef which equals in Gallic popularity and stability the 'roast' of England and the States.

'What's the matter with you?' 'My leg's smashed,' says he. 'Can't yer walk?' 'No.' 'Can yer see?' 'Yes.' 'Well,' says I, 'you're a —— Rebel, but will you do me a little favour?' 'I will,' says he, 'ef I ken.' Then I says, 'Well, ole butternut, I can't see nothin'. My eyes is knocked out, but I ken walk. Come over yere. Let's git out o' this. You pint the way, an' I'll tote yer off the field on my back.' 'Bully for you,' says he. And so we managed to git together. We shook hands on it.—1863.

Mr Rees (N. York) says: 'Bully' is used as indicating satisfaction amongst lower English classes—as 'Never mind, as they say in the waxey crowd, he's a bully boy.'

Captain Townshend saw an omnibus pole strike a gentleman's horse in the flank, knocking over both steed and rider, and the man, calling out 'Bully for you,' drove away laughing.

Bully about the muzzle (*Dogfanciers'*). Too thick and large in the mouth.

'Angelina [a terrier] is bully about the muzzle,' said Maulevrier ; we shall have to give her away.'—Miss Braddon, *Phantom Fortune*.

Bully-fake (*London*, 1882). A compound of 'bully'—here meaning advantageous and 'fake' action, or result. Fake is said to come from *facto*.

It's a bully fake for a dona when she has the fair good luck to snap hold a husband who will cut up to rights.—*Newsp. Cutting*.

Bully-rag (*Peoples'*, 19 cent.). To scold at length ; said of a woman. Probably suggested by the irritation caused to the bull in the ring, or perhaps pit, by being driven frantic with a perpetual red flag—the rag. 'Don't bully-rag *me*, woman !'

Bum-boozer (*Theatr.*). A desperate drinker. It is to be feared that the following line has been seen in the advertisements for artistes in the commoner theatrical papers :

'Bum-boozers—save your stamps.'

Bumble puppy (*Provincial*). A tossing game used to cheat simpletons —hence bumble-puppy means idiot and idiocy. Origin unknown.

By-the-bye now that we are to be legalized into such goody-goodies that little or no sport is to be allowed except battledore and shuttlecock, egg-hat, push-pin, etc., I am about to offer a prize for the championship of Bumble puppy, *i.e.*, if the police authorities will allow it to take place.—*Newsp. Cutting*.

Bummaree (*Billingsgate*). A middleman at the fish auctions. Corruption of bonne marée. French seaside term for high tide or flood, and also for saltwater fish.

The 'bummarees' or middlemen whip up all the plaice, and carry them off to turn a penny on them by breaking them up into smaller lots.—*Newsp. Cutting*.

Bummarees (*Cooks'*). Corruption of Bain-marie, a cooking utensil consisting of a number of little pots in a bath, or 'bain', of water contained in a large pot. The French phrase is as difficult to comprehend as the corruption—for Marie is beyond analysis— unless it is the name of the inventor. English books of a later school making an effort to avoid the first syllable and be truly Parisian, call the contrivance a 'bang Mary'—a very alarming rectification.

Bummer (*Anglo-Amer.*, 1880). Originally a commercial traveller, from one who 'booms'. (Now—a noisy cad.)

'You are nothing but a third-class society bummer, fit only to associate with your own class of New York scum.' —*N. Y. Mercury*, 8th October 1883.

Bun Feast (*Boys'*). A woeful description of a very poor and meagre feast, where buns need not necessarily serve to swell up the juvenile stomach.

Bunce (*Drapers'*). Goods—probably from a proper name.

Bunch of Fives (*L. Class*). The fist simply—ingenious mode of proving the speaker can count up to five.

One of the associates of the eccentric Marquis of Waterford formed a collection of door-knockers, brass plates, bell pulls, little dustpans, golden canisters, and glovers' 'bunches of fives', of which, in the course of a roystering career, he had despoiled private houses and tradesmen's shop-fronts.—G. A. Sala, *Illust. Lond. News*, 27th January 1883.

Buncombe or Bunkum (*Amer.-Eng.*, 19 cent.). Politically, or possibly any publicly, spoken flattery. This word is an admirable instance of a name at once passing into a language and even yielding to phonetic spelling. The press, both in the U.S.A. and in England, accepted immediately the name as a synonym for humbug. From a celebrated orator of honied phrases named Buncombe. Vulgarised rapidly into Bunkum ; but the Americans, permanently accepting the word, have restored the original spelling. This name-word has as absolutely passed into the English language as 'burke', or 'boycot'. Mr Rees (New York) says of this word :—

The origin of this expression was in the lower house of Congress. A member from North Carolina, and from the county of Buncombe, was speaking when some of the members showed disapprobation, manifested in the usual manner by coughing and sneezing. The member was not long in making the discovery that he was making himself very obnoxious, nor willing to yield an iota of his time to any one, and fully determined to have his 'talk', addressed the disaffected members thus:—'Go, gentlemen, if you like; clear out, evaporate, for I would have you to know that I am not addressing the house but—Bunkum!'

Bundling (*Welsh*). Courting—in a reclining position.

That peculiar Welsh institution, 'bundling' has almost disappeared, a son of the Cymry tells me, from the Principality. It was a sort of union by which a man and woman agreed to take one another on trial for twelve months. If at the end of that time harmonious relations still subsisted between them, they usually took one another, for better for worse, in the orthodox manner. But, if they separated, no sort of disgrace or stigma attached to either; they went their ways, and the world thought none the worse of them for having lived in open adultery.—*People*, 17th January 1897.

Bung (*Peoples'*, 1850 on). A landlord—sometimes endearing when used by dearest friends, but generally and increasingly suggestive of contempt and superiority on the part of the speaker. Used by a client towards a publican whilst he is holding his court in his own particular gin palace; might lead to an immediate call upon the chucker-out to eject the traitor. Only a complete 'pal' could afford, with an elegant but risky sense of fun, to say, 'Dear Bung, I'll take another bitter'—beer being understood.

Bung (*Public Schools*). A lie—probably from some notorious liar's name, known in some leading school, whence it has drifted to most schools.

Bung Ball (*London Tr.*). A great annual Terpsychorean meet of the bungs, or publicans. Celebrated for the grandeur of the diamonds — or what are said to be diamonds—and other precious stones. At this function artificial hops and grapes are never worn, they being too suggestive of the bar. (*See* Blood Ball.)

Bungaries (*Peoples'*, 1870 on). Public-houses. As taverning came to be looked down upon, the landlord, once mine host, honest John Barleycorn, etc., became a 'bung'—whence, as general contempt for pubs. increased, bungary for his house came to be good English. 'Bungs and bungaries must pass away.'

Buniony (*Art*, 1880). Term to express lumpiness of outline, from a a bunion breaking up the 'drawing' of a foot. 'He has still go, but he's getting very buniony.'

Bunk (*Peoples'*). To retreat judiciously. 'I shall bunk', very common in public schools.

Bunker (*L. Class*). Beer—Anglicizing of 'bona-aqua'—an idea of some light-hearted Italian organ-grinder in the Italian quarter behind Hatton Garden.

Bunko (*Amer. - Eng.*). Doubtful, shifty. From S. America. Heard in Liverpool.

At Mackinao they took him for a lord, and at Cleveland he was taken for a bunko man, and had to identify himself by telegraph.

Bunter (*Thieves'*). A woman thief of the lowest possible kind. The very gutterling of crime to whom no 'perfect lady' would condescend to fling a ''ow d'ye doo?'

Bunting - tosser (*Navy*) Signalman. The signals are small flags made of bunting, and they are run up at or near the mast-head.

Bupper (*Peoples'*, 19 cent.). Universal infantile reduction of bread and butter used, as a rule, until the specimen gets his first paternal spanking over his first pair of breeches, when the word passes into 'toke' for the whole term of his natural boy's life, *e.g.*, 'Bit o' bupper, p'ease'—too often heard in the watches of the night. Said to be of royal descent. 'Upon my word', said the old general, 'I think I prefer bup to anything.'

Burgle (*Soc.*, 1880). To commit burglary. Introduced (at all events to London) by Mr W. S. Gilbert in *The Pirates of Penzance.*

Burick (*L. Class*, 19 cent.). A wife —said to be Romany. To administer manual correction to her is 'to slosh the burick'.

When your burick gets boozed, smashes the crookery, and then calls in her blooming old ma to protect her from your cruelty, that's the time to do a guy.—*Cutting*, 1883.

Burke (*Polit.*, 19 cent.). To stifle, quash, abate—from one Burke, who with another, Hare, for some years early in the nineteenth century, systematically murdered persons of all ages, in Edinburgh, for the purpose of selling their bodies to medical men for hospital purposes. Their mode was by stifling with pitch-plasters, which prevented outcry. Their victims were first generally made drunk, except in the case of women. Hence the appositeness of the word for silencing. First used in Parliament by way of attack; afterwards accepted as a good verb full of meaning.

Burst (*Policemen's*, 1879). Outpour of theatrical audiences about eleven (of course P.M.), into the Strand. 'The burst gets thicker every month,' said the sergeant. 'All the world goes to the play now.' The sudden popularity of the play-house began about 1879, and went on increasing in the most marvellous manner.

Burst her stay-lace (*London*). A sudden bust-heaving feminine indignation, which might even literally, and certainly does figuratively, bring about this catastrophe.

Burst your crust (*Prize-ring*, 1800, etc.). Breaking the skin. Went to America.

It is not good manners to do so, and you might slip and burst your crust by so doing.—*American Comic Etiquette for Children.*

Bury (*Low Life*). To desert.

Buryen' face (*Amer.*) Solemn, serious countenance—burying face.

Soon's I could git my buryen' face on, I takes Spider in ter whar the fuss wuz goin' on.—*Tobe Hodge.*

Bus (*Soc.*, 1881). Dowdy dress. Applied only to women; when a badly-dressed victim enters a drawing-room this fatal word may be used—meaning not so much that the lady has come by bus as that her style of dress is not fitted to any sort of vehicle higher in character than the once popular one named.

Bus-bellied Ben (*Street*, E.C., 1840 on). An ordinary name for an alderman, who used to be frequently corpulent. The wave of abstinence, however, has swept even over the corporations of the City of London. The satire was completed by a couplet—
  Bus-bellied Ben;
  Eats enough for ten.

Bush-ranger (*Austral.*). Highwayman. Interesting as a comparative term; for while the word is fairly equivalent to our highwayman, it is significant to compare both with the American evasive 'road-agent'.

Bushy Park (*Rhyming*, 1882). A synonym for ' lark '.

Oh, it is a bushy park to see the Salvation souls toddling about arm-in-arm. —*Cutting.*

Business end of a tin tack (*Amer.*). The point.

The joke about the pin in the chair, and the suggestion that the business end of a tin tack would be preferable, are essentially American.—*D. N.*, 1882.

Persons unaware of the existence of such agents as buckram or crinoline muslin might be forgiven for supposing that such flounces were maintained in order on the principle of an air cushion, and that the introduction of the business end of a pin would produce sudden collapse.—*D. N.*, 27th March 1883.

Busker. He who goes busking. ' Now, gentlemen, don't break out the bottom o' the plate with the weight o' silver you 'and this old busker. I'd send round my 'at as more civil, but yer liberality 'ud knock the bottom out.'

Busking (*Street - singers'*). Going from pub. to pub. singing and reciting, generally in tow with a banjo.

' Hang it, I hope I shall never come down to regular busking; yes, now and again when bis. is bad, but for ever—Lord forbid.'

' That pub's no good—don't you see the notice—no buskers after 7. They've got their evenin' reglers.'—*Cutting.*

Busnacking (*Navy*). Equals Paul Prying—unduly interfering.

I wish old Nobby wouldn't come 'busnacking' about, worrying a chap out of his life. I wasn't doing any harm! To 'busnack' is to be unnecessarily fussy and busy.—*Rev. G. Goodenough, R.N.*

Buss me—bub (*London*, 18 cent.). Baise - moi—evidently. (*See Country Girl.*)

Bust (*Street*, 1875). Burst, or explode with rage, and so join the majority. As a noun it means a heavy drink.

A vulgar critic asserts that Poe must have been on a bust, and raven mad when he wrote his famous poem.

A sculptor can be on a bust without losing cast.—*Newsp. Cutting.*

Busted (*Amer.*, 19 cent.). Bankrupt.

'We're busted miners, missus,' began Black Dan, with a wink to his comrades, 'completely busted, an' can't pay. What you give us to eat must be fer charity.'—*Newsp. Cutting.*

Buster (*London*, 1844 on). A penny loaf. This word has rather a pathetic origin. When the abolition of the corn laws reduced the price of bread, it increased the size of the penny loaf, which at once obtained this eulogistic title—a corruption of burster, a loaf large enough to rend the enclosing stomach. This term remains, but not in its appositeness, for whereas the baker in those early free trade days took a pleasure in showing how much bread he could give for a couple of halfpence, the more recent baker has practically abolished the object. Even his penny roll is not overpowering as to size.

Buster (*Music Hall*, 1882). A special giantess, called Maid Marian. For some time after she left London the word was applied to big women, and for some years the boys in the Leicester Square district would shout at a big woman, 'My high—yere's a Maid Marian for yer!' Marian was a Bavarian giantess brought to London in this year. She appeared at the Alhambra in the autumn so successfully that the dividends paid to shareholders were doubled. She was sixteen only, more than 8 feet high, and was 'still growing'. The use of the word 'Maid' before Marian grew out of the suggestion the two words formed—that of the sweetheart of Robin Hood. Doubtless this title accelerated the popularity of the giantess, who died before she was twenty.

Bust yer (*Street*, 1880 on). A recommendation to ruin; *e.g.*, 'Bust yer, what do I care about that?'

Busy Sack (*Travellers'*). A carpet bag. Good word, and capital equivalent to the American 'hand-grip', given to the small hand-bag.

Butcher (*Public House*). One of the synonyms for 'stout'—obtained probably from general observation that few butchers are thin and narrow.

Butter, To (*Cricket*, 1898). To miss, fail to catch — from butterfingers, or rather buttered, so that they have no hold. In cricket generally applied to the miss of an easy catch.

Butter-churn (*Music Hall Artistes'*). Rhyming for 'turn'—the short appearance of the performer on the stage, which he or she occupies about a quarter of an hour.

When the dona's finished her butter churn, he fakes his way to her, and if there's no other omee mouchin for the music why he takes her to her next flippity flop.—*Biography of a Toff Bundle Carrier.*

Butter-fingers (*Household*). A servant careless in all her ways — especially as to crockery. As though the fingers are so greased that no grip can be made.

Butter upon Bacon (*Household English*). Extravagance — resulting out of the condemnation of eating bread and butter with bacon, instead of the plain loaf. 'What—are you going to put lace over the feather — isn't that rather butter upon bacon?'

Buttock and File (*Thieves'*, 18 cent.). Shop-lifter, evidently French; *filer*—meaning 'to escape quickly'.

Button-maker (*London*). A nickname of George III.

The King was familiarly called the 'Button Maker' by one generation of his faithful subjects, and 'Farmer George' by another. His son is still sarcastically referred to as the 'First Gentleman in Europe'.—*Newsp. Cutting.*

Buxton Limp (*Buxton*). Reference to the hobbling walk of invalids taking the waters. Borrowed from the Alexandra Limp (*q.v.*, also Grecian Bend, Roman Fall).

If walking is too severe exaction just at first and the 'Buxton limp' is too decided, the patient secures a seat in the omnibus.—*D. N.* (Harrogate), 31st August 1883.

Buy your Thirst (*Amer.*, passing English 1894). To pay for drink.

Buz (*Oxford Common Room*). Turn of the don or visitor to whom this word is addressed to fill his glass—the liquor, as a rule, being priceless port. 'It's your buz!' Very ancient—

supposed to be a corruption of 'bouse', or booze, common London for 'a drink', and to drink.

'In bousing about 'twas his gift to excel,
And from all jolly topers he bore off the bell.'

Buz-faker, Buz-faking (*L. London*). One of the applications of 'booze'—a buz-faker being an individual, generally a woman, or rather one that was a woman, who makes the victim drunk before the robbery is effected.

Buzzards (*Amer.*). People of Georgia — probably from the wild turkeys which once abounded there. Singular return to Red Indian customs, the Red Indian being always designated by the name of something in natural history associated with his surroundings. Nearly every state has its inhabitants named after this system. (*See* Blue Grass.)

Buzzer (*Peoples'*, 1898 on). A road-motor of any kind, from the noise made during progress.

Byblow (*Lower Peoples'*). An illegitimate child. Suggested by an aside breath. May be from Carolian times, and a corruption of 'bibelot'—(a valuable small art object)—a term which any one of the famous French 'beauties of the Court' might apply to her nursling—and one that may have been translated satirically into byblow. The *bas peuple* of France to this day style an illegitimate—'un accident'.

By the Holy Grail (*Hist.*). The blood of Christ. A solemn invocation to this day in thoroughly Catholic countries, and heard in provincial France now and again—'Par le sang real.' It is heard in England, in the west only, and there very naturally reformationised into 'By the Holy Grill' — for Grail has no meaning, while 'grill' has a deal. Probably here the grill refers to St Lawrence, who was completed by being grilled. In Paris this invocation is represented by 'Sacré', and 'Sacré Dieu'—'Sang Real de Dieu.' The English phrase has much exercised English etymologists. Many have assumed that the 'grail' was a round dish in which the Redeemer broke the bread. Nay, there has been published a drawing of this very dish. The phrase is derived from 'sang real' in this way. The 'g' of 'sang' thrown upon the following 'r'—we have greal; then the remaining 'san' has been taken for 'saint' — holy, and then some blundering early printer has taken the verbal phrase 'san greal'—and translated it 'Holy Grail'—and thus it remains to this day a phrase utterly without meaning. (*See* More Blue).

By th' good Katty (*Lancashire and North generally*). An ancient Catholic oath, evidently—By the good Catherine —St Catherine of Alexandria, whose popularity in England is probably proved by the number of wheel-windows in Gothic architecture. 'By th' good Katty, aw feel like as if aw should ne'er ha' done.'

C

C. B. U. (*Commercial*, 1897). Legal initials of Court of Bankruptcy, Undischarged. Arose from the process of one H. H. who obtained goods while an undischarged bankrupt by letter headed with these initials which he held, freed him from a charge of fraud.

The superintendent of police stated that there were hundreds of cases against the accused, who pleaded that the letters 'C. B. U.' which appeared on his notepaper informed his creditors that he was an undischarged bankrupt, the exact interpretation of the letters being 'Court of Bankruptcy, undischarged'.—*D. T.*, 23rd March 1897.

C. H. (*Popular* from Nov. 1882-83). Conquering Hero. The term took its rise consequent upon the incessant reception of the soldiers engaged in the Egyptian War (1882), by the playing of 'See the Conquering Hero Comes.'

It will soon be a military distinction not to be a C. H.—*Ref.*, 19th November 1882.

C. O. (*Military*). Soldiers' Greek for 'the Colonel'.

C. S. (*American Civil War*). Abbreviation of Confederate soldiers.

U. S. and C. S. slept together on blankets.—*Newsp. Cutting*.

Cabbage, The (1883). A familiar name given to the Savoy Theatre, opened in 1881, and named after the old 'Savoy' liberties, within which it was built.

When I saw the Cabbage Theatre full I thought to myself, etc.—(1883).

Cabbage Garden Patriots (*Polit.*, 1848 on). Cowards.

The phrase 'cabbage garden patriots' refers to the way in which Smith O'Brien, the uncrowned king of forty years ago or so, was discovered hiding in a bed of cabbages after his followers had fled in all directions, when they were informed as to the coming of the horrid Saxon's minions.—*Ref.*, 20th October 1889.

Cackle (*Theatrical*). To cackle is neither to gag, nor to pong—it is both, with cackle added. A ceaseless unpunctuated flow of words and phrases more or less unconnected and meaningless.

'Cackle' is a convertible substantive or verb which carries a meaning for which it would be most difficult to substitute any other word nearly so effective, and there is a world of satire in its application to a human goose.—*Stage*, 21st August 1885.

Cackle-tub (*Thieves'*). A pulpit. The dangerous classes evolved this term in prison, where they probably see a pulpit for the first time.

Cackling Cove (*Cadgers'*). An actor—the cadger seeing no difference between observing Shakespeare, and whining floridly for pence.

Cadaver (*Anglo-Amer.*). A financially 'dead 'un.'

Three fresh Cadavers. Last week the Crawford Mutual Relief Association, of Ohio, notified the Insurance Commissioner of that State that it was in the throes of dissolution. The day following the Northern Ohio Mutual Relief Association and the Eureka Life surrendered their hungry ghosts.—*Newsp. Cutting.*

See Dead 'un.

Cad-mad (*Oxford*, 1880). The vain glory and superciliousness which overcome, and permanently, the better sense of *nouveaux riches*, *parvenues*, mushroomers (*see*), 'Poor devil—forgive him — he's a cad-mad emancipated haberdasher.'

Cads on Castors (1880). Bicylists.

It will come as a severe blow to fastidious people, who, adopting and freely using the rather stupid phrase that stigmatised all bicyclists as 'cads on castors', fondly thought that they could kill by ridicule a pastime to which they took exception. — *D. N.*, 10th September 1885.

Cady or Kadi (*Whitechapel*). A hat—probably from the Hebrew. It has the distinction of offering one of the rare rhymes to lady. In 1886 a song-chorus began—

Met a lady!
Raised my cady!

The lady probably being of insufficient virtue — the context borne in mind.

Caesaration (*American*). A remarkable shape of evasive swearing—really damnation.

'Ow! ow! Caesaration! I'll kick the head off you!' he roared, catching hold of a fence and glaring at the boy.—*Newsp. Cutting.*

Cake (*London*, 1882). A foolish stupid fellow. Used in good society, Borrowed by Mr Emanual Duperré for a comedy of English manners called *Rotten Row*, produced at the Odeon (Paris, 1882).

Cake-walk (*Music Hall*, 19 cent.). Negro step-dancing.

The science of 'cake-walking' does not appear to be a particularly abstruse one. Indeed, it may be said to have been anticipated by the English minuet. Cake-walking is, in fact, a graceful motion, conducted upon the toes and ball of the foot. Yet there must be an unsuspected amount of merit in it, for we are informed that the Farrells won first prize at the Madison Square Gardens in New York before 10,000 interested spectators. . . . As the reward to the dancers generally consists of an elaborate cake we are at once enlightened as to the genesis of a colloquialism, which has become quite acclimatised in our own land.—*D. T.*, 14th March 1898.

Calf Round (*Amer. Agricultural*, 1870). To dawdle about, asking for some kind of help—suggested by a calf worrying its mother.

'No, sir; I'll die first. Integrity in business transactions is the rule of my life. When I set a time to pay you, calf 'round.' — *Kentucky State Journal*, 1882.

Calico Hop (*Amer.-Eng.*). A free and easy calico ball. This function was invented to evade expenditure by providing that all the dresses, ordinary or fancy, should be strictly of cotton. However cunning people held cotton velvet to be within the bounds of a calico ball, and so contrived to make rare displays of themselves.

The Pleasure League gave a calico hop to their numerous friends on Wednesday evening, at Gerstner's Hall, which was largely attended.—*N. Y. Mercury*, April 1883.

Calicot (*French*). Originally a trade phrase for a linen-draperman both in France and England—used to describe a 'snob' or cad. 'What a calicot he is!' E. Zola in *Au Bonheur des Dames* (1883) uses the word in its original acceptation — 'Hein—des calicots qui vendent des fourrures!' Derived from linen-drapers' young men dressing expensively, but not purchasing good manners.

Call it 8 Bells (*Nautical*). Early drink. It is not etiquette in good nautical circles to have a drink before high noon; 8 Bells. So the apology for alcoholics before that hour takes this form: 'Come along — I fancy the bar is this way. Call it 8 Bells.' And they do.

Call-money (*Police*). Money paid to policemen for calling artisans early in the morning at a given hour.

Attention to 'call-money' appeared to receive more favourable consideration, and sixpences per week for rousing sleepy shopkeepers were matters not to be lightly estimated, even though it is written in the rules, we believe, that no fees are to be received from the citizen who requires to be roused.—*Papers on Metrop. Police.*

Calloh (*Hebrew-Yiddish*). A bride. Proper spelling of the ordinary term, kollah (*q.v.*).

Camberwell Death-trap (*Camberwell*, 19 *cent.*). Surrey Canal.

Mr Powell, whose little nephew was recently drowned in the Surrey Canal, has called attention in a contemporary to the dangerous condition of that waterway. He regards it as a pitfall for little boys who walk on or play about its banks, and he tells us that it is locally known as 'the Camberwell Death-trap'. —*D. N.*, 27th September 1883.

Cambric (*Soc.*, 18 *cent.*). A shirt of fine linen; later a handkerchief of cambric. Derived from name of place of manufacture of fine linen. 'Cambray' or Cambrick, after the fashion of calico. (*See* Lully.)

Cambridge lot (*Oxford Univ.*). General term of scorn for men of the more eastern of the two universities.

The distinction of this 'Cambridge lot' is of a kind which is not merely official but individual, and of an individuality specially suitable for recognition by a University.—*Newsp. Cutting*, 1883.

Camera Obscura (*Amer. - Eng.*). *Le queu.*

The Arkansan walked behind the stooping darkey, swung his right boot into the air three or four times, and then sent the sole whizzing against the darkey's camera-obscura.—*Newsp. Cutting.*

Came up (*Street*, 1890). Come up. Amongst the masses it is a common shape of small wit to replace the present by the past tense. 'Came' for 'come' is very common and used by most drivers—who invariably say 'Came up'.

Camp (*Street*). Actions and gestures of exaggerated emphasis. Probably from the French. Used chiefly by persons of exceptional want of character. 'How very camp he is.'

Can (*Navy*). A. B.'s familiar abbreviation of Canopus. Why classic when you can be colloquial, and 'can' is still very colloquial in the Navy.

Can I help you with that? (*Peoples'*, 1895 on). Said generally to a man with money, or eating, or more especially drinking. Drolly begging, in fact—mean invention. When said to the fairer sex the import is different.

Can you say uncle to that? (*Dustmen's*). To which the usual answer appears to be (in a dust-yard) 'Yes— I can.' Uncle in this relationship appears to equal 'reply'.

Can you smash a thick 'un? (*Peoples'*). Can you change a sovereign. A grim sign of woe—suggesting the common experience that the moment a sovereign is changed, it is 'smashed' or gone.

Canader (*Oxford* 'er'). A Canadian canoe—this word being canoer. Accent on the second in Canader.

Canaries (*London*, 1882). Charity subscription papers. This term took its rise from the use of the word by Booth, the General of the Salvation Army. The colours of the Army were red and yellow, probably in close imitation of the scarlet and gold of the officers of the Guards. The idea of using yellow paper for subscription lists probably arose from the combined facts that yellow paper is cheap and that yellow was one of the Army colours. On the other hand, red paper is very expensive. General Booth, who had a marked tendency to very simple forms of humour, named these papers 'Canaries'. The word 'took' at once.

Canary (*Music Hall*, 1870). Chorus-singer amongst the public—generally in gallery. Invented by Leybourne, a comic singer, probably to give him rest between his verses, he being pulmonary. 'Go it, canaries', he flatteringly would say, meaning that they sang like canaries.

Chorus-singing by the canaries has long been a South London Institution.—*Ref.*, March 1886.

Canary (*Costermonger*, 1876). An ideal hip adornment.

Upper Benjamin built on a downy plan, velveteen taoc, kerseymere kicksies, built very slap up, with the artful dodge, a canary, very hanky panky, with a double fakement down the side.—*Cutting*.

Very difficult of explanation, and in true descent from the cod-piece, though not so glaring in its declaration. It has also some association with 'Il Ruossignuolo', as spoken of in the sprightly pages of Boccacio.

Canary Bird (*Peoples'*). A sovereign. Canary, as something charming, is often associated with pleasant things that are yellow. 'Yes, it's a canary bird, but it will soon fly away to my landlord. He gets them all!'

Candid Friend (*Soc.*, 1860). Equivalent of the damned kind friend of Sir Peter Teazle's. One who says what a mere acquaintance would studiously avoid. Man who urges what he should only admit with reluctance.

Mr Foster has for a long while taken upon himself the unpleasant rôle of 'candid friend' with regard to the Government, and every now and again considers it his bounden duty to chide the members of it when even those who are in open Opposition would remain silent.—*Ref.*, 8th March 1885.

Candle, To (*Peoples'*, 18 *cent.*). To investigate or examine minutely. Figure of speech derived from the use of candles to test eggs, and to ascertain if a second sheet or other enclosure was included in a letter. In the last century the candle was practically the only mode of illumination—a common object. Now, except in the 'wax' division of society, a candle is frequently not seen from year's beginning to end.

It requires a stretch of fancy to picture forth an old-fashioned post-office, with clerks 'candling' the letters as if they were doubtful eggs. The conditions of a single letter were that it should be written 'on one sheet.' The letters were held up to the light to show whether they required a surcharge for an enclosure.—*D. N.*, 1st August 1883.

Candle-shop (*Broad Church*). A Roman Catholic chapel, or Ritualistic church—from the plenitude of lights.

Canister (*Street*). A preacher. Evidently a corruption of a street preacher whose name was something like, for instance, 'Kynaster', and popularly Anglicised. (*See* Sky Pilot.)

Cant. Sneaking, mean, lying, faced with assertion of religion. Probably first used opprobriously after the Reformation, when Canterbury fell out of grace for the time being, as the metropolis of the English Church. Long after the destruction of the monasteries Kent was the headquarters of English beggars. It is so perhaps to this day. Dickens, who died in 1870, was always accompanied in his walks from Gad's Hill House by several mastiffs, which he declared were for his protection from beggars. The author certainly cleared the roads about Gad's Hill from beggars—and the lieges as well for that matter, for the dogs were as fierce as Bismarck's. The abbey-loupers always begged with canticles in their noses and mouths, especially with the prayer to S. Martin, patron saint of beggars. Cant may be from Kent, Canterbury, or canticle, or all three, but it certainly means, as it meant, whining imposture on a basis of religion, as 'He doesn't preach—he cants.' 'Don't cant, Bert, or I won't pay a doit of your debts.' All the great writers of the eighteenth century use this word—Swift, Addison, Dryden, and many others. Dr Johnson, of course, gives the word a Latin origin —'Cantus'—but does not say how the journey was made. In Scotland they believe the word came from two Andrew Cants, father and son, time of Charles II., and both very violent

Presbyterian preachers. But the word went north to them, the Cants did not send it south, 'I write not always in the proper terms of navigation, land service, or in the cant of any profession.'—*Dryden.* 'A few general rules, with a certain cant of words, has sometimes set up an illiterate heavy writer for a most judicious critic.' The word in Ireland is still used for selling by bids. 'Numbers of these tenants or their descendants are now offering to sell their leases by cant.'—*Swift.*

Terra del Fuégo is, as the cant phrase goes, beyond the sphere of British influence for either ambition or greed, but it has not been forgotten by the British missionary societies.—*D. N.*, 14th May 1889.

Cant of togs (*Beggars'*). A gift of clothes. Here the mode of begging for clothes affords a word to describe the present or benefit gained by canting. Good example of low satire satirising itself.

Can't see a hole in a forty-foot ladder (*Colloquial*). Drunk in the extreme degree, for such a ladder offers quite forty opportunities.

Every night does my husband come home blue, blind, stiff, stark, staring drunk, till he can't see a hole in a forty foot ladder, sure.—*Comic Song*, 1882.

Can't see it (*Peoples'*). Reply in the way of objection, such as 'Do lend me five pounds!' 'Can't see it.'

Can't show yourself to (*Peoples'*, 1880). Not equal to; as thus: 'You can't show yourself to Jack Spicer'—or of a play—'It can't show itself to *The Golden Prince.*'

Can't you feel the shrimps? (*Cockney*, 1877). *I.e.*, Smell the sea. Heard on a Thames steamboat when approaching Gravesend, the metropolis of shrimps. (*See* Speak the Brown To-morrow, Taste the Sun, See the Breeze.)

Cantillory Realism (*Soc.*, 1897). Onomatope applied to singing. The linguistic 'find' of 1897. Means singing in which the sounds suggest the words sung. Very open to ridicule, but intended quite gravely. At once burlesqued — where 'kiss' was used the lips were smacked. If 'thunder' came in the words, the singer used all his bass voice, etc., etc.

Owing to his powers as a vocalist, Mr Louis James, of Walthamstow, may be on the high road to fortune; but unless he promptly ceases to follow what the new-fashioned jargon calls cantillatory realism his rosy prospects may become overshadowed. — *D. T.*, 1st February 1898.

Cap (*Eng.-Amer.*). Equivalent to 'Sir' — but really abbreviation of 'Captain'. Common in America—gaining ground in England.

'Fact, Cap,' asserted a bystander.

Cape Smoke (*Cape Town, S. A.*). Indigenous whiskey of the colony, which is very cloudy in tone.

Mr Cecil Ashley strongly insists on the terrible effects of the 'Cape Smoke'. At present this evil vapour may be bought at sevenpence a bottle, and traders wander about the country with waggon loads of it, which they almost force on the natives.—*Newsp. Cutting*, 1878.

Captain Bates (Been to see)? (*Thieves' and Street*). A satirical enquiry of the 'How d'ye do?' character — applied to a gentleman once more restored to ungrateful society after a term in jail. Captain Bates was a well-known metropolitan prison-governor.

Captain Macfluffer (*Theatr.*). Sudden loss of memory on the stage; *e.g.*, 'He took Captain Macfluffer awfully bad.' Its origin is beyond the hope of discovery. Cut down to Fluff and fluffy.

The prompter's voice is dumb in America. Actors and actresses there are alert and ready for their work; they don't 'fluff'. — Clement Scott, October 1900.

Captain Swosser (*Peoples'*). Naval cousin of the military Captain Jinks, both blustering specimens of the services. Derived from a character of Marryat's.

The inducements of Captain Swosser, of the Royal Navy, to have his portrait taken are far less than they were.— (1882).

Carachtevankterous (*Amer.*). Desperately wanting in self-possession. Perhaps an intensification of cantankerous, which in its turn is a term beyond investigation. Both probably wild onomatopes.

I have seen folks upon this river—quiet-looking chaps, too, as ever you see—who were so teetotally carachtevankterous that they'd shoot the doctor who'd tell them they couldn't live when ailing, and make a die of it, jist out spite, when told they *must* get well.—*Newsp. Cutting.*

Carambo, Caramba (*Span.-Amer.*, going north, and passing to Eng.). Hearty good wishes—but more honoured in the breach than the observance. In fact honestly translated, and loudly expressed to a departing friend—might lead to the interference of any policeman with salvationary or even merely denominational tendencies. Meaning elegantly evaded in Spanish-English dictionaries. Much used in the extreme south-west of France — especially at Tarbes. Implacable etymologists may apply at any Spanish embassy—perhaps the Spanish doorkeeper, if there be one, is the safest professor of Spanish to trust to, during this lingual search after useful knowledge.

Carara (*European* passing, 1898). A murderer who cremates his victim.

As she was conveyed to prison the Mantes people shouted 'A mort la Carara,' giving her the name of the Italian mushroom merchant now awaiting trial in Paris for the murder of the bank messenger at Bicêtre.—*D. T.*, 4th April 1898.

Carding (*Irish-Fenian*, 1867-82). A local torture.

Cardings have very likely been rare in county Wicklow. A carding is a highly-spirited operation. About twenty persons, more or less well armed and disguised, break into a cottage, and subject persons who have basely paid rent to a more or less severe form of torture. According to the old Parliamentary reports, carders 'tool' with a board stuck full of nails, but perhaps modern science has provided, or modern spirit suggested, some less severe instrument of correction.—*D. N.*, 1881.

Carlylese (*Liter.*, 19 *cent.*). Benevolent despotism, Tory democracy (1880-85).

To him' (Bismarck) says Mr Lowe in the middle-class Carlylese which he affects, 'to him the ballot-box was only a dice-box.'—*D. N.*, December 1885.

Carnival (*Amer.*, 1882). A fashion or sudden practice.

It not unfrequently happens that such prominent events are followed by an epidemic or 'carnival'—to use a much-abused word—of suicides and murder. (1882).

Caroon (*Peoples'*). A five-shilling or crown piece. From *Corona*, and nearer the mark than the modern word. (*See* Cart-wheel.)

Carpenter Scene (*Theatr.*). Cloth or flats, well down the stage, to allow of some comic dialogue while the next scene is setting.

The old, feeble device of 'forward', or, as they were sometimes derisively called, 'carpenter' scenes—because notoriously written only to give time for the building of more elaborate sets behind them— have now almost entirely disappeared from the stage.—*Newsp. Cutting*, 6th April 1885.

Carpet-bagger (*Amer.—coming to England*). A general term for a poor person who arrives with a carpet-bag, and becomes prosperous by audacity or unfair trading. Originated by the Confederates, as against the Federals, when after the civil war hungry and place-seeking political adventurers from the north were appointed to places in the conquered south, and, arriving in a poverty-stricken condition, soon showed signs of wealth and general prosperity.

Carpet Dance (*Soc.*, 1877). A familiar dance for a few unfortunates in a drawing-room, as distinct from a large dance to which everybody is invited. It was voted bad taste to offer champagne at a carpet dance— or indeed to drink any wine whatever, except claret. White soup was often served, and became as fashionable as rational, *e.g.*, 'Do come and christen our new carpet with a valse or two.'

Carried (*Rhyming*). Married; *e.g.*, 'He was carried yesterday, poor bloke' — very ominous, and searchingly graphic. The word is obtained merely by supplanting the 'm' by a 'c'—but what a suggestion there is of harrying and rallying on the part of the bride!

Carriwitchet (*Peoples'*). A puzzling question. Probably an invented word, in itself suggestive of bewilderment. Or it may be from the name of a woman notorious for asking difficult questions—say Carrie Witchet!

Carrots (*L. Class*). Red hair. This is an interesting instance of aggressive Anglicization. It has not in origin anything to do with 'carrots', the colour of which has never yet been seen in association with human, or perhaps any other hair, except, possibly, that of one of the 'lemurs'.

It is a corruption from Catholic times in England when a red man or woman was called 'Iscariot', the 'betrayer' in the Roman Church, and especially in Rome where red hair amongst the people has always been a rarity — because Judas Iscariot was historically supposed to have had red hair. The Protestant religion in England more or less parting with Iscariot, the historical name became associated with the vegetable, which, by the way, may have gained its name, seeing its colour, from the same source as did red hair.

'Hello—carrots—what cheer now, my lad!'

'Deceptive—what can you expect of her? Isn't she carroty?' Indeed to this day there is a firm belief that red-haired women are faithless and deceptive—probably from their frankness, possible rudeness, yet general desire to please. In Scotland 'carrots' has degenerated into 'sandy', invariably applied to red-haired men, but never to women. Supposed by correctly thinking people to be a nickname for Alexander; but really a substitute for Iscariot, and a good one, for there is plenty of 'sand', or 'grit', or 'go' in most men or women with hair more or less auburn.

Carry me out (*Peoples'*, 18 *cent.*). A satirical expression, pretending defeat, humiliation, and pardon. Sometimes 'carry me out and bury me decent.' The latter portion is possibly an Irish addition. Derived from the prize ring, when the senseless, defeated hero was, when quite vanquished, as scrappers once were, ignominiously carried out. Or it may be from cock-fighting, or both. The dead birds were certainly carried out.

Carry on proper (*Common Lond.*, 19 *cent.*). To behave well.

Carsey (*L. London*). A house; corruption of casa—from the Italian organ-grinders in Saffron Hill district.

If you're a bank director and broken up a thousand carsers of poor honest people, that's the time to do a guy.—*Newsp. Cutting.*

Cart (*Peoples'*, 18 *cent.*). A metaphor for the gallows — to which terminal its victims were jolted in a cart. Still heard in provincial places — 'You be on'y fit for the cart'— doubtless now used without the least idea of its original meaning. In London the cart travelled, only too often, several miles from Newgate to Tyburn Tree, whose site was that of the Marble Arch in Hyde Park. Used by all the dramatists in the last century.

'I care not—welcome pillory or cart.' —Garrick, *Abel Drugger.*

Now would I sooner take a cart in company with the hangman than a week with that woman.—Farquhar, *The Inconstant.*

Cartocracy (*Soc.*, 19 *cent.*). People distinguished enough to keep carts—especially dog-carts. (*See* Gigmanity.)

Carts (*L. London*). A pair of boots—generally those of noble size. Onomatopoetic—reference to the noise a young navvy can make with his understandings as equal to that of the passing waggon.

Cartwheel (*Peoples'*). A five-shilling piece. From its noble weight and thickness. (*See* Crown.)

Carve up (*Amer.*). To annihilate completely.

That dear grave holds a disappointed chap who cum out here from Reno to carve me up.—*Newsp. Cutting.*

Case (*Fast Life*, 1850 on). Abbreviated form of Casino, and referring to the rowdy cafés for which the Haymarket was once celebrated. The word has survived the abolition of late houses and the closing of public-houses at 12.30. The word is applied to any common public-house or confectioner's where the business carried on is not wholly one of stomachic refreshments. 'He kept a case for years in Panton Street'—may be from Casa. 'Case' is also thieves' English for a counterfeit five-shilling piece.

Though Neal kept what is vulgarly known as a case, and was assisted in his unholy work by Mrs Neal, and though both of them at different times were concerned in the management or direction of other cases, he seems to have considered it his wife's duty to remain,' etc. —*Ref.*, 16th March 1890.

Casket (*Amer.*). Evasion of 'coffin'. First mentioned in Webster, in edition of 1879. Coming to England slowly.

When he got to the house the child was laid out in a handsome white casket that must have cost at least twenty dollars.—*N. Y. Mercury*, 1884.

Cast-iron and double-bolted (*Amer.*, 1880). Samsonly strong.

Striking outcome of the spread of engineering work.

'Stranger, onless yer made of cast-iron and double-bolted, ye hadn't better go in till the row is over!'—1883.

Cast an Optic (*Sporting*). A paraphrase of 'look'.

Cast skin, To (*Soc.*). To rejuvenate — from the serpent throwing off its skin annually, and coming forth radiant. Still used.

'Why, sir, you've cast your skin.'— Farquhar, *The Inconstant*.

Castor (*Street*). A hat. Of course from the first hats being made of the fur of the castor, or beaver; passed down to the streets, where any hat is called a castor. Superseded by Gossamer.

Casuals (*Hotel*). One-day stayers in luxurious hotels at marine and mineral water stations. From the casual, or night pauper, as distinct from the superior settled unionist.

Another day the 'casuals' at the hotel were mystified exceedingly by a carefully printed programme announcing that a performance of wax-work would be given in the drawing-room. — *Newsp. Cutting.*

Casualty (*Peoples'*). A black eye. From the first Soudan war, when slight injuries were cabled under this head.

In one of these contests, in the affair of the Cross Causeway, indeed, Scott became what is now called a 'casualty'. He suffered a contusion.—*D. N.*, 21st March 1885.

Cat (*Thieves'*). Woman in general, and a bad one in particular. Suggested probably by her smoothness, the uncertainty of her temper, and the certainty of her claws.

Cat and Fiddle (*Hist.*). A very common sign for a tavern until words supplanted rebuses, which were for the ignorant. The country arrival who could neither pronounce 'The Bacchanals', nor understand these three dancing graces, could nevertheless know he 'was there' when he saw as a painted sign the 'Bag o' Nails'. The use of the house-sign was its power to paint the sound of a word or words by objects which had a relation of sound only to the actual meaning of the sign. Hence a goat and a pair of compasses, one of the Cromwellian signs after the Restoration, represented 'God encompasses us.' Probably all the old Catholic signs, especially those on the road to Canterbury, are still in existence. For instance, the rendezvous for the Blackfriars as distinct from the Southwark pilgrims was 'The Hand and Flower,' which lent itself readily to the painter's art. It refers to the Virgin and her emblem, the lily. This house was at the corner of Gravel Lane and Union Street, about half a mile from the Tabard, and it only lost this sign some thirty years since. The Cat and Fiddle is the 'Catherine fidèle', probably brought over with the Conqueror, for 'à la Catherine fidèle' is still a common sign in Normandy. Obviously the Anglo-Saxon knew nothing of the great saint of Alexandria—but a painted Cat and Fiddle was quite within his means. Necessarily these signs were in the old parts of London, which in time became all the low parts of London. For a hundred years or more 'Cat and Fiddle' has meant a doubtful house, where thieves and loose women abound.

He's come down in the world, has Jim. He keeps a Cat and Fiddle.

Cat and Mutton Lancers (*E. London*, 1870). Name given to the militia in the district of Dalston when drilling in Cat and Mutton Fields. When time, elegance, and the wave of progress have swept these 'fields' far away from their present elysium the term will remain an enigma. Probably from a chapel or chantrey (11th to 15th century) dedicated to Catherine Martyr (of Alexandria). It is a good instance of human stupidity in accepting sheer ignorance as gospel truth that within the precincts of these fields a publican had for sign a cat running away with a leg of mutton; his rebus perpetuated the absurdity.

Cat-lap (*L. Soc.*). Tea and coffee; terms used scornfully by drinkers of beer and strong waters. Cat-lap in club-life is one of the more ignominious names given to champagne by men who prefer stronger liquors.

Bell rings, and enter Emperor and Empress; and then there takes place the general presentation. A vast crowd, but not much animation; plenty of card tables, but few players; no supper, but plenty of soup; also 'catlap' in abundance. Empress retires very soon; Kaiser stays.—*Newsp. Cutting.*

Cat-meat pusher (*Street*). A merchant of cooked horse-flesh, the final term being derived from his truck—albeit pusher means generally a maker or doer of something. Linendrapers' young men are calico-pushers, while the trimmers up of old clothes are called faker-pushers.

Cat o' Mountain (*Peoples'*). A shrew. A very common example of confused origin, for whether this term comes from catamaran, a wild, over-sailed S. American craft, or from catamount (a panther) it would be difficult to say. Very common still in London street feminine statements. Yer catter mountin', go 'ome an' wash yer pore childring an' don't dare ter haddress *me*, mum!

Cat on testy dodge (*Soc.* 1870 on). A ladylike beggar worrying ladies at their houses for money—if only a sixpence (tester), and bringing testimonials in favour of some charitable institution. These 'cats', generally strong-minded ones, take commission on the sums they get.

Catafalque (*Fashion*, 1897). The high plumed hat—especially black feathered, which rose to its greatest height in 1897, towards the end of which year they were sometimes removed to laps by their wearers when in theatres and a good temper.

The ladies with the huge hats have capitulated, and George Alexander has added another to his many conquests. At the last Saturday matinée there was not a catafalque to be seen on any head, but towers of plumes in many laps.—*D. T.*, 25th November 1897.

Cataract (*Soc.*, '40's). Voluminous and many folded falling cravat, which swarmed over the length and breadth of the fashionable masculine chest.

Cat-sneaking (*Thieves'*). Stealing public-house pots. Probably an easy disguise for 'pot'. Creatures of a felonious turn so fallen as to take to this trade would have little invention.

Catch Cocks, To (*Low Military*). To obtain money by false pretences. Catch-cocks are contrived by characterless soldiers who address gentlemen, invent tales of distress, and often thereby obtain money. 'Joe, let's go cock-catching.'

In the Kensington Gardens a soldier told a gentleman that he lost his railway ticket, which was to take him to Windsor to join his battalion, and he would be punished if not at his quarters at a certain time. The gentleman gave him the money for his fare, but saw the man go in a contrary direction to that of the railway station. He followed him, but he ran into a public-house and got out by the back-door, and the gentleman saw no more of him. He ascertained that he was a Grenadier Guardsman, and that his battalion could not be at Windsor, as the Fusilier Guards were there. There is not a day but soldiers are guilty of such disgraceful acts of 'loafing', and they glory in it. They call it, in the Guards, 'catching cocks' and 'throwing the hammer'. These terms may have a far more cogent or obscure meaning.—*Newsp. Cutting*.

Catch on, To (*Amer.* probably from New Eng.). To make a hit; to succeed beyond question.

'Come down to The Bric-a-brac and I'll show you some of the gentlemen thieves; the fellows who have discovered a way by which they can commit highway robbery by daylight and in the presence of witnesses, and not to be amenable to the law', said Old Sport to the reporter. 'I don't catch on,' replied the reporter.

'I don't catch on worth a cent', sadly murmured the managing editor; 'but as you have worked on the great dailies, I suppose it's all right.'—*Newsp. Cutting*.

I hear that Miss Helen Dauvray is coming to the Prince's to play 'One of Our Girls', the comedy which Bronson Howard wrote expressly for her. The piece seems to have caught on in the States.—*Newsp. Cutting*.

Catch-penny (*Street*). Gutter Ballads.

The origin of the phrase 'catchpenny' is that after the execution in London of Thurtell for the murder of Weare (1824), a publisher named Catchpin printed a penny ballad entitled: *We are Alive Again*. When cried on the streets it sold to the extent of 2,500,000 copies, the persons buying supposing from the sound that the ballad had reference to Weare. It came, therefore, to be spoken of as a 'Catch-penny affair'.

Catechism (*Bankruptcy Court*). Interrogatories.

Caterpillar (*Soc.*, 1848 on). A ladies' school. (*See* Crocodile.)

Caterwauling (*Peoples'*). Cat-music. Johnson gives up the attempt to derive this word. 'What a caterwauling do you keep here.'—Shakespeare (*Twelfth Night*). Used now only by the vulgar.

'So I cannot stay here to be entertained with your caterwauling.'—Gay, *Beggars' Opera.*

Cats' Party (*Sporting*). Chiefly women. Probably from the high tone of women's voices.

Upon one occasion she was at a party given at 88 Adelaide Road. It was termed a 'cats' party', owing to the number of ladies who were present. (Laughter.) —Mr Justice Butt: Descriptive of the music, I suppose. (Laughter.)—Divorce Court, *Dunn* v. *Dunn & Wall*, 1st February 1888.

Caucus (*Amer.-Eng.*). Vehmgericht, or council of many tens, who secretly combine on a given line of action. The word came from U.S.A. about 1870. Primarily 'caucus' like 'gueux' in Flanders (16th century), and 'frondeur' in France (17th century) was a term of reproach, which was adopted by the party attacked with this word; and used by themselves to distinguish themselves. Very wide in its application. Mr Joseph Chamberlain has done much to popularise this very important word — not yet admitted into dictionaries.

Gordon, in his history of the American Revolutions, says, 'About the year 1738, the father of Samuel Adams, and twenty others who lived in the north or shipping part of Boston, used to meet to make a caucus and lay their plan for introducing certain persons into places of trust. Each distributed the ballots in his own circle, and they generally carried the election. As this practice originated in the shipping part of Boston, caucus may have probably been a corruption of caulker's meeting.'—(1830).

'The House of Lords', says Mr Chamberlain very truly, 'has become, so far as its majority are concerned, a mere branch of the Tory caucus—a mere instrument of the Tory organisation.'—*D.N.*, 9th October 1884.

'Then the noble lord says I am the Birmingham caucus. This description is flattering as to my influence and ability, but it is a total mistake.'—Mr J. Chamberlain, House of Commons, 30th October 1884.

Caucus-monger (*Political*, 1883). A political agitator. Introduced by Lord Randolph Churchill (1883), and accepted by the Conservative party as representing the average radical.

They now knew beyond all manner of doubt, that on the 4th of May last the Government of Ireland was handed over to Mr Chamberlain, the caucus-monger of Birmingham—and to Mr Sheridan, the outrage-monger of Tubbercurry — Lord Randolph Churchill. Dinner at Woodstock, 27th February 1883.

Caulk, Calk (*Naval*). Go to bed and to sleep, probably from tucking in the clothes under you in the hammock or bunk, and so suggesting the action of caulking a seam in the vessel's side; also used for a short sleep—forty winks:—' I'll caulk it out.'

From this word grows out 'caulker'. Four of Irish hot; *i.e.*, four pennyworth of Irish whiskey. Quite naval, and equal to the mere landsmen's 'nightcap'—caulk meaning to make all tight and weather safe.

Cave (**Cave of Adullam**) (*Polit.*, 1866-97 on). A secret political combination — distinct from illegal conspiracy.

You recollect a new institution brought into the House of Commons at that time (1886). It is called the 'Cave'. Into the 'Cave' entered, as was historically correct, all the discontented—those who did not like the Bill on the opposite side of the House, and some on our side who did not like it; and the result was that the Bill was destroyed, and the destruction of the Government followed it. We supposed the 'Cave' would come into office. They came into office, not all the 'Cave', but some of them.—J. Bright: Bright Celebrations, Birmingham, June 1883.

Many of you will no doubt remember that a strenuous effort was made by the Opposition in which they were joined by some 'Cave' men from our side to frustrate the Government Bill, which was rejected, and the Government itself overthrown. — John Bright, Leeds, 18th October 1883.

Cave Dwellers (*Soc.*, 1890 on). Atavists—people whose habits are on a par with those of the pre-historic races.

A certain mining camp of cave-dwellers was wont to beguile its Sabbaths by tying up in the same bag a cat, a terrier, a monkey, and a parrot, and speculating on the issue.—*Newsp. Cutting.*

Caved out (*Amer.-Eng.*, 19 *cent.*). Come to an end—finished. From the metal ceasing in a tunnel. The end of the vein.

Cawfin (*Marine*). A badly found ship. Corruption of 'coffin'—name given as suggestive of a sailor being as bad as dead who sailed in her. Became popular when Mr Plimsoll forced his Bill.

Celestials (*Theatrical*). Gallery occupants, a synonym of 'gods'—from their superior position to pit and even boxes.

One of the 'celestials' visiting Toole's Theatre (pulled down in 1897) recently complains that, although he was elevated, his seat wasn't sufficiently high to enable him, with Tam o' Shanters and Gainsboroughs on the heads of the ladies in the upper boxes, to see more than the top of the scenery.—*Ref.*, 5th October 1884.

Cellars (*Street*). Boots. Probably because these apartments are the lowest necessities in connection with ordinary sumptuary arrangements. (*See* Garret.)

Centipedes, The (*Military*). 100th Foot. From the insect of that name. One of the punning regimental cognomens. (*See* $\frac{2}{D.G.}$ and XL's.)

Cess. *See* Bad cess to ye!

Chain lightning (*L. Class, Lond.*). Potato spirit, imported from Germany. Filthy mess—poisonous to a degree. Smuggled chiefly.

On telling him the charge he exclaimed, 'It's all nonsense; I only gave her some chain-lightning,' which he understood to be some foreign spirit.—*D. N.*, 22nd December 1885.

Chair Days (*Soc.*). Old age.

Why should a cruel and humiliating malady torture the kindly, upright, conscientious spirit, and rack the strong, temperate bodily force spent in the service of his age, deserving, if any ever did, easy 'chair days' and the supreme blessing of the natural euthanasia of old age?—Sir E. Arnold, writing of Gladstone's death, June 1898.

Chair Warmer (*Theatrical Anglo-Amer.*). A beautiful or pretty woman who does nothing on the stage beyond helping to fill it.

Richard Whalen fired a pistol shot at Carrie Howard, a 'chair-warmer' at Esher's Alhambra, St Louis, at the close of the performance on Friday night. A 'chair-warmer' is a lady whose talent is comprised in her physical charms, and who can neither sing, dance, nor act. —*Newsp. Cutting.*

Chairmarking (*L. Industrial*, 19 *cent.*). Secret markings of licences and employés' characters by masters, foremen, and others. Probably marking by the chairman or master. On 4th August 1894 (*see D. T.*) a complainant, whose name did not transpire, by a solicitor, summoned a cab-proprietor for (through his foreman) marking a licence with secret signs.

What two witnesses for the complainant regarded as 'chairmarking' was some additional writing in the date column.

Mr Hopkins (the magistrate at Westminster) said it is possible that the licence is marked in a manner to be understood in the trade, but if cabmen are able to combine to make their terms —they have a powerful union of their own—why should not the proprietors also combine and by marking a licence in a particular way, let it be understood that the holder of it is not a desirable person to be employed? They are entitled to do it.—*D. T.*, 4th August 1891.

Chalk against (*Peoples'*). Resentment or desire for explanation. In the last century when very few of the smaller shopkeepers could write, a score was kept in chalk on a square of wood. (*See* Hogarth's *Distressed Poet*.) It is most figuratively used to designate an unsettled misunderstanding or grudge. (*See* Score.)

Chalk marquis (*Peoples'*). A false marquis. Never applied to any other title than this. Probably the result of some forgotten pun or play upon a name.

Chalk out (*Peoples'*). Distinct directions. Nothing so vivid as this in any well-known modern language. 'If you miss it now — you *are* a juggins. I've clean chalked it out.'

Challik it oop (*Theatrical*). A grotesque request to obtain credit— the primitive way of marking up a credit in public-houses before education was extended.

Chamber of Horrors (*Soc.*). The name of the corridor or repository in which Messrs Christie (King Street, St James's) locate the valueless pictures that are sent to them from all parts of the world as supposed genuine old masters; sent, as a rule, with directions to sell at certain prices most preposterously fixed very high. Phrase borrowed from Madame Tussaud's wax-work, where this chamber is coloured black, and filled with the effigies of murderers.

Chamber of Horrors (*City*). Room at Lloyd's (Royal Exchange) where are 'walled' notices of shipwrecks and casualties at sea.

Champagner (*Mus. Hall*, 1880). Lorette. Within the last twenty years the marvellous increase in the consumption of champagne — or what seems like it to the unlearned in wines —has been most marked. Directly the tap-stopper was invented and 'fizzing' wine came to be sold by the glass, the ladies who chiefly frequent the better parts of music-halls at once showed their elegance by deserting gin, rum, and other horrors for this less damaging, however adulterated, drink. Hence the poor souls who could not command the 'sparkling' and its adjuncts, either from want of good looks, good breeding, or good clothes, assimilated the new popular drink and its female consumers.

'Oh, bless you, she won't speak now—she's quite the champagner.' (*See* Tip-topper.)

Champagne Shoulders (*Soc.*, 1860). Sloping shoulders. From the likeness to the drooping shoulder of the champagne bottle as distinct from the squarish ditto of the sherry or port bottle.

Champagne Weather (*Soc.*, 1860 on). Bad weather—said satirically.

Champion Slump of 1897 (*London*, 1897). Motor car. On and after Lord Mayor's Day of 1896 the motor car claimed English highways for their own. On the 10th there was a procession from Westminster to Brighton, with such a lamentable result that the 'slump' or catastrophe prefaced 1897—for some time.

Has the great motor car demonstration, which was to revolutionize British humanity, fizzled off into this?—*D. T.*, 15th February 1897.

As this year wore on a dozen or so of pale yellow motor-cabs, which came to be satirically styled 'The Butter-coloured Beauties,' made their appearance. But they had not plied for hire three months before one of them killed a hanger-on boy with its back wheel gear, while in November a driver went drunk and amok with his motor-cab; the two in combination doing considerable damage.

By the end of November they were called the 'Margarine Messes', which grew out of their first satiric name—'The Butter Beauties'— from their colour.

Towards Christmas the motor once more took to its initial behaviour—and ran away.

The Champion Slump of 1897 was not appreciably modified by the natural history of the motor car in 1898.

Chancellor's Eggs (*Legal*). Day-old barristers.

Every term a new batch of what were once humorously called 'Chancellor's eggs' is incubated..—*D. T.*

Change breath (*Amer. tavern*). Take a 'go' of whiskey—this certainly does change the smell of the breath.

The other day as three or four of the old boys were sitting around the stove in Schneider's sample room stirring in the grated nutmeg, Bill Matson came in to change his breath.—1882.

Chant (*Sporting*, 1886 on). To swear—the last satirical popular verb to describe 'language'.

Chanting-ken (*L. London*). A music-hall.

Chapel (*Printers'*). Secret meeting and decision. The congregation of unionists in a 'shop', to confer upon any given matter of trade, or even personal importance. Little notes are sent about, a chapel never being called at a moment's notice. They generally take place at tea-time, when the assembly sit in some quiet corner, drink their tea quietly, and as quietly discuss the question. Probably from 'chapter'—especially as printing in England dates from the chapter-house, Westminster Abbey. (*See* Garret.)

Chapper (*L. London*). Mouth—from associations with chaps, chops, and cheeks.

Chapper, To (*L. London*). To drink.

Chappie (*Soc.*, about 1880). Replaced chum, which had become vulgar. There was quite a friendly meaning in the word; it was by no means contemptuous, and thereby varied from the meaning put upon 'Johnny', which appeared about this same time. Dropped rapidly in the world, and vanished from society in the '90's.

The hue of vine and mulberry just now is delicious, and makes us regret somewhat that the Mulberry Gardens liked by Pepys when the 'chappies' and 'Johnnies' of his day did not carry him off to 'Fox Hall,' have made way for the peculiar ugliness of Buckingham Palace.—*D. N.*, 1882.

Charity Bob. The quick, jerky curtsey made by charity school-girls, now (1883) rapidly passing away.

A little mite about eighteen inches high on the O.P. side wins loud applause for her correct rendering of the charity bob.—*Newsp. Cutting.*

Charley (*Street*, 1662-1829). London street watchmen.

In New Boswell Court might be seen until recently (1868) a relic of the light of other days in the shape of an ancient box (which used to be drawn up from the pavement during the day), fitted for the protection of those slow, antiquated, muffled-up guardians of the night, covered with their many-caped dark coats, called watchmen. . . . At length the Charley found himself one fine morning superseded by that admirably constituted and well organized body, the new police, as modelled by Sir Robert Peel, who appeared in the London streets for the first time, 20th September 1829.—*Diprose's Clement Danes*, vol. i. p. 101.

Between the bellmen and the London watchmen there was always a close alliance, and in the reign of the Merry Monarch, from whom the Charlies took their name, their identities were more or less merged.—*D. T.*, 17th January 1894.

This same word is used by 'the general' to describe women's breasts when well developed. It is said this term also comes down from Charles II., and refers to his many mistresses, who certainly displayed their charms as never women did before. Wilder etymologists assume the word to come from Carolian French—'cher lis'—referring to the painted whiteness of the attribute in question.

Charlie Freer (*Rhyming, Sporting*). Beer; *e.g.*, 'He can put down Charlie Freer by the gallon, he can.'

Chateau Dif (*S. Exchange*). A grotesque play upon Chateau d'If. Here the exchange is the castle of diff, or diffs—*i.e.*, 'differences' on settling days.

Chatham and Dover (*London public-house rhyming*). 'Over.' This phrase is generally used as a pacificating one —in a tavern quarrel, a friend will say, 'Come—Chatham and Dover it'—meaning give it over.

Cheap beer (*Police*). Beer given by publicans at night-time to officers.

'There are innumerable publicans who make a practice of allowing this "cheap beer", and it is tacitly understood that all cases will be treated leniently in which those houses may choose to form the scene of future action. The first enquiry of a constable whose beat is changed to his brother officer, who shows him "his new relief", is, which are the houses where "cheap beer" may be relied upon to be ready when punctually called for.'—*Newsp. Cutting.*

Cheat (*Thieves'*, 18 *cent.*). Gallows. Fielding's *Jonathan Wild*.

Check up (*Gallery, Theatrical*). To 'check up' is to obtain entry to the gallery, not by the ordinary mode of payment, but by waiting at the bottom of the gallery stairs and asking passers out, 'Have yer done with yer check, sir?'—the pass-out check, by production of which the holder obtains re-admission to the theatre. When the applicant gets the check, he 'ups' at once—the gallery stairs. Theatrical managers hold that these transfers are not legal, but magistrates, certainly in London, will not convict checkers-up if brought before them upon charges of fraud. 'I've checked up three times this blessed week!' said the youth. 'I checked it up—I wasn't goin' to pay no bloomin' shillin'.'

Cheek-ache (*Artisans'*). Blushing or turning red in the face rather for the meanness of another than your own. 'I got the cheek-ache over him.'

Cheeky (*Peoples'*). Adjective form of cheek—smart sauciness.

Cheese and Crust (*Low Classes*). Exclamation — perversion of Jesus Christ. Frightful at first sight, this phrase suggests a slight sense of respect by its veiling of the oath. Also a little touching as being a phrase associated with comfort to those amongst whom comfort is little known. (*See* Corkscrew.)

Cheri (*Soc.*, 1840-55 and on). A charming woman. Derived from Madame Montigny, of the Gymnase, Paris. Her stage name remained Rose Cheri. She was a singularly pure woman, and an angelic actress. Word used by upper class men in society, in the 'forties', to describe the nature of their mistresses. Word now forgotten.

Cheshire, The (*Peoples'* 19 *cent.*). Perfection. Figure of speech, a metaphor wherein the perfection of Cheshire cheese is made to stand for perfection itself. Good example of homely coining of words, *e.g.*, 'She's the Cheshire —I can tell you.' A variant is—'That's the Stilton.' Charles Steyne was very funny as the ratcatcher, who calls everything 'the Cheshire'.

Cheshire Cats (*Provincial*). Amiable result of adjacent county criticism, —that of Lancashire. Chiefly used in association with the comparison to 'grin like a Cheshire cat'. Cat may have been derived from kit— Christopher.

Chest Plaster (*Theatrical*, 1883). Satirical description of the young actor of the day by his much older and more 'legitimate' brother actor. From the heart-shaped shirt-front worn with a very open dress waistcoat, and starched almost into a cuirass. 'Bah—he is but a chest plaster humbug.' (*See* Shape and Shirt.)

Chesterfield (*Soc.*). A long, white coat—originally made with capes— now applied to white coats generally, but sometimes to blue (1840-50). Good example of qualifying name being used for the object qualified.

Chestnut (*Amer.-Eng.*). An old joke offered as new. Brought to England officially in 1886 by A. Daly's Company at the Strand Theatre in 'A Night Off', where the heroine tells the hero the play was found in an 'old chest'—to which he replies, 'Very old —chestnut!'

Chevalier Atkins. *See* Tommy Atkins.

Chevaux de frise (*Lit.*). Friesland Horse, or cavalry—a tangle of spikes set at right angles as a rule. The Dutch had no cavalry in the 17th century. Invention of the Frieslanders; named by the French (17th century) in scorn of Dutch enemies. Good example of a phrase by its construction suggesting an apparently more obvious meaning, for the frise suggesting 'friser', the temptation to write Cheveux-de-frise, as describing the tangle, has in many instances been fatal.

Chevy-chase (*Rhyming*). Face—in common use.

After listening for a while her chevy-chase gets serious looks.— *Newsp. Cutting.*

Chew into dish-cloths (*Amer.*, 1882). To annihilate.

The wolf came down with his ears working with delight, and had only reached the earth when the goose sprang upon him and chewed him into dish-cloths.—*New American Fables.*

Chic (*Franco-English*, 1865 on)— Dash, smartness.

'Chic' in its original acceptation meant simply 'trick' or 'knack', and was applied to dexterity of performance before it acquired its application to elegance of result. A painter, for instance, was said to have 'du chic'— that is, the knack or dodge of using his brush with effect. It was only later that a 'stylish' toilette was described as displaying the same quality. The phrase came in, if we remember rightly, in the early sixties, and with the vogue of Offenbachian opera-bouffe.—G. A. SALA.

Chicago Reform Lawyer (*Amer.- Eng.*, 1890 on). A lawyer of lawyers— from the fact that Chicago is supposed to be the most alert spot on the mere earth. 'No—he's not an American advocate—he's a Chicago reform lawyer.'

She devotes herself to finance, looks after railway interests and her bonds, assisted therein by her son and daughter, who lives with her, and she defies even a 'Chicago reform lawyer' to get the better of her.—*D. T.*, 10th February 1897.

Chickaleary - cove (*Costermongers*', 1860). A perfect personage. Introduced into society above the gutter by Vance, a comic singer, who used the word in a song-chorus. 'I'm the chickaleary cove, with my one, two, three'—the numbers probably referring to the mere trinity of blows required to floor the enemy.

The barrowman's one aim and ambition is to be chickaleary.—*D. T.*, 6th April 1893.

Enterprising clothiers at the East End make the construction of 'chickaleary' attire a leading feature of their business. —*Newsp. Cutting.*

Chi-ike (*Anglo-Amer.* 19 *cent.*). A distance call used by American trappers, and borrowed by them from the Red Indians. 'Hullo—don't chi-ike me like that over there—you'll wake Westminster Abbey.'

Mr G. A. Sala (*D. T.*, 28th August 1894) says of this phrase. 'Chi-ike!' I have not the remotest idea when this slang cry was first heard or what it means. Emitted, however, from a powerful pair of lungs, 'Chi-ike' could be made almost as far-reaching as the Australian cry, 'Coo-ee'. Often sent in unfriendly salute by street arabs along the street. 'Whoa-chi-ike' addressed to a 'toff'.

And then a crowd got round and began to chi-ike the couple.—*Cutting.*

Chinwag (*Hist.*). Talk.

I have not been out of my pyjamas all day and no further from the tent than to the next one for a 'chinwag'.—*People,* August 1898, Letter from near Klondyke.

Chin-music (*Costers' defiant talk*).

One of the toughest fights Geoghegan had ever was with Jim M'Govern. The two had indulged in a lot of 'chin music' on various occasions, and finally met in a saloon on the Bowery and Hester street one winter's night, when it was snowin' hard.—*Newsp. Cutting.*

Chin-chin (*Naval—passed into club society*). 'Hail!' 'Good health!' 'Here's to you!' 'Chin-chin, old chap.' The answer is 'Pa-pa'. Origin obscure, probably — 'Same to you!' Dates from the Chinese of Singapore. 'We went into the temples, and our pockets were not rifled; we went into the prisons, and we were not brained by manacled villains; we mixed in crowds and were never hustled; and the only cries we heard were 'Chin, chin!' or 'Pa, Pa!'—which means welcome or good fellows.—Clement Scott, *D. T.,* 1st August 1893.

Chip in (*Anglo-Amer.*). To join in discussion; to subscribe money.

'Gentlemen, let's chip in enough more to buy her a new dress. I'm a poor man, but here's a quarter for the old lady.'—*Newsp. Cutting.*

Chirrup, To (*Music-hall,* 1886 on). Applaud, cheer. The word was made classical on 5th March 1888, when a man was 'sent' for a month as the result of levying blackmail upon music-hall artists as they entered at the stage door to pay for applause, with the alternative of being hissed if they did not 'stump up'. This case killed the process.

Pike, the stage-doorkeeper at the Canterbury, proved seeing the prisoner for some time carrying on the system of obtaining money for what in the slang of the gang is called 'chirruping'. He had seen the prisoner receive money, and had cautioned him.—*Police Court Report,* 6th March 1888.

Chiv(e) (*Historical*). A knife. Said to be Romany, but it may be a curtailment of Shevvle, as the metropolis of knife manufacture, Sheffield, is called to this day. If so, on all fours with 'jocteleg'—Jacques de Liège — who manufactured in the 14th century a splendid knife, long before Sheffield rose to glory.

Chiv is used on the stage. 'I've had to be chivved.' Mr H. Marston (1870)—meaning stabbed in the course of the piece.

Presently Selby pulls out a chivy (knife), and gives Big Tim a dig or two —one on his arm and one at his face, and another at his leg. Big Tim says to me, 'Costy, I've got it a bit thick; suppose I give him a bit of chivy, and see how he likes it.' Then we all laughed, and Big Tim pulls out the chivy, and makes a dig or two at him.—*People,* 6th January 1898.

Chiv(e)-**fencer** (*Criminal*). One who harbours, fences, wards off from arrest—murderers.

'He's a chive fencer, the director of a railway, or a swell.'—*Newsp. Cutting.*

A chive-fencer is also a purveyor in the streets of cheap razors and knives.

Chivy (*Criminal*). Relating to the use of the knife.

Chivy Duel (*Thieves'*). A fight with knives.

A 'Chivy' Duel—Described by a 'Costy.'—At Southwark evidence was given in the charge of 'intentionally and maliciously wounding and inflicting grievous bodily harm on each other by stabbing each other', preferred against two men, etc.—*People,* 6th January 1895.

Chivy, To (*Hist.*). To hunt down, worry. A corruption of Cheviot (Hills), whence this kind of attention was much practised by the early English of the north when swinging into the Cheviots after the cattle stolen, or to use the more northern term— 'lifted'—by the Scotch more or less all along the border.

'Which a pore cove were never chivied as I'm chivied by the cops.'

Choice Riot (*Street,* 1870). A horrid noise, such as the festive marrow bones and cleavers. Mildly satirical. 'That there baby's making a choice riot.'

Choke off, To (*Peoples',* 18 cent. on). To get rid of. From the necessity of twisting a towel or other fabric about the neck of a bull-dog to make this tenacious hanger-on let go his biting hold. Used against persons of pertinacious application.

'Choke off' in the U.S.A. means to reduce a pleading man to silence.

Choker (*Peoples'*). A lie, in its most direct form. 'What a choker!' —such a bare-faced lie that the hearer is nearly choked. Also applied to very large neckties and for similar reasons —the huge adornment appearing to choke the wearer. The masculine choker was at its greatest in England in the time of George IV., and the fashionable lead of Beau Brummel, when it was over a yard in length. Now and again a choker breaks out about the masculine neck, but in the '80's and '90's it was steadily replaced by the 'ties'. The feminine choker is always with us, and assumes a new shape once a month.

Chokey (*Sailors'*). Imprisonment —derived from the narrow confines of the ship's lock-up and the absence of ventilation—chokey generally being fixed as near the keel as conveniently it can be managed. However, some authorities maintain that this word is an Anglicising of the Hong-Kong Chinese 'Chow Key'—a prison.

Been run in? Been locked up? Been in chokey? What!—what do you take me for? Who are you blooming well getting at? Who're you kidding?— *Cutting.*

In a very short time the whole of them were safely in the chowkey. The parties implicated have been brought up at the Fort Police Court, and committed for trial.—*Bombay Times.*

Chonkey (*Lond. Street*). A meat pie—derivation beyond the bounds of mere discovery. Probably from the name of a once historic pieman, whose fame remains a name alone.

Chop up (*L. Class;* last cry of the 19th century). To annihilate; a variant of cut up.

Chopping (*Nursery*). Big, lusty, handsome. Johnson says:

'A child which would bring money in the market' — suggested by chopping and changing. 'Perhaps,' he says, after admitting all the etymologies to be doubtful — 'a greedy, hungry child, likely to live.'

'Both Jack Freeman and Ned Wild
Would own the fair and chopping
child.'   —*Fenton.*

Chortle, To (*Peoples'*). To sing. Probably an onomatope. Chortled like the nightingale, and smiled like anything.

Many present on Boxing Night fully expected that when he appeared he would chortle a chansonnette or two.— *Ref.*, 29th December 1889.

Mr Wilford Morgan has been engaged to chortle the famous song, 'Here's to the maiden of bashful fifteen!'—*Ref.*, 18th August 1886.

Chortle also means to praise excessively. 'Joe chortles about his kid pretty loudly—it's 'is fust!'

It seems a curious time for an American critic to chortle over the recent success of Miss Minnie Maddern Fiske.— *D. T.*, 31st March 1897.

Chouse (*Peoples'*, 17 *cent.*). A cheat, to cheat. Henshaw derives it from the Turkish word chiaus, an interpreter, and referring to an interpreter at the Turkish embassy in London in 1609. He robbed the embassy right and left. In 1610 Ben Johnson in *The Alchymist* made the word classic.

'What do you think of me—
That I am a chiaus?'

Johnson has this word, but his modern fine brethren have rejected it, though Johnson gives Swift and Dryden as his authorities. 'Freedom and zeal have choused you o'er and o'er' (*Dryden*). 'From London they came, silly people, to chouse' (*Swift*). Butler also uses it in *Hudibras.*

Chow-chow (*Anglo-Ind.*). A hash, or resurrection pie, from Hindustanee word for mixed confectionery.

Christ-killers (*Peoples'*, 19 *cent.*). Jews. Passing away—chiefly used by old army men. 'What can you expect?—he's a Christ-killer. Pay up your sixty per cent., and try and look pleasant!'

Christen a jack (*Thieves'*). A grim use of baptismal ceremony—to replace the name on a stolen watch by another, to defeat detection. (*See* Church a Jack.)

Christmas (Oh) (*M. Class*). Evasive swearing. Used by Rudyard Kipling in *The Day's Work.* Of course it is 'Christ's Mass'.

Chronic (*M. Class*, 1896). Ceaseless, persistent. 'Oh! Joe's chronic.' 'Charley's Aunt's chronic'—said of a piece that ran perpetually.

Chronic Rot (*Peoples'*). Despairingly bad. Rot may or may not be from erotic; it is more likely an application of the original meaning of the word; but it is now quite understood. Chronic is used in its original application; but more widely as—'Oh, that theatre's chronic'—means that never is a good piece seen there. These two words intensify each other. 'Jack's swears to swear off' (drink) 'is chronic rot.'

Chuck (*Naval*). A biscuit—hard tack (*see*). Probably an onomatope from the noise made in chewing, or perhaps from the hand-broken biscuit (for to snap it with the teeth were out of the question), being thrown or chucked carelessly into the mouth, which is the tar's mode of coaling up.

Chuck, To (*Old Eng.*). To fling. Johnson gives half a dozen meanings to this word, but not fling, which is its most forcible meaning. Everything is chucked amongst the common folk, from a farthing or a chunk of bread, to a wife or a mistress. Now applied to the process of divorce.

She had three children by him and two by some other fellow, which is the habit of some great ladies, so Sir John chucked her.—*Newsp. Cutting.*

Jones and Dimsdale were arrested in court, as they were heard to say, referring to the evidence against the prisoner Foster, 'He's sure to get chucked'—a slang expression for discharged.—*Police Report*, November 1890.

So I takes the knives away and chucks them over a bridge. Selby then picks up an iron bar, and makes a drive at Big Tim, but I catches hold of it, and stops him. — *Chivey Duel, People*, 6th January 1895.

They would blush a maidenly pink if certain words were uttered in their presence, and then shake off with relentless severity and austerity any erring sister who has, in modern parlance, 'chucked everything'. — *D. T.*, John Strange Winter, 5th August 1899.

Chuck a Chest (*Street*). Generally said of a soldier who has a full bust. To throw forward the chest, as though prepared to meet the world.

Chuck a Dummy (*Tailors'*). To faint. Very interesting as illustrating the influence familiar objects have in framing new ideas—from the similarity of a falling fainting man to an overthrown or chucked tailor's dummy—a figure upon which coats are fitted to show them off for sale. 'I chucked a dummy this mornin', an' 'ad to be brought to with o-der-wee !'

'Chuck it out, Creswick' — then manager of Surrey.

'Yes, and chuck it out quick, cully,' observed Sir John Adamant.—*Cutting.*

Chuck a Shoulder (*Costers'*). To turn away—said chiefly by the male coster of the female; *e.g.*, 'Which she chucked me a shoulder, an' not the one I want—an' 'av been on hice ever the mortal since.'

Chuck a yannep (*Back Slang*). To throw a penny.

'The Lord loveth a cheerful giver'; but there's no use chucking a yannep into the collection plate loud enough to make the people in the back seats think the Communion service has tumbled off the altar.—*Cutting.*

Chuck his weight about, To (*Milit.*). To demonstrate his physical magnificence — generally said of any soldier who is showing off, but more particularly one of the household brigades. 'So 'e turned up, and chucked 'is weight about all over the blooming place—he did.'

Chuck out ink (*Press Reporters'*). To write articles.

Suddenly it came across my mind that the boss might be waiting about for me somewhere with a big boot and genteel language, and that it might be better for my health if I chucked out ink.—*Cutting.*

Chuck over the lug (*Peoples'*). To thwack over the ear—lug being high Scotch for the auricular. (*See* Poultice over the peeper, One over the gash.)

Chuck up, To (*L. London*). To abandon.

Did she mean, we says, to chuck us up? Of course she did, says she, flaring up like a mill on fire.—*Cutting.*

'But after all, cullies, being mashed on a dona is nothing; it's when the bit of jam chucks you up—that is the stinger.'—*Cutting.*

Chuck up the bunch of fives (*Pugilistic*). To die. The one poetic figure of speech engendered by the prize ring. The fives are the two sets of four fingers and a thumb—the fists — the 'bunches' — flaccid in death. 'Pore Ben—'e's been an' gorne an' chucked up 'is bunches o' fives.'

Chuck up the sponge (*Prize Ring*). To admit defeat—by way of a pugilist's attendant, at his chief's failure, throwing up the sponge with which he has been refreshing his principal. This custom was, and is, applied to death. All trades yield these figurative modes of referring to birth, marriage, death, and money.

'Bill chucked up the sponge this morning.'

Chuck your money about (*Street*, 1894 on). A satirical but good-tempered reproach cast at meanness, or insufficient reward. 'Jack—you've done me a real good turn—yere's the price of a pint.' To which Jack may reply, 'Well—you do just chuck your money about—you do!'

Chuck-barge (*Naval*). Cask in which the biscuit of a mess is kept. Also equivalent to bread-basket. (*See* Bread-barge.)

Chuck-bread (*Beggars'*). Waste-bread, that which would be thrown away but for mendicants. 'No chuck-bread for me.'

Chuck-out (*L. Theatrical*, 1880 on). This verb has the force of 'vigorous'. 'Can't he chuck it out?' would mean that a singer or actor has a powerful delivery. Therefore the recommendation 'Chuck it out' is equal to 'Louder—if you please' of the public dinner.

Chuckaboo (*Peoples'*). A name given familiarly to a favourite chum. No meaning; but probably the 'chuck' is a conversion of 'duck'.

Chuckaways (*London*). Lucifer matches — graphic description of the act of rejection after the match is done with. Bill—'I want a light — got any chuckaways?' (*See* Bryant and May.)

Chucked all of a heap (*Street*). Fascinated, ravishingly overcome, mashed, enthralled.

When he gazed upon her soft and gentle beauty, and heard the gurgling sound which smote his ear like the rushing of many waters he was chucked all of a heap.—*Cutting*.

Chucker-in-Chief (*Public-house*). A prince amongst mere chuckers-out.

The magnificent figure of the gentleman, who was late literary adviser to Gussy (Sir A. Harris, of Drury Lane Theatre) and chucker-in-chief, is now to be seen nightly at the Princess's, where its owner finds his services appreciated.

Chucker-out (*Public-house*, 1880). The name given to a barman who turns out noisy tavern customers. Chuckers-out are simple and compound. The first argues the case, he being generally not a giant of strength. The 'compound', who gets his name probably from his size—large enough for a 'compound' of men—'bounces' without a word—which he seldom has.

Chuckers-out are of two blooming sorts generally—simple and compound. The simple chucker-out is sometimes a bit barmy in the crumpet, and is only kept for the sake of show, and to prevent the sweet tarts behind the bar hollering out. . . . He's a warm 'un, is the compound chucker-out. You generally find him at music-halls and about the bars of pubs. which blokes use that aren't afraid of a couple of black peepers.—*Cutting*.

Chucking-out Time (*Lond. Public-house*). Half-past twelve, the closing hour for metropolitan taverns, when those who do not go willingly are 'chucked out'.

Chuffy (*Peoples'*; *rare*). Surly; *e.g.*, 'Don't be chuffy'—probably from the behaviour of one 'Chuffs'—who may have once been powerful in the cadger world.

Chum (*Universal*). A familiar friend. This term is probably the only one that has steadily remained patronised by all classes. Dr Johnson, who always sought the unexpected, says this word is 'Armorick'. He adds, 'a chamber fellow'; a term used in the universities.

'The princes were quite chums.'

'I had a chum, etc.'—Fielding, *Tom Jones*, book viii., ch. 2.

'The two actors were very, very friendly indeed. We dressed in the same dressing room, and were very friendly. In fact, Mr Crozier bought some colours from Mr Franks on Saturday, I believe.' The Coroner: 'They were what is called in vulgar parlance "chums".' Witness: 'Yes. I never knew them to have any quarrel or speak any angry words to each other.'—Evidence of Mr C. Lillford at an inquest upon Crozier, an actor accidentally killed at the Novelty Theatre, London (10th August 1896).—*D. T.*, 14th August 1896.

Chump (*Peoples'*). The head. Chump initially is a fine onomatope, being the sound made by horses in grinding oats. Hence the use of the word to represent head, of which the dentition is only part. Then extended to the human head. (*See* 'Orf Chump', 'Orf his Chump'.)

Spain had her flirtations, and Marie Antoinette was frivolous and fond of pleasure until she lost her chump.—*Cutting*.

Take off yer blooming 'at; take off yer blooming chump as well.—Said in a theatre.

Chump (*Ang.-Amer.*, 1895). Equivalent to Juggins. A youth (as a rule) who is in any way cheated of his money — especially by the so-called gentler sex.

What's a chump? 'Say, pa, what's a chump?' asked young Tommy as his father was taking him out walking. 'See that young man in there?' (they were just passing an ice cream saloon) said the father, pointing in. 'Yes, I see him; the one with the girl in the red dress?' 'Yes; well, he's buying ice cream for his girl with money he ought to save to buy his lunch with till next pay day. He's a chump.'—*Cutting*.

Chumps Elizas (*London*, Five Pounder Tourists', 1854 on). A grotesque pronunciation of Champs Elysés—still in Paris.

Church a Jack, To (*Thieves*'). To remove the works of a watch from its case, and put them in another, of course with the view of destroying the identity of the article. (*See* Christen a Jack.)

Church-bell (*Rural*). A talkative woman. 'Ah ca'as ma wife choorch bell, cas 'er's yeard arl over t' village.'

Church parade (*Soc.*, 1885 on). The display of dress after morning church. Quite the thing to carry prayer books. Began in Hyde Park; imitated now all over the country.

Mr Dutton asked, with respect to some wearing apparel which prosecutrix paid £4 for on delivery for Mrs Gardiner, whether she did not part with the money to enable 'the countess' on the following Sunday to accompany her to the Church parade in the Park. Prosecutrix: 'Church parade was never mentioned.'—*D. T.*, 17th March 1893.

Church-piece (*Soc.*). A threepenny piece—the smallest silver the genteel mean can put in the absurdly-named offertory.

Churched (*Com. Lond.*). Married —amongst the common; attendance at prayers after childbirth amongst higher-class women. The commonest possible term amongst lower classes for marriage, and singularly expressive as marking the distinction between ordinary come-together marriage, and the real ceremony.

He did grand before we was churched, and used to blarney and call me good-looking, and squeeze my blooming waist. —*Cutting*.

Churchyard Cough (*Peoples'*). A fatal cold — sometimes in these later times synonymised by 'cemetery catarrh'.

Churchyard Luck (*Peoples'*). The 'good fortune' which the mother of a large family experiences by the death of one or more of her children; *e.g.*, 'Yes, mum, I hev brought 'em all up —ten boys, and no churchyard luck with it.'—Said by a Liverpool woman to a district-visitor.

Cigareticide (*Soc.*, 1883). A word invented to meet the theory that the cigarette is the most dangerous form of smoking. More common in America than in Great Britain.

That young man's grit is indeed remarkable in this age of dudism and cigareticide.—*Cutting*.

Cinder (*Peoples'*, 19 *cent.*). Hot— especially alcoholic heat, *e.g.*, 'That's a cinder for him.'

He had been a teetotaller himself for seven years, and really left his last lodgings because the landlady was too fond of putting 'a cinder in her tea', that is to say, flavouring her Mazawattee with a plentiful supply of rum.—*D. T.*, 12th May 1896.

Cinder-knotter (*Navy*). A stoker — very descriptive, and necessarily modern, phrase; for he does knot the living coals into heaps.

Cinder-sifter (*Fashion*, 1878). A hat with open-work brim, the edge of which was turned up perpendicularly. On all fours with the poke bonnet, called 'coal-scuttle', or the high collars introduced by George III., and styled gills.

Cinderella (*Society*, 1880). A dance which ends at twelve — the name fancifully suggested, it is not known by whom, in reference to that successful young professional beauty who, at midnight, was by force major compelled to give up dancing. Adopted in France—1880.

N'ayez pas peur, ma chère, ce n'est qu'une Cendrillon; à minuit — finis et silence.

The hours at which balls begin grow later and later. The stroke which sends the last guest hurrying away from the Cinderella dance scarcely ushers the first arrival to a season ball.—*D. N.*, 27th March 1884.

Circlers (*Theatr.*). Occupants of dress-circle. Applied with envious derision by the pit.

Circs (*City*, 1860). Abbreviation of 'circumstances'.

The Duke and Duchess of Teck patronized the performance of *Iolanthe* at the Savoy Theatre on Monday last. Under the circs I am disposed to exclaim, 'What extravagance!'—*Cutting*, August 1883.

The royal couple at this date were about economising by leaving England and going to Bumpenheim.

Circuit Rider (*Amer., provincial*). A peripatetic preacher.

There was no 'circuit rider' or other evangelical authority to be relied upon. —*Cutting*.

Circumbendibus (*Peoples'*). Evasion —adopted probably from some author playing with Latin formation—based upon circumlocution. 'He allowed the accusation by a circumbendibus.'

Circus (*Amer.*) Excitement, adventure—from the pother created when a wandering circus heaves in sight. A circus is the most favourite form of American provincial amusement.

Lafayette got the check cashed and spent the money, and then Coghill found out that he had paid Lafayette just three times too much for the Louisiana lands. Then there was a circus.—*N. Y. Mercury*, 23rd May 1885.

The next day old Hays and young Hays started out in search of Reed's companion—Stephens. The pair found Stephens in his room. He made a desperate fight, but there was no 'circus' this time, the two Hays bein' too many for the one Stephens.—*Cutting*.

City Road Africans (*Street*, 1882). —Hetairæ of that quarter. Origin not known.

City sherry (*Peoples'*, E. London, 1880). Four ale, which in colour may be said to resemble the worst description of sherry or the highest quality of rectified varnish. The East London people have a modified mistrust of those living amongst them, who get their living in the city, especially of the great body of exclusive clerks, whose general poverty they satirise in many ways, of which this is one. 'City sherry' used to be the basis of a great perennial practical joke at the 'European,' once a prosperous tavern in the Poultry (E.C.), where this liquid was set out in imperial half pints and royal array on the counter awaiting the 'ready' pennies of the passing public. The humble little joke took its rise from this opportunity of helping oneself to these drinks without calling for a barman, and then planking the money down.

Country cousins were told that tumblers of city sherry were given away at this particular house all day long. The victim was taken in, was handed a glass of fourpenny from the counter, while the operator gave a well-known wink to the attendant barman who instantly comprehended this joke. When the wondering eye of the country cousin was off the counter the town relative paid for the drinks.

This 'sherry house,' the European, fell before the improver at the end of 1884, and the jocular 'halves' ceased to be drawn for ever. However, city sherry, *in* the City, is still cloaked satire for a pretended 'free drink'.

Clackbox (*Hist.*). Male or masculine of chatterbox—generally applied to a woman, and especially a girl. This word rarely comes to town.

Claim (*Ang.-Amer.*). To recognise in travelling. In a railway carriage one may frequently hear the enquiry— 'Surely I claim you—we met at Suez?'

Clamp (*N. Eng.*). A kick, from the name given to the heavy boots clamped or tipped with iron. Very formidable weapons.

Clap-trap (*Theatrical*). Commonplace. Trap to catch a clap from the audience, as:—

'The man who lays his hands upon a woman, except in the way of kindness, ought to be yard-armed.'

Clare Market Cleavers (*Strand*). They were the butchers in this once densely populated place—now a sixty yard street. The rival community was Seven Dials—half a mile away—with which country there were frequent wars. The glory of Clare Market began to pitch in '70, rocked in the early '90's, and was practically gone in '98. The Cleavers were great fighters, Princes in Clare, and heavy blackmailers of newly-married couples of that ilk—who were always obliged with a concert of marrow-bones and cleavers. These cleaver serenades had to be paid for. 'Oh—he's a cleaver bloke—I can tell you.' As it has been said, the glories of Clare Market and her cleavers began to fade in '70. Her commercial and butcherly bravery, beginning in the west at Drury Lane, and swinging south-east down to Temple Bar, with a dash over into Strand Lane (*see* Diprose's St Clement Danes), fell before the demands of the new Law Courts. Two-thirds of the parish were swept away; and with the old crowded houses the Clare Market customers. The butchers shared in the fall—but they still remained a combined power in the old slaughter-houses, until in the '80's their 'cleavin' propensities ended in a steel fight, which finished one of the later cleavers. Resulting precaution, and two School Board schools slowly suppressed the cleavers, who vanished, while the market faded into a mere street.

Clare Market Duck (19 *cent.*). Baked bullock's heart stuffed with sage and onions—which gave a faint resemblance to the bird. The term is one of those satirical associations of cheap food with luxurious dishes, of which there are several specimens. (*See* 'Billingsgate Pheasant,' 'Two-Eyed Steak,' etc.)

Clarkenco (*Polit.*). A new political party. When the Gladstone Government went out (June, 1885) and that of Lord Salisbury came in, Mr Ed. Clarke, Q.C., who was expected to get office was left out in the cold. He was supposed to lead a new party which took the place of that led previously by Lord R. Churchill.

'Mr Edward Clarke and Co.', as the new Fourth Party is called in the House, will let the Churchill lot 'have it' at every convenient, and at several inconvenient, opportunities—*Ref.*, 19th July 1885.

Claw-hammer (*Amer.-Eng.*). Tailcoat, accepted in England about 1880. Description of the divided tail, like in shape and lines to the claw of a hammer. (*See* Bobtail.)

Clean Time (*Amer.*). A figurative expression for honesty; derived from the old phrase, 'clean hands'. 'He never would do the clean thing.'

Clean tuckered out (*New Eng.*). Utterly exhausted—probably from the name 'Tucker'.

He was clean tuckered out all but his eyes (and he could just barely turn them in his head) and his bill.—*Newsp. Cutting.*

Cleavin (*Clare Market*). Boastful —from the Clare Market Cleavers (1750-1860)—the king-butchers of that once popular market who were the equal pride and terror of that place, —terror because of their readiness to fight, pride, because of the warfare, continual and unflagging, they carried on over the border amongst the Pictpockets and maurauding Scots of the adjacent Drury Lane. They made much coin by marriage in the neighbourhood, and far around by their rough marrow-bone and cleaver orchestras.

Clicker (*Printers'*). The sub-foreman in printing office. Gives out copy and conveys orders from foreman to men. Probably contemptuous, and from the French — Claqueur. The clicker also puts the type into pages. Most obscure phrases or words in printing come from France.

Climb in on, To (*U.S.*). To overcome easily, to get the better of another by cunning.

'I climbed in on him proper.'

Dr Hall says it is very unhealthy to live on the ground floor of a house. Doctor's right. A fellow's creditors can climb in on him with so little trouble.— *Newsp. Cutting.*

To lower pride.

Climb the Golden Staircase, To (*Amer.*). One of the U.S.A. equivalents to the Latin 'join the majority'.

Edward's Folly Dramatic Company is reported as having climbed the golden stairs. The cash assets are alleged to have been carefully secured in a pill box.— (1883.)

D'Arcy and his company, with Josie Batchelder as star, climbed the golden staircase last Monday. They are said to have been kindly assisted on their tour homeward by sympathizing citizens.— *Cutting.*

Climb the Mountain of Piety, To. To pawn; from the first governmental pawnshop being situated on a height in Rome called Monte di Pietà, so named, of course, from a group of the dead Christ and the Virgin called in art a Pietà.

Mr Candy: On one occasion, I think, you had to resort to what is called 'climbing the mountain of piety'?— Evelyn *v.* Hulbert, *D. N.*, 15th April 1896.

Clinger (*Ball-room*). A lady who holds on in waltzing; *e.g.*, 'She's a bad 'un to go, but she's a real clinger.'

Clobber (*Jewish, E. London*). Superior, or rather startling clothing. In Hebrew ' KLBR '.

' My high—look at Beck.'

Clobbered (*N. Eng. Prov.*). Well nourished and dressed. Common in Yorkshire.

' Eh, he looks well clobbered.'

Clock (*London*). A dynamite bomb, when carried in a small square Gladstone bag. Took its rise in the '80's, during the dynamite scare, when a dynamiter, being stopped by a policeman and asked what he had in his bag, replied—' A clock '.

Clock stopped (*London, Peoples'*). No credit. ' No *tick* '—hence the clock has stopped. ' No tick ' means 'no ticket'—given by master or other to obtain credit.

Cloddy (*Dog Market*). Aristocratic in appearance. Applied to human beings by some divisions of the lower classes.

''E's a cloddy bloke — don't yer make no mistake about it !'

A bull-dog should be low to the ground, short in the back, and thickset. An animal that possesses these qualifications is known as one of the ' cloddy ', the correct expression among dog-fanciers.—*D. T.*, 13th November 1895.

Close out, To (*Amer.*, 1883). To finish. Quite local until recently. Now sometimes heard in England.

Do not close out the last of your soup by taking the plate in your mouth and pouring the liquid down.—*Cutting.*

Clou (*Theatr.*). From the French. Equal to ' heart' or central idea of a tale or drama. Of course, literally ' nail '—upon which the piece or book hangs.

Whatever may be the decision arrived at, the case will be memorable as fairly placing before the world entirely opposite views as to the degree of copyright in the central idea, or ' *clou* ', as it is called in France, of a drama or romance.—*D. N.*, 4th August 1883.

'The field of the French writer is almost unlimited. He writes for men and married women. His first thought when hammering out the *clou* or mainspring of his play is " What shall I do with my adulteress ? "'—G. W. Gilbert, *D. N.*, 21st January 1885.

Clouded over (*American*). Overwhelmed by misfortune. (*See* Bound to shine.)

Clove-hunters (*Amer.-Eng.*) Frequent nip-drinkers, especially between the acts of a play, when the nibbled clove vainly sought to hide the higher perfume of the alcohol. Came to be used (1884) for the refreshment itself.

Pleasing example of modern metaphor.

A belief prevails among Union Square Theatre patrons that the trick chairs which adorn the auditorium were designed to trap and hold in place between the acts clove-hunters.—*N. Y. Mercury*, December 1884.

Coal-oil Johnny (*Amer. coal - oil fields*). The derivation of this word is interesting. Many of the uneducated and more wasteful men who struck oil squandered their money, while Johnny in American is the equivalent of English Sammy, Sappy, or Softy—hence a coal-oil Johnny was at first a suddenly enriched coal-oil miner, who wasted his easily-gained wealth. The term soon spread, and stood for a description of a stupid, extravagant, vulgar person.

He played a ' coal-oil Johnny ' career ; treated to champagne by the basket, had the handsomest carriage and pair in the city, and paid cabmen five dollars to drive him a few blocks.—*Newsp. Cutting.*

Coal Sack (*Peoples'*). Cul de sac—one of the most egregious Anglicisations in the language.

' Which we bolted up a blind alley, and found ourselves in a coal sack.'

Coal up, To (*Trade. Stokers'*). To feed. ' Let's coal up on bread and cheese—nothing better, sonny.'

Cock (*Printers'*, 1874). In throwing types to decide who shall pay for drinks or other matters, by the number of nicks which turn up, the types used sometimes catch together, and do not fall flat on the imposing stone, the general arena for these adventures. ' That's a cock ' is said—abbreviation of ' cock and hen '. The question is once more tried.

Cock and Bull Story (*Peoples'*). Every etymologist has had an attack of analysis of this phrase, which Sterne uses as his abrupt and unintended termination of ' The Sentimental Journey '. No one has solved this difficulty. Possibly a phrase on all fours with ' By hook or by crook,' ' A miss is as good as a mile,' etc., and meaning ' A. Cock, and D. Bull, story' —and may refer to two witnesses of these names in some once notorious case.

Dr Brewer of course goes off at score upon this phrase. He says : ' A corruption of "a concocted and bully story". The catch-pennies hawked about the streets are still called *cocks*, *i.e.*, concocted things. Bully is the Danish *bullen* (exaggerated), our bull-rush (an exaggerated rush), *bull-frog*, etc., etc.' All this is confused, contradictory, wanting in relation of parts. Probably corruption of perchance Cockaigne Bill—a forgotten teller of inconsequent tales — like the more modern Mrs Partington.

Sir Francis Jeune said the petitioner had shown a great deal of carelessness. His wife told him a cock-and-bull story about having been married before, and he took no steps to verify it until some years afterwards.—*Sir F. Jeune, Div. Court*, 29th October 1896.

Cock and Hen Club (*Soc.*, 1880). One of mixed sexes—then spoken of contemptuously probably because they had not at that date quite succeeded.

He takes advantage of his wife's absence from home to ' make a night of it', and take supper with a strange young lady at a club which, I believe, would be called of the cock-and-hen order.—*Carados*.

What are described as working men's clubs (often enough falsely described thus), very early breakfast clubs, cock-and-hen clubs, with one or two other clubs whose names and descriptions will to the initiated suggest themselves, are all flagrant and distinct violations of the Licensing Acts.—*Ref.*, 19th May 1889.

Cock of the Walk (*London, Sporting*, 18 *cent.*). Leader—derived from cock-fighting, or from farmyard, where one cock alone holds the central ground.

Directly you get up one or two steps in the ladder, you want to be cock of the walk—*Cutting*.

Cock one's chest (*Navy*). To throw the chest out, after the manner of vain creatures. Generally used with the addition—' like a half-pay Admiral '—not a full-pay, mark you.

Cockatoo (*Austral.*, 1880). A small farmer. The name is given by the squatters or sheep breeders to the agriculturists, from the cockatoos following the movements of the farmer over his land, especially at sowing time. The word is offensively used, for there is, or perhaps it is better to say was, bitter war between the settled farmer and the unsettled squatter, whose sheep often ruinously injured the unenclosed agricultural stretches, while too frequently, it is to be feared, the squatter made a path for his sheep, even where an enclosure had been made. The squatter still knows the cockatoo has the sympathy of the legislature, and he 'hates him accordingly'.

Cocked Hat, To knock into a (18 *cent.*). To conquer, tumble about in all directions. Perhaps no phrase is more obscure than this. It is probably one of the expressions which result out of a change in dress, especially where the change is associated with political movement. The hat which preceded the cocked was the cavalier, which possessed a flat flopping brim, above which showed the white feather, which swung round and trailed between the shoulders. Hence arose the Puritan term for cowardice —showing the white feather—this dancing adornment displaying itself very ineffectively when the cavaliers took to flight, which they did upon occasion. The cocked hat might figuratively be described as a cavalier hat, whose brim had been knocked up and in by three spaced blows round the circumference. Now as the cocked hat came in with the Guelphs and the Whigs, it can readily be understood that the Jacobites accepted the new cocked hat as a head-gear that had been assaulted by cavaliers—hence probably a Jacobite term, ' I'll knock the Whig into one of his own cocked hats '—an idea so practical that it was accepted by the people. It has lasted to this day, when the three-cornered cocked, or up-turned hat has absolutely vanished in England except amongst mayors and aldermen, and by way of the black cap worn by judges while uttering the death sentence. The tricorne is still worn in Germany, and even in France and Italy.

I thought that was the worst play I had ever seen, but *Nadine* knocked it into several cocked-hats.—*Newsp. Cutting*, 8th March 1885.

Wilson Barrett licks everything else into a cocked hat.—*Newsp. Cutting*.

Cock-linnet (*East London*). A dapper boy, a tiny buck from the East End of London, where bird fairs are held every Sunday morning. It is also rhyming slang for 'minute'.

'Hold on for a cock linnet—now barney.'—*Newsp. Cutting.*

Cocks (*Dispensing chemist*). Concoctions.

Cock-sure (*Sporting*, 18 cent.). Absolutely certain. In the good old days of cock-fighting the vanquishing bird always crowed—but never until he was quite sure, by various modes of proof, that his enemy was either dead or insensible. Then he gave gullet.

Used disparagingly in these later days.

In the identification of prisoners police constables sometimes blunder, and rarely, if ever, hesitate. They are very 'cock sure' in their evidence.—*D.N.*, 8th December 1884.

Cocker up, To (*Chaunters'*). To make a horse look young for sale. Evidently from the French 'coquet'; the more likely that Chaunter is certainly from Chanteur—an unscrupulous and daring cheat.

Cockowax (*Peoples'*, 18 cent.). Obscure — used satirically. 'Hullo my cock'owax.' Probably corruption of cock of wax, which may have been said in cock-fighting days of a bird which had no mettle in him—a poor soft, waxy, creature, opposite of cock of the walk.

Cock-pit (*Political*). A convenient place for settling a sanguinary quarrel. From the pit or enclosure in which the cocks fought, and which would become much blood-stained—hence the name was given to that portion of a warship to which the wounded were taken for treatment.

England cannot consent to make Egypt the cock-pit in which the diplomatic intrigues of Europe are to find a new arena.—*D. N.*, 21st January 1885.

Cocoa (*Nautical*). Comic shape of Toko—(*see*). Schoolboy expression, probably from Negronia. When a word has become time-weary, it is often newly editioned by being exchanged for a well-known word which rhymes with it.

Charlie Wyndham and W. H. Vernon must mind their eye, or Onesimus will give 'em 'cocoa' before long.—*Newsp. Cutting.*

Cocotte; Cocodette (*Franco-English* 1860-70). Non-virtuous French, or other young woman of large income. The second is to the first as a first officer is to the captain.

In the circle of cocottes, and cocodettes, by which the French Court has during the last fifteen years managed to surround itself, fast American women have furnished no inconsiderable contribution. —(1867.)

Cod (*Printers'*). A fool; *e.g.*, 'the fellow's a cod.'

Cod (*Peoples'*). Humbug, swindle, more generally coddem, cod em, cod them.

Cod, To (*Thieves'*, 18 cent.). To cod is to cheat meanly by way of familiarity in relation to eccentric erotics. To comprehend this term an intimate acquaintance with Balzac's *Vautrin* is required.

Cod, To (*Theatr.*). To flatter; *e.g.*, 'Don't try to cod me'—from Coddem —a game of deception.

Cod (*Trade. Tailors'*). A drunkard. The word is suggested by the fallen cheeks and lips' corners which are some of the facial evidences of a drunkard, and which certainly suggest the countenance of a cod, which fish, furthermore from its size, is typical of huge drinking. 'He's a bigger cod every day.'

Cod, Coddem (*Mid. Class*). To ridicule by appealing to the sanity of one codded.

'Cod' is peculiar as a word signifying ironical chaff, and perhaps it has not much to recommend itself beyond its brevity.—*Stage*, 21st August 1885.

I don't know all the perfessionals. Irving don't play coddem in our taproom.—*Cutting.*

I hear that at the end of Adelphi Terrace there is a theatrical club where coddem is now the favourite pastime. —(1882.)

Shoreditch isn't what it was; but there's some fun in the old village still. You can show off your Sunday togs in the Aquarium. You can play coddem.— (1883.)

Cod-bangers (*Great Grimsby and Billingsgate*). Gorgeously arrayed sailors. Good example of an obscure phrase or word having a solid foundation. The cod are brought in alive from the North Sea to Great Grimsby, and are knocked or banged on the head as wanted for market. The fishermen in this trade make, and waste, considerable money. They keep to the blue worsted jersey, but it is complicated with rich silk squares hauled round the neck, and by frequent rings. This gorgeousness has begotten the half-contemptuous, half-envious name. It has spread to Billingsgate and beyond the cod-trade. 'Whoa — yere comes a cod-banger.' The word may also have another meaning, easily sought and found.

Coddem (*L. Class*). A tavern game—for from two to say ten, and the equivalent of the American bluff or brag. All the shapes of this word come from Coddem, which is played by the operators dividing into two sets—each set seated opposite the other—a table between them. One side have a bean, or other small object—the hands belonging to this side are lowered under the table, the bean is placed in one of the hands, and all the fists are brought up in a row on the table. The other side now have to guess where the bean is. He must not touch the fists, but he points to one, and says either 'tip it' or 'take it away'. If he says 'tip it', the hand pointed at is opened, and if it is empty, the other side has lost one, and the holders of the bean score one. Then they begin again, and again bring up their fists. Now as to the other term 'take it away'; upon this direction, the owner of the hand pointed at takes it off the table—if it is empty. On the contrary shows the bean if it is in his hand—then the other side loses another point. This hand being lowered, the guesser begins again with the remaining hands, until he either guesses right, or again loses a point—all of which may appear to the reader very simple. On the contrary, it is one of the most psychological games ever invented. It calls for immense intelligence, and there is not probably a village in England without its champion codder—a man who invariably wins at this game. When a guess is right, the bean passes to the other side that has guessed rightly. Money is won or lost at this game—but the process is too complicated for clear explanation.

Codger (*Peoples'*). Roystering, ageing, boon companion. The earlier dictionaries will have nothing to say to this word, which does not appear to have come from the Persian or other equally next-door language. A modern dictionary describes him as a stingy, clownish fellow, whereas he is rarely stingy, and never clownish. There was, until perhaps 1880, a Codger's Hall for political discussion and drinks, under the shadow of S. Bride's, Blackfriars. Word probably invented itself, in the gutter, or near about. Byron first gave it house-room in an occasional address to 'Thomas Moore', 'Oh you who are all, etc.' Learned etymologists assume this word to come from cogito, but do not suggest the itinerary. Nor indeed do codgers ever think. They have no time for cogitation.

Codocity(*Printers'*, 1874). Stupidity —capacity for being codded.

Coffee-and-B. (*Night Tavern*, 1880). Coffee and brandy.

On being served the barmaid asked him to treat her. He inquired what she would have, and she said coffee and 'b.' He asked what she meant by 'b', and she said brandy, or as they called it 'coffee and cold water'.—*Newsp. Cutting.*

Coffee-sisters (*Germany*, 19 cent.). Malignant gossipers. From the women drinking in coffee and scandal at the same eager moment. Much after the use of the word tea-talker in England. 'What is she — a mere coffee-sister.'

A well-known society lady in Germany is credited with the statement that coffee not only keeps those who indulge in it wakeful and gay, but is likewise endowed with the mysterious 'virtue' of bringing to light all the vices of a not too-populous city. And it is well understood that herein lies the attraction it has for the critical sisterhood of mature German ladies known as 'coffee-sisters', or, as we should say, gossips.—*D. T.*, 26th September 1895.

Coigne (*Printers'*). A clever trade term for money. A play upon coin and coigne, or coin, or quoin, a wedge, generally named thus in printing offices. Pun suggested by the force of coin as a wedge, and a wedge as a coign.

Gascoigne, I am willing to believe, has little 'gas' about him, and not more coigne than he knows what to do with.—*Newsp. Cutting.*

Coker-nuts (*Low London*). Well-developed feminine breasts. (*See* Prize Faggot.)

Cold (*London Tavern*). The antithesis of 'warm with' and 'hot with' (sugar). Cold is short for cold water. Hence, the usual order in times of heat is 'Three of cold'—say gin.

Cold Coffee (*Artisans' Secret*, 1874). Beer. In some offices, especially in some printing houses, beer is only allowed at certain hours, while coffee is admissible at all times. Coffee-house mugs are therefore kept, and the errand boys go for 'cold coffee'. The coffee-house keeper has the beer ready, and to such an extent was the effort at deception carried that in some cases milk was mixed with the beer to complete the deception — many young printers being very moderate drinkers.

Cold Cook (*London*). An undertaker—for dead humanity being by the lower classes called 'dead meat', clearly the undertaker who looks after the dead is a cold cook.

Cold-creams (*Military*). Linesman's name for the 'Coldstreams', to designate their assumption of superior manners and distinction. 'Look out, mate—yere comes a cold cream.' (*See* Porridge Pots, Grinning Dears, Muck, Gee-gees.)

Cold Day (*U.S.*). Bad luck—good instance of climatic influence in producing phrases.

'It's a cold day when I get left anywhere that I can't find my way back. Well, good-bye, old potatoes.'—*Newsp. Cutting.*

This essentially American phrase (now common in England) intimates that he is very clever, adroit, and rarely bested. A cold day in America is indeed cold, the phrase therefore means—only a very dreadful state of weather would result in his discomfiture.

'It's a cold day when the trotting-horse reporter gets left,' said the law reporter to the managing editor.—*Newsp. Cutting.*

Cold Deck of Cards (*Californian*, 1849-80). Cards marked for the purpose of cheating.

During the early days of California, a witness giving evidence in court referred to the operation technically known as 'ringing in a cold deck' at poker. For the information of the judge, the witness explained that, at the game of poker, it was not uncommon to introduce a pack, or as the American phrase goes, 'deck' of cards, which was said by professional cardsharpers to be 'cold' when duly marked and arranged for the purpose of fraud. The judge asked if any person was present who could give an explanation of the *modus operandi*. To his amazement the audience rose like one man.—*Newsp. Cutting.*

He denied the alleged 'cold deck' business *in toto*, and made some vigorous remarks about the moral weakness of a man who puts up all he can raise on four aces, with a view to scooping in the parties of the other part, and then turns round and 'squeals' when another fellow takes the pot with a straight flush.—*Newsp. Cutting.*

Cold Four (*Public-house*). One of the more opprobrious terms for the cheapest description of beer. The cold does not refer to the low temperature of four-ale, or four 'arf-an-'arf, but to its fatal want of warmthful generosity.

Cold Meat (*L. London*). Dead humanity.

The wicked Scorcher says a dead wife is the best bit of cold meat in the house. —*Cutting.*

Cold Shake (of the hand) (*Amer.*). A new form of cold shoulder, or dismissal. 'Leave you,' he cried—' do you give me the cold shake?' 'No, no,' she said, 'only for a minute.' He watched—it was her false back hair. She fixed it and returned radiant.

Matsada S. Ingomar, a Japanese athlete, who had married a rich Quakeress—one Miss Lodge of Philadelphia—for a month or so forsook the arena, and gave his former companions the 'cold shake'.

Cold Shoulder (*English, coming from the Italian of Dante's time*). To turn the shoulder upon an applicant. It is interesting, as illustrating how personal wit will deflect a meaning, or add to it, that Douglas Jerrold totally changed the aspect of this phrase. He made it refer to cold shoulder of mutton, and 'cold shoulder' became synonymous with inhospitality, as it remains to this day. The climax was reached by the comicality (attributed also to Douglas Jerrold) of Paterfamilias (at dinner table). 'For what we are about to receive may we be truly thankful—cold shoulder again!'

Shakespeare used the phrase as turning the human shoulder from a suppliant.

If you are too clever, people are sure to find you out, and call you red-hot treats, and will give you the shoulder of mutton for ever.—*Cutting.*

Cold Snap (*Amer.-Eng.*). The first premonitory frost—figuratively a quick, markedly cool reception.

When the first 'cold snap', as the Americans call it, arrives, then many of us must wish to be hibernating animals. —*D. N.*, 20th November 1884.

Young Blunt had his overcoat in pawn during the cold snap and wanted to get it out, so he called on Mr Moses to see about it.—*Newsp. Cutting.*

Cold Tub (*Soc.*, 19 *cent.*). A cold morning bath. Good example of homely metaphor. Here the water gets dubbed by its containant.

The speech of the Chancellor of the Exchequer, so far from encouraging illusions in the mind of clever youth, was as bracing as cold tub.—*D. T.*, 11th November 1899.

Colder'n a wedge (*Western Amer.*). Dead—colder than a wedge, the iron quoin used for splitting timber, and which in American winters is cold enough to take the skin off upon touch.

Colinderies (*Soc.*, 1886). The Colonial and Indian Exhibition, South Kensington. The last of the droll names given to the series of four industrial exhibitions at South Kensington (1883-86).

The Colinderies was patronized by no fewer than 81,516 people, making a total since the opening of 2,240,536.—*Ref.*, 8th August 1886.

Even the authorities accepted this droll titling, which began with Fisheries, followed by Healtheries, continued with Inventories, and ended with Colinderies. Even the attendants bore upon their caps the legend 'Colindia'.

The epilogue was called 'Colindia', and was a very pleasant entertainment. It was a sort of ten minutes' pantomime. —*Ref.*, 8th August 1886.

At a Royal Commission of Inquiry into the Metropolitan Board of Works (7th August 1888) Mr Emil Loibl, a witness, added the last invention in 'ries'.

A song mentioned was *Ten to One on the Lodger*, and the songs were said to have put to the blush two Chinese mandarins. Witness replied: That was another trick of the briberies.—*Public Press*, 8th August 1888.

Collah Carriage (*Street Negro Minstrels*). A railway carriage filled with women — Collah being Yiddish for young girls. 'Git into a collah carriage.' Said while waiting on a railway platform by one negro minstrel to another, both with their musical instruments of torture, their banjos, ready. Until stopped by the police, these tiresome persons found it pay to take shilling third-class return tickets some way down a line, and change their carriage at every station—making a collection before every change. The victims fixed, and many of them nervous, it was a poor collection that did not produce threepence. Granted twenty stations there and back, five shillings was the result—a profit of three shillings—while they had their ride to some fair or festive occasion and back for nothing. Probably derived from Hebrew negro minstrels in the first place — practically all Jews singing from birth, while most acquire some aptitude on some musical instrument.

Collar (*London*). In work. Said of a horse when he gets into swing, or perhaps when he begins to get wet with work. Applied to human beings when in work, and therefore making money. 'Joe's in collar.'

College (*Poor Peoples'*). The workhouse. Term by no means satirical, and used to avoid the true expression.

'The old gent is gorne inter the college at last.'

'Mother ain't 'ome now—she's at the college.' (*See* 'Lump', 'In there'.)

Colleggers (*Oxford* '*er*'). Academical collections.

A ceremony at which the whole host of Dons, sitting in solemn boredom, frankly say what they think of you—are 'colleggers.'—*D. T.*, 14th August 1899.

Collie shangles (*Soc.*, 1884). Quarrels. Brought in by Queen Victoria, in *More Leaves* (1884).

'At five minutes to eleven rode off with Beatrice, good Sharp going with us, and having occasional collie shangles (a Scotch word for quarrels or rows, but taken from fights between dogs) with collies when we came near cottages.'

Colloquials (*Soc.*, 1890 on). Familiar conversation—good example of adjective passing into abstract noun.

Well—well—let us give up the higher culture now the teapot's here, and have some colloquials.

Colour (*Amer. Soc.*, 1860 on). Applied to negroes in American as more delicate than black or even negro. This euphemism commenced with the popularity of 'Uncle Tom's Cabin'.

Why there should be an objection to the word 'negro' is strange. It defines a person of a certain African origin and complexion, and it is gratifying to know that sensible black men are beginning to see it, and despise the studied over-politeness of some white people who talk and write of 'color' without knowing what it really means.—*N. Y. Mercury*, 1883.

'Color' at a Discount. — Attorney-General Brewster has bounced all the Africans in the Department of Justice. He found that the 'color' of money was a little too much for the 'man and brother.'—*N. Y. Mercury*, 1883.

Colour Ball (*Amer.-Eng.*, 1880 on). In England a vulgar black Sal and Dusty Bob kick-up. In U.S.A. a negro or 'dignity' dance.

Colour the meerschaum, To. Drinking to the extent of reddening the nose. 'Aint 'e colourin' 'is meerschaum?' The phrase arises from an association of ideas—those in the first place of darkening the colour of a meerschaum pipe by steady smoking, and in the second, intensifying the hue of the nose by steady drinking. The colour harmony between the pipe and the nose above it is very droll, the hintful phrase itself a singularly good example of the keenness of the common people masking itself in a mock politeness which is worse than the plain truth.

Coloured grave (*Amer. Puritanism*, 1882). That of a negro — striking instance of class prejudice creating phrases of its own.

Presently the undertaker came up, and I asked him. He said he didn't know; that he had told them to dig a coloured grave.—*Newsp. Cutting*.

Colt (*Anglo-Amer.*). A revolver. Good example of the name of the manufacturer being given to the manufacture. Colonel Colt was the inventor of the commercial as distinct from the historical revolver. 'I put down five pounds for my 'colt.' 'This is the colt that is bound to win.' Supplanted by one 'Derringer', a small pocket revolver, sometimes called a 'saloon' from its possible conveyance by way of the waistcoat pocket into polite society.

Colt Party (*Anglo-Amer.*). A soirée of all young people—no elders. Much more in vogue in United States than in England.

'I'll never give another all young party again,' said her grace—'it was too, too stupid.' 'Dear duchess,' replied Lord Claud, 'the colt party is impossible. The charm of maturity, to say nothing of age, dares everything.'

Com (*Business*). A commercial traveller.

I loved the good old 'com.' I have spent many a pleasant evening in commercial rooms with the shrewd men of the world who used to be bagmen, and who had strange tales of the road to tell. —G. R. Sims, *Ref.*, 28th December 1884.

Comb and Brush (*Rhyming*). Lush. At one time this word signified 'drink', and drink only. 'Won't yer lush us?' meant Will you not pay for some drink for us? Now the word has been extended in its meaning, and includes all shapes of liberality. 'Jack lushed us all three to the Surrey Theayter.'

Comb-cut (*Sporting*). Trimmed, manipulated; applied to a man who has been completely vanquished. From the comb of fighting cocks being removed to prevent the opponent from seizing it; may be suggested by the vanquished bird having had his comb torn across by the victor.

Come and have one (*Peoples'*, 1880). Drink is understood. A jocular application of the phrase ' One of those'.

Come and have a pickle (*Soc.*, 1878). An invitation to a quick unceremonious meal.

Come and wash your neck (*Navy*, 1860). Take a drink—from the liquor flushing the throat.

Come-day, go-day (*Military*). An extravagance, *e.g.*, 'It's come-day, go-day with him'—meaning that he receives on 'come'-day money or pay that is spent or goes the same day.

Come-down (*Common Life*). Disaster, ruin, degradation, humiliation, *e.g.*, 'What, no bonnet! What a come-down; an' I knoo 'er mum when she 'ad six of everything.'

Come down (*Theat.*). The act of moving towards the audience from up the stage.

Come off, To (*Amer.-Eng.*, 1892). To cease, refrain, desist, etc. Very graphic—probably from the American call to fighting dogs, or men.

'How much does yez ax for this book?' ('Six dollars,' replied the smiling clerk.

'Six dollars! Oh, come off!'—*N. Y. Mercury*, February 1892.

Come in, To (*Society*, 1880). To become fashionable; *e.g.*, 'You mark my words, the horrid old Victorian furniture, especially from 1840 to 1851, will come in. Already spindley Chippendale is a pill.'—(1883.)

Come on (*Theat.*). No invitation to fight, but a direction to appear upon or 'come on', the stage. (*See* 'Go off' and 'Go up'.)

Come over on a Welk (or Wilk) Stall (*Coster satire*, 1880). *E.g.*, 'Where did yer dad come from? Come over on a whilk-stall?' This may be a folk-satire upon 'Coming over with the Conqueror,' or the 'whelk' may have that broad reference which was applicable to 'He's got 'em on'—when first this satirically eulogistic phrase came out.

Come out, To (*Soc.*, 19 *cent.*). To appear in society—applied to young women in society. The crown which finishes the work of coming out is presentation at Court.

Mr Francis Knowles called, and examined by Mr Clarke, said: I have known Lady Durham ever since she 'came out'.

General Reilly, examined by Mr Clarke, said: I have known Lady Durham ever since she came out in society.—*Evidence in Lord Durham's Nullity Suit*, March 1885.

Come the old soldier over, To (*Peoples'*). Cajolery, pretended poverty, specious lying statement. 'Don't come the old soldier over *me*'—from fraudulent uniformed beggars after Waterloo.

A great amount of imposture practised by means of the 'old soldier' dodge upon the Duke of Wellington during the latter part of his life. To 'come the old soldier' is in some quarters still a familiar expression signifying the practice of an artful trick, and the 'old soldiers' after Waterloo were so numerous and so pestered the Duke of Wellington that he was fain to hand over all applications for alms to the Old Mendicity Society.—*D. N.*, 3rd March 1885.

Come to grief, To (*Sporting*, 1880). A riding man's term for a smash or spill; gradually accepted on all sides to depict failure.

'He tried Hamlet, but to the surprise of his family, though not of his friends, he came to distinct grief.'

Come to stay (*Amer.-Eng.*). Come to remain.

What he had to say about the origin and development of that remarkable institution, which, as the Americans put it, 'has come to stay', was very interesting.—*D. T.*, 20th May 1899.

Come up with (*Amer.-Eng.*). To be on equality; *e.g.*, 'I came up with him instanter and he took a back seat.'

Come up to the rack, or jump the fence (*Amer.*). To decide to do a thing or take departure. Rack is short for 'racket', this word representing noise. Racket gives a capital idea of the bustle of American life, while 'jump the fence' is singularly suggestive of new settlements, and enclosed homesteads.

'Well, I want to bring this young man to time. Fact is, he's either got to come up to the rack—or jump the fence.'—*Newsp. Cutting.*

Comfy (*Soc.*, 1880 on). An endearing diminutive of comfortable. Probable origin—a royal nursery.

Felice is lonely, homesick. These dear girls are very nice and kind; but the simple tastes and simple conversation of the truly rural is apt to pall on your *blasé* old Diogenes. She feels as if half only of her were here, and the sensation is not 'comfy'.—*D. N.*, 4th July 1895 (Craigie v. Craigie).

Comic-song faker (*Music Hall*, 1880). Music-hall way of describing music-hall song-writers.

Mr Joseph Tarbar tells me he is the boss author of this or any other country—as far as comic song-faking is concerned.—*Cutting.*

Coming bye-and-bye (*Amer.-Eng.*, 1876 on.) Eternity. The evangelical nature of the ballads, and other musical compositions for the voice, became very marked after 1870, and even preachers thought it elegant to refer to the second personage of the Trinity as 'our mutual friend J.C.'—evidently without any thought of offence; indeed with true sincerity. A ballad entitled 'In the coming bye-and-bye', very namby-pamby, and referring of course to the after life brought (about 1880), this style of composition into sudden contempt—more especially when Mr W. S. Gilbert imported it into a ballad for the Lady Jane (*Patience*), wherein, lamenting the lapse of her charms, she fears that in the coming bye-and-bye—meaning a few years—her charms will be gone.

It seems to me that there will be plenty of calls on that 'Actors' Benevolent Fund' in the coming by-and-by.—(1883).

Commandeer, To (*Transvaal War*, 1899). Required—in Dutch; but in England held to be robbery. To commandeer was to press unwilling men into the Dutch army, or 'take' whatever the Dutch came across, and with no concurrent effort to pay for the property annexed.

Some of the recruits from the inland districts were wild and uncouth beings, arrayed in rags and patches, and without boots or shoes. With these attractions were combined the external polish of uncombed bushy hair and beard, and skins rarely washed. Mausers and ammunition were all they possessed in many cases. One of them commandeered—otherwise stole—a native's horse, borrowing a saddle from one Britisher and stirrup leathers from another.—*D. T.*, 24th October 1899.

Mr Labouchere suggested that Sir Michael Hicks-Beach should make a commando among the melodramatic millionaires of Park Lane.—*D. T.*, 24th October 1899.

The 'last cry' of this term, and practically closing it and the war, was in the *D. T.* for 2nd March 1900—the day of the relief of Ladysmith.

Scores of them had commandeered the contents bills of the morning and evening papers announcing the 'Relief of Ladysmith', and, sticking them on their chests, they marched on, blowing trumpets and waving flags.

President Kruger, before leaving the capital, commandeered a quantity of gold.—*D. T.*, 7th June 1890.

Commander of the Swiss Fleet (*Polit.*, 19 *cent.*). An impossible title; satirical attack upon titles and positions which exist only for the money they produce. This is the best of them, Switzerland being not only in the centre of Europe, but generally two miles above the sea-level.

It sounds quaint enough to talk of an Admiral 'winning his spurs', articles not generally associated with seamanship, except in the case of the legendary Commander of the Swiss Fleet.—*D. N.*, 6th July 1883.

Commando (*Transvaal War*, 1899). A regiment. Name found by Dutch. In a few days it was in London differentiated from commandeering—which was found to be sheer pressing of men, and annexation of property.

I believe that the first attack will be made on the large Free State commando.—*D. M.*, 25th October 1899.

Commercial Drama (*Theat.*, Nov. 1900). Drama that pays—without relation to literature, art, wit, poetry, or any other comfortable quality. Generally depends upon surprise scenery and machinery, or the reproduction of well-known places, or common objects of street life. Used satirically, but started quite seriously in a lecture, with this title; given before the O. P. club, a society of patrons of the drama. The lecturer warmly applauded the commercial drama, of which he declared himself a successful producer (at Drury Lane), while he intensified his position by an attack upon Shakespeare, of whose plays he declared that some were so pervaded by horrors that they were thereby objectionable, while he maintained that some half dozen could not be produced on the modern stage.

'Oh, yes, quite a commercial drama—thousands of pounds in it, and not one sentence worth hearing.'

Commercial legs (*Recruiting sergeants'*). Bad ones—unfitted to drill.

A slender, awkward, shambling youth, with the 'confounded commercial legs', which show that he has never taken the Queen's shilling, etc.—*Newsp. Cutting*.

Common-roomed (*Varsity*). Had up before the head of the college—the common room being the principal's chamber of state. Good example of substitution of place for person.

The descendants of Mr Dickenson may not mind a story as to how he climbed the college gates, and was being 'common roomed', when cries were heard of 'Dickenson for ever!' from the Quad, and it was found that he had won the Latin verse prize.—*D. N.*, 7th October 1886.

Commonsensible (*Soc.*, 1890 on). The condition of common sense.

English jurisprudence has had a blunt and downright way of presuming a man's motives from the results of his conduct—a somewhat rough and ready method no doubt, but still eminently 'commonsensible'.—*D. T.*, 21st January 1898.

Compos, Non (19 cent.). Abbreviation of non compos mentis—and a very lame one too.

The churchwardens proved that he raised the disturbance before the collection had commenced. It was stated that this was not the prisoner's first appearance on a similar charge, and a doctor had certified that he was not altogether compos. — *D. T.*, 23rd February 1897.

Comstockism (*Amer. - Eng.*, 1885 on). Opposition to the nude in art. Comstock was quite a public man in America. He for some years had a formidable following in his attacks upon 'naked art'.

Comstock on Nudity.—He admits that it is not necessarily obscene — the proprieties observed. Anthony Comstock (in heated bath-room): 'Hello! Hello! I say, porter! Bring me a match. I can't see to fix my necktie.' Servant (hastening to the door): 'Did the gas go out, sah?' 'No; I put it out. I've been taking a bath' — (1889.) (*See* Horsleyism.)

Con (*Polit.*, 1883). An abbreviation of Constitutionals, a designation fugitively borne by the Conservatives in this year. This rather contemptuous word was bestowed by the Radicals in return for the discovery of Rad (*q.v.*).

Mr Wilson Croker in *The Quarterly Review* more than forty years ago recommended the Tory party to abandon that designation and call themselves instead the Conservative party. *The Quarterly Review* of the present day seems disposed to think that the title of Conservative should be quietly dropped, and that of 'Constitutional' adopted instead.—*D. N.*, 20th October 1883.

Con (*Thieves'*). Simply disguised convict.

Concertize (*Musical*). From America—to assist musically in concerts.

M. Ovide Musin, the great Belgian violinist, has returned to this city to concertize under Mr L. M. Rubens' management.—*Newsp. Cutting*, November 1885.

Concrete Impression (*Art.*, 1890 on) Conviction. One of the most absurd of the art critical 'finds' of the '90's.

Thus, Mr Peppercorn's 'Bosham, Early Morning', is all breeze and grey light, but not much else; the study is not distinctive enough to call up a definite and concrete impression.—*D. T.*, 4th January 1896.

Condemned; Condemnation (*Sporting*, 1870). Damned; a damn. A sort of jocular avoidance of even mild swearing.

David out-gagged even himself, and caused great laughter. Nobody else was worth a condemnation. — *Ref.*, 11th December 1884.

'Ducks!' I says; 'you condemned lunatic, them ain't ducks; them's mud hens!'—*Cutting*.

Confidence - queen (*Ang. - Amer.*, 1883). A female detective—outcome of American state of society.

The confidence queen of Miss Caroline Hill revealed that lady's stage qualities to great advantage, especially in the scene of the third act.—*N. Y. Mercury*, June 1884.

Confidence man (*Thieves'*).—He is a specious gentleman who asks his way of one who appears to be a promising victim, and whom he never meets, but overtakes, after allowing him to pass, and so take stock of him. He then enters into conversation, asks the victim to have a drink—as they approach the tavern where the confederate awaits results. If the victim accepts, the confederate, who appears to be a stranger, begins showing what appears to be gold, and making foolishly weak bets. The confidence man then whispers confidentially to victim that they may as well have the fool's money as another. If the victim is as much rogue as fool, he consents, and by some one of twenty dodges (*see* 365 Straightforward Ways of Cheating), he is robbed. If he is honest, however, his honesty saves his pocket.

Congo patois (*Amer.*, 1884). Slang. Term heard at Liverpool.

The professor had, probably, been reading those shockingly poor books, the Grandissimes, Dr Sevier and the Creoles, in which Congo patois, as it is called, is ascribed to educated white people.— *Newsp. Cutting*.

Considerable amount of united action (*Parliamentary*, 1883). Conspiracy. Early in this year Mr Herbert Gladstone charged the Conservative opposition with 'malicious conspiracy' to oppose the government. Called to account, he modified the statement into this phrase, which henceforth remained a satirical euphemism amongst the younger Conservatives for 'conspiracy' in general.

Mr Herbert Gladstone, however, is mildly of opinion that his words were 'stronger than the occasion justified', and that he would more accurately have expressed whatever amount of meaning was present in his mind by substituting for 'malicious conspiracy' the phrase 'a considerable amount of united action'.—*Globe*, 16th March 1883.

Conspiracy of silence (*Soc.*, 1885). Evasion of comment. Created by the silence of general press in relation to certain terrible articles in *The Pall Mall Gazette.*—(1885.)

Some of the clergy and some of the judges have at last been aroused to the danger of the situation, and many journals are now breaking through the 'conspiracy of silence', and boldly denouncing the shameless creatures, etc.—*Ref.*, 31st August 1885.

Constant-screamer (*Peoples'*, 1860 on). Concertina — A satirical onomatope of the musical instrument in question—which is a machine played by an upward pull, and a downward pressure of the construction, which has much the appearance of a tubular Japanese lantern.

Tommy of the Artillery and Army Service is brimful of music hall talent, and nightly upon the foredeck to the melody of a 'Constant-Screamer' he warbles, solo or chorus, 'Off to Ashantee'.—*D. T.*, 20th December 1895.

Constructive Assault (*Sporting*, 1880). Attendance at a prize-fight.

Some time ago the whole of the common law Judges met to decide the question, what is an assault? The point arose out of a decision of a Chairman at Quarter Sessions, who had ruled that any one 'assisting' at a prize-fight was guilty of a 'constructive assault'. The Lord Chief Justice of England agreed with the Chairman, and carried a majority of the Court with him.—*D. N.*, 14th October 1884.

Consume salt (*Theat.*). English equivalent of *cum grano salis*.

A recent Modjeska poisoning item in the country papers suggests that some stars must consume a great deal of salt if they read about their reported doings.—(1883.)

Contango (*Stock Exchange*). Practically, suspense or renewal of a transaction. (*See* Bull, Bear, and especially Backwardation.) These entries read and furthermore understood—contango may possibly be comprehended. No gain being made on a transaction, and the backwardation being paid, the contract is renewed, in the same terms, upon the price at the commencement of the transaction, and without reference to the price of the day when the contango is arranged. This process is more generally indulged in when there has been no, or very little, variation in the price of a given security between purchase-day and settling-day.

Context, To (*Printers' and Typewriters'*). To try to ascertain, or to discover a badly written word in 'copy', by its context, by studying the words on both sides of it; *e.g.*, 'Oh, context it, and do the best you can.'

Continent (*Amer.*, 1880). The latest shape of oath in the States; *e.g.*, 'What the continent do you mean by it?' It refers of course to the continent of America. Origin obscure. Not in any way the transmutation of a word like it.

Not one of them even looked up. Not one of them seemed to care a continental whether his old ore assayed 15 or 95 per cent. They had all 'been there'.—*Wall Street News* (1883).

Conversation, A little. Violent swearing.

Coo-ey (1860 on). Shout of goodfellowship. This cry, with a long accent on the 'ey' is an imitation of the Australian aborigines' friendly call to another from long distances in the bush. It is therefore naturally a friendly call here in the home country, and is never used in an inimical spirit. It is generally used to find a friend lost in a crowd, or far ahead by night in the street. Probably introduced by sailors, the starters of so much hearty, vigorous, popular passing English—probably miners who have tried their luck at the gold fields, and found it only trying. The gold diggers were the first to adopt the 'coo-ey'—which, properly pitched, appears to travel with exceptional vigour. The e-e-e-y is always half a tone below the 'coo', which is generally pitched as high as the individual voice will allow. The Australian starts upon the 'C' in alt, or that *ut de poitrine* which is the ambition of every operatic tenor in the world.

Cooking Day (*Navy*). Twenty-four hours devoted to Bacchus.

Cool (*Back-phrase*). Means look, 'c' being used in place of 'k', probably because being a true word it is more misleading.

Cool her on Sunday in a black velvet costoom, with boots, gloves, and gamp to match.—*Cutting*.

Cooper (*Nautical*). One who sells liquors on the sly; also one who buys illicit spirits. Applied (1884) to the vessels, generally Dutch, which follow English fishing smacks into the North Sea. Also applied to the cooper's vessel.

Another matter in which he took deep interest was the suppression of those floating grog-shops in the North Sea which have done so much injury, and no inconsiderable step was taken in that direction when he made arrangements by which duty-free tobacco is now supplied from the mission smacks in the North Sea to the fishermen, who have not now the inducement to board the 'Coopers' which before existed.—*Prince of Wales, Birkbeck Testimonial Fishmongers' Hall, 31st October 1885.*

There is a queer craft always hanging about. She is called a 'cooper', and no man cares whence she comes. She flies sometimes an English, sometimes a foreign flag, and is in fact defined by the Duke of Edinburgh as a floating grog-shop of the worst kind.—*D. N., 20th June 1883.*

Cooper (*Peoples'*). The name of a beer-mixture of common beer (3d. per quart) and stout (6d. to 8d. per quart). Named from the coopers who invented the mixture.

Cooper up, To (*Boer War*, 1899-1900). To surround, fix, render immovable—from the fixing of the staves of a tub by its hoops.

The pursuit of De Wet failed, and the swoop in a semi-circle from Pretoria to Pinnaar's Poort, miscarried in so far as 'coopering up' De la Rey, Theron, or any of the lesser Boer leaders and raiders was concerned.—*D. T., 20th October 1900.*

Cop (*Thieves'*). Complex rhyming. Taken, seized, thrashed, struck, caught by disease, well-scolded, discovered in cheating—a universal verb suggesting defeat or damage of some kind. There has been more discussion over this widely applied word than any other in the kingdom of phrase. It is a very obscure, complicated, abbreviated, back-phrasing example. It is to 'pocket' (in the shape of receiving)—the tek being elided—when poc being spelt backwards 'cop' appears. When the police cop a man he is practically 'pocketed'. So with all the many applications of this word—with a little indulgence—its vigour will be seen. Its common use is 'cop the yenneps', penny backworded, with an 'e' added for the sake of euphony, the plural being made in the ordinary way. 'I've copped the yenneps, and I'm off to the carse and the burick'—that is, home and wife. Cop has another meaning—to take too much to drink. In universal use.

Cop a mouse (*Artisans'*). Get a black eye. Cop in this sense is to catch or suffer, while the colour of the obligation at its worst suggests the colour and size of the innocent animal named.

Cop on the cross, To (*Thieves'*). To discover guilt, by cunning.

A good way of copping her on the cross is to pretend to go off into the country for a day or two, and come down on her in the middle of the night.—*Cutting.*

Cop the brewery, To (*L. Class,* 19 *cent.*). To get drunk.

Cop the curtain (*Music Hall, passing into the theatres*, 1880). To gain so much applause that the curtain is raised for the performer to appear and bow. 'The Basher copped the curtain twice, and was a great go.'

Copper (*Street*, 1868 on). A policeman. The term superseded Peeler, Robert, Bob, Bobby. From the common street verb 'cop'. 'There's a copper round the corner will (1884) scurry a covey of toddlers wrangling in the gutter more rapidly than a four-horse waggon.' Copper is perhaps the first word the infantile street arab thoroughly comprehends.

This word is also used as an exclamation amongst work-people when any one of their number is blustering. It means giving himself the airs of police authority.

'Copper! copper! we shall soon be a sergeant!'

The incident of the trial which will probably pass on and become history when the rest is forgotten was the enquiry of Mr Justice Hawkins as to the meaning of the word 'copper'. The witness kindly explained to the innocent judge that a copper is a policeman—one who 'cops'.—*Ref.*, 15th August 1888.

'A Lady' writes to a fashionable rag that the low-necked dress is an abomination, 'into which it is the duty of the press to look.' Look! No, old gal. If any of 'em come near me I shall cry 'copper!'

'I cry copper' was the refrain of a popular song (1882) in which the policemen 'got it'.

Copper Captain (*Queen's Bench Prison,* Southwark). A captain found in neither Army nor Navy List. An officer of self-promotion.

'The Affable Hawks and other varieties of copper captains have taken flight from the Borough Road. Flash songs are no longer heard behind the high walls, on the inner side of which the racquet courts are still marked out, and a ghastly stillness has fallen upon the once thickly peopled spot.'—Article upon Queen's Bench Prison (1881), then about to be pulled down. 'But the modern practitioner has made a notable advance in method from the copper captains, table knights, and Dandos of yore.'—*D. N.*, February 1882.

'The company contains many copper captains, brazen adventurers, and women whose character is advertised in their countenances.'—*D. N.*, 26th August 1883.

Copper-clawing (*Street.*) A fight between women. Probably a corruption of 'cap-a-clawing'—a pulling of caps—a phrase which ceased to be applicable when lower-class women ceased to wear caps.—(1820.)

Copper-rattle (*Navy*). Irish, generally Irish, or other stew—from the hubble-bubble of this boiling delicacy —called in London city restaurants, 'French Pie'.

Copper's Nark (*Thieves'*). A policeman's civilian spy.

Upon this the prisoner, who was standing by, accused witness of being a 'copper's nark' (*i.e.*, a police spy), and dealt him several severe blows.—*D. T.*, 18th October 1897.

Copper's Shanty (*C. L.*). A police station. Shanty is from the backwoods of America—a small, cosy house.

'Do you think I've arrived at my time of life without seeing the inside of a copper's shanty?'—*Cutting.*

Copper-slosher. An individual with the mania of 'going for' policemen.

Miss Selina Gripp, the well-known copper-slosher, returned to the buzzim of her family on Tuesday from Tothill, where she had been staying for some months.— *Mock Fashionable Intelligence,* 1882.

Copy (*Printers'*). The matter to be set up in type, and which must be one of two kinds, the ever legitimate MS. or manuscript, and the frequently stolen reprint.

The copy's bad, as though with skewer the author wrote, and watery ink. 'What word is this?' quoth one. 'Elephant, elegant, or telephone?' 'Oh, I don't know, at this time of night; put it what you like, and let the reader find it out.'—*Cutting.*

Coqcigrues (*European*). Utopias, impossibilities. The word evidently refers to something that will never happen. It is on all fours with the French folksaying: 'That will happen in the week of the four Thursdays.' May it be Coqs aux Grues—cock fowls that are half storks or cranes—more especially referring to the differences between the gallinaceous claw and the long leg and web-foot of the stork. The anticipation of arrival is also consistent with the migratory habits of storks, and also of the coqs de Bruyère. 'Coqcigrues' may have originally been booth clowns — professional jesters; applied afterwards generally to foolish people. They were dressed as cocks, with feathers and cocks' heads, and danced upon stilts, hence the reference to storks—'grues'; or cocks on storks' legs.

If reform can only come from within, the teaching of history warns us that we cannot expect reform till the coming of the Coqcigrues.—*D. N.*, June 1885.

The king sent John de Shoreditch to ask the Dean and Chapter for a loan of the hundred marks left by Bishop William de Marcia, and kept at Wells *usque ad generale passagium ad Terram Sanctum* —'till the general passage to the Holy Land;' that is to say, till the coming of the Coqcigrues, or *usque ad adventum Coqcigruorum.*—*Newsp. Cutting.*

Corfee-'ouse cut (*Cheesemongers'*). The back of bacon, without bones, and exceptionally used by coffee-house keepers.

Cork (*Workshop*). The cork (probably from the American caucas) is the complainant who brings a charge before the shop-constable and the garret. He may bring a complaint against a fellow-workman of a technical character, or of some social nature or even crime. The restraint upon the cork takes the shape of the rule which compels him to pay five shillings if he lose the case, while the defendant, when losing, is mulcted in but half-a-crown. Of these fines half is generally spent in drink in the shop, the other forwarded to the secretary of the Union, who applies it to the General Purposes Fund.

Corkscrew (*L. Lond.*). An evasive pronunciation of God's Truth—used satirically. (*See* Cheese and Crust.)

Corn-crackers (*Amer.*). The people of Kentucky; probably from the immensities of corn grown there.

Corner Boys (*Dublin*). Loafers, who generally affect street corners, as presenting more scope (1) for seeing, and (2) for bolting.

Kilmainham was reached a few minutes before five o'clock. There were only a few corner boys present in the neighbourhood of the prison, and there was no demonstration of any kind.—*Report of Arrest of Mr Dillon, M.P., 1881.*

The term comes from America.

Cornichon (*Soc.*, 1880). A muff. Direct from French—gherkin.

Yet are not all French sportsmen good shots; indeed, for every decent gun you must reckon twenty highly developed *cornichons*—French for muffs.—*Newsp. Cutting.*

Cornstalks (*Austral.*). The people of New South Wales; from this province growing quantities of corn. Given by the people of Victoria.

Being usually of good height, but wanting in depth and breadth, they have gained for themselves the epithet of cornstalks, which is saying a great deal for the value of their heads.—*Baden Powell, New Homes for the Old Country.* (*See* Gum-suckers.)

Cornucopia (*Amer.*). A rich individual.

We who dine at noon, live in one-story cottages with mortgages on them, and have wet blankets thrown over us as we slowly elbow our way through life, sometimes envy the old cornucopias as we see them go down to the bank to draw their dividends.—*Cutting.*

Correctitude (*Soc.*, 1900). Correctness. Latinised word first seen and heard in England in 1900. Probably from U.S.A.

M. Delcassé, it is true, has all along been a pattern of 'correctitude'; but the Waldeck - Rousseau Cabinet had a difficult people to deal with.—*D. T., 29th December* 1900.

Corroboree (*Nautical*). A drunken spree, in which there is much yelling. Supposed to be derived from a term used by some unknown South Sea Islanders to describe a wordy and excited interview. Every sailor knows the word, sometimes used disparagingly as 'It just *was* a corroboree.'

Gould (*Handbook of the Birds of Australia*) says it is the Australian native word for a discussion, or powwow. 'The males' (of an Australian bird) 'congregate and form corroboree places.'

Corpse (*Theat.*). To balk a fellow-actor on the stage while he is acting, by some by-play or facial action which attracts attention. Very emphatic. 'Look here, Joe, if you corpse me again to-night in the second act, while you are up, I'll pull your long nose!'

Corpse-worship (*Club*, 1880 on). The extreme use of flowers at funerals. This custom, set by the Queen at the mausoleum (Frogmore) immediately after the death of the Prince Consort, grew rapidly, until the custom had extended to quite the lower classes, amongst whom neighbours vied in forwarding expensive floral tributes. Finally, in the '90's, many death notices in the press were followed by the legend, 'No flowers'.

Corsey (*Sporting*). Stiff betting or play—not from race-course, as it might well be supposed, but from French *corsé*.

Baccarat may be played for any sums, from the *petit baccarat de santé*, the family baccarat, up to the sport which is usually described as *corsé*, or in stronger language, reckless.—*D. N., 18th January* 1884.

Cosey (*Slums*). A small, hilarious public-house, where singing, dancing, drinking, etc., goes on at all hours.

Cosh (*Amer.*). One of the veiled ways of naming the Deity.

The word 'Oshkosh' is the name of a town, and not a form of profanity in use by the Scandinavians, from whom the

Americans have obtained it in the modified form of 'Cosh! Good-morning'—said satirically, of course, as to Scandinavia.

Coss (*Hatters'*). A blow. Origin obscure — probably the name of a pugilist.

Coster (*Low Life*). Short for costermonger, a great being in low life, generally a sort of prince, and often a king o' the costers. To be really royal he must make money, but save nothing, dress beautifully (*see* Pearlies), be handsome in a rough way, be always flush of cash and liberal with it, possess a handsome girl or wife (generally the latter), and above all, fight well, and always be ready to fight. Reign generally extends to five years (nineteen to twenty-four), when he either takes a shop and does well, takes to drink and does worse, or growing ancient, grizzly, or broken with disease, loses a fight, abdicates, and sinks into the ranks. Said to be derived from 'Quatre saisons'—the 'Marchand des quatre saisons'—that is fruit and vegetables of spring, summer, autumn, and winter.

Costermonger Joe (*Com. London*). Common title for a favourite coster.

Costermongering (*Musical*, 1850). Altering orchestral or choral music, especially that of great composers. From the habit Sir Michael Costa sometimes showed of modifying the score of Handel. Happy hit, as contrasting the guerilla business of the coster with the proper professional and established tradesman.

But the costermongering was worse than ever this time, and, in mingled sorrow and anger, amateurs cried, 'Et tu, Brute!' Better things were expected of Mr Manns, but it was found that Cæsar and Pompey are very much alike—specially Pompey.—*Ref.*, 28th June 1885.

Costume Play (*Theat.*). A drama in which the dresses are any before those of the 19th century, but not before say the tenth; *e.g.*, 'Thank God,' she observed, 'I've got a costume play at last. I shall klobber in crimson and gold for the first act, blue and amber for the second, and pure white and silver for my death in the third. I shall make a great success. Redfern will make.'

A new play by Robert Buchanan is, however, being rehearsed at the Vaudeville. Like *Sophia*, it is a 'costume' piece.—*Ref.*, 5th February 1888.

Costume plays are, to the thinking of some folk, handicapped because they are costume plays. It is sneeringly said that the modern young actor cannot be at ease unless he can dive his hands into his pockets.—*D. T.*, 18th July 1899.

Cot so (18 *cent.*). An evasion of God's oath—the Redemption. Common in Richardson.

Cottages (*Fast youths'*). Vespasians; retiring points for half a minute. Said to be derived from the published particulars of an eccentrically worded will in which the testator left a large fortune to be laid out in building 'cottages of convenience'. Passing away in favour of the underground palaces dedicated to Cloacina—palaces generally termed 'Fountain Temples' or 'Palaces'.

Cough Drop (*Peoples'*, 1860 on). Poison, or even anything disagreeable. 'Lor', what a cough drop she are!' From the ominous motto used many years since with a cough lozenge—'Cough no more'. The gruesome *double entendre* here was first seen by W. Brough, who incorporated it in a burlesque—for when you are dead you *cough no more!*

'Honest John Burns,' who has been returned for Battersea by the skin of his teeth, and who would have benefited considerably had his constituents given him a holiday, objects to being called 'a cough drop'.—*Ref.*, 27th July 1895.

'Oh, he's awful leary—a very cough drop—a genuine red hot treat, make no blooming error.' 'Oh, she's a cough drop, a red hot treat, and no mistake.'—*Cutting.*

Couldn't speak a threepenny bit (*Street*, 1890 on). Utter temporary incapacity for speech. 'I couldn't speak a threepenny bit, but I made myself a luvverley cup o' tea, an' I were soon better.' The lady had probably been drinking—indeed the phrase may be an elegant evasion of the admission of, at least, partial intoxication.

Counting-house (*Street*, 1870). A stupid perversion of countenance—supposed to be comic. 'Just take a squint at his counting-house.'

We get into the shop and see a really fine-looking dona smiling all over her counting-house.—*Cutting.*

Country Cousin (*Rhyming*). A dozen, *e.g.*, '. They put away about three country cousins o' Bass.'

County-crop (1856). A closely-cropped head of hair, such as is imposed upon prisoners sent to the county jails. In 1856 when the Crimean soldiers returned with long heavy beards, which for many years remained a national fashion, it was found that longish hair, such as had been worn all the century, gave with the heavy beard too top-heavy an appearance. The hair was therefore cut down, and the result was dubbed a county crop, while the beard was called a doormat, shortened to mat. 'He's got a crop and mat' quite described the swell of 1856-1857. The door-mat has vanished—the 'crop' (1897) remains.

Couple of Flats (*Theat.*). Double meaning. In the old time, before the advent of elaborate set scenery, two scene screens run on from opposite sides and joining in the centre were called a 'couple of flats'. Applied to two bad actors. (*See* 'Camp at Olympia', by Planché.)

Course-keeper (*Winchester School*). A bully's bully. The Wykehamist strong enough to compel fagging officered the 'course-keeper'—a medium between the oldest and youngest of the scholars. He deputed his work to one of the smallest boys.

The offices which the Eton fag performs are amongst the lightest of the duties of the Winchester fag. Besides these he had to clean dirty boots, clean frying-pans, cook breakfasts, and fetch water. The infliction of some of the most offensive of these duties, as *e.g.*, cleaning frying-pans, was often deputed to a middle boy, or 'course-keeper' as he was called, who gratified any personal grudge he might have against any particular small boy by selecting him for the odious task.—*Letter to Daily News.*

The term remains, but fagging at Winchester is a thing of the wretched past.

Couscousou (*Algerian French*, 1840). The native rendering of qu'est-ce que c'est, the enquiry a French soldier always puts upon every possible occasion, and which the Algerian has supposed to be the name of a stew. Hence in imitating this dish they apply the enquiry it would elicit from a French onlooker—equivalent to our 'kickshaw'. Used to be used in London eating-houses — derived undoubtedly from the same French origin.

Cover to Cover, From (*Soc.*, 18 *cent.* on). Through and through. Good example of the spread of education and reading yielding new phrases, for of course this figure of speech is obtained from reading a book from first page to last.

I can vouch that Sir William White, who knew him 'from cover to cover', never entertained this view of his character.—*D. T.*, 12th June 1897.

Covered Brougham (*Peoples'*, 1870). A waggon with tarpaulin over the top. Given to the vehicles which once plied from the Bank to the East of London, taking up customers too late for even the last 'bus. They were in especial force on Saturday night, and were generally very convivial. The increase in the number of 'buses swept away the covered brougham. (*See* Virgins' 'Bus.)

Cow-boy (*Local Amer.*). A Texas farmer, from his cattle-raising — boy being a common term for men of all ages. 'The graziers of Colorado have come to the title of 'cow-boys'.

Cow with the iron tail (*Peoples'*). Pump. A way of attacking milkmen who until about 1865 sold extensively watered milk. This phrase was very familiar until certain municipal acts were passed which by penalties put down the watering of milk. (*See* 'Simpson', 'Hard Simpson', 'Liquor', 'Dill').

Cow-juice (*Amer.*). Milk — used by Buckstone, the actor, in *Our American Cousin*.

Cowlick (*Peoples'*). A wisp of growing hair, of different colour from the general tone. 'Lick' is evidently a corruption of 'lock', and cow has nothing whatever to do with kine. Good example how the Anglicizing of one word modifies another in association with it. The first word having been turned into 'cow', and lock having no meaning in connection with 'cow', it became lick, and the double error suggested a cow-lick which had turned the colour of the wisp of hair. Probably in the first place from a lock common to the head of a clan, the

Gow or Gough, Irish or Scotch. This wisp of hair in all probability frequently became a birth-mark, and was probably often imitated by art when nature arrested the inheritance. A very powerful French drama, in which Fechter was famous in Paris was built up on a cow-lick (*Les Fils de la Nuit*). A superstition of luck or ill-luck attaches to the cow-lick. 'Ha! he always had a lucky cow-lick.' The 'widow's lick' or 'lock' is a tuft of unmanageable hair which grows lower than the rest of the forehead hair, and is always at or near the centre of the top of the forehead. The belief that a woman possessed of this lock, generally of a greyish tone, must lose her husband has, in past generations, prevented many a good woman from getting even a worse husband. Johnson has nothing to say to this word.

Coxey (*Ang.-Amer.*, 1894). A wild political leader. From an American politician of this name who pioneered a number of out-of-work mechanics, who seized trains and invaded Washington.
The march of the 'tramps' in America is a very live thing. The 'Coxeyites' are having a tremendous amount of fun, and the eyes of the world are upon them. —*Ref.*, 29th April 1894.

Coxies (*Low Class*). Corruption of cock's eyes. A term at dominoes for double 1. A good example of rebus phrasing. Probably a translation from the French *œil de coq*—especially as a single one is called 'udder cock'—*œil de coq*, although rarely. 'Cock's eye' is the general term. The other names for dominoes are evidently French — 2, tray ; 3, duce ; 4, quarters ; 5, sinks. The whites are called 'blanks', while the sixes have become quite English. Interesting to mark that 'tray' and 'duce' are used still by old-fashioned people for 2 and 3 at cards, while even the French 'valet' is still 'varlet'.

Coy-gutted (*Devonshire*). Difficult in the matter of eating. Generally used with an addition more emphatic than elegant.

Crabby (*W. Eng.*). A carpenter—said despitefully. Origin vague.

Crack (*Jovial*, 18 *cent.*). A roystering meeting, derived from 'cracking' and finishing a bottle of wine.

'My poor old mother', he wrote, 'comes in with her sincere, anxious old face. "Send my love to Jane, and tell her" (this with a woeish face) "I would like right weel to have a crack" (conversation) "wi' her once more." '—FROUDE, *Carlyle's Life in London*, vol. ii., p. 96.

Crack (*London*). A narrow passage of houses; *e.g.*, ''Ave yer seen the grand duchess of our crack this blessed mornin'—gorne to the Cristial Pallis in 'lectric blue—she 'av.'

Crack a case (*Thieves'*). To break into a house. 'Case' from *casa* (Italian) anglicized.

Crack a wheeze (*Theatrical*). To utter the last thing out—'wheeze' probably from the alcholic guffaw which follows the tale, especially if it is erotic.

'Cracking a wheeze' is a phrase which has always struck us as extraordinary, especially as it has not the recommendation of brevity. It is synonymous with the sailor-slang phrase, 'spinning a yarn'.

Crack the bell (*Peoples'*). To produce failure by speech; or even act, to reveal a secret unintentionally; to muddle—the phrase in fact has many meanings. Derived from the necessity of being silent while casting a bell, the belief, coming down from monastic times, that a mere word spoken during casting may produce a flaw in the bell ; *e.g.*, 'What? told Tom—Jack's going to marry Jill? Then you *have* cracked the bell.' 'She dropped in the mud with all her new togs on, and cracked the bell in a jiffy.' (*See* Let the Cat out of the Bag.)

Crack the monica (*Music-halls*). The chairman, who once ruled in these places—he vanished in the '80's—had before him a table-bell, which he sounded after certain ways, one of which informed the audience applauding a singer who had retired that he or she would appear again. 'He cracked the monica, an' on she came smilin' like "jam"'—the monica is the bell.

Cracker (*American*). A biscuit. The English word, evidently meaning 'twice cooked', or baked, is a misnomer, while the States'-wide synonym is at least a good specimen of onomatope.

I, a lone bachelor, a lone fisherman, with infinite pains and great pleasure, first dipped these ink-pots in the freshest of eggs beaten up; after that into the finest and crisped cracker dust.—*Newsp. Cutting.*

This ink-pot is cuttle-fish, named after a protective secretion it throws out when pursued. Its more fishmongerly title is squid. It abounds in New York waters. They are capital eating when 'dusted' and fried.

Cracker (*S. Carolina*). Native—origin unknown.

Imagine a tall, gaunt, loose-jointed man, with long grizzled hair, deep-set eyes that glow like coals of living fire, high, square shoulders, a stooping, slouching gait; skin wrinkled and dirty beyond pen description; hands and feet immense, the former grimy and with protruding knuckles, the latter incased in cowhide boots with soles an inch thick and of astonishing width; clothes beside which Joseph's coat would sink into insignificance, so covered are they with patches of divers colours—this is a South Carolina 'cracker'.—*Newsp. Cutting,* 1883.

Crackpot (*Stock Exchange,* 1880). A doubtful company promoter, a man who has the appearance of prosperity and who is but an impostor. This word may come from New York. 'A crackpot in the city' is a term so familiar that it was taken for the chorus in a comic song. It appears even in France where a commercial crash of a swindling nature or a political breakdown is called a 'krach' (pronounced crack), which may represent either crack or 'crash'—more probably the latter—bearing in mind French spelling of most English words. 'Crackpot' replaced the phrase 'Lame Duck'.

They take the honours, and they should do some of the work. Besides, they might improve their minds by listening occasionally to 'The Crackpot in the City' and 'Tiddy-fol-lol'.—*Ref.,* 28th January 1883.

'We do a tremendous business in our bank,' said one crackpot to another. 'Why, through buying ink at a new place we save £200 a year. Fancy the amount of writing we do.'—*Cutting.*

Cracksman (*Thieves',* 18 *cent.*). A man who cracks buildings—a burglar, as distinct from a high toby man or a low toby fellow. (*See* High Toby.)

Craft (*Youths',* 1870). A bicycle, from liking the machine to a ship. (*See* Beast, Bone-Shaker, Craft, Crock.)

Crambo Song (*Peoples'*). Still heard in the remoter parts of England. Roystering ballad, of a cavalier, wine, and women swing. From the eternal Spanish carambo or caramba, shortened by the omission of the first vowel. Probably brought over by Philip of Spain; or a countess in the suite of Catherine of Braganza, or Charles II. may be answerable. This cry would be a beloved one in the mouth of a man who did not object to be called 'Old Rowley'—Charles II. indeed was rather proud of the distinction. Rowley himself was an étalon in the royal stables.

'The secret flew out of the right pocket of his coat in a whole swarm of your carambo songs, short-footed odes, and long-legged pindarics.'—Farquhar, *The Inconstant.*

Cranky gawk (*Chicago*). Equal to Scotch 'dazed gowk'—said of a stupid, awkward lad.

Crazy quilt (*Amer. Mid. Cl.*). A quilt of patchwork, made at random.

The old woman's dress looked like a crazy quilt, and two of the boys had only one trousers-leg apiece.—*Texas Siftings,* 1883.

Craythur, Craytur, or **Craychur** (*Irish*). Whiskey; *e.g.,* 'Oh, for the love o' God giv me now a taste o' the craythur.' The origin of the word may be of singular significance in considering the history of Ireland and the Irish if it is really 'creator' and not 'creature', as it is generally supposed. In the latter case 'creature' means Satan. This is certain, that for years after the middle of the 18th century whiskey was not known in Ireland, while during the period of Home Rule (1782-1800) Grattan himself in the Dublin House of Commons declared every seventh house in Ireland was a whiskey shop.

Cream Ice Jacks (*London Streets*). Street-sellers of ½d. ices. Jacks—probably from Giacomo and Giacopo. 'They've a bad time of it, 'ave the cream ice Jacks, for whenever a kid gits ill the mother goes for the jack an' 'as it out with 'im.'

Creams (*London Street*). Abbreviation of cold-creams, in its turn a droll mode of describing the Coldstream Guards. Intimates that they are dandies, and know how to get themselves up. 'Now then, my creams—gods of the essences,' he observed. 'Then there was a shindy!'

Credit Draper (*Peoples'*). A smooth-spoken seeming cheat—from the tallyman system, whose practitioners have bestowed upon themselves this evasive and hypocritically benignant name. 'Don't believe a word 'e 'ave to say— 'e's on'y a credit draper.'

Cremorne (*Society*, 1884). An open-air place of amusement frequented by doubtful women. From public London gardens of that name, long since built over. Applied in 1884 to the 'Inventories' (*see*) when that entertainment was so frequented by 'tarts' that it became in the evening scarcely a place to which a girl could take her mother. Now applied generally.

But as it is certain that no porter with a flaming sword can possibly stand at the gate to decline the shillings of persons not immaculately virtuous, so it is probable that some day a cry will be raised about a 'Cremorne'. When once that ominous word is whispered people begin to be shy of their natural pastime of letting the evening pass in the open air.—*D. N.*, 10th November 1886.

Creoles (*Amer.*). People of Louisiana—probably a satire by the north upon the illegitimate mingling of slave-owners' and slaves' blood previous to 1862.

Crib (*Street*, 1800-40). To conquer with the fists fairly. From Tom Crib, a celebrated pugilist early in the 19th century. To crib, meaning to thrash, is still heard in the slums of London and other great cities. In the nautical novel, 'Rattlin the Reefer' (chap. lxii.), is this paragraph :

Apt quotation!—you are cabined— you are cribbed — you are confined — *cribbed*—look at your countenance—as I said before, 'tis the hand of Providence. —*Cutting*.

Crime (*Army*). Small fault. Often intentional. ' Squinting on parade ' is a crime. ' What will a sergeant not go for to say—ain't you got a crime ? ' —that is to say, confinement to barracks or extra drill scored against a soldier.

Crimea (1856). The full-beard— given to the first long beards worn in England from the time of Elizabeth to that of Victoria. The fashion of shaving, which passed from France (Louis XIII.) to England, prevailed here long after Frenchmen had begun to grow hair. The severity of the winter 1854-55 (in the Crimea) caused the issue of an order to wear beards, and these were retained. Upon the return of the few survivors, their strange and fierce beards were thus dubbed, and amongst the people the term has remained. ' My eye, what a Crimeer Bill have got along o' the doctor for 'is bronkikkis (bronchitis).'

Before the invasion of the Crimea no man, ' unless an officer in Her Majesty's cavalry, ever ventured to wear a beard or moustache'.—Sir A. West, *Memoirs*, 1897.

Criss-cross (*Peoples'*). A corruption of Christ's Cross—one of the few religious exclamations which have not become vulgarized since the Reformation. Generally refers to right angles in textile fabrics, wood, and metal work. Sometimes used exclamatively. ' S'help me criss-cross ' (or crass), ' I didn't ! '

Not many who use this word appear to have any idea of its meaning, yet it is one of the few old Catholic oaths which have retained much of the original sound.

Croak (*Society*, 19 *cent.*). To be hypocritical, suggested by the lamentable declaration of a frog when he tunes up.

John Hollingshead for some time past has been telling his patrons how they croaked in 1807.—*Newsp. Cutting*, March 1883.

Crock (*Youths'*, 1870). A bicycle. One of the more obscure names for this apparatus. Perhaps from part of the name of a builder. (*See* Beast, Boneshaker, Craft.)

Crocks (*Art jargon*, 1880). Ornamental china. This term came in when, from 1870 to 1880, the porcelain mania raged, and huge sums were given for even poor specimens of china. This word of meek unobtrusiveness is an abbreviation of crockery-ware. (*See* Rags and Timbers.)

Crocodile (*Society*, 1850). A lady's school out walking. A ballad in the forties went :

' I'd rather meet a crocodile
Than meet a lady's school.'

Crocodiles' Tears (*Peoples'*, 19 *cent.*). Imitation sorrow.

Many visitors have probably passed by the alligator in the somewhat out-of-the-way corner where he at present sojourns ; but others know him well, and love to stir him up until he swells out with anger, and emits from the corners of his eyes the queer little bubbles which pass for crocodiles' tears. —*D. N.*, 21st March 1883.

Crocus (*Thieves'*). A mock doctor —a cheap-jack gentleman with a wonderful cure. Simple derivation: 'croak', to kill, or cause to croak, and 'us'.

Crony (*Peoples'*). A friend, or rather trusted and loved companion. Johnson says of this word: 'An old acquaintance, a companion of long standing.' Generally used with the qualifying adjective 'old'. Swift has this word:

'Strange an astrologer should die
Without one warder in the sky!
Not one of all his crony stars
To pay their duty at his herse!'

Pepys (30th May 1665) says:
'Died Jack Cole, who was a great crony of mine.'

Probably one of the few words came from one of the universities. If so, it is possibly derived from Chronos.

Crooked 'un (*Peoples'*). Crook. The reverse of a straight 'un. Generally said of a husband who turns out bad. 'He was about as crooked as they make 'em.' (*See* By Hook or by Crook.)

Crop up (*Society*, 1850). To suddenly appear, or introduced. 'Then Jack cropped up'—from geological term referring to a sudden stratum. Accepted when geology became modish.

Croppie (*Scottish*). Equivalent of Roundhead, and used precisely in the same way. Strangely enough, in the 1798 Irish rebellion, the rebel Irish were called croppies, equally from the shortness of their hair. A Hanoverian song was popular, called 'Croppies, lie down,' which suggestion of treating them as dogs made the rebels very wild. In one historical instance a servant of thirty years' standing shot at the family after hearing one of them singing this song.

Cross-bench mind (*Society*, 19 *cent.*). Undecided, hesitating; from the cross benches in both Houses of Parliament, upon which those peers or members seat themselves who have not made up their minds to which party they belong. 'Poor man, with his mother to the right of him, and his wife to the left of him, he has but a cross-bench mind.'

Lord Glenaveril is brought up partly in Germany, is born to great estates, and takes his seat on the cross-benches of the House of Lords. But poor Lord Glenaveril with his title, and his land, and his patronising disposition, and his 'cross-bench mind', is merely a puppet through whom, about whom, and starting from whom, Lord Lytton may expound his social and political philosophy.—*D. N.*, 30th March 1885.

Crosses (*Peoples'*). Woes, miseries, sorrows. This may be derived from 'across', or more probably from Catholic times, and a reference to carrying the cross.

Cross-grained (*Peoples'*). Ill-tempered, hard to manage. A trade metaphor, from the carpenter's shop, where cross-grained wood is hard to deal with.

Cross-life men (*Thieves'*, 1878). Men who get their living by felony. Used amongst themselves — rather plaintively it would seem, and in remarkable contrast with the 18th century term, 'gentlemen of the road', 'high toby men', and others.

Sir H. James—What do you mean by men of your class? Witness—Men of the world—(laughter)—men like myself. I did not tell him that I had seen gentlemen's servants there—I am certain of that. I did not use the term that the room was the resort of cross-life men (thieves).—*Bignell* v. *Horsley*, 1880.

Cross the Ruby (*Fast World*, early 19 *cent.*). A grotesque abbreviation of 'cross the Rubicon', with the same meaning. Ruby was then the name for port wine.

Crocheteer (*Society*, 1880). A patron of crotchets.

Within later years the ladies and gentlemen who feel so strongly on the subjects of vivisection, compulsory vaccination, teetotalism, Sunday closing, and other cognate topics, have been called crotcheteers.—G. A. Sala, *I. L. N.*, 12th May 1883.

Crotchetty (*Society*, 19 *cent.*). Eccentric, unexpected. Trade metaphor; from music. Probably from the time when solemn, slow church music was enlivened by the comparatively quick crotchet; or it may be from a man named Crotchet.

Crowbar Brigade (*Irish*, 1848). The Irish Constabulary. From the crowbar used in throwing down cottages to complete eviction of tenants.

After a while the whole *posse*—sheriff, sub-sheriff, agent, bailiffs, and attendant policemen—came to be designated the 'Crowbar Brigade'. — A. M. Sullivan, 1878.

Still used to deride policemen in Ireland.

Crowbar Landlord (*Ireland*, 19 *cent.*). Outcome of Crowbar Brigade.

I recommend my countrymen to shoot the crowbar landlord as we shoot robbers or rats, at night, or in the day, on the roadside or in the market-place!— T. Mooney, California, 1865.

Crowd(*Theatrical*, 1870 on). Simply the audience; *e.g.*, 'What sort of a crowd is it to-night?' Also a theatrical company; *e.g.*, 'Who's in the crowd?' 'Lal Brough and Arthur Roberts.' 'Oh, then, there will be at least half-a-dozen laughs.' Also said of the mass of supers, whose numbers increase yearly; *e.g.*, '*I*? What do *I* do? Oh, I go on with the crowd.'

Crows' feet (*Soc.*). Diverging Delta wrinkles at the outer angles of the eyelids.

Crow's nest (*Soc.*, 1850 on). Small bedroom for bachelors high up in country houses, and on a level with the tree tops; *e.g.*, 'Give me a crow's nest, and pray save me from the state bed-chamber.'

Cruel classes (*Soc.*, 1893). Used by the Duke of York, 6th February 1893, on the occasion of his first public speech, as chairman of a dinner in aid of the Society for Prevention of Cruelty to Children. At once took, as distinguishing the savages of the lowest classes from the lowest classes generally.

Until this Society came into existence the lives of young children belonging to the cruel classes of the community could not be considered secure. Their very helplessness made them an easy prey.

Crumb. See Bit o' Crumb.

Crumpet. See Barmy.

Crush the stur (*Thieves'*). To break from prison—stur being abbreviation of sturaban.

A short time after I ascertained from the jailor who payed me a visit, that my two 'fly' friends had 'crushed the stir', and were at large, ready to prey on the community again.

Crushed (*Soc.*, 1895). Spoony, in love with.

Quite new is the slang 'crushed'. It is used in place of the expression, 'mashed', 'struck', etc., and is quite *au fait* with the summer resort girls. One hears everywhere murmurs of Charlie Binks being utterly 'crushed' on Mabel Banks, and so on with regard to various things. Dora tells Flora that she is 'crushed' on Jim's new sailor, when she really isn't damaging his headgear at all, and so it goes. The English language is getting awfully queer!—*American Paper*.

Crusher (*Peoples'*). A policeman— evidently a word suggesting respect for the force. Mr W. S. Gilbert used this word in the *Bab Ballads*.

'One day that crusher lost his way,
    In Poland Street, Soho!'

Crushers (*Navy*). Ships' corporals, who are the rank and file of the master-at-arms. Descriptive term, borrowed from ashore, where this term is still applied satirically to policemen.

Crusoe (*Iron Trade*). A good example of anglicising; name given by English ironmasters and workmen to the great French ironworks at Creuzot —a reminiscence of Robinson Crusoe.

Cry! (*Peoples'*). Shape of Carai— probably introduced by English gipsies passing from Spain. One of the libidinous good-wishes at nightfall, similar to Carambo. Both words more or less known to the oi polloi. Now applied indiscriminately to express surprise of a satiric character.

Cry haro (*Jersey*). A synonym of justice. Word used by people calling upon their lords for interference. One of the first railway engines run out of St Helier's was named 'Haro'. Now used as a 'jollying'.

It is characteristic of the satirists of the hour that they make their victims' very sobriety a reproach. If he is perfectly well dressed, an excellent thing in youth, is exceptionally quiet and well bred, and goes frequently to the theatre, they dub him a 'masher', and 'cry haro' upon him.—*Newsp. Cutting*, 1883.

Cuff-shooter (*Street*, 1875 on). A clerk. Name invented after the introduction of shirt-cuffs wide enough to come down well over the hands; a movement of the arm to throw forward the cuffs was called cuff-shooting; said scornfully or enviously of young clerks popularly supposed to consider themselves leading gentlemen; *e.g.*, 'Well, what if I am a coster? I earns a dollar (5s.), where a blooming cuff-shooter don't make a 'og' (1s.).

This wide cuff was introduced by the late Duke of Clarence. He also invented the high collar. Indeed the prince's designation was familiarly 'cuffs and collars'—finally 'cuffs'.

Culver-head (*Lower Classes*). A fool; practically calf-head. Probably from Dutch fishermen (chiefly with eels) frequenting Billingsgate, once the matrix of so many vigorous phrases. If from Holland of course the word is a corruption of Kalver, which gives a name to one of the chief streets of Amsterdam.

When the culver-headed yeknods are down in the dumps, strike us pink if they're not as humble as a blackberry swagger.—*Cutting.*

Cum grano (*Anglo-Amer.*). Abbreviation of 'cum grano salis'—with the same meaning. To listen—with allowances.

Managers as a rule agree with Talleyrand that words were made to conceal thoughts, hence theatrical announcements are always received cum grano by the public.—*Newsp. Cutting*, 1883.

Cummifo (*Peoples'*). Cockney for *comme il faut.*

Were it not that she is a lady, and possesses the cachet of foreign and not home production, there are folk who might begin to have a dawning suspicion that she is within a couple of miles or so of being not quite as cummifo as she might be.—*Ref.*, 28th April 1889.

Cup o' tea (*Colloquial*, 1870). Consolation—probably suggested by a cup of tea being 'so very refreshing' to persons who do not drink any shape of alcohol. Used satirically of a troublesome person.

'Oh, don't yer though. You are a nice strong cup o' tea.'—*Cutting.*

Cupboard (*Lower Classes*). Hungry. Hunger suggested by mentioning a food receptacle.

A pleasant hour or so was spent here, and then we turned our faces back towards Valletta, full ready for the lunch on which in my mind's eye, Horatio, I had been feasting for some while before my internal economy set up its cry of 'Cupboard'!—*Ref.*, 6th June 1886.

Cupboardy (*Com. Lond.*). Close and stuffy.

I ain't one of them fellers as thinks that you can't keep healthy without yer drinks rose water and eats cream cheese, but, surely me, if the air of the alley ain't a-gettin' rayther too cupboardy for my stomach.—*D. T.* (Greenwood).

Curled Darlings (*Soc.*, 1856). A name given to military officers immediately after the Crimean War, which once more brought soldiers into fashion. Referred to the waving of the long beard and sweeping moustache.

But it is needless to cite instances to be found by the score in warlike annals, from the 'Gentlemen of the French Guard fire first' at Fontenoy to the well-fought field at Inkerman, when the 'curled darlings' approved themselves metal of the right temper. — *Newsp. Cutting*, May 1883.

Curmudgeon (*Anglicized French*, 17 *cent.*). Cœur méchant. Probably from court of Charles II. The phrase is colloquial in France.

But he would be a curmudgeon, indeed, who grudged the warmest praise for an entertainment light, lively, and melodious, appealing to the eye and grateful to the ear.—*D. T.*, 9th May 1899. (*See* Quandary.)

Cœur méchant is much objected to as the origin of this word. It is fully accepted here on the principle that the more obvious derivation is preferred to the more erudite, on the ground that corrupters of phrases are generally uneducated.

Curse o' Cromwell (*Irish*). One of the more vigorous civilities exercised by the lower Irish to their equals. No one seems to know what the 'curse' was—probably his presence in his lifetime—possibly tertian fever after the death of the Protector.

Curtain (*Theatrical*, 1860 on). A tableau at finish of act or play, to obtain applause.

It matters little for the purpose of romance whether or not Nelson saw Miss Emma Hart in Romney's studio before he met her a married woman at Naples. These things have to be done for stagecraft, for theatrical tricks, for what are vulgarly called 'curtains'.—*D. T.*, 12th February 1897.

It is singular, considering how excellently French dramatists write, that they so frequently fail in getting a good 'curtain'.—*Ref.*, 15th March 1885.

Also a 'call before the curtain' at the end of an act or a piece.

Edward Russell plays well as Peggotty. His acting, if a little too hurried, was full of power, and he revealed considerable pathos. He was rewarded with several 'curtains'.

(*See* Take a curtain—Quick curtain.)

Curtain-taker (*Theatrical*, 1882). An actor more eager even than his brethren to appear before the curtain after its fall. (*See* Take a Curtain, Lightning Curtain-taker, Fake a curtain.)

Curtains (*Regimental.*) A name given to one of the first modes of wearing the hair low on the military forehead (1870). The locks were divided in the centre, and the front hair was brought down in two loops, each rounding away towards the temple. The hair was glossed and flattened.—*Guiver.* (*See* Sixes, To put on the, Scoop, etc.).

Cut a finger (*Lower Classes*). To cause a disagreeable odour; *e.g.*, 'My hi! some cove's cut 'is finger.'

Cut and run (*Peoples'*). Make off rapidly, retire without permission. Trade metaphor. From sailoring, and act of cutting a vessel in the night-time from her moorings and then running before the wind. Very general; probably accepted from T. P. Cook in *Black-Eyed Susan.*

Cut one's stick (*Old Eng.*) To travel for work—the stick being cut or obtained for helpful and probably defensive purposes.

Cut the line (*Printers'*). To knock off work—for a time; origin obscure, but may refer to the line of type.

Cut the record (*Peoples' sporting*). Victory. Here cut is used as surpassing.

People are saying that the Inventions Exhibition is not so much talked of as previous displays at South Kensington have been; but I think that as soon as we get hot weather, the admission returns will cut all previous records.—*Entr'acte,* 30th May 1885.

Cut-throat (*W. Amer.*). Destructive, reckless—applied to card-playing.

It is not uncommon, therefore, to see merchants (especially American) having a social game of 'cut-throat monte', 'eucre', or 'poker', with piles of gold before them.—*All the Year Round,* 31st October 1868.

Cycling fringes (*Cycling,* 1897). Especially prepared forehead-hair to be worn by such women bikers as had not abjured all feminine vanities.

It may be, of course, both libellous and ungallant to suggest that there could be any possible connection with those wonderful 'cycling fringes', warranted never to come out of curl, at present filling the barbers' windows.—10th March 1897.

Cyclophobist (*Literary,* 1880). An invented word to describe haters of tradesmen's circulars.

The word 'cyclophobist' is still comparatively new to the English language, and perhaps it is not a very scholarly compound to express 'a man who hates and dreads tradesmen's circulars'.—*D. N..* 6th January 1882.

Naturally came to be applied to the opponent of the bicycle, as this vehicle became ubiquitous.

The chairman, on whose suggestion the communication was laid on the table in the first instance, explained that he was not a 'cyclophobist', but he did most emphatically object to scorchers, and racers, and pacemakers, and also to careless riders, of whom he and many other people went in daily terror.—*D. T.,* 9th December 1897.

Cyrano (*Soc.,* 1900). A huge nose. Due to the popularity of Rostand's play, *Cyrano de Bergerac,* whose hero had a phenomenal nose, imitated in pasteboard by French and English actors who played the part. Pronounced Sée-ra-no, with the accent on the first. A dactyl.

Miss Annie Hughes was as unlike Sam Weller as it is possible to conceive. The immortal 'man' was not a dandy 'tiger' with a Whitechapel accent and a Cyrano nose.—*D. T.,* 16th April 1900.

(*See* Boko, Duke.)

D

D. B. (*Theatrical*). A masked mode of condemnation.

Although Miss Deby was d. b.—which being interpreted means deucedly bad—some of those about her were deucedly good.—*Newsp. Cutting.*

D. D. (*Naval*). Discharged—dead. The usual way on board a man-of-war of writing a man's epitaph; as: 'Bill? Oh! he's D. D.—this year agone.'—Captain Chamier, 1820.

D. T. Centres (*Lit.,* 1880 on). Minor Bohemian, literary, artistic, and musical clubs—from the jollity, or supposed jollity, of a Bacchic character which continually proceeds within their walls. D. T. is a reduction to the absurd of delirium tremens—or 'tremenses,' as some comic folk style that self-imposed disease.

D. V. (*Atheistic*). A satiric and not very adroit application of the initials of 'Deo Volente', to 'Doubtful —very'.

Fred Hughes says that the letters 'D. V.' in his advertisement referring to his appearance at the Jumbo Theatre, mean 'doubtful—very'. I thought so.

D. V. (*Soc.*). Divorce. Another shape of satire upon Deo Volente—Heaven, of course, having certainly nothing to do with the performance, if papal authority is of any value.

Daddles (*Pugilistic*). Hands.

All was in readiness, and the men having shaken daddles, the seconds retired to their corners, and at 12.56 commenced the fight.—*Newsp. Cutting*, 1862.

Daisy (*Amer., passing to England*, 1870). A charming, fresh, delightful person or thing.

An enthusiastic admirer of 'The Silver King' lately, in the upper circle of the Grand Opera House audibly proclaimed Wilfrid Denver to be 'a daisy'.—*Newsp. Cutting*, October 1883.

This morning a young man walked into the office with a huge watermelon in his arms. Placing his burden on the counter he addressed the agent: 'Now, isn't that melon a daisy?'—*Newsp. Cutting*.

Specially used (and abused) as a sentimental basis; hence 'Daisy' came to be synonymous with humbug.

He took me by the ear and said I couldn't come no 'daisy' business on him.—*Detroit Free Press*, 1883.

Also a satirical term for a drunken man.

Detective Lanthier had hardly approached the platform where the 'Female Dudes' were on exhibition when a piping voice exclaimed familiarly: 'Vote for me, mister; I am a daisy!'—*N.Y. Mercury*, 8th October 1883.

Daisy Crown of Cricket (*Sporting*, 1883 on). Poets have their imaginary bays, warriors their imagined laurels—the field daisy, therefore, is the appropriate floral emblem given to the champion bowler, batter, fielder, *et hoc*.

Oxford, so far, is retaining her maritime supremacy, though the daisy crown of cricket is decorating other brows.—*D. N.*, 6th July 1883.

Daisy-five-o'clocker (*Amer.-Eng.*). A charming five o'clock tea. An extreme application of daisy, as a term of approbation.

Dam (*University*). Abbreviation of 'damage' in relation to payment for entertainment or entry to place of amusement; *e.g.*, 'What's the dam?' 'A sov. per fellow.'

Damager (*Theatrical*, 1880). A nonsense name for manager. Perhaps some covert reference to his autocratic power of sweeping out a comedian.

The green room became so crowded that at last the damager was compelled to put up a notice.—*Newsp. Cutting*.

Then a damager took him in hand and engaged him to come on first.—*Newsp. Cutting*.

Dame (*Eton*). A master who confines his attention to mathematics. To some extent a supercilious term.

'Badger' Hale went to this school as a mathematical teacher, and though for the last twenty years he took the classes in natural science, he remained, to use the Eton term, a 'dame'—that is to say, a house-master who did not teach the classics, and whose boys consequently always had a 'tutor' as well outside.—*D. T.*, 26th July 1894.

Damfino (*Anglo-Amer.*) The last instance of abbreviation and obscure swearing. 'I am damned if I know' is its origin.

A vicious college student being asked what he intended doing after graduating, replied: 'Damfino; preach, I s'pose.'

Damfoolishness (*Amer., passing to Eng.*). Intensification of foolishness, and abbreviation of damned foolishness.

'Now, Hennery, I am going to break you of this damfoolishness, or I will break your neck.'—*Newsp. Cutting*.

Damned (*Theatrical*, 18 and 19 *cent.*). Condemned utterly; *e.g.*, 'The piece was damned from the gods to the groundlings.'

Damned good swine up (*Peoples'*, 1880). A loud quarrel. Suspected to be of American origin. In the States the 'swine' are more demonstrative than at home. Here even the common pig is quarrelsome; *e.g.*, 'Tell Cecil to tone himself down a bit, or we shall have a damned good swine up.'

Damirish (*Amer.*, 1883). A disguised euphemism for 'damned Irish'.

When I read the story in the papers about the explosion in the British Parliament pa was hot. He said the damirish was ruining the whole world.—*A Bad Boy's Diary*, 1883.

Damp bourbon poultice (*Amer. Saloon*). A 'go' of whiskey.

'Postage stamps', replied the country merchant, as he slammed the door and went out to soothe his feelings with a damp bourbon poultice.—*Newsp. Cutting*.

Dampen (*Amer., Theatrical*). A euphemism for 'to damn'.

Most interesting, but the 'heroine' dying so soon, rather dampens the piece in her opinion.—*Newsp. Cutting*.

Damper (*Soc.*, 1886 on). A dinner-bill—a document which has steadily increased in importance through many years. Term recognised in the lines attributed to Theodore Hook.

Men laugh and talk until the feast is o'er;
Then comes the reckoning, and they laugh no more!

Curiously enough the French found a correlative title to Damper, viz., La Douloureuse.

La Douloureuse! Few know that in modern French slang it means the bill that is offered to a generous host after the dinner is over and the reckoning is at hand.—*D. T.*, 29th June 1897.

Dance (*Fashion*, 1890). A ball—this latter word being only used for solemn state and aristocratic functions.

The Duke and Duchess of Devonshire gave a large dinner party last evening at Devonshire House, followed by a dance reaching the dimensions of a ball, only that the word has fallen out of favour save for public functions.—*D. T.*, 6th July 1899.

Dance upon nothing (*Peoples'*, 18 *cent.*). To be hanged—the convulsive motions of the legs in the air suggesting the phrase. Probably took the place of 'Mount the cart' (*q.v.*), when the place of hanging was in the prison, or its shadow, and a cart was no longer in vogue. Passing away in appositeness, now that the hangman uses a long rope, so that the neck is broken, and the victim does not struggle. (*See* Hemp is grown for you.)

Dancing dogs (*circa*, 1880). A satirical title applied to 'dancing men' when dancing began to go out.

Then drop in those supercilious masters of the situation, the dancing young men, the 'dancing dogs', as they have been called.—*D. N. Leader*, 27th March 1884.

Dander riz (*Amer.*). Classic in *Sam Slick*. 'Dander' is indignation; 'riz', a diminutive of 'raised'. Dander is probably from the old Dutch of the early American settlers — the source of so much American droll phraseology.

I don't for a moment say that she would; but, quoting from one of the Claimant's own letters, 'Anna Maria has got a timper of her own', and there is no knowing what she might say if her 'dander were riz'.—*Entr'acte*, 1st November 1884.

Darbey (*Thieves'*). A haul (of course of stolen goods).

'Ben—You ought to be in London on the 10th of this month. The Prince of Wales will be married, every place will be luminated, and all the "lads" expect to make a good "darbey" (good haul, or robbery). Old Bill Clark expects about 24 reddings (gold watches), and old Tom and Joe expect twice as many.'—*Thief's Intercepted Letter*, March 1863.

In the plural this word represents the common name for handcuffs. It were curious to trace the first of these bracelets to Derby, which 'on the spot' is, or at all events was, pronounced 'Darby.'

Dark as a pocket (*Merchant Seamens'*). Very expressive.

Darkies (*Lower Lond. Soc.*, 1860 on). A synonym for the coal-hole, the shades, and the cider cellar—places of midnight entertainment in or near the Strand, all famous in the mid-nineteenth century.

The days of The Cider Cellars, and The Shades, called in slang terms 'The Darkies' and 'The Coal Holes', and the low music-halls with their abominable songs, and the Haymarket orgies and the dancing saloons disappeared.—*D. T.*, 20th November 1896.

Darn(*Eng.-Amer.*). A United States evasion of damn, and very suggestive of household occupation and equally innocent swearing. (*See* Dern.)

When Sacramento was being destroyed by fire some of the merchants managed to save some champagne, and, going outside the town, drank 'Better luck next time. This is a great country.' Next day a tavern-keeper had a space cleared among the ruins, and over a little board shanty hastily run up was this inscription: 'Lafayette House. Drinks two bits. Who cares a darn for a fire!'—*All the Year Round*, 31st October 1868.

Some writers maintain that this term went to U.S.A. from England, upon the argument of the phrase, 'Darn my old wig,' which cannot be American. Here a kind of pun was intended, for wigs were economically darned. Wigs have passed away, as a fashion, over a hundred years, yet this phrase is still heard at and about Plymouth, which suggests that the word may have crossed the ditch in due course, sailing long after the *Mayflower*.

Vance thinks that the management of Her Majesty's Theatre are a darned sight too particular.—*Newsp. Cutting*, March 1883. (V. was a very clever comic singer, and most comic in petticoats).

Dash my wig (*Peoples'*). Another version of 'darn' in the time of wigs. Still heard, though wigs are seldom referred to, if worn; rarely worn amongst men. Some wild etymologists hold this to be a perversion of 'Dish the Whigs', but they do not give the clue. Dishing the Whigs, by the way, may mean 'douching' them, though, on the other hand, there is a common expression, 'Well, I'm dished!' but this is supposed to be a corruption of dashed, in its previous turn a corruption of d—dash—d, the printer's moral evasion of 'damn' when the printing of this word was in bad taste, and was bad in law!

Daverdy (*Devon*). Careless. Probably from an individual notoriously untidy—possibly David Day.

Day-bugs (*Essex schools*). Day scholars; *e.g.*, ' Don't row with that fellow, he's only a day-bug '—said by a night-flea or boarder. This phrase is interesting as showing that the U.S.A. habit of using 'bug' for beetle went from England.

Dead as a door-nail (*Peoples'; from Ireland*). Dead as O'Donnel; on all fours with 'I'll smash you into smithereens'—that is to say, Smithers' Ruins—S. having had his house pulled about his ears. O'Donnel being dead and Smithers no longer alive, the two folk-phrases become, the one anglicized into 'door-nail', the other into a powerful word representing complete destruction, one which is heard to this day amongst the Irish lower classes wherever found. Probably many phrases, such as 'The Twinkling of a Bed-post ', etc., are built upon proper names which have faded from memory, while the phrases relating to them remain. Dickens begins his *Christmas Carol* with this phrase: ' Morley was dead as a door-nail—to begin with !'

Falstaff: What ! is the old king dead ?
Pistol: As *nail in door:* the things I speak are just. *Shakspeare.*

Dead-beat (*Amer.-Eng.*). A pauper —lost his last copper.

'Hang *me* ef I savvy! He didn't pungle, he ain't got no kit; and nobody don't know him ! Now it's my opinion he's a dead beat—that's how I put *him* up !'—*Newsp. Cutting.*

Dead broke(*Amer.-Eng.*). Another reading of dead beat.

' Cheap enough—dog cheap for the fun I had, but I'm dead broke. Had 60 dollars yesterday morning, but she's gone—all gone—not a red left.'—*Newsp. Cutting.*

Dead give away (*Amer.*). A swindle, deception.

He would seem to argue with her that a brood of chickens would be a dead give away on them both.—*Newsp. Cutting.*

Dead-eye (*Sailors'*, 19 *cent.*). Generally 'A bit o' dead-eye'. Figurative reference to esoteric effort. In ordinary nautical language 'dead-eyes' are the small clean-cut holes worked in rigging blocks, and in ships' woodwork generally. They certainly have an appearance of shadowed sight, which is very startling at times. Mr W. S. Gilbert gave this term to his hero, Dick Dead-eye, in the opera-bouffe *H.M.S. Pinafore*—(1878).

Deadhead (*Theatrical, from Amer.*). One who does not pay his or her entrance fee. Critics are professional deadheads. Hebrews are the great sinners in this connection, they getting their free passes, they themselves only knowing where. All 'theatrical people' are deadheads, for they never pay to enter a theatre. ' The female deadhead was in a red opera cloak—she always is.' This vermilion stain, however, has now vanished.

I have not paid a cent for a seat at the theatre in twenty years. I boast of this sometimes. Why is this? I am supposed to have 'influence'. I am one of the old ' men about town'. Really I am without influence. But no matter. Let me live out the remainder of my theatrical days in peace. I shall be a real deadhead soon.—*Soliloquy by ' Old Deadhead'.*

Mr E. V. Page has written a good song for Miss Tilley on the 'deadhead' lay. After this, how can I expect him to pass me into the Cambridge stalls ?—*Entr'acte,* 30th May 1885. (*See* Order deadhead.)

He wished also to add that there were quite 'Deadheads' enough visiting theatres. Mr Chance asked what that meant. Mr Parkes said it meant a class of persons who under various excuses obtained or attempted to obtain admission to theatres and places of public entertainment without paying.—*Newsp. Cutting*, 1882.

The experienced eye can always divide the deadheads from the 'plank-downers' in a theatre. The deadheads are always dressed badly, and give themselves airs when looking at the inferior parts of the house. The plank-downers never give themselves airs, mean business, and only look at the stage. Deadheads are very emphatically thus described by a theatrical official : 'Here come two more deadheads ; look at their boots.'

Dead-lock (*Street*, 1887 on). A Lock Hospital. Very significant; *e.g.*, 'Don't muck about—always go to the dead-lock.' Applied from the habit of stags clinching their horns, and fighting thus to the death.

Dead number (*Com. Lond.*). The last number in a row or street; perhaps the *end* of the street.

Dead 'un (*City*). A bankrupt company; e.g., 'The All Round Blessing Assurance is a dead 'un.' (*See* Cadaver.)

Dead wood (*Amer. forest*). Advantage. Origin very obscure. In clearing trees a skilful axeman so acts as to take every advantage from the hang of the tree that it may heel over and save him as much cutting as possible. The gain is 'dead wood'.

She extracted a twenty dollar bill, and remarked: 'I reckon I've got the dead wood on that new bonnet I've been sufferin' for.'—*Texas Siftings.*

Deal of weather about (*Nautical*). Bad meteorological times. For sailors fine weather is no weather at all. On the sea the word always means discomfort and struggle, as may be seen in its use, 'weather the storm'.

Deaner, The (*Oxford 'er*). The Dean.

The dean of a college is the 'deaner' or the 'dagger', while even this is reduced by some to 'the dag'.—*D. T.*, 14th August 1899.

Dear me (*Soc., passed to people*). Exclamation used by the best people; may be a corruption of Dio mio. Possibly introduced by Maria Beatrice of Modena, second wife of James II.

As a matter of fact, women do appeal a good deal, and often when they do not know it. What is the meaning of 'Dear me'? As English it is absolutely meaningless. It is a mere phase, an expletive, until we understand it as a corruption of 'Dio mio'.

Or it may be 'Dieu mais', an exclamation which came into use immediately after the Restoration—introduced by one of the French Court beauties.

Death on (*Amer.*). Determined, even at the risk of life.

Birmingham, to use the Yankee vernacular, which is well understood in that locality, is 'death on' Woman Suffrage.—*Newsp. Cutting.*

Death-promoter (*Amer.*, about 1880). An ominous synonym for alcoholic drink. This phrase is a very fine instance of the etymological landmarks sometimes — perhaps often— afforded by passing English. Here is seen subterfugal conviction of the danger of alcoholic indulgence, even taking possession of the intelligence of the very patron of whiskey himself. Throughout history there is no period before the end of the 19th century where alcohol is associated with death —if we except *L'assommoir*, a cudgel, and used in France to describe a drinking-bar. (*See* 'Pisen'.)

Decadent (*Soc.*, 1885-90). A synonym for degenerate (noun and adjective), and the antithesis of atavism, atavistic (*q.v.*).

The most extravagant guesses were made as to its authorship—the writer having for obvious reasons cloaked himself with anonymity—and it was even whispered that the book came from the hand of a famous decadent, who 'dropped out' some time back.—*Sun,* 7th November 1899.

Decencies (*Theatrical*). Pads used by actors, as distinct from actresses, to ameliorate outline.

Deck (*Gaming*). A pack of cards.

John Kernell tells of an actor who spouted his trunk for his board, claiming that it contained fifty-three pieces. When the landlady opened it she found a paper collar and a deck of cards.—*Newsp. Cutting.*

Deck (*Costers'; local*). The Seven Dials (W. London). 'He's a decker' means he lives in the classic dials. (*See* Seven Dials' Raker.)

Degenerate (*Soc.*, 1899). A libertine (male), a woman of gallantry (female). Its antithesis was regenerate, which probably meant a return to a reasonable life, and church at least once on Sunday. A play styled *The Degenerates*, by Sydney Grundy, with Mrs Langtry for lead, was set before the public in the autumn.

To-night you receive—and receive most hospitably and graciously—a member of the theatrical profession. Whether your taste in this respect is better or worse than your father's, whether you are degenerates or regenerates I must ask others to decide.—*Charles Wyndham* (at Argonaut Club), 13th November 1899.

Degrugger (*Oxford 'er*). A degree.

When you passed an examination you obtained a testamur or certificate, which was labelled a 'testugger', and thanks to it you could proceed to take a 'degrugger', which is Oxford for Degree.— *D. T.*, 14th August 1899.

Delo diam (*Back slang*). An old maid; in common use.

When a bloke's hard up it's the delo diam who is his friend. When a poor girl goes wrong it is the delo diam who gives her shelter until the kid is born. Delo diams are angels on this muddy earth, and if there is a heaven delo diams will take a front seat there.—*Newsp. Cutting*, 1883.

Delo nammow (*Back slang*). Old woman.

'If he doesn't pay that delo nammow eighteenpence for washing there will be a bankruptcy at his door.'—*Newsp. Cutting*.

Delo nam o' the Barrack (*Thieves'*). 'Old man', which is back spelling, and 'Master of the house'—barrack, used for house; probably being obtained from soldiers on furlough.

'Delphi (*Theatr.*). Mass pronounciation of 'Adelphi', the great house, through the Victorian era of melodrama in the Strand. (*See* 'Lane.)

Demijohn (*Peoples'*). Large measure, swingeing draught. Probably from a measure of the time of King John; *e.g.*, 'All gorne—well, that was a demijohn, that was.' Johnson has nothing to say about it.

Demons (*Austral.*). Old hands at bushranging; derived from men who arrive from Van Dieman's Land (Tasmania), some of whom are popularly supposed to have inaugurated bushranging in Australia.

Den (*Public-house*). A name generally given to a public-house frequented night after night by the same set, and bestowed by them half-ruefully, half-satirically.

Dennis (*Sailors'*). Nothing except below contempt; *e.g.*, 'Hullo, Dennis!' 'Oh, I'm Dennis, am I?' Sailors always call the 'pig' Dennis. This may have reference to a certain sister isle—and it may not. (*See* Mud.)

Derby (*Sporting*). To pawn. At a time when men still were foolish enough to take their watches to races, and especially the crowded Derby, they were frequently 'rushed' (that is, 'pushed at', but passing language is always industriously inclined to be lazy enough to save a word) for their watches. This became so common that men who pawned their watches would say they had been stolen on the Derby or other course. Satirical friends saw the point, and hence a new verb for 'to pawn' was added to the countless stores of changing English.

Dern (*Amer.*). Another of the evasive stages of 'damn'.

'Never held such derned hands in my life. Beat the game, though.'—*Newsp. Cutting*. (*See* Darn.)

The study of evaded swearing in English may be interestingly compared with the same process in French. In the former the evasion is always a concession to religious thought, in the latter it is always an attack. For instance, 'Sacré nom de Dieu' has fallen to 'Cré nom de Chou'. Any one can mark the sound similarity of the final words—the pronounciation of 'chou' being something like the mode in which 'dieu' is uttered by Alsacians and Auvergnats. But how needless is the offence of calling the Almighty a cabbage.

Desert (*Soc.*, 1892 on). Ladies' Club—from the absence of members.

Deuce. Dusius—the erotic God of Nightmare, passing (15th century in England) into Robin Goodfellow. Also applied to the four two's of a pack of cards—here from the French 'deux', playing cards having arrived from Paris, precisely as the three is called 'tray'—from trois. There is no association between dusius and the deuce of clubs say, or any other card deuce.

'It's true, I admit, that women have babies, but who the dooce has to keep 'em?'

The most familiar shape of Deuce is Robin Goodfellow, whose pictorial representation has long since been turned out of good society. If any curious reader is desirous of seeing him in his habit as he lived, he must be prepared to pay him five pounds for a copy of Mr Thomas Wright's remarkable little book upon Phallic worship. Its study will enable him to comprehend Shakespeare's allusions to this alarming personage—probably Robin Goodfiller.

Deucid or **Deuced** (*Peoples'*). Either corruption of decided, or meaning devilish in the more daily use of that word, as in 'He's a devilish good fellow'. In the latter case it is derived from deuce. George Eliot, in 'Felix Holt,' ch. 17, makes it 'deuced'. 'He has inherited a deuced faculty for business.'

Deuce o' denas (*Thieves'*). From deux, two, and dena, shilling.

If you ask them to lend you a deuce o'

denas, very likely you won't get it.—*Newsp Cutting*.

Deuce take you (*National*). Ejaculation desiring that Satan may fly away with you. Sometimes impersonal—'Deuce take it.' From Dusius—Dusii.

'They were in fact the fauns and satyrs of antiquity, haunting, as they did, the wild woods. As incubi they visited houses at night. They made their presence known as nightmare. They were known at an early period in Gaul by the name of dusii, from which, as the church taught that all these mythic personages were devils, we derive our modern word deuce used in such phrases as "Deuce take you!"'—R. Payne Knight, *Worship of Priapus*.

Devil doubt you, The (*Peoples'*). Very commonly used in this form, but in full, 'I don't' is added. Used to concede a violent assertion on the other side. 'I'm a scorcher, I am,' to which the reply would be, 'The devil doubt you—*I* don't;' probably from the time when compliments were still passed to Satan on the Persian plan. Means 'I am not clever enough to dispute your theory; it requires one as clever as Satan to question your assertion.' Probably the most familiar oath, if it is an oath, in the English language.

Devil's dinner hour (*Artisans'*). Midnight, the hour for all Satanic revels. Said in reference to working late.

Devil's luck and my own (*Peoples'*). No luck whatever. The demon having been lamed early in life, and frequently cheated of his prey, even of the Fausts of this world, his luck is not extensive; *e.g.*, 'Getting on? Bless me no; I've the devil's luck, and my own too. When I pay my way I fancy I'm somebody else.'

Devonshire compliment (*W. Country, except Devonshire*). Doubtful politeness; *e.g.*, 'Do 'ee 'ave this cup o' tea in the pot; 't'ull on'y be thrawed away!'

Dew o' Ben Nevis (*Lond. and Edin. Taverns*). A fortunate name discovered by a Scotch distiller to distinguish his whiskey. 'Dew' was poetic, and 'Ben Nevis' was already in the heart of the Scotch customer. The name is now used in place of the word whiskey, much like 'Guinness' for stout, 'Alsopp' and 'Burton' for ale, and 'Kinahan' for Irish whiskey. 'Twa o' bennévis' (the 'e' pronounced short) is a common request, always complied with in the hard-working land o' cakes.

Dick's hat-band (*Peoples', provincial*). A makeshift. The hat-band in general use, even in Mr Weller's time of widowhood, was a portentous sweep of crape, draped and bowed behind. It slipped into a band of cloth on the hat, and has now passed to the arm as a strip, in imitation of the mourning worn by the late Queen's servants for the Prince Consort. Who was Dick? 'Tis all that remains of him. 'What be that, gammer—that bean't a bonnet?' 'No, bless thee, 'tis a Dick's hat-band.'

Dicky, Dickey (*Peoples'*). Very doubtful; *e.g.*, 'It's Dickey, ain't it?' Origin obscure. May refer to Richard III. as conquered. A courtier of Henry VII. may have started the phrase as a flattery to the Conqueror.

The columbine was less fortunate in his opinion. 'She's werry dicky; ain't got what I call "move" about her.'—Greenwood's *Night in a Workhouse*.

Die in a horse's night-cap (*Thieves'*). To die in a halter. Supposed to be very brilliant satire.

Die Dunghill (*Sporting*, 18 *cent.*). Said of a cock that would not fight—and applied to human curs; *e.g.*, 'I never die dunghill—always game.' In our days the term has changed to 'die on a dunghill', meaning the person spoken of will have no home in which to die.

Diff (*Soc.*). Abbreviation of 'differences', *e.g.*, 'No—it is not I love her—she loves me.—That's the diff.'

Probably came from the Stock Exchange, the birthplace of so much passing English.

There is a great diff between a dona and a mush. You *can* shut up a mush (umbrella) sometimes.—*Newsp. Cutting*.

Diffs (*Theatr.*). A euphemistic abbreviation of 'difficulties', cruelly common with lessees until the prince, about 1870, completely brought the theatre into fashion.

Diffs (*Vulgar*). Abbreviation of 'difficulties'. 'For gentlemen in difficulties arrested in the county of Surrey there was a single spunging-house in a street somewhere off the Blackfriars

Dig   *Dish*

Road. I remember visiting a friend there once, who told me that the apartments were extremely comfortable. The sheriff's officer was an accomplished whist player, and he had a musical daughter who used to play and sing to the gentleman in "diffs".'— G. A. Sala, *Fifa and Ca Sa, in T. D.*, 15th August 1893.

Dig (*Mid. Class, Elegant*). Abbreviation of 'dignity'; *e.g.*, 'So I stood upon my dig, and told him his room was nicer than his company.' Sometimes 'otium dig' (from 'otium cum dignitate'; *e.g.*, 'Come and see me in my summer-house; there I am in my otium dig.'

Dig me out (*Soc.*, 1860). *I.e.*, call for me; tear me from lazy loafing in the house.

Digger (*Milit.*). The guard-room. Short for 'Damned guard-room'.

Digs. Short for 'diggings'. Australian for lodgings, from the time when gold miners lived on their claims, or diggings. In common use by theatrical touring companies.

The strolling 'mummers' have alighted from a cheap excursion train, and are imbibing hot whisky and water before commencing their chilly exploration of the quiet little country town in search of 'digs'.—*D. T.*, 23rd March 1898.

Dill (*Chemists'*). A disguised title for water—no such simple liquor as mere water being named before the public. 'Dill' sounds more medicinal than dill water. The word is a liquidising of 'distilled water'.

Dilly-dally (*Peoples'*). Hesitative. An equivalent of shilly-shally, both generally used as an attack upon the spoonery of lovers. Probably rhymed from the latter.

Dimber-damber (*Street*). Smart, active, adroit. One of the alliterative phrases with no absolute meaning—a false onomatope. Namby-pamby and nimmeny-pimmeny are on similar lines.

He is a bit dimber-damber, and up to everything on the carpet. — *Newsp. Cutting.*

Dime Museum (*Freak Show, applied to theatres*, 1884). A common show— poor piece. From New York, which has a passion for monstrosity displays, called Dime Museums—the dime being the eighth of a dollar.

Dimensions, To take (*Police*). To obtain information.

I said, 'Are you sure?' and he said, 'Yes; she's been murdered in a railway carriage.' At eleven that same night Sergeant Cox came to the house and took 'dimensions'.—*Newsp. Cutting.*

Dinah (*Com. London*). A favourite woman; *e.g.*, 'Is Mary your Dinah?' Corruption of 'dona'.

Dipping (*Thieves'*). Picking pockets —literally dipping.

Mr Selfe: What is meant by 'dipping'? The policeman: It's the last new word —it means picking pockets. — *Newsp. Cutting.*

Dirt Road (*Amer.*). The highway, as distinct from the railroad, which is gravelled. Probably railway official satire.

His Honour talked to him in a fatherly way, and told him to start for home by the dirt road, and David went out.—*Newsp. Cutting.*

Dirty Half-Hundred (*Milit.—O.S.*). 50th Regiment.

The gallant 'Fiftieth,' otherwise known as the 'Dirty Half-Hundred,' a regiment with a splendid record, retains its title as 'The Queen's Own', with a local habitation in West Kent.—*D. N.*, July 1881.

Disagreeable Bore (*Soc.*). The antithesis of Agreeable Rattle.

Discommons (*University*). To boycott, send to Coventry, exclude.

A man is supposed, on leaving school and going to college, to be learning to take care of himself. Except by 'discommonsing' dishonest tradesmen, a form of permitted Boycotting which might be more widely exerted, we fail to see how the Heads of Houses are to make extravagant young fellows careful.— *D. N.*, 20th March 1885.

Disguised (*Soc.*). One of the numerous evasive synonyms for 'drunk'.

Most of Bob Prudhoe's customers are noblemen disguised—in liquor.—*Newsp. Cutting.*

Bob was a very handsome and dashing licensed victualler in the 'neck of the Strand', between St Mary's and St Clement Danes—long since demolished.

Disguised Public-House (*Polit.*, 1886). Workmen's political clubs. First used in the House of Commons; *e.g.*, 'Call it a club if you like—this is a free country—but it's an after 12.30 p.m. public, and nothing else.'

Dish (*Parliamentary*). To overcome, to distance—figuratively, to present the enemy trussed in a dish, displayed before the conquerors and the nation.

It is alleged that Liberals have stolen a march upon the Conservatives, that non-political candidates have turned out to be Radicals in disguise, and, in short, that the Tories have been dished.—*D. T.*

The Whigs had been dished, to use the historic phrase of the great Lord Derby.—*D. T.*, 20th May 1899. (*See* Dash my Wig.)

Dismember for Great Britain (*Soc.* 1886). The last political nickname given to Gladstone. About the time of the Home Rule Bill.

They used to call him the Member for Midlothian. Now they call him 'the Dismember for Great Britain.'—*Ref.*, 18th April 1886.

Distinct(ly) (*Society*, 1880). Thorough(ly). The use of this word in this sense in many cases became a mania. 'He is a distinct fool.' 'She is a distinct fraud.' 'They are distinctly in the wrong.'

Ditch, the (*Local Lond.*, 1850). Abbreviation of Shoreditch, one of the chief eastern thoroughfares of London.

The Ditch is the oldest village in London. A bloke named Shore hung out there once. His missus went wrong with a King. When the King snuffed it the dona had to walk through the streets in her nightgown. She died in a ditch did Jane. Hence the name Shoreditch. —*Cutting*, 1883.

A frequenter of the Ditch is a Ditcher.

Ditch (*Anglo-Amer.*). The Atlantic. A playful allusion to its immense width (*See* Herring Pond.)

Ditch and Chapel (*E. London, street*). An abbreviation of Shoreditch and of Whitechapel

You only know me, maties, in Ditch parlours and Chapel bagatelle rooms.— *Cutting*, 1883.

Ditched (*Anglo-Amer,*). Off the highway; halted. Accepted by the States from old coaching days.

A portion of Doris's Inter-oceanic circus was ditched on Friday on the Missouri Pacific Railroad, near Booneville, Mo.—*Newsp. Cutting.*

Now figuratively used; *e.g.*, 'I was ditched completely, and did not know what to say.'

Ditto, Brother Smut (*Peoples'*). Your tongue is as coarse as you say mine is. Probably from chimney-sweeps.

Dive (*Amer. Eng.*). An underground drinking bar. Reached England through Liverpool—from 'diving under to reach it'. Equivalent to the lost London word 'Shades'—from the underground darkness of these resorts. The last 'shades' were in Leicester Square. The first dive is scarcely more than a gun-shot away in Piccadilly.

In many places (U.S.A.), especially in the cities, the existence of the law makes no real difference; in some few, by fits and starts, it is rigidly enforced, and the consequence is that the drinking is driven underground, into what they variously call 'dives', 'speak easies', and 'kitchen bar room' in the North; and 'blind pigs' and 'blind tigers' in the South. The liquor sold deteriorates at the same time. Little but spirits is dealt in, and much of it is of the vilest quality. —G. A. Sala, *D. T.*, 25th October 1893.

A grand entrance takes the place of the tavern, which is relegated to 'down below,' and is called a 'dive'.—*Ref.*, 10th May 1885.

Diver (*Thieves'*). A pickpocket— obviously from diving the hand down into others' pockets.

Divine punishment (*Naval*). Divine service.

Jack has little faith, and does not know, perhaps cares little, what to believe; and as to worship, it has long been known in the forecastle as 'divine punishment'.—*Newsp. Cutting*, 1869.

Diviners, or **Divvers**(*Oxford Univ.*). Reduction in Oxford 'er' of the Divinity Examination, which replaced the Rudiments of Faith and Religion.

Dixie (*Polit. Amer.*). The pet name given to the South, or Dixie-land. A popular negro song went, 'I wish I was in Dixie', that is to say, 'In heaven'.

Dizzy Age (*Soc. of a kind*, 19 *cent.*). Elderly. Makes the spectator giddy to think of the victim's years—generally those of a maiden or other woman canvassed by other maiden ladies—or others, *e.g.*, ' Poor dear; but though she is really very well, especially at a distance, on a dull day, she must be, the dove, quite a dizzy age.'

Dizzy flat (*Chicago*). A fool whose foolery makes the hearer giddy.

Do (*Peoples'*). In one capacity, as a neuter verb, praiseful, as 'He'll do'. Convert it into an active verb, 'He'll do you', and it becomes the most emphatic possible warning against a cheat. Rare instance of one word serving two distinctly opposite purposes. To 'do', as meaning to fight and conquer, has quite passed into common English life. 'I got done in three rounds', simply means that the speaker cried *Væ victis* after he had been grounded for the third time. A serio-comic singer, Bessie Bellwood, turned this word to great account while singing a song as a girl who boasts of her prowess, saying— 'Yoho, you come down our court. If I can't do yer, me and my sister Jemima 'ull do yer proper,'—proper in this case meaning completely.

Finally, this (the emphatic auxiliary verb of the eight auxiliary verbs) is used to describe murder.

Her ladyship replied: 'The two men have been trying to do for me.'—Lady Florence Dixie, concerning an armed attack upon her, 1883.

Quite classic in the criminal division of Irish society, and is even used to express—hanging by law.

'What sort of a *do* did Walsh get?' Asked by Patrick Joyce, the principal assassin in an agrarian outrage, when almost a whole family were swept away (Nov. 1882). He asked this question of a jailer immediately after he had been condemned to death. Walsh had some time previously been hanged at Galway.

Arthur Chewster, of Boston, U.S., was committed for trial from the West Ham Police Court on Saturday for severely wounding a labourer at Walthamstow with a bowie-knife. The prisoner informed the police that he was an Irish-American, and meant 'to do' for all Englishmen.—*Globe*, 5th October 1885.

In Lancashire is used to express suffering; *e.g.*, 'I've had a severe do this time—bronchitis, three weeks in bed.'

Amongst thieves to 'do' is to serve a term of imprisonment.

In middle-class life 'do' represents a joke, as, 'What a do!'

Chiefly applied to cheating, as—'I was done Brown'—that is, completely cooked.

Carlyle's favourite Cockney, who affirmed that every lottery had 'a do at the bottom of it', would find his rather cynical view of the gambling world strengthened by a case heard at the Guildhall Police Court. — *D. N.*, 25th May 1885.

Judge: Will you speak to what you know of the morality of Mr Doulton?—Well, I will only say that he has 'done' me out of my money. (The word 'done' aroused the curiosity of the Court, and the witness said, emphatically, 'Well, then, robbed me of my money.'—*Newsp. Cutting*.

Do again (*Navy*). Contemptuous reference to some one who never achieved much. Generally applied to marines, who, being neither enrolled sailors nor soldiers, are the 'buffers of both, and get pressed hard'.

'Pick him up and pipeclay him and he'll do again.'—*Newsp. Cutting*.

Do a bunk (*Public School*). To retire with precaution.

Do a bust (*Thieves'*). To burst a house open; burglary.

Redfern and his mate told him they were 'going to do a bust', meaning a robbery.—*D. T.*, 14th December 1897.

Do a Dutch (*prob. Amer. Knickerbocker*). To remove one's furniture without the preliminary of paying the rent due.

The Spitkinses did a Dutch with all their stock just before quarter-day.—*Newsp. Cutting*.

Do a moan (*Navy*). To growl. Moans are of frequent occurrence.

Do a smile (*Amer.*, 1860 on). To take a drink. Now rarely heard.

Do a stamp (*Amer., passing to England*). To go for a walk.

Do him a treat (*Pugilistic*). To give him a thrashing.

'He's a gee-gee of another colour. Whoa, my rorty pals, he's a hot 'un, though some of you can do him a treat when he gets a trifle cheeky.'—*Cutting*.

Do in (*Sport*, 1886 on). To adventure, bet, plank down, etc.

I am utterly unable to understand the unhealthy state of mind of a young fellow of one or two and twenty who in little more than a twelvemonth loses between three and four hundred thousand pounds, and who now rushes to 'do in' every spare fiver or tenner that comes into his possession.—*Ref.*, 19th May 1889.

Do one's bit (*Thieves'*). To carry out one's enforced contract as a felon with the Government.

It is not easy to persuade a wealthy employer who can buy what labour he requires in the cheapest and best market to take a man who has 'done his bit' in a correctional institution.—*Newsp. Cutting*.

Do oneself well (*Colloquial*, 1881). To make an effort to succeed in life.

He was heard to remark to the lady of the house, in confidence, that this was what he appreciated, that he adored domesticity and 46, and that he intended to do himself well.—*Newsp. Cutting*, 3rd February 1883.

Do over for (*Low London*). To extract money by flattery or threats.

When they comes back, Selby says to me, 'All I could do him over for was a couple of bob.'—*People*, 6th January 1895.

Do the aqua (*Public-house*). To put in the water, as ' Jo, do the aqua', and Joe pours the water into the held-out glass, observing ' Say when !' ' When', says the other—at the point he considers the dilution absolute.

Do the graceful (*Peoples'*). A paraphrase: to fasciuate, to charm by elegance of attention or behaviour.

On Saturday last, on the occasion of the 300th performance of *Iolanthe*, D'Oyly Carte did the graceful by presenting every lady visitor with a choice bouquet.—*Newsp. Cutting*.

Do to rights (*Lower Classes*). To effect perfectly; achieve quite satisfactorily. Has shades of meaning. ' Did me to rights.' May be said eulogistically of a meal. ' I'll do you to rights ' may be a promise of high delight, but it may mean, when addressed to a man, that the addressee will be thrashed awfully by the speaker.

Do ut Des (*Soc.*, 1883). Selfish people whose philosophy is 'I give' that thou 'mayest give'.

THE 'DO UT DES' AT HOME: Since the time of Bismarck's famous 'do ut des' policy, we have known that the statesmen of the Fatherland are not inclined to give favours for nothing.—*D. T.*, 29th December 1900. (*See* Doddies.)

Do yer feel like that ? (*Lower Classes*). Addressed to a person generally lazy who is being industrious, or who is doing some unusual work. Used satirically.

Do you know ? (*Peoples'*). The history of this initial phrase is very odd. It was first heard in the East of London, used by a popular preacher who often preached colloquially in the streets, and whose voice had very droll changes in it. The phrase spread (1883) over the East district, and reached the West towards the end of the year. It became public early in 1884 through its adoption by Mr Beerbohm Tree, in *The Private Secretary*. The piece was soon removed to the Globe when Mr Tree's part was taken by Mr Penley, who made the phrase more marked still throughout the year. It helped to make the piece popular. The oddity of the phrase was got out of its strange musical character..

The ' Do' was used short, as a grace note. Then followed the ' you' a third higher, and held about an ordinary crotchet's length. The 'know' was then taken a sixth below the 'you'. The whole had a most droll effect. Mr Penley began on the middle A, rose to C, and fell to E. The phrase was in common use in all stages of society. It went to America.

The Secretary has little more to say than ' Do you know', which is delivered in amazingly sepulchral tones, and which is likely to become a 'gag' expression on the street.—*N. Y. Mercury*, 1884.

Do you savey ? (*Half-society*, 1840). Mongrel French—Savez-vous ?

' All right—I shall savey in a minute.'
' I couldn't savey that in a month.'

Do you to Wain-rights (*Lower classes*, *c.* 1874). Intensification of ' Do you to rights,' by introduction of the name of a more than usually notorious murderer, one Wainwright. (*See* Wainwright you.) The phrase was used by men to women, meaning a threat of murder, sometimes used quite earnestly. Wainwright had killed a mistress who troubled him very much. Phrase still heard in East London, where the crime was committed.

Doc (*Amer.*). Short for doctor.

' Now, doc, I want you to tell me the worst. Is she dangerous?' The doc said it was not his nature unnecessarily to frighten any one, but he said doctors often had a duty to perform that they would prefer to transfer to other shoulders.—*Newsp. Cutting*.

Doctor Brighton (*Soc.*, 19 *cent.*). Brighton : said to be the invention of George IV. ; one of his few small witticisms.

' Doctor Brighton' is the prince of fashionable physicians, and does not dose his patients with nasty physic. The ' Doctor' has a pleasant face and an agreeable manner at all times.—*D. T.*, 13th August 1885.

Dr Jim (*Peoples'*, 1896). A soft felt hat, with wide brim. When soft felt hats began (1895) to overcome the eternal hard black or brown 'un bowler, they obtained several names of little account, the quotation of which was more honoured in the breach than the observance.

Upon the arrival, late in 1896, of Dr Jameson from the Transvaal, the wide rim of his soft Africander felt was at once accepted. For some weeks these models were called Jemmysons, but the hero in question becoming more popular as Dr Jim, the wide soft felter became a Dr Jim—very soon reduced to Jimmunt, sometimes a Jimkwim—the outcome of a coalescing between the earlier and later titles.

Do without (*Yorkshire*). To dislike. A Yorkshire man is generally too cautious to say he hates a man. He circumambulates, and says, 'Eh, ah could do wi'out him.' (*See* Nice place to live out of.)

Dod rabbit it (*Amer.*). In Charles II.'s time it was God rebate (assuage) it. This passed finally in England into 'Od rabbit it'. Going over to America the phrase was there further changed.

Doddies (*Peoples'*) Corruption of *Do ut des* ; reduction of Doddies-man ; *e.g.*, 'E's a doddies—give a sprat to catch a herring any day in the week, and any hour.'

Dodo (*Amer.*, beginning to be known in England). A human fossil, a man who clings to the past, and condemns future days and present—a *ganache*, to use a French term.

Dodo (*Press*, 1885). Scotland Yard —figuratively to express that the metropolitan police were fossil in their organisations.

The old dodo at Scotland Yard, roused into a state of feverish activity by the comments of the press and the public on the failure of Monday, yesterday converted itself by a tremendous effort into a gigantic turkey-cock, or, to use the much more expressive Scotch word, a great bubbly-jock—which strutted and rattled and stamped and made its guttural gobble all over the metropolis yesterday, with the most alarming result. —*Pall Mall Gaz.*, 11th February 1886.

Dodrottedest (*Amer.*, 1883). An example of evasive swearing.

The Apaches war well mounted, and I recko'nized the leader as a feller they called Chief Billy, the dodrottedest thief and cut-throat that ever pestered a community.—*Newsp. Cutting.*

Doesn't give much away (*Peoples'*, 1880). Yields few or no advantages—seizes all chances. Very cogent, and full of folk-keenness.

Edgar, who doesn't give much away, arranges to have Rayne drugged with a wonderful potion, two drops of which will make a man silly for the time being.—*Newsp. Cutting.*

Dog (*Peoples'*). Clever, cheery, hearty fellow—age not considered. Derived from the active, cheerful nature of dogs in general.

An Irishman has always been 'a dog at a ballad', as a Shakespearian character (oddly anticipating modern slang) calls himself 'a dog at a catch'.—*D. N.*

Dog-cheap (*Peoples'*). Very cheap. Who or what was the dog ? Certainly not canine, for the word would not be apposite—cat-cheap would be nearer the mark. Probably a pedlar, whose name might be Diggory, abbreviation to dig, and thence dog—'I bought it dog-cheap'. Johnson, who was cruelly puzzled by some of the compounds in 'dog', says, 'dog and cheap—cheap as dog's meat; cheap as the offal bought for dogs.' Dryden uses the word—'Good store of harlots, say you ? and dog-cheap !'

Dog-gone (*Peoples'*). Devoted ; from the pertinacious devotion of the doggie. In U.S.A. it is an evasion of 'God damn'.

Dog my cats (*Amer.*). An example of concealed swearing—God damn my eyes.

Dog my cats if she didn't make a nest of it and set three weeks on the buttons ! —*Newsp. Cutting.*

Dog's legs (*Soldiers'*). The chevron, designating non-commissioned rank, worn on the arm, and not unlike in outline to the canine hindleg.

Doggie (*Milit.*, 1850). Officer's servant, especially cavalry. The increase of education amongst the men has swept the term away. Men were proud of it in times when officers and their servants were more familiar than at present.

Doggie (*London Youths'*). All-round upright collar. (*See* Sepulchres, Poultice, Shakespeare navels.)

Doing (*Peoples'*). A thrashing ; *e.g.*, ' I'll give 'im a doin''—which 'e won't see out of 'is eyes for a fair week after I've done 'im over.'

' I've had a bad doing this week—lost thirty quid.'

Doing the bear (*Span.-Amer.*, *passing over U.S.*). Courting which involves hugging.

Courtship is carried on in a most extraordinary manner in Mexico. The part a man plays in a courtship is called 'doing the bear', which is a translation of 'hacer el oso'. It is quite a common expression in Mexico to say: 'I am doing the bear to Miss So-and-so'; or for the girl to say: 'That young man is doing the bear to me.'—*Newsp. Cutting.*

Dol (*Peoples'*). Abbreviation of dollar.

Dollars to buttons (*Anglo-Amer.*). A sure bet.

'She has got to put those clothes on, and she feels that it is dollars to buttons that when she picks up an under-garment from the floor by the table leg, that she will be blown through the roof.'—*Newsp. Cutting.*

(*See* Million to a bit of dirt.)

Dolly mop (*Peoples'*). An overdressed servant girl. Probably a form of Dollabella and Mopsa, both names used in 18th century for weak, overdressed, slovenly women.

Dolly worship (*Nonconformist*). The Roman Catholic religion. From the use of statues, etc.

Dominoes (*Tavern*). The teeth, when bad and yellow. When white, they are ivories.

Don Cæsar spouting (*Soc.*, 1850 on). Haughty public elocution—especially after dinner. Probably a satirical combination of 'the Don'—a memory of Mary Tudor's husband, and Julius.

Dona Highland Flingers (*Rhyming—Music Hall Singers*). One of the names of the serio-comic—generally one who sings or flings high notes—hence the term. 'Many a dona Highland Flinger gets nailed when she thinks she marries a toff, and finds out that he's a bad egg.

Dona Jack (*Lower Classes*). Lowest description of Jack—man who lives on the dona, a man who preys upon men of all designations.

Done (*Texas*). Completely. Done is the commonest of adjectives; e.g., 'We are done tired';
    'The kitchen is done swept';
    'The baby is done woke up.'

Done Fairly (*Sporting*, 1860). Completely cheated.

Fairlie has taken the Novelty Theatre. Let's hope that nobody will be able to say he's done Fairlie.—*Cutting.*

Donkey's breakfast (*London*, 1893 on). A man's straw hat. Satiric reference—a protest against the then new fashion, with suggestion as to the wearer. Died out as the century wore to an end. 'Which when a gent puts a donkey's breakfast a-top of his nut—he wants jollying.' It took several years for the streets to accept the straw hat. Even now it is far from universal.

Donnybrook (*Anglo-Irish*). Riot, disturbance, down to a shrew's squabble. Applied in a thousand ways. On 19th February 1900 the *Daily Telegraph* had a paragraph about a number of torpedo-boat destroyers, one of which broke away in harbour from her moorings, and did much mischief. This par was headed 'The Destroyers' Donnybrook'.

From the historical conviction that Donnybrook Fair (Ireland) is *all* noise.

Don't be a chump (*E. London*, 1889). Do not lose your temper. Derived probably from the act of fixing the teeth in passion as though chumping—that is, biting hard.

Don't care a Pall Mall (*Club*, 1885). A synonym for a damn. In July 1885 the *Pall Mall Gazette* gained wide notoriety by the publication of articles entitled 'The Maiden Tribute'. Hence the phrase, 'He may say what he likes; I don't care a Pall Mall.'

Don't dynamite (*Peoples'*, 1883). Avoid anger. Result of the Irish pranks in Great Britain with this explosive. Their chief result was to add a word to the army of phrases.

Don't know who's which from when's what! (*Street*, 1897). Total sentence of stupidity. Speaks for itself.

Don't lose your hair (*Peoples'*, 19 cent.). Don't lose your temper. Came in when wigs went out, and replaced 'dash my wig'. From the tendency to tear the hair in a rage, or, at all events, to seize it. (*See* Keep your hair on.)

Don't mention that (*Common London*, 1882). A catch word which prevailed for some time in consequence of Mr Baron Huddleston's frequent use of the phrase during the endless hearing (for over forty days) of a libel case between sculptors—Belt *v*. Lawes.

Don't seem (*Colloquial*). Equivalent to 'incapable of'; *e.g.*, 'I don't seem to see it, my dear fellow; where does the advantage come in?'

Don't sell me a dog (*Soc.*, 1860). Do not deceive me. Derived from the experience that the purchase of a dog, most fanciers being thieves, was ever a deception. Very popular until 1870.

Don't think, I (*Mid. Class*, 1880). Emphatically meaning *do* think ; *e.g.*,

'So you've nailed my young woman— well that's a nice thin job, I don't think' —simply because he's quite sure of it.

Don't turn that side to London (*Peoples'*). Condemnation of any kind —of a patched coat or boots, the worst side of a joint of meat, some injury to the body, etc., etc. From the supposition that everything of the best is required in the metropolis. (*See* Turn the best side to London.)

Doogheno (*London, Back*, 19 *cent.*). This is a remarkably complicated specimen. It is composed of 'good' backwards, the letter 'h' to prevent the softening of the 'g' when brought next an 'e'. 'Eno' is of course 'one'.

It can't be denied that Booth has made a doogheno hit, and you ought to nark his bucket.—(1882.)

Edwin Booth was an American actor who (1881-82) obtained considerable success in London in Shakespearian characters.

If a chap happens to be a dab tros he gets on better than a doogheno who keeps himself quiet and never lets anybody Tommy Tripe know how clever he is.—*Cutting*.

Dook (*Peoples'*). A huge nose. Corruption of 'duke,' and referring to *the* 'Duke' — time of Wellington, who during the first half of the 19th century was, with intervals of unpopularity, styled 'the duke'. His Grace's high nose was hereditary. The title became shortened to this one word, and his nose being so exceptional, the title of the owner came by metaphor to represent a huge nose. To this day it is used. (*See* Boko.)

Dookin (*Thieves'*). Fortune-telling. Sixpenny horoscopes in by-ways and cast upon the lines of the palm of the hand, the left, that being nearest the heart. Hence the word—dook, dookes, being ancient slang for hand; generally used in plural. 'Put up yer dooks.' 'Dookin' has now become fashionable, and is called palmistry. Where all the hand is concerned (this in telling character), the term is chiromancy.

Door and hinge (*Lond., Peoples'*). Neck and breast of mutton, a joint which bends readily amongst the cervical vertebræ. Very graphic and humorsome. (*See* Stickings, Hyde Park Railings.)

Door-knocker (*Peoples'*, 1854). A ring-shaped beard formed by the cheeks and chin being shaved leaving a chain of hair under the chin, and upon each side of mouth—forming with moustache something like a door-knocker.

Charles Dickens had a moustache and a door-knocker beard.—E. Yates, *Recollections*, vol. i., p. 256.

Door-mat (*Colloquial*, 1856). The name given by the people to the heavy and unaccustomed beards which the Crimean heroes brought home from Russia in 1855-56, and which started the beard movement, much to the astonishment of French excursionists. By 1882 the term came to be applied to the moustache only, probably because about this time the tendency to shave the beard and wear only a very heavy moustache became prevalent.

While writing, a pal comes in and tells me that the City peelers are to be allowed to grow doormats.—*Cutting*.

The Corporation of London, always very conservative, only allowed the City police to wear moustaches in 1882.

He was a little joker with a red smeller and a small red doormat over his kisser.—*Cutting*.

Doormat (*Common Lond.*, 1880). Victory (*see* Grease - spot), meaning that the enemy was overcome, and so fallen that the victor wiped his feet upon the conquered—Væ Victis !

I guess that chucker-out won't hit me any more. I made a doormat of him.— *Cutting* (1883).

Doping (*Racing*, 1900). Hocussing rather than poisoning racehorses when about to run. In 1899-1900 large sums of money had been made by American betting-men at English race meetings. Gradually the conviction gained ground that runners were being tampered with in new and dangerous ways, resulting in more than temporary injury to the horses. Especially in the U.S.A. it was remarkable how frequently racers either died at or shortly after a race, or that they so went back that they were never raced again. In the U.S.A. the term used for the exercise of this nefarious usage of horses was called 'doping'—said to be derived from a proper name. The term came to be heard in England in the summer of 1900. In November of this year the Animals' Aid Society held a weakly organised meeting to devise means to meet these fraudulent practices. But it turned out that nobody present knew anything at all about the matter.

Dorothy (*Soc.*, 1888). Rustic love-making. From the mode of an opera-comique of this name (1887-88).

Those (letters) of the defendant were of the most amatory character, containing repeated promises, in Dorothy style, to be true to the plaintiff.—*D. N.*, 7th July 1888.

Dorsay (*Soc.*, 1830-45). Perfect. Count d'Orsay, of an old French family, led the fashion generally during these years; so much so that it was the highest praise to say he was a dorsay.

Dose of Locust (*N. York Policemen's*). A beating with fists.

Mullaley, smarting under the pain of the wound, gave Mr Supple a dose of locust, which induced him to accompany the officer to court.—*Newsp. Cutting.*

Dossy (*Street*). Elegant. Probably from Count d'Orsay (*q.v.*).

Dot and carry one (*Street*). Person with a wooden leg.

The 'dot' is the pegged impression made by all wooden legs before the invention of the modelled foot and calf. The 'one' is the widowed leg.

Dotted (*Tavern*, 19 *cent.*). Black-eyed. To 'dot' a gentleman is to punctuate him emphatically with a black-eye.

The chucker-out he dotted,
He got so blooming tight.
—*Cutting.*

Dotties Man (*Peoples'*). Greedy, grasping—giving a sprat to catch a herring.

Double-breasted water-butt smasher (*Street*). A man of fine bust —an athlete.

The Bobby said that Joey Fanatty (aged), described on the charge-sheet as the double-breasted water-butt smasher, was charged with a salt.—*Newsp. Cutting.*

Double intenders (*Peoples'*). Knock-down blows—labial or fistful.

Double-plated blow-hard (*Amer.*). A loud and contemptible boaster.

They went away believing I was an old liar and a double-plated blow-hard, and in a week no one would stop here.—*Newsp. Cutting.*

Double Scoop (*Military*, 1890). Hair parted in centre, and worn low— gave way to the quiff.

Dough-nut (*Amer. passing to England*). A baker, especially the German variety.

'Shut up, thou dough nut, or thy last moment may be thy next.'—*Cutting.*

Probably from the too frequent pale, flabby, doughy face of this sickly operative.

Dover Castle boarder (*Prison; Debtors'*). A circumscribed district around the Queen's Bench prison (Southwark Bridge Road), pulled down in 1881, was called the 'rules of the Bench'. Certain debtors, not imprisoned in the Bench itself, were compelled to sleep in this district, and they were thus called because the most prominent tavern in the neighbourhood was styled 'The Dover Castle'—much frequented by these poor debtors, who were therefore called 'boarders'. The house still exists. It was not a stone's-throw from the prison.

Down the banks (*Irish colloquial*). Failed; *e.g.*, 'I got down the banks for my pains'—meaning I failed only as a result. Probably the outcome of life amongst the bogs, which are scored with deep ditches, as the peat is cut perpendicularly. The water at the foot of the banks is frequently quite deep, often enough to go over a man's head.

Down the Lane and into the Mo (*Central London, Low*). Here the Lane is that called Drury; the 'Mo' is abbreviated 'Mogul Music Hall' (established 1850), and afterwards baptized The Middlesex. But the Lane clung to 'Mo'—probably a name given to the place generations since, when a public garden there was kept by some wonderful Indian.

What was the good, thought we, of saving your rhino, if you've got no girl to take for trots down the Lane or into the Mo.—*Cutting*, 1883.

Down the Road (*E. London Streets*). Showy, flashy. The road is the Mile End Road, which to frequent on a Sunday, in a good cart or 'shay', is the ambition of every costermonger and small trader in that district.

Down to the ground (*Peoples'*). Completely—from head to heels.

The character suits Rignold 'down to the ground'.—*Newsp. Cutting.*

Drag (*Theat.*) Petticoat or skirt used by actors when playing female parts. Derived from the drag of the dress, as distinct from the non-dragginess of the trouser.

Mrs Sheppard is now played by a man —Mr Charles Steyne, to wit. I don't like to see low coms. in drag parts, but must confess that Mr Steyne is really droll, without being at all vulgar.—*Ref.*, 24th July 1887.

Also given to feminine clothing by eccentric youths when dressing up in skirts.

Dragon (*Cornish*). Opprobrious distinction conferred on the men of Helston by their Cornish neighbours— especially the nearest.

A neighbourly legend of Helston— formerly Hellstone—in Cornwall, says that the borough was dropped from the clouds by the Evil One in the course of a provincial tour over the western county. To this moment, I understand, it is a deadly affront to call a Helston man a 'dragon'.—*D. T.*, 20th August 1896.

Drapery Miss (*Com. Class*). A girl of doubtful character, who dresses in a striking manner. Libellous generally. Degenerated from the time of Byron, who says in a note to st. 49 ca. xi. of *Don Juan*:—

'Drapery Misses': This term is probably anything now but a *mystery*. It was, however, almost so to me, when I first returned from the East, in 1811-12. It means a pretty, a high-born, a fashionable young female, well instructed by her friends, and furnished by her milliner with a wardrobe upon credit, to be repaid, when *married*, by her *husband*.

Drasacking (*Devon.*) Draw-sacking —idle, slow, dragging.

'Drasacking' is a common and cheap pastime, consisting of an aimless, pointless, shambling sauntering. The 'drasacking' householder, while an absolute tortoise himself, believes that a wise and just dispensation intended his servant-girl or hired man to be a hare.—*D. T.*, 19th October 1895.

Draw iron (*Amer.*). To present a pistol.

If every person who fancied himself aggrieved by his cabman were to 'draw iron', the nature of the cabman's shelter would have to be altered and made to correspond with the iron huts familiar to Irish police.—*Newsp. Cutting.*

Draw the Badger. (*See* Badger.)

Draw the dibs (*Bootmakers'*). To take wages—dibs being a trade term for money. Dibs are small nails, hence coins.

Draw the line at tick (*Serio-comics'*). A euphemism for declaration of virtue on the part of a serio-comic lady singer. 'I may sing a hot line or two, or take a present here or there, but I draw the line at tick,' the material in question being not a scheme of credit or 'tick', but a covered allusion to the textile fabric used for the covering of beds and mattresses.

Dree his weird (*Lancs.*). To bear trouble sadly.

Little do the unthinking youths who nowadays assemble at a wedding to 'guy' the 'best man' suspect that a generation ago a victim of this description would not have had to 'dree his weird' alone. His weird would have been dreed conjointly with him by a 'second best', a third best, down sometimes in a descending scale of excellence to an eighth best man.—*D. T.*, 3rd September 1895.

Dress for the part (*Society—drawn from Theatre,* 1870).—To act hypocritically.

The only two authors of real celebrity whom I can remember as having looked 'like themselves'—I mean their books— were Douglas Jerrold and Alexandre Dumas the Elder. Sham celebrities, on the other hand, 'dress for the part', and contrive to look that which they are, really, not.—G. A. Sala, in *Ill. Lond. News*, 16th December 1882.

Dressed up to the nines (*Com. London*). A eulogistic or sarcastic expression of opinion as to another's dress—according as the accent and manner of the speaker go. Corruption of 'Dressed to the eyen'. When 'eyen' (pl. of 'eye') was departing English, an 's' was added to give 'eyes' a modern plural—while the knowledge of 'eyen' remained. After a time 'eyen' lost its meaning, and the old plural was colloqualized into a comprehensive expression, and 'nines' followed. Concurrently, the expression 'dressed to the nines' took form, and is still used.

Drilling (*Workpeoples'*). Punishment by way of waiting, applied to needlewomen who make errors in their work.

There is a common punishment in these sweating warehouses when work is wrongly done. It is termed 'drilling'.

The woman could not, it seems, be sufficiently 'drilled' by merely being sent home to undo the work and do it again. She must be taught to be more careful by punishment a little more drastic than that, and accordingly she was told her bundle would be sent down to her, and till it came she must wait. 'The woman stood there expecting the parcel every minute for three days.'—*D. N.*, 26th February 1885. (*See* Sweater.)

Drinkitite (*Peoples*': *East London*). Thirst. The struggling populace, who chiefly joke (when they joke apart from abuse) over their struggles, having discovered 'bite-etite' as a jocose conversion of appetite—came naturally to give it a correlative in 'drinkitite'. There is also grim satire in the application of the last syllable, which is the common word for 'drunk', hence 'drinkitite' as a pendent to 'bite-etite' is positively perfect. An East London gentleman gently referring to his continued libations would evasively but emphatically observe : ' I've been on the drinkitite right through the week.'

Driving at (*Peoples*'). Energetic action. Good example of phrase coming out of general characteristic vigour of the race. ' He must be driving at something.' Even the word drive, without the progressive 'ing' or the emphatic 'at', is a perfect English word.

Drop (*Amer.-Eng.*). To cause to drop.

About two minutes after he had the revolver his body was swung a little on one side, when I pointed my revolver and fired where I thought I could drop him.—*D. N.*, 5th September 1884.

Self-defence of a burglar named Wright. Also, to understand.

'Ah ?' sobbed the girl, 'you do not drop.'—*Newsp. Cutting.*

Drop (*Society and Sporting*, 1850). To lose (money). A racing man or society man who fails to win money on a race never loses it—he always drops it; *e.g.*, ' I dropped awfully on the Leger.'

Drop (*Thieves*'). The modern gallows. A very significant word to describe modern capital punishment. At Tyburn tree the man stood in the cart, which was drawn from under him. Afterwards, at Newgate, the sufferer was pulled up. But when some genius invented the falling flap, which dropped from under the feet of the victim, the significance of the word became evident.

Drop the cue (*Billiard-players*'). To die.

Drouthy (*Scotch*). Wavering person ; one of no settled will.

Leading citizens were occupied the greater part of the night before the polling-day watching doubtfuls, known locally as ' drouthies ' ; every voter was pledged ; not a few were 'nursed' ; the halt, the blind, and the deaf were escorted to the polling-booth.—*D. N.*, 27th October 1884.

Drum (*Thieves*', 1860). A house.

Close to the gardens the prisoner said ' What do you think of those "drums" there ?' and witness said, ' I don't think much of them.'—*Felon's Queen's Evidence.*

Drum is not usually applied to a respectable quaker-like house, but to any one frequented by, say, soldiers. Fielding uses this word in *Tom Jones*, Bk. xvii., ch. 6.

Drum (*Thieves*'). A cell—precisely because a drum is an enclosure.

Drunk as a lord (*Streets*). Very intoxicated. Descent from 18th century middle-class—when drunkenness was honourable.

'Drunk as a lord ' and 'Sober as a judge' have ceased to have any recognisable application to the nobility and the Judicial Bench. Judges, in these later days, are as sober as other folk, take them as a class, no more and no less, and the same applies to the Peerage.—*D. T.*, 27th May 1888.

Drunk as Floey (*Peoples*'). Who it appears was dead drunk—may be a corruption of Flora, but probably a confusion between that comparatively familiar name and 'Chloe'. If the latter, good instance of the power Swift had to popularize. In the dean's poems Chloe is always more or less under the influence of drink.

Drunk as a polony (*Lond.*). At first sight this expression might be accepted as very literal, seeing that a sausage cannot stand, and that a polony (corruption of Bologna—celebrated for its sausages) exists under the same conditions. But it is more probably one of frequent but obscure expressions derived from the French, who to this day say : 'Soul comme un Polonnais'—this probably took its origin in reference to Maurice Maréchal de Saxe, who, in his drinks, was more

Polish than French. On the other hand, the Pole, for drinking comparisons, has long held in France the position maintained in England by the cobbler—'drunk as a cobbler'.

Druriolanus (*Theat.*, 1885). Drury Lane Theatre. Playful outcome of calling Mr Augustus Harris, afterwards Sir Augustus Harris, the Emperor Augustus. The word also suggests that other directorial personage, Coriolanus.

The vast stage of Her Majesty's is not a whit less advantageous for the display of its spectacular effects than that of the house which gives to Mr Harris's telegraphic address of 'Druriolanus' its special fitness and significance.—*D. N.*, 12th October 1886.

Augustus Druriolanus is their president, and they are going to bring off a four-oared race from Barnes to Hammersmith on October 31.—*Ref.*, October 1886.

Dry Bobs (*Eton*). A cricketer. (*See* Wet Bobs.)

Dry canteen (*Milit.*). (*See* Wet canteen.)

Dry guillotine (*Franco-English*). Severe imprisonment. From the penal French colony at Cayenne, a fearful place.

Cayenne is so malarious that transportation thither used to be styled the dry guillotine.—*Graphic*, 1st November 1884.

Dry land (*Rhyming*). To understand.

Whenever you see a chap after your judy, the best thing to do is to go up to her and tell her that you don't mean to stand her blooming kid, that you dry land her emag.—*Cutting*.

Dry up (*Anglo-Amer.*). To cease because effete—from mining districts of W. America, where, when the mountain torrents dry up in summer, mining operations necessarily cease.

Duca di Somevera (*Peoples'*). Liberal Italian translation of Duke of Somewhere. On a par with the Earl le Bird, Sir Tinly Someone, and Swift's Lord Nozoo.

The unhappy purchaser of a supposed masterpiece must be prepared to hear that his picture is a replica of one in the Isle of Wight, or at Madrid, or in Lord Blank's gallery, or in the Palazzo of the Duca di Somevera.—*D. N.*, 16th June 1883.

Duchess (*Silk trade*). The shapely girl upon whom mantles and jackets are tried to enable ladies to judge of the effect.

The Duchess—living lay figures receive that title, in addition to a whole pound a week.—Besant & Rice, *The Golden Butterfly*, vol. i., ch. 11.

Duchess (*Peoples'*). Mother — invariable title given between familiar friends when the mother of either is being asked after. 'How's the Duchess, Bob?'

The wife, under similar conditions, would be asked after as 'The Old Clock'—a title whose derivation a sharp-witted man may find in the first chapter of Sterne's *Tristram Shandy*.

Duck-pond (*Navy*). The shallow bathing-place on the lower deck, effected by a rig-up of sail-cloth, made watertight, fixed to the deck, and in which the cadets wash and roll themselves, in batches, under the watchful eyes of a warrant officer.

Ducks (*Soc.*, 1840). White trousers of a peculiarly woven cotton fabric—mentioned here because it has been said to be a corruption of 'dux', the name given to the material by the Scotch manufacturer who discovered it. Dux was, if not is, used much by the Scotch. (*See* Lindley Murray's *English Grammar*).

Duffer-fare (*Lond. Cabmen's*). In the neighbourhood of the theatres, as closing time approaches, the police will not allow cabmen to drive empty cabs through the Strand highway. In order to get past the police, and so obtain a chance of a fare when the theatres vomit their thousands, cabmen will ask a pedestrian to be 'chummy' enough to jump in, and be driven into the Strand. Here arrived the 'duffing-fare', quits the cab, the driver is in the Strand—and keeps there till 11 P.M., when the theatres disgorging, he gets a fare that is no duffer, and who pays more or less nobly.

Duffing (*Soc. and Peoples'*, 1880 on). The outcoming adjective of 'duffer' and 'duff'. By 1897 this word became one of the most active qualitatives in the language. As a verb it had by this time come to be thoroughly conjugated; *e.g.*, 'He duffs everything he touches.' 'He is the most duffing duffer that ever duffed.' 'He has duffed, he does duff, and he will duff for ever.'

Duke (*Street*). Nose. (*See* Dook.)

Duke o' Seven Dials (*Low Class*, 1875). Satirical peerage bestowed upon any male party dressing or behaving above or beyond his immediate surroundings. There is no corresponding duchess. A young person of airs and graces is generally spoken of as about to marry the peer in question; *e.g.*, 'I'm going to be the duchess of the Dook o' Seven Dials.'—*Parody Song, Drury Lane Pantomime*, 1884.

Duke's (The) (*Lond.*, 19 *cent.*). A nickname of the Argyll Rooms in Windmill Street, Haymarket, W., now replaced by the Trocadero. In allusion to the Duke of Argyll.

Why should the Argyll be suppressed and the Pavilion be tolerated? Of the two 'the Pav.' is far worse than 'the Duke's'.—*Newsp. Cutting.*

Dukey (*Street, Boys'*). A penny gaff. The four-farthing theatre obtained this title from a Jewish proprietor of one of these temples of art. His nose was very prominent (1840-50). In these days such a feature begot its owner the title of duker, from the hero of Waterloo, emphatically 'the duke' from 1815 to 1850. The 'y' here is an instance of endearing addition.

Dumbed (*Amer. Puritanic*). Evasion of 'damned'.

The man who believes that the Jews are such a pack of dumbed fools, as to seriously entertain any such plan, should be shut up in an asylum for the feeble-minded.—*Newsp. Cutting.*

Dummy (*Thieves'*). Loaf—probably from the softness of the crumb.

Dumplin' on (*L. Classes*). Enceinte.

Dun (*Peoples'*). To worry for money. One of the forcible words gleaned from proper names. Of course lexicographers trace it to Early English, Anglo-Saxon, or some other remote source. Webster says it is taken from the Saxon *dynan*, to claim. But the Saxons did not dun—they recovered their debts by more forcible means.

Here is its true origin: It owes its birth to one John Dun, a famous bailiff of the town of Lincoln; so extremely active, and so dexterous was this man at the management of his rough business, that it became a proverb when a man refused to pay his debts, 'Why don't you dun him?' It originated in the reign of Henry VII.

Durn (*Amer.-Eng.*). Another evasion of 'damned'. (*See* Darn.)

Worms that rise early are caught—gobbled up by birds every time. The worm's a durn fool to get up so early.—*Newsp. Cutting.*

Dust (*American Teamsters*). A mere light touch of anything.

The visiting, the music, the marching, the cheering and the excitement of the reunion, with a little dust of liquor, had made him feel quite excited.—*Newsp. Cutting.*

Dust (*Amer.*, 1880). To walk quickly—suggested by the dust thrown up in the act. Indirect proof of the dry nature of American weather.

One grabbed a rope that was on the sidewalk where they was moving a building, and pa got up and dusted. You'd a died to see pa run.—*Newsp. Cutting.*

Dusting (*Boer War*, 1899-1900). Finishing the war — complement of 'Sweeping up'.

North of Pretoria there is still a good deal of dusting to be done.—*D. T.*, 2nd November 1900.

Dustman's bell (*Nursery*). Time for bed. Origin obscure. Is it Dowseman's bell—curfew bell—time to put out ('dowse') the lights? Has it any association with 'dowse the glim'? Johnson gives: 'To fall suddenly into the water'—which would certainly put out the light.

Dust out (*Amer.-Eng.*). To retreat quickly, 'levant'. Suggested by dust thrown up by rapid walking.

I quickly got inside, locked the door, and dusted out the back way.—*Newsp. Cutting.*

Dust up (*Milit.*, 19 *cent.*). An engagement—from the dust made by the movements.

A member of the Royal Army Medical Corps, who, in his own words, 'got through the Graspan dust-up nicely', was sent, etc.—*D. T., Boer War*, 16th January 1900.

Dusty (*Navy*). A ship's steward's assistant—probably because this hard-worked official looks it.

Dutch (*Peoples'*). Retreat—especially from a creditor, and still more especially when accompanied by furniture removed from a tenancy, the rent of which has not been handed over.

'We did a dutch with everything—even down to the coal-hammer.'

Dutch Cheese   *Early Riser*

'Yere comes 'Anner's young bloke—I think I'll do a quick dutch.' I make myself agreeable, and then say, 'I must do a Dutch'.—*Cutting*.

Dutch cheese (*Low London*, 1882). A bald-head; derived from the fact that Dutch cheeses are generally made globular.

Dutch daubs (*Amer.*, 1883). Common paintings of still-life, imported into America by the ten thousands. Introduced by the *New York Herald* (April 1883) in reference to a political measure which placed a 35 per cent. *ad valorem* duty upon imported pictures. The term soon came to mean a bad picture of any kind.

The term 'Dutch Daub' has fetched me a little. I call to mind that in almost every refreshment buffet and miner hotel bar in the Southern and Western States you come across oil-paintings of still-life.—G. A. Sala, *Ill. London News*, 28th April 1883.

Dutch row (*Street*). A got-up unreal wrangle. Rarely heard. On all fours—with 'une querelle d'Allemand'.

Dutchman (*Soc. of a sort*, 1870 on). Name for champagne of Deutz and Gelderman. Here the first name is pronounced Dutch, and the last syllable of the second name is added.

Duty (*Lower Class, Respectable*). Interest on pawnbrokers' pledges. Evasive synonym for interest.

Dying duck in a thunderstorm (*Peoples'*). Lackadaisical.

'Whoa, call her good-looking? That dona with a mug like a dying duck in a thunderstorm, and smiling as if she'd had a dose of castor oil and didn't like it.'—*Cutting*.

Dynamite (*Mid.-class*, 1888). Tea. Early in February two men, Americans, were tried in connection with Irish-American attempts to do injury in this country with dynamite. In the course of the trial (*D.N.*, 4th Feb. 1888) it came out that dynamite was always called 'tea'—for the purposes of concealment. The word took at once.

Dynamite Racket (*Amer. - Eng.*, 1885). Invented contemptuously to describe this sort of explosion.

New York loves a show, whether a parade, a big funeral, a blazing fire, or a dynamite racket.—*Newsp. Cutting*.

Dynamiter (1882). A user of dynamite for illegal purposes. It soon came to be a synonym for any violent man or woman, especially the latter; *e.g.*, 'My eye, ain't she jest a dynamiter?' When 'tart' came to be common passing English, it was applied to this word; *e.g.*, 'Well, she may be tasty, but to my mind she's a dynamitart.' (*See* Petroleuse.)

Dyspepsia (*Milit. Hospital*). Drink delirium. D.T.s.

E

E.C. Women (*Snob Soc.*, 1881). Wives of city people, so named from the city forming the East Central postal district of the metropolis.

E.P. (*Theat.*). Experienced Playgoer.

The experienced playgoer will readily guess that Branson compasses the (apparent) destruction of Gerald, and anon returns to Ballyvogan to personate the heir—and the e.p. will be right.—*Newsp. Cutting*.

E.R. (*Oxford 'er'*). Suffix applied in every conceivable way to every sort of word. Began early in the Queen's reign and has never lapsed. A new word in 'er' is generally started by some quite distinguished Oxonian—generally a boating man, sometimes a debater.

There has been a furore at Oxford in recent years for word-coining of this character, and some surprising effects have been achieved. A freshman became a 'fresher' in the earlier Victorian era, and promises to remain so for all time and existence.—*D. T.*, 14th August 1899.

Ear-mark (*Parliam.*, 19 *cent.*). ?—Note of interrogation, or enquiry. Used by M.P.'s when reading Bills and other papers to draw their future attention. A sort of rebus, from this character being something like an 'ear'. Word often heard in Parliament.

Nervous reference is made to the assertion of the Chancellor of the Exchequer that certain items of Transvaal revenue would be ear-marked for the purpose of the war contribution. —*Newsp. Cutting*.

Early riser (*Anglo-Amer.*—returning emphasized to England). A sharp, business-like person. Probably from 'Early to bed and early to rise, Makes a man healthy, and wealthy, and wise,' or again "'Tis the early bird catches the worm' (who unfortunately is for himself, too early a riser). In U.S.A. this phrase takes several shapes—the best being 'You'd have to get up early to be before me!'

The general idea is that anybody who is going to over-reach Hetty Green (New York), or do her out of a fraction of those millions, will have to be a very early riser indeed. She gives no costume dances, and never will; she would be better liked if she did.—*D. T.*, 10th February 1897.

Early purl (*Street*, 19 *cent.*). A drink made of hot beer and gin, so named because taken early on a cold morning. A song ran—
'I'm damned if I think
There's another such drink
As good early purl.'

When princes and princesses are born there is a lavish distribution of 'caudle', a mysterious beverage of the nature whereof we confess ourselves as ignorant as of that of 'early purl'.

Early-turners (*Music-hall*). Scornful reference to an inferior artist who takes his 'turns' early in the evening, before the audience is thrang, or fashionable, or both. From 8.0 to 8.30. (*See* Enders.)

Earth-hunger (*Political*, 1880). Greed to possess land. Supposed to have come from Ireland, and in that relation to refer to the desires of peasants to obtain a bit of land. In England used to define the passion of landed proprietors to add to their land at any cost.

East of the Griffin (*W. London*). East London. Replaced 'East of Temple Bar'. Outcome of the city Griffin on his wonderful pedestal replacing Temple Bar.

At the Pavilion Theatre, you ought to know by this time, even if you never go east of the Griffin. they do things in a way that is not excelled at many West End theatres that I am acquainted with. —*Ref.*, 11th October 1885.

Eat strange meat (*Soc.*, 19 *cent.*). A delicate evasion of cannibalism.

We feel much less horror than in face of the naked fact of cannibalism practised by civilized men for the sake of dear life. Life is not worth the imputation of having 'eaten strange meat'.—*D. N.*, 14th August 1884.

Eat the leek. To apologize. From Shakespeare.

Eat vinegar with a fork (*Peoples'*). The extreme of acid sharpness—in conversation. The vinegar alone would set teeth on edge, the fork intensifies the condiment.

Eatings (*Peoples'*; old). An ancient word now represented by board; *e.g.*, 'The room 'ull be 'arf-a-crown a week, without eatin's'—for there are lodgers who would expect banquets thrown in with a sixpenny bed for the night.

Eautybeau (*Music-hall transposition*). Beauty.
Do I know him? Do I rumble the eautybeau? What do you think?—*Cutting*.

Ebenezar (*Puritanic*). An exclamation of rejoicing—from the Hebrew. George Eliot often uses this word in her diary.

Eccer (*Oxford 'er'*). Exercise—both c's hard.

Every man after lunch devotes himself to 'eccer', which is, in ordinary parlance, exercise. This may take the shape of 'footer', or a mild constitutional known as a 'constituter', while if any one lounges idly about he is, of course, a 'slacker'.—*D. T.*, 14th August 1899.

Edgarism (*Club*, 1882). This was the new satirical name given to agnosticism, or rather atheism upon the production of Tennyson's prose play *The Promise of May*. The villain-hero, Edgar, is an educated man of position, who bases his arguments for free love and free will upon a denial of the deity. This bit of historical passing English died with the play, which, while never successful, was most unfairly damned by critics and public. The former appear to have resented the poet's despotic associations of free thought with immorality —as a necessary outcome of atheism.

Edge (*Criminal*). To bolt, escape. Probably from 'dodge'—and retire.

One of the other two called out 'Edge' (a slang term to be off), and they ran away.—*D. N.*, November 1886.

Eekcher (*Peoples'*, 1882). Inversion of cheek—audacity.

Well, modesty is not marketable nowadays, and perhaps Tippy is right to pin his faith to the doctrine that there's nothing like 'eekcher'.—*Newsp. Cutting*.

Eel-skin (*Soc.*, 1881). A name given to the tight skirt worn at this date; *e.g.*, 'She wore an eel-skin of London smoke.' (*See* One leg.)

Eenque (*Streets; transposition*). Queen. A very popular example of this queer mode of word-making.

So shout, you beggars, shout; God save the Eenque.—*Cutting*.

Eetswe (*Transposition*). Sweet—a very common word in low life; *e.g.*, 'Lord, I *am* eetswe on that udyju' (judy).

Eff., Effy. (*Theatr.*) Abbreviation of Effingham, a small theatre once in E. London.

Efficient effrontery (*Soc.*, 1885). Clever audacity—brought in by J. W. M'N. Whistler in February by a lecture at Prince's Hall, called 'Ten o'clock', from the hour at which it began—P.M. It was an attack upon art-critics in general, and Ruskin in particular. The lecturer used this term, which at once became familiar in society in a hundred ways.

Mr Whistler's lecture is distinctly a surprise. He deprecates the tone in which such subjects are too frequently handled. The commonplace world endowed with 'efficient effrontery' no longer reverently approaches Art as a dainty goddess, but 'chucks her under the chin'.—*D. N.*, 21st February 1885.

Eicespie (*Transposition*). Pieces. An interesting example of the rough logic used in phrase-making. 'Pieces' is a figure of speech for money, and there is the ordinary transposition. But that is not all. The *i* being left as the initial would destroy the ordinary vowel sound of 'piece'; therefore the *e* is placed before the *i*.

Does the artful, and he draws the eicespie.—*Cutting*.

Eighteen-carat lie (*Amer.*, 1883). A good. sound lie, 18-carat gold being good, thorough metal.

Eighty Club (*Soc.*). A club formed in the year ''80', shortly before the general election, with the object of promoting political education, and stimulating Liberal organization by supplying Liberal meetings in London and the country with speakers and lecturers.

Eiley Mavourneen (*Commercial*). A non-paying debtor. Refers to the line in Moore's song, 'It may be for months, and it may be for never.'

Elaborate the truth (*Soc.*). To lie.

Elderly Jam (*Peoples'*, 1880 on). Aging woman. Qualified jam; *e.g.*, 'Elderly jam is—elderly jam, and heaven preserve it, for man turns from it.'

Electrate (1890 on). To describe locomotion by electricity.

They go by train to Bourne End, where they take to the river and 'electrate' to Medmenham Abbey and Henley. Electrate is one of the recently-invented verbs to express the new mode of locomotion, to which the words sail and steam are inapplicable.—*Newsp. Cutting*.

Applied more recently to violent and eccentric meetings; *e.g.*, 'They electrated from 8 to 11.15 P.M. Everything was amended, and then they amended the amendments.'

Electrocution (*Amer.-Eng.*, 1890). Execution by electricity. Built upon execute.

Elephant's Trunk (*Street; rhyming*). Drunk. The phrase became incomprehensible by the dropping of the rhyming. 'Oh, he's elephants' (*i.e.*, intoxicated) will, in time to come, exercise many an etymologist.

(Daddy) And what am I to be? (Mother G.) Get out—you're drunk. (P. Char.) You shall be—let's see—Baron Elephant's Trunk.

A capital example of a common bit of slang phrase locally applied, for this line is found in an Elephant and Castle Theatre Pantomime. It should be added that 'daddy' was a satire upon the Blue Ribbon movement—he belonging to it, and yet always being 'elephant's trunk'.

Elevator (*Soc.*, 1882 on). The crinolette. For some years the dress below the back of the waist was almost flat, when in this year bows were seen there, and then followed the crinolette, which, throwing up the dress, obtained this satiric name amongst young men, and was afterwards accepted literally.

Elijah Two (*Amer. - Eng.*). A false prophet. From one Dr Dowie, an American peripatetic preacher who first gained this title. His son was dubbed Elijah Three.

Ellersby (*Peoples'*, 1870 on). The initials of the London School Board. No particular point beyond brevity—said to be the soul of wit.

L.S.B. Extravagance: The extraordinary extravagance of the London School Board is strikingly shown by the constant increase in the amount paid by the Strand Board of Works.—*People*, 20th September 1896.

Ellessea (*L. Compositors*). The initials of London Society of Compositors.

Elongated kisser. A wide mouth. 'Yer looks like a lady,' I says; 'then why do yer wipe yer elongated kisser with a whopping great red stook?'—*Cutting.*

Empress Pidgeon (*Naval*, 1876 on). Pigeon is discussion, and Empress Pigeon was a palaver with Queen Victoria for a basis. Now Emperor Pidgeon.

Endacotted (*Socialist*, 1887). Illegally arrested. Attributed to Mrs Annie Besant. Derived evidently, by partial similarity in sound, from Boycott, and referring to a policeman of the name who was tried and acquitted (1887) upon an indictment for illegal arrest of a young dressmaker, whom he swore was a well-known woman of the town. After a time the term was reduced to 'cotted' following the common tendency to shorten phrases and even words.

Ender (*Music-hall*). A performer of inferior quality, even inferior to an 'early-turner,' (*q.v.*) who only 'goes on' after the great hours. Enders perform from 11 to 11.30—when most musichalls are emptying—except on 'bens'.

End-men (*Negro Minstrels*). The two comic black souls who enliven with small wit a negro entertainment, and sit at either end of the line of seated performers. Now passed to black comics who even sit in the midst.

On the stage there are sixty of these dark coloured minstrels, whose voices are interposed with striking effect in many of the choruses. The 'end men' are numerous, and amply endowed with a boisterous humour.—*Newsp. Cutting.*

Engineer (*Amer.-Eng.*, 1880). To manage, manipulate, direct. Outgrowth of railway and steam era generally.

Afterwards you may look out for Daly's Company from New York, engineered by Terriss.—*Ref.*, 8th June 1884.

English pluck (*Peoples'*). Money, figuratively; *e.g.*, 'Got any English pluck to-day?' (Have you any money with which to gamble by means of tossing?)

Enobs (*Back slang*). Bone, in ordinary plural. A very favourite specimen because by chance the inversion is a sort of rebus, bones showing affording a study of 'knobs'.

But he swallowed a box of matches one day which burnt away all the fat and left the mere enobs you see now.—*Cutting.*

Enthuse (*Amer.*). Abbreviation of 'create enthusiasm'. Not yet accepted in England.

An entirely new play, called *Uncle Tom's Cabin*, with muzzled bloodhounds in their stellar rôle, did not enthuse the manager nor his patrons of the past week.—*Newsp. Cutting.*

Enthuzimuzzy (*Soc.*, 19 cent.). Satirical reference to enthusiasm. Attributed to Braham the terror.

Entire Squat (*Amer.*, *reaching Eng.* 1883). A houschold, including wife, children, servants, and furniture.

Espysay (*Stable*, 1880 on). A word composed of the letters S.P.C.A.—initials of the Society for the Prevention of Cruelty to Animals. Secretive in its nature, being created by people about horses and cattle, many of whom go about in savage fear of this valuable society.

Essex calves (*Provincial*). A contemptuous designation of Essexmen, always looked down upon by more prosperous Suffolk.

Essex lion. Lion is a variant of calf. Not used in Essex, but against it; especially by superior Kent, over the way, on the south side of the Thames. Interesting as showing intercounty hostilities, now passing away. The men of Kent or Kentish men (between whom there would appear to be great differences) have always belonged to an advanced part of England, and have escaped satire by reason of their superiority. Probably they gave their county neighbours their well-known sobriquets—Hampshire Hogs, Sussex Sows, Surrey Swine. Middlesex they avoided, but Essex, separated from them by the Thames, and inferior, as a county, to Kent, as indeed it remains to this day, was specially honoured with a title.

Establish a funk (*Oxford*). To create a panic—invented by a great bowler, at cricket, who enlivened this distinction with some cannon-ball bowling which was equivalent amongst the enemy to going into action. Funk for panic, dismay, alarm—is superior to origin. Probably from establish a suit in whist.

Euro! (*Navy*). Seamen's name for the Europa—a happy example of the sailor's love of getting in a final *o*, as in 'what oh!', 'what cheer oh!', etc.

Europe on the chest (*Army*). Home-sickness. Used chiefly by soldiers in India, who commit offences sometimes in order to be sent home.

Sir, they are not all bad at the bottom of them, but they have had at times the fever, and ague and their heart grows faint for England, and then they get what the driver terms Europe on the chest, and at the same time he is not particular what he does as long as he has a chance of coming to England.—*Letter by Convict, D. N.*, 3rd November 1885.

Even with, To get. A vigorous use of this word, to procure equality with one who has bested the speaker, *e.g.*, 'Never fear, I'll get even with him yet.'

Evening wheezes (*Peoples'*). False news, spread in evening halfpenny papers in order to sell them.

Eventuate. To result. A direct importation from America, and not at all wanted.

'It appeared as though we were committed to a conflict with the House of Lords of a nature so strenuous and so exciting that it might possibly have eventuated in something like a revolution.'—*H. Richard, M.P., Speech*, 1st January 1885.

Everlasting knock (*Amer.-Eng.*). The stroke of death.

And so he closes his career. He may be far happier as a man than he has ever been, but as a ruling prince he has taken the everlasting knock.—*Ref.*, 10th March 1889.

Everything is nice in your garden (*Soc., passing to People*, 1896 on). A gentle protest against self-laudation; *e.g.*, 'I don't wish to praise myself, but I believe I'm the greatest living tenor, in this world at all events!' Reply: 'Yes, yes, everything is nice in your garden!' This is said to be derived from one of the young princesses (probably a daughter of the Princess Beatrice) who made this reply when something in her garden at Osborne was praised by Her Majesty. If this is a true statement, it forms one of the very rare phrases that have come down from the precincts of the throne.

Ewigkeit (*Soc.*, 1880). This German word for 'eternity' came to be used not so much in adulation of Carlyle as in order to fall in with the bantering spirit of treating religious speculation, which began to grow rapidly in this year. It spread slowly, and by 1883 was found in popular journals.

All these things have vanished temporarily into the 'ewigkeit', to yield the field to beer and spirits—the people's drink, the birthright of every free-born Briton.—*Ref.*, 17th May 1885.

Exceedings (*Oxford*). Expenditure beyond income. A delicate evasion.

Extra (*Theatrical*). An individual of the great brigades who 'go on', but do not speak, sing, or dance. An extra does but fill the eye. Generally a pretty girl, of no talent, perhaps with a passion for the stage—perhaps with ulterior intentions.

Extra pull (*Operatives'*). Advantage, or disadvantage, as the case may be. As an advantage, it is a figure of speech from the extra pull of the handle of the beer engine in public-houses (*See* Long Pull)—a pull which flushes a spirt of beer into 'their own jugs' after the proper measure, in the publican's pewter, has been shot in. As a disadvantage—refers to the extremely troublesome tooth in the dentist's grip. All depends on the context.

Extradition Court (*Polit.*). The second justice-room at Bow Street (London). Name given jocularly by officials. Good example of the mode in which passing English grows out of the history of the day.

The case was taken in the second court, which is commonly called the Extradition Court, because nearly all the extradition cases are heard in it.—*D. N.*, 10th April 1883.

Extreme Rockite (*Clerical*). One who believes in the Rock newspaper, and preaches on its basis.

In a recent issue of a contemporary, for instance, we find a 'liberal' rector asking for a fellow labourer, who among other qualifications must be 'an extreme Rockite'.—*Newsp. Cutting.*

Eye in a sling (*Peoples'*). Crushed, defeated. From the doleful appearance presented by a sufferer with a bandage over the suffering eye.

Eye peeled (*W. Amer.*). Eyes well opened; peeled away from drooping lids; on the watch.

The Librarian was instructed to keep his eye peeled for a stray copy of a Chinese hymn book which might be bought cheap.—*Newsp. Cutting.*

F

F.C.'s (*Theat.*). False Calves (*i.e.* paddings used by actors in heroic parts to improve the shape of the legs).

F.F.V. (*Anglo-Amer. Soc.*). Distinguished. Initials of First Families (of) Virginia. Used quite seriously in the South of the U.S.A. and satirically in the North. The origin of the use of the letters may be traced to Massinger's *City Madam*, Act V., sc. 1 (acted in 1622).

Face the music. To fearlessly meet difficulties.

Before sailing Mr Cecil Rhodes gave a brief interview to some reporters. He stated that he would not resign his seat in the Cape Parliament. 'I shall meet my detractors. I will face the music.'—*D. T.*, 18th January 1896.

Face ticket (*British Museum*). A ticket is required for the Reading Room. It is never asked for when a constant reader passes the janitors. Nothing is said—the passer-by has a face ticket.

Fade (*Pure Amer.*). Antithesis of masher and dude. Either of these ornamental beings gone shabby.

A young lady employed at one of the Exposition displays rather took the shine off of a fade the other day. The fade, recently a dude, walked up to the place where she was stationed, etc.—*Newsp. Cutting.*

Fair cop (*Thieves'*). Undoubted arrest; 'fair' here means 'thorough', while 'cop' is from Early English for 'catch'.

Fair herd (*Oxf. Univer.*). Good attendance of strangers.

Foreigners are sometimes busy, or indifferent, or afraid of the Channel, and many promising schemes for a 'fair herd' on Commemoration Day have broken down owing to this cause.—*D. N.*, 13th June 1883.

Fair itch (*Street*). Utter imitation. Equally vulgar and vigorous.

Fair trod on (*Street*, 1887 on). Most ill-used.

'Oh, the yeroines o' them penny novelettes—yer good old penny ones—none o' yer 'apenny ones for me—o' them yeroines—arn't they fair trod on?'—Bessie Bellwood (serio-comic, Jan. 1891).

Fair warning (*Street*). Manly and frank intimation.

Faire Charlemagne (17 *cent.*, *Court*). To know when to leave off—especially at cards. A corruption of 'faire chut la main'—to make quiet the hand; that is, do not go on manipulating the cards, 'chut' being the equivalent of the English 'hush'. Said to be used by Louise de Querouilles, known as Mother Carwell, and afterward as the Duchess of Portsmouth—a very economic and long-headed Bretonne.

That feat which the French describe by the mysterious expression, 'faire Charlemagne'—the feat of leaving off a winner—is one of the most difficult in the world to perform.—*D. T.*, 22nd April 1896.

Fairy (*Lower Peoples'*). A debauched, hideous old woman, especially when drunk.

Fairy, To go a (*Theat.*). To toss for a penn'orth of gin, meaning that a fairy takes very little. In use amongst the minor literary men.

Fairy tales (*Mid. Class*, 1899 on). Untruths.

Mr Kruger, for the information of his sympathisers in America, has told a Chicago journalist one of his pretty little fairy tales, the only truth in which is that some burghers are again taking up arms.—*D. T.*, 4th July 1900.

Fake a curtain (*Theat.*, 1884). Reference to 'Take a curtain', 'Curtain-taker', and 'Lightning curtain-taker', will alone enable the student to comprehend this term. To fake a curtain is to agitate the act-drop after it has fallen, and so perhaps thereby induce a torpid audience to applaud a little, and justify the waiting actor to 'take a curtain'. The manager himself may direct this operation, but it is generally the stage-manager who manipulates the manœuvre.

Fake a picture (*Artistic*, 1860 on). To obtain an effect by some adroit, unorthodox means. In this sense it is difficult to say where swindling ends and genius begins. It is much used by inferior artists.

Fake a poke (*Thieves'*). To pick, or manipulate, a pocket. This phrase is a singular revival. Johnson has 'Fake—amongst seamen a pile of rope,' and as to poke—'a pocket or small bag'. 'I will not buy a pig in a poke!'—Camden.

He denied that when entering the music hall he was accused by a lady of picking her pocket, and further said that when called out he did not say he had never 'faked a poke' in his life.—*People*, 6th September 1896.

Fake pie (*Straitened Soc.*, 1880).— A towards-the-end-of-the-week effort at pastry, into which go all the 'orts', 'overs', and 'ends' of the week. *See* Resurrection pie—a term which this has superseded.

Fakement Chorley (*Dangerous Classes*). A private mark, especially on the outside of houses and in thieves' kitchens.

Fal (*Rhyming*, 1868). Represents 'gal' (girl).

Fall in the thick (*Street*). To become dead drunk. Full of metaphor. Black beer is called thick, so is mud; the phrase suggests equal misery whether the patient plunged in the mud, or rambled into drunkenness.

Fall-downs (*Street*, 19 cent.). The fragments of cookshop puddings which fall down while rapidly slicing up the puddings for sale; fragments which are finally collected on a plate, and sold for a halfpenny. A boy will rush in, and, with the air of a general at least, say: ''A'porth o' fall-downs'. Conquered when the reply comes, 'Hall sold!'

Fancy oneself (*Mid. Classes*). On good terms with oneself.

They had never known a Government which, if he might use the language of the street, 'fancied itself' to the extent to which the present Government did.— *D. T.*, 14th December 1897.

Fanned with a slipper (*Amer.-Eng.*, 1880 on). Simply spanked, the vibratory action suggesting the fanning.

Miss Lulu Valli made a hit at once as the demon child, Birdikins, who is threatened to be 'fanned with the slipper' of her devoted but erratic mother.—*D. T.*, 2nd February 1897.

Fanning the hammer (*W. Amer.*, 1886). Brilliantly unscrupulous. Instantaneously active, equal to energetic in the highest. Example of application of one term to varying meanings. Derived from West American gamblers wiring back the trigger of their revolvers, so that its stop-action is arrested. The six barrels of the revolver are discharged by rapidly striking back the hammer with the outer edge of the right hand, while the revolver is held in the left. This vibratory action of the right hand is the fanning. No aim can be taken, and fanning is only successful in a crowd. Six bullets will generally clear a crowd. So rapid is word adaptation in the States that already the term 'fanner' is used to describe an unscrupulously brave man.

Far away (*Lower Classes*, 1884). Pawned. From a song, a parody upon 'Far, far away'. One line ran, 'Where are my Sunday clothes?' To which the singer answered, 'Far, far away'. The 'far away' is mine uncle's. Passed into a verb; *e.g.*, 'I far-awayed my tools this blessed day —I did!'

Far gone (*Theat.*, 1882). Exhausted, or worn out, figuratively.

Miss Gilchrist, who has now matured into a well-formed young woman, is what I should call a vocal defaulter, her singing being 'far gone'. — *Entr'acte*, April 1883.

Farcidrama (*Theat.*, 1885). A failure comedy of a farcical character, tied with a thread of serious interest. Discovered by Mr Ashley Sterry to describe a posthumous half-finished comedy by H. J. Byron, and named *The Shuttlecock*—one which Mr Sterry quite finished. It failed, and this word at once came to be used to describe a failure of any light piece. 'It was a farcidrama' — meaning a 'frost'.

To begin with, the description of *The Shuttlecock* as a 'farcidrama in three acts and a song' may be set down to the living rather than to the dead dramatist. —*Ref.*, 17th May 1885.

Farthing-faced chit (*Peoples'*). Small, mean-faced, as insignificant as a farthing. Chit also means small and contemptible.

Farthing-taster (*Street Children's*, 1870 on). Lowest quantity of commonest ice-cream sold by London street itinerant ice-cream vendors.

In other shops may be seen hundreds of the thick, small glasses in which the 'farthing-taster' will be dealt out to their juvenile consumers.—*Newsp. Cutting*, 27th June 1898.

Fastened (*Lancs.*). Pawned.

Fastidious cove (*London*, 1882). A droll phrase for a fashionable swindler, who pretends to be of the upper ten.

You can always tell the 'fastidious cove' by his sending twenty-seven cuffs and collars to the laundry accompanied by a single shirt.—*Cutting*.

Fat ale (*Peoples'*, early 19 cent.). Strong ale—as distinct from weak ale, which is 'thin'.

'I was stupefied as much as if I had committed a debauch upon fat ale.'—Marryatt, *Rattlin the Reefer*, ch. 58.

Fat will burn itself out of the fire (*Peoples'*). Antithesis of 'All the fat's in the fire'.

After a while, however, the fat burnt itself out of the fire, and the happy couple seemed to get on very comfortably.—*Cutting*.

Favourite vice (*Jovial*, 1880). General habitual strong drink.

'I have watched the Prince's progress,' says His Worship, 'and I am glad to say there has been progress; for at one time I did not entertain a particularly high opinion of him. I rather thought that the Prince cared more for his pleasures and, I may as well say, for his vices, than for the duties of his high position.' Of course, the word 'vices' is here used in a harmless sense: for example, when the bottles and the cigar-case are to the fore, even a bishop may enquire of you, with a jovial smile of boon companionship, What is your favourite vice?—*D. N.*, 6th October 1885.

Fearful frights (*Peoples'*). Kicks, in the most humiliating quarters.

I shouldn't like to be in James Carey's boots—his trousers either, if all I hear is true. He's had some fearful frights, you bet.—*Cutting*.

Fearful wild fowl (*Soc.*). From Shakespeare's line, any extraordinary creature not often seen; even applied to men making antic fools of themselves.

A full programme of the Show is a formidable study, but a patient plodding through it shows that the fearful wild fowl mentioned are really to take a part in the pageant.—*D. N.*, 10th November 1884.

Feather in her mouth (*Marine*). Capable of showing temper, but holding it in. Poetical description of the merest idea of foam at the point where a ship's cut-water touches the wave, and which shows there either has been, or will be, dirty weather.

So to Elba the *Foam* was now directing her course, dancing lightly along upon a sparkling and nearly smooth surface, with only just enough movement during the later portion of the day to keep a very small 'feather in her mouth'.—Sir E. Arnold, in *D. T.*, 31st March 1897.

Feather in the cap (*Hist.*). Probably from Scotland, where only he who had shot an eagle dared to wear a feather in his cap.

Features. Practically no features worth talking about. Satirical-like expression, *e.g.*, 'Hullo, Features!' 'Face' is used similarly.

Fed (*Amer.*, 1860-65). Abbreviation of federal, given to themselves by the Northerners, whereupon the Southerners cut themselves down to Confeds, and met the Northerners at that.

Fed up with (*Boer War*, 1899-1900). Overdone, oppressed, filled with.

'Oh, I'm about fed up with it' is the current slang of the camps when officers and men speak of the war.—*D. T.*, 20th October 1900.

Feeder (*Theat.*, 1880). Actor or actress whose part simply feeds that of a more important comedian. Took the place of the 'confidante' in opera.

Feeding birk (*Thieves'*). Cook-shop — 'birk' being possibly a corruption of 'barrack'.

You have to be a bit cheeky to go into a feeding birk to order pannum good enough for a prince without a D in your clye.—*Cutting*.

Feel cheap (*Peoples'*, 1890). Humiliated, *e.g.*, 'Every other girl was in white, and I felt quite cheap.'

Feel like (*Amer.-Eng.*, 1884). Inclined towards.

'Do you feel like brandy and water?' is certainly an incorrect question (even grammatically) in England. Across the sea we believe the observation means, 'Do you feel inclined to partake, at my charge, of the refreshment of cognac and water?'—*D. N.*, 16th April 1885.

Feel like accepting it (*Amer.*). To repent, be humble.

In his death we has lost a good man, but we has at de same time gained some waluable experience, in case we feel like accepting it.—*Lime-kiln Club*, 1883.

Feel one's oats (*Amer. - Eng.*). Certain to be active. Figure of speech from the work got out of a well oat-fed horse, *e.g.*, 'You needn't be afraid—he's a man that feels his oats.'

Feel the collar (*Stable*). To perspire in walking.

Feel very cheap (*Mid.-class Eng.*, 1885 on). Antithesis of self-sufficiency. Generally refers to condition when recovering from dissipation.

Does some brother officer adjacent 'feel very cheap' after some midnight revelry; or how comes it that my host is not in the way?—Clement Scott, in *D. T.*, 21st January 1893.

Female personator (*Music - hall*). Another misnomer (*see* Male impersonator), for the performer is a male who impersonates female appearance, singing, and dancing. A man who dresses and acts like a woman, while the male impersonator is a woman who dresses and acts like a man. These interchanges of sexual appearance are still much relished on the music-hall stage.

Fenian (*Peoples'*, 1882 on). Three cold Irish, *i.e.*, threepence worth of Irish whisky and cold water. Brevity is the soul of cruel as of brilliant wit. In this instance the wit is very cruel, for it refers to the hanging and therefore coldening of the three Fenians who were hanged for the murder of Lord Frederick Cavendish and Mr Burke, Under-Secretary for Ireland, in the Phœnix Park, Dublin, on 6th May 1882. Other authorities say that the three Irish, here referred to with such grim humour, were the Fenians Allen, Larkin and O'Brien, hanged at Manchester for the murder of Police Sergeant Brett. They are called by the Irish national party 'the Manchester martyrs'. In Manchester itself the '3 cold Irish' became at public-house bars — 'Give me a Fenian'. The term spread all over England. (*See* Got a clock.)

Fewer of him (*Amer.-Eng.*, 1880). Expression of congratulation at absence of numbers in the given case.

An English judge is a much more conspicuous personage than a judge in any foreign country. His salary is higher, his social position is better, and there are, to use an expressive Americanism, 'fewer of him'.—*Newsp. Cutting.*

Fiddle-face (*Peoples'*). A doleful face, widening abnormally at the temples and jaws, and sinking at the cheek bones.

Put on a fiddle-face and jaw to him about his future, and it's most likely he and his mates will slosh your mug for you and sneak your yack.—*Cutting.*

Fiddler (*Racing*). *Fille de l'air*—a French horse. The Anglicization of the names of foreign horses is a positive study in itself. English racing men who speak French always accept the English baptism.

Another stud horse, Peut-Etre, always called in the English betting ring 'Potater' was, as well as a few other lots, bought in.—*Newsp. Cutting.*

In the case of Volodyovski (Derby winner, 1901) no Anglicization was possible, so the pencillers tried an assonance, and styled him Bottle o' Whisky, and it is interesting in this connection to observe that in all professions and trades uncommon proper names are always Anglicized—roughly, absurdly, no doubt; but this process clears away all doubt as to pronunciation. For instance, in the Navy sailors always simplify a hard-named ship. A person had a vessel named the *Spero*, which was corrupted into Sparrow. As for *Psyche*, what they called her can scarcely be mentioned in decent company. Another person bought a vessel called the *Dædalus*, which was called the Deadloss.

Field Lane duck (*Holborn, Lond.*). Baked bullock's heart. A good example of lower peoples' habit of satirising their own poverty. This bake is made savoury, and is the nearest approach to duck possible, exactly as baked liver with sage and onions is called 'poor man's goose'. Field Lane was a near neighbour of Saffron Hill, where Dickens's Fagin reigned; London improvements have nearly swept it away. Field Lane is great in the annals of charity as the locality where first a night refuge was opened.

Field-running (*Builders'*, 1860). Building rickety houses rapidly over suburban fields. Introduced when the district railways brought small suburban houses into fashion.

Fiery cross (*Liter.*, 19 cent). Warning of danger. Probably from Scott—who introduces this flaming mode of carrying news of clan-risings.

The Police send round the Fiery Cross:—'Idle Panic' was the headline by which we described in our later editions of yesterday the extraordinary alarm which seized upon the metropolis, and nothing which occurred during the evening calls for any modification of that description. — *P. M. G.*, 11th February 1886.

Fifteen puzzle (*Mid.-class Eng.*). Complete confusion. The fifteen puzzle was an arrangement of moveable cubes bearing numbers which were to be arranged in a square, so that every line counted fifteen. It was very difficult and became a rage (1879). It soon came to represent confusion, incomprehensibility.

The syrup cup was, for a while, a fifteen-puzzle for the bear.—*American Bear Story*, 1883.

Fight space with a hair-pin (*Oxford Univ.*, 1882). A figurative way of describing the impossible.

Fighting Fours (*Milit.*). The 44th Regiment.

The 44th East Essex loses nothing of its identity in being called 'The Essex Regiment' except, perhaps, that the signification of The Fighting Fours is hardly so clear as it was.—*D. N.*, July, 1881.

Fighting the tiger (*San Francisco*). Gaming, with all its consequences; some of which are desperate. Practically applied—desperate game.

He asked me if I had ever heard of Faro, and if I knew the meaning of 'fighting the tiger'. Soon afterwards I learned that I was conversing with the keeper of one of the most notable among the gaming hells of San Francisco.—*Cutting*.

Figure-head (*Nautical*). The head simple, and suggested of course by the prow-terminal of most English ships.

A cove can, too, if he likes, spend the half of his bob in pongelow and the other tanner in bread and cheese, but we think he's likely to stop out of collar longer than a cove who doesn't cloud his blooming figure-head with booze.

We have once or twice landed our blooming figure-head on the kerb.

Filbert (*Street*). Head—variety of 'nut' to describe the same. Probably applied to a long-shaped head. Derived from prize ring.

'Yere—come and look at the bloke standin' on his filbert,' said the boy.

Filibuster (*Amer.*). To obstruct, impede business.

The Senate had an all-night sitting, the Republicans filibustered from six P.M. till early morning. To 'filibuster' means in its Parliamentary sense to obstruct.—*Newsp. Cutting*, 1882.

Filing-lay (*Thieves'*, 18 cent.). Pocket-picking. Fielding's *Jonathan Wild*. Probably from the French 'fil' —thread—from threading the fingers in the pocket.

Fill the bill (*Amer.*) To suit.

I have a tree claim and homestead, am a good cook and not afraid to work, and willing to do my part. If any man with a like amount of land, and decent face and carcass, wants a good wife, I can fill the bill.—*Newsp. Cutting*.

Fill, To give a (*Thieves'*). To deceive, *e.g.*, 'I gave the blue belly a fill'—would mean that you sent the policeman on a wrong scent.

Fills a gentleman's eye (*Sporting*). Shapely—possessed of thoroughly good points.

What do we not suffer from other people's dogs? Our own, of course, is a treasure of love and loyalty, he has a splendid nose, is perfectly purely bred, and, in short, as doggy people say, 'he fills a gentleman's eye'.—*D. N.*, 1875.

Filly (*Ball-room*). A lady who goes racing pace in round dances, *e.g.*, 'She's the quickest filly in the barn.' Either from French 'fille', or in reference to the use of the word in stables. 'Colt' is often applied to an active boy.

Filly and foal (*Peoples'*). A young couple of lovers sauntering apart from the world.

Fin de siècle (*Soc.*, 1897 on). Extreme in literature, art, and music. From Paris—adopted here in a condemnatory spirit. Within a year in London was introduced the phrase 'New Century'—first applied in a public manner to the 'New Century Theatre Society'—whose plays were based upon the Ibsen theories of life. The authors appear to have thought these words typical of the 20th century, whereas Ibsen towards the close of the 19th century had been writing for more than fifty years, and had long been a classic in Scandinavia and, in a less degree, throughout Germania.

Find cold weather (*Public-house*). To be bounced, or expelled; *e.g.*, 'Yere you—if you ain't quiet you'll soon find cold weather *I* can tell yer'.

Finger and thumb (*Rhyming*). Rum.

Finger in the pie (*Peoples'*). Obvious—and based upon the philosophy of too many cooks spoiling the broth.

Finish (*Soc.*, 1830). A house where the night (which was next morning about 4 A.M.) was finished by the exhaustion of the *débauché*.

'We are writing of the days when the Elysium, Mother H.'s, The Finish, Jessop's, etc., were in their zenith and glory.'—Diprose's *Clement Danes*, vol. i., p. 98.

'Let us go to a finish—say Jessop's'. Jessop's finally expired about 1885. It was the building afterwards occupied by the *Echo* newspaper. Opposite was the celebrated place of accommodation, 'The Fountain' — significant title, which had then been established hundreds of years.

In 1896, King William Street, Strand, saw the opening of a brilliantly-appointed lounge entitled 'The Finale', assuredly good Italian for finish ; a sign the proprietor had brought with him from South Africa.

Fire (out) (*O. Eng.; now Amer.— reaching Eng.* 1896). To eject. Probably from 14th century, the phrase being invented from the summary process of the first cannon. 'Let us fire him' is equivalent to 'bounce him'.

Then they thought his objection to the spending of £20 on a lecture—and its necessary or needful accompaniments— on the interesting and entertaining subject of 'Bacteriology' too much of a good thing, so they had him 'fired' from the meeting.—*E. N.*, 10th Feb. 1899.

The Americanism 'to fire out' is seen in a sonnet of Shakespeare's:

'Yet this shall I not know, nor live in doubt,
Till my bad angels fire my good one out.'

This instance shows that in the matter of the mother-tongue common to both countries, Yankees are even more conservative of the 'well of English' than Britishers themselves.—*Rees, U.S.A.*

Fire-box (*Passionate Pilgrims'*). A man of unceasing passion.

Fire-new (*Prov. Potteries'*). 'Brand-new', absolutely new—from drawing pottery from the oven or furnace.

It seems an incongruity, an impossibility, for the sculptor and painter of such forms as those we owe to Watt's genius to become suddenly a 'fire-new' baronet.—*D. N.*, 1st July 1885, referring to offer of baronetcy to Mr Watts.

Fire-proof coffin (*Amer.*). A last house which will resist the action of the nethermost region. Said of a bad man that he will need one.

'My pa says that if your pa would stay at home from prayer meetin' to mix a little more sugar with the sand he sells for fourteen cents a pound, p'raps he might not need a fire-proof coffin when he dies'.—*Newsp. Cutting.*

Fire the question (*Amer.*). To propose marriage.

First on the top-sail and last in the beef-skid (*Navy*). Truly perfect able-bodied seaman. More in praise could not be said of him.

Fish-bagger (*Suburban*). Suburban resident who working in the city, or in town, generally takes home food, especially cheap fish, in that respectable black bag which looks so very legal.

The tradesman shook his head, and explained that 'fish-bagger' was a contumelious term applied to those who live in good suburbs without spending a penny there beyond rent.—*Graphic*, 27th September 1884.

Fishy about the gills (*Street*). Appearance of recent drunkenness. Derived from very acute observation. Drink produces a pull-down of the corners of the mouth, and a consequent squareness of the lower cheeks or gills, suggesting the gill-shields in fishes.

Fit in the arm (*Street*, 1897). A blow. In June 1897 one Tom Kelly was given into custody by a woman for striking her. His defence before the magistrate took the shape of the declaration that 'a fit had seized him in the arm', and for months afterwards back street frequenters called a blow a fit.

Fit-up towns (*Theat.*, 1880). Poor, behind-the-times places which cannot boast a theatre amongst them.

Perhaps you don't know what the 'fit-up towns' are. Let me tell you. They are the towns which do not possess a theatre, and which are therefore only visited by small companies carrying portable scenery, which can be fitted up in a hall or an assembly room.—*Ref.*, 22nd July 1883.

Fitz (*Peoples'*). Royal natural children — derivation obvious. Broadly applied amongst old theatrical people to the invasion of the stage by educated persons of position or fortune.

'I wish all the fitzes in the world were at the bottom of the sea.'—*Said by a young stage manager*, October 1883.

Five-barred gate (*London Streets*, 1886 on).—A policeman, from the force being chiefly recruited from the agricultural class.

The evidence against the defendant, given by Constable 308 A, was that whilst in company with a woman he abused him (the policeman) without reason, asking how long he had been away from a 'five-barred gate' (the country).—*D. N.*, 2nd July 1890.

Five o'clock tea (*Soc.*, 1879). Strictly tea, and nothing beyond, except a wafer biscuit, a little more wafery bread and butter, and perhaps a microscopic cake, if it is a society holiday. Came to be added first to the ordinary refreshmentless call between three and five P.M. Five o'clock tea has gradually stolen up to a four o'clock teapot, for people came in a crowd, and the old exclusive puritanic plan of one visitor retreating as another came, or retired, even if solus-visiting at the end of a quarter of an hour was abandoned.

Five or seven (*Police; London*, 1885). Drunk. From 'five shillings or seven days', the ordinary police magisterial decision upon 'drunks' unknown to the police, and reduced by Mr Hosack, a metropolitan magistrate, to five or seven.

Another is, 'Arthur Roberts in dress allegorical of five or seven, as Mr Hosack.' Mr Hosack, as many of my readers may not be aware, is a magistrate, and 'five or seven' means——but no matter.—*Ref.*, 17th January 1886.

Fiveoclocquer (*Paris-Eng.*, 1896). Afternoon tea.

Every one, we suppose, has heard of the delightful French phrase, 'five-oclocquer à quatre heures', which is, perhaps, the noblest achievement of the art of word-coining in sublime contempt of meaning.—*Newsp. Cutting*, 24th June 1898.

Five-pounders (*Jersey*). Not a piece of ordnance—but cheap excursionists, who fall upon Jersey in high summer-time, and who make a stay of three or four roaring days, having this sum when they start, and nothing by the time they reach London.

The five-pounders are usually of the genus 'Arry. They are not unwelcomed in Jersey, so long as their five pounds last.—*Graphic*, 31st March 1883.

Fiz (*Society*). Champagne.

Pat Feeney has sworn off fiz, and will never touch a drop for the rest of his life. Not even a drop of whisky. Another injustice to Oireland.—*Cutting*, 1883.

Pat was a patriotic singer of Irish songs, and constantly wailing over the 'green sod' of his native land.

Fizzle (out) (*Peoples'*). To fail, and a failure; from the noise made by the gas escaping from ærated waters when the corks fail, so that the water has no effervescent quality when opened.

Gale and Spader's 'Fizz-Bang-Boom' company has fizzled out in San Francisco.—*Newsp. Cutting*.

It is a foolish, highly-peppered story of love, intrigue and politics. It was little better than fizzle.—*N. Y. Tribune*.

Flabbergast (*Briv. Class*). To astound. Rejected of most lexicographers, but accepted of all men. Probably a proper-name word, possibly Phil Applegarth or Applegast.

The goings on of Cock-Eyed Sal flabbergasted him much, but he was spliced to her, and he couldn't help it.—*Cutting*.

Flag (*Printers'*). Woeful expression referring to an 'out'; that is to say, some missed words in setting up a piece of 'copy'. This may involve over-running a number of lines at a frightful expense of time. Taken from the aspect of the 'out' words written at the side of the proof and enclosed in a loop; a line leading from the nearer end of which concludes in the caret which marks the point in the copy where the missing words are wanting.

Flag of distress (*Street*). A boy's shirt through a too-open trousers-seat. From the flag of a distress on a ship being white—because more easily seen; though perhaps the flag in question is only more or less white.

Flag unfurled (*Rhyming*). A man of the world—passing into flag, after the mode of rhyming English of a passing character.

A cove who fancies himself a flag unfurled is very now or never we don't think.—*Cutting*.

Flam (*Soc.* 18 *cent.*). Fib—rather than lie. Quite passed away from London, but still heard in the counties. Probably from a proper name. Johnson says, 'a cant word of no certain etymology'. Words from proper names really have no etymology. Butler (*Hudibras*) uses this word :

A flam more senseless than the roguery.
Of old aruspicy and augury !

Miss Wilhelmina Skeggs (*Vicar of Wakefield*) is great in the use of this term. May be from Flamborough Head, whence, in the 17th century, came false continental news, exactly as 'Humbug' came to be the term applied to continental false news from Hamburg.

Flannel - jacket (*Contractors'*). Familiar name for the gigantic navvy who, without exception, wears this garment. Generally pronounced 'flannin', *flannel* being a hard word from Wales. Tom Taylor used the term in a scene of the *Ticket of Leave Man*. 'Hey - sup (drink) thou dear flannin-jacket.'

Flap - jack invalid (*Amer.*). A victim of dissipation.

'Reduce the nation to a vast hospital of flap-jack invalids.'—*Texas Siftings*.

Flapper (*Lower Class*). Hand—sometimes flipper. Possibly from the slapping movement of the hand suggesting the striking tail or fins of a fish—when the word would be an onomatope—its sound being that of the flap of a fish on wet sand or stones. Said by some authorities to have a very disagreeable meaning.

Flapper (*Society*). A very immoral young girl in her early 'teens'.

A correspondent of *Notes and Queries* has been troubling his mind about the use of the slang word 'flapper' as applied to young girls. Another correspondent points out that a 'flapper' is a young wild duck which is unable to fly, hence a little duck of any description, human or otherwise. The answer seems at first sight frivolous enough, but it is probably the correct solution of this interesting problem all the same.—*E. N.*, 20th August 1892.

Flare-up (*Peoples'*, 19 *cent.*). A stir, riot, disturbance—obviously from a house on fire.

'Flare-up' at the present time is a purely jocular interjection. A noisy revel is very often spoken of by bacchanalians as 'a jolly flare - up'; but sixty - three years ago 'flare-up' had another and a very sinister signification. To it was added the admonition 'to join the Union'. 'Flare-up and join the Union !' The Union part of the cry is associated in my mind with processions of working men, yelling and cursing and bearing banners embellished with death's - heads and cross - bones, and inscriptions about 'Bread or Blood'; while 'flare-up' had a direct bearing on incendiarism.—G. A. Sala in *D.T.*, 28th July 1894.

Flash (*Thieves'*). Imitation gold coins—the name probably suggested by their glitter. Sometimes called 'Hanoverian' sovereigns — a term originating probably upon the accession of the House of Brunswick—looked upon by all true Jacobites as counterfeit. The last occasion where these terms were in transitory use was at the trial (1881) of one Lefroy, for murder. The attorney-general, Sir Henry James (afterwards Lord James of Hereford), prosecuted. In his opening speech he said :

'Precisely similar coins—the 'flash' or Hanoverian sovereigns found in the carriage, which Lefroy repudiated, etc.' —*Newsp. Cutting*.

Flash (*Milit.*). A ribbon decoration of the 23rd Royal Welsh Fusiliers.

It is easy to imagine the indignation which would be displayed at any attempt to deprive the officers of the 23rd Royal Welsh Fusiliers of their right to wear what is called 'the Flash'. This ornament consists of a black ribbon sewed on to the back of the tunic-collar, and allowed to flutter in the breeze in imitation of the tie of the old pig-tail.—*D.N.*, July 1881.

Flash (*Street*). Grand, splendid. Evidently derived from strong flash of lightning.

They're so flash that it's a blooming wonder they know themselves.—*Cutting*, 1883.

Flash dona (*Thieves'*). A high-class low-class lady.

'I was always a real lady, as much as any flash dona what gets her portrait took and then goes on the boards.'—*Cutting*.

Flash o' light (*New Cut, S. London*). Complimentary description of a woman dressed upon the model of the rainbow.

Flat as a frying-pan (*Peoples', old*). Flat indeed. Probably derived from the first implement of this kind which was level compared with the crocks of Elizabethan days.

'Egad—I'm struck as flat as a frying-pan'.—Farquhar, *The Inconstant.*

Flat chicken (*Lower Class*). Stewed tripe. All common foods have fine satirical names.

Flat-foot (*Navy*). A young sailor less than twenty-one. (*See* Shellback).

Flatty (*Thieves'*). A greenhorn. An endearing diminutive of flat, who would be more despised than the less contemned flatty.

Flaxation (*New Eng.*). One of the more remarkable American hypocritical evasions of actual swearing. Equal to damnation.

'Then, what in flaxation do you want of those things?'—*Newsp. Cutting.*

Fleet (*Old Eng.—gone to Nantucket, where it stays*). To trifle, idle. Heard sometimes in mid-counties, *e.g.*,

'He fleets his life away. Many young gentlemen flock to him every day, and fleet the time carelessly as they did in the golden age.'—*As You Like It.*

Fleshy part of the thigh (*Peoples',* 1899). Evasive military hospital phraseology to describe a wound on that part of the human frame which 'goes over the hedge last'. Came into use upon the news from S. Africa of Lord Methuen having been wounded in this region.

Flier (*Sporting, 19 cent.*). A breeder of carrier and other homing pigeons.

'Fliers', a term given to the individuals whose sportsmanlike instincts induce them to spend considerable time and money on the training of homing pigeons. —*D. T.*, 17th December 1897.

Flight o' steps (*Coffee-house*). Thick slices of bread and butter. Royal order in relation to steps—at least four ridge and furrows.

He asks for a pint of mahogany juice, a flight of doorsteps, and a penny halligator.—*Mankind* (Surrey Theatre), 1883.

Flimsy (*Press*). Copy on very thin tracing paper. A dozen sheets of flimsy are interleaved with as many sheets of carbonized or charcoaled paper, when by writing heavily in pencil on the mass of flimsy, twelve copies are obtained. Passed into a verb— 'Flimsy me that par', means 'make half a dozen copies on tracing paper'.

Had the questions to be copied out?— Yes; and the answers to be flimsied.— Sir C. Dilke, Crawford Divorce Suit, July 1886.

Fling out or flung away (*Peoples'*). Angry retreat.

Wardlaw whipped before him and flung out of the room. (Charles Reade.)

Theodore flung away and was rushing off. (Miss Yonge.)

Flip-flap (*Street boy*, 1898 on). Broad fringe of hair covering the young male forehead. This fashion, revived from the time of George IV., began with the quiff (*q.v.*), expanded to the guiver, and widened to the flip-flap, a name evidently gained from its motion in the winds.

Flop (*Low Lond.*, 1881). When the lower classes of women adopted the 'cretin' or 'poodle' style of wearing the hair low down over the forehead, they gave it this name.

Flounce (*Theatrical and Society*, 1854 on). The thick line of black paint put on the edge of the lower eyelid to enhance the effect of the eye itself. When under the second empire painting the face (*see* Mind the paint), became common, this term came to be heard in society.

Fluff in (*Lower Peoples'*). Deceive by smooth modes.

Fly cop (*Anglo-Amer.*). Detective (*see* Tec). Cop is abbreviation of copper (*q.v.*). Fly is quite an old word for adroit.

Fly donah (*Street*). Adroit lady— not perhaps too honest.

Fly loo (*Student*, 1850). Summer game. The players stand round a table, each having a lump of sugar or touch of honey well before him. The owner of the sweets upon which a fly first settles takes the stakes. (*See* Kentucky Loo.)

Fly me (*Ancient*). Exclamation against mistrust or doubt. From flay.

Fly member (*Com. Peo.*). Clever, adroit man—fly being used to give the idea of speed in apprehending, and lighting on what passes. (*See* Hot member.)

Fly rink (*Peoples'*, 1875). A polished bald head.

Flying the kite (*Soc.*). Making public—in the 90's. Earlier in the century it was issuing accommodation bills. Now, however, it has the other meaning, as—

He would be very sorry to do entirely without the interview, and politicians were said to use it as a means of 'flying the kite'.—*Anthony Hope, April* 1898.

Foal and filly dance (*Soc.*). Dance to which only very young people of both sexes are invited.

Fog in (*Soc.*). To see a place by chance, or to achieve by accident.

Foot! foot! Now and again this expression is cast after the respectably dressed person who wanders into strange and doubtful bye-ways. Phrase obtained much attention by its use by Emile Zola in *L'Assommoir*, where it is found even in the mouth of a priest. It is difficult to say when this term passed into England. The word is to be found as 'foutre' in Shakespeare (*Henry VI.*). Probably reintroduced into England by the French court of Charles II.

Foot-and-mouth disease (*Lancashire*). Swearing followed by kicking.

Foot-bath (*European.*) Overflow from glass into saucer. Said in England of a full glass.

It is customary throughout Spain for the waiters of cafés to fill a glass with wine or liquor so that it overflows upon the saucer. This custom, in which it is desired to show an appearance of liberality, is called 'the foot-bath'.—*People,* 28*th July* 1895.

Foot - rot (*Public - house*). Contemptuous name given by the contemners of fourpenny ale. (*See* Brown.)

Footless stocking without a leg. (*Irish*). Nothing—zero. (*See* What the Connaught man shot at.)

Fopper (*Parvenus'*). Mistake. Perversion of 'faux pas'. In its extreme application an 'event', if you accept the word's Latin meaning. Equivalent to what the French call *brise du soir*.

Forcing the hand (*Soc.*). Compel admissions. From whist, where to force the hand of an adversary is to play high in order to compel him to play higher. Much used by lawyers—always great whist-players.

Sir C. Warren agreed with the assessor that it was hardly fair to put a question of this character.

Mr Wontner observed that it was forcing his hand.—*Cass Case, July* 1887.

Fore God (*American*). Shape of old English oath — 'Before God, I swear.'

Foreign line (*Railway*). Any line which is not that on which the speaker is employed.

Foreigneering coves (*Low London*, 1860). Most graphic description of dislike to others than British that has perhaps been invented.

We have no passion for ribbons, and orders, and all the tinsel trappings of aliens or 'foreigneering coves', as they are termed in the simple language of 'Those in the Know'.—*D. N.*, 1883.

Foreigner (*Negro*). Elegant evasive title given by negroes to describe themselves, in order to avoid the hated word black.

Forest of fools (*Literary,* 17 *cent.*). The World.

Amongst all the wild men that run up and down in this wide Forest of Fools, etc.—*Decker's Gull's Horn-Book,* 1609.

Forever - gentleman (*Soc.*, 1870). A man in whom good breeding is ingrained. (*See* Half Hour Gentleman.)

Forrader (*Soc.*, 1880 on). Forwarder—adopted from the gutter, one night, in the House of Commons. Used in many jocular ways.

Whether the Liberal Forwards will get any 'forrarder' over the light claret which we have no doubt is all that they can conscientiously allow themselves remains to be seen. — *D. T.,* 15*th December* 1898.

Fortnum and Mason (*Soc.,* 1850 on). Complete, luxurious hamper for picnic or races. From the perfection of the eatables sent out by this firm of grocers in Piccadilly.

49ers (*W. - American*). Earliest Californian miners—from the year in which the movement to California commenced.

Forum (*Birmingham*). The 'Forum' is the Town Hall, and known by that name through all Warwickshire.

Earl Granville, who was received with most enthusiastic cheers, said : I rise a stranger in this famous Town Hall—(cries of 'No')—known in Birmingham, I believe, by a still more classical name.—Bright Celebration (B'rgham), June 1883.

Forwards (*Polit.*, 1897). Radicals—last cry of the 19th century in discovering a new name for the advanced sections in the House of Commons.

Sir Charles Dilke leads a knot of Radical 'forwards' on questions of foreign affairs, whose views are, probably, at least as distasteful to the leader of the Opposition as the policy of Lord Salisbury.—*D. T.*, 21st June 1898.

Foundling temper (*London*). A very bad temper—proverbially said of the domestic servants poured upon London by the metropolitan Foundling Hospital.

The ladies who are conducting the Metropolitan Association for Befriending Young Servants are perpetually thwarted and discouraged by the singular incapacity for self-control of the girls who have been bred in the great pauper schools. Their chief characteristic is an ungovernable temper. This is popularly recognised as the 'Foundling temper'.—*D. N.*, 9th September 1885.

Foundry (*Peoples'*). Shop, but chiefly applied to a pork butcher's—probably because of the noisy vibration of the sausage machine.

Fountain temples (*London*, 90's). Places of convenience, sunk below the roadways. Remarkable for lavish marble, mosaic, and clear running water. (*See* Cottages.)

Four arf (*Costers'*). The costermonger's favourite beverage is a pot o' four arf.

Four-legged fortune (*Soc.*, 1880 on). Winning horse.

They talk Turf slang ; they back 'four-legged fortunes', and his lordship owns a steed which brings him to utter grief.—*D.T.*, 22nd April 1898.

Four liner (*Soc.*). Very important. From 'whips' or messages to M.P.'s, which have from one to four lines drawn under them, according to importance.

Four-lined whips have been sent out on both sides of the House of Commons urging members to be in their places this evening.—*D. N.*, March 1890.

Four thick (*Public-house*). Fourpence per quart beer—the commonest there is (in London), and generally the muddiest.

Fourpenny cannon (*London Slums*). Beef-steak pudding—price, a groat. Named possibly from its shape, that of a cannon-ball (cut down to cannon), but possibly referring to the cast-iron character not only of the beef, but its integument.

Fourpenny pit (*Rhyming*). Fourpenny bit—now antiquarian phrase—since this silver coin has been absolutely withdrawn in favour of the threepenny bit.

Foxes (*American*). People of Maine—probably owing to the foxes which prevail there.

Frame (*Artists'*, 1890). Picture.

Franc-fileur (*French*, 1870). A cur, a freebolter—in contradistinction from franc-tireur, the volunteer light infantry of the defence. Used now and again in England in society for a man who gets away quietly and won't dance.

Freak (*Theatrical*, 1885). Actors who lose professional cast by aiding in eccentric shows. From New York.

Actors who play in dime museums are now called 'freaks'.—*Ref.*, 18th April 1906.

Freakeries (*London*, 1898). Barnum's freak and acrobat shows at Olympia.

Free (*Peoples' and School*). To make free. Process never of a very elegant kind — especially amongst school-boys. Expectoration enters into the process as a rule. (*See* 'Lynch').

Free hand (*Political*, about 1880). Plenary powers, *carte blanche*.

General Gordon has been given, if we must use a detestable piece of slang a 'free hand'. In plainer and better English he has been allowed to do as he pleased.—*D. N.*, 5th May 1884.

French (*S. of N. Amer. Soc.*). Term used in Maryland and Virginia for any fashion that is disliked. Probably from 18th century when the people of these states very much disliked the French population of Louisiana.

Frenchman (*Soc.*, 19 cent.). Bottle of brandy — from this spirit being French.

Frenchy (*Street*, 19 cent., to 1854). A term of contempt addressed to any man with a foreign air in the streets.

Fresh-whites (*Peoples'*, 19 cent.). Pallor.

Freshers and toshers (*Oxford*, 1896). Freshers despised as freshmen, and toshers being men who have no sympathy with the Church. Combined term of contempt.

Fretted (*American*). Vexed to do a thing.

Friars (*L. C. and D. Railway passengers'*, 1860). Hurried short for 'Blackfriars'.

Friction (*Polit.*, 1885). New satirical term for political or international quarrel.

The letter from Lord Granville which Lord Edmund Fitzmaurice read in the House of Commons contained an expression of Lord Granville's hope that the 'friction' with Germany may now be considered a thing of the past.—*D. N.*, 10th March 1885.

Fried carpets (*London Theatrical*, 1878-82). Given to the exceedingly short ballet skirt, then especially seen at the old 'Gaiety'.

Friendly pannikin (*Australian gold-fields*). An amicable drink together out of the small tin pot—one which serves the outlying Australian for most purposes.

Fright hair (*Theatrical*). A wig or portion of a wig which by a string can be made to stand on end and express fright.

Frisk at the tables (*London*). A moderate touch at gaming.

My object is fulfilled if I have made it clear that 'a frisk at the tables' is now rendered easy to Londoners, and that those wishing to enjoy one have but to attend the first well-managed sporting meeting, to receive encouragement and respectful protection at the hands of the police.—G. A. Sala.

Frisky (*Com. London*, 1880). Bad-tempered, and a euphemism for the same.

Frivoller (*Soc.*, 1879 on). Person with no serious aim in life. Substantive derived from Lord Beaconsfield's celebrated phrase 'hair-brained frivolity'.

'Junius' contains plenty of fine stirring lines, even if they awake no more than an occasional echo in the bosoms of the cynical 'frivollers' who exclusively occupy 'the best parts' at all our theatres.—*Ref.*, 1st March 1885.

Frochard (*Theatrical*, about 1870). Savage old woman part—from the demon-hag in *Les Deux Orphelines*.

Augustin Daly's *Under the Gaslight* was more or less a 'bobtail' piece, and thoroughly American in tone. We had a New York blood; a low-comedy character called Bermudas; a 'side-walk merchant prince, with a banjo swarry'; a Wall Street dealer; a judge of the Tombs Police Court; and a vile Frochard sort of person called Old Judas.—*D. T.*, 9th June 1899.

Froncey (*Low. Lond.*, 19 cent.). Français—protest in the interests of things English and of England.

Front (*Soc.*, 1888). Audacity—from the forehead, pushing forward. Equals affront.

There is another rendering of the word 'front' in use among some clever folk, but I wouldn't for the world suggest that the promoters have any of that—to say nothing of 420 ft. of it.—*Ref.*, 9th March 1890.

Front name (*Universal Street*, 19 cent.). Christian name, and always considered as *the* cognomen.

Front piece (*Theatrical*, 1880). Dramatic trifle which precedes the *pièce de resistance*.

The new front piece, *Written in Sand*, turned out to be a pretty little idyllic affair.—*Ref.*, 31st August 1884.

Frosy (*Devonshire*). A delicacy in food eaten quietly by not more than two, after the children are in bed—the couple generally man and wife.

Froze out (*Amer.-Eng.*, 1880-96). Conquered, made the other a nonentity.

Fruit of a gibbet (*Peoples'*, 18 cent.). Hanged felon. The gibbet, as distinct from the gallows, was the frame upon which the hanged man was swung in chains.

I found thee a complete emblem of poverty, resembling the fruit of a gibbet seven years exposed to wind and weather —Gay's *Beggars' Opera*.

Frump (*Soc.*, 1871 on). High cut bodice. When the second French Empire fell (1870), the low-cut bodice, which the Court of the Tuileries had maintained for eighteen years, was swept away. London society led with the high, and afterwards the square cut bodice, which still very generally prevails. Young men in society at once dubbed the high bodice patroness a 'frump'—a badly dressed woman.

Full as a goat (*Tavern*, 18 *cent.*). Drunk. This phrase is evidently 'Full as a goitre', the word often used for the huge throat wen which, common in the last century, is now rarely seen. The word having no distinct modern meaning, has been naturally changed to goat. The idea of fulness is complete in contemplating a huge goitre, which always looks upon the point of bursting.

... New Arrival—'I want a bed.' Clerk: 'Can't have one, sir; they're all full.' N. A.: 'Then I'll sleep with the landlord.' Clerk: 'Can't do it, sir. He's full, too; fuller than a goat, and has been for three days.' — *N. Y. Mercury*, 1888.

Function (*Soc.*, 1880 on). First used for grave musical performances; but the æsthetes began to apply the word to all kinds of meetings—even afternoon teas.

The drenching showers of Thursday night in no way damped the ardour of Haymarket reopeners. The ceremony was, in its way, almost a function.—*Ref.*, 18th September 1887.

Fury (*Navy*). Crew's name for the *Furious*.

Fuss (*Anglo-American*, 19 *cent.*). Dispute, row, wrangle, without any serious consequences.

Fuss and feathers (*Amer.-Eng.*, 1880). Bosh, pretence, froth. Probably from 18th century English; and referring to cock-fighting where the birds only pulled feather and threatened.

Well, as an American critic says of the notions of the solar mythologists, this was 'all fuss and feathers'.—*D. N.*, 10th February 1898.

Fuz-chats (*Beggars'*). The people who camp out on commons amongst the 'furze'. Generally show-people, and gipsy cheap-jacks, also gipsies proper.

G

G. O. M. (*Political Popular*, 1882). Grand Old Man. In this year Mr W. E. Gladstone, when Premier, was described in this way. The satirical journals took up the phrase, and reduced it to initials.

I knocked the G. O. M. down, Northcote sat on his head, and he gave in.— *Ref.*, 7th December 1884.

G. T. T. (*New York*). Gone to Texas. Confession of flight put on office door.

Gads O (*Hist.*). Evaded swearing. Equals God's oath—probably refers to the promises made to the patriarchs.

Gadsbud (*Queen Anne*). God's blood, or God's bud, meaning the Infant Saviour. Another shape is Od's Bud (*q.v.*), 'Gadsbud! I am provoked into a fermentation.'—Congreve, *The Double Dealer*.

Gaelically utter (*Soc.*). The Scotch accent when trying to produce English.

'*West* of England!' cried a supporter of the majority, in an accent too Gaelically utter for London ink to reproduce. 'I don't believe there are any solicitors in the *West* of England. Only a set of clerks.'—*S. T.*, 1st February 1883.

Gaiety girls (*Stage*, 1890 on). Dashing singing and dancing comedians in variety pieces — from their first gaining attention at the Gaiety Theatre.

One of the most interesting features of the Nellie Farren benefit is the promised re-appearance of Miss Marion Hood, one of the brightest and most graceful of 'Gaiety' girls.—*People*, 27th February 1898.

Gaiety step (*Theat.*, 1888-92). A quick, high dancing pas, made popular at the Gaiety Theatre. Term spread to America.

Galbe (*Thieves'*). Profile of a violent character, and even applied to any eccentricity of shape above the knees. This is from the French, and doubtlessly came into fashion at the Court of Charles II. The word is one of the proper-name series, and comes from the Emperor Galba, who lived long in Gaul, where his pronounced profile and terrific nose begot the word. Galbe is used daily all over France, but especially in Paris.—"*Quel Galbe.*"

Gallersgood (*Thieves'*, 18 *cent.*). Corruption of gallows' good. So bad that it is worthy of the gallows.

Gally-pot baronet (*Soc.*, 19 *cent.*). Ennobled physician—outcome of the scorn of birth for even the scientific parvenu.

Gal-sneaker (*Common Lond.*, 1870). A man devoted to seduction.

Gambetter (*International*, 1879). To humbug—'Don't you try to Gam Better *me!*' From Gambetta, of Italian and Jewish origin, who was very popular in France from 1870 to about 1876, when politicians began to suspect his sincerity. In 1879 his popularity was rapidly waning. In this year the verb in question was invented. It is still used in French politics when accusing an opponent of double-dealing.

Gamblous (*Soc.*, 1885). Gambling —invented by Mr J. Chamberlain. (29th April 1885. Speech at dinner of the Eighty Club.)

I suppose Lord Salisbury thinks that if this country only blustered enough we might attain all that we desired from the fears of foreign Powers. There is something to be said for the game of brag, but in this case the stakes are so high, the risk so great, that I do not believe that any sensible men will commit their fortunes to a party or a statesman who would run such tremendous hazards in such a gamblous spirit.

Gander (*London*, 1815-40). Fop. It is a perversion of Gandin, the Parisian description of a fop from the Restoration to the '40's.

Ganymede (*University*). Freshman, or man in his second or even third year, of an effeminate tendency.

Gaperies, The (*London*, 1902). The very last outcome of entertainments ending in 'ies' (*see* Colindiries, etc.) It is simply a rendering of 'Gay Paris'.

Garbage (*Naval*). Clothes, etc.— probably from the appearance of a box of clothes waiting the wash.

Garbed (*American*; *passing to Eng.*). Full-dressed. Would appear to be an intensification of the ordinary use of the word dressed.

Garret (*Hatters'*, 19 *cent.*). A consultation of the members of a shop in relation to some trade or social difficulty of the moment.

Garret (*Street*, 19 *cent.*). Mouth— probably suggested by the mouth being high up in relation to all the body.

Gas-pipes (*Street*). Name given to trousers when tight. In France when fashion causes the hem of the trouser to widen out, this style is called *pied d'elephant*, to which it has a fair resemblance.

Gaul darned (*American*). Modern opposition to too plain bad language— 'God damned'.

Gawblimy (*Street*, 1870). Ceaseless apostrophe by the lower orders to heaven, in reference to some declaration. This is 'Gaw Bli Me'. Gaw from the street shape of the word 'God'—this shape being Gawd, 'bli' an ellipsis, and 'me'.

Gawd forgive him the prayers he said (*Peoples'*). Evasion of saying the sinner swore consummately.

Gaze at the melody (*American*). Look a thing in the face. Another form of 'Face the music'.

Gee-gees (*Infantry*). Cavalry. This term, from the nursery, for a horse is directed at the cavalry by the infants. (*See* Coldcreams, Porridge pots, Grinning dears, Muck.)

Gee-ru (*American*, 1880). Extension of amazement. The 'Ge' is for Je'rusalem, a word once much used; accent on first syllable and on second. Often used, 'Je—you don't say so!'

General (*Com. Life*). Chandler's shop — where everything may be obtained.

General (*Mid.-class*, 1880 on). Maid of all work.

That the race of generals threatens to become extinct is a proposition which is not really so startling as it sounds at first.—*D. T.*, 18th January 1898.

General (*Middle-class*, 19 *cent.*) Shilling. 'Can you generalise?' A delicate mode of saying 'Can you loan me a shilling?'

General Backacher (*Military*, 1899). General Gatacher — modulation of his name to designate this soldier's love of hard-working his men. (*See* Bobs.)

Genitrave (*Peoples', Hist.*) Farthing — or smallest coin. Was in use before maravedi, which probably came to England with Philip of Spain.

Gentleman (*Liverpool*). There are no men in Liverpool; all are gentlemen.

Gentleman in blue (*London*, 1840). One of the satirical names for policeman.

Gentleman super (*Theatrical — about* 1884). A theatre-super of some position or standing — the ordinary super being a person of no standing whatever beyond earning about a shilling or two per evening. In 1884 Mr Wilson Barrett (Princess's Theatre) invented the gentleman super with a view to creating a school of actors, who began on the lowest rung of the ladder. Their price was about twelve to fifteen shillings per week.

Gentleman who pays the rent, The (*Irish peasantry*, 19 *cent.*). Pig —Milesian variety. Origin obvious.

The Irish pig, the gentleman who pays the Irish rent, if not exactly a willing immigrant into this country, has always proved a quiet one after his arrival. He has generally been *cured* before leaving home.—*D. T.*, 17th December 1897.

Gentlemen of the long robe (*Historical*). Term applied by warriors who wore short tunics, satirically to designate mere lawyers, who waged wars with but words.

George (*Military*, 1880-96). The Commander-in-Chief, George, Duke of Cambridge. Good evidence of the duke's popularity, which never waned to the moment he resigned the command.

Georgium Sidus (*Soc.*). The Netherlands — figuratively speaking. The Surrey side of the Styx.

Geranium (*Street*, 1882). Red nose.

German gospel (*Peoples'*, November 1897). Bounce, vain boasting, megalomania. From a phrase addressed in this month by Prince Henry of Prussia to his brother of Germany at a dinner: 'The gospel that emanates from your Majesty's sacred person, etc.'

Get away closer (*Coster, Hist.*). Invitation to yet more pronounced devotion.

Get curly (*Tailors'*). Troublesome.

Get fits (*Peoples'*). *Væ victis*— suffer rage from being conquered; impatient under defeat. Generally 'git fits'.

Get in (*Low London*, 19 *cent.*). Victoriously strike.

And then you goes and gets in both fists — one, two, three — afore I knew where I was. Then o' course I ups and gives you a one-er, and off I goes.— *D. T.*, 18th October 1897.

Get inside and pull the blinds down (*Low London*, 19 *cent.*). Gross verbal attack delivered on the highway at a poor rider.

Get it down the neck (*Lower Peoples'*). To swallow.

Get left (*Anglo-Amer.*). Abbreviation of 'in the lurch'.

Get outside (*Street*). Swallow.

Get religion (*Peoples'*). Become religious.

Get the drop (*Amer.-Eng.*). Outcome of the use of the revolver in U.S.A. The muzzle of the revolver is dropped down to the aim from a higher level—hence the term, which means to obtain victory.

Get the g. b. (*Amer.*). Dismissal —g. b. being 'go by'.

'Won't he feel cheap when he gets the g. b. ?'

Get the heels on it (*Amer.-Eng.*). Victory, success—from the American habit (rapidly passing away) of resting the heels, when their proprietor is seated, on a level with his head, if not above it.

Get the shillings ready (*Street*, 1897). Be prepared to ladle out money. From the rush of charity which characterised the sixtieth year of Queen Victoria's reign, and especially referring to the *Daily Telegraph* shillings charity lists towards the fund for the payment of the debts of the London Hospitals.

Get the shoot (*Peoples'*). Dismissal —probably from the mill shoot turning out the flour.

Get the spike (*Low London*). Lose one's temper.

'O' course Chris git's the spike !'— *People*, 5th January 1895.

Get to onest (*Amer.*). Retire immediately.

Get up early (*Street*). Be clever.

Get up steam (*Peoples'*, 1840 on). Be energetic. Outcome of the initiation of the railway system. Even George Eliot, who hated anything approaching slang, used this phrase so early as 1846.

'I do not know whether I can get up any steam again on the subject of Quinet —but I will try.'—George Eliot's *Life*, vol. i., p. 150.

Get your eye in a sling (*Peoples'*). Warning that you may receive a sudden and early black eye, calling for a bandage—the sling in question.

Getting a big boy now (*London*). Of age. The line was the leading phrase of the refrain of a song made popular by Herbert Campbell. It is applied satirically to strong lusty young fellows about whose manhood there can be little or no question.

Getting all over a man (*L. Life*, 19 *cent.*). Handling and examining him—not necessarily for theft, but in all probability feloniously.

The only reason witness could give for the attack was that a few days previously he prevented Regan 'getting all over a strange man' whom he had brought into the lodging-house.—*D. T.*, 8th October 1895.

Getting before oneself (*Peoples'*). Personal emphasis of any kind — of vanity, boastfulness, threat, anger.

Getting behind yourself (*Peoples'*, 19 *cent.*). Lapse of memory in reference to events.

Getting it down fine (*American*, 1880). Successful by adroitness.

Getting it down fine on burglars. It is getting so that even burglars are seriously interfered with in the practice of their professions. A recent invention, etc.—*Albany Argus*, 1883.

Getting ox-tail soup (1867-83). Refers to the maiming of cattle, exercised by Fenians and other disaffected Irish, against the property of cattle-owners who displeased them.

In Ireland there have been no experiments at all, for the cutting off the tails of living cattle—'getting ox-tail soup', as some Irish facetiously styled this practice—is not a scientific experiment. *D. N.*, 7th June 1883.

Good example of historical phrase.

Giants (*Restaurant*). Huge asparagus.

I was startled by hearing the player call the waiter and order, as he pointed to the carte, 'Two Giants'. I arrived at a solution of the mystery when presently I saw the gourmands devouring 'giant' asparagus.—*Ref.*, 1882.

Gibby (*Navy*). Spoon.

Giddy young whelp (*London*, 1896). Youth about town. Rather contemptuous. Sometimes giddy young whelk — pronounced Wilk. Giddy kipper was the first development—from probably giddy skipper.

Gigglemug (*Street*). An habitually smiling face.

Gigmanity (*Soc.*). People who keep gigs — therefore respectable. Took its rise from the trial of one Thurtell for the murder of a Mr Weare, as to whom it was asked by counsel of a witness:—'Was Weare a respectable man?' the answer being 'Yes—he kept a gig'.

Gilt on the gingerbread (*Peoples'* —*almost obsolete*). The past - away annual rural fairs were made ghastly gay with flat gingerbread cakes, covered with Dutch metal, which tried to look like gilt.

Gin and fog (*Theatrical*). Peculiar hoarseness, generally believed to be caused by the abuse of alcohol.

Dr Lennox Brown has been delivering an interesting lecture on the effects of alcohol on the voice. There is a broken-down voice known in the profession as 'the gin and fog'.—G. R. Sims, *Ref.*, 11th January 1886.

Gin bottle (*Street*). Dirty, abandoned, flabby, debased woman, generally over thirty, the victim of alcoholic abuse, within an ace of inevitable death.

Gin crawl (*London, Fleet St. and Strand*). Beaten street tracks haunted by drunken or broken down literary men, journalists, reporters, and inferior actors out of employ.

Phil Benjamin was taking his daily constitutional, which consisted in what is called 'a gin crawl'—in this instance between Drury Lane and Covent Garden. —*Bird o' Freedom*, 7th March 1883.

Gin - sling (*Public-house*, 19 *cent.*). Practically cold gin-punch. Generally supposed to come from U.S.A., and named thus from slinging the mixture from glass to glass.

Ginger blue (*Amer.-Eng.*, 1855). Exclamation protesting against caddishness. Ginger was applied on the plantations of S. U.S.A. to over-eager negroes. Blue was added as a satirical reference to blue blood.

Girl of the period (*Soc.*, 1880 on). Term invented by Mrs Lynn Linton in a series of articles in *The Saturday Review*, attacking the self-emancipation of the young lady of this generation.

After Naseby, by Mr Briton Riviere. The reader, even if he has not visited the Academy, can imagine for himself the young lady of the period, bowed down with grief, and holding the fatal letter, below a tall window of the Royalist hall.—*D. N.*, Academy Crit.

Git a bit (*L. London*). May refer to woman, but generally means obtaining money.

On the day this 'ere job came off Chris comes around to me and says: 'I 'aint going to work to-day; you had better come out and see if we can't get a bit.—*People*, 6th January 1895.

Git the ambulance (*Street*, 1897). Declaration of incapacity, generally of a drunken character, cast at the sufferer. Took the place of 'git the stretcher'—which was (and is) maintained by the police. Took its rise from the introduction amongst civilians of ambulance service.

Git the sads (*Peoples'*). Vulgar synonym for 'to have the vapours'. (*See* Smokes).

Give a lift (*Amer.-Eng.*). A sharp quick kick.

Give it hot (*L. Life*). Severe castigation.

Remember, remember,
Next month of November,
The boycotting, treason, and plot—
For condoning this treason
(To win votes the reason)
We'll give it Lord Salisbury hot!
—*Ref.*, 18th October 1885.

Give the crock (*Peoples'*). Yielding victory—the crock must have been a jug.

I have been making a long calculation, and I find that this sum will only just cover ex.'s, so I am simply *giving* you the crock.—*Our Boys*, No. 2, December 1883.

Give away the racket (*American*). Unintentionally to reveal.

Give him rope enough (*Old English*). This phrase is abbreviated from the addition, 'and he'll hang himself'.

Give way to booze (*Street*). Mode of describing habits of drinking.

Give it a drink (*Theatre and Musichall*, 1897). Fin de siècle shape of condemnation conferred upon a bad piece, or some poor turn at the music halls.

Give out (*American*). End—finish; from a mine giving out as to ore.

Give way (*Ladies'*, 19 cent.). Weep, break down, resolve in tears.

Unhappily the infection appeared to extend its influence even to Mr Barrymore, who, when Mr Forbes-Robertson was preparing to bring the scene to a close by 'taking the measure of an unmade grave', had begun to exhibit in his turn an alarming tendency to 'give way', as the ladies say.—*D. N.*, 11th November 1882.

Give the shake (*American*). Abbreviation of shaking hands upon departure.

Give us a rest (*American*, 1882). A figurative way of asking a long talker to curtail his sermon.

Give him a rolling for his all over (*Street*). Corruption of give him a Roland for his Oliver.

Giving one. The one here mentioned may be a kiss or a blow.

Glim (*Thieves'*). Candle.

Glory-oh (*Navy*). Name given by the crew to the *Glory*.

Glory hole (*Street*). One of the names found for the places of meeting of the salvationists—in their early days.

The 'Glory Hole' Disturbances at Maidstone.—The 'Glory Hole' disturbances were continued last night at Maidstone.—*D. N.*, 24th October 1887.

Glow (*Com. Class*). Blush.

Go and eat coke (*Back Street*). Direction implying contempt.

Go around (*American*). Drift; go with current in life; live thoughtlessly.

Go-away (*Soc.*, 1886). The dress into which a bride passes before she departs with her husband.

Go close (*Sporting Anglo-American*). To the winning post. Abbreviation.

Go down one (*Com. London*). To be vanquished.

Go in (*Peoples'*). Act with absolute vigour. 'Go in and win' is the best known of the applications of this phrase.

The person who jumped on the communion table at St Paul's Cathedral the other day, pulling down the crucifix, knocking over the flowers and other adornments, may be said to have had a very inexpensive 'go in'. He had been fined £5.—*Entr'acte*, April 1883.

Go off (*Theatrical*). Go off—the stage.

Go off (*Soc.*). Not to take place.

Mr Matthews: 'There is something cut out of the diary?' 'That was an engagement that went off.' 'Whenever an engagement goes off you cut it out?' 'Yes.' 'What do you mean by an engagement going off?' 'When a person says he will call and does not, I cut it out.'—Sir C. Dilke, *Crawford Divorce Suit*, July 1886.

Go on the æger (*Oxford*). Signs the sick-list.

If a man is ill, or thinks he is—the will often being father to the thought—he 'goes on the æger'—that is to say, he puts his name down on the sick-list and obtains the luxury of a hot dinner in his rooms.—*D. T.*, 14th August 1899.

Go on tick (*Hist.*), Credit—short for ticket. Fallen very low in the world.

This phrase is derived from the French word 'Étiquet,' a little note, breviate or best—*i.e.*, a ticket or note being made or taken instead of payment; consequently, to go on trust or credit. "We'll play on tick, and lose the Indies; I'll discharge it all to-morrow."—Dryden, *An Evening's Love*.

Go on with the funeral (*American*). Continue the ceremony.

Go out foreign (*Thieves'*). To emigrate under shady circumstances.

Go one better (*American*). Superiority—from a term at 'poker', or 'brag'.

The merry Duchess can see the late Mrs Lydia Pinkham, and go her one better.—*N. York Puck*, September 1883.

Go solid (*American-Eng.*, 1884). Thorough.

The Irish Nationalist vote, whatever it may amount to, will, in American phraseology, 'go solid', against the Liberal party.—*D. N.*, 10th Sept. 1885.

Go to Hanover (*Jacobite*, 18 *cent.*). Paraphrase of 'Go to Hell'—Hanover being quite on a par with the hotter place in the opinion of the Jacobites.

Go to bed (*Printers'*, 1860-80). Phrase used by printers in reference to printing a newspaper on the bed of the printing-press.

Go to Hell or Connaught (*Hist.*). Be off. From the time of Cromwell, but still heard, especially in Protestant Ireland. Means utter repudiation of the person addressed. The Parliament (1653-54) passed a law, driving away all the people of Ireland who owned any land, out of Ulster, Munster, and Leinster.

Go to sleep (*American-English*). Fail, expire, come to an end, now generally accepted; but in the first place used as to wandering theatrical and other amusements companies about the U.S.A.

Go up (*Oxford and Cambridge*). To go, academically, to one 'Varsity or the other.

Wiclif went up to Oxford between 1335 and 1340. Balliol was his college naturally, as he was a North Countryman.—*D. N.*, 30th December 1884.

(*See* Go down).

Go up (*Theatrical*). The action of going up—the stage—that is to the back boards of that platform. (*See* Go off, Come on).

Go up one (*Peoples'*). Applause. Derived from the school class — the scholar going one nearer the top as he goes up one.

Go-aheaditiveness (*Amer.*) Success.

Go-between, The (*Holborn, W.C.*, 1897). St Alban's Church, Holborn. This high church used to be called 'Machonichie's'—from the name of its first spiritual director, who, dying in the snows of Scotland, was succeeded by Father Stanton, when the church came to be called 'Stanton's'. It acquired the title here given from a police-court case.

Mr Horace Smith: What is your religion?

The Woman: Well, my boy was christened at St Alban's, Holborn.

Mr Carr (second clerk): Is that Church of England?

The Woman: I don't know. You ought to know; you're more learned than me.

Mr H. Smith: Is it a Roman Catholic Church?

The Woman: Well, it's between the two. It ain't Roman Catholic, and yet it's very High. It's a go-between.—*D. T.*, 5th February 1897.

Go without passport (*Amer.* 1860). Commit suicide.

Go wrong (*Soc.*, 1870). Antithesis of prosper.

Goes Fanti (*Scientific*, 19 *cent.*). Tendency to return to primitive life—atavism.

Another sort of man simply 'goes Fanti,' like the Rev. John Creedy, M.A., Oxon, and reverts to savagery.—*D. N.*, 25th August 1887.

Going 'ome (*L. Class*). Dying.

Going into laager (*Colonial*, *passing to England*). Taking precautions against danger. From S. Africa, where the farmers in a given district, when fearing an attack from natives, assemble their waggons and form them into a zigzag circle or square, and pitch their tents within it. This is going into laager.

The news from Bechuanaland this morning is more serious. The magistrate and farmers at Kuruman have gone into laager.—*D. T.*, 9th January 1897.

Going ter keep a peanner-shop (*Street, London*). Evidence of complete grandeur, said aloud of and to a neighbour or other person passing in all the flaunting array adapted to holiday-making.

Going to Calabar (*Naval*). Dying —from Calabar being situated on the marshy estuary of Cross River, West Coast of Africa, and particularly one of the spots called white men's graves.

Going to buy anything? (*Streets*, 1896 on). Evasive request for a drink. One man who wants refreshment badly meets another, and puts this minute inquiry.

Going to see a dawg (*Sporting*). Meaning a woman, whose social position may be assumed by her association with ' dawg'—always thus spelt or pronounced.

Going to see a man (*Anglo-Amer.*, 1883). Going to get a drink.

A young fellow, who had a pretty young woman in tow, got up after each act and went out. When he came back the second time his companion asked: 'Did you see him?' 'See whom?' he demanded. 'The man you went to see.' 'I didn't go out to see a man; I wanted to get a drink,' was the candid rejoinder. The chronicler adds that the frankness of this admission so overpowered her that she could only squeeze his hand and say, 'Oh, George! and was it good?'—*Ref.*, 6th September 1885.

Gone coon (*Amer.-Eng.*). Raccoon, which has taken refuge in a tree, and thus offers a perfect aim to the sportsman. Conquered, trapped.

Gone over a goodish bit of grass (*Peoples'*). Tough—referring to a very hard leg of mutton, presumably old. Good example of evasive satire.

Gone through Hades with his hat off (*Amer.—just understood in England*). Bold.

Gone through the sieve (*Managers'*). Bankrupt—lost from sight.

Gone to Chicago (*Eng.-Amer.*). Vanished, levanted. Last outcome (1884) of G. T. T. (*q.v.*).

The spectacle of half a score of gold-laced and brass-buttoned generals in full uniform gravely discussing whether a fellow-officer was or was not wanting in proper respect for a civilian now shorn of official station and 'gone to Chicago' cannot fail to be inspiring.—*New York Mercury*, April 1885.

Gone to Rome (*Obscure*). Become silent.

Catholic Spain still keeps up her old traditions of Holy Week observances and religious ceremonies. When the clock strikes ten on the morning of Maundy Thursday all carriage, cart and tramway-car traffic ceases, even in the streets of Madrid; and the capital of Spain becomes a Silent City for forty-eight hours, until ten o'clock strikes on Saturday morning, and the bells of the churches 'return from Rome', as the popular saying has it, and announce High Mass.—*D. N.*, 4th April 1890.

(*See* Sent to Coventry.)

Godfer (*Peoples'*). Troublesome child. Short for God-forsaken.

God-forbids (*Rhyming*). Kids — a cynical mode of describing children, by poor men who dread a long family.

God-speed (*Nautical*). Hospitable meal given when a vessel is about to sail.

Mr Sutherland at a God-speed party on board the *Valetta* said, etc.—*D. N.*, 3rd March 1884.

Golblast (*Amer.*, 1883). A mild oath.

Gold hunters (*American*). Californians.

Gom (*Political*, 1883). G.O.M. became a word. Coined on the initials of Grand Old Man — Mr Gladstone, who in this year was quite the idol of the people.

Gonnows (*Women of Lower Class*, 19 *cent.*). God knows—with the 'd' elided. 'Gonnows I'm innercent Mrs Biffley—gonnows that.'

Gonoph (*E. London*). Thief—this word being Hebrew for the same.

Good curtain (*Theatrical*). Good ending to an act.

Good hiding (*Peoples'*). The good refers to the hider, not the hided. The second word refers to the hide, or skin of the victim.

Good strange (*Queen Ann*). God's strings, that is, the cords which bound — string having possibly been pronounced strang, as it still is in some parts of England.

Good strange — I swear I'm almost tipsy.—Congreve, *The Double Dealer.*

Good thing out of it '(*Peoples' Hist.*). Success—probably not wholly unaccompanied by smartness.

Meantime it is as well to put in a word of warning against the notion that the British Government seeks — to use a common commercial phrase—to make a 'good thing out of it' from a financial point of view.—*D. T.*, 18th January 1898.

Good young man (*L. Peoples'*, 1881). Catch phrase for hypocrite. Brought in by Mr Arthur Roberts in a song. (*See* Bad young man.)

Goose (*U.S.A.*). Practical joke. Has nothing to do with goosing in theatres.

Gooseberry-picker (*Soc.—old*). A confidant in love matters, who shields the couple, and brings about interviews between them.

Gorblimeries (*Police*). Seven Dials.

Gorblimy (about 1875). A gutter phrase A corruption of 'God blind me'.

Gord keep us (*London-Jewish*). A vulgar translation of one of the most beautiful Hebrew ejaculations.

Gordelpus (*Street*). A 'starver,' or casual, who has obtained this name from his ordinary exclamation — 'Gordelpus (God help us)—what's a cove ter do?'

Gosh ding (*Anglo-Amer.*). God damn.

Gospel according to St Jeames (*Soc.*, 1847 on). Snobbery, abject devotion to persons of position. Derived from Thackeray's *Jeames de la Pluche.*

Gospel of gloom (*Anti-æsthetic*, 1880). Satirical description of æstheticism which tended to doleful colours, gloomy houses, sad limp dresses, and solemn, earnest behaviour.

As what was called 'the artistic dress' was never adopted by acknowledged beauties or ladies of rank and fashion so did that theory of house decoration familiarly known as 'the gospel of gloom', completely fail to obtain any grip in Grosvenor, Berkeley, St James's, or Belgrave Square.—*D. N. Workers, etc.,* 17th September 1898.

Gospel of the tub (*Society*, 1845). The mania for the use of cold water.

A bath was, all over Europe, a luxury, or a remedy for illness, until what has been called the gospel of the tub was commenced in England. Athletics, tubbing, and the Broad Church seized on the English mind together, and cold water was preached as the great preserver of strength and beauty.—*D. N.*, 9th February 1883.

Got a clock (*Peoples', Historical*). Carrying a handbag. The creation of this phrase is quite historical. The first serious explosion by dynamite in London (Victoria Terminus, 1883) was effected by dynamite in connection with an American clock whose hammer struck the trigger of a pistol whose charge fired the explosion. (*See* Fenian.)

Got a collar on (*Street*). Stuck up.

Got a face on him (*Peoples'*). Evasion of ugly.

Got the crop (*Military* — up to 1856). Short hair. Until after the Crimean War, when the long beards the men brought home resulted in the hair being close cropped as a matter of natural taste; hair in the British army was worn somewhat long.

Got the glow (*Com. London*). To blush.

Got it (*General*, 19 *cent.*). The 'it' here is very emphatic, and means punishment *in excelsis.*

Got line (*Theatrical*, 1870 on). Shortly 'go'; but the words mean more than this. They infer vigour, grace, strength and charm in movement, especially in dancing. Only applied to women.

Got right (*Sporting*, 19 *cent.*). Cured.

Mr C. Hibbert has, we understand, sent Kirkhill to Jesse Winfield to be got right. Jesse is a good trainer and rider, but he has theories.—*Ev. News*, 23rd January 1896.

Got swing (*Artistic generally*, 1880). Equivalent to 'go', vigour—or the French *avoir la ligne*.

Got thar (*Anglo-Amer.*, 1880). Got there—completion, triumph, victory.

Got the morbs (*Soc.*, 1880). Temporary melancholia. Abstract noun coined from adjective morbid.

Got the pants (*Common*). Panting from over-exertion. Figure of speech.

Got the perpetual (*Peoples'*). Chiefly confined to vigorous and go ahead young men.

Got the shutters up (*Peoples'*). Surly—from the silent appearance of a closed shop.

Got the woefuls (*Peoples'*). Miserable, wretched, in the dumps.

Got up and dusted (*Amer.-Eng.*). Escaped—from a man when running away throwing up the dust behind him.

Got up no end (*Peoples'*). Magnificent personal display, appertaining to all parts of the dress and person.

Götter-dam-merung (*Soc.* 1862). Grotesque swearing which was used after Wagner had allowed his *Ring* to be performed in London (1862).

Gowned (*L. Fashion*, 1890 on). Evening dressed.

The diamonds worn by Mrs Raleigh, exquisitely 'gowned'—we believed that is the word—would not bear the scrutiny of the experts of Hatton Garden.—*D. T.*, 26th September 1895.

Grab-bag (*Anglo-American*). Tombola, or lucky bag, filled with small and large prizes disguised in sawdust.

Grabber (*Thieves'*). Evasive term amongst the fraternity for a garotter.

Grabbies (*Country*). Infantry. Probably disguised grubbies, from the evident fact that the infantry are not out of the mud as are the cavalry.

Grace o' God (*Financial*). Term given to the copy of a writ issued upon a bill of exchange.

Grandfather Clock (*Peoples'*, 1868). High eight-day clock. Never had a name before this date. From an American song called 'My Grandfather's Clock,' which became popular and gave this title.

Grand Old Man (*Pol.*, 1880-90). Mr W. E. Gladstone. Mr Bradlaugh, although claiming no originality for this phrase, was the cause of its popularity, through introducing it, in reference to Mr Gladstone, in a speech at Northampton.

Five minutes later an almost painful silence, followed by a craning of necks and a general rising from chairs and benches, proclaimed the fact that the 'Grand Old Man' had been seen emerging from the central doorway at the back of the stage.—*D. T.*, September 1896. (*See* G.O.M.)

Grand Young Man (*Pol.*, 1885). Rt. Hon. Joseph Chamberlain — in contradiction to the Grand *Old* Man.

Granite-boys (*American*). People of New Hampshire, which is a granite-producing territory

Grass before breakfast (*Irish*, 18 *cent. and early* 19 *cent.*). Duel. May be a jocular derangement of grace before breakfast.

Dick Dawson had a message conveyed to him from O'Grady requesting the honour of his company the next morning to 'grass before breakfast'. — Lover, *Handy Andy*, ch. xix.

Grasses (*Printers'*). A cry directed at any one particularly polite; probably from French *gracieuse*. (*See* Bridges.)

Grave-digger (*Anglo-Ind.*, 19 *cent.*). Strong drink.

Too much 'route marching, pipe-claying, and starching' tends to dulness and apathy, whilst it leads the British soldier, when off duty, to make too free an acquaintance with the 'grave-digger', as it is termed in India.—*D. T.*, 21st August 1896.

Graved (*Sheer adopted American*). Buried. (*See* 'Nuptiated.')

Gray-mare the better horse (*Peoples'*). Praise of a wife, as more able than her husband.

Gray-mite (*American*). Vegetarian. From one Graham, who advocated severe vegetarianism. Grahamite offered an irresistible opening.

Grease (*Westminster School*).— Struggle, contention, or scramble of any kind, short of actual fighting.

Grease. See Bit o' Grease.

Grease-spot. The imaginary result of a passage-at-arms.

Greaser (*Navy*, 1860-82). A scornful way of describing naval engineers.

Great bed of Ware (*Peoples'*). Anything very large in the furniture way. The great bed of Ware was at Ware, in Hertfordshire, until near 1870. Shakespeare speaks of the Great Bed of Ware in *Twelfth Night*.

Great bounce (*Am.*, 1883). Death. Everyday Americans, disgusted possibly with the sentimental fashion of describing death for some years (*see* Rocked to sleep, Joins the angels, Sweet bye and bye, etc., etc.) invented several grotesque paraphrases of death — (*see* Set to music). This was one of the attempts.

Experience has shown that iron steamships are very dangerous in case of collisions, so the only plan now to increase ocean travel will be to build vessels entirely of india-rubber. A collision between vessels would hardly do more than give the passengers the grand bounce.—*Detroit Free Press*, 1883.

Great horn-spoon (*American—probably from the Dutch*). The Deity.

Great Seizer (*Amer. satirical*). The Sheriff.

Greater Britain (*Polit.*). Annexation. Term seriously invented by Sir C. Dilke (1885) to include all colonies.

Greater London (*Soc.*). Popular, well-known. 'He belongs to Greater London'—meaning that he is more than known to a mere division of society. Originally invented to describe the vast modern increase in suburbs.

Grecian Bend (1865-70). A satirical description of a stoop forward in walking noticed amongst women of extreme fashion during the last years of the Second French Empire, and which was due to the use of enormously high-heeled French boots. The fashion fell with the Empire. (*See* "Roman Fall," "Alexandra Limp," "Buxton Limp.")

Greedy Scene (*Theatrical*). An acting scene in which a principal actor or actress clears the stage in order to have it for himself or herself, and bring down the curtain upon himself.

Green mountain boys (*American*). People of Vermont—a droll translation).

Green, To be (*Railway*, not yet come to people). Be cautious, from green through the railway world being the colour signal for caution. Good example of changed meaning—green still in one sense meaning foolish, inexperienced. (*See* All over Red.)

Greenery-yallery (*Soc.*, 1880-84). Distinctive term applied to the æsthetes who affected this peculiar 'colour-tone'. Derived from W. S. Gilbert's *Patience*.

When we all admired maidens clad, like the Goddess Venus in an obscure minor poem, 'in mourning raiment of green and grey', when, in fact, the 'greenery yallery' view of life prevailed, then blood was at a discount, and albumen ceased to be firm in the market.—*D. N.*, 11th June 1885.

Greens (*Hist. Pre-reform*). Corruption of groans, no longer comprehensible after the reformation. This word has got coalesced with 'agreeings'—these referring to domesticity, and thus the inexplicable 'greens' become comprehensible.

S'elp me greens, yer washup, I don't know what booze is. I'm a most ill-used bloke.

Grey (*Thieves'*). Evasive name for silver—from its colour presumably; and figuratively, money.

Griminess (*Literature*). Eroticism in literature, especially French.

Attempt to write a novel in which the characters are 'all good' was no doubt a spirited reaction against the prevalent 'griminess' of French fiction.—*D. N.*, 19th January 1895.

Grin like a Cheshire cat (*Peoples'*). Fearfullest grin of all.

Grinning at the daisy roots (*Anglo-Indian*). Dead—singular reminiscence of home fields, daisies being absent from the Hindustanee flora.

For thin potations are fortunately in favour, and the old-fashioned gormandizers of twenty dozen of oysters and unlimited stout are like the beer-swilling 'nabobs' or 'old Indians', all, in Calcutta language, 'grinning at the daisy-roots' now. — *D. N.*, 25th September 1884.

Grinning dears (*Military*). Linesman's nick-name for 'Grenadiers'.

Groceries sundries (*Trade*). Wine and bottled spirits sold furtively on credit to women—the bills sent in to their husbands including the cost of these liquids, itemed as (groceries sundries).

Grogging (*Peoples'*). Adulteration. Took its rise from making false grog by pouring boiling water into empty whisky barrels, impregnated with the spirit. Thence passed as a well-understood word to represent adulteration in general.

Groping for Jesus (*Peoples'*, 1882). Public prayer. Derived from one of the imitative military orders of General Booth, the creator of the Salvation Army. They did actually use the cry 'Grope for Jesus—grope for Jesus', when the followers fell upon their knees.

Groundling (*Theatre*, 16 *cent.*). Occupier of the pit, probably came out of the bear-pit.

Grouse (*Army*). Grumble and growl. This is a provincial word still in extensive use for worrying and scratching.

Growler-shovers (*Peoples'*). Cabmen.

Grub-hamper (*Public Schools'*). Consignment of sweet edibles from home.

Gruel (*American*). Sloppy poetical effort.

Guanoing the mind (*Soc.*, 1847). Reading French novels. Invention of Disraeli, published in *Tancred*. Accepted by Geo. Eliot. "This is a piece of impiety which you may expect from a lady who has been guanoing her mind with French novels. This is the impertinent expression of Disraeli, who, writing himself much more detestable stuff than ever came from a French pen, can do nothing better to bamboozle the unfortunates who are seduced into reading his *Tancred*, than speaking superciliously of all other men and things."—*Life*, vol. i., p. 163.

Guess (*American-English*). Think; as 'I guess not'. Supposed to have come from U.S.A. to England, but it seems in the first place to have gone there from here. Escalus, in Shakespeare's *Measure for Measure*, replies to a question, 'I guess not'.

Guffoon (*Irish*). An awkward, shambling fellow. From Italian.

Gugusse (*French—used by certain English Catholics*). An effeminate youth who frequents the private company of priests. In Paris (1880) the word was taken from the name of one of the novels specially directed about this time at the French priesthood.

Guinea gold (*Peoples'*, 18 *cent.*). Sincere—perfect. The gold coin of the whole eighteenth century was made of gold from the coast of Guinea. It was of a magnificent yellow and gave the name to the new twenty-one shilling coin.

Guiver (*Street Boy Swells*, 1890 on). The tignasse or sweep of hair worn down on the forehead, lower and lower as the '90's proceeded. (*See* Quiff.)

Gum (*Lower Peoples'*). Said to be abbreviation of 'God Almighty'.

Gummed (*American-English Boys'*). American boys' ways of referring to age. 'He's gummed'—meaning that he has no teeth left—that he is only fit to die.

Gummed (*Amer.-Eng.*). Equal to damned. Disguised swearing. Term very common in U.S.A.

Gum-suckers. A native of Tasmania, where gum-trees abound; a fool.

Gummy (*Sporting*, 1870). Swell, a grandee. Imported by English racing book-makers who infested and infest Paris. A translation of 'gommeux'.

Gummy composer (*Musical*). Old and insipid.

Gun-flints (*Amer.*). People of Rhode Island.

Gunnery Jack (*Naval*). Gunnery lieutenant—very popular in the Navy during the Boer War, and especially after the relief of Ladysmith.

Gunning (*Amer.-Eng.*). Shooting,

Gyle (*Fast Life*, 1850-78). Shortened familiar, and secretive title for Argyle Rooms, Windmill Street.

H

H. O. G. (*American*). Satire upon titles of honour—High Old Genius.

H. Q. (*Volunteers'*, 1860, etc.). Abbreviation of Head Quarters.

Had enough (*Street*, 19 *cent.*). Way of saying a man is drunk.

Haggis debate (*Parliamentary*). Referring to Scotland and Scotch affairs.

Hail up (*Australian*). Put up, as at an inn. Also an order by a bushranger—an intimation to throw up the hands, so that no weapon shall be used.

Haines (*American-Eng.*). Intimation of sudden retreat. Heard in Liverpool, whence it arrived from New York.

Hair raised (*American - Eng.*). Feminine quarrelling.

Hairpin (*American Soc.*, 1882). A simpleton.

Hake (*Cornish Local*). Offensive description of a man of St Ives—probably because hake is a very common fish, or possibly because it and St Ives smell equally fishy.

It is an unpardonable sin to describe a gentleman of St Ives as a 'hake'.—*D. T.*, 20th August 1896.

Half-a-brewer (*Low Street*, 1850). Drunk.

Half-a-doz (*Theatrical*). Short for half-a-dozen.

Half-a-foot o' port (*Strand*, 19 *cent.*). Glass of that wine at 'Short's'—opposite Somerset House. From the height of the glass, its shape being that of the champagne beaker of the '40's.

In the front department we have the 'ladies' who are the life-long companions of hard work, and enjoy their port of uncertain date, at 3½d. the half foot, for the size of the long glasses warrants this description. — *People*, 20th November 1898.

Halfalfanalf. *See* Arfarfanarf.

Half-and-half. *See* Arf-an-arf.

Half a pint of mild and bitter (*Tavern*). Intimated by a whistled phrase, well known to bar tenders, and quite as readily accepted as a spoken order throughout London — except the West district.

Half a ton of bones done up in horsehair (*Sporting*). A thin ill-conditioned young horse.

Half - a - yennork (*Com. London*). Half-a-crown.

Half-crown ball (*Mid.-Cl.*, 1880). A respectable, commonplace hop.

Half - go. Three pennyworth of spirits, for mixing with hot or cold water.

Half-hour gentleman (*Soc.*, 1870). A man whose breeding is only superficial. (*See* For-ever gentleman).

Half - past nines (*Lond. Streets*). Very large feminine boots and shoes—nines being a large size even for men of moderate feet.

Halfpenny howling swell (1870-79). An imitation howling swell—a pretender. (*See* Brown.)

Halfpenny-lot day. (*See* 'Apennylot day.)

Half-rats (*Peoples'*, 1897). Partially intoxicated.

Half up the pole (*Street*). Half drunk. (*See* Up the pole.)

Hallelujah galop (*Salvationists'*). A quick hymn in $\frac{2}{4}$ or $\frac{6}{8}$ time, to which they marched — invented by General Booth to attract the multitude.

Hallelujah lass. (*See* Ally Luja Lass.)

Halligator (*Coffee-house*). One of the variety of names for herring.

Hamburg (*Anglo-Indian*). Bazaar rumour.

Hamlets (*Theatrical*, 1885). Omelettes—started on Ash Wednesday by the actors of the Princess's Theatre, where Mr Wilson Barrett was then playing *Hamlet*. These gay souls dined and supped at the Swiss Hotel, Compton Street, and necessarily therefore found themselves before omelettes. They were dubbed 'Hamlets' — and they have kept the name in 'the profession'.

Hammered (*N. Country Iron Trade*). Married—very local word.

Hampshire hog (*Sussex*). Hampshire man. (*See* Sussex Sow.)

Hand - me - down shop (*Poor*). Illegal pawnbroker's—where halfpence are advanced upon property which the Lombardians will not look at. Used to designate the shop. (*See* Ammedown.)

Hand of Trumps (*Mid. - Class*), Bound to win. Victory.

Handful (*Mid. - Class*). Trouble, difficulty. Much to contend with.

Handy Jack (*Peoples'*). Contemptuous form of 'Jack of all trades'.

Handy man, The (*Boer War*, 1899-1900). Sailor. When the Boers (October 1899) overran Natal, the sailors who went to the front with cannon showed themselves very active.

The handy man. High praise for the naval brigade.—*People*, 1st April 1900.

Hang up (*Amer.*). Hold your tongue.

Hang up the ladle (*Soc.*, 18 *cent.*). To marry.

Hanover jacks (*Peoples'*). Imitation sovereigns. Probably originally false coins bearing the effigy of Jacobus, or James II., sent over from Germany, and passed as genuine in William III.'s reign. It may be doubted if the issuers could have been prosecuted— for their coins were not imitations of really current coin.

On searching the prisoner I found twenty-five 'To Hanover' sovereigns usually carried by magsmen, several 'Bank of Engraving' notes, and two duplicates relating to coats. — *Police Report*, 1888.

Happen on (*People's, Old*). Discover.

Happy dosser. (*See* 'Appy dosser.)

Hard and fast line (*Parliamentary*). Equal to obstinacy, argument which refuses to hear reason.

Mr Henley did not after 1870 take any prominent part in the debates. Some of his sayings will probably be always recollected in Parliament. The 'hard and fast line' and the 'ugly rush' are destined apparently to become stock phrases in our Parliamentary controversy.—*D. N.*, 10th December 1884.

Hard on the setting sun (*Anglo-Saxon Hist.*, 19 *cent.*). Phrase indicating utter scorn of the Red Indian.

'Hard on the setting sun' is a characteristic bye-word with which to signalise his humiliation.—*People*, 13th June 1897.

Hard Simpson (*Milk-sellers'*). Ice. Simpson was the general name for water up to the time when the introduction of the system of market inspectors put an end, or almost an end, to adulterated milk. This phrase came out in a police court—1865.

Hard tack (*Sailors'*). A sea biscuit. In passed-away times it *was* hard. Tack is the diminutive of tackle, to encounter. (*See* Soft tack.)

Hard up (*All Classes*). Impecunious.

Harder (*Anglo-Amer.*). Higher, in reference to betting.

Hardware (*Army and Navy*, 1880). Ammunition in general, and shells in particular. Jocular description.

If King Theebaw has had the precaution to lay in a supply of torpedoes, he may be able to give the expedition some trouble, but the chances are that the authorities at Rangoon may have had an eye on such kind of 'hardware'.—*D. N.*, 12th November 1885.

Harlequin Jack (*Low Class*). A man who shows off equally in manner and in dress; *e.g.*, 'What is 'e?—on'y a 'arlequin Jack.'

Haro. To yell. (*See* Cry haro.)

Harrico veins. (*See* 'Arrico veins.)

Harriet Lane (*Peoples'*, 1875). Australian canned meat—because it had the appearance of chopped-up meat; and Harriet Lane was chopped up by one Wainwright.

Harvested (*Amer.*). Guarded, watched over.

Hash dispensary (*Amer.*). Boarding house.

Hash-slingers (*Amer.*, 1880). College-student waiters in up-mountain hotels.

Hasty pudding (*Peoples'*). Literal —for it is flour and water boiled and completed in five minutes. (*See* Stirabout; Turn-round pudding.)

Hatter? Who's your (*See* Bad hat.)

Haussmannisation (1860-70 on). Imperious action in relation to the improvement of cities—without reference to the liberty of the subject. From Haussman, the minister of Napoleon III., under whose administration half Paris, for political purposes, was pulled down and rebuilt.

But, after all, the possibilities of improvement in this direction are strictly limited; land is too valuable, and the

Have a cab (*London*). Paraphrase for admission or reproach of intoxication.

Have a down (*Australian*). Bear a grudge. Very significant Saxon.

Also, the handicapper would 'have a down'—as the phrase goes in Sydney—on that owner for all forthcoming races.—*Ref.*, 26th September 1886.

Have a turn (*Pug.*, 19 *cent.*). A bout of fisticuffs, a pugilistic skirmish.

Ansburgh even told one of the officers that he would have liked to 'have a turn with him', placing himself at the time in a sparring attitude.—*D. N.*, 10th April 1885.

Have out (*Peoples'*, 1860). To hold a frank discussion, verging upon personalities.

But she cannot forego the satisfaction of 'having it out' with her husband.—*D. N.*, 2nd April 1883.

Have to rights (*Lower Peoples'*, 1880). To vanquish—frequently used in the passive voice.

Have to wait for the honey (*Devonshire*). Wait until hungry.

Havelock's saints (*Military—Indian Mutiny*). Teetotallers, abstainers.

Having (*Leicestershire*). Greedy.

Mrs Deane was proud . . . and having enough—she wouldn't let her husband stand still for want of spurring.—George Eliot, *Mill on the Floss*.

Haw-haw toff (*Street*). Swell, aristocrat—'haw-haw' being an expression very common as to the opening words of upper class men, while toff is almost the sound caused by haughtily drawing in the breath with the lower lip on the edge of the upper teeth.

Hawk and pigeon (*Soc.*, 19 *cent.*). Villain and victim.

The station-sergeant on duty, not knowing the detective, supposed him to be the accused. 'But I am the officer in the case.' It was not until the real captive intervened with an explanation that hawk and pigeon were sorted out properly for the occasion.'—*D. T.*, 17th June 1897.

Hawking (*Amer.*). Pouncing. Derived from the action of birds of prey crashing on their quarry.

Hawkins, Sir Frederic. (See 'Awkins.)

Haymaking (*College and Army*). Practical joking.

A number of men go into a friend's room, find him absent, and testify to their chagrin by disturbing the arrangements of his furniture. But haymaking of this sort is comparatively harmless and inoffensive.—*D. N.*, 1882.

He lies at the Pool of Bethesda (*St. Beghs?*). This comes from the German. *To lie at the Pool of Bethesda* is used proverbially in Germany, in speaking of the theological candidates who are waiting for a benefice.

He never does anything wrong (*Music Hall*, 1883). Satirical mode of describing a man who never does anything right. 'What — bankrupt again? Oh, impossible—he never does anything wrong.'

He worships his creator (*Soc.*). Said of a *self-made* man who has a good opinion of himself.

Heap o' coke (*Thieves'*, *Rhyming*). Bloke—which means a comrade.

Some heaps o' coke haven't got an ounce of cheek in them until they're flatch kennurd, but they ain't worth calling into account.

Heap o' saucepan lids (*Rhyming*, 1880). Rhyming with dibs—money. This is one of the trade titles for money, and comes out of the hardware trades.

Heaping in (*Amer.-Agri.*). Accumulating an argument, or debt. From heaping in produce.

Heapy (*Rhyming*). Bloke (a chum). Short for heap o' coke.

Heated term (*Amer.*). Name for the short but fierce American summer.

Hearthstone (*Coffee Palace*). Butter. It results out of the term 'door-steps', as a description of the flight of three or four thick slices of bread and butter on a small plate. The action of rubbing hearthstone over house-steps, and of spreading butter thinly on the slices of bread yielded this grotesque figure of speech.

Heaves (*Com. Class*). Spasms. Graphic description of the complaint.

Heavy hand (*Com. Peoples'*). Deep trouble.

Heavy merchant (*Theatr.*). Man who plays the villain.

Heckling (*N.B.*, 18-19 *cent.*). Mild bullying — from cock-fighting, heckling being the process of pecking out the neck-feathers.

Heckling (*Polit.*, 1850 on). Searching enquiry by way of questions asked of political candidates. From passing hanks of raw hemp through carding machines.

There was some timid heckling, to which Mr Gladstone good-humouredly replied.—*D. N.*, 11th November 1885.

Hell and Tommy (*Old English*). Said to be Hal and Tommy, *i.e.*, Henry VIII. and Thomas Cromwell—this couple, after the fall of Woolsey, playing havoc with church property. 'I'll play hell and tommy with you!' In all probability this phrase is a corruption of 'hell and torment'.

Helter-skelter (*Historic*). Full speed. Reid says: 'Helter-skelter is a contraction of the Latin, Hilareter celerter—cheerfully and quickly.' Probably an onomatope—very fortunately applied when Van Tromp's fleet fled before the English—some ships north towards the Helder, others south towards the Scheldt (Dutch Skelder).

> And helter-skelter have
> I rode to thee,
> And tidings do I bring.
>
> Shakespeare, *Henry IV.*,
> 2 part, Act 5, Sc. 3.

He-male (*Com. London*, 1880). A full shape of male, and resulting from calling female she-male (*q.v.*).

Hemp's grown for you (*Peoples'*, 17 *cent.*). Periphrastic prognosticate of the gallows—flax coming from hemp and rope from flax. Meaning that already the executioner's cord is in existence for the beneficiary referred to. (*See* 'Dance upon nothing', 'Mount the cart'.)

Henri Clark (*Drury Lane*, 1883). Flatter. From the flattering stage-mode of a singer of this name.

Her Majesty's naval police (19 *cent.*). Sharks—whose presence all over the world prevents sailors from deserting by way of harbour water.

Hercules pillars (*Lit. and Soc.—from Latin*). Limit of belief. Gibraltar and the corresponding rock on the African coast, were, for the Roman, the limits of the world of waters, and, colloquially, of any extreme statement.

Hero-hotic (*Bohemia*, 1897). Grotesque pronunciation of 'erotic' and applied to the more eccentric novels of the day.

He's saving them all for 'Lisa (*Peoples'*). Said of a good young man who will not use oaths or strike blows. This phrase arose in consequence of a row between a violent beggar and a frank young man of the people. The mendicant asked for a copper, the frank youth intimated he was saving them all for 'Lisa. A fight followed.

Hess-u-hen (*Lower Middle Class*). A way of asking for a copy of *The Sun* newspaper.

Hey lass—let's be hammered for life on Sunday! Probably, in the first place, from the work of the blacksmith at Gretna Green. It was said of him jocularly that he hammered couples together rather than married them.

Heye-glass weather (*Street*, 1860 on). Foggy — requiring the help of an eye, or rather eye-glass. Attack upon young men wearing single eye-glasses, which became common in this year.

Hidgeot (*Street*). Gutter translation of idiot.

High (*Oxford*). High Street.

Why, Oxford has laid out more than £100,000 in adding a barrack for purposes of examinations to the 'High', already sufficiently modernised by the tramway.—*D. N.*, February 1885.

High collar and short shirts (*Music Hall*, 1882). This was an attack upon the cheap swells of the period.

High time, or (intensified), **High old time** (*American*). Jovial period, enjoyment without much control.

'Look to your safes—the burglars are having a high old time of it.—G. A. Sala, *I. L. News*, 10th February 1883.

High part (*Dublin Theatrical*). Satirical phrase for the gallery.

High shelf (*Peoples'*). The ground.

Highflyer (*Nautical*). Slave-ship.

High-grade (*American-Eng.*, 1895). Superior. From railway world—meaning steep—above the general level.

High-toned coloured society (*American*, 1882). Negro-astheticism.

Higher culture (*Soc.*, 1885 on). Catch word of enthusiastic society people interested in education, who assume that all persons are capable of advanced education.

Moreover, even if we neglect to organise in this way the force which appears to be thus mysteriously making for 'the higher culture,' its mere appearance among us is a highly encouraging sign.—*D.T.*, 11th February 1897.

Highland fling (*Political*, 1881). Series of speeches in Scotland. When Gladstone (1879-80) delivered his famous Midlothian speeches, this term was applied to the statesman's efforts, and has since been accepted as representing a political speech delivered in Scotland.

Hill-top literature. Solid advice. Derived from danger-board warnings to cyclists on the summits of steep hills.

The attention which is now being given to that form of 'hill-top literature', known as 'danger-boards', has resuscitated some stories concerning them. It is said that in Ireland a tourist went down a steep and dangerous hill and was astonished to observe that it seemed to be without the necessary warning. However, when he got to the foot of the descent he found the notice, 'This hill is dangerous to cyclists'.—*D. T.*, 14th July 1898.

Hinchinarfer (*Streets*, 1880 on). Gruff-voiced woman, with shrieking sisterhood tendencies. Obscure erotic.

His hand was out (*Peoples'*). Ready to take all and everything at all times.

Histed (*American, outlying*). Vigilance committee evasion for hanged. Corruption of hoisted — pronounced high-sted.

Historical (*Society*, 1882). Old-fashioned—said of a costume or bonnet which has been seen more than three times.

Now, though dinner-dresses are rich, costly, and elaborate, if a lady appears at a fourth dinner or even a third in the same gown, it is immediately dubbed historical. — *Fashion as it was and is, D. N.*, 26th December 1882.

Hitch up (*Anglo-American*). Start. From harnessing two horses to run abreast.

Ho — he's got the white coat (*Provincial*). Meaning he is drunk.

Hold a candle (*Peoples'*). Be humble. Serve abjectly, as seen in the proverb. Took its rise from the habit of a host receiving an honoured guest by holding a candle in each hand and walking backwards before the arrival.

Hold stock (*Eng.-American*, 1879). Assertion of possession. From the money brokering operations in New York.

I do not come as a grievance monger or complainant. I do not ask for your pity, and have not the faintest feeling of revenge. Those were the passions of youth—a delightful period in which, as our American friends phrase it, no longer 'held any stock'.—Mr E. Yates, at Dinner given to him, London, 31st May 1885.

Hold up (*Society*, 1860 on). To be cheated or turned to account. From the American highway - man's habit of calling upon his victim to 'hold up' his hands, that he may not fire.

Holding up the corner (*Anglo-American*). Satirical description of a leaning idler.

Hollanders (*S. London*, 1875-85). Pointed waxed moustache. When Napoleon III. became popular in England (1854) many adopted the chin-tuft or goatee he wore—a tuft to which the necessary name imperial was given. During the first half of the 19th century no face hair in England was possible below the mutton-chop whisker—probably from national horror of the over-bearded faces of the French revolutionaries. A Mr W. Holland became a popular lessee—he at last reaching Covent Garden Theatre. Throughout his public life he grew, and always had on hand, or rather on upper lip, the finest pair of black-waxed sheeny moustaches ever beheld.

Holler Cuss (*London*, 1899). From Holocauste—a French horse in the Derby of 1899. There is here also a little satire, for the horse in question showed several faults in form.

Holocauste, colloquially 'Holler Cuss', excited some ribald remarks by reason of his peculiar hue.—*D. T.*, 1st June 1899.

Holloway Castle (*Peoples'*). Prison at Holloway (chiefly for debt), in the north of London; hence, sometimes called North Castle, as more evasive than Holloway.

It may be taken as highly improbable that Her Grace (of Sutherland) will be subjected to the indignities which are alleged to have been suffered by persons who have purged their contempt of Court by terms of imprisonment at Holloway Castle, as the gaol is called.—*D. T.*, 20th April 1893.

Hollow thing (*Racing*). Failure; no chance of success.

Holly (*Soc.*, 1880). Philippic. Mr John Hollingshead, as lessee of the Gaiety Theatre, for many years issued scathing proclamations signed with his name, printed in the house bills. (*See* Sacred lamp.)

Holy cod (*Atheistic*, 1890 on). Good Friday. The free-thinkers of France called the day of the crucifixion ' La Sainte Morue '.

Holy dynamite (1883). This term was given to the substance by American Irish Fenians.

Among the many senseless and wicked crimes which have been attempted with 'holy dynamite', the explosions in the Underground Railway are the most wicked and the most senseless.—*D. N.*, October 1883.

Holy Ghost shop (*L. Class*). Church — sometimes Theatre Royal, Amen.

Home rulers (*London*, 1882). Roast potatoes, as baked in the streets.

Homely (*American*). Ugly.

A Brooklyn man who saw Robson and Crane's company during the past week asks the *Mercury* if the ladies of the cast are the same who won the prize for homeliness at Bunnell's Museum.—*N. Y. Mercury*, February 1883.

Homesters (*Cricket*, '90's). Home team.

Honest broker (*Lower Mid. Class*). Matrimonial agent.

Marriages are not all made in heaven; some of them are made by marriage brokers . . . though the 'honest broker' does not seem to find the trade very remunerative.—*D. N.*, November 1884.

Hoodoo (*Amer.* 1883). Evil genius — or some object bewitching the sufferer. Comes from negro superstition.

Hookum snivey (*Street*). Nobody.

Hooley (*London*, 1897 on). Fur-lined and fur-collared overcoat—from its magnificence suggesting million-airism, the word being the name of a well-known financier. In 1898 this financier became bankrupt, and the word Hooley acquired a new and condemnatory meaning.

Hooley, To (*City*, 1894 on). To pile success upon success. From a millionaire of this name.

But, you know, when you apply, if I may use the phrase, 'Hooleying' finance to any good industry, there must be a certain finality about it. — Mr H. Bottomley, 10th December 1897.

Hooligan boys (*Street*, 1880 on). Street roughs—always youths, or even boys. This word is Hooley Gang, a name given by the police in Islington to a gang of young roughs led by one Hooley.

William Lineker, described as a Hooligan, sets upon an inoffensive man, of whom he had asked money, and beats and kicks him black and blue.—*D. T.*, 6th August 1898.

Horizontal (*Anglo-Fr.*, 1886). Lorette.

Une horizontale à huit-ressorts arrive l'autre soir devant, etc.—*Almanach des Cocottes*, 1887.

Hornpipe (*Theat.*, 19 *cent.*). Cry of condemnation.

There can be little doubt that after a while the person in the pit who loudly called upon the performers for 'a horn-pipe'—unseemly as was his interruption —gave accurate expression to the general feeling of depression which prevailed.—*D. N.*, 6th May 1885.

Horror (*Soc.*, 1896 on). Objectionable person.

You do not suppose that a 'horror' would have been able to settle with the natives. (Hear, hear.) You do not suppose I would have trusted my skin amongst them unless I felt perfectly sure of what they thought about me. — C. Rhodes, 22nd April 1898.

Horse and cart (*Rhyming*). Heart.

Horse of another colour (*Peoples'— proverbial*). Admission of an error in comprehension.

Horse's leg (*Military Band*). The bassoon—from its shape

Horse's meal (*Street, Hist.*). Meal without drink. Contemptuous expression, inferring the absence of beer.

Horsleyism (*Art*, 1885). Anti-nude in art. In the autumn of this year Mr Horsley, R.A., who never painted the nude, lectured against it very severely, and was thereupon himself very severely handled.

As an artist Mr Horsley insulted his art; as a man he insulted his manhood. How anatomy is to be studied, how painters and sculptors are to learn the first principles of their art, if Horsleyism is to prevail, it is difficult to say. Perhaps artists will in future be compelled to study the human form from the undraped dolls in the Lowther Arcade.—*Ref.*, 18th October 1885.

Hospital game (*Peoples'*, 1897). Football—from the harvest of broken bones it produces.

Hot blanketer (*Peoples'*, 19 cent.). Hot blanket woman. Refers to a woman who pawns her blankets while they are warm from being slept in— she redeeming them before night-time.

Hot corner (*Peoples'*, 1854 on). Figuratively—a position in which one is threatened, or bullied.

The 'hot corner' which was occupied by a crowd of helpers. . . . —*D. N.*, 26th September 1883.

Hot - heads (*Anglo - American*). Antithesis of cool-heads.

The news of the loss of the *Maine* caused intense sensation at Washington. The hot-heads talked wildly about the explosion being due to foul play.—*D. T.*, 17th February 1898.

Hot member (*Peoples'*, 1880-82). A troublesome, quarrelsome man. The phrase was rarely applied to a woman, probably because it appears to have taken its rise about the time when the Irish obstructionists in the Commons drew general attention to the vigour of the Nationalists—as they afterwards came to be called. This phrase remained popular for years.

Hot potato (*False Rhyming—Music Hall*, 1880). Waiter.

Hot water play (*Theatrical*, 1885). Farcical comedy. Came from America. From the actors in the play always being in difficulties until the fall of the curtain.

Hotel - beat (*Anglo - American*). Frequenter of hotels with no means of payment; a cheat in relation to board and lodging.

Hotel Lockhart (*Peoples*, 1890 on). Satirical attack upon doubtful grandeur.

House (*Middle - Class*). Exclusive set at parties and dances—a group whose members sit together and dance together.

House (*Poor Lond.*). The union poor-house.

House broke up (*Military*, 1870 on). Total despair.

House of distinction. (*See* Tench.)

House of Parliament (*Tailors'*). Convention of workmen in their shop.

House-proud (*Lancashire*). Weaver generally, who lives in his own cottage.

Considerable numbers of workmen own their houses, and those who know the place thoroughly assure me that the tendency towards small proprietorship of this kind is steadily on the increase. 'House-proud' is a very common expression in Oldham, and may be peculiar to it. The word explains itself.—*D. N.*, 29th October 1885.

Housebreaker (*Industrial*, '90's). Breaker up of houses—not a burglar. This term appears to have been created in perfectly good faith.

Sophia Ashton stated that her husband was a housebreaker.

The Coroner: What? Do you mean a burglar?

Witness: No, sir; he breaks up houses.

The Coroner: Oh! — *D. T.*, 11th October 1897.

Howdy (*Amer.*, 1880). Contraction of How do you do?

Howells-and-scrape (*Lit.*, 1883). Weak, purposeless fiction. From two American novelists.

. . . a repetition of the usual American novel, the two species of which have been irreverently described by a vulgar person as respectively 'James - and - water' or 'Howells-and-scrape'. — *Sat. Rev.*, 5th December 1885.

Howler (*London*, 1896). A swell, a fop, a fashionably-dressed man. Abbreviation of howling swell. May have been suggested by the annoyance contrived by howling curs.

Howling comique (*Music Hall*). Very bad comic singer indeed, with no particular qualities.

Hubris (*Academic*). Accomplished, distinguished insolence. Compare with 'grit'.

Boys of good family, who have always been toadied, and never been checked, who are full of health and high spirits, develop what Academic slang knows as *hubris*, a kind of high-flown insolence. —*D. N.*, 28th October 1884.

Hug centre (*Amer.—passing to England*). Head-quarters of public love-making.

Central Park as a hug centre. The amount of love made visible in Central Park is simply appalling. — *N. Y. Mercury*, December 1882.

The word was soon taken up in London, Hyde Park doing duty as a 'hug centre'.

Hullabaloo (*Peoples'*). Noise, disturbance. It would appear to be a corruption of the French *hurluberlu*—the accent on the two 'lu's'.

Hullo, features! (*Com. Peoples'*). Friendly salute upon meeting an acquaintance.

Hullo, my Buck! (*Peoples'*). Exclamation of approbation. Possibly from Villiers, Duke of Buckingham, or from the idea of a fine deer. Or it may be from buckram, the first stiffening used in making men's clothes. In that case it is a metaphor from the man to his fashion.

Hum (*Navy*). Crew's name for the *Hermes*.

Hum (*Lower Classes, 19 cent.*). Smell evilly. This is an application from the humming of fermentation in an active manure heap.

Hum (*Peoples', Hist.*). Attract attention.

Mr Douglas Sladen has given new life to an old and somewhat decrepit annual; a new life that makes it 'hum' in the very direction the reading world desires. —*People*, 4th April 1897.

Hunder-hand (*Street Boys*, 1880). Sudden blow given with advantage.

Hung (*Artists', 19 cent.*). Picture accepted and hung at an Exhibition. "I'm hung at the Ac." (*See* Walled.)

Hung up (*Soc.*, 1879). Said where in lower classes stuck up would be used. From the American — where personal catastrophe is referred to by this phrase. (*See* Screwed up.)

Hunkered down(*American prairie*). Stooped, anchored down.

Hunter (*Soc.*, 1880). Hunting watch.

Jennings was on Friday presented with a gold hunter and chain, by a few of his kind friends in front, who took this opportunity of expressing their opinion of his form as man and manager.—*Ref.*, 9th August 1885.

Hupper sukkles (*Soc.*, 1846-70). Upper circles. Introduced by Thackeray in the *De la Pluche Papers*.

Hurry up (*Anglo-Indian*, 1850). Be quick—originated in the river steamer navigation of U.S.A.

Hustler (*Amer. Circus*). Name invented for flaming advertisements.

Hyde Park railings (*Streets of W. London*). Breast of mutton—from the parallel bones suggesting the parallel railings.

Hyking (*Peoples'*). Calling out at or after any one.

I

I. T. A. (*Peoples'*). Euphemism for Irish toothache (*q.v.*).

I believe you, my boy (*L. Class*). Certainly. Accepted by middle-class about 1850—from the drama of *The Green Bushes*, in which Paul Bedford, then a most popular actor, used the phrase as a catch line.

'Tis forty years since Buckstone's drama *The Green Bushes*, was first played at the Adelphi, and since Paul Bedford's 'I believe yer, my boy!' found its way on to tongues of the multitude. —*Ref.*, 18th October 1885.

I refer you to Smith (1897). Synonym of Ananias—champion long bowyer, etc. From a character named Smith with an affliction of lying in *The Prodigal Father* (Strand Theatre, 1897).

'I refer you to Smith.' This will be the new London catchword. Whenever anyone has been drawing the long bow, as Harry Paulton does in the new play, whenever a boaster has been telling tarrididles or lying with extra vivacity, he will be met with the quick rejoinder, 'I refer you to Smith'.—*D. T.*, 2nd February 1897.

I say (*Peoples', 19 cent.*). Protest.

Ichabod (*Nonconformist*). Lamentation. From Biblical source. 'Ichabod —Ichabod—I have lost my wealth. The Lord be praised.'

Idle fellowships (*Oxford and Cambridge*). The old as distinct from the new fellowships. Parliamentary action swept away towards the end of the

19th century most of these fatal sinecures.

Much has been said against what are called idle Fellowships. — *D. N.*, November 1884.

Ietqui (*C. L. — Sporting*). A remarkable shape of phrasing, where the first letter or so is removed from the beginning of the word and added at the end. The word is 'quiet'.

Ile (*Complicated rhyming*). Dance—Isle of France—dance. 'Can't he ile?'

I'll give you Jim Smith (*Street*, 1887). Thrashing. Sudden adoption of the name of a prize fighter to designate fighting.

Imperial pop (*Street*, 1854). Pop is ginger beer, derived of course from the sound made when drawing the cork. The adjective was added by street sellers of this refreshment when Napoleon III. passed in state through London.

Imperialists (*Polit.*, 1888 on). Name found by the Radicals (who were in favour of the abandoning of the colonies) for the Conservatives, who wished the Empire to remain intact.

Impressionist (*Soc.*, 1884). Intensely appealing directly to the emotions.

Of late years we are accustomed to take our notions of French dramatic art from something more 'impressionist'; more vivid and rapid and startling; depending more on sudden effects and bold splashes of light and shade.—*D. N.*, 29th April 1885.

Improve the occasion (*American*). Take advantage of it.

In (*Peoples'*). Gain. 'I'm nothing in by that deal.' (*See* Out.)

In and out (*Common*). Pauper who gives notice frequently to leave the poor-house, and who returns after a short holiday, say a day, or from Saturday to Monday.

There are considerable numbers of paupers, it seems, who find the workhouse a convenient retreat on emergency, but have a strong aversion to permanent residence there. They are known familiarly as 'the ins-and-outs'.—*D. N.*, 10th December 1884.

In for a bad thing (*Peoples'*, 1880 on). To have ill luck.

'You are in for a bad thing, Phil, my boy.'—*E. N.*, 23rd February 1896.

In Paris (*Soc.*, 19 *cent.*). Eloped.

In the drag (*Tailors'*). Behindhand.

Incident (*Amer.—accepted in England*). An illegitimate child.

Indorse (*Amer.*). To sanction.

Inferior portion (*Polit.*, 1885). Eighties party of younger Tories. From a letter written by Mr W. E. Gladstone, which commenced

My Dear Sir,—In 1879 and 1880 the inferior portion of the Tory party circulated a multitude of untruths concerning me, etc.

The phrase took at once, and was satirically used.

Ink-bottle (*Artisans'*). A clerk.

Inkslinger (*Navy*). Purser's clerk. Term of sovereign contempt.

Innocent (*Thieves', Hist.*). Referring to a term of undeserved condemnation.

An ex-convict, who admitted having undergone long terms of penal servitude, applied to Mr Denman, at Westminster, complaining that his worship gave him three months' 'innocent' in May 1893 at South-Western Police Court. — *D. T.*, 16th October 1896.

Inquiry note (*Theat.*, 1860). Term came into use when provincial companies were replaced by travelling ones. It is a letter asking for information as to what nights a theatre may be had for performance.

Ins (*Political*, 19 *cent.*). The Ministerial side of the House of Commons. (*See* Outs.)

Inside (*Thieves'*). Abbreviation of 'inside a prison'.

Beaufort's duke trots by, and then dashes past a once member of the dangerous classes, who has been 'inside' many a time and oft, but who, having run into a bit of ready, will now go straight while straightness pays.—*Ref.*, 14th October 1888.

Inside of (*American*). A very emphatic synonym for 'within'.

Inside the mark (*Anglo-Amer.*). Moderate.

Inside the probable (*American—reaching England*). Within probability.

Introduce shoemaker to tailor (*Peoples'*). Evasive metaphor for fundamental kicking.

Inventories (*Soc.*, 1885). Play upon the word inventions. In the previous year a series of industrial exhibitions had been started in the then gardens of the S. Kensington Museum. This initial display was the 'Fisheries', and from that time the successive exhibitions had their titles changed into plurals in 'ries'. Hence the 'Inventions' became the Inventories.

As all the world knows by now, London was very near losing its 'Inventories' on Friday, for about noon a fire broke out there, and for some time threatened to be a big thing.—*Ref.*, 14th June 1885.

This is the close of the season. I suppose the Kensington Inventories has had the best of it, and owing to this fact I imagine many of the managers may be deprived of that great pleasure—paying income-tax. — Mr J. L. Toole's closing speech, Toole's Theatre, 7th August 1885.

Inveterate Cockney (*Political*, 1885). Ignorant of country life — a mere townsman.

. . . Now, gentlemen, there are three assumptions in this calculation, every one of which I, an 'inveterate Cockney', can see at a single glance to be totally inaccurate.—Mr Joseph Chamberlain, 14th October 1885.

Invincibles (*Fenian*, 1883). Short for Invincible Brotherhood.

Irish draperies (*Peoples', England*). Cobwebs.

Irish toothache (*Peoples'*). Enceinte. (*See* I. T. A.)

Irishman's rest (*Peoples'*). Going up a friend's ladder with a hod of bricks.

Irons (*American*). Pistols.

Irvingism (*Lond. Soc.*, 1880 on). Imitation on or off the stage of the mode of speaking and bearing of Sir Henry Irving.

Mr William Felton may also be heard of again. The 'Irvingism' of his voice was obviously natural and in no way assumed.—*D. T.*, 12th October 1896.

Islands (*London*). Refuges (*q.v.*) or raised pavements in centre of roads, to facilitate road-crossing by pedestrians.

The statue (Charles I., Charing Cross) being situated on an 'island,' a certain amount of skirmishing was necessary in order to reach it.—*D. T.*, 31st January 1899.

It snowed (*Peoples'—from America*). Catastrophe, misery.

Italian quarrel (*Soc.*). Death, poison, treachery, remorselessness.

It's doggéd as does it (*Pugilistic*). Perseverance.

Mr Benjamin's race and nation have generally shown themselves perfectly alive to the truth of the principle that 'it's dogged as does it', and they are not as a rule devoid of wits.—*D. N.*, 10th February 1883.

J

J. (*Peoples'*). Lost reduction of Juggins (*q.v.*)—which in 1884 was quite exceptionally popular.

By means of this knowledge we find the greatest of all differences between the raid on betting men in 1869 and the raid on professional gamblers and their J.'s twenty years after.—*Ref.*, 19th April 1889.

J.A.Y. (*Peoples'*, 1880 on). Fool, over-trustful person, one of easy belief.

Our business is not, however, with them or their intentions; what we have to do is to think of the jays who offered about ten times the market price for a ten-round spar.—*Ref.*, 17th November 1889.

J. S. or N. or D. (*Divorce Court*). The initials of the three forms of disturbance amongst married folk.

Whether it was an application for a divorce, a judicial separation, or for nullity of marriage, no one outside the parties interested will, probably, ever be any the wiser, since the letter indicating this (either 'J. S.', or 'N.', or ' D.', as the case may be) was not added in this instance, for some inscrutable reason.—*People*, 16th August 1896.

Jack (*Lambeth*, 1865-72). A policeman—quite local.

Jack-a-dandy (*Rhyming*). Brandy. This evolution has something probably to do with brandy, as being the most expensive of the ordinary spirits.

Jack ashore (*Peoples'*). Jack elevated — practically drunk, and larky.

Jack up (*Street*). To quit — especially in love affairs.

Jacked it (*Obscure*). Died.

Jacket (*Military*). A soldier who wears a jacket (chiefly cavalry or horse artillery).

Jacket, To (*Peoples'*). Threat to have you locked up as a madman.

Jag (*Spanish - American - Eng.*). Desire to use a knife against somebody —to jag him.

Jaggers (*Oxford*). Men of Jesus College.

Jesus College men were called 'Jaggers', long before a certain messenger - boy played the part of Mercury across the Atlantic.—*D. T.*, 14th August 1899.

Jailed (*Peoples'*, 1879). Sent to prison. From America, through Liverpool, over England.

Jakkitch (*Provincial*). Term of opprobrium. Probably corruption of Jack Ketch.

Jam (*Lower Class*, 1880 on). Pretty girl—presumably of easy habits. The history of this word is very interesting. A girl of notoriety in Piccadilly was named 'Tart'. She, in compliment to her sweetness, came to be styled jam tart, and the knowing ones would ask— 'Would you like a bit of jam tart?' Then the tyranny of brevity asserting itself, the phrase became 'jam', which lasted twenty years.

Here's a timely warning for all burlesque writers. The Examiner of Plays, which his name is Pigott, has determined that he will not give his sanction to the production of any piece in which the word 'tart' occurs. It is not yet known whether orders have been issued from headquarters to all dictionary publishers to wipe the word out of the English language; but the order has been sent, or will be, first to the burlesque makers, and to the dictionary-makers it may be sent tart-er.—*Ref.*, 27th October 1889.

Jam-pot (*Political*, 1883-84). One of the opprobrious names cast at Mr Gladstone—*apropos* to his recommending to Englishmen the cultivation of fruit and the exportation of jam.

Mr Gladstone is insulted day after day and week after week in Tory prints. He is a jam-pot, a wood-cutter, a hopeless lunatic, a Jesuit, an Atheist, a windbag, a storyteller, an idiot, and a humbug.— G. R. Sims, 28th September 1884.

Jammiest bits of jam (*Com. Lon.*, 1883). Absolutely perfect young females.

Jane Shore's fate (*Provincial—very ancient*). Death in penury and shame.

Jap crock (*Soc.*, 1860 on). Any piece of Japanese porcelain of a value from £10,000 to a mere 10d.

Japanned (*Soc.*, 1897-98). Dressed or furnished in Japanese fashion. Play upon the old word for lacquering.

The play is 'japanned' by Mr Arthur Diósy of the Japan Society. — From Daly's Theatre, London, play - bill, 1897-98.

Jarbee (*Navy*). Able seaman.

Jaundy (*Navy*). Master-at-arms. Supposed to be from 'gendarme'.

Jaunty (*Peoples'*). Self-sufficient in appearance or words.

Jawkins (*Club*, 1846). A club bore. Name-word derived from Thackeray's 'Book of Snobs'.

Jay town (*Anglo - Amer.*, 1889). Valueless.

A brother-journalist who has spent some years in the United States has written explaining to me the meaning of a '*jay* town'—term alleged to have been used by Mrs Kendal in describing San Francisco. A *jay* town is a *country* town. A 'jay' or a 'yapp' is the American equivalent of an English yokel or country bumpkin.—*Ref.*, 25th November 1894.

Jayhawkers (*American*). People of Kansas.

Jee (*American*). Oath-like expression. First syllable of Jerusalem. 'Jee! You don't dare to do it!'

Jeff (*Anglo - American*, 1862 - 83). Master, superintendent, director, manufacturer.

Jenny, To (*Thieves'*). Comprehend.

Jeremiah, To (*Peoples'*). To complain — from the character of that prophet.

Jeremiah-mongering (*Soc.*, 1885). Deplorable and needless lamentation. Invented to describe the social behaviour of those who after the fall of Khartoum went around maintaining that England had indeed come to a finality.

Jerking a wheeze (*Theatrical*, 1860). Telling a wheeze (*q.v.*) with brilliant effect.

Jersey hop (1883). An unceremonious assembly of persons with a common taste for valsing; from Jersey, U.S.A.

Jesus'-eyes (*Papal*). Forget - me - nots.

Jettisonise (*Col.*, 19 cent.). Imported—placed on a jetty.

Jeune siècle (*Soc.*, 20 *cent.*). Conversion of *fin de siècle*, and describing people equally of the same social behaviour. Of course from Paris.

Jib (*Soc.*, 1848-80). Flat-folding, 'chimney-pot' hat, closed by springs set in centre of vertical ribs. Name from that of the French inventor 'Gibus'.

Jib, Big (*Navy*). Good wishes — 'Long may your big jib draw' ostensibly refers to a valuable sail, but furtively has an erotic meaning. Practically it is wishing a man, who has served his time and is leaving the service, health and happiness.

Jiggot o' mutton (*Thieves'*). French —gigot.

Jimmies (*Hist.*, 17 *cent.*). Guineas —in the reign of James II. Remains to this day.

Jimmy Bungs (*Navy*). Coopers.

Jimmy Rounds (*Nelsonic Period*). Frenchmen—according to the Jack Tar of the wars with France in Nelson's time. From the cry of the French sailor when face to face with the English mariner—*je me rends*.

Joburg (*Military*, 1900 on). Johannesburg.

Jinks the Barber (*M. Class*, 1850). Secret informant. Idea suggested by the general barber being such a gossiper. Jinks is a familiar name for an easy-going man. Invented by Pierce Egan.

Job (*Peoples'*, *Hist.*). Hen-pecked husband. Patient origin obvious. Douglas Jerrold gave this Biblical name to Mr Caudle.

Jobanjeramiah(*Peoples'*). Maunderer — combination of the two doleful patriarchs.

Jockies, By (*American-Provincial*). Said to be survival of early English; 'By Jesus' cries.

Jockeying (*London Streets*, 19 *cent.*). Vehicular racing.

Joey (*Theatrical*). To mug, or attract the attention of the public, while the 'mugger' is up the stage, and should be quiet, letting actors "down the stage" have their chance.

John Fortnight (*Workmen's London*). The tallyman — from his calling every other week.

The tallyman, or 'John Fortnight', as the humorists call him, and the caller for the club-money secure varying receptions.

Johnny Crapose (*Peoples'*). Frenchmen. The second word is 'crapaud', but how comes it that this word has been accepted in conjunction with Johnny to describe a Frenchman?

Johnny Horner (*Rhyming*). Round the corner—meaning a public-house.

Joined the angels (*Amer.*, 1880). One of the ways of mentioning death. 'Do not ask me after my dear John Thomas—he has joined the angels.'

Joint (*Street*). Wife.

Jolly (*Middle Class*). Rally, a shout, a chevy. This word is evidently very old.

He chanced to come where was a jolly Knight.—*Spenser.*

Those were jolly days.—*Dryden.*

While the jolly horns lead on propitious day.—*Milton.*

The jolly hunting band convene.
—*Beattie.*

Jolly utter (*London*, 1881). One of the phrases resulting out of Punch's attack (1881) upon the Æsthetic School. This is to be found in Sir W. S. Gilbert's piece *Patience*.

Broken Hearts is rather a ticklish piece to tackle. Badly or even carelessly played, the love-sickness and the moonstruckness would be quite too jolly utter for the ordinary Philistine mind to stand.—*Ref.*, 18th February 1883.

Jonah (*Theatrical*, 1883). An actor who brings bad luck to a theatre. Suggests the superstition of the evil eye. From Jonah's supposed ill-luck —bringing catastrophe, when at sea. Apt antithesis to Mascotte.

Joseph and Jesse (*Polit.*, 1886). Political satiric cry against Mr Joseph Chamberlain and Mr Jesse Collings, raised immediately after the latter took office (February 1886).

The amendment did not expressly contain the principle of compulsion, and the speech of Mr Collings is not binding upon the House of Commons or the Government. But, as Mr Chaplin rather neatly put it on the night of his last appearance as Chancellor of the Duchy, 'the voice is the voice of Jesse, the hand is the hand of Joseph.—*D. N.*, 26th February 1886.

Josser (*Hong-Kong*). A swell, a grandee. From joss, the name of the figures of Chinese gods, with the personal 'er' added. Suggested by observation of the request paid by the Chinese to the 'joss'.

Jubilee (*Mid. Class*, 1887). The Jubilee (1887) came to be applied in many ways — but one, satirically descriptive of supremacy chiefly survived.

Judaic superbacey (*C. Garden and vicinity*, 1897). Jew in all the glory of his best clothes—generally a young Joseph, or a young old David.

Judy-slayer (*London, Jewish*). Lady-killer.

Juggins's boy (*L. Lond.*, 1882). The sharp and impudent son of a stupid and easily ridiculed father.

Juggins-hunting (*Tavern*). Looking for a man who will pay for liquor.

Jumbo (*London*, 1882). Anything particularly large and striking became a 'jumbo'—there being at this time a large elephant of that name in the Zoo.

The vulgar assert that Epsom is a very hotbed of training theories, and it must be admitted that it has its peculiarities in this direction. Nay, did it not produce the genial Mr Ellis, whom the wicked called 'Jumbo'?—*E. N.*, 23rd January 1896.

Mr Ellis was a big, heavy, solemn official. Some months after Jumbo's expatriation, a very tall man appeared in Drury Lane Theatre, and all the boys on hand yelled 'Jumbo'; an amiable Bavarian eight-foot giantess was trotted out at a music hall—she was at once baptised Jumba by the very press itself.

Jumbo (*Tavern*, 1882). The Elephant and Castle Tavern, S. London. (*See* Animal.)

Jumboism (*Polit.*, 1882). The Liberals having invented Jingoism to describe the warlike tendency of the Conservative party, this latter took advantage of the Jumbo craze to dub the hesitative policy of the Liberal Whigs jumboism.

Jump bail (*Anglo-American*). To run away from it. Both jumped their bail.

Jumped up swell (*Street*). Sudden leap from rags to royal raiment; also a toff in a hurry.

Jumping Moses (*Amer. - Eng.*).
Exclamation equivalent to Great Heaven.

June too-too (*Peoples'*, 1897). June 22 in 1897—the celebration of the sixtieth anniversary of the Queen's reign. Survival, or rather resuscitation of the phrase 'too-too', satirically directed against æstheticism in the '80's — meaning (satirically) too, too good. Here used as a comic variation of '22'—two two.

Jupiter Scapin (*Parisian*, 1810). Napoleon I. Used in England now and again to indicate a tricky minister.

Just ached (*American*). Longed.

Just too sweet for anything (*American*). Highest form of praise.

K

K.A.B.G.N.A.L.S. (*Mystic*). The letters of back slang (less the needless 'c'), and uttered rapidly to indicate that this mode of conversation will be agreeable to speaker. Another form is Kabac genals.

Kangaroo (*Nautical in origin*). A tall, thin man, especially ill-shaped and round-shouldered.

Kansas neck-blister (*American*). Bowie-knife.

The same with a knife. Horsemen, when travelling, carry it in the boot, and footmen down the neck; hence a bowie-knife is popularly known as a 'Kansas neck-blister'. — *All Year Round*, 31st October 1883.

Kapswalla (*N. American-Indian*). To steal—adopted from the original by American thieves.

Katterzem (*Scotland*). Quartorsième. A man willing to go out dining at a moment's notice—a parasite.

Kee gee (*E. London*, 1860). Go, vigour.

Keep off the grass (*Peoples'*). Be cautious.

Keep the boiler clear (*Engineers'*, 1840). Watch your stomach — in reference to health.

Keep the devil out of one's clothes (*American — probably from Dutch*). To fight against poverty.

Keep up, old queen (*Street*). Valediction addressed by common women to a sister being escorted into a prison van.

Keep yer 'air on (*L. Class*, 1800 on). A favourite monitory proverb recommending patience as distinct from impatience, and tearing the 'air off.

Keep your nose clean (*Army*). Avoid drink.

Keep yourself good all through (*Soc.*, 1882). Modern paraphrase of Keep yourself unspotted from the world.

Keeping Dovercourt (*E. Anglia*). Making a great noise. Dovercourt (Essex) was once celebrated for its scolds—this we have on the authority of Halliwell. On the other hand the term may come from the great noise made by a local insect called the Dovercourt beetle.

Kemble pipe (*Hereford*). Last pipe of the evening. An ancestor of John Kemble, a Catholic priest, suffered martyrdom at Hereford, in the seventeenth century. On his way to execution he smoked his pipe and conversed with his friends.

Kenealyism (*Soc.*, 1874). Social method composed of alternate profound humility and complete rebuke — supposed to have been invented from Dr Kenealy, who in this year defended Arthur Orton, called 'the claimant', upon a charge of perjury. Orton claimed to be Sir Roger Tichborne.

Kentucky loo (*Students'*). Summer gaming operation. (*See* Fly loo.)

Kepple's snob (*Naval*, 1870). Expression of scorn by superfine naval young officers. 'The Kepple's Head', named after the admiral. The naval clubmen have converted knob into snob. 'Cut him—he puts up at the "Kepple's snob".'

Kerwollop (*Amer.*, 19 *cent.*). To beat, or wallop. 'Ker' is also frequently used before words implying movement, as kersmash, kerbang, kerash (crash), kerflunimux, kerslap. (*See* Artemus Ward—'I went kerwallop over the fence.')

Kew (*Reverse Slang*). Week—spelt with one 'e'.

Key-vee (*Peoples'*, 1862). Alert, on the key-vee—of course a corruption of 'qui vive,' the French sentry challenge.

Khaki is a tint once called Devonshire grey. It was recommended by a military convention (1882) to replace the scarlet cloth of the British army—this scarlet being condemned in consequence of its offering a ready mark for the distant bullet.

Khaki (*Military*, February 1900). Volunteer—especially yeomanry volunteer for the Boer war, 1899-1900. Applied in all ways—to pease-pudding amongst many, from the colour. Hence resulted in common eating-houses the order, 'Cannon and Khaki,' *i.e.*, round beef-steak pudding and a dump of pease-pudding.

Kibe? (*University*). To whose benefit? Abbreviation of 'cui bono'.

Kick (*Anglo-American*). To succeed in pleasing audience.

Kick (*Costermongers'*). Trousers—short for kicksies, probably from the garment being that in which the wearer uses his boots at angles. Or it may be from 'quelques choses'.

'That dona's dotty,' said Obadiah, as he gazed upon his half-a-dollar, and put it carefully away in his only kick; 'and now for a jolly spree.'

If the burick (wife) wears the kicksies, that's your luck, not ours.

Kick is also used by thieves for 'pocket', probably because the kicksies or trousers have pockets. Fine example of application of the title of a whole to a portion.

When your kick is empty, and your mouth is dry, your blooming pals will not give you a yannep to get a drop of four thick.

Kick (*Trade-tailors'*). To seek for work — probably suggested by a barbarous mode of kicking at a door, before knocker or bell was invented.

Kick a lung out (*Anglo-Amer.*). Severe castigation.

Kick into dry goods (*American*). To dress—clothes being dry goods.

Kick up my dust in the park (*Soc.*). Promenade there. From French 'Faire ma poussière aux Champs Elysées'.

Kick out (*Anglo-American*). Die —from the frequent nervous movement of the legs as death approaches.

Kicked the cat (*L. Class*). Shown signs of domestic dissatisfaction.

Kid-catcher (*L. School Board*, 1869 on). L.S.B. official who beat up school tenants.

Coroner: How did you escape the school board officers?—Witness: I don't know how I managed to escape the 'kid-catcher', sir, but I did it.—*People*, 30th August 1896.

Kill who? (*Peoples'*, 1870 on). Satirical protest against a threat, and an assertion of quiet bravery.

Kill with kindness (*Peoples'*). This phrase is not generally understood; supposed to be literal. Really means to cause shame by overwhelming with satirical attentions a person who has misbehaved himself. It is not forgiveness, but retaliation.

Killing the canary (*Bricklayers'*). Shirking work.

Kilmainham (*Political*, 1882). Compromise. Said of an arrangement in which each of two parties concedes something to the other in order that a third party may be defeated. Took its rise early in 1882, when the Conservative opposition unintentionally brought about the Kilmainham Treaty.

Kin'd (*Soc.*, 1884). Satirical pronunciation of kind. Result of Barrett's production of *Hamlet* (October 1884) wherein he made this reading 'A little more than kin and less than kin'd.'

Kingsman of the rortiest (*Sporting*, early 19 *cent.*). Square, folded necktie of high colours.

Kippers (*Navy*). Stokers. Very probably because they are so smoke-dried, and dark of complexion.

Kiss-curl (*Peoples'*, 1854-60). Flat temple curl, abandoned by middle-class in 1860 or about. Still seen in S.E. London, where it is patronised by the street belles of that locality.

Kite (*American*, 19 *cent.*). The face.

Kite, Blow out the (*Com. Lond.*). To have a full stomach — suggested either by an inflated bladder, or a soldier's full 'kit'.

Klobber (*E. London*). Jewish for best or state clothes generally.

Kate Vaughan was perhaps a trifle too dainty, and I fancy any Kitty so circumstanced, on the sudden return of master in the midst of unlawful revelry, would have taken some pains to cover up the resplendent and unaccustomed 'klobber' —I believe that is the aristocratic term, Kate ought to know, now—donned for the occasion.—*Ref.*, 17th May 1885.

' And belted knight
Isn't such a sight
As Becky Moss in her klobr.'

' So I klobbered myself up as well as circs would permit.'

K' mither (*Provincial*). Corruption of "Come hither"—a woman of the town.

Klondyke (*Peoples'*, 1897 on). Mad —not fit to be trusted. From the craze that set in August 1897 around the Klondyke gold-bearing district.

Klondyke fever (*July*, 1897). Rush for gold in British Columbia. Began in this month, increased as the year waned.

Klondike gold fever has 'caught on' in the City. . . .—*D. T.*, 31st July 1897.

Knapsack descent (*Peoples'*). Soldiers in a family, either on the father's or mother's side, and very possibly both.

Knee-drill (*Peoples'*, 1882). Hypocritical praying. Derived from the military terms introduced into prayer meetings by the Salvation Army.

Knickerbocker (*N. York*). Man or woman in best society in New York. Accepted from opponents and made a class word.

Knife (*Lowest Lond.*, 19 *cent.*). A shrew—suggestive of being 'into you' in a moment.

Knife (*Theatrical*, 1880 on). Condense a piece. Knife is now modified into blue pencil.

Knife and fork tea (*Middle Class*, 1874). Vulgarisation of high tea (*see*).

Knights of the Jemmy (*Soc.*, 19 *cent.*). Burglars—the arms of the cavaliers in question being jemmies; the modern name for short crow-bars.

Some seasons ago the place was overrun by knights of the jemmy, who committed their depredations on other people's property in the coolest manner possible, and yet contrived to evade capture.—*D. T.*, 8th August 1896.

Knock about drolls. (*See* Athletic drolls.)

Knock along (*Austral.*). To idle.

There is an Australian phrase, isn't there, with reference to an idle fellow? they say he goes 'knocking along'.—I am not aware that it is an Australian phrase. We get our bad language from England.

The Lord Chief Justice: 'Knocking along' is not an English phrase. It is 'knocking about'.

Dr Kenealy: Well, it is 'knocking along'. I don't think it an improvement on the English phrase.—Tichborne Case, 1874.

Knock fairly silly (*Lower Class*). Almost, if not quite annihilated.

Capt. Thatcher said that when they first came in touch with the Boers they expected to be attacked, and they were. But they 'knocked the Boers fairly silly' and then made for Krugersdorp at a hand-gallop all the way.—*People*, 16th February 1896.

Knock in (*Costermongers'*). To make money—into the pocket understood.

Knock in (*Club*). Make one at a card table.

Knock off corners (*Music Hall*, 1880). Be successful.

Just as Arthur Williams had commenced to 'knock corners off' at the music hall, he is once more summoned to the Gaiety. More study!—*Entr'acte*, 16th April 1885.

Knock-upable (*Soc.*). Open to being knocked up.

For some time I have been weak and knock-upable.—G. Eliot's *Life*, vol. i., p. 440.

Knocker on the front door (*Peoples'*). Achieve respectability.

Knows how many go to a dozen (*Hist.*). Sharp. Even to this day many things are sold thirteen to the dozen — especially books and newspapers. 'Thirteen' is generally called a baker's dozen from thirteen loaves being sold as a dozen, exactly as thirteen rolls in our days go to the dozen.

Knuckle end (*Cornwall*). The extreme west of the duchy—the Land's End, so named from its shape.

Kodak (*Soc.*, 1890 on). To surreptitiously obtain shape-information. From the snap-shot photographic camera—named after its inventor.

We are watching him (Sir Henry Irving, *Richard III.*), our eyes are riveted on his face, we are interested in the workings of his mind, we are secretly kodaking every expression, however slight.—*D. T.*, 21st December 1896.

Kollah (*Hebr.-Yiddish*). A bride. Often spelled calloh (*q.v.*).

Kop-gee (*Peoples'*, 1899). Last discovery of the century for head—from the Transvaal kopje or mound.

Kosal Kasa (*Hebrew — Trade*). 1s. 6d.—the Hebrew words for '1' and '6'.

Kosher (*E. Lond., Judaic*). Pure —undefiled. Word used by the Jews in reference to eatables, and especially alcoholic drinks at certain feasts of the year, especially Passover and Pentecost. The word is here written phonetically, but in actuality the vowels are omitted K SH R, or rather R SH K, to be very precise. The antithesis of this word is Trifer — unclean, unholy, written T R F R.

Kruger-spoof (*Peoples'*, 1896). Lying. From the promises of fair dealing forwarded in January 1896, made by the President of the Transvaal republic, and not kept.

Kwy (*Fast Life*, 1800-40). First syllable of 'quietus'—death.

Kyacting (*Navy*). Jocularity during work.

'Here, knock off that "kyacting", will you?' an irate P.O. will say if he sees a youngster playing the fool instead of attending to his work. — Rev. G. Goodenough, R.N.

Kypher (*L. Class*). To dress hair —from the French 'coiffer'.

L

L., The (*N. York*, 1880 on). The Elevated Railway.

We have in New York a rich man who is almost the counterpart of Hetty Green. I refer to Mr Russell Sage. He was once associated with Jay Gould, and between them they engineered the 'L,' or Elevated Railroad of New York, much to their advantage, as most people imagine.—*D. T.*, 18th February 1897.

L. L. (*Dublin Tavern*). Best whisky. Initials of Lord Lieutenant.

L. L. (*Financial*, 1870 on). Initials of Limited Liability, and used satirically to suggest fraud.

La! (*Suburban London*). Nimminypimminy for the vulgar 'lor!' which is an abbreviation of the exclamation 'Lord!'

La-di-da (*Street*). Elegant leisure, and liberal expenditure.

Laagered (*S. African*). Waggon-defence. The waggons are zig-zagged in line or in square, so that the head of one waggon is half way down the side of the next—thus giving an extended firing line, while the length of the waggon is used to offer its fullest protection as compared with its width.

For several hours after we were laagered in position on Monday to receive the attack, concealed behind trees and tall grass, their sharp-shooters kept up a scathing fire.—*D. N.*, 29th January 1885.

Lady from the ground up (*American*). (*See* Perfect Lady.)

Lady in the straw (*Hist.*). 'Our Lady in the Straw'—referring to the stable in which the Redeemer was born. An old popular oath.

Lady Jane (*Soc.*, 1882). A stout, handsome, cheery woman.

Lally-gagging (*American Peoples'*). Flirting—origin probably Dutch.

You see, Pa has been in a habit lately of going to the store a good deal and lally-gagging with the girl clerks.—*Bad Boy*, 1883.

Lamartinism (*Literary*). Goody-goody. Lamartine introduced the novelty, in historical writing, of maintaining that everybody has always acted for the best, whatever his action, in the best of possible worlds. Term used scornfully since 1848 in French literature. Now sometimes exercised deprecatingly at Oxford, and in London.

Lambeth (*Peoples'*, *S. L.*). Wash. From the popular cleansing place in S. London being the Lambeth baths.

Lambies (*Navy*). Mizzen-top men.

Lame as St. Giles Cripplegate, As (*Peoples' Hist.*). Very lame — applied to a badly-told untruth. St. Giles was the patron saint of cripples, as distinct from St. Martin, who was the patron of all beggars. Cripples, therefore, had two saintly patrons. St. Giles's, London, was just under London Wall at its most northern point, and was St. Giles's Without—that is, outside the city. It abutted on the great north gate, and the church being frequented (in Roman Catholic times) by cripples in great numbers — many of them being fraudulent limpers — the gate came to be called Cripplegate; and this phrase suggested a lame excuse. The great bastion near the north gate is still represented by about half of it.

Land Navy (*Cadgers'*). Imitation sailors.

Land o' Cakes (*Historical*). Scotland.

It was my firm intention when I returned from my little Scotch tour to write glowing accounts of the scenery of 'the land of cakes.'—G. R. Sims, *Ref.*, 5th October 1884.

Land o' Scots (*Eng. - American*, 1884). Heaven.

'Lane (*Theatrical*). Classic term—became popular for Drury Lane Theatre.

Langtries (*Society*, 1880). Fine eyes. Mrs Langtry, whose portraits as a celebrated beauty had been seen for years in shop windows, suddenly became popular (1882) by appearing on the stage in England and America, where immense crowds were attracted.

Language (*Peoples'*), Sheer swearing. Satire upon violent expressions.

Meanwhile a scramble has been taking place between two omnibuses behind for the lead of the road, illustrated by a free use of what is called 'language.'—*D. N.*, 1st August 1890.

Language of flowers (*Bow Street Police Court*, 1860-83). Ten shillings —or seven days; the favourite sentence of Mr Flowers, a very popular and amiable magistrate at this court for many years.

Lap (*Coffee-house*). Tea.

Lapsy lingo (*Peoples'*). Corruption of *lapsus linguæ*.

Lard - king (*Anglo - American*). Typical Cincinnati millionaire, whose fortune is based upon pig.

Lardy - dardy (*Peoples'*, 1862). Affected.

Large - heads (*Anglo - Amer.*). Drunkards.

Large-sized scare (*Amer.*). Wild panic.

Lassitudinarian (*Soc.*, 1894 on). Satirical evolution from valetudinarian.

Evasive term for a constitutionally lazy man.

... an occupation, by the way, exactly suiting a 'lassitudinarian' temperament.—*D. T.*, 4th February 1897.

Last bit o' family plate (*Artisans'*). Final silver coin.

Last shake o' the bag (*Peoples'—old*). Youngest child.

Latch - key (*Irish Constabulary*, 1881-82). Crowbar — name given by the Irish Constabulary to the crowbar, as the too frequent key with which they had to open house doors when in the process of eviction.

Law (*Police*). Advantage, start, privilege. Invented by the police.

The defendants were placed in the police van and driven off under the very noses of their would-be persecutors, who were quite unaware that their prey had escaped them. Having given the van a good extent of 'law', the crowd were allowed to go where they wished, but only in time to find that they had been outwitted.—*D. N.*, 15th September 1885.

Law's - a - me (*Hist. — now chiefly used in U.S.A.*). Lord save me.

He's full of the Old Scratch, but laws-a-me—he's my own dead sister's boy!—Mark Twain, *Tom Sawyer*, p. 19.

Lay (lie) on the face (*Peoples'*). Dissipate exorbitantly.

Lea toff (*Local Lond.*). A youth of social aspirations, chiefly in relation to Sunday; one who displays his distinction, in a hired boat, rowing up and down the River Lea.

Lead poisoning (*W. America*). Active bullets.

Very recently a gentleman who was at once editor of a local newspaper and town constable found it necessary to relinquish the latter post in consequence of a disease which he euphemistically termed 'lead-poisoning', the result of being shot through part of the lungs by a desperado of the township under his care.—*D. N.*, 27th March 1883.

Leaden pill — sometimes **Leaden favour** (*Anglo-American*). Bullet.

Leadenhall market sportsman (*Sporting*, 1870). Landowner who sells his game to Leadenhall market poulterers.

The true foxhunter loathes the preserver of pheasants as 'an old woman', or 'a Leadenhall-market sportsman'; while the latter rages at the wholesale destruction of his costly game by the fox.—*D. N.*, 11th November 1885.

Leaderette (*Press*, 1875). When, probably borrowing from the French, the idea of lightening journalism, short pithy 'leaders' were introduced, a technical name was to be found for them, and 'leaderette' was the result.

Leading article (*Trade*, 1870). A term used to denote the best bargain in the shop—one that should lead to other purchases.

Leading heavies (*Theat.*). Middle-aged women's serious rôles.

I am an actress. I was in Mr O'Connor's company during his engagement at the Star Theatre, playing the 'leading heavies' throughout that engagement. I was to receive 12 dollars a week and expenses.—*N. Y. Mercury*, 9th June 1888.

Leak (*Anglo-American*, 1880). To lie.

Leaky (*Peoples'*). Talkative when drunk.

Learn by rote (*Scholastic*). Learn by the road, route, or rut—that is to say, without intelligence, perfunctorily.

Learning shover (*Com. London*, 1869 on). Schoolmaster—took its rise at the institution of the London School Board.

Leather and prunella (*Middle-Class—ancient*). Expresses flimsiness. A corruption of 'All lather and prunella'—the 'lather' being whipped cream, the 'prunella' probably damson *purée* or plum jelly. Sometimes used to express humbug.

Then who shall say so good a fellow,
Was only leather and prunella.—*Don Juan*.

The Foreign Office regards all the organised cheerfulness of the last few days' Chinese diplomatic blandishments and promises, edicts and telegrams, alike, as so much leather and prunella. —*D. T.*, 24th July 1900.

Leave them to fry in their own fat (*Plantagenet English*). This phrase is equal to—Give him rope enough and he'll hang himself. The phrase was brought into fashion again by Prince Bismarck, who (1871) after the partial retirement of the German forces, applied it to Parisians and their politics.

Leave yer 'omer (*L. Class — Women's*). A handsome, dashing man. This is derived, very satirically, from 'That's the man I'm goin' to leave me 'ome for'. Good example of street sentiment.

Leccers (*Oxford 'er'*). Lectures—both 'c's' hard.

Each man attends as cheerfully as he can his 'leccers'.—*D. T.*, 14th August 1899.

Left centre (*Polit.*, 1885). Whig. Bestowed by advanced Liberals on cautious Liberal party.

Thiers used to say that France was essentially Left Centre, and that power would come to the party of the most prudent.—*D. N.*, 20th October 1885.

Left her purse on her piano (*Peoples'*, 19 *cent.*). Satirical hit at self-sufficiency.

Left the minority (*Soc.*, 1879). No longer with the living.

Poor 'Benefit Thompson' has left the minority.—*Entr'acte*, 30th April 1885.

Leg (*Fast Society*, 1860). Footman —from the display of the lower limbs.

Leg maniac (*Stage*, 1880 on). Eccentric, rapid dancer.

Mr Fred Storey holds a unique position as a 'leg maniac'—horrible term!—*D. T.*, 3rd December 1896.

Leg up (*Peoples'*). Help.

Legit (*Theatrical*). Shortening of legitimate, in its turn the curtailing of the legitimate drama.

Leisure hours (*Rhyming*). Flowers.

Leisured rich (*Soc.*, 1885). Invented by Mr Gladstone.

Lemon squash party (*Soc.*, 1882). A meeting of young men, initially at Oxford, when nothing was drunk but this preparation.

Lemoncholy (*Transposition — London*). Melancholy.

Lend us your breath to kill Jumbo (*Low London*). Protest against the odour of bad breath.

Length of the foot (*Irish*). Comprehend and manipulate the victim.

Does the enterprising tradesman who thus shields himself behind magisterial patronage undertake to teach the district the length of Mr Bushby's foot? —*D. N.*, 18th August 1884.

Lengthy (*Parl.*, 1875). Used by both houses for 'long'.

The fine people who think it elegant to say 'lengthy' when they mean 'long', though they have not yet come to say 'strengthy' when they mean 'strong', are fond of saying 'utilise' when they mean use.—*D. N.*, April 1883.

Let, To (*Art*). Sparsely-filled canvas.

Let 'em all come (*Peoples'*, 1896). Cheery defiance. Outcome of the plucky way in which the British, in the first days in the new year, accepted the message of congratulation by the Emperor of Germany to President Kruger on the repulse of the Jameson raid; followed next day by the imperial message sent by President of the U.S.A., *apropos* to the English boundary dispute with Venezuela; both followed by some defiant comments in the French press.

Let her rip (*English-American*, 1840 onwards). Let her go as she wants. This phrase has a very striking history. When rival river steam-boats were fully established on the Mississippi and other American rivers, the rival captains would put on every ounce of steam in order to keep ahead. Too frequently the boiler would burst, or 'rip', as emphatically it would when bursting. 'Let her rip' came to be a common expression amongst these captains when more timid passengers or sensible sub-officers urged him to lower the steam pressure.

Let out (*American*). Releases — very emphatic.

'Well, sah, I wanted to ax how many kinds of religun you had up dat way?'

'Oh, about a dozen, I guess.'

'Cracky, golly!' he whispered, 'but dat lets me out!'—*Detroit Free Press*, 1883.

Let out your back-band (*American*). Be more familiar and friendly in your statement.

I ax you let out your back band a little on that last statement.

Let through (*Peoples'*). (1) Escape; (2) Cause injury.

Let up (*Anglo-American*). Make an end. From 'letting' or lifting up the engine bar which, down, puts all steam on. To end pressure.

Lethal (*Press*, 19 *cent.*). Mortal. From the waters of Lethe. Now applied by careless writers to any mode of violent death.

It is always understood among the most distinguished members of the profession—the higher burglarious circles, as they are called—that nothing but the direst necessity shall ever make them use a revolver or other lethal weapon.—*Ref.*, 3rd February 1889.

Letter - fencers (*London*). Postmen.

Levenses (*E. Anglican*). Lunch—the meals of the elevens, whence this pleonastic plural has been evolved. (*See* Bever.)

Liberal forwards (*Political*, 1898). Modified Radicals—without fads.

'Liberal forwards'—as Mr George Russell's party styles itself—are notoriously suspicious of the reactionary designs which they attribute to Lord Salisbury.—*D. T.*, 2nd February 1899.

Lick into shape (*Com.*). To get ready. Obviously — from animals, especially bears, licking their young.

It had not been thought necessary to lick the piece into shape. The result was most laughable; the last act created more laughter than has done any farce for years.—*Stage*, 21st August 1885.

Lie down and die (*Anglo - American*). Despair.

Lie down to rest (*Amer. - Eng., Street*). Fail, come to an end, a dramatic company which has collapsed. Often seen, in the past tense, in American graveyards; finally it passed into a colloquialism. (*See* Climb the golden staircase.)

Henderson's *Uncle Tom* Company laid down to rest at Dunkirk, Ohio, on Tuesday.—*N. Y. Mercury*, December 1884.

Reached England about 1883.

Life and everlasting (*Peoples', Hist.*). Complete, final, without appeal—especially applied to sales.

His Honour: Why didn't you jib, and take the horse back then?
Defendant: I took it back the next morning. When he sold it he said 'it was for life and everlasting'.—*D. T.*, 23rd November 1897.

Lift up (*N. Eng. Methodists'*). To pray.

Lifter (*Stable*). Kicking horse, one which lifts.

Lifu (*Motor car*, 1897). Reduction of liquid fuel (paraffin or other oil).

Starting punctually to time, the Lifu, which takes its name from the liquid fuel (oil) which it uses, as the odour proclaims, arrived at London Bridge.—*D. T.*, 17th December 1897.

Light - comedy merchant (*Theatrical*). Comedian pure and simple.

Despite its title, *The Mormon* has no connection with the followers of Brigham Young, and the scene is laid not at Salt Lake City, but at Ramsgate; a very light-comedy merchant, the Hon. Charles Nugent, being heavily in debt.—*Ref.*, 13th March 1887.

Light - food (*Lower Peoples'*). Tobacco for chewing as a repast—very light.

Light-house (*Navy*). Pepper-castor.

Lightning curtain - taker (*Theatrical*, 1884). A curtain-taker (*q.v.*), who does not wait for much applause (which he may not receive), and who therefore rushes on upon the least approbation. (*See* Take a curtain, Fake a curtain.)

Lights up (*Theat., circa*, 1900). Condemnation of a new piece on the first night of its production (*see* Boo). Chiefly the decision of the gallery.

Like to meet her in the dark (*L. Class*, 1884). Plain.

Lime - juice (*Theatrical*, 1875). Lime light.

Limerick (*Peoples'*). Queer and coarse rhymes, like 'There was a young lady of Lea,' etc. Some say this style of rhyme was called Limericks because all the specimens go to a tune to the original words,

'Won't you come up—up—up
Won't you come up to Limerick?'

Lincoln & Bennett (*Soc.*, 1840 on). Superior hat. From makers' name. (*See* Dorsay, Nicholls, Poole, Redfern.)

Lined (*Low Life*). Passive voice of active verb to line, and derived from certificate of marriage.

Link and froom (*Street, Hebrew*).

'Dolly', who was a Jewess, but one who was link rather than froom, was about forty years old at the time of her death.—*Ref.*, 3rd February 1889.

Linkman (*W. London*). General man-servant about kitchen or yard.

Lion Chang (*Fugitive Ang.*, 1896). Jocular Anglicising of the name of Li Hung Chang — and referring to his fleeting popularity. He arrived in the beginning of the month, went to America before the end of it, and in the meantime was dubbed long Lion Chang. His *entourage* also obtained, in several instances, droll names. Lo Feng Luh became Loafing Loo, Viscount Li became Lud Lulliety, and Seng became S'eng-song.

Lion comique (*Music Hall*, 1880). This term was a way of describing a leading comic singer.

Changes of fancy and taste have abolished the 'lion comique', as he was known to an antecedent generation, and the death of Mr Macdermott practically snaps the last link.—*D. T.*, 9th May 1901.

Liqueur of four ale (*City, satirical*). Precisely as the common folk make fun of cheap food and give it impressive titles such as calling sheep's head broth turtle soup; so middle-class young city men chaff their drinks. The most expensive liqueur, green Chartreuse would be eighteenpence—while four ale (City sherry) is the cheapest. Phrase really means, 'a glass of bitter'—beer understood.

Liquor (*Public-house keepers'*). Euphemism for the water used in adulterating beer.

Listening to oneself (*Irish, old*). Thinking.

Little beg (*Pub. Sch.*). Abbreviation of little beggar—friendly term applied by upper form to lower form boys.

Little bit o' keg (*L. Class*). Kegmeg meat, that is, common meat—erotic.

Little bit of sugar for the bird (*Peoples'*, 1897). Premium, unexpected benefit, surprise, acquisition.

She applied for five Ordinary shares at £1 premium, paying £2, 10s. with her application, and on allotment she paid up the balance, £7, 10s. in full. She held all the shares when the corporation was wound up, and received nothing for her money.

You didn't get anything of Goodman's 'little bit of sugar'? (Laughter.)—No. —*D. T.*, 24th December 1898.

Little deers (*Soc. Anglo-American*). Young women—generally associated, or declaring themselves to be associated, with the stage. New spelling of 'dears' to form a feminine to stags.

Little go (*Thieves'*). First imprisonment, first invented by a fallen university man.

Little Ireland (1879). The then Home Rule brigade in the House of Commons.

Little more Charley behind (*Theatrical*). More lumbar width—speaking of feminine dress or costume.

Little season (*Society*, 1880 on). London season between 6th January and Shrove Tuesday. The real season begins about 15th April and ends with July.

London has been during the last few years not only full of visitors after Easter, but has developed a pre-Lenten or 'little' season, as it is called.—*D. N.*, 6th July 1884.

Little whack (*Drinking men's*). Small quantity of spirits.

You may choose for the moment of illustration either your going into or your coming out of the Carnarvon Arms; where you intend to have or where you have had your little whack.—Besant & Rice, *Golden Butterfly*, vol. i., ch. xii.

Live down (*Soc.*, 1870). To overcome by strenuous patience.

When it took six months to go from India to England they made the most of a bad situation, and tried to live down heat and care. — (Indian Hospitality) *Graphic*, 17th March 1883.

Live messages (*Telegraphers'*, 1870). Messages in course of transition.

In the telegraph department dining accommodation has been provided, because it is thought undesirable that those who are engaged in the transmission of telegraph messages should leave the premises during their period of duty. With what are called 'live messages' fresh in their minds, there is felt to be an objection to their adjourning to neighbouring restaurants.—*D. N.*, 27th September 1883.

Live on (*L. Peoples'*). Fine girl or woman. (*See* Leave yer 'ome.)

Live up to (*Æsthetic*, 1878-83). Exist purely up to a pure standard. Invented by Du Maurier (*Punch*). Phrase used quite seriously by the Burne Jones school. (*See* Apostle of culture.)

Living bache (*Soc.*). Life in chambers—living like a bachelor.

Living with mother now (*Music Hall*, 1881). The refrain of a doubtful song, in which this answer is made by the young person to all the blandishments of her inamorato.

Lizards (*American*). Men of Alabama.

Loaferies, The (*E. London*). Whitechapel Workhouse — from the tenderness shown towards the inmates. In 1898 the guardians even wished to do away with the term workhouse.

No very luminous suggestions were forthcoming as to a new title, though one of the guardians thought 'Paradise' a fitting change. The others, however, seemed to consider this a little previous. Perhaps 'House of Repose' or 'The Loaferies' would be considered appropriate. Mr Perez remarked that whatever the new name, in a few years it would be as unpopular as the old one.— *D. T.*, 10th February 1898.

Loan (*American*). Lend, now becoming English. Has been accepted probably as a euphemism.

Such a term as 'I will loan you my dog Schneider' is hardly British.—*D. N.*, 1882.

Loathly (*London Club*, October 1897). Offensive.

This savage sacrificial feat, performed with horrible frequency by Bitchlieli and his reverend subordinates on the 'teocalli', or green stone, surmounting the shrines of the loathly idols that were eventually overthrown and destroyed by Hernan Cortes.—*D. T.*, 24th December 1898.

Lobby (*Amer.—coming to Eng.*). To corrupt by process. To attempt to exercise an influence on members of a legislative body by persons not members —who attend the session of a legislative body for the purpose of influencing the debates.

Lobby through (*Amer.—passing to Eng.*). Is to get a bill accepted by influence.

Loblifer (*Cornwall*). Luck-bringing mannikin. Probably a corruption of Lob-lie-by-the-fire—from this genius being fond of warmth after his damp cave abode.

'Lob-Lie-by-the-Fire,' is a pretty story of farm life and rustic folk, in which mysterious agrarian services rendered by an unseen benefactor awaken all the old country superstitions. — *D. N.*, 17th December 1885.

Local pot. (*See* Pot.)

Locate (*American*). To settle.

Locked up (*Street*). Arrested.

Locust (*Soc.*). Extravagant person who sweeps everything away.

Locum (*Doctors'*). Deputy—short for *locum tenens*. Sometimes 'loke' —a medical man who performs for another who is ill or away.

Lolliker (*Durham—old*). Tongue.

Lollipop dress (*Theatrical*, 1884). Stripy dress, generally red and white, suggestive of sticks of confectionery.

London, Best side towards (*Peoples'*). Making the best of everything. Good example of the national desire to battle through adversity. Derived from the desire of all country people to visit London for themselves, and make their fortunes, though its street are not paved with gold.

London ivy (*Colloquial*). Dust— sometimes used for fog.

London smoke (*Soc.*, 1860). A yellowish grey; became once a favourite colour because it hid dirt.

Long last (*Eng. Prov.*). Time or period spaciously waited for.

At long last Sir George White and his gallant garrison are free. Lord Dundonald rode into Ladysmith on Wednesday night.—*D. T.*, 2nd March 1900.

Long pull (*Public-house*). Overmeasure, either as a custom, or to induce trade.

Long-shore (*Maritime*). Landlubber; coast people who have the misfortune not to be sailors.

But what would have been the alarm of those timid 'long-shore' races if they could have imagined the present dangers of the deep.—*D. N.*, 6th January 1886.

Long stale drunk (*American-Eng.*, 1884). State of depression owing to physical inability to throw off the effects of intoxication.

... recovery from what our American cousins describe as a 'long stale drunk'.— *Ref.*, 9th April 1885.

Long-tailed bear (*Peoples', Hist.*). One of the evasions of saying 'you lie'. From the fact that bears have *no* tails.

Long 'un (*Poachers'*). Pheasant— referring to the length of the tail. (*See* Short-'un.)

Long's (*Strand*, 19 cent.). Short's wine-house opposite Somerset House.

Look into the whites (*Peoples'*)— 'Of each other's eyes' understood. To be about to fight—from the fact that the eyes protrude, or the lids recede more than usual when a set-to is about to commence.

It would be absolutely impossible for any adjustment of the boundary question to be made if the Russians and Afghans kept advancing until they could look into the whites of each other's eyes.—*D. N.*, 14th March 1885.

Look old (*Street*). Severe. Very fine eulogy of the wisdom of age, as compared with the carelessness of youth.

Look slippery (*Naval*). Hurry up, be quick — from the association of slipperiness and speed.

Look through the fingers (*Irish*). To evade; to pretend not to observe and see.

Looking as if he hadn't got his right change (*London*). Appearing mad or wild.

Looking round the clock (*American*). Getting appearance of age—parallel between life and completion of the orbit of the hands of a clock.

Looking seven ways for Sunday (*Lower Middle London*). Squinting.

Looks like a widder woman (*Amer.*, 1883). Appears old.

Loose bit o' goods (*Street*, 1870 on). Young woman who has abandoned the proprieties. (*See* Straight bit o' goods.)

Loosing a fiver (*Peoples'*). Having to pay extravagantly for any pleasure or purchase.

Loosing French (*Street*). Violent language in English.

Lord Blarney (*Irish*, 1885). Aristocratic flatterer. First given to Lord Carnarvon, who after his appointment as Lord Lieutenant of Ireland (1885) made many flattering speeches.

Lord Carnarvon's plausible and soothing, or to adopt the Irish expression 'soothering', speeches appear only to have won for him the nickname of Lord Blarney.—*D. N.*, 14th November 1885.

Lordy me (*Prov. Hist.*). Exclamation. Corruption of Lord have me! One of the sacred ejaculations of early reform days.

Lost a cartful and found a waggon-load (*Peoples'*). Getting stout.

Lot's wife's back-bone (*Peoples'*). To suggest extreme saltness, as 'Salt as Lot's wife's back-bone'.

Lottermy (*Mid. Counties — rarely used*). Corruption of Lord take me!

Lotties and Totties (*Theatrical*). Ladies at large.

If time and space permitted I should like to tell you all about the Lotties and the Totties and the other out-of-work pets who pervaded the stalls, and showed a liberal proportion of their backs—backs and bosoms, too—as bare as they were born.—*Ref.*, 15th November 1885.

Lotus (*L. Class*, 1885.) Rhyme to hocuss.

Love curls (*Society*, 1880). This term came in when women began to cut their hair short and wear it low over the forehead.

For the defence the respondent, Mr Robert Nathaniel Latham, was called. He gave a positive denial to the charge of cruelty. He had objected to his wife wearing what she called 'love curls'.— Latham v. Latham, Probate and Divorce Division, 9th February 1883.

Lovely as she can be and live, As (*American*, 1882). Superlative praise of beauty. That is to say—she could only be more lovely when raised to the condition of an angel.

Lovey dovey (*Low London*). Example of nonsense rhyming.

Low comedy merchant (*Theat.*, 1883). Farcical actor.

The success of *Indiana* mainly depends upon the extravagant humours of the chief low-comedy merchant. — *Ref.*, October 1886.

He won't be able to box Mr Fred J. Stimson, the low comedy merchant, for some weeks to come.

(*See* 'Shop'.)

Lully (*L. Class*). Shirt.

Lumberer (*Soc.*). Lying adventurer —obscure.

Mr Gill felt instinctively that there was something wrong with this man's appearance; and when this man came, in cross-examination, to give an account of himself, it accorded with the well-known expression 'lumberer'. — Lord Dunlo's Divorce, July 1890.

Lump of ice (*Rhyming*). Advice— in common use.

Lump of school (*Rhyming*). Fool.

Lump o' jaw on (*Street*). Talkative.

Lump o' stone (*Thieves'*). County jail.

Lumpy-roar (*Low London*, 1855). A grandee, a swell of the first water. Said to be an anglicization of 'l'Empereur' — Napoleon III., who became popular in 1885 by his visit to England, owing to the excitement produced by the Crimean War, and his encouragement of English trade.

M

M. D. (*Bridgewater*, 1857). Money down — referring to electioneering bribery.

McKinleyism — McKinleyise (*American-Eng.*, 1897). Protection. From President Mackinley, U.S.A., the great apostle of protection.

Meanwhile Congress is hearing from the people in no uncertain tones as to certain schedules which Mr Dingley proposes to 'McKinleyise'.—*D. T.*, 23rd March 1897.

Macing (*Peoples'*, 19 *cent.*). Severe, but regulated thrashing by fists. Early in the 19th century Mace was for an exceptional time a leading prize-fighter.

Mackinaw (*American Hunters'*). A very strong and ingeniously-woven blanket, said to have been first made and sold by a Scotch wool-stapler called MacInor.

Mad as hops (*American*). Excitable.

Made in Germany (*London*, 1890 on). Bad, valueless. Outcome of the vast quantity of inferior goods imported from Germany. Term increased in force from the date when this phrase had, legally, to be printed on the object.

Maffickers, Early.

Japanese merchants in New York met at dinner last night 'to celebrate the Japanese victory'. — *Star*, 10th February 1904.

Several days after the first naval success of the Japanese.

Mafficking (*Street*, 1900). Street rowdyism. April 1, 1900, added this word to the English language. It is quite as likely to stay as boycott. On the evening of that day the news of the relief of Mafeking arrived at about 9 P.M.—by eleven o'clock the streets were absolutely riotous.

Magdalen Marm (*Southwark*, 19 *cent.*). A servant from the Magdalen, a refuge for fallen women in the Blackfriars Road, which existed there until about the middle of the century. The women who went out as servants from that place had been too often pampered there, and gave little satisfaction — hence the Surrey side found this satirical term.

Mailed fist (*Peoples'*, 1897). Needless threats, boasting. From a send-off dinner speech by the Emperor of Germany when sending forth his only brother, Henry, to conquer China with a fleet of two sail—all of which ended in leasing a coaling-station by China to Germany.

Mailing (*Anglo-American*). To post for the mail.

After mailing, I returned to the Capitol, and rejoined Agneni on the balcony of the Senator's hall.—*D. N.*, 1870.

Maintenon (*Soc., Hist.*). Mistress who affects piety. From the position and life of Madame de Maintenon, the last favourite of Louis XIV.

Major MacFluffer — or **Fluffy** (*Theatrical*, 19 *cent.*). Sudden lapse of memory, and use of words to call the attention of the inattentive prompter. It is said to have arisen from an actor, in this strait, yelling half a dozen times as he looked off on the prompt side—'Major MacFluffer —where the devil is Major MacFluffer.'

More than one of the principals were foggy with the text, and were reduced to fluffing or to waiting for 'the word' from the wings.—*Ref.*, 13th November 1887.

Major Methodist (*Soc.*, '80's on). Extremely precise person. Intensification of Methodist.

Make a fun (*Irish*). Exercise fuss.

The villagers make a fun over every sister leaving, but we don't like it in any instance. Being externs, they might express their gratitude that way, but we wish to avoid it. It was done in the case of Sister Mary Clare. — *Miss Saurin's 'Nunnery' Case.*

Make a stuffed bird laugh (*American*). Absolutely preposterous.

Make all right (*Election*, 19 *cent.*). Promise to pay for vote.

Make - it (*London Poor*). Corruption of make-weight, the piece of bread added by bakers when weighing a loaf, to make up the weight — few loaves being baked of the correct weight.

Make it warm (*London*, 1880). Punish.

Mr Firth remarked that he himself was engaged in the icy latitude of the north endeavouring, as some one had said, to make it warm for their good friends on the other side, and to help to carry the flag of progress once more to victory.—*D. N.*, 7th October 1885.

Make leg (*Com. Lond.*). To become prosperous.

Make up (*Soc. and Peoples'*, 1860 on). To make love to.

Make up my leg (*Costermongers'*). To make money. From the time of smalls, stockings and buckled shoes, when making up the leg was a necessary prelude to going into society. (*See* Pull up my boot.)

Making your coffin (*Tailors'*). Charging too highly for an article. Said when a tailor charges a heavy price for a first job, and so probably loses a second.

Male impersonator (*Music Hall*). A misnomer—for the performer is a female who personates a man — and sings like one.

Mall (*Metal Trades'*). Credit.

Man of Sedan (*Political*). Last nickname given for Napoleon III.— from his fall at that city.

Man-killer (*Abstainers'*). Porter, stout, cooper—the black beers.

Manchester school of nutrition (*Soc.*, 1860). High-feeding, emphatically introduced by certain medical men of that city.

Mandamus (*Legal*). Verb invented from a writ of mandamus.

The court was not dispensed from considering this part of the case, as it would have been if Mr Bradlaugh had been trying to 'mandamus' the Speaker or the Serjeant-at-Arms.—*D. N.*, 28th January 1885.

Mange, letty, bevy and clobber. Italian — through the organ-grinders' lodging-houses. Eating, bed, drink, clothes—this last word being Hebrew.

Manny (*Jewish E. London*). Term of endearment or admiration prefixed to Jewish name, as 'Manny Lyons'. Apparently a muscular Hebrewism.

Mantalini (*Mid. Class*, 1840 on). A man-milliner—from the milliner's husband in Dickens's *Nicholas Nickleby*.

A famous Mantalini, one who will very shortly open a palatial branch establishment in London town, has draped and adorned the feminine form divine of handsome Jane Hading. — *D. T.*, 2nd January 1897.

From about 1860-90 this name was superseded by that of 'Worth', the English man-milliner of the second empire, and afterwards of the third republic.

Marcus Superbus (*Theat.*, 1896). Grandee. This was the name given to himself by Mr Wilson Barrett in his play, *The Sign of the Cross* (1896). Soon after the success of this morality, a variety piece called *The Gay Parisienne* was produced; therein Miss Louie Freear made an immediate success as a burlesque actress, who invented a grotesque name—Marcus Superfluous.

Margery (*L. London*, 19 *cent.*). Effeminate.

Mark time (*Mil.*, 19 *cent.*). Wait, hold on, be patient, don't be in a hurry. From the military order when soldiers are halted for a short time on march, or drill, and which is done that step may not be lost.

Marking M. (*Irish Peoples'*). Rapidity. The M. is the initial of the Virgin Mary, still a very sacred symbol in Ireland. Usually used in describing rapidity of action.

Marksman (*Old*). Legal term for a man who cannot write, and who makes his mark.

Marm - poosey or **Marm - puss** (*Public-house*, 1863). Applied to a showily-dressed landlady.

Marmalade country (*Scotland*). Music hall reference to the orange marmalade made in Dundee and other Scotch places.

Marriage face (*Middle Class*). Sad one—because generally a bride cries a good deal, and so temporarily spoils her looks.

Married the widow (*French — known in England*, 19 *cent.*). Made a mess of things. Derived from a man going to the guillotine, which makes widows, while the idea of marriage is suggested by the momentary association with the guillotine, which is called in French slang 'the widow'.

Married to Brown Bess (*Mil.*, 18-19 *cent.*). To serve as a soldier. Brown Bess was of course the musket.

You can tell her that you are safe and married to Brown Bess (that is to say enlisted). Thackeray, *Barry Linden*, ch. v.

Martialist (*Soc.*, 1885). Soldier holding a commission.

The marvel was 'that the colonel stood it'. He was, indeed, a long-suffering martialist.—*D. N.*, 31st December 1885.

Marwooded (*Peoples'*). Hanged. This term prevailed while Executioner Marwood held office. He died in 1883.

Mary Ann (*L. London*, 19 *cent.*). An effeminate man.

Mash, Made a (*Soc.*, 1883). Effected a conquest—struck somebody all of a heap.

Mash that (*Com. Lond.*). Hold your tongue. Probably from macher to chew, or figuratively—keep to yourself in your mouth.

Mashers' corners (*Soc.*, 1882). The O.P. and P.S. entrances to the stalls of the old Gaiety Theatre.

Masonics (*Soc., Hist.*). Secrets— from the secret rites of Freemasonry. Not that there are either secrets or rites in Freemasonry—at all events in England—where combined secrets are neither wanted nor expected.

Massites (*Soc.*, 1897). Members of the Anglican Church who believe in transubstantiation. These believers accept the term gravely; but it was invented by the representative, or Low Church, party.

Masterpiece o' night work (*Street*). Admiringly said of a handsome unfortunate.

Match (*Soc.*, 19 *cent.*). Society classic for marriage throughout the reign—giving rise to the compound matchmaker, a woman who brings about marriages.

Mrs Gerard did her best to make the match, and although she afterwards conceived doubts as to whether her sister really loved him, she said nothing to Lord Durham to that effect. — Lord Herschel, *Lord Durham's Nullity Suit*, March 1885.

Materials (*Irish*). Evasive term for whisky-punch.

Matinée (*Theatrical*, 1870). Morning theatrical performance. This entertainment came from New York, and was speedily adopted not only in England, but in France, which accepted the word.

Matinée dog (*Theatrical*). Sufferer experimented upon. From vivisection of canines, or testing food for poison by submitting it to tykes. Of course a figure of speech in relation to the frequent dramatic rubbish which is submitted at matinées, as distinct from evening performances.

Arrangements have been made by Irvine Bacon and Charles Groves to try it ere long on the matinée dog—probably at the Haymarket.—*Ref.*, 3rd February 1889.

Matineers (*Soc.*, 1885). Frequenters of matinées. Outcome of the rage for matinées, 1884-85. They are composed of quite 80 per cent. of ladies.

Matineers on the look out for a really excellent and varied show will thank me for calling their attention to a matinée to be given in compliment to Mrs Robert Reece.

Maty (*London Workmen's*). Mate.

Maungo (*N. Country*, 1869). Shoddy. This word is said to come from the term 'it maun go'—that is to say it must sell from its cheapness.

Maw-sang (*Northumbrian*). Blood —a corrupted oath — probably mort saint, holy death.

Mawther (*E. Anglican*). Not only mother, but applied to even a girl baby, girl, maid, wife, and childless widow.

Mawwormy (*Peoples'*). Fault-finding, dismally anticipating wretchedness. From the character Mawworm.

Augustus Harris insisting on Carl Rosa accepting the wreath thrown on the stage last Saturday night was a delicious and touching spectacle. Here is a glorious subject for one of our figure-painters. Without being mawwormy, I fail to see why a wreath should be presented to any man who makes a business of giving opera.—*Entr'acte*, 6th June 1885.

(*See* Pecksniffian.)

May God blind me (*Street*). The original invocation of the gutterling, reduced to 'Gaw blin' me', 'bly me', 'blyme', 'bly'.

Mayhap (*Peoples*). Abbreviation of may happen.

'Your widow? Mayhap not.' — Garrick, *Abel Drugger*.

Mean to do without 'em (*Music Hall*, 1882). The ''em' infers to women. The phrase was first made popular by the singer Arthur Roberts.

Mean white (*Anglo-Indian*). A poor Englishman.

Meater (*Street*). Coward. Said of a dog who only bites meat, that is to say, one who will not fight. Thence applied to cowardly men.

Meddle and muddle (*Political*, 1879). Came in during contest between Beaconsfield and Gladstone— unmasterly policy which harries and does nothing.

The Board is pursuing a policy of meddle and muddle, and is getting itself most cordially hated all round,—*Ref.*, 26th April 1885.

Meddling duchess (*Peoples'*, 1880). Intensification of duchess (*q.v.*). Ageing, pompous woman who fusses about and achieves nothing.

Melt (*Financial*). To discount a bill.

Melton hot day (*Sporting and Club*, 1885). Equivalent to melting hot day. Created Derby Day (3rd June), which was very sultry, and *apropos* to the winner of the day— 'Melton'.

Several who came near me after the big race remarked that it was a Melton hot day, and seemed to think they were saying something original and something funny.—*Ref.*, 7th June 1885.

Memugger (*Oxford*). Martyrs' memorial. A satirical and even profane application of 'er'.

The triumph of this jargon was reached when some one christened the Martyrs' Memorial the 'Martyrs' Memugger'.— *D. T.*, 14th August 1899.

Mended (*Street*, 19 *cent.*). Bandaged.

Menkind (*Soc.*, '90's). Male relatives simply.

The great pull which Pekin had, over other Eastern or over South American Legations was that it is the traditional custom that the ladies of the Corps Diplomatique, who can rarely be prevailed upon to venture so far from Paris as Chili and Peru, accompany their menkind forth to the Celestial City.— *D. T.*, 4th July 1900.

Mentisental (*Syllable traversion— E. of London only*). Sentimental.

Merchant (*Theatrical*, 1882). The theatre coming to be called the 'shop', actors dubbed themselves 'merchants', qualified by their line.

Merely moral man (*Soc.*, 1890). Started by Ritualistic incumbents. Attack upon men who are moral without expressed Christian belief.

Mervousness (*Polit.*, 1885). Satirical synonym for nervousness invented about 1876 by the political party who did not believe in the advance of Russia towards India.

Messengers (*Country*). The small dark, rapidly-drifting cloudlets which foretell a storm.

Micky. See Bob, Harry and Dick.

Microbe of sectionalism (*Soc., and Parl., circa* 1896). Social fad in the House of Commons. As gradually the 'microbe' was discovered to be the cause of all disease, or the effect of all tendency to disease, the phrase was used figuratively. In this case it is applied to the total break up of the Liberal party in the '90's, by the divided feeling upon most extreme points. Such as total abstinence, local veto, vaccination, voluntary schools, etc.

The abdication by the Radical party of its proper functions has an unfortunate tendency to foster what we have called the microbe of sectionalism. — *D. T.*, 21st June 1890.

Mid vire (*Sporting, Paris*). Midday wires, giving last prices in the coming-on races. Heard in London.

Middle cuts (*Slums'*). These are the prime cuts of fried fish at fried fish shops.

Midge (*Devon, old*). A tell-tale.

Mighty roarer (*Yankee*). Niagara cataract.

Mikey (*Corrupt Rhyming*). Sick after drink. (*See* Bob, Harry and Dick).

Milikers (*Com. London*, 1870). Militia—probably a corruption of the true word, upon the basis that publichouse is idiotically called shuvlycowss.

Military (*Tavern*, 1885). Porter. One of the later baptisms.

Milk-bottle (*Com. Peoples'*). Baby.

Milken (*Thieves'*, 18 cent.). Housebreaker. (*See* Fielding's *Jonathan Wild.*)

Million to a bit of dirt (*Sporting*, 1860). A sure bet requiring no caution. 'It's a million to a bit o' dirt the Plunger pulls it off.' (*See* Dollars to buttons)

Mimodrama (*Theatrical*, 1897). Drama of dumb show, as distinct from melodrama, wherein the more noise the better.

He had found the argument of this minodrama in an artic e of criticism written by Theophile 'Gautier.—*D. T.*, 3rd March 1897.

Minchin Malacho (*Peoples'*, 18 cent. on). Whatever this may mean it is evidently still understood by the vulgar. In April 1895 the present writer heard a man in the gallery of the Palace of Varieties (London), after several scornful phrases, say derisively, 'Oh—ah—minchin maleego.'

Mind the grease (*Peoples'*). Let me pass, please.

Mind the paint (*Peoples'*). Said of passing girls who have painted their faces. Adopted from the ordinary phrase used by house-painters who flourish this legend on floor, pavement, and wall. (*See* Aristocratic veins.)

Mind the step (*Peoples'*). Veiled or satiric suggestion that the victim addressed is drunk.

Mine (*Low Life*). Husband—of a kind. Sometimes really applied to a husband.

Mine-jobber (*City*, 1880 on). Cheat. When English copper mining became comparatively valueless by reason of the import of Australian and other ore as ballast, all the rascals on change floated mine companies, which had not a chance of success.

Minnie P. play (*Stage*, 1885 on). Drama in which a little maid variety actress is the chief motive. She must sing, dance, play tricks, and never wear a long dress. From Miss Minnie Palmer's creations, chiefly in *My Sweetheart*. Now obsolete.

Misery (*Old Eng. and American*). Pain.

Misery bowl (*Tourists'*). Reliefbasin—at sea.

Misery junction (*Music Hall Singers'*). The angle forming the southwest corner of the York and Waterloo Roads. So named from the daily meeting here of music hall 'pros' who are out of engagements, and who are in this neighbourhood for the purpose of calling on their agents, half a dozen of whom live within hail. (*See* Pro's Avenue.)

Misleading paper (1876 on). Name given to *Times* newspaper when it began to lose its distinctive feature as the 'leading paper' in Liberal policy.

Probably the critic of the leading—I should say the misleading—morning paper did not see the show.

Miss (*American*). To be unlucky.

Mistaken (*Birmingham*, 1885). Lie. From a satirical paragraph by Mr Chamberlain (9th November), at Birmingham.

Mitching (*Canadian*). Common term for playing the truant. Comes from Devonshire, where the term is still in use.

Mitten (*Amer., Hist.*). Refusal of marriage by a lady. 'She gave him the mitten.'

Mixologist (*American Saloon*). Outcome of the complicated nature of American drinks—a learned mixer.

Mo'. (*See* 'Arf a mo'.)

Mock litany men (*Irish mendicants'*). Sing-song beggars who utter plaints or requests in a chanting manner.

Modernity (*Soc.*, '90's). Obvious. This word was invented early in the '90's — first as a satire, then as a perspicacious descriptive.

Nothing seems to be wanting to the perfect 'modernity' of the process by which Clerkenwell is endeavouring to discover its most fitting 'shepherd of souls' save the presence of a few bookmakers and a daily report of the state of the odds against the various competing candidates.—*D. T.*, 16th June 1898.

Moll-hunters (*Street*). Men, of all ages, who are always lurking after women.

Monaker (*Com. Lond.*, 1870). Title or name. From Italian lingo for name, Monaco being the Italian for monk.

Monday mice (*L. Str., Hist.*). The processions of black eyes, in both sexes, and in back streets—as the result of the week-end closing at 11 P.M. on

Sunday nights — a black eye getting this name from its ordinary size and rounded shape suggesting a huddled up mouse.

Monday pops (*Soc.*). Abbreviation of popular and put in plural. Refers to celebrated long-established concerts at St James's Hall, London.

We have been to a Monday pop this week. — Geo. Eliot, *Letters*, 26th November, 1862.

Money bag lord (*Soc.*, 19 *cent.*). Ennobled banker. (*See* Paint brush baronet and Gally pot baronet.)

Money bugs (*Amer. - Eng.*). Millionaires. Beetles are called bugs, or were, in the U.S.A. The golden bug is a beetle that has the appearance of a lump of dead gold.

It is estimated, I see, that the Vanderbilt family of millionaires control among them 20,000 miles of American railways, which in one way and another afford employment for three millions of human beings. . . . The happiness or the misery of three millions of people wholly dependent on the whims and caprices of, say, half a dozen 'money bugs'.— *People*, 20th March 1898.

Monkey (*Mechanics'*). Clerk.

Monkey and parrot time (*American*). Equivalent to cat and dog life.

Monkey motions (*Military*). Extension drill. Used satirically by the men in reference to the manœuvres of this really droll drill.

Monkey on the house (*Soc.*). Expression current in Cambridgeshire. It means that the owner of the house has raised money on it. The natives also say, 'A monkey on the land', the word 'monkey' being exactly equivalent to 'mortgage'.

Monkey, To (*American - Eng.*). Prance and carry on effusively — especially towards a pretty girl.

Monks. Sickly parrots. They hold their heads down and in.

Monos (*Westminster School*). King's scholar who at 4 P.M. announces, in Latin, the finish of the day's work.

Moo (*L. Class*). Common woman.

Moocheries (*Peoples'*, 1885). One of the names given to The Inventions. (*See* Muckeries.)

Moony cove (*Peoples'*). The word is derived from the tendency of persons suffering from incipient insanity to keep the eyes raised when walking. Moon-struck is another form of the word.

Moorgate - rattler (*Clare Market*, 1899). Startlingly - dressed passerby — a swell of that district, or in it. Perhaps a corruption of Moorgate, or possibly Margate.

Mops and brooms (*Peoples'*). Drunk — probably suggested by the hair getting disordered and like a mop. From a time when hair was worn long.

'Mops and brooms' doubtless express a sense of confusion.—*Daily News*.

Moral Cremorne (*Soc.*, 1883). Fisheries Exhibition, Royal Horticultural Gardens, 1883. So named because there had been no illumination fêtes since the closing of immoral Cremorne Gardens.

The Fisheries Exhibition is over. The lights of the moral Cremorne are out.— *Ref.*, 3rd November 1883.

More blue (*Devon, old*). Exclamation. Absolute pronunciation of 'mort bleue', and coming down probably from the Frenchified court of Charles II., when Exeter was a western metropolis. (*See* Big beck, Zounds, Zooks, Odd's fish, Please the pigs, Maw sang.)

More war (*Street*, 1898). Street quarrel or wrangle, especially amongst women. Outcome of the somewhat discussive warfare carried on between U.S.A. and Spain in this year. Satirical to some degree.

Mother (*Complicated Rhyming*, 1868). Water. Abbreviation of 'mother and daughter' — rhyming with 'water'.

Mother of the modern drama (*Theatrical*). An actress who took up high matronly ground in a lecture delivered (1884) at Birmingham. The lady, successful early in life, and married to a rich, prosperous and devoted husband, spoke very *ex cathedra*, and during her oration pitied the strugglers, and announced her intention of quitting the stage when '40'. Calculating people arrived at the conclusion that the lady never therefore intended to leave the stage, as no one can be '40' twice.

177

Mother's help (*Mid. Class*, 1883 on). Nursery governess. Term invented for the accommodation of people who want a governess, and do not want to pay for one.

Motor (*London Soc.*, 1896). Fast, hard-living; said of a man about town.

Motor (*Oxford*, 1897). Coach, cram tutor for exams. Origin obvious. Simply the conversion of the old-time coach into the new-time motor—without the car.

Motor (*Soc.*, 1896). The motor-car, immediately shortened to motor, was first shown in London streets on 10th November 1896. Before the end of the year a score of phrases were built up around it.

Byron had shown the true origin of the Motor long before the gentlemen who thought they invented it were born. Did he not say in his famous riddle:

'Twas whispered in Heaven, 'twas Motor'd in Hell. — *D. T.*, 19th November 1896.

Motter (*Street*, 1896). Name given to the motor carriage on its very first official appearance in London on Lord Mayor's Day, 1896.

Mount the cart (*Peoples'*, 18 cent.). Be hanged—from the then habit of carting culprits from Newgate to Tyburn tree, or gallows — the cart being drawn from under the wretch when the rope had been attached to the beam.

Mourning coach horse (*Middle Class London*, 1850). A tall, solemn woman, dressed in black and many inky feathers. (*See* Sala's B.)

Mouth-pie (*Street*). Emphatic name for feminine scolding.

Move the previous question (*Soc., from Parliamentary Life*). To evade; to object to explain.

To 'move the previous question' is in Parliamentary phraseology simply to say that the present is not the most convenient moment for discussing any particular motion. Another time, it says—another time, by all means; but not just now.

Move the procession (*American Mining*). To incite a crowd against some unpopular person.

Mowrowsky (*Anglo - American*). Interchange of initial consonants of two adjacent words, by accident or intention, as bin and gitters for 'gin and bitters'. Very common, 1840-56. Brought into fashion by Albert Smith from hospital life. Now chiefly patronised in America.

A mowrowsky is often a transfer of two words, as in the *Taming of the Shrew*, where Grumio cries, in pretended fright, 'The oats have eaten the horses'. During the Donnelly discussion (1888) wherein it was contended that the plays of Shakespeare had been written by Lord Bacon, an intended satirical mowrowsky was invented by an interchange of initials between the two names, Bakespeare and Shacon.

Muck (*Military*). Scornful appellation bestowed upon all infantry by all cavalry.

Muck and halfpenny afters (*Middle Class*). Bad, pretentious dinner — spotted at the corners with custard powder preparations, and half-dozens of stewed prunes, etc., etc.

Muckeries (*Youths*, 1885). Name given to the 'Inventories' (Inventions Exhibition at S. Kensington) as the season went on, by the youthful frequenters.

Mucking (*Westminster School*). Idling, hanging round.

Mud island (*E. London*). Southend—watering-place on the mouth of the Thames, whose estuary still produces a deal of mud.

Mud show (*Soc.*). An agricultural, or other out-door show.

Mud - hovel argument (*Political*, 1879-84). Term given to Tory argument against extension of political liberty in Ireland.

A great part of his speech, however, consisted only of what we may call the 'mud - hovel' argument, an argument which he applied to Ireland, and on which it will be remembered he had recently an opportunity of expatiating in Ireland.—*D. N.*, 4th March 1884.

Mud-pusher (*Street*, 1870). Crossing sweeper.

Muff (*Soc.*, 1840 on). A stupid, dilatory, inactive, and generally amiable young man.

Muffin - puncher (*Street*). Muffin - baker.

Muffin - wallopers (*Middle Class London*, 1880). Scandal-loving women, chiefly spinsters, who meet over a cup of tea.

Mug (*Theatrical*). To show variety of comic expression in the features.

Multa bona fakement (*Tavern*, 1800-35). Very good trick — from the Italian molto bono, and abstract noun made from fake—to manipulate adroitly if dishonestly.

A hand truck was procured, and drugged Charley (watchman) and his box were then transferred to another locality, so that when Charley awoke he found himself and box ready for doing duty in another parish. This trick was estimated to be a multa bona fakement.—Diprose's Clement Danes; Pierce Egan, *Life in London*, vol. i., p. 101.

Mumchance (*Peop.*, *Hist.*). Dolefully silent.

The man or woman who can sit 'mumchance', and with faces as long as a yard measure, over a well-acted farce do not deserve to be ranked in the noble army of all-embracing playgoers.—*D. T.*, 11th March 1897.

Mumming booth (*Lower Stage*). A wandering marquee in which short plays are produced.

Munching house (*City*, 1850). Onomatope for Mansion House—from the lusty-feeding going on there.

The distinguished artists who repeated *The Masque of Painters* at the Munching House the other day do not seem to have been quite satisfied with their treatment.—*Ref.*, 5th July 1885.

Mundane (*Franco-Eng.*, 1890 on). Person of fashion.

The Comtesse de Maupeou, a mundane who has recently risen upon the musical horizon, rendered several songs.—*D. N.*, 12th April 1897.

Murder an' Irish (*Peoples'*, 19 *cent.*). Exclamation intimating that things are at a climax. Sometimes more emphatically used as 'murderin' Irish'.

Museum headache (*Authors'*, 1857).

Many a student avers, whether candidly or not, that it costs him less to buy rare books than to hang about the Museum, waiting the leisure of the attendants, and struggling against a 'Museum headache'.—*D. N.*, 11th December 1882.

Mush, gush, and lush (*Amer.-Eng.*, 1884). Mean interested criticism —critiques paid for either in money or feastings.

Mushroom (*Public-house*). Name given by frequenters (presumably in contempt), to the great clock to be seen in most taverns, and which gives warning as to closing time.

Music Hall howl (*Musicians'*). The peculiar mode of singing in music-halls, the result of endeavouring rather to make the words of a song heard than to create musical effect.

Music Hall public (*Soc.*, 1884). Satirical description of public who do not care for high-class compositions.

Next time M. Rivière organises a benefit let him make up his mind whether he will seek the suffrages of the musical or the music hall public. He might be happy with either, but he will never get both at once.—*Ref.*, 3rd May 1885.

Musk-rats (*American*). People of Delaware—given because those animals prevail in this division.

Must know Mrs Kelley? You (London, 1898 on). Joking exclamation with no particular meaning, generally shot at a long-winded talker. Phrase used for two years at all times and places by Dan Leno.

Mustard plaster (*Peoples'*). Dismal young man. Put a mustard plaster on his chest. Said of a doleful and dismal pallid young man. Derived from a comic song, in association with Colman's mustard, written by the celebrated pantomime writer, E. L. Blanchard, and sung in one of his pantomimes at Drury Lane.

Mustard pot (*Peoples'*). Carriage with a light yellow body. Obvious outcome of mere relation of colours.

Mutton shunter (*Policemen*, 1883). Policeman.

My elm is grown (*Peoples'*, 18 *cent.*). Prognostication of one's own death—figure of speech depending upon the practical fact that elm is used throughout the land for coffins.

N

N.—A.—D. (*Military Hospital*). Shamming in any way. Initials of No Appreciable Disease.

N. D. (*Soc.*, 19 *cent.*). Initials of No Date, used by librarians in making their lists. Applied to a woman who tries to look young.

N. F. (*Artisans', masked*). Initials of No Fool.

N. G. (*Peoples'*, 19 *cent.*). Emphatic initials of No Go—which in its turn implies failure.

N. N. (*Soc.*). Necessary Nuisance —generally applied to husband.

N. Y. D. (*Military Hospital*). Evasive for drunk. Initials of Not Yet Diagnosed—found on military hospital bed-cards as a direction to visiting medical men and to nurses. In this case the true diagnosis would lead to a confinement to barracks.

Nail a goss (*Thieves'*). To steal a hat—industry gone out since hats became so cheap. The silk plush hat which succeeded and killed the beaver was so comparatively light that it was called a gossamer, soon naturally reduced to goss.

Nail a strike (*Thieves'*). To steal a watch.

Nailed up drama (*Theat.*, 1881). Satirical title found for the drama which depends upon elaborate scenery. Said first in relation to *The World*, produced at Drury Lane about this time.

Nana, Nanaish (*Club*, 1882). Outrageous, overstepping decency—from the French romance *Nana*, by Zola.

Theodora would be an unpresentable being to a London or a New York audience, and is almost too 'high' in the sense poulterers attach to the word for even a Boulevardier public. In the name of history, Zola's *Nana* is out-Nana-ed.—*D. N.* (criticism on *Theodora*), 29th December 1884.

Nancy (*Low London*, 19 *cent.*). Effeminate in a slight degree. Also used in the U.S.A.

Nancy tales (*Lit.*, 1890). Humbug, bosh.

The negroes of the West Indies call an old wife's fable 'a Nancy story', derived from Ananzi, the African spider who told tales.—*D. N.*, 17th January 1891.

Nanny (*Street boys'*). Banana. (*See* Tommy Rabbit.)

Nanty (*Italian organ-grinders'*). Nothing—corruption of *niente*.

''E's a nanty cove.'

Nanty narking (*Tavern*, 1800 on to 1840). Great fun. (*See* Egan's *Life in London.*)

Nanty worster (*Common London*). Nanty (Italian) here means 'no'; worster an intensification of 'worst'. The phrase means therefore a 'no-worse'.

Nark the titter (*Dangerous Classes*). Watch the woman. 'Nark' is probably a rhyming word to 'mark'. Titter is the very lowest mode of describing a woman—one who has teats.

Nap (*London*, 1855-70). A very pointed moustache—the two points forming a long line which 'cut' the face. It was re-introduced by Napoleon III., and is still worn by Napoleonists in Paris.

Nap or nothing (*Club*, 1868). All or naught.

Nap (knap) the regulars (*Thieves'*). Receive or grab the customary portion of the money resulting from the sale of stolen property.

Narrative (*Middle-class*). Dog's tail. A tale is a narrative—tale = tail in pronunciation.

Nathaniel, Below (*Old English*). Even lower than Hades—Nathaniel (like Samuel, or Zamiel in Germany) and Old Nick, or Nicholas, being familiar synonyms for Satan.

Throughout my life I have always had a burning desire and a dogged determination to get below the surface of things, and Eugène Sue's masterpiece took you, as the saying is, 'down below Nathaniel', as regards the basements and the subterraneans of society.—G. A. Sala, *D. T.*, 18th July 1895.

Nattermy (*Peoples'*). Word for a thin human being. From anatomy.

Natural, All your (*Peoples'*). Ellipsis of all your natural born days. Natural probably here meant as 'ordinary', which phrase would exclude your 'extraordinary' days.

Nautical triumvisetta (*Music Hall*). A singing and dancing nautical scene by three persons, of whom two are generally women.

Near and far (*Public-house Rhyming*). The bar.

Neat (*Low Peoples'*). Unadulterated, unmixed—in relation to drink: *e.g.*,

Two o' gin neat is quite an improvement upon a similar quantity of 'raw'.

Nec Ultra (*Soc.*, 17-19 *cent.*). West side of Temple Bar.

To the Countess Blushrose, Nature herself had written *Nec Ultra* on the west side of Temple Bar.—D. Jerrold's *The Story of a Feather*, chap. ix.

Neck oil (*E. London*). Beer generally.

Ned Skinner (*Rhyming*). Dinner.

Neddyvaul (*Street boys'*). 'Ned of all'. Chief, commander, conqueror.

Neecee peeress (*Soc.*). An E. C. or city bride of little or no family, and an immense fortune, both of which are wedded to some poor lord or baronet.

Needful (*Peoples'*, 19 *cent.*). Money —and one of the most urgent terms for it. In use by all classes.

Needle (*Tailors'*). Got the needle, *i.e.*, irritated, as when the needle runs into a finger. Has spread generally over working classes, who have accepted the graphic nature of the phrase.

Needles and pins (*Peoples'*). Warning against marriage. The rhyming runs—

Pins and needles—needles and pins
When a man marries his trouble begins.

Common also to America, to which land it passed from Devonshire, where the phrase is still very common.

Neetrith gen (*Back speech*). Thirteen shillings. The first word is thirteen spelt backwards—the 'th' very properly being taken as one letter. 'Gen' is the short for general (a shilling).

Negus (*Queen Ann's reign*). Port wine and hot water, heightened by grated nutmeg. One of the name words—from a Colonel Negus who invented the beverage.

Never fear (*Peoples'*). Don't be anxious.

Never squedge (*Low. London*). A poor pulseless, passionless youth — a duffer.

Neversweat (*Common English*, 19 *cent.*). A graphic, one-word description of a lazy, or even a slow individual, used only towards men and boys.

New (*Britannia training ship*). Fresh arrival, last addition. Used in the plural.

New (*American*). News. 'Oh, is that the new?'

New cut warrior (*S. London*, 1830). An inhabitant fighter, in or near the New Cut, a road made only in the 19th century through the Lambeth Marshes from Blackfriars to Lambeth.

New departure (*Soc.*, 1880). Synonym for change of any kind.

We have often pointed out that the electoral changes which have just been accomplished must produce a new era— or, as the Americans would call it, a new departure—in legislation.—*D. N.*, 9th August 1885.

New pair of boots (*Mid.-class*). Another question altogether — later shape of another pair of shoes.

Once they have the concession made to them, then it becomes a 'new pair of boots' altogether.—*Entr'acte*, 17th March 1883.

Newcastle programme (1894 on). Extreme promises, difficult of execution. From a speech of extreme Radical promise made by Mr John Morley at Newcastle.

Next parish to America (*Irish*). Arran Island—most western land of Ireland.

Just sixteen miles beyond Barna, and at the mouth of the Bay of Galway, is Arran island, which the people here call the 'Next Parish to America'.—*D. N.*, December 1887.

Next thing to the judgment day (*wholly American*). Absolute social shock.

Nice as nasty (*Lower Peoples'*). Evasive way of declaring the opponent objectionable.

Nice blackberry (*American*). Satirical phrase, intimating that the other is a bitter weed or fruit.

Nice joint (*Street*). Charming, if over-pronounced, young person.

Nice place to live out of (*Peoples'*). Evasive way of condemning a locality.

Without corresponding to the idea of 'a nice place to live out of', Harrogate is assuredly one of those spots which owe much to their surroundings.

(*See* Do without it.)

Nice thin job (*Peoples'*, 1895). Mean evasion of a promise. 'Thin'—to be seen through, comes from America — and in England antithetically suggested thick—now very prevalent for ill-usage and misbehaviour in general.

Nicholls (*Soc.*, 1860 on). Complete riding habit. From the splendid habits made by Nicholls, of Regent Street.

Nickel-plate (*American*). An equivalent to our German silver—a swindle, a social fraud.

The name 'nickel plate', as applied to the New York, Chicago & St Louis Railway, came into use in this way: speaking of the road by its initial letters—a common practice among railroad men—N. Y. C. L. suggested nickel, and from that to 'nickel plate' was an easy transition.—*Detroit Free Press*, 1882.

Niggers' duel (*Anglo-American*). A never-intended encounter. Each behind a mile-stone, therefore a mile apart.

Night flea (*Essex School*). Boarder —in contradistinction from Day-bug (*q.v.*).

Niminy-piminy (*Soc.*, 19 *cent.*). Effeminately affected.

Mr Beckford wrote in Leigh Hunt's *Story of Rimini*:

Nimmini Pimmini
The Story of Rimmini.
—*D. N.*, 11th December 1882.

Nimshes (*American Federal*, 1860-65). One of the contemptuous names describing the Secessionists. Origin not known.

Nine mile nuts (*Japanese pigeon*). Anything to eat or drink very sustaining. From the nutritive qualities of chestnuts—especially in Japan.

Nine tailors make a man (*Old Eng.*). Said derisively of a small man, whether tailor or not.

Nines, Up to the (*Common*). Perfect.

90 dog (*Street*). Pug. Referring to aspect of tail.

97 champion frost (*Peoples'*). First motor cars. The expectations raised on 10th November, 1896, by the procession of motor cars from the Embankment to Brighton, were disappointed by the immediate results.

No. I. (*New York*, 1883). When the U.S.A. were interested, early in this year, as to whether the 'No I.' of the Invincible Brotherhood (Fenian) was or was not in America, the term No. I. was often applied to noisy, or even merely evident, Irishmen.

No. I. (*Political*, 1883). Mysterious. This phrase took its rise early this year, consequent upon the collapse of 'The Brotherhood of Invincibles'.

No better than they ought to be (*Peoples'*). Worse than many.

There are fireworks on certain nights now at the Crystal Palace, and they are about the most successful of the displays given here; though it may be said they attract very many persons whom Mrs Grundy says are no better than they ought to be.—*Entr'acte*, 6th June 1885.

No beyond jammer (*Street*). Perfectly beautiful woman.

No church (*Peoples'*). When the great wrangle took place between the High Church party and the Low Church party, this phrase, which at once took, and has remained popular, was deftly discovered by Douglas Jerrold to represent the religious condition of the utterly outcast. The phrase was first published by the wit in a page of *Punch*.

No class (*Street*, 1893 on). Commonplace.

He proposed to Sal and she knew he was gone on her a bit—
Although I knew quite well it couldn't last;
But when she said, 'I love him, Bill,' it fairly knocked me sick,
Cos I seemed to know 'e wasn't any class.

'Soldiers! Why, soldiers ain't no class.'—*D. T.*, June 1897.

No earthly (*London*, 1899). Abbreviation of 'no earthly chance'.

The actors who have not booked their seats *viâ* Mr Henry Dana, are hereby notified that they have now no earthly, as all seats have been allotted.—*Ref.*, 22nd October 1899.

No grease (*Engineers'*). Absence of behaviour, of politeness.

No rats (*Peoples'*). Scotchman. Evasive reference to that native, it being supposed that a Scot is always associated with bagpipes, and that no rat can bear the neighbourhood of that musical instrument.

No return ticket (*Common, London*). Abbreviation of ' He's going to Hanwell and no return ticket '—said of a man who shows signs of madness.

Nobby (*Navy*). Anglicization of the 'Niobe'.

Nolled (*American*). Form of *nolle prosequi*. Used by lawyers.

Non compos. See Compos, Non.

Non me (*Peoples'*, 1820-30). Lie. 'That's a non me for one.' Took its rise from the trial of Queen Caroline, wherein the Italian witnesses observed 'non mi ricordo' (I do not remember) to every important question put to them in cross-examination.

Nonsensational (*Critical*, 1897). Sensational nonsense.

With a piece of nonsensational extravagance entitled *The MacHaggis*, Mr Penley on Thursday night re-opened his theatre.—*People*, 28th February 1897.

Norfolk Howard (*Popular*). A bed-bug. Due to a man named Buggey advertising a change of name to this phrase, a combination of the family name and title of the Duke of Norfolk. Produced much press comment and even sympathy for all persons with objectionable names. The following list of vexatious names was compiled and published in the *Times*.

Asse, Bub, Belly, Boots, Cripple, Cheese, Cockles, Dunce, Dam, Drinkmilke, Def, Flashman, Fatt, Ginger, Goose, Beaste, Barehead, Bungler, Bugg, Buggey, Bones, Cheeke, Clodd, Cod, Demon, Fiend, Funck, Frogge, Ghost, Gready, Hagg, Humpe, Holdwater, Headach, Jugs, Jelly, Idle, Kneebone, Kidney, Licie, Lame, Lazy, Leakey, Maypole, Mule, Monkey, Milksop, Mudd, Honeybum, Maydenhead, Mug, Piddle, Paswater, Pisse, Pricksmall, Pricke, Phisicke, Pighead, Pot, Poker, Poopy, Prigge, Pigge, Punch, Proverbs, Quicklove, Quash, Radish, Rumpe, Rawbone, Rottengoose, Swette, Shish, Sprat, Sheartlifte, Stiffe, Squibb, Sponge, Stubborne, Swine, Shittel, Shave, Shrimps, Shirt, Skim, Squalsh, Silly, Shoe, Smelt, Skull, Spattel, Shadow, Snaggs, Spittle, Teate, Taylecoate, Villain, Vittels, Vile, Whale.

North Castle (*Slang of the impecunious*, 1880). Holloway Jail, in the north of London.

Nose (*Boating*). The extreme tip of the bow of a boat.

Nose and chin (*Rhyming*). One of the modes of referring to gin.

Nose-bag (*Mid.-class*, 19 *cent.*). A hospitable house.

'These gulls', remarked the keeper before referred to, 'come now in larger numbers from year to year. The fact is they are like a good many of the people you see walking about—if they once find out where there's a good nose-bag they take care to be near it.'—*D. T.*, 22nd December 1898.

Nose-bagger (*Seaside Soc.*). A day visitor to the seaside, who brings his own provisions, presumably in a bag—one who is of no monetary value to the resort visited. Contemptuous comparison to the cab-horse, or even the shore-donkey.

'Last season was a bad one; there were plenty of visitors, but nearly all "nose-baggers"—people who come for the day and bring their own provisions,' said a Southend butcher in his examination at the Chelmsford Bankruptcy Court. — *Lloyds'*, 24th November 1807.

Noser (*Covent Garden*). Said of visitors to the market who inspect the flowers and fruits, sometimes quite closely, and who do not buy.

Nosper (*Low London back*). Common word for stranger. It is 'person'.

Not a feather to fly with (*Colloquial—from Universities*). When the word 'plucked' was used to designate failure to pass an examination, the figure of speech was carried out by describing a very doleful failure as being plucked 'without a feather to fly with'—meaning that no success whatever was obtained. Applied in many ways.

Not dead yet (*Theatrical*, 1883). Ancient—generally said of an antique fairy.

Not enough written (*Authors'*, 1870). Not sufficiently corrected for style.

Not in it (*Sporting*). Failure—referring to a horse in a race as having no chance.

The gentleman who declared that gold-mining was not in it was strictly correct. The gold production in the United States is worth between nine and ten millions, but the profit upon it is nothing like that on sugar.—*D. T.*, 26th February 1897.

Not on borrowing terms (*American*, 1882). Not in friendly relations—said of next-door neighbours.

The families of the two young souls were not on 'borrowing terms'.—*Texas Siftings*, 1883.

Not the cheese (*Peoples'*, *Hist.*). Not satisfactory. Dr Brewer absolutely refers this word back to the Persian and the Hindoo—cheez, thing; though he says nothing of the journey. May be from the French, 'Ce n'est pas la chose'—chose being used a great deal for thing in the sixties.

Not to-day, Baker (*Peoples'*, 1885). Said at a youth who is paying attentions which are obviously unwelcome. Term used by housewives refusing bread when the morning baker calls. But satirically applied in reference to a military man of this name who was given into custody for pressing his attentions upon a young lady travelling by accident alone with him.

The gentleman signs himself 'Baker', and wants to try an experiment on my family. In the words of the poet, I reply, 'Not to-day, Baker!'—*Ref.*, 8th March 1885.

Not too nice (*Soc.*, 1870 on). First degree of condemnation—equals bad. Outcome of the frequent use of nice.

Not up to Dick (*Common Respectable Life*). Not well; ill and wretched.

Not worth a rap (*Irish*, *Hist.*). Worth nothing. In the early years of the 18th century, from 1721, notwithstanding the savage Drapier Letters, copper money was so rare in Ireland that a quantity of base metal was in circulation in the shape of small coins. They came to be called raps—probably the short of *rapparee*, a good-for-nothing fellow—hence the word came to be applied to describe valuelessness.

Note (*Soc.*, 1860 on). Intellectual signature, polite war-cry.

Culture is the 'note' of Boston.—*D. N.*, 18th November 1884.

Notergal Wash, or N. Wash (*L. Class*, 1857 on). No wash at all—grubbiness. Very interesting if from Nightingale. Miss Nightingale, the creator (1855-56) of rational nursing, had the misfortune to incur the lower public satire for stating that a person could keep himself clean on a pint of washing water per day. She did not say he was preferably to do this.

Nothing to do with the case (*Peoples'*, *Hist.*). Elegant evasion of 'you lie!' Made very popular by Mr W. S. Gilbert's *The Mikado*, wherein Mr G. Grossmith had a capital song which began:

'The flowers that bloom in the spring Have nothing to do with the case.'

Nottub (*Back phrasing*). Button.

Now or never (*Rhyming*). Clever.

Well, these Tommy Rotters kid the poor judy they're very rich, and if they're now and never they get carefully carried (married) to her.—*Biography of Cheap Heiress Hunters*, 1882.

Now we're busy (*Peoples'*, 1868). To suggest action. Also an evasive intimation that the person spoken of is no better for his liquor, and is about to be destructive.

Now we shan't be long (*Peoples'*, 1895 on). Intimation of finality. Origin obscure. Probably from railway travellers' phrase when near the end of a journey.

'Now we shan't be long', said Henry Martin to Thomas Hiom, as the couple equipped themselves with a pair of double-barrelled catapults and a copious supply of indiarubber pellets, and started off on a partridge-shooting expedition to the Finchley Road.—*D. T.*, 8th September 1896.

Now we shall be shan't (*Dec.* 1896). Another jocular shape of 'Now we shan't be long'—and purposely having no meaning.

Nudities (*Critics*, 1890 on). New shape of 'nude studies' or 'nudes'.

The nudities, though of the usual class, are fewer and less fragrant than usual, the horrors less horrible, and what may be called the medical pictures less repulsive.—*D. N.*, 19th April 1898.

Nuf ced (*From America*). Contraction of 'enough said'—absurdly spelt. Warning to say no more. Used in Liverpool chiefly.

Number one (*Navy*). Strictly naval for first lieutenant.

Nuptiated (*Wilful American*). Married.

Nurse the hoe-handle (*Agricultural American*). Lazy.

Nursery noodles (*Literary*). Critics who are very fastidious.

O

O (*Peoples', Hist.*). Most emphatic form of liking and satisfaction—always used as a suffix. "What O!"

O (*Printers'*). Emphatic, and abbreviation of overseer.

O. B. (*Criminal*). Old Bailey, City Criminal Court.

O. P. H. (*Polit.*, 1886). Old Parliamentary Hand—meaning Gladstone. Invented by *Times* (February 1886).

O. T. (*Street, Satirical*, 1880). One way of observing that the weather is warm.

O. V. (*Booth*). Abbreviation of oven—the name given to the open space below the stage in which the Pepper's ghost illusion is worked. This apparatus, which is at an angle of 35, and upon which the phantomised comedians lie, is surrounded by lamps, and is very hot — hence the title. (*See* Phant.)

OVO (*Low Class, Hist.*) Quite inexplicable. No solution ever obtained from the initiates.

O Bergami, or **O Begga me** (*London Peoples'*, 1820). Still used in the streets as intimating that the person addressed is a liar, or worse. From one Ber'gami—a lying witness at the trial of Queen Caroline—whose denial of everything brought about this phrase, with his eternal 'non mi ricordo'. (*See* Non me.)

O chase me (*Streets*, 1898 on). Satiric invitation, or pretended satiric, by a maiden to a youth to run after her and hug and kiss her.

O Cheese and Crust (*Lower Peoples'*). O, Jesus Christ!

O cricum jiminy (*Peoples', Hist.*). An exclamation of pretended fear.

O! cry! (*Peoples'*). Exclamation of satiric surprise, confounded with cry, but probably nothing to do with it. 'O! crickey!' may be another shape of the expression. May be an evasion of 'O! Christ!'

O dear me! (*Peoples'*). Exclamation of regret. Probably from the Court of Katharine of Arragon (Henry VIII.), or perhaps from that of Catherine of Braganza (Charles II.).
'Ay di mi!' as the Spaniards say, we shall have no Pomard this year! The storms of yesterday and of Monday have devastated the vineyards.—*D. N.*, 1874.

O Gomorrah to you! (*Com. Life*). Play of a word upon 'to-morrow', and said either savagely or jocularly.

O—good night! (*Low English*). Meaning, 'This is too much—I think I must be going.'

O! la! (*European—almost historical*). O! law! The influence of the Crusades upon European society was notoriously immense. Surely some expressions were imported? What more likely than that of 'Allah!'—which is in the mouth of every Mahomedan at all times, and always at the beginning of a sentence? 'Hullo!' may be from the same source.

O my eye (*Peoples'—Old Catholic*). Corruption of 'Ah mihi'—the opening words of the prayer to St Martin, the patron of beggars. Implies doubt, and a suggestion of deceptive utterance.

O. P. H. (*Street*, 19 cent.). Off.

O Pollaky! (*Peoples'*, 1870). Exclamation of protest against too urgent enquiries. From an independent, self-constituted, foreign detective, who resided on Paddington Green, and became famous for his mysterious and varied advertisements, which invariably ended with his name (accent on the second syllable), and his address.

O soldiers! (*Peoples'*). Exclamation —not now often heard.

O Smith! (*Peoples'*, 1835 - 50). Cavernous laugh, very popular, for nearly a score of years. 'What an O Smith' would be the comment upon hearing a grim 'Ha-ha'. O Smith always did the frequent Adelphi villains of that day, also the unscrupulous villains.

O the language! (*Peoples'*). Generally said to a drunken woman using violent or spluttering English.

O Willie, Willie (*Peoples'*, 1898). Term of satiric reproach addressed to a taradiddler rather than a flat liar.

Oak (*Rhyming*). Joke — very common. Now passed into chestnut.

Oaky-pokeys (*Devonshire*). Cockchafers.

Oat-stealer (*Country Tavern*). Ostler. A play upon the original word.

Obvious (*Soc.*, 1897). Fat, stout. Origin evident.

'Mary, you are becoming too obvious.'

Obviously severe (*Soc.*, 1890 on). Hopelessly rude of speech.

Occifer (*Colloquial imbecile,* 19 *cent.*). Officer.

Ochorboc (*Italian organ-grinders'*). Beer. The word is here found by taking the first letter of the word 'bochor' and adding it to the end, also adding 'oc'. The original word is 'Bocca' (mouth).

Odd job man (*Trade*). Modified description of the Shyster, who professes to do anything and only does his employer.

Odd-fellows (*Peoples'*). Name of a mutual benefit society. Corruption of God-fellows.

Odd's Bobs (*Peoples'*). *God's Babe* (the Redeemer). May be found in *Roderick Random*.

Od's death. The Crucifixion—His death; long since passed into 'Sdeath.

Od's fish (*Peoples', Hist.*). Scotch exclamation, probably brought south by James I. 'Od' is an evasion of 'God', while fish is a Scotticism for fash, which in its turn is from *faché*, one of the French terms brought into Scotland through French influence.

Od's my life (*Lower Class*). One of the religious adjurations—'God's my life.'

Know Lieutenant Bowling—odd's my life! and that I do.—*Roderick Random*, ch. xxiv.

Odsbud (*Peoples'*). Is probably God's Bud—and meaning the Redeemer, or it may be God's Blood. (See *Tom Jones*, bk. xvi., ch. viii.)

Odso (*Provincial*). Now only heard in country places. One of the evasive religious ejaculations of 17th century —'God's oath'.

Young Mirabel: 'Odso — the relics, madam, from Rome!'—Farquhar, *The Inconstant*.

Off chump (*Stable*). No appetite— onomatope of the noise made by horses in eating.

Off the rails (line) (*Peoples'*, 1840 on). Unsteady.

Officers of the 52nds (*Irish—City of Cork*). Known generally in Irish garrison towns. Young men, chiefly clerks and shopkeepers, who make a rigid official appearance on Sundays. There are fifty-two Sundays in a year.

Officers' wives (*Army,* 19 *cent.*). Prosperity.

The bugle sang out 'Officers' wives have puddings and pies, while soldiers' wives have skilly', that is the soldiers' translation of the call to mess.—*Ref.*, 10th April 1885.

Ofters (*Sporting*, 1884). Frequenters.

We may almost assume that the principle of heredity has once again asserted itself, and that the youthful 'ofters' whom I saw in the Haymarket the other night, all shirt front and fur collar, are the offspring of the very same sort of springalds who exploited themselves thirty years ago in the very selfsame neighbourhood. — *Ref.*, 23rd December 1888.

Og-rattin (*Lond. Restaurant*). *Au gratin*—anglicization.

Ogotaspuotas (*Street, S. L.*, 1897). Bosh, nonsense. At once dubbed 'Oh, go to spue'. Legend upon a Radical flag carried on Sunday, 7th March 1897, to Hyde Park and to a meeting in favour of the Cretans.

Old boots, To fight like. Fight like Marlborough—the first English general to wear immense jack boots. William III. preceded him in this display—but the Orange's were lighter boots. For several generations Marlborough was the people's hero. Indeed he was only displaced first by Nelson, and then by Wellington. The heroes have given several boots to society— Wellington and Blucher amongst others. 'My dawg can fet like old boots, and shoon too.'

Old boys (*Soc.*, 1880). Old schoolfellows.

An 'Old Boy's' Dinner. — An 'Old Boy's' dinner of Amersham and Amersham Hall School was held last night at the Freemasons' Tavern, when about 130 were present.—*D. N.*, 9th April 1885.

Old Ebenezer (*American - Sport*). Grizzly and grisly bear. Probably applied from its appearance.

The hunter on the lonely heights of the Rocky Mountains is far too well armed to-day to fear either a 'mountain lion', as the panther is locally called, or 'Old Ebenezer', the renowned grizzly bear himself.—*D. N.*, 2nd February 1883.

Old gal (*Peoples'*). General term of affection describing a wife.

Old gang)*Parliamentary*, 1870-1900). Ancient Tory party—uncompromising Tories, generally old men.

Lord Randolph Churchill has probably not gained all the points on which he was disposed to insist. But, in deference to his opinion, there will no doubt be a clearance out of some of those whom the Fourth Party is in the habit of politely designating as the 'Old Gang'.—Mr J. Chamberlain, 17th June 1885.

Old geyser (*Street*). Elderly man.

Old hat (*Old English and new Australian*). Modern anatomical reference —very cogent, but not explainable.

I shall conclude this note with remarking that the term 'old hat' is at present used by the vulgar in no very honourable sense.—Fielding, *Jonathan Wild*.

Old Mother Hubbard (*Common English*, 1880). Fictional—said of a story which is past belief.

Old moustache (*Street*, 1880). Elderly vigorous man with grey moustache.

'Prisoners of War', two English middies, one of them with his arm in a sling, on a bench in a French seaport. An old moustache guards them.—*D. N.*, 9th April 1885.

Old put (*Soc., early* 19 *cent.—now Peoples'*). A pretentious, stupid, aged gentlemanly man. Derived probably from a proper name.

It is quite credible that such a man, meeting in an omnibus an elderly gentleman of antiquated air and costume, should consider it funny to insult the 'old put' by pretending to be an intimate acquaintance, and accosting him with a familiar 'How's Maria?'—*St James' Gazette*, 7th August 1883.

Old Shake (*Amer. Press*, 1870). Shakespeare.

Old shoes. Rum. (*See* Old boots.)

Old Shovel-penny (*Military*). The pay-master, who is generally an ancient.

Old slop (*London*, 19 *cent.*). A corruption of 'saloop', derived from the French 'salope'. Applied to the *Times* newspaper from 1840-50, to intimate that it was bowing and smiling on all sides, and trying to attract, while having no will of its own.

Old splendid (*American*, 19 *cent.*). Splendid in the highest.

Old Whiskers (*Street*, 19 *cent.*). Cheeky boys' salute to a working-man whose whiskers are a little wild and iron-grey.

Old Wigsby (*Middle - class*). Crotchety, narrow - minded, elderly man, who snappishly can see no good in any modern thing. Same in French —equivalent *perruque*.

M. Halévy, whom he welcomed at the Academy, is also no *perruque*, or solemn big wig, and it may be said, with some emphasis, that he is no prude—*D. N.*, February 1886.

Olds, middles, and youngs (*Provincial*). Scotch, English, and Irish.

Some one who had studied the idiosyncrasies of the three chief component parts of the United Kingdom, summed up his experiences of them by comparing the Scotch to old people, the English to middle-aged, and the Irish to children. —*D. N.*, 5th March 1885.

Oldster (*Slang, Clubs*, 1884). Ageing man. Gift from U.S.A.

You mustn't trust the oldsters too implicitly when they endeavour to persuade you, as they always will, that there never was such a time as their time.—*Ref.*, 7th March 1886.

Olive oil (*Music Hall*, 1884). English pronunciation of *Au revoir*.

Oliver (*Compound Rhyming*). Fist. As thus: Oliver Twist. Derived from Dickens.

Omnes (*Wine Merchants'*). Word for the mixtures of odds and ends of various wines.

On dig (*School*). Abbreviation of 'on his dignity'.

On for a tatur (*Peoples'*). Fascinated, enraptured. Said of a man talking to a barmaid, and making eyes at her. Evidently from *tête-à-tête*.

On his ear (*Amer.-Eng.*). In disgrace—from American handy mothers grabbing their boys' ears while battling in the streets with other boys.

On his feet (*American*). Ruined.

On ice (*Amer.-Eng.*). Dead. From placing body on ice to aid in 'faking it'.

On (a bit o') toast. 'He had me on (a bit o') toast'; figuratively to say he absorbed or swallowed me so readily that the act was no more trouble to him than swallowing anything that will lie on a fragment of the toast in question.

On the back seam (*Tailors'*). Another elegant evasion. Flat on the floor.

On the beer (*Peoples'*). Evident.

On the bias (*Dressmakers'*). Illegitimate. On the cross.

On the deck (*Costers' local*). Living in Seven Dials. (*See* Deck.)

On the marry (*American*). Looking out for a wife or husband.

On the nail (*Peoples'*). Immediate payment—no trust. From the habit of ancient shop-keepers having a square-headed, large nail driven through the counter. Upon its head the money in payment was laid.

On the pig's back (*Irish*). In luck's way. Comes from Rome. During the reigns of the Twelve a golden amulet in the shape of a pig was supposed to bring good luck.

On the pounce (*Irish*). Preparing to spring, verbally. Brought into sudden fashion by Mr E. Harrington, H.R., M.P. (13th September 1887). Upon his being suspended he observed, 'You, Mr Speaker, have been on the pounce for me since I rose—you have been on the pounce waiting for me all the evening, and I claim my right to speak.

Mr Smith has the further function of keeping ready—'on the pounce', as the irreverent phrase goes—to clap on the closure whenever he and his colleagues think they have had enough of a debate. —*D. N.*, 10th October 1890.

On the run (*Anglo-American*). Escaping.

On the slate (*Lower Peoples'*). Written up against you — from the credit-slate kept in chandlers' shops.

On the square (*Peoples'*). Totally honest and straightforward. From Freemasonry, where the square is typical of everything that is good.

On the tapis (*Diplomatic*). Rumour, equivalent to 'on dit'.

On velvet (*Mid.-class* 1860), Luxurious success.

Once (*Street*). Vigour, go, cheek— the substantivizing of 'on' — most emphatic.

I like Shine—I cannot help admiring the large amount he possesses of what is vulgarly called 'once'. — *Ref.*, 24th October 1886.

Once a week man or **Sunday promenader** (*London*, 1830-40). Man in debt. Could only go out on Sunday, because on that day no arrests for debt could be made. (*See* Egan's *Real Life in London*.)

Onces (*Artisans'*). Wages — abbreviation of 'once a week'.

One and a peppermint drop (*Com. London*). One-eyed person.

One bites (*Lond. Costers*, 1870 on). Small, acrid apples — which, being tested with one bite, are thrown away.

One consecutive night (*Soc. and Stage*). Enough.

The second lecture is almost invariably a dismal failure. 'One consecutive night' is the limit of the funny man's course.— *D. N.*, 15th August 1890.

One drink house (*Common London*, 19 *cent.*). Where only one serving is permitted. If the customer desire a second helping, he has to take a walk 'round the houses' after the first.

One leg trouser (*Soc.*, 1882). Tight, feminine skirt of the period.

. . . and ladies in the latest 'one-leg-trouser' fashion from Paris. — *D. N.*, 18th April 1883.

(*See* Eel-skin.)

One of them (*Streets*). A shilling.

One of those (*Peoples'* 1880). An obscure phrase, coming probably from a comic song entitled, 'I really must have one of those'. No ascertained meaning above the class in which it originated—but evidently quite understood by its patrons. Remained in gutter fashion for about four years, when it fell from its high intent.

1.30 (*Tavern*). That is to say, 'one hour and a half'—derived from railway mode of counting time.

One-eyed city (*American*). A poor, inactive place.

One-light-undershirt-and-no-suspenders weather (*American*). Very hot.

One-two (*Peoples'*). Familiar figure of speech for rapidity.

Oner over the gash (*Peoples'*). A blow over the mouth.

Oolfoo (*Low. Class*). Fool.
He'll make the judy think that you're the biggest oolfoo that ever was started on the blessed earth.

Oons (*Provincial — Romanesque*). Evasion of 'God's wounds'. Once pronounced 'ouns'. (*See* 'Tare an' ouns', 'Hounds').

'No—hang it. 'Twill never do—oons.' —Farquhar, *The Inconstant*.

Op (*Soc.*, 1870). Opera.

Open-airs (*Salvationist*). Meetings beyond roofs.

We have had some blessed heart-rejoicing times. Last week three sinners wept their way to Calvary, and enlisted to fight under the blood-stained banner. Our open-airs are glorious.—*War Cry*, 1884.

Open door (*Polit.*, 1898). Colonial free trade. Heard long before this year, but took form in the autumn of this, due to the discord in China—when England urged that Chinese commerce should be equally free to all nations—hence the term, which at once passed over Europe.

Open eye (*Trade*, 1899). Correlative and completion of open door—meaning that though the foreigner may trade with the whole empire, a sharp eye must be kept on him. Invention of Mr Stuart Wortley (at Stoke-upon-Trent, December 1899), who said in a dinner-speech: 'For our commercial prosperity we needed the open eye as well as the open door.'

Open to (*L. London*). To tell—confess.

I knew then that Selby had got a bit more (money) than he opened to (told) me.—*People*, 6th January 1895.

Opera (*Amer.*, 1880). Perversion of 'uproar'.

Operation (*Tailors'*). Patch, especially in relation to the rear of trousers.

Opportunism (*Polit.*, 1860 on). Shaping ways to most available means. Used rather in contempt, as subserving conscience to convenience, or to personal advantage.

Opt (*American—passing to England*, 1882). Abbreviation of verb 'optate'.

Food and treatment are much better at lunatic asylums than at gaols, or in casual wards; therefore Mr Wickham 'opts' for lunatic asylums. — *D. N.*, February 1882.

Order (*Theat.*). Free pass.

Order dead-head (*Theat.*, 1880). Patron of the theatre—the dead-head —who passes on with an order. 'Dead-head' (*q.v.*) comes from America, and is there unqualified by the word 'order' (*q.v.*).

On Monday the house was quite full of what looked like money, leavened by a faint sprinkling of the order dead-head. —*Ref.*, 17th April 1885.

Order of the Boot (*M. Class*). A species of violent assault. The order of knighthood is bestowed by a tap with a sword on the shoulder. The Order of the Boot is conferred by the toe of the boot—farther down.

Orf chump (*Peoples'*). No appetite. 'Orf' is a variation of 'off'. Derived from stablemen's tongues in reference to their horses—'I'm orf chump altogether.'

Orf his chump (*Peoples'*). Mad, cranky. It has nothing to do with 'orf chump'. Means 'off his head' —his brain not in order.

Ornary (*American*). Expression for contemptible. Corruption of 'ordinary'.

But I was roused by a fiendish laugh
That might have raised the dead—
Them ornary sneaks had sot the clocks
A half an hour ahead!

Ornin' (*L. Class*). Boasting, praising oneself. Probably from the bombastic self-assertion of the hunter's horn. Chiefly provincial.

Otamies (*Lower Peoples'*). Surgical operations of all kinds. Probable corruption of anatomies.

And now, poor man, he is among the otamies, at Surgeons' Hall.—Gay, *Beggars' Opera*.

Other arrangements (*Theatrical*). Defeat—retreat.

Wherefore Hartt, though still by no means bowed down by weight of woe or otherwise, thinks it now time to make other arrangements. — *Ref.*, 5th July 1885.

Other side (*Anglo-American*). In U.S.A. it is G. Britain. In G. B. it is U.S.A.

Ouah (*Erotic, Peoples'*, 1882). Exclamation of delight.

Ought to know (*Soc.*). Expression of belief in capability of person spoken of.

Out (*Peoples'*). Loss. Sometimes used in the plural.

Out (*Soc. and Peoples'*, 19 *cent.*). Quarrelled.

Nor is Russian statesmanship our only trouble at the present moment. Prince Bismarck is or has been 'out with us', as the children say.—*D. N.*, 6th March 1885.

Out of commission (*Clerks'*). Requiring an appointment.

Out of the cupboard (*Peoples', Boys'*). Turn out in the world.

Out of mess (*Military, Hist.*). Dead—he eats no more.

In the Eastern Soudan, in 1884, at El Teb, many of our men were wounded—indeed, I believe, some killed—by the wounded, wily enemy; and it became necessary, as we searched the field for our own dead and wounded, to put some of these treacherous foes out of mess; but there was no unnecessary butchery. —*D. T.*, 7th January 1899.

Out of sorts (*Printers'*). Literally, out of sorts of types — some of the composing compartments empty. This term is quite obsolete—now that composing machines are universal.

Out of the tail of the eye (*Irish*). Furtive observation.

Out of the whole cloth (*Amer.*). Untruth in the deepest degree. Equivalent to 'Whole hog' (*q.v.*).

Out of the wood (*American*). Out of the difficulty. Derived from pioneers and others in the West.

Outs (*Polit.*, 19 *cent.*). The Opposition.

While the Outs look upon this discovery as a tremendous blow to the Ins, while Tory newspapers insist that all this is the outcome of Liberal concessions, there is little or no chance of our getting the remedy that is so necessary.—*Ref.*, 25th February 1883.

Outs (*Anglo-Amer.*). Out of friendship. Probably old provincial English.

It is currently believed that Mrs Willie K. Vanderbilt, *née* Alva Smith, and the Baroness Fontenilliat, *née* Mimi Smith, are decidedly and emphatically on the outs.—*New York Mercury*, 1892.

Outside Eliza (*Low. London*). Drunk again, Eliza. Applied to intoxicated, reeling women. Derived from a police case where a barman stated that he said to the prisoner over and over again, 'Outside, Eliza'—but she would not go, and finally smashed a plate-glass window.

Outward man (*Devon*). A guzzler, one who does not stop at home.

Ovate (*American - English*, 90's). Verb derived from ovation.

An acute stage of the troubles in China seems to have been thoughtlessly ended by the Allies without their Commander-in-Chief, who was really very busy being received and ovated. — *N. Y. Times*, August 1900.

Over the bender (*Old English*). Implying that the statement made is untrue, *e.g.*, 'You'll pay me cock sure on Monday?' 'Yes—over the bender.' The bender is the elbow. It is historical in common English life that a declaration made over the elbow as distinct from not over it, need not be held sacred. Probably from early Christian if not from Pagan times. The bender is always the left elbow, and may therefore have something to do with 'over' the left.

Over the lefter (*Poachers'*). A partridge before 1st September, or a pheasant before 1st October.

Over the stile (*Rhyming*). Committed for trial.

Over-eye (*Peoples', old*). To watch.

Owl, Biled (*Eng.-Amer.*, 1880 on). Bad complexion—signs facial of dissipation.

But Christmas scooped the sheriff,
  The egg-nogs gathered him in;
And Shelby's boy, Leviticus,
  Was, New Year's, tight as sin;
And along in March the Golyers
  Got so drunk that a fresh-biled owl
Would 'a' looked 'longside o' them two
  young men,
Like a sober temperance fowl.
  —Col. Hay, U.S.A., Ambassador
    to Eng., 1897.

Oyster months (*Peoples', Hist.*). All the months (8) in which there is an 'R'—oysters being quite 'out' in May, June, July, August.

Oysterics (*Mid.-class*, 1900-04 on). A coined word, suggesting hysterics, to satirize the panic in reference to oysters creating typhoid fever.

Once again the public is thrown into a state of what is grimly known in the trade as 'oysterics', owing to reports of deaths at Portsmouth from infected oysters. It is two years since the great oyster scare followed on the deaths following the mayoral banquet at Winchester.—*D. T.*, 11th November 1904.

P

P. C. (*Soc.*, 1880). Initials of 'poor classes'.

P. P. and **C. C.** (*Irish*). Parish priest; Catholic curate.

P. P. C. (*Middle-class*). Snappish good-bye. Of course from departure card, *Pour prendre congé*.

P. P. C. (*Soc.*, 19 *cent.*). *Pour prendre congé*. Used in two ways, when sending a card. If without addition, it means good-bye—if with future date added, it means *au revoir*.

P. P. C., To (*Soc.*, 1880 on). To quarrel and cut.

P. P. M. (*Soc.*, 19 *cent.*). Initials of *Pour P'tit Moment*, a modification of P. P. C.

P. R. (*Sporting*). Initials of Prize Ring.

P. R. B. (*Soc.*, 1848 on). Pre-Raphaelite Brotherhood. Sometimes ironically styled 'the Purby'. In 1848 three artists, D. G. Rosetti, Holman Hunt and J. E. Millais, formed a brotherhood, with these letters following their names. Several other painters joined them, together with T. Woolner, the sculptor. Theirs was a revival of religion in art, religion which the brotherhood maintained had been swept out of Italian art by the materialistic force of the Renaissance.

The Pre-Raphaelite brethren, or 'P.R.B.'s,' as they are familiarly called, brought skill, earnestness, and thoroughness to the purpose of overturning established beliefs in matters artistic.—*D. N.*, November 1885.

P. S. (*Theatrical*). Prompt side—first entrance left hand of the stage, when facing the audience.

P. S.'s (*Hatter's term*). This secret trade phrase is called as here written, but is always described in the trade by 'x'. It represents a sum of money which the master is willing to advance to a valuable workman in addition to his statement of weekly account, when he has made a short week, and which P. S. he will repay when a 'long' week arrives.

P. W. Abney (*Streets'*, 1897). A high, feminine hat which first appeared in 1896, and grew. The phrase is a reduction of Prince of Wales Abney Cemetery; it is got from three black, upright ostrich feathers, set up at the side of the hat in the fashion of the Prince of Wales's crest feathers. (*See* 'Catafalque'.)

P. Y. C. (*Baltic Coffee-house*). Pale yellow candle—from this establishment persistently rejecting gas.

Pa (*Peoples'*). Relieving officer of a parish.

Pack (*Navy*). Curtailment of 'Pactolus'.

Pack (*Texas*). To carry.

Packing (*Peoples'*). Food.

Packing-ken (*Low. Class*). Eating-house—because you pack the food in your stomach then and there.

Padder (*Oxford*). Short for Paddington Terminus.

Paddington Station, dearest of all the London termini to the undergraduate heart during term, is Padder.—*D. T.*, 14th August 1899.

Paid shot (*Old Scotch*). 'Shot' is a common mode of expression to denote a reckoning, etc. 'I have paid my shot,' or rather 'scot', from 'scottum', a tax or contribution, a shot.

Paint a proof (*Printers'*). To make a number of corrections on a proof, and so paint it with ink on both margins.

Paint the town red (*Amer.-Eng.*, 1890). Originally to produce a sense of danger by night rioting. From railway system, where red is the danger signal. Now applied in a thousand ways.

The delegates from California are full of Chicago firewater, and are in the streets howling for Blaine and threatening to paint the town red.

An effectual stop has been put to the last eccentricity of the facetious ex-Communist Maxime Lisbonne, who had lately, it will be remembered, endeavoured to 'paint the town red' by promenading the streets of Paris in a scarlet brougham.—*D. T.*, 6th November 1894.

After a time variety was gained by the use of vermilion.

There are no dreary exhibitions of 'comic' drunkenness—as if drunkenness could ever be comical—nor any representation of 'racketty' young bloods painting the place vermilion.

Paint-brush baronets (*Soc.*, 1885). Title invented for ennobled artists.

The two paint-brush baronetcies are also sure to be popular. Mr Watts has his admirers in the circles of 'culture', and is a magnificent artist of the imaginative school. Mr Christmas Number Millais is, however, a household word, and popular with all classes. Now he is a bart. he will be more popular still, and his pictures will fetch bigger prices than ever.—*Ref.*, 28th June 1885.

Painter stainers (*Soc.*, 1883). Artists. At the Royal Academy Banquet, 1883, remarkable for much erratic observation, the Lord Mayor endeavoured to obtain a lift for the then threatened glories of the city by declaring that 'in earlier times the Corporation was the means whereby art was fostered in this country, and we have still amongst us a body which has devoted itself largely to the encouragement of Art — namely, the Painter Stainers' Company, which existed in the reign of Edward III., and is still in a flourishing condition. This company may really be described as having been the Royal Academy of England until the foundation of the present Academy in 1761'.

For the remainder of the season artists were in society jocularly called painter-stainers. Indeed the term lasted for many seasons.

Pair o' compasses (*London*, 1880). This term for a couple of human legs (in connection with a human body) came into vogue when the narrowness of the trousers brought out the stretched, compass-like effect of a pair of long legs. (*See* Gas-pipes.)

Pair o' round-mys (*Low Life*). Trousers.

Palpitate with actuality (*American-Eng.*, 1885). Intensely evident.

As no one of any influence is at present proposing a separation between Church and State, the vow does not, in the beautiful phrase which has been wafted to us across the Atlantic, 'palpitate with actuality'.—*D. N.*, 12th November 1885.

Pan out boss (*American Miners'*). Successful. Pan out is derived from the process of washing for gold.

Panic (*Stock Exchange*, 19 *cent.*). Sudden alarm, followed by fall in prices.

Pannum (*Thieves'*). Bread, dinner.

Panny (*Low Peoples'*). A familiar house.

Panny (*Low Peoples'*). Fight amongst women.

Panorama (*Lower Class*). Paraphrase of paramour.

Mr Branson, the bank forger, murders his wretched panorama, Mary Power, and departs for Australia.—*Ref.*, 17th November 1889.

Pantile Park (*London*). View of roofs and chimney pots. Used by Charles Dickens upon viewing the scene from Foster's back windows at 58 Lincoln's Inn Fields.

Panto (*Theatrical*). Brief for pantomime. Who would call a pantomime by any other name than this, would be voted an outsider at a blow. 'I now hear that this house is not to be altered until after the panto.'

Pantry Politics (*Soc.*, 1884). Servants' talk.

The case has laid bare one side of 'Society journalism', or, if we may suggest an amendment, 'pantry politics', and very curious the revelation is.—*Sat. Rev.*, 21st March 1885.

Pants-shoulder (*American*). The broadest part of a pair of trousers.

Paper house (*Theatrical*). No money—all free admissions.

Paper trunk and twine lock (*Figurative Anglo-American*). The least possible amount of luggage—packed in an old news sheet and stringed.

Paperer (*Theatrical*, 1879). The official who issues 'paper', or free passes, and so 'papers the house'.

Results showed that the 'paperer' understood his business. — *Ref.*, 14th June 1885.

Par-banging (*Street*). Tramping, seeking for work. Origin obscure—but probably French.

Par-leader (*Press*, 1875). A short, commenting article, in which no break occurs. A little essay of perhaps a score of sentences, but all in one paragraph.

Parable (*Amer.-Eng.*). Long, dreary egotistical statement.

Parish pick-axe (*Peoples'*). A prominent nose.

Parker (*Local L.*, 1850 and on). Street description of a very well-dressed man in the neighbourhood of the parks.

Parliament Whiskey (*Irish*). Satirical description of potheen which has paid inland revenue dues.

If you are very ignorant, you must be told that poteen is the far famed liquor which the Irish, on the faith of the proverb, 'stolen bread is sweetest', prefer, in spite of law, and—no—not for lawgivers, they drink it themselves, to its unsuccessful rival, parliament whiskey.—*Mirror*, 1829.

Parlour-jumper (*Police*, 1870 on). From jump, to thieve, to start property from you to him.

A constable explained that the prisoner was known as a 'parlour-jumper'. This, in ordinary language, meant that he went in for robbing rooms.—*D. T.*, 4th August 1898.

Parnelliament (*Soc.*, 1886). Invented and accepted name for 'Parliament'—from the astounding success of Parnell in throwing the Conservatives and Liberals into confusion.

Parrot and monkey time (*Amer.-Eng.*, 1885). Period of quarrelling. Started from a droll and salacious tale of a monkey and a parrot. Soon shortened to parroty.

There is no work to be had for them and the unfortunate creatures are likely to have what has graphically been called 'a parroty time' in their new home.

Leonard and the chairs have had what Leonard's gay countrymen call 'a parroty time'.—*D. N.*, 12th October 1886.

Parsley bed (*Peoples'*, *Hist.*). The supposed matrix of the new baby, as chronicled in nurseries. (*See* Visit from the stork.)

Part that goes over the fence last (*American*). Evident.

Parts his hair with a towel (*American*, 1882). Bald.

Pas de Lafarge (*Soc.*, '40's). Tabooed subject—as the result of its being over discussed. Did or did not Madame Lafarge poison her husband? The dinner discussions became as great a bore as did, long after, the Tichborne case—which by the way, led to the yell at dinner tables—'No Tich'. In Paris, for years, when a man showed himself a bore, the protest ran 'Pas de Lafarge'. Now 'Pas de Dreyfus'.

Pass round the arm (*American*). To apply open-handed castigation to children—after the manner of applause.

Pass the Rubicon (*Classic*). Venture everything, no going back.

Pattern (*Irish*). Delightful, brilliant. Abbreviation of 'pattern fair', which is a corruption of 'patron fair', which is short for 'patron saint'.

Paul capstan (*Navy*). Expression of admission of excellency on the other side—as 'Well, you paul my capstan'.

Paulies (*Transvaal War*, 1899). Followers of Oom Paul Kruger—a pun between this word and 'poor lies'.

'The writer calls the Boers 'Paulies'.—*E. N.*, 9th December 1899.

Pawked up stuff (*Sporting*). False goods—bad horses, or dogs, or valueless sportsmen.

Pay out (*American miners'—passing to England*). Derived from a mine ceasing to be productive, when it was said to have paid out. Passed into general use amongst English-speaking people.

Peabody (*L. Class*). Short for block of houses built under the Peabody Bequest to the poor of London.

Peacock (*Anglo-Indian*). Walk up and down in full fig while the band plays.

Peacock and the ladies, Before the (*Old Eng.*). A solemn promise—an appeal to knightly honour.

In olden days the peacock was a favourite dish with lords and ladies of high degree. It was customary to skin the bird without plucking, and send the roast bird to table with its natural envelop. The peacock was considered in the days of chivalry not simply as an exquisite delicacy, but as a dish of peculiar solemnity. When it was brought to the table, decorated with its plumage, its comb gilded, and a sponge in its bill, wet with spirits of wine and lighted, it was the signal for the gallant knights present to make vows to accomplish some deed of chivalry 'before the peacock and the ladies'.

Peacock horse (*Street*). Mourning coach horse—which generally has much parade in his movements.

Pear (*Parisian*, 1830-48). Name given to Louis Philippe—from the shape of his head. (*See* Jupiter Scapin).

Peas in the pot (*Low London*). Rhyming phrase — meaning 'hot', erotic.

Big Tim says you are very peas.— *Peoples'*, 6th January 1895.

Pecksniffian (*Peoples'*). Hypocritical — from Dickens's *Martin Chuzzlewit*.

Peel off (*City*, 1860). To obtain money by a Stock Exchange transaction.

Peel the patch off the weak point (*American*). Expose a man's weakness.

Peep o' Day tree (*Theatrical*, 1862). In this Exhibition year, one Edmund Falconer produced a piece called *Peep o' Day*, at the Lyceum, and made out of it a great fortune, chiefly by the ingenuity displayed in a stage tree, on the edge of a quarry. Its chief branch moved on a pivot by the use of which the hero swung down on to the stage just in time to prevent the murder of the heroine. From that time forward this providential stage machinery has been thus called.

The hero and heroine escape by a *Peep o' Day* tree, which enables them to descend from the cliff, amidst the enthusiastic and unanimous applause of the audience.—*Era*, April 1883.

Peg (*Theatrical*, 1884). Sensation point or effect of a piece. Something upon which the actors, or more probably an actor, can build up a scene.

Pegging away (*American, Military*). Used by General Grant for heavy artillery attack. Previously known as a careless phrase, but after the Civil War accepted gravely.

Penances and leatherheads (*American*). People of Pennsylvania —probably from their early puritanic origin—still very marked.

Pencil, open, lost, and found (*Com. Lond.*, 19 *cent.*). Rhyming phrase, means £10.

Pencil dates (*Theatrical*, 1896 on). Make engagements to perform.

The fourth D'Artagnan is Mr Charles Warner, who, full of spirit and energy, intends to bombard Suburbia and the provinces with the already successful Hamilton version, and is, as the phrase goes, 'pencilling in dates' as fast as a manager can who knows his business.— *D. T.*, 6th August 1898.

Pennorth o' treacle (*L. London*, 1882). A charming girl—the final outcome of the use of 'jam'.

Pennorth o' treason (*Newsvendors'*). Copy of a notorious penny Sunday London paper, which attacks every party, and has no policy of its own.

Penny death-traps (*L. London* 1897). Penny glass paraffin lamps— made in Germany. Fragile and easily upset; they caused many deaths.

Penny gush (1880-82). Exaggerated mode of writing English frequently seen in a certain London daily paper.

This, published in an English paper would probably be described as penny gush.—G. A. Sala, *Illustrated London News*, 16th December 1882.

Penny loaf (*Thieves'*). Cur — one afraid to steal; a man who would rather live on a penny loaf than steal good beef.

Penny locket (*Rhyming*). Pocket.

While he's got his peepers on the penny locket, you know, perhaps, how to be a bit careful.

Penny pick (*London, circa* 1838). Cigar. From *Pickwick*, Dickens's first popular creation.

Penny puzzle (*Street*, 1883). Sausage—because it is never found out. (*See* Bag o' mystery.)

Penny starver (*Street*). Lowest description of cigar—commercial value three for twopence.

Penny toff (*London*, 1870 on). The lowest description of toff—the cad imitator of the follies of the *jeunesse dorée*.

Perfect lady (*Street*). Not at all one — anything but. Satirically applied to any woman drunk and misbehaving herself in the streets. The phrase took its rise from a police court case, in which a witness deposed that, though the prisoner did get her living in the streets and drank a little, she was otherwise a 'perfect lady'.

Perfumed talk (*Anglo-American*). Satirical synonym for vile language.

Perhaps (*Old Eng.*). Equivalent to most decidedly.

Permanent pug (*Printers' and Tavern*). Fighting man around the door of the premises. Originally applied to the door-porter of editorial offices.

Perpetual staircase (*Thieves'*). The tread-mill.

Perpetuana (*Norfolk*, 18 *cent.*). A very strong dress fabric, which lasted an immense time. Still applied to describe old women in Norfolk.

Norfolk folk want a little fresh impulse now, to restore the flourishing condition of their textile manufactures. Beauty arrayed herself in bravery that *was* cheap and was *not* nasty. *Perpetuana* lasted for ever.—*Athenæum*, 1870.

Perplexed and transient phantom (*Politics*). Politician who fails and vanishes.

Lord Salisbury hopes to be something more than a 'perplexed and transient phantom'.—*D. N.*, 1st July 1885.

Perseus (*Soc.*, 1883). An editor. From a phrase used by Professor Huxley at the Royal Academy Banquet, 1883.

Petit bleu (*Franco-Eng.*, 1898). Forgery. From the colour of the French telegraphic paper.

Then, with regard to the *petit bleu* which Picquart is accused of forging. It is true that the address on this telegraphic post card was scratched out, the name of the addressee being effaced, and that of Easterhazy written over it. —*D. T.*, 28th November 1898.

Peto (*Soc.*). Evasion of P.T.O.—initials of Please turn over.

Petticoat interest (*Literature*, 1860 on). Those portions of fiction referring to womankind.

Scott did not trouble himself much about Maid Marian. He had enough of what is now called 'petticoat interest' in his story without her.—*D. N.*, 29th March 1892.

Phant (*Showmen's*). The sheet of plate-glass placed sloping, or diagonally, on the stage, to reflect from below or from the side the illusion known as Pepper's ghost. In order to keep the secret as far as possible, the word glass was never used, but the first syllable of phantom. Sometimes fant', at other times, in the North, 'peeble'—a new evasive name.

Pheasant (*Common London*). Dried herring. (*See* Two-eyed steak.)

Phil and Jim (*Oxford*, 1890 on). Church of S. Philip and S. James. This phrase is sometimes pronounced 'Fillin Jim'.

Philistine (*Soc.*). Formerly an outsider, but with no offensive meaning; but now with an offensive meaning.

In 1840 Liszt's reputation was at its highest, but he met with indifference here, and no doubt regarded us as given over to philistinism.—*Ref.*, 11th April 1886.

Physic-bottle (*Peoples'*). Doctor.

Piano (*Soc.*, 1870). To sing small, to take a back seat.

Piccadilly fringe (*Low. Class*, 1884). Front hair of women cut short and brought down, and curled over the forehead. Fashion originated in Paris about 1868.

By Mr Russell—When Jarrett talked about cutting my hair, she asked me if I wanted a 'Piccadilly fringe'.

What is the 'Piccadilly fringe'!—Cut your hair on your forehead.

Is there anything objectionable about that?—It makes you look ugly.—*Armstrong Abduction Case*, October 1885.

Piccadilly window (*Street*, '90's). Single eye-glass worn by some men of fashion—hence the Piccadilly.

Pick of the basket (*Sporting*). Best—derived from market baskets.

Some of Sir Watkin's horses are of extraordinary build and value. Comet stands out foremost, and 'is the pick of the basket'.—*World*, 1878.

Picker-up (*Thieves'*, 19 *cent.*). Woman of the town.

Picking its eyes (*Stock Exchange*, '90's). Getting the best, or top, of a good thing. From S. Africa mining, there applied to obtaining the immediate and easily obtained gold.

It is to be feared that more attention would, naturally, be paid to extracting the richest ore from the mines ('picking its eyes', as the popular term is) than to proceeding with the regular course of development.—*D. T.*, 26th July 1900.

Pickled dog (*Provincial*). Term of contempt—rarely now heard.

Pickles (*Peoples'*). Exclamation of good-tempered mistrust, or even want of belief.

The promoters say that benefit will accrue to our Indian fellow-subjects by bringing before the English people actual representations of the methods of manufactures, amusements, etc., of our vast Indian empire, and will thus serve imperial interests. That, of course, is all pickles.—*Ref.*, 5th July 1885.

Pickpocketienne (*Anglo-French*). Woman pickpocket.

Picnic (*American-English*). A treat—from the frequency of picnics in America, where there is always room for them.

Native dramatists for the past week have enjoyed what the street gamins would call a picnic. — *N. Y. Mercury*, January 1884.

Pidgin (*World's Sea-shore*). Simplified mixture of two or three languages, of which English is generally one. Lingua Franca, the common tongue of the Mediterranean, has Italian chiefly for its basis, mixed with French and Arabic. The word started in the Chinese waters. The chief English pidgin, sometimes erroneously called pigeon, is the mixture of English with Hindostanee, and of English with Chinese—but there must in all be scores of pidgin in the world, negro specimens being the more curious. Pidgin is a corruption of business.

According to Herr Leo Wigner, this mysterious Yiddish is not the mere barbarous trade-jargon, the 'pidgin-Hebrew', of the indigent alien of Whitechapel.—*D. T.*, 6th July 1899.

Pie (*Eng.-American*, 19 cent.). Delightful—very enjoyable.

At the depôt the light was dim, and so it was in the sleeper, as it generally is; but as she got into the car a neat leg in a white stocking showed plainly enough to make Jim murmur to himself, 'Well, this is pie'.—*N. Y. Mercury*, 3rd January 1885.

Piebald eye (*Peoples'*). Black one—black by a blow.

My! Bill—where was yer piebaldered?

(*See* Mouse, Eye in a sling.)

Piebald mucker sheeny (*E. Lond.*). Low old Jew.

Pie-pusher (*Streets*). Street pieman, who ceaselessly recommends, or pushes, his wares.

Pieces, All to (*Soc., from Sporting*, 1880). Exhausted—generally said of horses.

She was as pale as death, and trembling from head to foot. He was perfectly satisfied that what she had described took place, for when she came in she was 'all to pieces'.—Statement by Sir Beaumont Dixie concerning an attack on his wife, Lady Florence Dixie, March 1883.

Pie-shop (*London*). Dog—from the supposition (1842), when one Blauchard first started a penny pie-shop, that the pies were made of dogs.

Pieuvre (*Anglo-French*, '60's). Prostitute. When Victor Hugo published his *Les Travailleurs de la Mer*, his terrible description of the octopus—the *pieuvre*—as a creature which overcame a man by embraces, was at once seized upon by the boulevardier-journalists as an apt description of the woman of the town.

Pig months (*Peoples', Hist.*). All the months (eight) in which there is an 'R'. These pig months are those in which you may more safely eat fresh pork than in the others—the four summer months in fact.

Pig-bridge (*Trin. Col., Cambridge*). The beautiful Venetian-like bridge over the Cam, where it passes St John's College, and connecting its quads. Thus called because the Johnians are styled pigs (*q.v.*).

Pigeon pair (*Familiar*). A boy born first, a girl following, within not more than two years. Probably from the known fidelity of winged pigeon pairs to each other.

Pigs (*Trin. Col., Cambridge*, 19 cent.). Name given by the men of Trinity to their neighbours of St John's.

Pigs, An't please the (*Pre-Reformation, Eng.*). Corruption of 'Please the Pyx'. Still common in West England, where 'x' becomes 'gs'. (*See* Please the pigs.)

Pigot or Piggot (*Hist.*, 1888-89). Lie—unblushing, obvious lie. Passed into verb, generally passive — to be pigotted. From the forger Pigot.

I must print the verses, and leave the reader to judge if I have been Pigotted or not.—*Ref.*, 17th March 1889.

Pigtail (*Street, obsolete* about 1840). An old man, from the ancients clinging to the 18th century mode of wearing the hair.

Pill (*Street*). Dose, suffering, sentence, punishment. Endless in application.

Pill (*Sailors'*). Custom-house officer. Because both are so very searching.

Pill-pusher (*Peoples'*). Doctor. Fine example of the graphic in phraseology.

If the pill-pushers will only chuck it out now that diamond rings are poisonous, broughams pestilential, oysters and champagne deadly, and villas in Singin's Wood fatal in every case, many a man will be happy, many a pal will be saved.

Pillow securities (*City*, 19 cent.). Safe scrip, shares that rarely vary in price.

The shares of the earliest cable companies did not enjoy their present character of 'safe', or, as Mr Draper, Secretary of the Eastern Telegraph Company, who was associated with Sir John Pender thirty years, aptly terms, 'pillow securities'—those which do not trouble an investor's dreams at night and which a man need not worry about.—*D. T.*, 8th July 1896.

Pin (*Peoples'*). To pawn clothes.

When Lantier was doing up his bundle to send to the pawnbroker's, one intelligent pittite shouted out 'Pin!' Evidently that pittite knew something. —*Ref.*, 1882.

Pin pricks (*Hist.*, 1898). Slight attacks—assaults.

Our friendship with France is not to be obtained by a policy of pinpricks—a phrase, by the way, which is not, as some suppose, of English origin, but was first employed by a responsible French journal, *Le Matin.*—*D. T.*, 9th December 1898.

Ping (*Sportsman*, to 1854). To speak in a quick singing high voice. From the sharp ping of the old musket.

Pink 'un (*Sporting Times*, 1880). Sporting life—from the tint of the paper, and to distinguish it from the Brown 'un, Sportsman.

Before doing so, I took the advice of one John Corlett, who propriets a paper called the *Pink 'Un.*—*Ref.*, 31st July 1887.

Pink wine (*Military*). Champagne.

Pinnacles (*Peoples'*). A corruption of 'barnacles', eye-glasses, spectacles.

Pint o' mahogany (*Coffee-house*). Coffee.

Piou-piou (*Soc.*). Tommy Atkins translated into French.

Pip-pip (*Streets'*). Hue and cry after any one, but generally a youth in striking bicycle costumery. Onomatope of the horn warning which sometimes replaces the bell of the bike.

Pipe-opener (*University*). First spurt in rowing practice—to open the lungs, and get that kind of pipe in working order.

Pirate (*Low London*). Emphatic person — man or woman — especially the latter, and in music halls, where the actresses and singers of great force obtain this distinction.

Pistol-pockets (*American - Eng.*). Warning not to fool.

Pitch in (*Scotch*). Railway collision.

Pith (*Hospital*). Sever the spinal cord.

Pittite (*Theatrical*). Frequenter of the pit. Took the place of groundling (*q.v.*), when seats destroyed the force of the Shakespearian term.

A correspondent wishes me to ask Mr Irving if, when he has finished looking after the interests of Lyceum pittites, he will be kind enough to turn his attention to Lyceum dress-circlers. — *Ref.*, 10th May 1885.

(See *Stall-pots.*)

Pizen (*American, circa* 1875). Corruption of poison, and here describing alcohol—generally in its whiskey form. (*See* Death promoter.)

Plain as a pipe-stem (*Peoples'*, 17 cent. on). Utterly plain — nothing could be plainer than the stem of the white clay pipe from the cutty of the time of Charles II., to the long churchwarden—*tempo* George III.

Plank the knife in (*L. Class, Hist.*). Stab deeply.

Planter (*Anglo - Indian*). Bad-tempered horse.

Plaster (*Peoples'*, 1890 on). A collar—a huge shirt or applied collar, said to be introduced by the late Duke of Clarence.

Plasterer's trowel and seringapatam (*Rhyming*). It means 'fowl and ham'.

Plates o' meat (*Low London— Rhyming*). Feet. (*See* Barges.)

Platform ticket (*Railway*). Phrase uttered by friend who has been to see a friend off by train, and is stopped as a passenger.

Play camels (*Anglo-Indian*). Get drunk, or drink too much. Playful reference to the drinking habits of the camel, who stores his drink rather than drinks it.

Play consumption (*American — becoming English*). This is the equal of malingering, or shamming.

Play dirt (*American*). Deceive.

Play for paste (*Billiard-room*). For drink — probably from 'pasta' (Spanish)—a meal, or perhaps 'vino di pasta'—a light sherry.

Play low (*American-Eng.*). Act meanly.

Farewell banquets have lately been played a little low down, but the 'send-off' supper given to Wilson Barrett at the Criterion, on Thursday night, was an exception.—*Ref.*, 15th August 1886.

Play owings (*Sporting phrase*). Living on credit.

Play the bear (*Lancashire*). Damage.

Played out since '49 (*W. American*). Ancient untruth.

If he further informs you that 'this has been played out since '49', he means that since the first colonization of the Pacific coast by 'smart men', such a thing was never believed in: 1849 being the year of the commencement of the Californian gold digging.—*All the Year Round*, 31st October 1868.

Playing a big game (*Criminal*). Trying for a daring success.

Prior to his finally leaving her, he had often spoken about 'playing a big game'.—*D. T.*, 31st March 1897.

Playing for a sucker (*American*, 1880). Attack upon the innocence of a youth.

Please I want the cook-girl (*London*). Said of a youth haunting the head of area steps.

Please mother open the door (*Street*). Expressed admiration of a passing girl. Always said in a high monotone, except 'door', which is uttered in a falling minor third.

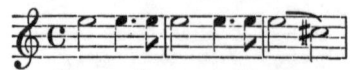

Please mo-ther o-pen the door.

Please the pigs (*Old Catholic*). *Deo volente*—God willing. Corruption of 'An it please the pyx' (Pyxis). A very interesting form of this phrase is to be found in Devonshire—'An it please the pixies.'

Pleinairists (*Art*, 1885 on). Open-air artists — the school of pleinair, which is utterly antagonistic to shadowed or claustral art.

These pretty illustrations, from the designs of the well-known French *pleinairiste* and figure painter, Raphaël Collin, are delicate and graceful even to the verge of effeminacy.—*D. T.*, 10th February 1897.

Plimsoll (*Nautical*). The 'cargo' line in merchant shipping. Plimsoll, in the House of Commons, forced the Bill for the better regulation of merchant shipping.

Plon-plon (*Parisian*, 1855). Name given to the despised Prince Jerome Napoleon after he hurried away from the Crimean War.

Pluck (*Peoples'*). Daring, as distinct from slow courage.

Plucking (*Peoples'*). Robbing.

Plug (*American*). To get into difficulties.

Ply (*Mid.-class*). Tendency, kink, inclination, leaning. Probably from the French 'pli'.

Pocket artist (*Critical*, '90's). Small actor or actress. Meant kindly, but not liked by the victims.

To the prettiness and grace of Miss Cutler *Florodora* owed not a little. She is quite a 'pocket' artist.—*D.T.*, 13th November 1899.

Pod (*Commercial*). Practical short for Post Office Directory.

Podsnap (*Soc.*, 1865 on). A Sir Oracle; whose word is sufficient—for himself. From Dickens.

Podsnappery. Wilful determination to ignore the objectionable or inconvenient, at the same time assuming airs of superior virtue and noble resignation.

Oppressed nationalities have not been accustomed to expect sympathy or assistance from Austria. But the question is a very grave one, and no amount of diplomatic Podsnappery can keep it any longer in the background.—*D. N.*, 8th July 1889.

Poet of the brush (*Art*, 1890 on). Artist. Outcome of the eternal search for new phrases.

Mr T. Hope M'Lachlan is the painter of night skies, through which the moon sails with an opalescent halo round her disc. He is in his truest conceptions a poet of the brush.—*D. T.*, 4th January 1896.

Poke (*Thieves'*). Purse. This word for sack, pouch, satchel, is to be found in Shakespeare.

Poked up (*Anglo-American*). Embarassed, inconvenienced.

Poker (*American-Eng.*). Game of cards.

Polka, To (*Anglo-Amer.*). Another of the forms of expressing rapid retreat.

'Boss, dis woman neber raise dat money in dis world;' and with a plaintive farewell, she polkaed from the office, and once more deep silence prevailed. — *Providence Journal.*

(*See* Balley, Skip, Valse.)

Pomatum pot (*Soc.*, 1885). Small specimens of pot-shaped and covered china.

Mr Gladstone at twenty-five minutes to five was fairly embarked on his speech. The familiar throat mixture commonly known as the pomatum pot was at his side, only on this occasion there were two pots instead of one.—*D. N.*, 9th May 1886.

'Pon my life (*Com. Lond. Rhyming, 19 cent.*). Wife.

Pongelo (*Anglo - Indian Army*). Pale ale—but relatively any beer.

Poole (*Soc.*, 1840 on). Perfect clothing—from Poole, a leading tailor, in Saville Row. (*See* Dorsay, Lincoln & Bennet, Redfern, Nicholls, etc.)

Poor as a Connaught man (*Irish, Personal*). Poorest even amongst Irishmen.

Marrying Mr Cecil Devereux, who is as poor they say as a Connaught man.— Miss M. Edgeworth, *Ennui*, ch. xi.

Poor man's goose (*Low. Classes*). Bullock's liver, baked with sage and onions and a bit of fat bacon.

Poot (*Hindostanee*). Shilling—use confined to E. London where once E. Indian beggars were common.

Pop goes the weasel (*Street*, about 1870). Phrase — a great mystery of passing English. In the '70's every etymologist wrote about this phrase— and left it where it was. Activity is suggested by 'pop', and the little weasel is very active. Probably erotic origin. Chiefly associated with these lines—

Up and down the City Road,
In and out the Eagle,
That's the way the money goes,
Pop goes the weasel!

Pop on (*Sporting*). Quick blow— generally on the face.

Then big Tim popped it on Selby's face, and they had a bit of a spar round like.—A Chivy Duel, *People*, 6th January 1895.

Pop visit (*Soc.*, 18 cent.). Short ones.

I have a dozen friendly pop visits to make in less than an hour, and would not miss one for the universe.—Garrick's *Abel Drugger.*

Pope (*Com. Eng.*). Abbreviation of pope o' Rome, the rhyming for 'home'.

Poppa (*Amer. - Eng.*, 1890 on). Papa.

But even those who have never seen or read the American play can guess how an old Kansas millionaire, vulgar, bombastic, dictatorial, and good-hearted, the typical Yankee 'poppa', came to New York with his 'gals'.—*D. T.*, 15th February 1897.

Popping-crease (*Railway Officials'*). Junction station.

Popsy wopsy (*Low. Lond.*). A smiling, doll-like, attractive girl.

Pork pie hat and crinoline (*Street*, 1866 - 71). Satirical reference to women's appearance in the streets.

Suppose my Œdipus should lurk at last Under a pork-pie hat and crinoline.
— R. Browning, *Prince Hohenstiel Schwangau*, 1871.

Porky (*Low. Class*). Name for a pork-butcher, and sometimes satirically for a Jew.

Porridge-hole (*Scotch*). The mouth.

Porridge-pots (*Military*). Linesmen's satirical mode of naming the Scotch guard. (*See* Cold creams, Grinning dears, Gee-gees, Muck.)

Port wine don (*University*). Scornful description of the college professorial grandee, who leans to the Manchester school of nutrition.

Mr Mark Pattison was a very remarkable character. . . . He was extremely unlike the port wine don of fiction and caricature.—*D. N.*, 6th March 1885.

Portable property (*Doubtful Soc.*). Easily stolen or pawned values—especially plate.

The testimonial consisted of a silver tea-pot, coffee-pot, and chocolate-jug— all of which would doubtless have been considered by my friend Wemmick very fine specimens of portable property.— *Ref.*, 7th June 1885.

Portuguese pumping (*Nautical*). Not to be learnt. Ask sailors the meaning of this phrase, and they may laugh a good deal, but they give no etymology. It is probably nasty.

Possle (*Low. Class*). Earnest advocate. Corruption of apostle. Used satirically.

Post the blue (*Racing*). Gain the Derby.

Post haste (18 *cent. English—survival*). Rapid—from the post-chaise being the most rapid mode of travelling before 1840. (*See* Motor.)

Postage stamp (*Tavern*, 1837-85). Facetious name given to hotels and taverns signed the 'Queen's Head.'

Postern gate (*American*). Widest part of the trouser.

Postman's sister (*Mid.-class*, 1883). Secret informant.

For any little inaccuracy of detail which may have crept into the above paragraph I am in no way to blame. I tell the tale as 'twas told to me—by the postman's sister.—*Ref.*, 18th October 1885.

(*See* Jinks the barber, Boy Jones.)

Pot (*Naval*). Executive officer—as distinct from Greaser and Scratcher (*q.v.*).

Pot of all (*C. London*, 1883). Pot *in excelsis*, pot of exaltation, a perfect leader-hero, demigod.

Pot o' beer (*Abstainers'*). Bottle of ginger beer.

Pot o' bliss (*Public-house*, 1876). A fine tall woman.

Pot of O' (*Rhyming*, 1868). Short for 'Pot of O, my dear,' which is the rhyme for beer.

Potty (*Low Class*). Tinker.

Pot-au-feu (*Polit.*, 1885). Domestic policy. Due to Clémenceau, who invented it, and named it in antagonism to the Chauvinist principles of Ferry.

M. Clémenceau's rapidly - increasing influence is the most significant fact in the current politics of France. One might imagine that the *pot-au-feu* principle, as he himself has named it, would fail, as a cry, among a people like the French.—*D. N.*, 8th August 1885.

Pot-house (*Club Life*). Easy-go club. Suggestive of a licensed victualler's house.

Potching (*Hotel Waiters'*). Taking fees against rules. Probably from the French to 'pocher' or 'empocher'.

Good-natured customers may imagine that if they have given a fee to the waiter who presents the bill, they may hand another to the usual man who has attended upon them; but head-waiters are alive to the perils of this practice, which they call *potching*, and dismissal will be the punishment of the waiter who is caught taking vails on the sly.—*Graphic* (Restaurant Management), 17th March 1883).

Potentially (*Polit.*, 1883). To all intents and purposes.

This person considered that Russia was through her railway system practically, or as it is the fashion to say potentially, mistress of Herat.—*D. N.*, 29th April 1885.

Potsheen (*Irish*). Whiskey. Word varies in various districts—generally Potheen.

Potsheen, plase your honour—because it's the little whiskey that's made in the private still or pot; and *sheen*, because it's a fond word for whatsoever we'd like, and for what we have little of and would make much of.—Miss Edgeworth, *The Absentee*, chap. x.

Potter's field (*American*). Portion of graveyard appropriated to unpaid burials.

Poultice (*Soc.*, 1880). Fat woman.

Poultice (*Soc.*, 1882). Very high collar, suggestive of a neck poultice, ring-like in shape.

Poultice-mixer (*Navy*). Sick-bay man, or nurse.

Poultice over the peeper (*Peoples'*). A blow on the eye.

Pound to an olive (*Jewish*). This is a phrase resulting out of the Hebrews' love of olives, and is equivalent to the sporting term, 'It's a million pounds to a bit o' dirt.'

Powdering hair (*Tavern*, 18 *cent.*). Getting drunk—still heard in remote places. Euphemism invented by a polite landlord to account for lengths of time such as dressing and powdering hair required.

Pow-wow (*Anglo-American*). Convention or tentative meeting. From North American Indian — this word meaning in that language Congress.

Prairie. (*See* Bit o' prairie.)

Prairie comedians (*U.S.A.*). Poor, ranting, talentless actor.

Nothing can be more painful to a city summer audience than the wild rantings of barn-storming tragedians, or more aggravating than the inane drivel of prairie comedians.—*N. Y. Mercury*, 1883.

Prayer-book (*Sporting, circa* 1870). Ruff's *Guide to the Turf*.

Predeceased (*Legal—become satirical*). Used to ridicule the statement of some obvious fact, such as two and and two make four.

Premiere (*Press*, 1884). Abbreviation of *première* representation, an ordinary Paris phrase. First used in London press for first night in 1884.

Prescot (*Rhyming*). Waistcoat.

'Spot his blooming prescot.'

Prester John (*Peoples'*). The unknown.

He's no more related to our family than Prester John. — Farquhar, *The Inconstant*.

Preterite (*Soc.*, 19 *cent.*). Ancient — especially applied to women. 'Young? She's quite a preterite—nevertheless, intense.' (*See* Has been.)

Pretty-boy clip (*Soc.*, 1880 on). Hair brought flat down over the forehead, and cut in a straight line from ear to ear.

We happen to know that the style termed by irreverent mashers the pretty-boy clip, the style sometimes called the upward drag, and the quiff which ranges from a delicate fringe to furze-bush proportions, at first amazed and amused the neat Japanese damsels.—*D. N.*, 26th January 1885.

Pretty fellow (*Peoples'*). Fine, handsome, sometimes satirical.

Polly thinks him a very pretty man.— Gay, *Beggars' Opera*.

Pretty steep (*American*). Threatening.

Previous. (*See* Behind yourself.)

Price of a pint (*Workmen's*). Any sum below sixpence.

Prince's points (*Soc. and Club*, 1877). Shilling points at whist. Takes its origin from about this date. Very keen reasoning on the part of the then Prince of Wales, an eager whist-player. H.R.H. laid down the theory that the best whist-players were not necessarily the richest of men, and therefore if he played high points he might deprive himself of the pleasure of meeting the best players. Prince's points became very rapidly fashionable.

Printing House Square (*Club*, 19 *cent.*, to 1880). Powerful—crushing, *ex cathedra*, from the *Times* being published in that locality.

Prize faggots (*Street*). Well developed breasts in women. Faggots are savoury preparations of minced bullocks or sheeps' viscera—or plucks, mixed with oatmeal, shaped into rounded lumps and baked until the outside forms a crust. They are sold in all the busy lower parts of London at a penny. Prize faggots would be those larger than usual.

Problem novel (*Literary*, 1888 on). Title bestowed upon novels with a purpose—generally as affecting women, their aspirations and wrongs.

It was impossible to resist the question whether the 'problem novel' had had its day, and it appears 'not quite, but it is considerably less in demand than it was.' —*D. T.*, 2nd October 1896.

Process-pusher (1880). Lawyer's clerk. Satirical description.

Process server (*Artists'*, 1886 on). Photogravure printers.

Perhaps many of our artists have not yet learned the technique which best suits processes, or perhaps our process-servers are not yet adepts in their business.—*D. N.*, 9th December 1890.

Procesh (*American-Eng.*). Abbreviation of procession — growing common in England (1884).

I was removed on a plank, escorted by a torchlight procesh of the local fire brigade.—Besant & Rice, *Golden Butterfly*, vol. i., ch. xviii.

Pro-donnas (*Music Hall*, 1880). Professional ladies—actresses.

Professional beauty (*Fashionable slang*, 1879-82). This term arose in one of the Society papers, and was at once accepted by the best people, and even by the best of the Press. It referred to women in society, sometimes the very highest, who 'professed' their beauty by permitting any number of their photographic portraits to be sold in infinite varieties of poses.

Promoted (October 1890). Dead. From the public funeral of Mrs Booth, wife of General Booth, the originator of the Salvation Army.

Propers (*Low. Class*). Meaning refused—but thoroughly comprehended by the coster classes. Erotic.

Proper donas and rorty blokes (*L. Peoples'*, 1880). Good and true men and women.

Properties (*Theatrical*). Theatrical adjuncts.

Propper bit of frock (*Com. Lond.*, 1873). Pretty and clever well-dressed girl.

Prospect (*American Miners'*). To search for new gold-fields.

Prostituted (*Patent Law*). Made common. Said of a patent, so long on the market, waiting to be taken up by a capitalist or company, that it is common, and known to one and all.

Pros' Avenue (*Theatrical, circa* 1880). The Gaiety Bar (Strand). From this bar being the resort of gentlemen of 'the profession'.

Prosser (*Theatrical*, 1880). Pro passed into 'prosser'.

Protean entertainer (*Theatrical*). Artiste whose exceptional ability consists in rapid changes of dress.

Few will deny that Leopoldi Fregoli is an artist to the tips of his fingers, alert, versatile, neat in his business, quick as lightning in his changes, and, when all is said and done, the best 'protean' entertainer that the oldest playgoer has ever seen. — *D. T.*, 10th March 1897.

Proud nothing (*Provincial.*). Obvious.

Prudes on the prowl (*Soc.*, 1895 on). Hypersensitive women who haunted music halls to discover misbehaviour either on or off the stage.

Prudes on the prowl have long ceased to minimise the much too meagre fund of human enjoyment left in the world, and their place has been taken by a body who may be described as Guardians on the Growl. — *D. T.*, 16th December 1897.

Pschutt (*Parisian*, 1883). Ton, fashion, distinction. Reached America in 1884, and at once became ridiculous as pasha.

Psha (*Peoples'*). Exclamation. No derivation.

Psychological moment (*Soc. and Literary*, 1894 on). Opportunity. Nick of time. Became very popular in 1896.

I seized the p. m., and nailed him for a tenner.

It can afford to bide its time, and strike a decisive blow when the psychological moment has arrived.—*D. T.*, 6th March 1896.

Pub (*Theatrical*). The public—sometimes P. B.

Publican (1883). One of the names of General Booth after buying the Grecian Theatre and Tavern in the City Road (1883). (*See* Salvation Army.)

Publicaness (*Tavern*, 1880). The wife of a publican.

Puff-puff (*Children's*, 19 *cent.*). Railway engine. (*See* Gee-gee.)

Puffing billy (*N. Eng.*). Steam-engine, given contemptuously to Stephenson's first engine, still at Darlington, and accepted seriously by him.

Pull (*Peoples'*). Anxious moment. (*See* Extra pull.)

Pull-down (*Soc.*, 1870, etc.). Name given to the moustache which succeeded the nap. (*q.v.*).

Pull down the blind (*Low London*, 1880 on). This was addressed in the first place to spooney young couples who in public were making too great a display of their love.

Pull down your basque (*American—amongst women*). The 'basque' is the spine of the corset. The recommendation is a suggestion to behave properly.

Pull down your vest (*American*). Be well bred, behave yourself.

Pull leg (*Peoples'*). Satirize, humbug, mislead, ridicule.

Young Chinny hinted that they must be pulling his leg.—Rudyard Kipling, *The Tomb of his Ancestors.*

Pull oneself over (*Com. London*). To feed.

I took one for myself, and essayed to pull myself over it. But there, I will spare further recital, beyond that, burnt outside, the chops were raw inside, and like iron all over.—*Ref.*, 6th June 1886.

Pull the string proper [*Theatrical*]. To know how to succeed with the public. Suggested by manipulating marionnettes.

Dressed in the uniform of the London Scottish Rifles, he hides from his mother-in-law in a shower-bath, and is swamped by that awful lady, who knows how and when to 'pull the strings'.—*Ref.*, 5th October 1884.

Pull-up (*American—becoming English*, 1870). Wave of prosperity following disaster; chiefly used in theatrical life.

Pull up my boot (*Costermongers'*). To make money. When a man prepares for his day's work, he pulls on and strings up his boots. (*See* Make up my leg.)

The Strand people are pulling the string with the *Comedy of Errors*, I am told (1883).

Pull your ear (*Peoples', Hist.*). To produce memory.

Pulling a pop (*Anglo-American*). Firing a pistol.

Pulling the right string (*Cabinet-makers'*, 1863). Before calipers were in use by carpenters and others, small measurements were made with string. Hence arose the term, 'Are you pulling the right string?' Some maintain it refers to the pulling of puppet-show strings.

Pumblechook (*American - Eng.*). Human ass.

Pumpkin - face (*American*). A round face with no expression in it.

Puncheous Pilate (*Peoples'*). Corruption of Pontius Pilate, jocosely addressed to a person in protest of some small asserted authority.

Punkah one's face (*Anglo-Indian*). Fan the features. From the Hindostanee.

Push-buggy (*American—heard in Liverpool*). Perambulator.

Pushing (*Peoples'*, 1885). Endeavouring to induce a man to propose marriage. Early in 1885, in the suit brought by Lord Durham to obtain a nullity of marriage (Durham v. Milner, otherwise Durham), the Hon. Mrs Gerard, the sister of the defendant, said in evidence:

Lord Durham joined my sister at Buxton.

What was her bearing towards him? —I thought she seemed shy, but I considered that was chiefly on account of there being only one sitting-room in the house. I had a conversation with my sister as to the propriety of visiting Lambton. She was nervous, and said it looked 'rather pushing' to go.—28th February 1885.

Pusley (*American—heard in Liverpool*). Most mysterious — who *was* Pusley?

Pa is better, thanks to careful nursing. You see, Pa began finding fault with me again because I didn't play more jokes on him. I told him that people were getting an idea that I was mean as Pusley, because I played jokes on him, and I had quit. Pa said 'never mind what people say. I am your father, and it pleases me to have you practise on me.' —*Peck's Bad Boy*, 1884.

Pusserspock (*Naval*). Corruption of 'purser's pork' — bad, hard salt-meat, name being given to it because the purser was the purchaser.

Put a steam on the table (*Peoples'*). To earn enough money to obtain a hot Sunday dinner. A figure of speech. Refers chiefly to boiled food, the phrase having been invented before domestic ovens.

Put down (*Low London*). To eat.

Put it on (*L. London*). Extract money by threats, or whining lying, as the case may best be met.

Arter all the brass was nearly all gone, Selby says, 'I'll go round to the Mug agin, and put it on him (make him pay) for another bit.'—*People*, 6th January 1895.

Put on (*Street*). Old woman mendicant who puts on a shivering and wretched look.

Put on (*Theatrical*). To produce.

Put on a boss (*Street*). Take a look—of a malevolent character, so that a squint is suggested—for squinting suggests malevolence.

Put on a cigar (*Peoples'*, 1850 on). Assertion of gentility, to the injurious exclusion of the pipe.

Put on the flooence (*Peoples'*, 1850-83). Attract, subdue, overcome by mental force. Corruption of 'fluence —from influence.

Put on the pot (*All Classes*). Be grand.

Put oneself outside (*American-English*, 1860). To eat or drink.

Put out (*Low Class, Hist.*). Killed —abbreviation of 'Put out his lights' (*q.v.*).

Brien, on the way to the station remarked to the officer, 'I am not in this, but I know they meant to put you out to-night.'—*D. T.*, 14th May 1901.

Put the gloves on him (*Scotch Thieves'*, 1868). Ameliorate him.

Put the light out (*Criminal and Street*), Kill.

In the days of Shakespeare wise men called 'stealing' conveying; now a malefactor does not murder, he pops a man off, or he puts his light out.—*Graphic*, 24th September 1884.

Put the miller's eye out (*Peoples'*). To use too much water in making grog or tea.

Put the windows in (*Street*). Smashing them.

Put to bed (*Music Hall*). To conquer, to annihilate, figuratively.

Put to find (*Low Class*). Prison.

Put you on your back seam (*Tailors'*). To seat a gentleman suddenly, not only on the ground, but on the seam which hemispheres the 'shoulder' of his trousers. Very local.

Put your hat up there (*Peoples'*). Friendly accusation of courting there—meaning you are resolved to make one of the family.

Put your clothes together when you come (*Provincial, Peoples'*). Shape of inviting for a long visit, stretching over time, requiring many changes of garments.

Puts a 'and in a pocket (*Lower Classes*). Hospitable, given to charity.

Putting a poor mouth (*Irish*). To complain moaningly.

The Irishman, putting a poor mouth on his position, declared that at his house 'whin they had a red herring it was Christmas Day wid 'um'.—*D. N.*, 1884.

Putting the value on it (*Artists'*). Signing a canvas. Satirical — meaning the work has no real value, and sells only by reason of the name attached.

Putty-medal (*Peoples'*, 1856). No medal at all. Satirical recommendation to reward for mischief or injury. A tailor makes a misfit; *e.g.*, 'Give him a putty medal.'

Pyrotechnic pleasantries (*Soc.*, 1897). Dynamite explosions of a feeble and harmless character. Probably the work of semi-idiots. Sign that destructive anarchy was abating.

There is, indeed, a growing impression that if he is found out, it will at once be perceived that he is a monomaniac, who has acted out of sheer silliness in indulging in these 'pyrotechnic pleasantries'.—*D. T.*, 17th June 1897.

Q

Q. B. (*Law*, '90's). Queen's Bench. Now King's Bench.

Q. S. (*Peoples'*). Initials of Queer Street — a figure of speech, even a metaphor, whereby a gentleman in difficulties relegates them to his district.

Quagger (*Oxford 'er'*). Queen's man — student of Queen's College. Also called 'gooser'. Quaggers is possibly goose, duck, quack—quaggers.

Quandary (*Peoples'*, 17 cent.). Difficulty, fix. Probably from the half-French court of Charles II., who was half French by his mother. Qu' en dirai-je? Skinner gives this derivation. Possibly a frequent expression of Louise Querouille (the Mother Carwell of the streets), who afterwards became Louise, Duchess of Portsmouth, when she built Portsmouth Place, S.W., corner of Lincoln's Inn Fields—some seven houses, those remaining still showing on the pilasters alternate roses of England, lilies of France, double flanked with torches of Hymen that look like rams' horns — which insignia would probably be more appropriate. Johnson calls 'quandary' a 'low word'. (*See* Curmudgeon.)

Quarter pound bird's eye (*Low. Class Smokers'*). Quarter of one ounce —a pennorth. Asked for quite seriously. Probably begun as a joke. (*See* Sherry.)

Quarter sessions (*Legal*). Jocose swearing.

Quarter stretch (*Thieves'*). Three months' imprisonment. 'Saucy Sall's got a quarter with hard.' (*See* Stretch.)

Quartern o' bliss (*Low London*, 1882). A taking small woman. Diminutive of 'Pot o' bliss'—a fine woman.

Quartern o' bry (*Complicated Rhyming*, 1868). Short for Bryan o' Lynn—which rhymes with gin.

Quartern o' finger (*Complicated Rhyming*), 1868). Short for finger and thumb, which rhymes with rum— the refreshment called for.

Queenie (*Street*). Mock endearing name called after a fat woman trying to walk young. 'Queenie, come back, sweet' (Drury Lane Panto., 1884). Addressed to Mr H. Campell, one of the heaviest men on the stage, and then playing 'Eliza', a cook. (*See* Poultice.)

Queen's bad bargain (*Military*). A recruit who turns out a bad soldier —from Queen's shilling.

Queen's weather (*Soc.*, 1837 to end of reign). Fine sunshine—from the singular fact that through her reign the Queen almost always had fine weather when she appeared in public.

Queer-bit makers (*Police*). Coiners.

Queer shovers (*Police*). Queer is bad money — shovers any kind of industrials; the whole—passers of bad money.

Queer the pitch (*Music Hall*, 1880). Spoil business, impede applause. This phrase comes from the patter of street performers, whose 'pitch' for performance is 'queered' by a severe policeman. In its application in music halls it means any act which injures a performance—the pitch. For instance a jeer, a cough, a sneeze will queer the pitch, but it is chiefly applied to the band, when by a sudden stoppage, or error in accompaniment, the singer is, or might be, brought to grief.

At home, if an actor or actress dared to act whilst some one else was speaking, he or she would be fined or dismissed as 'queering somebody's pitch', whereas every gesture, every animated movement assists the speaker instead of spoiling him.—*D. T.*, 29th June 1897.

Queue (*Theatrical*). Tail-piece, last word, upon which another actor has to reply. Evidently from French, and quite clear from 'queu', as it is often lamentably spelt.

Quick-change artiste (*Theatrical*). Translation of protean entertainer.

England has boasted a goodly supply of what were once called 'quick-change artists', from the days of the elder Charles Mathews until the more decadent and mechanical times of W. S. Woodin. —*D. T.*, 10th March 1897.

Quick curtain (*Theatrical*). Rapid descent of curtain.

Quid-fishing (*Thieves'*). Skilled thieving—quid being a sovereign.

Quid to a bloater (*Street*). Sovereign to a herring — commonest shape of street cock-sure betting.

Quiff (*Anglo-Indian*). Idea, fancy, movement, suggestion.

Quiff (*Army*, 1890 on). The sweep of hair over the forehead.

Quifs (*Military*, 19 cent.). Manœuvres.

Quit off (*American*). To refrain.

Quite a dizzy (*Mid.-class*). Very clever man—evidently from Disraeli.

Quite the don (*Peoples' Hist.*). Perfect, magnificent. Probably from the name given to the husband of Queen Mary Tudor—Philip being a very magnificent Spaniard.

R

R. C. (*Catholic*, 1880 on). Roman Catholic.

R. M. D. (*London, Lower Financial*). Ready money down.

Racial atavism (*Society*, 1897). Atavism. Came from Paris. It is a synonym for heredity.

We prefer to believe that it is a case of what might be scientifically described as 'racial atavism'. It is simply that 'fault of the Dutch' which Canning discovered in the course of treaty negotiations at an early period of the century, and which has now broken out in a fresh place among their colonial descendants. — *D. T.*, 19th February 1897.

Rad (*Political*). Abbreviation of Radical, and bestowed by the Conservatives probably from its suggestiveness of 'rat'.

Rag (*Oxford*, 19 cent.). Disarrangement of another man's furniture, but with no damage.

If you return and find your rooms in a state of chaos, your friends have been indulging in a 'rag'.— *D. T.*, 14th August 1899.

Rag-stick (*Peoples'*). One of the names for umbrella, said of a loose and unreefed implement.

Ragged edge (*Amer.-Eng.*, 1884). Deserted.

It seems fair to assume that father, daughter and her child sailed yesterday for Paris, leaving poor Tom on the ragged edge. — *N. Y. Mercury*, 10th January 1885.

Raggies (*Navy*). Steady chums. The term, however, seems to be generally one of disparagement.

Rags (*Art Jargon*, 1880). Old lace used for decorative purposes. (*See* Crocks and Timbers.)

Rags, Daily (*Printers'*). London lower class daily newspapers.

A man in the country wants to sell his old kicksies, Charley Prescotts and coats, and seeing the advertisements in the respectable daily rags, he sends them all up to the buyer, and gets five bob in return, which, he is told, is all they're worth.

Rail-birds (*Racing*, 1890 on). Watchers of race-horses when exercising. From their perching on five-barred and other gates while on the wait.

The 'rail-birds', as certain people are called who closely watch the work of horses on the race tracks, would do well to keep an eye on Tommy Ryan.—*N. Y. Mercury*, December 1891.

Railroad Bible (*Amer. Travellers'*, 1880). Pack of cards.

Railways (*Railway Servants'*). Red stockings—of course worn by women, and resulting out of 'signal red'—used throughout the British dominions; *e.g.*, 'She's a pair of smart railways—ain't she?'

Rain-napper (*Street*). Umbrella—because it catches the rain. From 'knap'—to catch quickly.

Raise (*Amer.*, 1880). Kick—vigorous instance of replacing cause by effect.

Rajah, The (*Drury Lane*, 1850 on). Synonym for the Mogul.

Raked fore and aft (*Mariners'*). Desperately in love. Figure of speech from damage done to the whole of rigging by a well-directed shelling.

Raker (*Common Classes*, 1840-56). Comb.

'Ral (*Navy*). Strict naval for admiral.

Rampers (*London Street*). Noisy street-rangers, chiefly young men.

Randy-voo (*Army*). Tavern which is the headquarters of recruiting sergeants. Also synonymous with noise and wrangling—from Rendez-vous.

Rank and smell (*L. Peoples'*, 19 *cent.*). Common person.

Rare old water-bruiser (*Nautical*). A tough, hard-working old shore-man.

Rarified (*Soc.*, 1860 on). Tamed. Usually applied to tamed women—from one Rarey, a horse-tamer.

Rasher and doorstep (*L. Classes*). Coffee-house phrasing — the rasher speaks for itself. The doorstep is a thick slice of bread and butter.

Raspberry. (*See* Bit o' raspberry.)

Rat (*Artisans'*). A man who has not served his time, and therefore who has no indentures. He may, however, be a very fine workman; but he can enter no society or union.

Rat back clip (*Peoples'*, 1856). Short hair.

Rational costume (*Society*, 1895). Trousers for women. Early in the fifties these appendages were called Bloomers—from an American lady of that name. A generation passed, when they loomed up again as divided skirts and Bectives (probably from Lady Bective having approved the fashion). Next, about 1890, they took over the name for young boys' knee-trousers, and were styled knickerbockers—the name of which probably came from Washington Irving. Finally, in 1895, the female trouser was known as rational costume.

Rattle (*Sporting*). Good news of certain reliance, and in relation to a horse entered for a given race.

Rattle-belly-pop (*American Saloon*). Whiskey and lemonade. Changed, when speaking to the more elegant sex, to rattle-blank-pop.

Rattle, With a (*Racing*) Unexpected rapidity.

The only approach to a sensation was caused by Warrington and Kettleholder, the former coming 'with a rattle' in the morning to the price taken about him in the excitement caused by his forward running in the Cesarewitch. — *Newsp. Cutting.*

Raum method (*Anglo-Amer.*, 1890). Nepotism, corruption.

The 'Raum method' is simply the method by which Mr Commissioner Raum is said to determine the fitness of candidates for clerkships in the Pension Office. It consists in simply 'looking them in the face and giving a judgment'. He looked his own son, Green B. Raum, jun., in the face and formed a judgment of him.—*D. N.*, 17th July 1890.

Raven (*Public-house*). Small bit of bread and cheese—2d. From the idea that the ravens could only carry small quantities to Elisha.

Readied the rosser (*Lower Classes*). Bribed the police. Readied, past tense of to ready, from the 'ready'-money. *Rosseur*—French—one who harries and worries.

Ready-money betting (*Racing*). Where the backer at once pays his money to the bookmaker, and awaits the result.

Real healthy (*American—passing to England*). Well-brained.

Real Kate (*London Local, Clare Market*, 1882 — *swept away*, 1900). Kind matron. In this year a charitable queen of the market, one Kate, died.

Real lady (*Music Hall*, 1881). A lady *in excelsis*.

Real Peacer (*Street Boys'*). Final shape of Charley Peace, a hero-murderer.

Real raspberry jam (*Street*, 1883). Climax of the use of 'jam' to describe lovely woman.

Real razor (*Westminster School*, 1883). A defiant, quarrelsome, or bad-tempered scholar.

Real Rugby (*Public-school*). Cruel. Derived from the Rugby rules of football, which are more likely to lead to accident, it is generally held, than the more modified rules of the 'Soccer'.

Real scorcher (*Street*). Vigorous, active personality—but without vice.

Real sweet (*Eng.-Amer.*) Perfect.

Reb (*American Civil War*, 1862-65). Abbreviation of 'rebel', given in scorn by the Federals to the Confederates, and afterwards adopted by them.

Reconstituting an epoch (*Lit.*, 1875). Misrepresenting history. Devised when Mr Wills produced Charles I. at Lyceum Theatre.

M. Sardou lays the scene of his story in a historic period, introducing more or less authentic historic personages; or, as the phrase goes, reconstituting an epoch. —*D. N.'s* Criticism of M. Sardou's *Theodora*, 13th July 1885.

Receipt of fernseed (*Proverbial superstition*). Ability to be present invisibly. The statement that if you held fernseed you were invisible was based upon the supposition that you could not do so, because fernseed had no existence—ferns showing no flowers.

Rifle green, the dark artillery blue, and the dark grey of the service greatcoat were as bad, or nearly as bad, as black; so that at present the British soldier of all arms must be admitted to be singularly destitute of the 'receipt of fernseed'.—*D. N.*, March 1883.

Recently struck it (*Amer.-Eng.*). *Nouveau riche*—man of sudden wealth. That is—he has recently struck gold. Common to U.S.A.—growing in England.

Re-dayboo (*Music Hall*, 1899). Re-début. Absurdity, of course—being a first appearance a second time.

This welcome 're-dayboo', as Dan Leno would doubtless call it, was made, etc.—*Sun*, 29th November 1899.

Red. (*See* Bit o' red.)

Red, All over. (*See* All over red.)

Red heart (*London Tavern*—about 1870. Short for 'redheart—rum'.

Red herring (*Soc.*). Intended deceit. From dragging a red herring, at the end of a string, over the track of a fox — whereby the hounds are thrown out.

The Conservative candidate gravely stated that if Home Rule is granted, Irishmen will come over in such numbers that instead of the labourers' wages being 12s. or 13s. a week, they will be reduced to 6s. and 7s.; and this red herring has been implicitly believed.— *D. N.*, 17th July 1886.

Red-handed (*Hist.*). In the fact— *flagrante delicto*.

George Wallis, 30, was charged on remand with stealing some cloth from a shop in Whitechapel.—The prisoner was caught almost redhanded.—*People*, 27th December 1896.

Red-hot miracle (*Sporting*, 1882). Startling paradox of the very day.

Red-hot treat (*Lower Peoples'*). Extremely dangerous person.

Red peppers (*American*). Form of swearing.

Red-shirts (*Colonial and American Mining World*). The name given to gold and silver miners, all of whom wear red flannel shirts. Garibaldi while in America adopted the red shirt for life, introduced it upon the continent of Europe, and made it historically famous.

Red-tie (*Univ.*, *Oxford*, 1876). Synonym for vulgarity.

Redding up (*N. Country, Hist.*). Tidying, putting the house in order. From the habit of rubbing red ochre over the cleaned doorsteps, side-posts, and hearth-stones. Passing away rapidly.

Reddings (*Thieves'*). One of the words for watches. Probably from the name of a receiver of that name, who gave the best prices.

Redfern (*Soc.*, 1879). Perfectly-fitting lady's coat or jacket. From the vogue obtained, 1879 on, by Redfern, Maddox, W. Regent Street, whose lady's tailoring became celebrated over the whole world.

Redundant (*City*, 1898). Impudent. Arose from the invention of Mr H. Bottomly in a speech.

Personally, and speaking entirely for myself, I regard the attitude taken up by Dr Alexander as a little redundant, having regard to the appointment of the committee.—*D. T.*, 2nd June 1898.

Reelings (*Rhyme*). Feelings.

Ref. (*Political*). Abbreviation of Reformer. Invented by the Tories as a term of brief contempt.

Refuges (*London Mid.-class*). The lamp-islands centred at wide crossings as half-way oases in the desert of London roads.

Reg. duck egg! (*Sporting*). A cypher of no value. From cricket—when a batter going out on nothing at all is marked 'O' — playfully described as a 'duck egg'. The 'reg' is a common abbreviation of 'regular'.

Regenerate. (*See* Degenerate.)

Regionalism (*Political*, 1880 on). Sub-nationality. Word to describe differences of political and social feeling between differing races or subraces under one government—as N. and S. of North America, Hungary and Austria, Poland and Russia. Adopted in England during the Home Rule struggle in House of Commons.

As platinum and silver do not melt at the same degree of heat, so, too, diversity of disposition, which in Italy is more marked than elsewhere, will not allow of the Southerners being educated by the same method as the Piedmontese. The twenty-six years which have elapsed since our unification have proved this abundantly. Regionalism is still a profound sore.—Signor Fazzari, *D. N.*, 21st April 1886.

Regular oner (*Peoples'*). Individual past praying for—a scapegrace. Sometimes used in satirical praise.

Reign of Queen Dick (*Peoples'*). Never—a quibble.

Removal (*Political*, 1883). Assassination. When the exposure of the Phœnix Park and other assassinations (1882) took place Carey, one of the chief informants, in his evidence, always referred to a political murder as a removal. The word at once took.

Umbrellas as Weapons.—In reading the evidence which Town Councillor Carey gave as to the Phœnix Park murders—or 'removals', as the Irish Invincibles call them—it is impossible to avoid wishing that the heroic victims of hired stabbers had been armed. — *Graphic*, 24th February 1883.

Reparty (*Soc.*, 1874). Satirical pronunciation of *repartee*.

Just as the young Gaiety lady favoured by royalty who had a speaking part presented to her on that account was not good at reparty, so artists are not, as a body, good at spelling.—*Ref.*, 7th March 1886.

Repentance curl (*Soc.*, 1863). It was a solitary, heavy curl made of a portion of the back hair, and brought over the left shoulder and allowed to fall over the left breast. The Princess of Wales brought this fashion into England (1863), where it held good for many years. (*See* Zarndrer.)

Repetitious (*Literary*). Repetitional. First applied by the *Daily Telegraph*.

It was just as well, for the scheme of 'Self and Lady' had a tendency to become monotonous and to be repetitious in its effects.—*D. T.*, 20th September 1900.

Reprint (*Printers'*). Printed matter for putting in type, as opposed to manuscript.

Resistance - piece (*Press*). Chief dish, or leading stage-piece. From the French—*pièce de resistance*.

The Christmas treat was a great success. About sixty sat down to the banquet. After this, the resistance-piece, was over, etc.—*Ref.*, 10th January 1886.

Responsible (*Theatrical*). Fee'd to lead. He is an actor more of common sense than parts, who steadily obeys the lead—and takes that leader's place when not acting.

Wanted, for a first-class portable, Entire Co., including Gent. for Entire Lead, Juveniles, Responsibles, etc.

Resting (*Theatrical*, 1890 on). Obvious—but it has another satirical meaning — that of 'out of an engagement'.

This is the period of the year when the actor casts off his stage - mantle, and settles down to that easy, indefinite, unemployed time which comes under the description of 'Resting'.—*D. T.*, 11th August 1898.

Resurrection pie (*Peoples'*). All sorts pasty.

Revolveress (*Soc*, 1885). A woman who uses a pistol.

The details of the career of the charming Lucille, the latest revolveress, are romantic, though slightly mixed.—*Ref.*, 8th February 1885.

'Ria (*Maria*). Passing to 'Aryet (Harriet). The typical name of the costermonger's young lady—a coster herself.

Rib-shirts (*Street*, 1880). Fronts, or dickeys, worn over a grubby shirt to give the air of a fresh one.

Rice Christians (*Soc.*, 19 *cent.*). Natives in rice-bearing countries, who accept the missionaries in order to gain rice or food. Now used generally of people who make of religion a business.

It is extremely doubtful, in these circumstances, whether such converts as the missions boast are ever more than the dregs of Chinese society, coolies without family, home, or pedigree, 'rice-Christians' as they are scornfully named.—*Ref.*, 11th August 1895.

Rich as crazes (*Irish*). Of course —Crœsus.

Rich-one (*Upper Hetairiæ*). A wealthy wife. Said of the luckless spouse of a man who finds home not to his liking.

Richmonds in the field (*Peoples'*). Satirical description of rivals in active work—no matter of what kind. From Shakespeare's *Richard III*.

I think there be six Richmonds in the field.

There were so many Richmonds in the field, so many pretenders to the throne, that it was quite impossible to discover the real king. I cannot tell you how it is going to end. Wars of disputed succession are proverbially long and bloody.—Sir W. Harcourt (June 1885) in House of Commons.

Ricing (*Mid.-class*). Throwing rice over the bride when in her go-away carriage. From the East Indies, where this custom intimates the hope of children—rice being a prolific growth.

Ride square (*Racing*). Square here means 'fair'.

Riding (*Sporting*, 19 *cent.*). Adroitness, ability — from racing, where a jockey's riding is a great factor in working out success. Applied in every possible way.

Nobody questions the guilt of William Palmer. But there was some truth in his remark that 'the riding had done it', and if Mrs Bartlett were acquainted with the language of the turf, she might pay the same compliment to Mr Clarke as Palmer paid to Sir Alexander Cockburn.—*D. N.*, 19th April 1886.

Rig sale (*London*, 19 *cent.*). Swindle—a false sale.

Right, About (*Peoples'*). Modest self-depreciation, or depreciation in general; not absolutely right, but nearly so, *e.g.*, 'I thrashed him about right'. (*See* To rights.)

Right gee-gee (*Sporting*, 1880). The horse certain to win.

Right off (*Peoples'*, 1897). Rejection, failure, determination.

Right racket (*Amer. - Eng.*). Successful public declaration. Chiefly refers to entertainments and publishing.

Right tenpenny on the cranium (*Peoples'*). Good phrasing. A new rendering of 'Right nail on the head'.

Messrs Robertson and Bruce, at Toole's Theatre, with 'M.P.', seem to have hit the right tenpenny on the cranium.

Rights (*Thieves'*, 1860). Perfection.

Ring dropping (*Peoples'*). Equivalent to 'Tell your grandmother to suck eggs'. Said in scorn of weak attempts at deception. From the stale cheat of the operator pretending to pick up a ring in the street in front of the intended victim.

Rip (*Anglo-American*). Creation of a word from the initials of *Requiescat in pace*—in Catholic cemeteries, the pious wish being declared by these initials.

Ripper (*Thieves'*). Daring murderer of women. Very common noun devised from rip, the ripper making his wound with a knife in the human body. In 1888-91 a number (ten) of murders of women were perpetrated, presumably by the same man, as the ripping treatment of the victims was common to all or almost all the cases.

Ripping slum (*Tavern*, 1800-30). Capital trick. (*See* Egan's *Life in London*.)

Rise bristles (*Anglo. - American*). Excite to resentment.

Risky (*Soc.*, '90's). Adulterous—but not openly so.

There are plenty of ladies living, as all their world knows, lives which are generally called 'risky', who are personally most scrupulous in observing all the minor conventionalities.—John Strange Winter, *D. T.*, 5th August 1899.

Rit (*University, passing to Peoples'*). A ritualistic clergyman. (*See* Tec, Cad, Pot.)

Ritualistic knee (*Doctors'*, 1840-50). When genuflection came in, with the success of Dr Pusey's church theories, the ritualistic knee really became known to medical men. It was caused by severe untrained momentary kneeling—when passing the altar, etc.

Road combination (*Anglo - American Theatrical*). Congregation of variety artists moving rapidly from town to town.

Road-starver (*Mendicants*, 1881). Long coat made without pockets, especially without a fob for money. Road meaning generally the mass of beggars — the starver is that which deprives the road of food.

Roader (*Local London*). Sunday splendour of the youthful persuasion, who displays himself in the Mile End Road. Superior to Whitechapel streeter (*q.v.*).

Roast 'and an' noo (*Eating-house waiters'*). Short for 'roast shoulder (of mutton) and new potatoes'. 'And, or hand used for shoulder shortens the word by more than one-half, while ' noo' is quite a reasonable reduction.

Robbing the barber (*Peoples'*, 19 *cent.*). Wearing long hair.

Robin (*Street*, 19 *cent.*). Little boy or girl beggar standing about like a starving robin.

'Robin Dinners' are due to the kindly suggestion of the Rev. Charles Bullock, editor of *Home Words* whose appeals to the generosity of his readers to enable him to entertain 25,000 or 30,000 London children every year.—*D. T.*, 7th January 1899.

Robin Goodfellow (*Peoples'*, *Hist.*). In Shakespeare's time he was a merry urchin boy. See *A Midsummer Night's Dream*. Previously he was associated with the dusius, and even with Satan —for in the drawings of the 15th century frequently he had horns and hoofs added to his peculiar qualifications. Descendant of the fauns. Probably his pre-Shakespearian title was Good-Filler. This term Robin Goodfellow would result out of the national tendency, as Puritanism spread over the land, to veil the erotic by Anglicized euphemism.

Robustious (*Peoples'*). Pompous.

Mr Barnes's unfortunate tendency on this occasion was to a rather 'robustious periwig-pated' style that sits ill upon the shoulders of so sentimental a personage as Lord Lytton's Claude Melnotte.—*D. N.*, 29th October 1883.

Rocked to sleep (1880). One of the sentimental American modes of describing death, one which began to prevail about this time.

Rockiness (*Low. Class*, 1887 on). Want of foundation, unsteadiness. Used chiefly of a drunken man.

Rogers (*Soc.*, 1830-50). A ghastly countenance — probably from Rogers the banker-poet, who in his age looked very old; or from the pirate flag, the Jolly Roger, which showed a skull.

Rogues' walk (*Soc.*, 1882). The 'Walk' in the '90's was the north of Piccadilly—from the Circus to Bond Street.

Roman Fall (1865-70). A droop in the back produced by throwing the shoulders well behind. A fashion of the last years of the French Empire, borrowed from French military officers, who were compelled to accept this attitude as the result of tight lacing, one of the more ominous excesses of French life in those terrible days. The fashion being accepted in England, it was dubbed the Roman Fall, as a counterpoise to the Grecian Bend (*q.v.*). Said to have been invented by Mr F. C. Burnaud, in *Punch*. 'Proud? Not proud? Spot his Roman fall.' (*See* Two inches beyond upright.)

Roof scrapers (*Theatrical*). Gallery boys—especially those standing behind the highest row of seats—and therefore nearest the roof.

Rooster (*Parliamentary*, 1860). M.P. who makes himself heard, who is not a silent member.

Whether the returned member be a rooster or not time will tell.—*Bird o' Freedom*, March 1883.

Roosters (*River Lea Anglers'*). Followers of the gentle craft, who do not move from one spot — probably because they ground-bated it the night before.

Rope-yarn Sunday (*Mercantile Marine*). Thursday. On Sunday the food being at its best, Sunday and feasting well are synonymous. Thursday, as the half-way day, is distinguished by duff, or pudding, which is always made long, roly-poly shape, which suggests rope-yarn hanks — hence Rope-yarn Sunday.

Rorty bloke (*Costers'*). Vigorous, strong.

Rorty toff (*Costers'*). Variation of rorty bloke—an inferior rorty bloke.

Rortyness (*Street*). Vitality.

Before that she reminded me a little too much, in her rortyness, of the seriocomic lady who sings 'What cheer "Ria", Ria's on the job!'—*Ref.*, 23rd August 1885.

Rose, Under the. (*See* Sub rosa.)

Rose-coloured spectacles (*Soc.*). Optimism. Free translation of *couleur de rose*.

In these days, when the mind's eye is less apt to observe things through rose-coloured spectacles, a good many of the grand old crusted adages have broken down badly.—G. R. Sims, *Ref.*, 1st February 1885.

Roses and raptures (*Lit.*, 1830 on). Satire of the Book of Beauty style of literature, the precursor of æstheticism. Attributed to Dr Maginn.

The social and religious life of Hellas was by no means what a vain people supposes. It was no more all roses and raptures than our modern existence is all beer and skittles.—*D. N.*, June 1885.

Rossacrucians (*Press*, 1885). Followers of O'Donovan Rossa. Satirical term invented by Mr G. R. Sims.—*Ref.*, 8th February 1885.

Rot-funks (*Cricket*). Panics.

Rothschild (*Soc.*). A rich man. (*See* Vanderbilt.)

Rotten orange (*Lower Peoples'*, 1686). Term of contempt. Historical—from the name given by the Jacobites to William III.—Prince of Orange.

Rotten-apple (*American, Theatrical*). To condemn an actor by hissing him. Figurative expression.

The last new American verb is 'To rotten-apple'. Actors, it seems, in some of the minor New York theatres, are not infrequently rotten-appled, much in the same way as our legislative candidates in the old hustings days used to be 'rotten-egged'.—*London Figaro*, March 1883.

Rotten row (*Rhyming*). Bow.

Rotter (*Theatrical and Street*). Failure in any way, especially on the stage. Presumably from rot.

Rotting about (*Soc. of a kind*). Wasting time from place to place.

Roughs and toughs (*Peoples'*). Beautiful rhyming coalescing, for 'rough' is English and 'tough' is the New York equivalent observation.

All the way down, whenever there was a stop, they were insulted by Boers, and we in the truck had to mix with sixty or more of the 'roughs' and 'toughs' of a score of nations.—*Sun*, 7th November 1899.

Round (*Ball-room*). A valse, galop, or polka. (*See* Square.)

Round the corner (*Street*). Drink. Figurative expression—not as the high road.

The barmaid replied: 'It's good enough for you; go into the other bar, where the men are.' Mrs Montgomery retorted: 'You're wrong all round the corner,' meaning that she had had something to drink.—*D. T.*, 16th July 1898.

Rovers (*American*). People of Colorado—given in consequence of their prospecting habits.

Row in (*Peoples'*). Unfair conspiracy. From Thames life through centuries. A man 'rowed in' in a river robbery, or even a murder.

It's very likely the sellers and the general public concerned in auction sales are anything but satisfied with the results of sales by auction where a 'knock-out' is arranged, and especially where the auctioneer 'rows in' with the crew.—*D. T.*, 12th February 1897.

Row-de-dow (*Irish*, 19 *cent.*). Riot—term applied scornfully by Irish to a disturbance. From a chief portion of the chorus of 'British Grenadiers'.

With regard to the Prince and Princess's visit to Ireland, the 'row-de-dow'—that is, we believe, the Hibernian term for it—which took place, etc.—*Ref.*, 9th March 1885.

Rubbing it in well (*Police*). Giving fatal evidence.

Rubbish (*Military Anglo-Indian*, early 19 *cent.*). Luggage of any kind, and especially furniture, which was frequently very shabby. (*See* Garbage.)

Ruck down (*West Provincial*, 19 *cent.*). To courtesy very low.

Ruckerky (*Soc.*, 90's). Grotesque pronunciation of *recherché*.

It was a security which a member of the Asylums Board had described, in a glowing adjective, as 'ruckerky'.—*D. T.*, 4th April 1898.

Rudders (*Oxford*). Rudiments of Faith and Religion (now abolished)—irreverent statement in 'er'.

Ruffer (*Peoples'*). One who is rough.

Rugger (*Oxford Football*, 1880 on). Rugby rules. (*See* Soccer.)

Rule the roast (*Old Eng.*). To govern noisily.

Rule was granted (*Lawyers'*). Another chance.

Rum-bottle (*Navy*, 1860). Sailor—from the liquor affected by mariners.

Rumbo (*Middle-class*, 1860). This is an exclamation of congratulation, probably obtained from the gipsies, as amongst them 'Rumbo' is a common cry upon the meeting of two men. Women never interchange this cry. It is a corruption of the Spanish carambo, the accent of which is upon the second, the word becoming almost k'rambo.

Rumourmongers (*City*, 1897). New coinage. Hitherto there have been iron, fish and cheesemongers. Newsmonger was the first modern discovery in this direction, and now the debased 'rumour' follows suit.

It would almost seem as if the once ingenious class of rumourmongers were losing its power of skilful imagination, and the method of the new school is to cover one blunder by a still greater blunder.—*D. T.*, 19th November 1897.

Run amok (*Asia*). Amok means homicidal mania — accompanied by running blindly forward. Passing from India to England it has got Anglicized into 'Running a muck', probably from the fleeting destroyer showing himself in a muck sweat. This corrupted phrase is now applied in England in a score of ways—all of which imply a good deal of action. In Malacca, Siam, Java and adjacent places the mental state which leads to amok is equally well known and dreaded. The perpetrator shows signs of moroseness for days, more or less in number, before he is seized with amok, when he dashes up, with a drawn knife, and lays about him amidst the scudding people until he himself is killed by a general onslaught. In the more civilised spots where this custom prevails, especially in Batavia, precautions are taken which prevent the destruction either of the victim to 'amok', or those near him when the murderous moment arrives. Every policeman is armed with a catch-fork. Directly a patient starts upon amok, supposing the police are not ready for him, as, being warned of the symptoms, they generally are, the spearing of this strange fish commences. Overtaken, the springed points of the amok-spear are pushed round the neck, which passed, the incurved articulations once more expand, and the victim is held at spear's length, when all the damage he can do is to himself. Thus hooked he is 'run in', where, if he has not wounded himself fatally, he is treated for 'D.T.'s'—the origin of most amok—when he either recovers or is passed into an asylum.

Run home on the ear (*American*). Entirely defeated.

Run through (*Parliamentary*). Rapid in action—especially official.

Runner (*Thieves'*). Technical name for dog-stealer.

Rushing business (*Thieves' and Public-house*). Robbery by adroitness, cheating under the semblance of fair treatment.

They go out on the rushing business, and a very profitable emag they find it.— *Rag.*, 1882.

Rushlight (*Peoples'*). Very thin man. Derived from use of candles— of which the forgotten rushlight was the slimmist.

Rusted in (*American*). Settled down. Suggested by rust fixing in a nail or screw.

Ruttat-pusher (1882). Keeper of a potato car.

S

S. A. These are the initials and sign of the Salvation Army.

S. D. (*Theatrical*). Stage door.

S. M. (*Theatrical*). Stage manager.

S. P. (*Press*, 1870 on). Letters equalling special correspondent, being first two letters of first word.

S. S. (*Street*, 1883). These initials originally stood for sinner saved. The letters were revived, with a similar meaning by some of General Booth's enthusiasts (1882) in the Salvation Army.

Sacred lamp (*Theatrical*, 1883). Ballet-girl burlesque. The origin of this term is quite historical. Mr John Hollingshead, lessee for many years of the Gaiety Theatre, Strand, London, issued one of a series of remarkable lessee's ukases, in which he cynically referred to the burlesques he had produced as keeping alight the sacred lamp of burlesque.

Sad, and bad, and mad (*Soc.*, 1880). Fashionable Jeremiah-mongering.

Philosophers and sages, and people who speak of the 'fatal gift of beauty' would say, with Mr Browning's half-repentant lover, this was all very 'sad, and bad, and mad'.—*D. N.*, 10th March 1885.

Sad vulgar (*Soc.*, 18 *cent. and earlier* 19 *cent.*). Synonym for cad, snob.

He is a 'sad vulgar', as the ladies' expression was in the days of George III.; and there is something very droll about the poetical retribution he meets with.—*St James' Gazette*, 17th August 1883.

Saddling - paddock (*Australian*). Place of amusement or rather place of assignation.

Saffron Walden God-help-ye (*Provincial*). Beggars, outcasts, mendicants of that place. (*See* Gordelpus.)

The triumph of scornful nomenclature was reached in the case of Saffron Walden, nicknamed 'Saffron Walden God - help - ye', from the presumed wretchedness of its inhabitants. . . . In the heart of the New Forest occurs a similar instance of nomenclature to that of Saffron Walden, with the difference only that it is accepted by the inhabitants instead of being thrust upon them by the surrounding population. The village of Burley is always spoken of by the native as 'Burley God-help-us'.—*D. N.*, August 1884.

Sag (*Amer.-Eng.*). Sinking, cessation, non-success—from mining, where a sinking of the bed, or roof, of a mine, has this term applied.

Still more when Mr Matthew Arnold or Mr Irving appears in the States, then there is 'no sag in the popular boom', which, being interpreted, means that there is no lull in the general excitement.—*D. N.*, 5th October 1886.

Sage hens (*American*). People of Nevada — probably from the multiplicity of prairie fowl which frequent the sage bushes which cover the prairie in that state.

Sail in (*American - Eng.*). Equivalent to 'Go it', and taking its place in England.

Sailor's champagne (*Peoples'*). Champagne on the *do ut des* principle —an easy-go sailor shoots all his pay in a day, and then reminds you all the rest of his run on shore that you only exhibit beer—and mere board and lodging.

St Alban's clean shave (*Church*). Appearance of the ritualistic or high church clergymen's face.

St Alban's doves (*Electioneering*, 1869). Two active political canvassers, so called from attending a certain church of which they were shining lights.

St Giles' carpet (*Seven Dials—old*). A sprinkling of sand.

St John's Wood donas (*Public-house*, 1882). Immoral women of the better class, living at St John's Wood generally.

St Lubbock (*Lower London*, 1880 on). An orgy, a drunken riot. From the August Bank Holiday, the first Monday in the month, chiefly invented, in the parliamentary sense, by Sir John Lubbock. The tendency on the part of the more violent holiday-makers produced the satirical 'St', and its accompanying meaning.

St Lubbock, Feasts of (*Public*, 1871 on). Bank holidays as established by law — Easter Monday, Whit Monday, first Monday in August and Boxing Day, 26th December. From Sir John Lubbock's Act, 1871, by which the first, second, and fourth were made legal, and the third created.

The feasts of St Lubbock—*i.e.*, Bank Holidays—established in consequence of the exertions of Sir John Lubbock, M.P. (afterwards Lord Avebury), in 1871, are regarded with the highest favour. Their influences upon the commercial world and whole community have been remarkable.—*D. T.*, July 1899.

St Peter's the beast (*Oxford*, 1890 on). St Peter's in the East.

All who have dwelt near St Peter's-in-the-East and been tortured by its fearsome bell will understand why, despite its pleasant situation and curious crypt, it should be referred to as 'St Peter's the Beast'.—*D. T.*, 14th August 1899.

St Stephen's hell (*Parliamentary*). No. 15 Committee Room, House of Commons. When the Parnellite 'split' took place, the Irish Nationalist members 'discussed' in this chamber for many days—the noise resulting in the bestowal by the lower officials of this title upon the room in question.

Sal hatch (*Peoples'*). Umbrella—origin quite obscure, but probably salacious.

Sal hatch (*Prob. Hist.*, 17 *cent.*). Dirty wench. Probably one of the court of Charles II. French phrases of a certain fashion. Of course a corruption—from 'Sale Ange', which is itself a French corruption of Sallanches, a town in Savoy whence spread over France, as from all other Swiss towns, women servants. The French have historically always considered the

Swiss less cleanly than themselves; they still use the phrase to worry servant girls from Savoy, now, of course, part of France. Sal Hatch is applied in exactly the same way to dirty - looking young English girls. This word, however, may come from the Italian—Salaccia—a dirty, ugly, big woman. If so, it reaches us from the Hatton Garden division of London.

Sal slappers (*Costers'*). Modification of a vigorous name for a common woman.

Salad march (*Ballet*, 19 *cent.*). March of ballet girls in green, white, and pale amber—from the usual colours of salads.

A 'salad' march, with the *coryphées* dressed as lettuces and spring cabbages, is an admirably harmonious arrangement.—*D. T.*, 7th May 1899.

Sally B. (*American*, 1880 on). A very thin, tall woman in evening dress. This phrase, which fleetingly passed through London, is quite historical. Derived from Madame Bernhardt, who, though at the end of the Victorian era, she became a well-developed comedian, was for many years the most absolutely thin woman on the stage.

Sally Lunn (*Peoples'*). Bun, invented in the 18th century by a Chelsea industrial of that name. (*See* Simnel.)

Saloon (*Amer. - Eng.*). Tavern—applied to a brilliant establishment.

Salt, Barrel of. (*See* Barrel.)

Salt-cellars (*Peoples'*). The cavities behind the feminine collar-bones.

Salt-horse squires (*Naval*, 19 *cent.*). Warrant, as distinct from commissioned, officers. Name used to suggest the parvenu grandeurs of the warrant officer, who was dined upon salt beef—the salt horse in question.

Salt-pen (*Lit.*, 1860 on). Nautical. Figurative description of the pen of a writer of sea-stories.

Salt junk (*Music Hall*, 1897). Last rhyming cry for drunk—passing into 'salt'.

Salt's pricker (*Naval*). Thick roll of compressed Cavendish tobacco. Used sometimes very figuratively.

Salvation Army (*Street*, 1882). Drunk.

Salvation Army of politics (*Polit.*, 1885). Radicals. Invented by Mr Goschen in this year.

For us Radicals, the Salvation Army of politics, as Mr Goschen denominated us, the keen desire for social improvement, the great and healthy efforts for actual and immediate reforms, the enthusiasm of social progress; but for him the better part, for the educated and thinking men the nobler mission of the candid friend, the duty of criticising the work in which his culture and refinement prevent him from taking any part.—Mr J. Chamberlain's Speech: Dinner of the Eighty Club, 28th April 1885.

Salvation jugginses (*Com. London*, 1882). The early aversion exhibited towards the more violent members of the Salvation Army led to the addition of the word juggins.

Salvation rotters (1883). Final term of scorn levelled at the early Salvationists.

Salvation - soul - sneakers (1883). This was one of the last terms applied, before General Booth (February) yielded to circumstances and with almost papal authority forebade outdoor processions in London. (*See* Skeleton Army.)

Sam (*Peoples'*). Abbreviation of Stand Sam—pay for a drink.

Sam Hill (*American*). Some hell, replacing the name of a notoriously wild-tongued man.

Same o. b. (*Peoples'*, 1880). Abbreviation of 'old bob'—this standing for shilling. Phrase has reference to the universal shilling entrance-fee to most ordinary places of information or amusement.

Same old 3 and 4 (*Workmen's*). 3 shillings and 4 pence—which, multiplied by six working days, gives £1 per week.

Sampan (*Navy*). Historical name, from Nelson's time, of the *Sans Pareil*.

Sandford and Merton (*Press*). Didacticism—from the lofty tone of the speakers in this once celebrated boys' book.

It would, we think, have been more attractive but for an occasional tendency to fall into the *Sandford and Mertoun* or directly didactic vein, as when we are reminded that 'an undue concession to narrow prejudice or cowardly convention should be unsparingly denounced, because it is insidiously and subtly destructive'.—*D. N.*, 2nd February 1885.

Sandwich board (*Street*, 19 *cent.*). Police station stretcher, used chiefly for conveying drunken persons.

Sandwich men (*Street*, 1860 on). The doleful, broken-down men employed at one shilling per day to carry pairs of advertisement boards, tabard-fashion, one on the unambitious chest, the other on the broken back.

Sangster (*London*, 1850). Umbrella. A Mr Sangster, of Fleet Street, invented a light and elegant steel-ribbed umbrella, which he called Sangster's patent umbrella.

Sanguinary muddle (*Polit.*, 1884). Policy of Europe—which seemed always destructive. Invented by Lord Derby.

Lord Derby used a very strong expression the other day about the diplomacy of Europe. He called it a 'sanguinary muddle', and recommended that England should keep out of it.—*D. N.*, 17th October 1885.

Sans-culottes (*Peoples'*, 1793-1830). San skillets—such was the translation by the people for the people in the loyal later times of George III. This phrase came to be immediately applied to the most wretchedly-clad men in the revolutionary streets of Paris.

Sapheadism (*Agricultural, Amer.*). When the sap is rising, the bark is soft—hence this term for weak-headedness.

Sapper (*Music Hall*, 2nd French Empire). Gay, irresistible dog. From 'Rien est sacré pour un sssapeur!'—the chorus of a song by Theresa, a great Paris music hall cantatrice, 1860-70. She came to London about 1866.

Mr Clement-Smith, the well-known theatrical bill printer, being captured the other day by another of those evening paper sappers to whom nothing is sacred, was irreverently christened by his tormentor 'the Bill-poster King.'—*Ref.*, 3rd February 1899.

Sappy (*Low. London*). Weak-headed. Origin obscure.

Saratoga (*American-English*). Anything large, huge. Saratoga is an example of new word-growth. Saratoga Springs being the most fashionable inland station for New Yorkers, necessarily the largest amount of personal luggage accompanied the fashionable frequenters, while size was required that ladies' costumes might not be crushed in travelling. But the most remarkable development of Saratoga was that of being used to describe anything of unusual size.

Sarcasm (*Soc.*, 19 *cent.*). Satirical assumption of the meaning of a stupidly-said thing.

Sardine-box (*Peoples'*). A jocular name given to the prison-van, in which the prisoners were stowed away or packed, as it were. (*See* V.R., Black Maria, Virtue Rewarded, Vagabonds Removed, etc.)

Sarey Gamp (*London*, '40's). Huge market umbrella. Now not seen out of museums, and mostly bought up for their mines of valuable whalebone.

Sargentlemanly (*Peoples'*, 19 *cent.*). Satirical perversion of 'so gentlemanly', and importing that the person has taken rank above a mere private.

Sarkaster (*Press*, 1880). Invented word; synonym for satirist—derived from sarcastic.

Sarken News (*London*, 1860-83). The common term for *Clerkenwell News*—a journal which was begun in a small way in Clerkenwell, and became one of the chief metropolitan mediums for advertising.

Sashay (*Anglo-American*). Slide, skip, dance, skirt, walkingly haunt, etc. From term used by French and other dancing-masters — *chasser* — to glissade from one side to the other.

Sat (*Univer.*, 1860). Satisfaction.

Satellite (*Public-school*). Modern synonym for 'fag'—a boy who revolves round a bigger one, whom he has set up as his model and hero. Sometimes 'Sat'.

Saturday middles (*Soc.*, 1875). The article on the left of the middle of the *Saturday Review* — where it opened in the centre.

Saturday pie (*Peoples'*). Pasty, within which is interred all the disjecta membra of the week.

Sauce-box (*Peoples'*). The mouth.

Sausanmash (*Jun. Clerks'*). Lowest common denomination of 'one sausage and mashed potatoes'.

Saveloy Square (*E. London*). Duke Place, Aldgate—so named satirically on the *lucus a non lucendo* principle—because, being wholly inhabited by Jews, no ordinary sausages are ever found there.

Say (*American colloquial*). Commonest form of 'listen'. Probably descended from the Plymouth Brethren who crossed to the States. 'Say', equivalent to 'do', is a common form of expression in Devonshire to this day.

Say howdy for me (*Amer.-Eng.*)' Remember me to, etc. (*See* Howdy). Passing rapidly into English every-day expression.

Say soldi (*Italian—through organ-grinders'*) Six shillings.

'Sblood (*Cath. Exclamatory*). His blood. Will be found in *Tom Jones*, bk. xviii. ch. 10; where also will be found Od zookers — God's hooks, or hooker, which equals 'nails' — the three used in the Crucifixion.

'S'bodlikins (*Cath. Exclamatory*). His bodily-kins! Meaning obscure. Some say it refers to the earthly kin of Jesus — His brothers and sisters on Joseph's side. Others, extremists say the word is His body leakings—meaning the blood flowing from the side.

Scaffold-pole (*Common London*). Is the fried potato chip sold with fried fish.

Scaling down (*American-English*). Repudiation of debt.

Scalp (*American-Eng.*, 19 *cent*). Victories.

After securing all the amateur scalps in San Francisco, Corbett became a professional pugilist.—*D. T.*, 18th March 1897.

Scalper (*American - English*). A savage horse, suggested by the Indian habit of achieving the scalp, and the tendency of the scalper to snap at the head of his groom. Now extended to describe briefly any human being of merciless tendencies, especially in his financial dealings.

Scalps (*Soc.*, 1896). Jewel chain charms worn upon bangles, and given by young men to young girls.

Scandal village (*Sussex*). London Super Mare or Brighton, where the virtuous natives assume their London patrons to be all libellous.

Scare (*American - English*, 1880). Grow frightened.

Scare-crown (*American, Boys'*). Intensification of scare-crow, and adapted to a woolless old man. (*See* Bald head, Bottle nose.)

Scent of the hay (*Theatrical*). Sneer at false pastoral writing for the stage. From the protest of Mr Pinero upon being accused, in *The Squire* (a pastoral comedy), of plagiarising a book of Mr Hardy's. Pinero urged that his chief desire had been to waft a scent of the hay across the footlights.

M. Mayer's company have been engaged in wafting the scent of the hay across the footlights. It is French hay, but good of the sort. — *Ref.*, 21st February 1886.

Schlemozzle (*E. London, Jews'*). Riot, quarrel, noise of any kind. Colloquial Hebrew.

I had espied W. A. P., sitting not far off, and partly with a desire to prevent bloodshed, partly in the hope of promoting a schlemozzle, I notified Jones accordingly.—*Ref.*, 1st December 1889.

School Board 'ull be after you (*London Streets*, 1881). Practically meaning — 'Look out—or the police will have you.'

School-marm (*Soc.*, 1886). Schoolmistress. (From U.S.A.)

Celibacy of the clergy is a familiar doctrine, both for banning and for blessing. But the celibacy of the 'school marm' is a heresy which as yet only exists in the pious dream of school managers and school boards, by whom marriage is regarded as an even more ruthless enemy than death.—*Pall Mall Gazette*, 12th January 1888.

Schoolmaster is abroad (*Peoples'*). In other times the country may have heard with dismay that 'the soldier was abroad'. It will not be so now. Let the soldier be abroad if he will; he can do nothing in this age. There is another personage abroad—a personage less imposing—in the eyes of some, perhaps, insignificant. The schoolmaster is abroad; and I trust to him, armed with his primer, against the soldier in full military array.

Schooners, frigates, and full-masters (*Naval*). Degrees of comparison as to the capabilities of apprentices in the Navy — the least accomplished being the schooner, the frigate the youth who is handy at his business, and the full-master the achieved youngster who can learn no more of the art—of navigation understood.

Scoop (*Military*, 1880). One of the modes of wearing the hair when the mode of bringing it down flat upon the forehead came in. (*See* Curtain.)

Scooped (*Amer. - Eng.*, 1880). Swindled—money being scooped out of the pocket.

Score (*Peoples'*). Reckoning — figuratively used. 'I've got a score against you, and some day you'll pay' —from the custom in old times of drawing lines upon a board with a bit of chalk—the number of marks in a line being a score. (*See* Chalking against.)

Scorpions (*Theatrical*). Babies— whose observations do not help the performance.

Scorpions (*Army, Hist.*). Scornful reference by officers to the civil inhabitants of Gibraltar. Originally referred to the natural children of English soldiers by Spanish mothers. Sometimes 'Rock scorpions', the 'Rock' being Gibraltar.

A military correspondent writes from Gibraltar complaining of want of houses for officers attached to the garrison. The 'Scorpions', as the inhabitants are facetiously called, have all the best houses in their hands. — *D. T.*, 5th November 1897.

Scotch (*Rhyming*). Abbreviation of Scotch-pegs, the catch-rhyme for 'leg'.

Scrag-hole (*Theatrical*). Gallery. Probably suggested by the stretching of the scrag or neck, and the resemblance of the gallery to a dark hole.

Scrape along (*Poor Peoples'*). To live somehow from day to day, to scrape off a living.

Scraper (*Soc.*, 1880). Short one to two-inch whisker, slightly curved, and therefore differing from the square inch.

Scratch down (*Street*). The public scolding of a man by a woman.

Scratch me (*L. Lond.*, 19 *cent.*). Lucifer match.

Scratch - rash (*Artisans'*). Face scratched—presumably by wife.

Scratchers (*Lower Class*). Lucifer matches. Splendid example of peoples' onomatope — always going on. The lower classes never took to the absurdly pompous word—lucifer; and even the middles added matches, from the old sulphur matches, probably a corruption of 'meche'.

Scratchers (*Naval*). Pay-masters and their subordinates. Comes down from the noisy times of quill pens.

Scratching poll (*Peoples'*). Pole for cattle to rub their sides against. A reference to a skin disease erroneously said to be prevalent amongst Scotchmen.

An exhibition of Scotchmen's knees took place at the Castle, and was attended with great success. Mr Sandy M'Alister MacDonoughloch took the first prize and a cold in the nose. The prize consists of a scratching poll.

Screamer (*Press*). Alarmist article or leader.

Screaming gin and ignorance (*Sporting Reporters*, 1868). Bad newspaper writing.

Screed (*American - English*). A pelt, or muck running. Widely applied.

Side by side with these garrulous 'screeds' about what took place six or seven weeks ago comes news of what is doing to-day.—*Ref.*, 9th March 1885.

Screw your nut (*L. London*). Dodge a blow aimed at the head.

When we gets there, the Mug says, 'How did he get that?' looking at Selby's eye, and I says, 'He got it because he could not screw his nut.'— *Peoples'*, 6th January 1895.

Screwed up (*Oxford and Cambridge Universities*). To be vanquished. The term takes its rise from the ancient habit of screwing up an offender's door, generally a don's. The action was only complete by breaking off the heads of the very thin screws.

Screwed up (*Artisans'*). Without money—can't move. More emphatically—screwed up in a corner. (*See* Hung up, Stuck up.)

Scribe (*Press*, 1870 on). A poor writer.

Scribley (*Provincial*). Screw-belly, *i.e.*, sourish small beer.

Script (*Authors'*, 1897). Short for manuscript—especially in the theatre.

Scripturience (*Literary*, 1900). Rage for writing; *cacoëthes scribendi*. Presumably invented by Mr William Archer, who wrote—

It is true that Mr Stedman's net is one of very small meshes, which hauls in the minnows as well as the Tritons ; but what an amazing harvest, even of mediocrity ! There is a serious danger, it seems to me, in this universal scripturience. — *M. Leader*, 27th October 1900.

Scrummage (*Youths'*, 1860). Struggle. Derived from foot-ball term.

Scrunging (*Country Boys'*). Stealing unripe apples and pears—probably from the noise made in masticating.

Scug, or Smug (*Schools'*). A new —that is new boy.

In regard to the general charge, it is well known that everywhere bullying has been reduced to the smallest proportion. In our fathers' time every new boy, 'scug', or 'smug', or whatever the generic name may have been, was kicked and knocked about as a matter of course for the first part of his curriculum.—*D. T.*, 12th June 1897.

Sculps (*American*). Convenient abbreviations of pieces of sculpture.

Permit no statue, except the unfortunates in Trafalgar Square, and the melancholy meeting of 'sculps' in Parliament Square, was more sharply criticised at the time of its erection, or more heartily laughed at afterwards than the gigantic equestrian effigy of the late Duke of Wellington.—*D. N.*, 18th January 1883.

Sculpt (*American Artists'*). Verb from sculptor—as writer—to write; dancer—to dance; singer—to sing; sculptor—to sculpt.

Sculptor's ghost (*Art*). Sculptor whose name is not associated with the marble upon which he works. May be the actual creator of a work which goes in another's name, or may be engaged only for his speciality which may be hair, or bust, or legs, or hands, or drapery.

Scurry around (*American*, 1876). Be active.

If you care to lynch him there are barrels of tar, and one of us might scurry around and get some feathers.—*Detroit Free Press*, 1883.

Scuttler (*Manchester*, 1870 on). Young street rough.

Might it not be possible to teach manners, and to enforce their observance, even by means of the rod and the cane, at the Board schools? It is in those expensive seminaries, we apprehend, that the majority of the juvenile 'scuttlers' are educated.—*D. T.*, October 1893.

'Sdeath (*Poetical*). Abbreviation of His death—meaning the Crucifixion. (*See* 'Sflesh.)

Se Tannhauser (*French-Eng.*, 90's). Bore oneself—as 'Que je me tannhause'.

Sea William (*Naval—early 19 cent*). Civilian.

'For d'ye see—I'm a Sea William, and not in no ways under martial law,' said the pilot.—Marryat, *Rattlin the Reefer*, ch. lviii.

Sea-side moths (*Mid.-class*). Bed vermin.

Seats Bill (*Political*, 1884). Short name suddenly given to the Redistribution of Parliamentary seats. Due to Mr Gladstone, and instantly accepted as a brevity, clear in meaning.

Further progress was made in the settlement of the main outlines of the Redistribution scheme, or the Seats Bill as it has now become the fashion to call it.—*D. N.*, 27th November 1884.

Sec. (*Commercial*, 1860). Abbreviation for second.

Second-hand sun (*Poor Folk*). Nothing much to be proud of—suggested where sunlight is only reflected into a given room from a neighbouring wall.

Second-hand woman (*Anglo-Indian Army*, 1859). Widow.

Second liker (*Tavern*, 1884 on). Repetition drink — another like the first. Now applied generally to repetition.

Second picture (*Theatrical*, 1885). Tableau upon the rising of the curtain to applause, after it has fallen at the end of an act, or a play.

Secrets of the alcove (*Soc.*, 1890 on). Most intimate influence of the wife over the husband. Outcome of analytical fiction. Phrase invented by Dumas *fils*.

It may be what Dumas called 'the secret of the alcove', but when perfectly represented, and with absolute purity, on the stage, it is very delightful to witness. Here we see a married woman using every feminine art and charm to tempt her husband back to companionship and love.—*D. T.*, 29th June 1897.

Sedition-mongers (*Polit.*, 1886). Name given to supporters of Home Rule. Started by Lord R. Churchill, 22nd February 1886, at Belfast.

See (*American*). To 'bet'. In the card game of poker each player 'sees' an opponent for so much—that is, bets so much upon cards which he holds, but has not yet shown. It is a word which now may often be heard in Liverpool commercial cotton circles.

Stearn Carpenter, the Heracles of the *Troy Times*, would have 'seen' Achilles, 'and gone ten dollars more', to employ the language understood by the countrymen of Mr Charles Dudley Warner.—*D. N.*, 13th February 1883.

See the breeze (*Cockney*, 1877). Expression of summer enjoyment at escaping from London to an open common. (*See* Taste the sun.)

Seek a clove (*American*). Take a drink.

Seen better days (*Middle-class*). Euphemism for saying a person is poor.

Seen the elephant (*American - English*, 1880 on). Climax—witnessed the finish. From the universal American circus—whose chief attraction in country places *is* the elephant. Therefore the phrase means proud exultation, and is applied to boastful persons.

Selah (*American - English*). The Hebrew 'vale', 'God be with you'. Probably the origin of the London artisan phrase, 'So long'. (*See.*)

Happy, happy England! Everybody has got plenty of work to do except the judges of the Divorce Court. Selah!—*D. T.*. 29th October 1896.

Senal pervitude (*Com. Street Satire*). Penal servitude.

Send for Gulliver (*Soc.*, 1887 on). Depreciatory comment upon some affair not worth discussion. From a cascadescent incident in the first part of Dr Lemuel Gulliver's travels.

Send off (*Anglo-American Lit.*). Poem, tale, or article written specially to attract attention—direct opposite to pot-boiler.

Mr English, then a journalist in active harness, promised the firm a 'send-of' poem.—*N. Y. Mercury*, 1888.

Sensation scene (*Theatrical*, 1862). Exciting scene of action in a play. Title invented by Edward Falconer. (*See* Nailed up drama, Peep o' day tree.)

Sensation-mongering (*Polit.*, 1888). Searching for effect.

Mr Chamberlain has resolved to take no part in a controversy raised and maintained either for party purposes or in pursuit of sensation-mongering.—*D. N.*, 26th February 1886.

Sensational (*American Press, passed to Eng. about* 1870). Omniscient adjective used wherever extraordinary might be a possible equivalent.

Sensational writing (*Lit.*). Crude, frank, banal description, or dialogue, intended to excite or dismay.

Sent (*Peoples'*). Evasion and contraction of 'sent to prison'.

At Northwich William Flynn was sent for seven days for begging. — *People*, 20th March 1898.

Sent across the Herring - pond (*Lower Class*). Transported to Botany Bay.

Sent to Coventry (*Rural*). Cut—not spoken to. Origin so obscure as not to be within view of any known etymologist.

Sent to the skies (*L. Mid.-class*). Killed—evasive accusation of murder.

Sent up (*American-Eng.*). Exposed, publicized. From the New York Police Court term for imprisonment. 'Sent up for a month'—up to the prison that is.

Sentimental hairpin (*Soc.*, 1880). An affected, insignificant girl.

Sentry go (*Military*). Mounting guard.

The Volunteer billets himself now preferentially in forts and in barracks, enjoys compliance with the stern regulations enforced in such places, and would rather be on 'sentry go' than in a public-house carouse.—*D. N.*, 28th April 1886.

Sepulchre (*Middle-class, London*). Name given to the flat cravats covering the shirt front between the coat and throat. Satire upon their effect in covering over and burying the shirt-front, when no longer immaculate. Afterwards called chest-plasters. (*See* Doggie, Poultice, Shakespeare-navels.)

Serio-comic (*Music Hall*, 1860-82). The title given only to lady-singers of a lively turn, and in distinction from 'comics', who are always men.

Serve (*Thieves Soc.*). Euphemism for passing through a term of imprisonment.

Sessions (*Peoples'*). Noise, quarrelling, disturbance, from the fact that at sessions there are conditions not peculiar to quietude.

Set (*Street*, 1880). Conquered, put down.

Set about (*Peoples'*). To assault.

The present assault was committed on the 20th ult. As frequently happened, they 'had words' about money matters, and because she would not accede to his demands he 'set about her'.—*People*, 4th April 1897.

Set the Hudson on fire (*New York*, 1884). Instance of imitation, of 'Set the Thames on fire'.

'Mme. Boniface' is not likely to set

the Hudson on fire, as it is original in neither plot nor music.—*N. Y. Mercury*, 1884.

Seven Dials raker (*Costers'—local*). A girl of the town who never smiles out of the Dials. (*See* Deck.)

Seven times seven man (*Peoples'— Satirical*). Hypocritical religionist.

Seventy-five cent. word (*Amer.- Eng.*, 1884). Sesquipedalian.

'Sflesh (*Provincial*). His flesh—a very rare Catholic exclamation, descended from before the Reformation. (*See* 'Sdeath.)

Shack-per-swaw (*Sporting*). Every man for himself. French — *chaque pour soi*. Introduced in England by a French gentleman rider.

Shadder (*Work.-class, 19 cent.*). A thin, worn person.

Shadow of a shade (*Polit.*, 1886). More than immaculate, when used in the negative, as it always was. Invented by Lord R. Churchill.

But of confiscation, of taking away a man's property without paying him for it, there is not, as Lord Randolph Churchill would say, the shadow of a shade of a hint or suggestion or implication or inference.—*D. N.*, 26th February 1886.

Shadow of the owl (*Athenæum Club*). Cellar smoking-room (until 1899, when the Council added a floor, part of which was the new *fumoir* of the Athenæum), where the visitor was at once met by the topaz eyes of the highperched owl, raised in honour of the tutelary goddess of that ilk, Minerva.

Shadwoking (*Soc.*). Grotesque rendering of shadowing.

Shake a flannin (*Navvies', 19 cent.*). To fight. (*See* Flannel-jacket.)

Shake fleas (*Old Eng.*). To thrash.

Shake leg (*Peoples'*). Remove.

Shake old fel (*American*). Greeting—'Shake hands, old fellow.'

Shake-out (*Stock Exchange*, 19 *cent.*). Sudden revulsion and following clearance—due to panic, the result of discovery of fraud, or of stupendous bankruptcy, or even the death of a powerful financier of known speculative turn of mind.

After Saturday's heavy shake-out in New York, occasioned by the news of Mr Flower's death, the market has settled down a little in consequence of the evidences afforded that the big financial houses were fully prepared to grapple with the situation.—*D. T.*, 16th May 1899.

Shake-up (*Peoples'*). Start, beginning, spurring.

The first French Revolution, with all its attendant horrors, was entirely due to the fact that in a little preliminary shake-up the Paris masses found themselves, to nobody's surprise more than their own, fully equal to cope with the gendarmerie.—*Ref.*, 27th November 1887.

Shake yer toe - rag (*Beggars'*). Show a clean pair of heels—run away.

Shakespeare-navels (*Lond. Youths'*, 1870). Long - pointed, turned - down collar.

Sham-abram (*Peoples'*). Pretend illness. Very common use still in the Navy. The captain is shamabraming again — he wants a day on shore, to see—a doctor.

Sham - ateurs (*Sporting*). People who are not even amateurs.

The amateurs of Pancras Road showed themselves distinctly different from the sham-ateurs of Her Majesty's Theatre. —*Ref.*, 16th December 1888.

Shamrock (*Military*, 19 *cent.*). A bayonet prick.

Shan von Voght (*Irish Peoples'*). The Pasquinado, Mrs Harris, or Paul Pry of Irish life.

Can anything as spirited and stirring as the 'Shan von Voght' be rhymed in favour of declining to pay rent ?—*D. N.*, 5th November 1883.

Shanghai gentleman (*Naval*). The very reverse of a gentleman.

Shank (*American*). Centre or heart. From the shank or grip of a button.

Why, you ain't going home already? It's right in the shank of the evening.— *Texas Siftings*, 1883.

Shank yersels awa (*Scotch*). Take yourselves off—move your shanks.

Shant of bivvy (*Hatton Garden*). Pint of beer.

Shan't take salt (*Theatrical*). Small returns. Good example of an elision creating obscurity. Means, 'We shall not take enough money to pay for salt, let alone bread.'

Shape up (*Peoples'*, 18 *cent.*). Show fight—from the aspect of a prizefighter when prepared to kill.

When Fred called him an all-round ass—he shaped up !

Shapes and shirts (*Theat.*, 1883). Satirical name given by young comedians of the present day to distinguish old actors, who swear by the legitimate Elizabethan drama, which involves either the 'shape' or the 'shirt'—the first being the cut-in tunic; the other, or shirt, being independent of shape. (*See* Chest-plaster.)

Shave (*Peoples'*, 1884). Drink.

Shaves (*Services*). False news—sometimes mere jokes.

Belgrade is getting livelier because of the influx of miscellaneous foreigners. It still maintains its pre-eminence for 'shaves'.—*D. N.*, 1876.

Shawl (*Mid.-class*). Symptom of engagement.

Lady Clonbrony was delighted to see that her son assisted Grace Nugentin in shawling Miss Broadhurst.—Miss Edgeworth, *The Absentee*, 1809.

She (*Soc.*, 1887). Queen Victoria. From *She*, the African romance by Mr Rider Haggard—produced early in this year.

She didn't seem to mind it very much (*Peoples'*, 1885). Cant phrase, intimating jealousy on 'her' part.

Sheckles (*Peoples'*). Money. From the Hebrew.

Shed a tear (*Peoples'*, 1860). Take a short drink—not a draught.

Shedduff (*Mid.-class*). Corruption of *chef d'œuvre*.

Sheet o' tripe (*Streets'*). Plate of this dish.

She'll go off in an aromatic faint (*Soc.*, 1883). Said of a fantastical woman, meaning that her delicate nerves will surely be the death of her.

Shellback (*Navy*). Sailor of full age. (*See* Flatfoot.)

She-male (*Common London*, 1880). Synonym for female, and pairing with he-male. (*See* He-male.)

I love the she-male sex.

Sheol (*E. London*). Evasion of 'Hell'—the word being Hebrew for this place.

In our own channels or in the great Australian bight we who would go to sea for pleasure would go to Sheol for pastime.—*Ref.*, 4th October 1887.

Shepherd, To (*Boer War*, October 1899-1900). To surround, to drive into a crowd—from surrounding the enemy.

Since Cronje was shepherded with his army into the bed of the Modder by a turning movement, the remaining Boer commanders have been very nervous lest a similar manœuvre should be tried against them.—*D. T.*, 2nd April 1900.

Sherry (*Tavern*). Four ale—that is, ale at fourpence per quart.

She's been a good wife to him (*Streets'*). Satire cast at a drunken woman rolling in the streets.

Shet down (*Engineers', American*). Thoroughly commenced; suggested by 'shetting' or 'shutting' down a safety valve.

Shet up, Sossidge (*Peoples'*, 1896). Recommendation to a German, noisy in public, to be quiet—really, 'Shut up, Sausage'.

Shettered (*Low Life*). Complete ignominy. Word derived from shopshutter.

Shevvle chap (*Sheffield*). A man of that city.

Shift (*Irish*, 1800). Blow up.

Shiftmonger (*Tavern*, 1882). Very remarkable expression. When the chappies and Johnnies became notorious for frequenting the old Gaiety Theatre stalls (1879-82), they were remarkable for the display of very large, rigid shirt-fronts. Indeed, this shirt became a specialty—hence the word.

The shiftmonger rolled into the Roman's (Romano's—an Italian restaurant in the Strand) blind, speechless, paralytic. Staggering up to the well-known slate, he wrote thereon, in trembling characters, 'Coffee and soda for one. Wake me in time to bress for Baiety Gurlesque'.—*Bird o' Freedom*, 7th March 1886.

Shillelagh (*Irish, Hist.*). Knobbed stick carried for fighting.

What did he hit you with? Witness: An Irish shillelagh—a crinkled and thick stick—a kind of Irishman's truncheon.—*D. T.*, 31st December 1895.

Shilling tabernacle (*Peoples'*). Wesleyan or Baptist tea-meeting—at twenty-four halfpence per head.

Shin stage (*Peoples'*, 18 *cent.*). Journey on foot—or by propelling the shins.

Shine (*American*). Smiling look.

Shingle (*American*). Close-cropped hair—ridge and furrow. When (1880) following a London fashion, the hair of American men of fashion was cut close, this term came to be applied. It is derived from the name of thin wooden tiles — shingles, which, of course, lie flat and close to the roof-rafters.

'There will be no more parting there',

said the man when he looked into the mirror after having his hair shingled.—*Texas Siftings.*

Shipwrecked (*E. London*). Drunk. (*See* Floored.)

Shirtsleeves and shirt-sleeves (*Peoples'*). Poor and rich, work and luxury. The first are rolled up to the shoulders. 'I do *my* work in my shirtsleeves.' The shirt-sleeves are fair, white, smooth, and only displayed, as a rule, at the cuff.

Shoe's on the mast (*Sailors' and Peoples', Hist.*). 'If you like to be liberal, now's your time.' Originally typical of homeward-bound and pay-off. In the 18th century, when near the end of a long voyage, the sailors nailed a shoe to the mast, the toes downward, that passengers might delicately bestow a parting gift.

Shofel (*E. London*). Hansom cab. Said to be derived from the peaked bonnets in use about 1850-53, which Jewesses dubbed by this name. Shofel, it seems, is a common word for hood, peak, or eave—even a hook nose.

Shool (*E. London*). Church or chapel—from this Hebrew word representing synagogue.

The beadle's eye was all over the shool at once. — Zangwill, *Children of the Ghetto.*

Shoot (*S. Exchange*). To give a man a close price in a stock without knowing whether there will be a profit or loss on the transaction.

Shoot (*S. London*, 1868). Walworth Road Station, L. C. & D. Railway. Because of the immense number of persons 'shot' out there.

A recent writer on the condition of Italy adduces the wretched character of most of the railway stations as evidence of the poverty of the country. I would give something to know his opinion of Walworth, as evidenced by the condition of the 'Shoot!'—*South London Press,* November 1882.

Shoot, Blooming (*Common London,* 1880). Cursed crowd.

Here's bad luck to the whole blooming shoot.—*Cutting.*

Shoot into the brown (*Volunteers', circa* 1860). Figuratively—to fail. The phrase takes its rise from rifle practice, where the queer shot misses the black and white target altogether, and shoots into the brown—*i.e.*, the earth butt.

Shoot the chimney (*American*). Chimney is figurative for talking, and derived from movement of chin. Shoot here means stop.

Shoot t' wood to t' hole (*Yorks.*). Be secret. Let no one hear you. Translated thus: 'Shut the wood to the hole;' or, in other words, 'Shut the door'.

Shoot your cuff (*Peoples'*, 1875 on). Make the best personal appearance you can and come along—from the habit of wearing wide cuffs. (*See* Cuff-shooter.)

Shooter (*American - Eng.*, 1870). Pistol.

Shooting at sight (*American*). Instantaneous homicide — without warning.

Shop (*Theat.*, 1880). Theatre. One of the mock-modest affectations of actors, putting themselves and their work on a trade basis. (*See* Low comedy merchant.)

Shop, To (*Low. London*). To be instrumental in sending an individual to prison. Generally used to describe imprisonment.

Sullivan shopped him — real landed him.—*People,* 6th January 1895.

Shop-constable (*Workshop*). He represents the first principle of justice, the most primitive type of the magistrate. He is appointed for a day; he takes his turn with the rest of his shop companions, and commands one day, only to obey the next. When there is a trade or a personal quarrel, an appeal is made to the 'constable', who has the case tried.

Shopped (*Theatrical*). Verb derived from shop. Engaged for piece.

Short (*Bankers'*). A cheque paid in as few notes as possible.

Short (*Public-house*). Raw spirits —to distinguish it from spirits and water.

Short turn (*Hatters' men*). A particular ring at the warehouse bell requires that the boy shall answer it. Upon his return he gives to the shop constable (*see*), of the day the message he has heard at the gate. 'Gentlemen, a short turn', he may say, or 'a long turn'. In the first case, the applicant is presumably a well-authenticated 'Unionist'.

Short 'uns (*Poachers'*). Partridges —referring to the almost complete absence of tail feathers. (*See* Long 'un.)

Short week (*Artisans'*). Not a full six days' wages to take.

Shortage (*Anglo-American*, 1880 on). Abbreviation of defalcation.

Sho's (*American*). Abbreviation of 'sure as'.

Shot (*Peoples'*, *Hist.*). Freed—from past tense of a verb rarely used in the singular in police society.

It was a horse that didn't mean work, and witness was very glad to 'get shot of him'.—*D. T.*, 14th December 1897.

Shoulder-dab (*London*, 1800). A warrant officer or bailiff, who tapped the debtor on the shoulder as a legal arrest.

Shouldering (*Undertakers'*). Carrying corpse in coffin.

It appeared that at a late hour on Monday night the prosecutors were 'shouldering' a coffin, containing a corpse which they had just brought away from the Westminster Hospital.—*D. N.*, 20th August 1890.

Shov (*Thieves'*). Knife, or rather dagger or dirk. Said by some to be an application of 'shove'—the movement made with the knife; by others a corruption, very cogent, of 'chiv'—the Romany for knife.

Shove (*Street*, 1880—*adopted generally*). Bounce, gas, self-glorification, preposterous patriotic yell.

You only get to know what a nice place England is by going abroad, and finding what a lot of 'shove' there is about the glorification of most other places.—*Ref.*, 24th July 1887.

Shove in (*Common Class*). Pawn —requires no elucidation.

Shove off (*Navy*). To quit, go, flee, depart—from shoving off a boat from land or ship.

Show drink, To (*Amer.-Eng.*). Obvious.

Show-houses (*Soc.*, 18 and 19 *cent.*). Mansions containing valuable works of art.

Show-houses is a very appropriate term for such of the mansions of our nobility and gentry as are open to public inspection.—*Mirror*, 1829.

Show the hand (*Peoples'*). To reveal unintentionally. From card-playing, where showing the hand is sure to lose the game.

Showy (*Society*, 1880). This word for overdressed and over 'made up' began to be common in this year.

Shulleg-day (*Street*, 1880). Corruption of show-leg day—referring to muddy day in London when the ladies carry their skirts high and expose their ankles.

Shunt (*Railway Officials'*). To kill or move out of the way—from shunting carriages and engines.

Shut down (*Amer.-Eng.*). Ceased —from closing the lid of the cash-box.

But Coghill didn't want any more of the lands at any price. Then Lafayette tried to get the balance of the money due in honour to Coghill from Barin' by selling Baring some more of the lands. But Baring by this time had got enough of the lands himself, and shut down.— *N. Y. Mercury*, 23rd May 1885.

Shut down (*Anglo-American*). Forbidden — very emphatic form of opposition.

Dr Oliver and Dr Myrtle—what pretty names!—have 'shut down' on 'monopole' and 'extra dry'.—*Harrowgate D. N.*, 31st August 1883.

Shut up your garret (*Street*). Hold your tongue.

Shuvly kouse (*Street*). Perversion of public-house. This phrase spread through London from a police-court case, in which a half-witted girl used this phrase.

Sick in 14 languages (*American Marine*). Very ill indeed.

Sick man of Europe (*Polit.*, 1853 on). Any reigning sultan of Turkey. The phrase, as applied to Turkey, is said to have been given currency by the Emperor Nicholas I. of Russia. Conversing in 1853 with Sir George Hamilton Seymour, the English Ambassador at St Petersburg, he used the words:—'We have on our hands a sick man—a very sick man. It will be a great misfortune if, one of these days, he should slip away from us before the necessary arrangements have been made.'

Side-scrapers (*Middle-class London*, 1879-82). This was the name given to the square inch or two of whisker parallel with the ear which came in about this time.

Sieve-memory (*Peoples'*—*old*). Bad memory.

I pray you, sir, write down these charms, for I have but a sieve-memory. All runs through. — Garrick, *Abel Drugger*.

223

Signed all over (*Artists'*). Said of a good picture which instantly reveals its creator in every inch.

Silence-yelper (*Thieves'*). Usher in a court of law—this word being his chief shape of speech.

Silly dinner (*Soc.*, *Anglo-American*, 1897). Free and easy feasts. Took its rise in an evasive paraphrase of the name Seeley. Mr Herbert Barnum Seeley gave (20th December 1896) a dinner in New York which was concluded by a femimine music-hall entertainment.

Instantly the news of the Seeley dinner got into the newspapers, Mr Oscar Hammerstein put a clever burlesque of the whole business on the stage of Olympia—a music hall in Broadway.—*D. T.*, 28th January 1897.

From this time a doubtful dinner was spoken of as a Silly one. Became quite colloquial. 'There will be a silly snack on Sunday, 11.30, T. W. B. F.

Silly moo! (*Provincial*, *Rural*). Evasion of silly cow. Said generally of a stupid woman.

Silver streak (*Patriotic*). English Channel.

The silver streak shelters England from those direct consequences of a great war on the Continent which might be expected to overtake France.—*D. N.*, 14th October 1885.

Simnel (*Scarborough*). Cake of two kinds set one on the other, and so baked. The result of an accidental baking. There is a legend in Scarborough, however, that this name refers to the pretender Simnel, and that this cake was first baked by him in Henry VII.'s kitchen.

The day was termed 'Mothering Sunday', because all children in service repaired to their homes, taking with them a spiced cake, called a simnel, to which quaint ceremony, still observed in many rural districts, Herrick alludes in the lines—

A simnel also will I bring
'Gainst thou goest a-mothering.

—*D. T.*, 16th March 1901.

Simpson *v.* Hard Simpson.

Singing drolls (*Music Hall*). Comic male duettists who invented this title to distinguish themselves from comic singers, who were not droll, and who rarely wore costume. (*See* Athletic drolls.)

Singing Spanish (*Old Eng.*). Making a wild, crooning noise—probably suggested by the church services of Queen Mary Tudor's husband.

Sinjin's Wood (*Streets'*, 1882). Satirical way of announcing St John's Wood.

You have tasted the bad lush called wines from the wood. Well, there is worse tipple than that, cully—the wines of Sinjin's Wood. They generally run you in about a dick a bottle.

Sip (*Com. Lond.*, 19 *cent.*). Synonym for kiss.

Sissies (*Soc.*, 1890 on). Effeminate men in society.

Sissy men in Society. — Powdered, painted and laced. They swarm at afternoon teas. Of late, says a London writer, a certain type of man has become protuberant — a languid, weak-kneed, vain, and lazy specimen of humanity who has literally no redeeming points that can be discovered, and who yet gives himself all the airs of one to whom the universe ought to do unquestioning homage.—*N. Y. Mercury*, May 1893.

Sit down supper (*Soc.*, 1860). When about this date the medical press began to agitate against high feeding, one of the economical results was the invention of the 'stand up' supper, a necessarily thinner meal than the old ball-banquet. Old-fashioned people thereupon adopted this term.

Sitter (*Cricket*, 1898). Easy catch.

Sivvy, Upon my (*Common London*). A polite way of taking or making oath—possibly a corruption of asseveration.

I'll not disgrace your toffish lot. I'll be a great man, upon my sivvy.—*Cutting*, 1882.

(*See* Thuzzy-muzzy.)

Six buses through Temple Bar (*Peoples'*, 1840-50). Impossibility. Originated by the celebrated M.P., General Thompson.

Everybody who asks the Government to go on with the Suffrage Bill and the Seats Bill as one measure, and at one time, will be committing that great mistake which our old friend General Thompson used to describe as being made by the man who insisted on driving six omnibuses abreast through Temple Bar.—John Bright, Leeds, 18th October 1883.

Six-cornered oath (*Anglo-American*). Complicated swearing.

Since we are going to have German opera this season, it is high time to explain that *Die Gotterdammerung* is not a six-cornered German oath, but an opera.—*N. Y. Mercury*, September 1883.

Six feet above contradiction (*American*). Completely imperious.

Six feet and itches (*Peoples'*). Over six feet. Corruption of inches, usually written 'ichs'— hence the word.

Six mile bridge assassins (*Tipperary*). Soldiers—from the fact that once upon a time certain rioters were shot at this spot, not far from Mallow.

Six of everything (*Workwomen's*). Said by workwomen and workmen's wives in praise of a girl who marries with a trousseau meeting the respectable requirements of this phrase.

Six - monthser (*Police*). A stipendiary magistrate of a savage nature who always gives, where he can, the full term (six months) allowed him by law.

Six-quarter men (*Cloth Drapers'*). There are two widths of cloth—six quarter and three quarter. The superior employés are called 'six-quarter men'— the inferior 'three-quarter men'—a term of contempt.

Sixes, Put on the (*Military*, 1879). Small hook curls, hence 'sixes' gummed by some privates on their foreheads, and composed of their forehead hair.

'Ain't the 3rd putting on the sixes,' said by a private at Dover of another regiment in reference to the 3rd, whose colonel allowed this style of hair-dressing.

Skalbanker (*Paper-makers'*). An outsider paper-maker, one who has not served seven years to the trade.

Skeleton Army (*Street*, 1882). Street fighting. The origin of this term for fighting in public took its rise about the end of 1882, when the Skeleton Army was formed to oppose the extreme vigour of the early Salvation Army.

Serious Affray between the Skeleton and Salvation Armies.—A man named Timothy M'Cartney is at present lying in the London Hospital suffering from a severe wound in the back, which he received from one of the members of the Skeleton Army.—*D. N.*, 10th January 1883.

Skettling (*Naval Officers'*). Full dressing.

Ski (*Westminster School*). Street Arab, road boy.

Skilamalink (*L. London*). Secret, shady, doubtful. If not brought in by Robson, it was re-introduced by him at the Olympic Theatre, and in a burlesque.

Skin-changers (*Peoples'*). Appertaining to metamorphosis. It referred, and refers generally, to the wehr-wolf throughout Europe.

Lycanthropy (a charming subject) is by the late Mr J. F. M'Lennan. The wolf is the animal, as Mr M'Lennan says, into which European 'skin-changers' commonly turn themselves. — *D. N.*, 7th August 1883.

Skinners (*Street*). Mental torture —figure of speech. From the agony endured by being flayed alive.

Skins a wicked eye (*American*). Evil-looking eye — the skinning referring to the wide opening of the lid.

Skip (*Anglo-American*, 1870). A rapid retreat, quick march to avoid consequences. Also to run away meanly. (*See* Balley, Polka, Valse.)

Skippable (*Soc.*, 1882). To be avoided—from skipping in reading.

Mrs Oliphant's contessa is not so odious nor quite such a bore as some contessas we have known, but she is skippable, too.—*D. N.*, 26th December 1884.

Skipper (*Criminal*, 1870). One retreating.

Skipper (*Military*). Naval way of describing a military captain.

Skivvy (*Navy*). Japanese—equivalent to rumbo.

Sky-pilot (*Naval*). Chaplain —brought in about the time of Dibdin and Tom Bowline. (*See* Holy Joe, Devil-dodger.)

While some of the members of the Congregational Union were enquiring the way to the hall where refreshments were served, the doorkeeper shouted in a stentorian voice: 'Sky-pilots' beanfeast!'—*D. T.*, 4th October 1895.

Skying a copper (*Peoples'*, 1830 on). Making a disturbance—upsetting the apple-cart. From Hood's poem, *A Report from Below*, to which this title was popularly given until it absolutely dispossessed the true one.

Slagger (*Low Life*). Fellow who keeps a house of accommodation.

Slam (*American—passing to England*). To skurry or chevy, probably from the vigour displayed in slamming a door.

Slam-slam (*Anglo-Indian*). To salute—taken from Eastern salaam.

Slanging (*Music Hall*, 1880). This is a term for singing, and is due to the quantity of spoken slang between the verses.

Slap (*Theatrical*). Paint used in creating a stage complexion. Probably from its being liberally and literally slapped on.

Slated (*London Hospital*, 19 *cent.*). To die. Visitors to their relations and friends in hospital are only admitted on certain days—until a patient is doomed, when he is 'slated'—that is to say, his name is placed on the doorporter's slate, in order that his relations and friends may mention his name, and obtain entrance to the hospital at any reasonable hour.

Slaughter-house (*Thieves'*). Name for the Surrey Sessions-house. (*See* Steel, X.'s hall, jug.)

Sleeps like a top (*Old English*). From taupe—a mole, which is practically always in bed.

Slice off (*Military*). Paying part of an old score.

'Slife (*Ancient*). Catholic exclamation—His life. (*See* Odd's my life.)

Slightly tightly (*Fast Life*). Bemused with beer; not drunk.

Sling a slobber (*Low Life*). To kiss, or rather sling a kiss—the salute itself being the slobber.

Sling hook (*Peoples'*). Dismissal. From the mining districts. Refers to a hooked bag which is hung up in dressing-room, and contains such things as the miner does not require down the shaft. When dismissed the miner removes his hooked bag, and takes it away.

Sling in (*American—now English*, 1860). Very common American verb to recommend action.

'Sling in your feet', said to a breakdown dancer.

'Sling us in something hot in your rag', said to a newspaper critic.

Sling joints (*American*). Gain a living rather by physical than mental effort.

Sling over (*Soc., from Amer.*). To embrace emphatically.

Sling your body (*Low. London*). Dance with vigour.

Slipper (*Tailors'*). Sixpence.

Slippery or slippy (*Marine*). Active.

Sloan, To (*Peoples'*, 1899). Hamper, baulk, cut. A word that lasted only as long as a summer's leaves. From an American jockey (Archer), who, riding a French horse (Holocaust) in the Derby this year, attempted to slant him across the course inside Tottenham corner and hamper the race. It was a fearless trick, invented by Archer at the risk of his life—one that Sloan imitated at the expense of his horse's life.

When the rider of a mare named Nursemaid finished à la Sloan, the Devonshire labourer expressed his mingled surprise and admiration at the daring of the feat.—*D. T.*, 12th August 1899.

Slop-made (*Australian*). Disjointed.

Slosh the burick (*Common London Life*). Beating the wife.

Slosh the old gooseberry (*Low. London*). Beat the wife.

Sloshiety paper (*Press*, 1883). A satiric imitative, equivalent to Society paper—invented to attack the 'sloshy' gushing tendency of these prints.

Sloshing around (*American*). Hitting out indiscriminately.

Slow (*Cricketting*). Slow ball.

Slow curtain (*Theatrical*). Curtain lowered gradually.

Slug (*Thieves'*). Hard drive of the fist into a face. Probably an onomatope.

Slumming (*Soc.*, 1883). Visiting the poorest parts or slums of a city with a view to self-improvement.

The results of a little experiment, which has been tried with the kindly consent of the Benchers of the Inner Temple, are well worth the attention of people who interest themselves in what is cynically called 'slumming'.—*D. N.*, August 1884.

Slung (*Art Students'*). Rejected—probably derived from rhyme to hung.

Slush (*Com. People*). Coffee and tea served in common coffee-house.

Small and early (*Soc.*, 1877). A carpet dance to which only a few intimates are invited. It is begun about eight and ends about eleven.

The Earl of Northbrook had a dinnerparty at his official residence yesterday.

A small and early party assembled after dinner.—*D. N.*, 6th March 1884.

Smash a brandy peg (*Military*, 1880). Drink the spirit in question.

Abdullah Bey would smash a brandy peg with any one of us, and on the present occasion quaffed his laager beer like a stolid old Dutchman.—*D. N.*, 7th May 1884.

Smash the teapot (*Street*). Break the abstinence pledge.

Smash-up (*Military*, 1854 on). Defeat.

Every one who was present at the 'smash-up' and victory at Tamai used to say that no battle like it would again be witnessed in the Soudan.—*D. N.*, 28th January 1885.

Smashed (*Navy*). Reduced in rank.

Smell hell through a gridiron (*American*). Reference to drink-madness.

Smell the foot-lamps (*Historic survival*). Stage-struck; but in many ways referring to the stage. Of course referring to the whale oil lamps used as the foot-lamps, where candles could not be conveniently snuffed.

Smilence (*Peoples'*). Word-disguising—with a suggested point.

Smilence, ladies, if you please.

Smithereens, Smither's ruins (*Irish*). Destruction. 'Faith, I was smashed entirely into smithereens.' May be an Irish word, but probably corruption of 'Smither's ruins'—as typical of complete smash. Though who Smithers may have been seems not to be known.

Smoke-waggons (*W. American-English*, 1890). Revolvers—pistols. They certainly do carry condensed smoke.

Smoker (*Social*, 1878). Club or corps concert, where the members sing, play, and smoke, and, as a rule, recite.

Upon Mr A. D. Sturley and Mr M. G. Dearin devolved the pleasant duty of presiding at the 'smoker'. — *D. T.*, February 1894.

Smoking (*School*). Blushing.

Smole (*Word disguise*). A grotesque variation of smile.

S'mother evening (*Music Hall* 1884). Cynical refusal.

Among the items was Roberts's song, 'S'mother evening'. — *Ref.*, 7th June 1885.

Smothering a parrot (*French*). Draining a glass of absinthe neat. Derived from the green colour of the absinthe.

Smouge (*American-English*, 1880), To steal—probably Dutch.

While grace is being said at the table, children should know that it is a breach of good breeding to smouge fruit-cakes just because their parents' heads are bowed down.—*American Comic Etiquette for Children*, 1882.)

Snaggle-tooth (*Street*). Woman of lower order, generally a shrew, who, lifting her upper lip when scolding, shows an irregular row of teeth.

Snake out (*Amer.-Eng.*, 1835-40). Hunt down. From rattle-snake hunting. Now dead in U.S.A. cities, where the force of the verb is lost. Comes from early settlers. Heard sometimes in rural England.

The present is a fair opportunity to snake Thompson out. — Proclamation, Boston 1835, against the English Abolitionist, Mr George Thompson, then visiting America.

Snakes (*Anglo-American*). Drink-madness—*delirium tremens*.

Snakes (*Eng.-American*, 19 cent.). Danger.

Mr Cluer asked if anybody was chasing the prisoner when he cried out, 'They're after me'?

The witness replied in the negative.

Mr Cluer: Then I suppose he saw snakes.—*D. T.*, 2nd January 1900.

Snakes alive (*American*). Much worse than snakes.

Snaky (*American Backwoods*). Evidently suggested by the backwoodsman associating untruth with the doubtful and uncertain behaviour of the serpent.

Snakes also have the vice of developing mendacity in the human race so conspicuously that in the Far West 'snaky' is the term applied to a tale more vivid than probable.—*D. N.*, 19th February 1883.

Snap-manager (*Anglo-American*). One who hurries a company together.

A snap-manager in Canada lately exemplified the ultimate of check by asking James Herne to loan him his lithographs to advertise the playing of a filched copy of Herne's 'Heart of Oak'.

Snapping your head off (*Society*, 19 cent.). Brusqueness of manner.

Anthony Trollope seemed a singularly gruff and ponderous personage, rather

Snapping *Soccer*

blundering in converse, and slightly addicted to 'snapping your head off' if you differed from him. — *Illustrated London News* (G. A. Sala), 16th December 1882.

Snapping (*Colliers'*). Eating—very good suggestion of hungry man devouring.

Snappy (*Soc.*, 1893 on). Attractive. Applied in all ways.

I must send you a few lines to tell you to take care of yourself, and be a good little boy, and keep out of mischief. I am going to keep the spotted jersey, and it looks quite snappy.—*D. T.*, 4th July 1895.

Sneaking-budge (*Thieves'*). Shop-lifting. (*See* Fielding, Jonathan Wild.)

Snide and shine (*E. London*). General description of the common Jews of the East of London by their Christian brethren. Both words bear the same meaning, but taken together are most emphatic.

Snide-sparkler (*Trade — Jewish Jewellers'*). False diamond.

Snippety (*Literature*, 1890 on). Journals made up of snippings from other and generally ancient journals. Used satirically. From the noise made by scissors in the operation of editing.

Men-folk may buy the 'snippety' publications, but this fact never appears to deter women from getting copies for themselves.—*D. T.*, 2nd October 1896.

Snossidge (*Commonest London*, 1880). A nonsense mode of pronouncing 'sausage'.

Snubber (*Public-school*). Reprimand.

Snuff a bloke's candle (*Thieves' English*, 18 *cent.*). To murder a man.

S'elp me, Bob (*Pre-reformation*). Corruption of 'So help me, Babe'. An appeal to the mediation of the infant Saviour. Following the rule of peoples' colloquial, which always finds a new meaning for an exploded word, Bob has here been substituted. Some writers insist upon Bob being the diminutive of Robert, a policeman—as though the classes using such a phrase as this would ask assistance from the nearest constituted authority ?

The City coppers can't leave the poor costers alone. It riles the coppers, *s'elp me bob*, to see a cove trying to get an honest living.—*Cutting*, 1883.

S'elp me greens (*Pre-reformation*). 'So help me, groans'—groans being aids to repentance after the manner of Jeremiah. To-day the word has a very remarkable meaning—'may I lose the attributes of masculine vigour if I am diverging from the line of rectitude.' A close study of Balzac's *Vautrin* will throw much probable light upon phrases of this kind.

Here's a nice little story, and it's all true, s'elp me greens.—1883.

S'elp me never (*Modern Low London*). Meaning, probably, 'May God never help me if I lie now' 'Never', however, may be a corruption of a distinct word.

So and so (*Military*). Short for Senior Ordnance Store Officer.

So'brien (*Mariners'*). Corruption of *Sobraon*, a well-known favourite Australian steam-ship, named after one of Wellington's victories. Good example of anglicizing.

So glad (*London*, 1867 on). Catch word from William Brough's *Field of the Cloth of Gold*.

His song is as likely to take the town as the French King's catch phrase, 'So glad', which was all over London twenty years ago.—*D. T.*, June 1867.

So long *v.* Aspect.

So very human (*Soc.*, 1880). Apology, originally for conduct, but applied finally in so many ways that it fell into disuse 1884.

An attempt to exclude foreign material would in all probability be met by retaliatory measures. This would not be a wise policy on the part of other countries, but then it would be, in the slang of the day, 'so very human'.—*D. N.*, 27th October 1884.

Soaked the mill (*American*). Sold all his property through drink.

Soap. Girls. (*See* Bits o' soap.)

Soccer (*Oxford Football*, 1880 on). Association football — saves three syllables.

'Soccer', however, is an excellent example of Oxford minting, whether or not she can claim the credit of its invention. For the rule is as follows: Take any word in common use; knock the end off and add 'er'. If it should sound acceptable, it suffers no further mutation. If it is still harsh and cacophonous, see what it will look like by striking off its head and the casual removal of an intermediate syllable. All these processes appear to have been gone through in order to produce 'Soccer' from Association. Rugby was more fortunate. It had only a tail to lose.—*D. T.*, 14th August 1899. (*See* Rugger.)

Social E. (*Mid.-class*, 19 *cent.*). Evasion of social evil.

Society (*Artisans'*). A synonym for workhouse.

Society journal (*Soc.*, 1878). Evasive name for a scandal-publishing newspaper.

It seems that Mr Legge is the proud inventor of the phrase *Society Journal*, and he may further plume himself on having rendered it much the same service as Hyperbolus performed for ostracism. Probably no paper will be ambitious of the title *Society Journal* after the account which Mr Legge gave in the witness-box of the way in which the business is conducted. — *Sat. Rev.*, 21st March 1885.

Society journalist (*Press*, 1875). A contributor to the *Society Journal*.

Society maddists (*Soc.*, 1881). Term to describe people not born in society, who devote their whole lives, and often fortunes, to get into society.

Sodgeries (*London*, 1890). Latest outcome of fisheries, colindries, etc. Started by *Punch* (April 1880). A Military Exhibition, Chelsea Barracks.

Soft sawder to order (*Anglo-Amer.*). Tailor's clothes ordered and not ready made.

There is a fine opportunity for any bishop who will fearlessly get in the pulpit, and tell a few truths to those eminent personages whose preachers supply them regularly with soft-sawder to order.—*Entr'acte*, 7th April 1883.

Soldier's farewell (*Garrison*). 'Go to bed', with noisy additions.

Soldier's supper (*Garrison*). Nothing at all—tea being the final meal of the day.

Some (*Anglo-American*). Is this word or not a pun? The question put 'Are you an American?' he will reply 'Some, sir'. Is this sum, Sam, or some, used with satire for out and out?

Some pumpkins (*American farmers'*). Considerable importance.

Some when (*Soc.*, 1860-70). Some time.

Some one has blundered (*Soc.*, 1860 on). Emphatic yet evasive mode of complaint. From Tennyson's *Charge of the Light Brigade*.

I am sure the Lord Mayor will be very sorry to learn that on this occasion some one has blundered.—*Ref.*, 5th July 1885.

Something in the city (*Peoples'*). Evasive suggestion of doubtfulness as to the person spoken of.

(Something) please (*Amer.-Eng.*). Substitution of 'dam-well' please.

We cannot all go to learn English accent and style in Boston or New York, and must try to be intelligible without hoping to be accurate or elegant. We are told not to say 'above his strength', but 'beyond his strength'. We shall do as we (something) please, to quote another Transatlantic authority.—*D. N.*, 16th April 1885.

Sooper (*Theatrical*). Common pronunciation of 'super', contraction of supernumerary, the name given to the rank and file of a theatrical company.

Sossidge - slump (*Polit.*, 1896). Failure — derived from sossidge (a German), and slump (failure or pay-out of a mine-vein), and referred to the telegram of the Emperor of Germany in January, to President Kruger, congratulating him on repulsing Dr Jameson's raid. This telegram made the Germans unpopular, and caused German trade in England to fall off woefully.

Soul-faker (*Peoples'*, 1883). One of the early names given to the Salvationists before their value was in any way recognized.

Souper and slang (*Thieves'*). Watch and chain. Probably the first word is soup-plate from the once huge size of the watch, while the second may be a wilful corruption of sling, because the old long chain, worn round the neck would habitually sling about a great deal.

Soupy (*Low Peoples'*). Drunk to sickness.

Soured on, To be (*Anglo-American*). To dislike thoroughly.

South Chicago rough (*U.S.A.*). Typical rough of American cities.

Souvenir egg (*American*). Ancient specimen—hence cogency of 'souvenir' always associated with time—which an egg should never possess.

Souvenir'd (*Theatrical*). Gratis picture or pamphlet, celebrating a centenary, or bicentenary, or even a tercentenary of a new piece or variety show.

First anniversary of *The New Boy* at

the Vaudeville next Thursday, when all the audience will be magnificently 'souvenired', as the Americans now say. —*Ref.*, 17th February 1895.

Sovereign not in it (*Nautical*). Jaundiced—said of a man whose complexion has suffered from yellow fever or other illness which leaves the skin chromy.

Spangle (*Theatrical*, 19 *cent.*). A sovereign.

Spank the kids (*Common London*). Figurative way of describing bad temper. (*See* On his ear.)

Spark (*Peoples'*). Man of fashion. Now and again heard in country places. Still very common in U.S.A., where it comes from Carolian times. Then chiefly used as a verb — 'to spark about'—equal to our once common, 'To beau about'. Evidently a figure of speech derived from the brilliancy and movement of a fire spark. Used as verb by Spenser, 'In her eyes the fire of love doth spark.' In Prior's time it was quite commonly used in place of beau. He says 'The finest sparks, and cleanest beaux.' Dryden has 'A spark like thee, of the man-killing trade, fell sick.' Farquhar (*The Inconstant*) says : 'Then the ideas wherewith the mind is preoccupate—but this subject is not agreeable to you sparks, that profess the vanity of the times.

Sparrer (*Dustman's*) (Sparrow). Finds in dust-bins—generally silver spoons, thimbles, etc.

I give you my word, sir, that I had never stole—in a regler sort of way, I mean—as much as a sixpence in my life. Course I had took plenty o' sparrers, but that you'll own is different.—James Greenwood, *D. T.*, 19th October 1895.

Speak (*Lower People*). To court, or make love.

Speak a piece (*American*). Recite. This phrase was taken, especially by Artemus Ward, from the schoolboy's way of referring to his own oratory.

Speak brown to-morrow (*Pure Cockney*, 1877). To get sunburnt. (*See* Can't you feel the shrimps, Taste the sun, See the breeze.)

Spellken (*Thieves'*, 18 *and early* 19 *cent.*). Cock-pit.

Booze in the ken, or at the spellken hustle. — Byron, *Don Juan*, canto xi., stanza xix.

Sperrib (*Middle-class, Lond.*). Wife of his bosom. Corruption of spare-rib, and derived from the legend of the creation of Eve.

Speshul! (*Street*, 1884-85). Lie. During the Soudan War the afternoon and evening papers were perpetually issuing special editions with extravagant news, rarely repeated in the next morning's editions.

Sphere of influence (*Diplomatic*, 1898). Nascent colony, range of country under a foreign eye, which so far has no real *locus standi*. Came out of the abortive scramble for China (1897-1900).

A rumour is current that France has offered the Pekin Government to suppress the revolt, considering the southern provinces within her sphere of influence. —*D. T.*, 14th July 1898.

Spieler (*Australasia*, 1890 on). Swindler.

Spieler, it would appear, is the Antipodean synonym for the professional swindler, whose business—and pleasure —it is to take in his fellow-man, to whom he contemptuously applies the generic term 'mug'.—*D. T.*, 14th July 1897.

Spierpon orchestra (*Soc.*, 1885 on). Public restaurant musical. This is Spiers and Pond, and the transmutation was due to a French musical conductor, who converted his employers' names into *Spière et Pon.*

Criterion.—Grand Hall, 3s. 6d. Dinner, at separate tables, 6 to 9, accompanied by the celebrated Spierpon Orchestra.— *D. T.*, 8th October 1894.

Spill (*Jovial*). Drink.

Spill and pelt (*Theatrical*, 1830, etc.). The name given to the practical fun at the end of each scene in the comic portion of a pantomime. Supers rush on with mock vegetables, meat, poultry, fish, etc., spill them all, and then pelt them at each other and altogether off the stage.

Spill milk against posts (*Lowest Class*). Extreme condemnation of the habits of the man spoken of.

Spilled in the big drink (*American-English*). Drowned in the Atlantic. (*See* Ditch.)

Zeus threw a thunderbolt at the rock, and, as the American says, Ajax was 'spilled in the drink'. — *D. N.* 8th August 1884.

Spin (*Anglo - Indian*, 1800 - 50). Short for spinster — the brigades of unmarried and poor young ladies who once went out habitually to India for husbands.

Spin a cuff (*Navy*). Bore a mess with a long, pointless story, which the narrator is finally, as a rule, recommended to cut.

Spin the bat (*Anglo-Indian*, 19 *cent.*). Used figuratively for remarkable military language.

Spit amber (*Amer.*, 1870). To expectorate while chewing tobacco.

Spits on his hands (*American*). Goes to work with a will—suggested by this habit on the part of energetic workmen when about to start work.

Splinters fly (*American Pastoral*). Riot—derived from the kicking experiments of the mule.

Split (*Low London*). Souteneur.

Split soda (*Tavern*, 1860 on). A bottle of soda water divided between two guests. The 'baby' soda is for 'one' client

Sponge it out (*Anglo-Amer.*, 1883). Forget it.

A new phrase is destined to become popular, viz.: 'Sponge it out'.—*N. Y. Mercury*, November 1883.

Spoof—oof (*Theat.*, 1896). Money. Mr Shine sings of Mashonaland, the land of British spoof, where the niggers do the digging and the white men get the ' oof '.—*People*, 16th February 1896.

Spooferies (*L. Peoples*', 1888 on). Sporting clubs of an inferior kind.

About half-past one this morning I was in the 'Spooferies'. — Where? In the 'Spooferies' in Maiden Lane.—*People*, 6th January 1895.

Spoon, Big (*Amer.*). An oath— the origin of which is lost. Sometimes 'By the great horn spoon'. Probably Biblical.

Rolling—roll—hold on ! By the big spoon you've hit it !

Spooning the burick (*Thieves'*). Making love to a friend's wife.

Spoony stuff (*London Theatres*', 1882). Weak, sentimental work, below contempt.

Sport (*Anglo-American*, 19 *cent.*). Eccentric, physical aberration, chiefly relating to human beings.

It is still undeniable that a child who is not interested in animals, especially of the larger and wilder species, must be wanting in some of the most graceful and endearing instincts of the childish nature. Such infantile 'sports', however, are happily rare. — *D. T.*, 29th December 1896.

Sportsman for liquor (*Sporting*, 1882). A fine toper.

We never knew what a sportsman Algernon Charles Swinburne was for his liquor till we took up his last volume of poems.—*Sporting Times*, 1882.

Spot winner (*Sport and People*). Lucky, or capable — perhaps both. From racing — spotting meaning judgment.

Some of them may have 'spotted winners', and were perhaps reflecting pleasurably on a success which they felt to be much more due to their own sound judgment than to mere good luck. — *D. T.*, 14th June 1898.

Spotted dog (*Street Boys'*). Plain plum-pudding — spotted dough. The dog here is one of the pronunciations of dough—the ' h ' being removed and the ' g ' made hard.

Spotted duff (*Street*, 19 *cent.*). Another shape of spotted dog. Duff has always been a street pronunciation of 'dough'.

Spotted leopard (*Street Boys'*). Another variety of spotted dog.

A penny's worth of spotted leopard is not a bad way of filling up the space of the internals, though spotted leopard may make you have to squander some rhino in pongelow.—1883.

Spout (*Peoples'*). Large mouth — ever open. (*See* Boko.)

Spread (*Anglo - American*). Take great, self - satisfied aims in doing anything.

Spring like a ha'penny knife (*Peoples'*). Floppy, dumpy, no resilience—from the absolute want of Sheffield perfection in the make of pen-knives at sixpence the dozen.

Sprung up (*Middle - class*). A parvenu—in the nature of a ready-made or self-made man.

Spurrings (*Yorkshire — Old*). Marriage banns. Origin vague ; but ominously suggestive of the bridegroom being goaded to the church-door.

Square (*Ball-room*). A quadrille or lancers. (*See* Round.)

Square up-and-down man (*Amer.*). Square-shouldered, upright, tall man, with no fat or superfluous flesh about him.

Squash (*Club and Hotel*, 1877). A temperance drink of lemon, soda-water, ice, and sugar—came into fashion during a panic against spirits and, in modified form, against wine. Onomatope, from the noise made by pressing the lemon.

By ten P.M., at the latest, you may be in the smoking-room of your club sipping lemon 'squash'. — *Illus. London News* (G. A. Sala), 17th February 1883.

Squash ballads (*Peace Party*). Ballads prompting war and personal devotion.

The new laureate has started off on a squash ballad *apropos* to Jameson's stir-up. — London Correspondent of *N. Y. Clipper*, January 1896.

Squasho (*American—passing into England*). Negro—a title probably resulting from the negro's love of melons, pumpkins, squashes, etc.

Squat (*Com. London*). A seat—probably derived from squatter.

Squat on (*American*). To oppose.

Squeaker, The (*Press*, '90's). Burlesque name given to the paper called *The Speaker*—a journal of representative Radicalism.

Squealer (*Fenian*, 1867, etc.). Informer.

Squeejee (*Streets'*). Mud-clearer; plate of vulcanized india-rubber fixed at right angles to a long handle. Onomatope—the cleaner in question actually saying the word now and again.

We were more than once awakened by the avalanche of the deck bucket and the noise of sandpaper and 'squeejee'.— *D. N.*, 27th April 1897.

Squeezability (*Polit.*, 1884). Political pressure. Word invented long since, but only accepted politically about 1884.

They could not realise the change which the Franchise Act had made in the counties; or they believed too implicitly in the squeezability of the newly-enfranchized electors. — *D. N.*, 3rd December 1885.

Squeeze-box (*Navy*). The ship harmonium—used in the hasty Sunday service. From the action of the feet.

Squilde (*L. Class*, 1895-96). Term of street chaff. Word designed from a Christian name and a surname coalesced.

Squint (*S. Exchange*). Man who hangs about the market with a paltry order, and who will not deal fairly.

Squirt (*L. Class*, 18 *cent.*). Doctor. Very suggestive of Molière in general, and of *Le Malade Imaginaire* in particular.

Squirt (*Doubtful Soc.*, 1870). One of the onomatopoetic titles of champagne suggested by its uppishness.

Stable Jack (*Infantry*). Cavalry—a scornful description, as intimating that the miserable man has incessantly to be the slave of his horse, an oppression from which the happier infantry man is free. (*See* Jack Tar, Jack in the water, Jack of all trades, Hulking Jack, Dona Jack.)

Stable mind (*Soc.*). Devoted to horses.

Stage, To (*American*, 1860). To stage a piece is to put a piece on the stage.

Stagger (*American*, 1883). Effort.

Staked out (*Mining*, 1880 on). Divided, measured.

When the first discovery of gold was made at Klondyke, in August 1896, the creek was staked off from end to end in claims.—*D. T.*, 21st July 1897.

Stalked unchecked (*American origin*). Freed from the attentions of the criminal classes. Satirically said to have been invented by a West U.S.A. criminal upon being about to be lynched, and in reference to the villain public, who moved around him without being ordered by him to hold up their hands.

The thieving and ruffianism of Moscow took its country holiday; and at the Coronation and its attendant festivities respectability, in the bitter words of the Western American desperado, 'stalked unchecked'.—*D. T.*, 29th April 1897.

Stall off (*Peoples'*). Damp, impede, hinder, warn.

Stall-pots (*Theatrical*). Occupants of the stalls. Applied by the gods derisively to these well-dressed patrons of the drama.

Stalwarts (*Conservatives'*, 1886). Satirical name for Radicals, used by Mr Chamberlain seriously; accepted satirically by Conservative party.

Stamps (*Thieves'*). Boots—a sort of onomatope.

Stand (*Colloquial—all Classes*). Pay for—only used in a general way for drink or eatables.

Stand pat (*American*, 1860). Satisfied. Taken from a game of cards called poker. 'Stand pat' means, 'I have got sufficient cards—go ahead!'

Stand-up supper (*Society*, 1860). About this date the 'stand-up' ball supper came into vogue—probably as the result of modern medical condemnation of late feeding. Necessarily more economical than its antithesis—the sit-down supper. It took immensely, so that very rapidly the term came to suggest anything of a mean and paltry character.

Star company (*Theatrical*). A wandering dramatic company, composed of one well-known person and a number of nobodies, all of whom appear in but one piece, as a rule, with which they travel.

A popular local leading lady writes for information regarding a Mr Henry C. Warren, of Troy, N. Y., who is alleged to load recognized actresses with propositions to take them starring next season.—*N. Y. Mercury*, February 1884.

Stars and stripes (*New York*). Contemptuous phrase applied by the younger New York society to the Puritanic habits still clinging to New England, and above all to Boston. It refers to the solemn Sunday cold dinner of the 'hub' of the universe, which distinctively consists—or *did* consist—of cold boiled belly of pork (stripes) and Boston beans (stars).

New Englanders are proud of their national dish of pork and beans, eaten cold on Sundays in Boston, and derisively called 'stars and stripes' in New York.—*D. N.*, 13th July 1883.

Start a jolly (*Theatre and Music Hall*). To lead the applause, and effect a diversion in favour of a given performer.

State tea (*Soc.*, 1870). Tea at which every atom of the family plate is exhibited. Name probably suggested by State ball. (*See* Five o'clock tea.)

States can be saved without it (*Pol.*, 1880). Condemnation. Origin not known.

In short, Mr Stephenson may be advised to take away *Séverine*. States can be saved without it.—*Ref.*, 10th May 1885.

Stay and be hanged (*Peoples'*). Still heard amongst lower middle-class. Probably started by Captain Macheath (*Beggars' Opera*): 'If you doubt it, let me stay and be hanged.'

Steal thunder (*Soc.*, *Hist.*). Annexing another man's idea, or work, without remunerating him, and to your own advantage. Said to be derived from—

John Dennis, a play-writer in the 17th century, who invented stage thunder for a piece of his own which failed. But the manager translated Dennis's thunder into another piece. It was highly applauded, when Dennis started up in the pit, and cried out to the audience: 'They won't act my piece, but they steal my thunder. Hence the origin of the phrase.

Steam on the table (*Workmen's*, 18 *cent.* on). Boiled joint—generally steaming, on Sunday.

Steel v. Bastile.

Steeple Jack (*Builders'*). Climber of steeples and shafts for fixing scaffolding when repairs are required.

Steeplechase (*Sporting and Soc.*). Direct line, defying and overcoming all obstructions.

Mr Fowler was one of the oldest inhabitants of Aylesbury, not forgetful of the historic cross-country ride to Aylesbury church-steeple from Waddesdon Windmill, which gave the name to the very modern sport called steeplechasing. I apprehend that the name of steeplechase arose from Aylesbury Church steeple being the goal of the famous race, in which Mr Peyton acted as starter, the Marquis of Waterford, of facetious memory was nearly drowned, Jem Mason finished third with Prospero, and Captain Beecher won on Vivian.—*D. N.*, 13th July 1885.

Steever's worth of copper (*Streets'*, *E. Lond.*). One penny—from Stuyver.

Stellar (*American-Eng.*, 1884 on). Leading Latin shape of 'starring' in relation to acting.

William Terriss and Miss Millward, of London, and their company made their stellar *début* at Niblo's garden to a tolerably good attendance.—*N. Y. Mercury*, October 1889.

Stellardom (*Anglo - American— Theatrical*). The condition of being a star, or leading actor or actress.

Impossible to form a company of actors and actresses who have not sought the divorce courts, and who do not aspire to stellardom.—*N. Y. Mercury*, November 1883.

Stem-winder (*American — Liverpool*). Keyless watch.

Steps (*Low. London*, 19 *cent.*). Thick slices of bread and butter, overlaying each other on a plate—thus suggesting the idea of a flight of steps.

Stern ambition (*City*, 1898). Determination. Brought in by Mr H. Bottomley in speech (1st June 1889):

I will invite you to pass the necessary resolutions for getting the Market Trust out of the trouble into which it has got, and out of which it will be my own very stern ambition, as well as that of my colleagues, to extricate you at the very earliest possible moment.

Stick a bust (*Thieves'*, 19 *cent.*). Commit a burglary.

Mr Paul Taylor: What were his exact words?
Witness: I am going to 'stick a bust.'
Mr Paul Taylor: What does that mean?
Detective-sergeant Fitzgerald: Commit a burglary.—*D. T.*, 28th December 1899.

Stick and bangers (*Sporting*). Billiard cue and balls. A phrase having also an erotic meaning.

Stickings (*Lower Peoples'*). Butchers' cuttings laid on a board, to which they clammily cling. (*See* Door and hinge, Hyde Park railings.)

Sticks (*Navy and Army*). Drummer.

Still (*Anglo - American*). Quiet drunkard.

Still as a mouse (*Peoples'*, 18 *cent.*). Quite still. But a mouse is never still! Good example of a bad translation. No doubt from the half-Dutch Court of William III. Mr Rees (U.S.A.) says very keenly:

Expressive of noiseless action. The Dutch phrase is evidently its origin: *Als stille als in mee hose*, i.e., as still as one in his stockings—a listener.

Or it may be, 'Still as Amos'—though what Amos is beyond ken.

Still he is not happy (*London*, 1870 on). Satire shot at a man whom nothing pleases or satisfies.

In 1870, a catch phrase used by Mr J. L. Toole in a burlesque at the Gaiety Theatre, 'Still I am not happy', enjoyed for some months considerable acceptance among sportive youths in the metropolitan thoroughfares.—*D. T.*, 28th July 1894.

Stilton (*Peoples'*, 1850 on). Distinction. Synonym for cheese (*see*). She was the real Stilton, I can tell yer.

(*See* Cheshire.)

Stinker (*Working Boys'*). Penny cigars. Frequently so named in taverns. Also the most emphatic term for the high-smelling dried herring.

Stir-about (*Peoples'*). Pudding or porridge made by stirring the ingredients—generally oatmeal or wheat-flour — when cooking. (*See* Hasty pudding and Turn-round pudding.)

Stir up (*Peoples'*). Equivalent to beat up in society. To visit on the spur of the moment.

Stolypin's necktie (*Europ. Politics*, 1897). The final halter. This term was brought into fashion in 1907 (Nov.-Dec.), at a Duma then recently assembled in St Petersburg. One Rodicheff, an extreme Radical, brought in the term on 30th November 1907.

Stone and a beating (*Sporting*, 18 *cent.*). The speaker offers to weight himself with 14 lbs. avoirdupois, and then outrun his opponent.

Canis vulpis is, as a rule, able to give, intellectually speaking, and in language germane to the matter, 'a stone and a beating' to the majority of his pursuers. —*D. N.*, 4th February 1885.

Stop-gap (*Theatr.*). Piece rushed on between a failure and the production of a carefully-prepared new piece or new arrival.

After the first act *The Denhams* was well received, the adaptor receiving a call; but, except as a stop-gap, we do not think it will prove of much service to the management.—*Ref.*, 21st February 1885.

Stop-gap administration (*Polit.*, 1885). The Conservative Government formed June 1885. Name given by Mr J. Chamberlain (17th June 1885).

Stork, Visit from the (*Soc.*, 1880 on). Arrival of a baby. From the German.

She was in the habit of receiving visits from the Stork—as the Germans put it to the children—by which it is meant that she occasionally presented her husband with an infant.—*D. T.*, 15th February 1897.

Stote-an'-bottle (*N. York Theatre*). Audience who neither applaud nor laugh. Probably corruption from Dutch.

We had but a stote-an'-bottlish crowd last night.

Stow (*Streets'*). Abbreviation of bestow.

Strad (*Musicians'*). Abbreviation of Stradivarius violin.

Straight (*Theatr.*).

In the United States the expression 'straight' is very generally used in theatrical circles to signify a part in which the actor or actress has but to be him or herself upon the stage.

Straight as they make 'em (*London Streets, from America*). Upright and honest.

Straight bit o' goods (*Streets'*, 1870 on). A young woman of good character. (*See* Loose bit o' goods.)

Straight drinking (*Low. London*, 19 *cent.*). Drinking without sitting down—bar-drinking.

Straight up and down the mast (*Irish*). Calm. An Irish sailor's way of describing a calm—when the mast is fairly perpendicular.

Strapped (*Amer.*). Without money —possibly suggested by the impossibility of removing when without money, as when strapped and bound.

Straps (*Streets'*). Sprats. One of the rhyming shapes of passing English.

Street yelp (*Low. Class*, 1884). Evolution of passing street cry, such as 'Walker', 'Does your mother know you're out?' Every few weeks some new street yelp is invented, and eagerly taken up as a substitute for wit by the class that enjoys these things.

Stretch (*Navy*). Outstay leave.

Stretch his breeches (*Peoples'*). Said of a boy who has been thrashed. It comes down from the time when the tight leather breech might be fairly said to be stretched when flattened.

Stretcher, The (*Irish*). Layer out of dead men.

Stretching (*Anglo-American*, 1895). Helping oneself at table without the help of servants.

Strict Q.T. (*Peoples'*, 1870). The letters being the first and last of 'quiet'. The phrase is an invocation to secrecy.

Strike (*Anglo-Amer.*). To come across a person, or thing.

Strike a bargain (*Sporting*, 18 *cent.*). To conclude it by the act of striking the butt ends of the riding whips of the seller and buyer as a mutual agreement — equal to the stipulation of the Roman buyer and seller, who exchanged straws.

In the end I agreed to charge him 26s. per week, and we then struck the bargain.

Strike a bright (*Peoples'*). Have a happy thought.

Strike legislation (*Amer. - Eng.*, 1897). Enforced bribery of legislators —the pressure being applied by the legislators themselves — to burke enquiries. 'Sir, this is not fair trading; it is nothing less than strike legislation.' Known slightly in England.

Strike me pink (*Soc.*, 18 *cent.* on). Literally an exclamation to declare truthfulness. Cover me with my own blood. Sometimes God, etc. From duelling times—when to pink was not so much to pierce as to draw blood.

Strike oil (*American — becoming English*). To be successful. 'I've struck oil at last.' This expression comes from the paraffin districts of North America, where sometimes numerous expensive artesian borings are made without the least success.

Strike us up a gum tree (*Low. London*). Bring to grief.

Yes, and strike us up a gum tree, she says, if you won't give her sardines and bloaters for her tea instead of winkles she'll go back to her old man.—1850.

Australian — probably meaning 'terrible'. The gum tree is enormously high, 100 feet of clear, smooth trunk without a branch, so that a man up a gum tree could not descend without help.

Stricken field (*Soc.*, 1898). Field where lie the vanquished. Term found in several poets. Re-introduced upon the fall of Omdurman in, the autumn of this year.

Colonel Holden's happy idea of organizing in the museum of the Royal United Service Institution an exhibition of the trophies brought home from 'the stricken field' of Omdurman has brought a vast number of visitors to see the collection.—*D. T.*, 25th November 1898.

Struguel (*Peoples'*). Struggle.

Stuck up (*American - English*). Moneyless—very figurative expression derived from being 'stuck up' by highwayman, after which you have no money left in your pocket.

Stuff. Girl. (*See* Bit o' stuff.)

Stuffed monkey (*Jewish Lond.*). A very pleasant close almond biscuit.

Now the confectioner exchanges his

stuffed monkeys, and his bolas . . . for unleavened palavas, etc. — Zangwill, *Children of the Ghetto*.

Stun (*Reversed word*). Nuts.

Sub (*Editorially*). Abbreviation of subject. Very common in U.S.A.

With Captain Williams, her namesake, as chairman, would be the judges here. The Mercury will be pleased to hear from Mrs Williams on this sub.—*N. Y. Mercury*, May 1885.

Sub rosa (*Soc.*). In secret. Sometimes 'under the rose'. Used by the author of Junius's *Letters* as his motto, the rose being above. Confounded with 'under the rows'—a sort of rebus. When houses were built floor out above floor, so that the ground floor was some feet within the front of the garrets, talkers, say lovers, could not be seen from the floors above—therefore 'under the rows' (rows of superposed jutting floors) implied 'secretly'. There still exists (1907) in London, a group of 'rows', forming the north side of Staple Inn (Holborn)—where it can be seen that a maiden on the first floor might almost shake hands, from the window, with a grenadier on the pavement, while from the second floor, an observer could not catch a glimpse of the military heels 'under the rows'.

The rose, a symbol of silence, gave rise to the phrase, 'under the rose', from the circumstance of the Pope's presenting consecrated roses, which were placed over confessionals to denote secrecy, whilst others contend that the old Greek custom of suspending a rose over the guest table was employed as an emblem that the conversation should not be repeated elsewhere.—*Cutting*.

Sub rosa look (*Anglo - Amer.*). Doubtful aspect. Perversion of the Latin proverb.

The business had a sub rosa look throughout.—*Newsp. Cutting*.

Submerged tenth (*Soc.*, 1890 on). Tenth of London, which is always in utter poverty. Originated by General Booth. First accepted satirically but now quite received as a serious phrase.

If the population of London is reckoned roughly at 4,000,000 and 'the submerged tenth'—as the phrase goes—is taken as the basis of the calculation of recipients, 400,000 meals will have to be given, and at a shilling a head £20,000 at least will be required.—*World*, May 1897.

Such a dawg (*Theatrical*, 1888). Tremendous masher. First used by E. Terry in a Gaiety burlesque.

The next time Mr Biggar thinks fit to leave these shores, perhaps he will try to be less fascinating, bearing in mind that women are weak and not always able to wrestle successfully with the blandishments of such a Lothario. 'Such a dawg!'—*Entr'acte*, 17th March 1883.

Suck the mop (*Cabmens'*). To wait on the cab-rank for a job.

The man who gives his horse a rest on the rank is, in cabmen's phraseology, 'sucking the mop'.—*D. N.*, 10th June 1889.

Sucker (*American*). A young and confiding youth.

Suffolk punches (*Provincial*). Descriptive name for Suffolk folk, much on all fours with Norfolk dumplings. A punch is a comfortable kind of cob-like horse. This is rather a complimentary term.

Sugar (*Low. Class*). Grocer.

Sugar-shop(*Electioneering*). Money shop, literally; but figuratively a head centre of bribery.

Suggestionize (*Legal*, 1889 on). To prompt.

Many witnesses were called to establish his identity, and for the defence it was alleged that these people might have been 'suggestionized' by the influence of the crime on their minds.—*D. T.*, 16th October 1896.

Suitable for electioneering purposes (*Polit.*, *Historic.*). Bad eggs. From the exercise of projecting them at antagonistic candidates.

Leather Lane supplies the greater proportion of the eggs, and if not to be classified as 'suitable for electioneering purposes', would probably be of that order curtly set forth as 'eggs', without any subtle grading as 'Fresh laid', 'Breakfast', or 'Cooking'.—*D. T.*, 27th June 1898.

Sum. (*See* Some.)

Summer, Another (*Devonshire chiefly*). Butterfly — generally the first - seen 'Oh! — here's another summer!' Very poetic. Remarkable that Devonshire offers most of the poetic phrases. (*See* Any birds can build in my bonnet.)

Sun, Been in the (*Peoples'*). Drunk. Fine figure of speech. Drink and hot sun both produce red face. Good example of *double entendre*, or rather perhaps of direct satire by indirect means,

'I see you've been in the sun, Tom!'

Sun over the fore-yard (*Navy*). Evasive mode of observing that So-and-so is pretty well dead drunk.

Sunclear (*Lit.*, 1885). Very clear. What there is in Royal subjects to paralyze the genius of a painter we fail to divine, but it is sunclear that Mr Haag could no more resist this unfortunate influence than the greater Landseer—*D. N.*, 10th November 1885.

Sunday (*Soc.*). To pass Sabbath with a given person.

Sunday face (*Irish*). Holiday countenance.

Sunday - flash - togs (*Street*). Sabbath garments.

A Sunday-flash-togs young man,
A pocket-of-hogs young man,
A save-all-his-rhino,
To cut-a-big-shine, oh,
Will soon-have-a-pub young man.
—Parody of a song in *Patience*, 1880.

Sunrise London (*London*). East London.

And, indeed, it cannot be denied that what has been spoken of as the 'sunrise' division of the great metropolis has of late years been greatly favoured. Thanks mainly to the advocacy of the most influential of the newspaper press, the aspect of the whole poverty - stricken area, in its length and breadth, from the Minories to Mile End, and from Spitalfields to Shadwell, has been vastly improved.—*D. T.*, 30th July 1896.

Surrey side (*London, exclusive*). Transpontine portion of London. The northern portion of London bounded by the Thames, and especially the more western quarters, have always spoken of this division of the metropolis (Southwark and Lambeth) to the south of the Thames, as the 'Surrey side'.

Susanside (*Idiot Phrasing*). Suicide.

Sussex sow (*Hampshire*). Probably a return compliment for the name of Hampshire hog (*q.v.*).

Swagger man (*Soc.*, 1880). Person of position. Used rather with praise than not.

Swaller a sailor (*Port and Harbour*). Get drunk upon rum.

Swallered the anchor (*Marine*). Said of a sailor who comes home, loafs, and does not show signs of going to sea again.

Swank (*Printers'*). Small talk, lying.

Swanny (*American Provincial*). Corruption of 'swear now'.

Swear off (*American—passing to Eng.*). To abandon, in relation to drinking habits.

Swearing apartment (*Tavern*). The street.

Sweat (*Thieves'*). To unsolder a tin box by applying fire, or a blow-pipe.

Sweater (*Work-peoples'*). One who 'middles' between the manufacturer, or tradesman, and the worker. He is answerable for the value of the work, and is therefore preferred to the worker himself. The middle levies a heavy blackmail upon the worker. Probably he pays no more than 50 per cent. to the worker of the money he receives from the tradesman.

In the second number of the *Charity Organisation Review* there is a short account of a co-operative needlework experiment, the object of it being to emancipate poor workwomen from the 'sweaters'.—*D. N.*, 21st February 1885.

Sweeping up (*Boer War*, 1899-1900). Grew out of the end of the war, when the dispersed Boers harassed the English very much.

Though the time has come when Volunteers, Yeomen, and Guards should be sent home, there is still a good deal of sweeping up to be done in the Transvaal.—*D. T.*, 2nd October 1900.

(*See* Dusting.)

Sweeps and saints (*City*, 19 *cent.*). Stockbrokers and their surrounders, from the First of May (Sweeps' Day) and the First of November (All Saints' Day) being holidays on the Exchange.

Sweet waters (*W. England*). Illicit spirit made from the residue of the cider press. Fearfulest drink in the world. Term well known in all the apple counties.

Swell donas (*Low Life*). Great ladies—in their way.

Swell donas lushes up on port wine, and that sort of pizon.

Swig Day (*Jesus College, Oxford*). St David's Day—so called because a drink called swig, composed of spiced ale, wine, toast, etc., is dispensed out of an immense silver-gilt bowl holding ten gallons, and served by a ladle of half-pint capacity — presented to the college in 1732 by the then Sir Watkin Williams Wynn.

Swipe (*Thieves'*, 18 *cent.*). Stealing. When silk pocket handkerchiefs (Indian bandannas) were used by all men of position and were worth stealing (*see* Dickens's 'Oliver Twist')—they were called 'Wipes'—hence to 'Swipe a Wipe' was to steal a bandanna.

Sworn at Highgate (*Peoples'*). Convenient asseveration whereby the declarant undertakes never to accept anything offered while he can obtain a better. The phrase took the shape of a coloured cartoon in 1796, when it was published (12th September) by Laurie and Whittle of 53 Fleet Street. A good impression of this print is now to be found at the Old Gate House, at the top of Highgate Hill—the locale of the toll-gate—where the swearing at Highgate was held to be only properly administered. The oath-taker is accompanied by a herald who holds aloof the significant horns, which are reproduced in letter-form on the front of the tavern before which the operation is completed. The 'maid' pins meanwhile a ragged clout to his coat-tail, while the mistress waits with a foaming pot of beer, or rather gallon measure, for the garnishing of everybody after the oath is complete. This declaration runs as follows:—

'Pray, sir—lay your right hand on this Book, and attend to the Oath—you swear by the Rules of Sound Judgment that you will not eat Brown Bread when you can have White, except you like the Brown the better; that you will not drink Small Beer when you can get Strong, except you like the Small Beer better—but you will kiss the *Maid* in preference to the *Mistress*, if you like the Maid better—*so help you Billy Bodkin*. Turn round and fulfil your oath.'

Sympathetic truth (*Art*, 1890 on). True, but not too true—some concession to the artistic ideal.

Mr James S. Hill has less experience, less power, perhaps, of making or seeing a picture, than some of his friendly rivals; but few, if any, of them surpass him in the sympathetic truth with which he renders some of the less obvious, the less showy aspects of nature. — *D. T.*, 4th January 1896.

Synagogue (*Covent Garden*, 1890 on). Shed in the north-east corner of 'the Garden'. So called from this place (erected 1890) being wholly 'run' by Jews.

Synthetic breadth (*Art*, 1890 on). Probably means 'harmony of treatment'.

Syrup (*Druggists'*). A trade word amongst dispensing chemists for money.

T

T. O. (*Printers'*). Turn-over, short for a turn-over apprentice from one master to another.

T. and O. (*Sporting*, 1880). New form of 2 to 1.

The betting to-night (Saturday) against the Empire's chance of getting the music hall licence is two and one (t & o).—*Ref.*, 4th August 1887.

T. W. B. F., also **C. W. D.** (*New York*). Mystic initials understood in certain New York society, but quite beyond the outer world. Placed at the foot of invitations, only one of these two series is used. When the recipient is a gentleman the arcana are T. W. B. F.; while the lady's masonics are C. W. D.

T. W. K. (*Military, Anglo-Indian*, 1840 on). Condemnatory initials of 'Too well-known'.

Tab (*L. C.*). The ear, amongst tailors and other workmen.

Tabby meeting (*London*). May meeting of the evangelical party at Exeter Hall (Strand, London—now turned to other uses). Probably contraction of Tabitha—generic name for quakerly persons.

Table beer (*Peoples'*). Poor beer. Commonly applied to any ordinary thing or proceeding.

The Spartan hosts entertained the visitor with cold beef, table beer, cheese, and pickles.—*D. N.*, 6th November 1884.

Table companions (*Oxford*). Men of the same College are called 'table companions' in one of the reports, which we take to be analogous to the 'stable companions' of our sporting contemporaries, and in certain cases are said, somewhat unintelligibly, to make the running for one another.

Table part (*Theatrical*). Rôle which is played only from the waist upwards, and therefore behind a table. Term in association with the protean

Table-Talk   *Take Gruel Together*

entertainer, and the quick change artiste.

The whole of the 'table parts', as they were called, were, as usual, by Charles Mathews himself, but he was relieved in the dramatic acts by Yates, who undertook a series of rapid changes of dress and character then originally introduced.—*D. T.*, 10th March 1897.

Table-talk (*Soc.*, 1883). Talk bordering on the unkind.

In summer we have the new pictures, and some critics will say 'the old are better'. But they are not better stuff to table-talk, because spite can get little pleasure out of condemning Sir Joshua or Rubens.—*D. N.*, 1st February 1884.

Tabled (*American Legislation*). Short for placed on the table.

Mr Forster spoke the other day of the amendments on the English Education Bill which he had just 'tabled', meaning which he had just laid on the table.—*D. N.*, 1st February 1884.

Taboo (*Soc.*, 19 *cent.*). Prohibited, forbidden. Sacred, not to be touched.

The King of Dahomi is not allowed so much as to see the gold in the Fetish House where the remains of his dead forefathers lie. That gold is taboo.—*D. N.*, 22nd July 1887.

Tabs (*Theatrical*). Ageing women. Abbreviation of Tabby, one of the common names for the cat, always associated with ancient women.

Tacking (*Peoples'—from Seamens'*). Obtaining end by roundabout means, from the mode of sailing against wind by zigzag courses. May be from tact.

Tacks (*Art*). Artist's apparatus. From tackle, taken from angling.

Tadpoles (*American*). People of Mississippi—probably from the superabundance of water there.

Tail out (*Amer.-Eng.*, 1880). To run away, scuttle, bolt. From the tail of birds and animals being last seen as they retreat.

Next I made out a brown thing, seated on the table in the centre, and in another moment when my eyes grew accustomed to the light, and I saw what these things were—I was tailing out of it as hard as my legs could carry me.—Haggard, *King Solomon's Mines*.

Tail tea (*Soc.*, 1880 to death of Victoria). The afternoon tea following royal drawing-rooms, at which ladies who had been to court that afternoon, appeared in their trains—hence tail teas. The King relegated drawing-rooms to the late evening.

Tail-twisting (*American*, 19 *cent.*). Worrying England — figuratively, twisting the tail of the British lion. Generally a political process in order to deflect the conviction of the voter.

We must, of course, be prepared for a little 'tail-twisting' from time to time whenever the domestic concerns in the States are turning out uncomfortably for the party in power.—17th October 1896.

Taits (*Church*). Moderate clergymen—from their following in the footsteps of Dr Tait, Archbishop of Canterbury, who sought, vainly, to assimilate all parties. (*See* Anglican inch, St Alban's clean shave, No church.)

Taj (*Boys'*). Lucious, ripping.

Take (*Printers'*). The bit of copy the printer's compositor 'takes' at one time.

Take a curtain (*Theatrical*, 1880). Appear before the curtain in answer to sufficient applause.

Written in Sand was well received, and Broughton had to 'take a curtain'.—*Ref.*, 31st August 1884.

(*See* Curtain-taker, Lightning curtain-taker, Fake a curtain.)

Take a squint (*Low Class*). Look. 'Take a squint at the donah, now!' (*See* Cast an optic.)

Take a trip (*Trade*). To discharge oneself from a situation—which act would be followed by movement searching for a new situation.

Take and give (*C. L.*, *rhyming*). 'Live', generally referring to man and wife.

Take care of (*Police*). To arrest.

Take care of dowb (*Political*, 1855). New reading of Take care of No. I.

Take gruel (*Low Classes*). To die —from the fact that gruel general accompanies any long illness which ends in death.

Take gruel together (*Low Life*, 1884). To live together as man and wife. Derived from a case where a housekeeper to an eccentric clergyman was 'inquested' as the result of death from want of medical attendance. The police newsmonger put a severe construction upon the case.

'They took their gruel together!' This is a charming euphemism perpetrated by an old clergyman to explain his relations with an elderly female who lived alone in his house with him. 'We take our gruel together!' is likely to become a fashionable expression.—*Ref.*, 14th December 1884.

Take in (*Anglo-American*, 1882). Patronize—from taking in papers.

Take it fighting (*American-Eng.*, 1880). Be courageous, antithesis of take it lying down.

But if we intend 'to take it fighting', then the most ordinary economy and plain sense demand that the construction and supply of the proper depôts be commenced without an hour's delay.—*D. N.*, 5th March 1885.

Take it lying down (*American-Eng.*, 1880). To be cowardly—on the basis that a self-respecting fighter will not strike a prostrate enemy.

If we mean to 'take it lying down', like the preacher threatened by Colonel Quagg—then every penny we spend on the volunteers, and every hour they give to drill, is so much wanton waste.—*D. N.*, 5th March 1885.

Take my Bradlaugh (*Peoples'*, 1883). New phrase for 'take my oath'. Humorously, or perhaps satirically adopted at the time when Mr Charles Bradlaugh's name was intimately associated with the Affirmation Bill.

Take off corner pieces (*Com. Classes*). To beat another, generally one's wife. (*See* Knock off corners.)

Take off my coat (*Street*). Challenge to fight. (*See* Blood or Beer.)

Take soles off your shoes (*Anglo-American*). To surprise utterly.

'But ah, my dear sir,' with another engaging smile which took the soles off the shoes of the interviewer, 'I did not know what was coming. I did not know what that initiation really was.'—*N. Y. Mercury*, 1884.

Take the egg (*American*). To win.

Take the flour (*American.-Eng.*, 1885). Outcome of Take the cake, which was followed by Take the bun.

There is a woman in Fargo who takes the flour.—*N. Y. Mercury*, 1885.

Take the kettle (*Com.*). Obtain the prize. It is said at one time a kettle was the reward (U.S.A.), of village spelling bees.

Take the number off the door (*Peoples'*). Said of a domestic establishment where the wife is a shrew, and by scolding draws attention to the domus. The removal of the number would make the cottage less discoverable.

Take the pastry (*Amer.*). Lead.

Take the tiles off (*Soc.*). Extreme extravagance.

He flings his money about with a lavish recklessness, sufficient to take, as they say, the tiles off the roof of a house.—*Truth*, May 1878.

Taken in and done for (*Peoples'*, 1880 on). Absorbed.

As it is, they are literally 'taken in and done for'. They visit a theatre, where they have no notion that the presence of tobacco-smoke will be felt, and find themselves only separated by a curtain from a saloon where noxious cigarettes poison the atmosphere.—*Entr'acte*, 1883.

Take time by the forelock (*Peoples'*). Be in time — probably suggested by long forehead tuft of hair, now and again worn by old men. Certainly time is always represented with one tuft on the head.

Taken stripes (*U.S.A.*). Equivalent to our 'wears the broad arrow'. Evasion in reference to an U.S.A. state prisoner.

After 4th July the convicts with a good record in the Kansas State Penitentiary will wear suits of cadet grey instead of striped suits.—*D. T.*, 4th June 1897.

Taken to the stump (*Polit.*). Public oratory. From the tree stump on which the wandering puritans preached. Good example of freedom of opinion, existing long since in England, when wayside stumps could be used as points for public speaking.

According to our correspondent at Sofia, General Kaulbars has now taken to the stump.—*D. N.*, 4th October 1886.

Talk by a bow (*Com. London*, 1860-82). Periphrase of quarrel.

Talk to his picture (*Suffolk Peoples'*). Admonish so gravely that the admonished one will be no more able to speak than could his portrait.

Tall 'un (*Com. Life*). Pint of coffee, half a pint being a short 'un.

Tall weeping (*Amer.*, 1883). Deep grief.

Tamarinds (*Chemists'*). Sometimes used by chemists for 'money'. Not general.

Tamaroo (*Irish*). Noisy.

Tammany (*American - Eng.*, 19 cent.). Bribery—from Tammany Hall, a place where for forty years the corrupt manipulators of the municipality of New York have held their meetings.

Not long ago there was an election on the other side of the water, and we were all full of contemptuous denunciation of Tammany. What was this but Tammany? This was a Tammany Government. — *D. T.*, 14th December 1897.

Tandem (*Cambridge*, 1870 on). Long. Used in speaking of a tall man.

Tangle - leg (*Anglo - Amer.*). Whisky. Derivation obvious.

Tangle - monger (*Soc.*, 19 cent.). Application of word 'monger'. Speaks for itself—an individual, generally a woman, who fogs and implies everything.

Tanky (*Navy*). Foreman or captain of the hold—which looks like a tank.

Tannery (*Anglo-American*, 1880). Large boots—also absolute reference to feet almost as capacious.

Tanter go (*Provincial, Mid. Hist.*). End, finish, departure. May be from Catholic times, and the 'Tantum Ergo'—the last division of a mass.

Tap (*Peoples'*). Draw blood, by a blow, from the nose. Derived from the beer barrel.

Before the magistrate one of them explained that they were simply engaged in a friendly, good-humoured contest, the one whose nose got 'tapped' first paying for a round of beer for the company.—*D. T.*, 19th July 1897.

Taper (*Polit.*). Seeker after profitable office. Abbreviation of Red Taper—from the colour of official tape.

We have our Tadpoles and our Tapers, it is true, and our greedy party-men clamouring for rewards, but our disappointed seekers after job, place and pay do not snarl and fight for their prey in public like hungry dogs over a bone. —*D. T.*, 27th April 1897.

Tare an' ouns (*Irish - English*). Corruption of 'Tear and wounds'—created when wounds rhymed with pounds. (See Oons, Zounds?)

Tart (*Street*, 1884). A common girl — the outcome of 'Bit of jam' (*q.v.*). Also a rhyming phrase — agreeing with 'sweet heart'. (See Banbury.)

I have to do my needlework
To make myself look smart,
But yesterday I'm glad to say
I found a little tart.

Taste of his quality (*Peoples'*, 19 cent.). Obvious. From the prize ring. Widely applied.

A fair 'taste of his quality' is afforded by a comparison between pp. 40 and 43. John Storm, who has become curate to a Canon of an outrageously caricatured type of worldliness, is being taken by him to call upon one of his lady parishioners, etc. — *D. T.* (Crit. *The Christian*), 1898.

Taste the sun (*Cockney*, 1877). Used as an intensifier by Londoners out in the country for the day. (See Speak brown to-morrow, Can't you feel the shrimps, See the breeze.)

Tatur-trap (*Irish*, 19 cent.). The mouth; tatur being short for potato.

Tax - fencer (*Com. Lond.*, 1878). Disreputable shopkeeper — as distinct from the honest pusher.

Tea and toast struggle (*Peoples'*). Said of Wesleyan tea-meetings where the supply is rarely adequate to the demand.

Tea and turn out (*Peoples'*, 19 cent.). A roundabout way of saying there is no supper.

Tea in a mug (*Irish*). Suggestive of bad breeding.

Tea - bottle (*Mid.-class*). An old maid — from the ordinary drink of spinsters.

Tea-kettle purgers (*L. London*). Total abstainers. 'Purgers' would appear to be a reminiscence of attacks upon Puritanism.

Tea-pot (*Peoples'*). Total abstainer. This phrase is a reduction of tea-pot sucker.

Tea - pot ('*Varsities*, 1880). Tea party — antithesis of wine (*q.v.*). About this year the more earnest life at the universities then commencing took as one shape that of temperance.

Tea-room party (*Parliament*, 1866). A Radical party in the House of Commons, whose members first foregathered in the tea-room. Gladstone and Bright were in favour of some limitation of the franchise, one which would exclude the so-called residuum, and it was proposed to draw a line somewhere above household suffrage pure and simple. Hereupon forty-eight Radicals held a meeting in the tea-room of the House of Commons.

Teatchgir (*Coster*). Right.

Tec, Teck (*Peoples'*). Detective—cut down after an ordinary fashion.

I'm told that Jack Shaw, the smartest and best tec in London or anywhere else, thinks of retiring from the force.—*Cutting*.

Teeth-drawing (*Med. Students'*, 19 cent. to 1860). Wrenching off door-knockers with club-like sticks. Headquarters, Lant Street, Southwark—street now cleared away, but until 1860 the bowers of St Thomas's and Guy's students.

Teetotically (*Peoples'*, '90's). Comic intensification of teetotally.

Tekram (*Inverted word*). Market; very common usage.

Telescope (*American Railway*). To collide and close in like a telescope —applied to the running into each other of railway carriages in collision. Now applied in various ways.

The excursion train, of twenty cars, came into collision with a goods car. The shock was so severe that five crowded cars were completely 'telescoped'.— *D. N.*, 1878.

Temporiser (*Polit.*). Shiftless uncertain man. From a speech by Mr Gladstone (17th November 1885) in Scotland.

Ten bob squats (*Theatrical*). Stalls in a theatre. About 1880 going to the theatre had become so fashionable, owing possibly to the steady patronage of the Prince of Wales, that the price of stalls in most of the best houses was raised.

Ten stroke (*Billiard-players'*). Complete victory—from the fact that ten is the highest stroke at billiards that can be made; cannon off the red, all three balls in.

10 wedding (*Peoples'*, 1897). '1' the wife, and '0' the husband=10 wedding.

Tenderfeet (*American mining*, 1849 on). Doubtful roving industrials. Given to the mining rabble in California, during the gold-rush (1849), and now classic in U.S.A., and all Colonial mining districts. Applied in all ways.

Numbers of prospectors and tenderfeet started for the then unknown goldfields, and when a steamer reached San Francisco with some of these miners who had 'struck it rich' aboard, the fact that gold had been found in abundance along the Klondike again excited public interest in the matter.—*D. T.*, 21st July 1897.

Tenip (*Public-house, inverted word*). Pint. As suggesting natural euphony.

Terrier (*American*). Troublesome boy.

A policeman came along and the dude told him I was a terrier, and the policeman jerked my coat collar off.—1883.

Terror to cats (*American—passing to England*). Most troublesome—chiefly applied to over-active and mischievous boys.

Pa says I am a terror to cats. Every time pa says anything it gives me a new idea. I tell you pa has got a great brain, but sometimes he don't have it with him. —*Detroit Free Press*, 1883.

Testril (*Hist.*). Sixpenny piece, and another shape of tester. Shakespeare proves that the testril was of the value of sixpence in the poet's time.

Sir Toby (to clown): Come on, there is sixpence for you. Let's have a song.
Sir Andrew: There is a testril of me too!—Shakespeare, *Twelfth Night*, Act ii., scene ii.

Testugger (*Oxford*). Testamur—a certificate.

Thames butter (*Poor London*, 1870). Very bad butter. A Mr W. Sawyer, then editor of *South London Press*, published a paragraph to the effect that a Frenchman was making butter out of Thames mud at Battersea. In truth this chemist was extracting yellow grease from Thames mud-worms.

Thank the mussies (*Peoples'*, 1870). Equivalent to 'Thank the gods'.

Thank you for the next (*Hist.*) Lancashire expression of gratitude for something given.

That gets me (*Amer.*). Defeat—from the game of poker, the other side getting the stakes.

That kind of thing will not answer (*Peoples'*, 1885). Poverty — from a fragment of evidence given by the Hon. Mrs Gerard, sister of the defendant in the case 'Durham *versus* Milner (otherwise Durham)' — the celebrated suit brought by Lord Durham (1885), against his wife for nullity of marriage, on the ground that the lady was insane at the time of the ceremony. Mrs Gerard said—

In the season of 1881 Lord Burghersh paid her a great deal of attention. I did not think it would be a suitable marriage. It was one that would be distasteful to her family. That was made pretty plain to my sister. I don't think she was very

That moan's soon made (*Scotch and Peoples'*, 19 cent). Grief easily consoled.

There is no more to be said on the subject; as the Scottish saying has it 'that moan's soon made'.—*D. N.*, 10th March 1885.

That won't pay the old woman her ninepence (*Bow Street Police Court*). Condemnation of an evasive act.

That's a cough lozenge for him (*Peoples'*, 1850 on). Punishment. Arose from an advertisement, 'Cough no more lozenges'. It was to be inferred that they might kill the patient, who would then certainly cough no more.

That's gone to Pimlico (*W. London, Streets'*, 1888). Smashed—ruined. Derived from the fact that Pimlico became a favourite residential centre of women who fell.

That's the ticket (*Peoples'*, 18 cent.). Proper thing to do — corruption of 'etiquette' — that's the etiquette. Diprose in his *St Clement Danes* says:—This term arose in 1717 when Spiller, a comedian, used the expression upon seeing the card of admission designed by Hogarth, then a very young man, for a benefit at Drury Lane Theatre, in favour of the celebrated Joe Miller. However, a good authority says: — 'Ticket' is from Norman French. The rules of 'etiquette' were written upon cards—hence the name 'ticket'. The 'etiquette' or pass-card was also affixed to a bag or bundle, to show it was not to be examined.

That's up against your shirt (*Street*). Significant of victory.

That's where you spoil yourself (*Peoples'*, 1880-81). A very popular catch-sentence applied to smart individuals who went a little too far.

Theatre Royal amen (*Low. Class*). Church. (*See* Holy Ghost shop.)

Theatricality (*Soc.*, 1888 on). Anything generically theatrical. Arose when theatres ceased to be a luxury.

And as if this 'terrible acting', these 'terrible frowns', and these 'terrific impressions', were not enough, as if the tinfoil, and the tinsel, and the theatricality were not sufficient, they must needs call in good old Colley Cibber to improve on Shakespeare, and enable the gifted actors to rant and storm the more.—*D. T.*, 21st December 1896.

Then comes a pig to be killed (*Peoples'*). Expression of misbelief—based upon the lines of Mrs Bond who would call to her poultry — 'Come chicks, come! Come to Mrs Bond and be killed.'

Then the band played (*Parliamentary*). Climax, finality. Derived from the use of brass bands on the nomination day, which immediately sounded when the opponent of their employer attempted to address the people.

There, All (*Street*, 1860 on). Exclamation, declaring perfection. 'I'm all there, completely happy'. 'She *is* an all there bit o' jam'.

Mrs Saker has done great things at the Liverpool Alexandra with 'Aladdin', the scenery and company being alike excellent. Miss Jenny Hill is all there, as she ever was, and I suppose ever will be.—*Ref.*, 18th January 1885.

There's 'air (*London Streets*, 1900). Shortened 'there is hair!'—meaning a quantity, and shaping out of the pulled up side hair, and fringe being about this time deserted in favour of packed masses, coming down over the forehead.

Thick (*Peoples'*). Severe, also too daring in cheating.

Selby says: 'I've got it thick this time. So I looks at his leg, and sees he was ableeding'.—*People*, 6th January 1895.

Thick ear (*Street*, 19 cent.). One swelled by a blow.

Thick end of a hundred years (*Yorks.*). Nearly a century.

Thick starch double blue (*Common Soc.*). Rustling holiday dress for summer — white dress very severely laundried.

Thick tea (*N. England*). A tea as solid as a dinner. Long known in the Ridings before high tea was thought of.

Thick 'un (*Peoples'*). Sovereign.

Thieves' kitchen (*London Street*, 1882), The name satirically given to the then new Law Courts.

Thin as a rasher of wind (*Com. London*). Complete skeleton of a man.

Thingembobs (*Com. Peoples'*). One of the idiotic names for trousers—like inexpressibles, unmentionables, etc.

Think and thank (*English-Jewish*). Translated from the first words of the ordinary Hebrew morning prayer. Implies gratitude.

Think some (*American*). Mature consideration.

Thinking part (*Theatrical*). That of a supernumerary who has nothing to say. Satirical.

Thinks he holds it (*Sporting, becoming general* 1875). Said of a vain man. As obscure as emphatic. It refers to any sort of championship in athletics.

Thirteenth juryman (*Legal*, 19 *cent.*). A judge who, in addressing a jury, shows leaning or prejudice.

No English Judge would have so far forgotten the impartiality of the Bench, prone as one here and there may be to convert himself into a 'thirteenth juryman'.—*D. T.*, 10th October 1895.

This is all right (*Peoples'*, 1896 on). With accent on the *all*. Satirical—meaning everything is wrong.

Mrs Harris was not there, and Harris remarked: 'This is *all* right, nothing to eat or drink, and no one to speak to'.—*People*, 7th November 1897.

Thistle down (*Irish*). Children of a wandering nature generally, but more particularly in open breezy places, describing the children who gather thistle down in autumn—the down with which the Irish peasant, especially in Donegal, makes pillows.

Thistle seed (*Peoples'*). Devonshire for gipsies, because they drift carelessly —like winged thistle seed.

Thorough-handed man (*American*). Candid, open specimen of the genus.

Thou (*Society*, 1860, etc.). Abbreviation for thousand.

Three acres and a cow (*Peoples'*, 1887). Satirical exclamation directed at illogical optimism. This was the panacea suggested for the renascence of agriculture in England. Every peasant was to have these blessings—but no one discovered where the money was to come from to meet the expenditure. Mr George Smith of Coalville claimed the invention of this phrase in a letter to the *Daily News* (27th August 1887), wherein he says:—

I also brought the subject before the Select Committee on Canals in 1883, and about which Lord Wemyss good-humouredly made some fun in the House of Lords in 1884, which fun gave new life to the phrase living to-day.

Three and sixpenny thoughtful (*Soc.*, 1890 on). Satire upon the feminine theory novel, which became dominant, 1890-96. Antithesis of the shilling shocker, which was so full of action that it had no time to think.

Fielding, according to the theory which has apparently suggested this undertaking, is so constantly in the hands of his countrymen of mature years, they show so marked a preference for him as a novelist over the author of the latest 'shilling dreadful' or 'three and sixpenny thoughtful', that they long to admit the younger generation to a share in their enjoyment.—*D. T.*, 27th May 1896.

Three a'porth o' gordepus (*Streets'*). A street Arab.

Three B's, The (*Clerical*). Bright, brief, and brotherly—the modern protest against the sleepy nature of a majority of the 19th century church services.

Three cold Irish (*Tavern*). Three-penny-worth of Irish whiskey with cold water. Because (1867) of a passing pun between this order and three hanged Fenians. The three cold Irish were Allen, Larkin, and Gould, who were executed at Manchester (1867), for the murder of Sergeant Brett in the attempt to rescue from him certain Fenian prisoners.

Three cornered constituency (*Soc.*). House where an only child or mutual friend throws in the domestic casting vote, and so gives victory to husband or wife. From the parliamentary arrangement (1867), whereby certain boroughs returned three members while the voter was only allowed to vote for two members.

Three d. masher (*Peoples'*, 1883). Young men of limited means and more or less superficial gentlemanly externals.

Three is an awkward number (*Soc. and Peoples'*, 1885). Paraphrase of 'three are company, two are not', and brought in with surprising rapidity from a line of evidence given by the Hon. Mrs Gerard in the celebrated Lord Durham's nullity of marriage suit.

On the ride to Raby in the pony carriage did not your sister get as far away from Lord Durham as she could?—I did not notice.

But you said that Lord Durham was

very nice while your sister was very silent?—Three is an awkward number under the circumstances of the case. (Laughter.)

Three out brush (*Public-house*). A glass shaped like an inverted cone, and therefore something like a housepainter's brush, especially when dry. The glass holds one-third of a quartern —a quartern being just half of half a pint.

Three planks (*Com. English*). A coffin.

In France the coffin is spoken of as— la machine à quatre planches et quatre clous.

Three-quarter man (*Cloth-drapers'*). An inferior employé. (*See* Six-quarter men.)

Three wise men of Gotham (*Peoples'*). Meaning that they were not wise. Generally applied to a trio of male fools. In the twenty-fourth year of the reign of Henry VIII., 3rd October, a law was passed by the magistracy of Westham, for the purpose of preventing unauthorised persons from setting '*nettes, potties, and annoyances*', or in anywise taking fish within the privilege of the march of Pevensey. The King's commission was directed to John Moor, of Lewes; Richard, Abbot of Begeham; John, Prior of Myehillym; Thomas, Lord Dacre, and others. Upon the proceedings of this meeting, which was held at Gotham, near Pevensey, the facetious Andrew Borde, a native of that town, founded his *Merrie Tales of the Wise Men of Gotham*.

Threepenny shot (*Artizans'*). Beefsteak globular pudding at that price, sold in common cook- and coffeeshops.

Throat - latch (*American*). The larynx, as outwardly developed.

Throw it up (*Theatrical*). Don't repeat it; figuratively. Really means reject it, as something not fit to be retained.

If Miss Hodson ever revises and compresses the piece, she must take heed that she removes the 'throw it up' lines, and the references to Somebody's virgin vinegar and Somebody else's soap.—*Ref.*, 20th December 1885.

Throw mud at the clock (*Peoples'*). Despair — even to suicide. Means defy time and die. Mostly used figuratively.

Throwing the hammer (*Low Military*). Erotic. Obtaining money under false pretences. (*See* Catch cocks.)

Thumper (*American*). Man who steals by misrepresentation—thumper being 'a big lie'.

Thusly (*American*). In this manner. The word was the invention of Artemus Ward (about 1860).

Thuzzy-muzzy (*Low. London*). Wilful corruption of enthusiasm. Said to come down from the tenor Brahan, who either invented the term or thought he was using the true word. His English was not great, as witness—

'Twas in Trafalgar Bay
We saw the Frenchman lay.

Ticket o' leave (*Peoples'*, '70's). Holiday, vacation, outing.

The expression, 'Ticket o' leave', is probably the invention of the criminal intellect, which, as everybody knows, delights in giving utterance to its own ideas in its own peculiar way.—*D. N.*, 27th October 1886.

Ticket-skinner (*New York*). Opera and theatre ticket speculator, who buys for a rise. Sometimes sells a 2-dollar ticket for 5 or even 10 dollars.

Innocent people regard the high rates announced by the managers as final, and only discover at the entrance that the advertised price for seats is a ruse to lure them to the merciful treatment of middle men, called ticket-skinners, who, having temporary possession of nearly all the tickets, exact just what they please for a seat.—*N. Y. Mercury*, October 1883.

Tickle one's innards (*Anglo - American*). Indulge in a drink.

Thankee, mister; that war well thought of. It's Sunday; but come, let's steer for a side door, and tickle our innards, ye know.—*N. Y. Mercury*, 16th January 1885.

Tickle to death (*U.S.*). Delight in the extreme.

Ticklers (*Transvaal War*, 1900). Peacock feathers, which were sold to the youth of both sexes on 'Mafeking Night' for the first time, at one penny a piece, and so named by the vendors.

It appears that the peacock feathers —'ticklers', for short—which were such an important feature in the popular rejoicings of the last few days, come from France. The cheaper kind of Union Jacks come from Germany, the better kind from Scotland.—*D. T.*, 28th May 1900.

Street genius immediately raised the word to an endearment by changing it into tiddler.

Ticklish (*Peoples'*). Easily excited, or spurred to resistance.

Tiddle-a-wink (*Rhyming*). A drink.

Tie o' mutton (*Irish, London Tailors'*). Thigh of — meaning leg; and refers to the hopes of a hot Sunday dinner.

Tie up your stocking (*Oxford Univer.*). Finish your tumbler of champagne — don't leave any. No heel-taps.

Tie up with a curly one (*Cricketing*, 1890). Bowl out with a screwed or rifled projection of the ball, sent from the shoulder on a parabolic curve produced by simultaneous swing of the arm and turn of the wrist.

Tied down (*American*). Crushed by the force of circumstances.

Tiger (*American*). Prostitute. Never tigress. Shadwell, London, was called by sailors Tiger Bay—long since swept away.

Tiger (*Boys', 19 cent.*). Tough-crusted bread. Probably from both offering a deal of fight.

Tiger (*San Francisco*). The guardian —inside the inner door of a gaming-house—equivalent to the chucker-out of a London tavern.

Tiger (*Political*, 1895). Hon. J. Chamberlain. Bestowed by the Radical party. Sir J. Kitson quoted this verse in a political speech:—

There was a young lady of Riga
Who went for a ride on a tiger;
They finished the ride with the lady inside,
And a smile on the face of the tiger.

The young lady was presumably Britannia.

Tiger bit him hard (*American gamester*). Meaning that he had lost a good deal of money at a sitting.

Tight as a biled (or boiled) owl (*American*). Completely drunk.

Tiled (*Masonic*). Closed—from the tiler closing in a house by way of the tiles. The outer-door paid officer of a masonic lodge is the tiler.

What is a 'tiled lodge of the Antediluvian Order of Buffaloes?' One of the Bristol lodges saw fit to meet together in a room in a public-house, and at this gathering there was singing and playing. Thereupon a constable entered and knocked at the door whence the sounds of revelry were proceeding. Here we get our first glimpse of the mystery attaching to the word 'tiled'. In one of the panels of the door there was a slide. Somebody looked through this aperture, shook his head, and the slide was closed again. Was the somebody a 'tiler'?—a term derived, like that of 'mason', from the old trade guilds.—*D. T.*, 2nd July 1896.

Timbers (*Art jargon*, 1880). Cabinets, bookcases, escritoires, elaborate tables—worked wood in general. (*See* Crocks and rags).

Timbers (*Gutter commerce*). Lucifer matches.

Timothy grass (*American*). Cat's tail grass.

Tin hat (*Anglo-Port Said*). Drunk —two tin hats very drunk—three, incapable, and to be carried on board.

Tinman (*Sporting*, 1880). Millionaire; from man possessing tin.

Too many of the big swells found profit in the Tinman to allow him to pass into retirement while able to earn winnings for them if conditions were modified for his benefit.—*Ref.*, 14th November 1886.

(Referring to F. Archer, a popular and rich jockey, who had some days before committed suicide.)

Tin-shin-off (*American*). Tin is money; shin is to walk; and together with the third word means—abscond with money.

Tinder-tempered (*Peoples', old*). Hot-tempered—from the tinder sometimes taking fire in a moment from the flash of the flint and steel.

'Tis both your faults, you tinder-tempered knaves.—Garrick, *Abel Drugger*.

Tintamarre (*Devon*). Noise, hubbub. One of the French phrases common, and only common, to Devon.

Tip the velvet (*Crim. Classes*). Kiss with the point of the tongue.

Tipping the office (*Soc.*, 18 *cent.*). Revealing a secret — frequently in connection with some doubtful proceeding.

Titotular bosh (*Music Hall*, 1897). Absolute nonsense—made up by an absurd play upon the word teetotal, and one of the terms for 'humbug'.

Tittimatorterin (*E. Anglican*). See-saw.

Tius (*East London—reversed word*). Suit of clothes.

To away (*Theatrical*). Creation of a verb from the dramatic exclamation 'away'.

To Christmas (*Soc.*, 1880). To make high holiday with plenty of feasting.

The associations of Christmas for the young and for the people are almost wholly of a festive character. They conjugate actively the verb 'to Christmas'.—*D. N.*, 25th December 1884.

Toast *v.* **On (a bit of) toast.**

Toast your blooming eyebrows (*Peoples'*). Probably a delicate way of telling a man to go to blazes.

Toby (*Soc.*, 1882). Lady's collar—from the wide frill worn round the neck by Mr Punch's dog.

Toe-path (*Cavalry*). Regiment of infantry. Eminently suggestive of the contempt in which the cavalry hold the infantry, who as a rule are much smaller men than the gee-gees (*q.v.*).

Toe-rag (*Peoples', Prov.*). Beggar. Most country people ride or drive, hence the contempt enclosed in 'toe', with which the possessor walks. Another term (Devon) is footpad—without reference to robbery. Rags speak for themselves.

Toff bundle-carrier (*Music Hall*, 1870 on). He is the gentleman in attendance upon a serio-comic, and see her from hall to hall—a prosperous serio-comic often having to sing at three or four music halls in the course of one evening. Her changes of dress, etc., call for a large assortment of flying luggage, to which the devoted one gives all his attention—hence the term.

Toff-omee (*Thieves'*). Superlative of toff.

Toff-shoving (*London Rough*, 1882). Pushing about well-dressed men in a crowd.

Tog-bound (*Peoples'*). No good clothes to wear.

Tog-fencer (*Com. Lond.*, 1870). A tailor.

Toga-play (*Theatrical*). Classical play.

Togies (*Public-school*). Knotted ropes' ends carried about hidden by elder boys to beat their fags with—once-called 'colts'.

Toileted (*American - Eng.*, 1884). Dressed. Conjugated throughout.

Pretty Martha Springsteen brings suit against her husband for separation. The lady is young and good-looking and is exquisitely toileted. — *N. Y. Mercury*, January 1885.

Tom (*Street*, 19 *cent.*). A masculine woman of the town. In higher ranks one who does not care for the society of others than those of her own sex.

Tom and funny (*Rhyming*). Figurative description of money.

Tom o' Bedlam (*Provincial*). A wild, maddish fellow—from the name once given to inoffensive imbeciles who were licensed to go about begging.

Abram-men, otherwise called Tom o' Bedlams, are very strangely and antickly garbed, with several coloured ribbons or tape in their hat, it may be; instead of a feather, a fox-tail hanging down a long stick with ribbons streaming and the like. Yet for all their seeming madness they have wit enough to steal as they go. —*The Canting Academy*, 1674.

Tomahawk (*Street*). Policeman's staff.

Tomasso di rotto (*Middle-class Youths'*). Italian shape of Tommy rot.

Tomb-stone (*Com. Lond.*, 19 *cent.*). A pawn-ticket—the shape and printed heading of which do give the idea of a doll's tombstone.

Tommy (Bobby) Atkins (*Popular*, 1882). The friendly name found about this year for a soldier of the line—presumably invented amongst line soldiers, and certainly adopted by them. Tommy Atkins first appeared in print in the correspondence sent home during the Egyptian campaign (1882).

This time it was some other member of the family of Thomas Atkins who resumed the colloquy of which our friend Bill had dropped the thread.—*D. N.*, 28th September 1882.

Tommy and exes (*Workmen's*). Bread—beer, and 'bacca.

Tommy make room for your uncle (*Music Hall*). Suggestive of the uncle being a better man than the nephew, and accepted very willingly by the less juvenile of music-hall patrons. Adopted as the leading line of a chorus to a comic song. Said, however, to have a recondite meaning.

Tommy pipes (*Navy*, 19 *cent.*). Boatswain — because he pipes or whistles all hands.

Tommy rabbit (*Street Boys'*). Pomegranate. (*See* **Nanny**.)

Tomtug (*Rhyming*). Bed insect.

Tone - painting (*Soc.*, 1890 on). Referring to programme music.

Mr Silas points out that even great musicians do not appear at their best in tone-painting.—*D. T.*, 31st March 1897.

Tony (*American — coming to England*, 1890). Adjective, formed upon the abstract noun.

As for fashionable matters, there was less 'society', of course, in point of numbers in Hone's time than in ours, but it was just as 'tony' of its kind, if anything a little more so.—*N. Y. Mercury*, 18th May 1890.

(*See* No class.)

Too all but (*London*, 1881). One of the phrases resulting out of *Punch's* trouvaille 'too-too' (1881), and to be found in Mr W. S. Gilbert's extravaganza, *Patience*.

Too cheap (*Peoples'*). Under valued. Used in every possible way.

Too damned good (*Military*). Second Dragoon Guards. From the regimental indication on the shoulder-straps.

2
D.G.

Too full of holes to skin (*W. America*). Very much riddled with bullets.

Too mean to raise (*American*). Utterly contemptible.

Too much with us! (*Soc.*, 1897). Boredom, incubus.

Klondyke is 'too much with us' just now. It has long been dragged into conversation with the persistency of a pantomime gag.—*D. T.*, 14th January 1897.

Too numerous to mention (*London*, 1882). Angrily drunk.

Too too (*Soc.*, 1881). More than perfect. Too-too was first found in *Punch* in the height of the æsthetic craze (1881).

Too utterly too (*Society*, 1883). Final phrase resulting from the satirical use of 'too-too'.

Tooled (*Soc.*, 19 *cent.*). Murdered. Satirical metaphor. Invented by De Quincey.

Sir Edward Reed's suspected assassin is thought to have 'tooled', as De Quincey says, with a Japanese dagger. —*D. N.*, 12th February 1885.

Tooleries (*Theatrical*, 1885). Toole's Theatre—now swept away.

Toothpick (*American-Eng.*). Clasp knife—or bowie knife. Satirical description of its formidable appearance.

Toothpicks (*American*). People of Arkansas.

Top-drawing-room (*Low. London*). A garret.

Topical allusion (*Political—Music Hall*). Direct or indirect reference to passing events.

When Miss Victor, exclaiming, 'Noble nation, the Russians!' a faint laugh, broken by a faint hiss, indicated that a perception had somewhere dawned upon somebody of what burlesque writers call a 'topical allusion'.—*D. N.*, 27th April 1885.

Topical vocalist (*Music Hall*).[1] One who sings concerning the events or topics of the day.

Tora - loorals (*Theatrical*). Feminine bust. Generally used in reference to a dress very *decolletée*.

Torch-light procession (*American*, 1883). One of the more fiery American drinks.

Tory democracy (*Polit.*, 1885). Impossibility, absurdity.

Lord R. Churchill had given a new combination in the words 'Tory Democracy'. A Tory could not be a Democrat, and a Democrat could not be a Tory.— Mr H. Labouchere, Finsbury, 13th October 1885.

Tory rory (*London*, 18 *cent.* to 1845). Name given to those who wore their hats fiercely cocked.

Tosh (*Cricket*, 1898). Fatally easy bowling.

Tosh (*Thieves' — old*). Pocket— probably a corruption from the French *poche*.

Tot - hunter (*Low Life*). Bone-collector — generally used offensively in quarrels, and in reference to parents.

Tot-hunting (*Low. Class*). Scouring the streets in search of pretty girls.

Totty all colours (*London Streets'*). Young person who has contrived to get most of the colours of the rainbow into her costume.

Totty one lung (*Street*, 1885). An asthmatic, or consumptive young person who, whether good or bad, thinks herself somebody.

Tough as tacker (*Peoples'*). Tough in excelsis.

Tourney (*Pugilistic*). Mill or encounter of two fighters. Word coined after the Eglintoun tournament.

Concerning the present tourney — I think that's the word — arrangements for a special train were attempted to be made.—*Morning Star*, 1862.

Tournure (*Dressmakers'*, 1882). Happily invented name for the dress-improver of that year.

Town (*Rhyming*). Halfpenny. Thus—town—brown—so named from colour.

Tra la la (*Peoples'*, 1880). Parting benediction—not too civil; possibly contemptuous. Died out about 1890. The phrase took its rise with a comic singer named Henri Clarke, whose speciality was imitating Parisians. Whether he invented 'tra la la', or heard it in Paris, or uttered by a Frenchman in London—he made a great hit with it as the burden of a chorus.

Thanks. I hate personalities. Good-morning. So tra, la, la!—*Funny Folk*, No. 519.

Traffy (*Navy*). Portsmouth's seafaring reduction of the *Trafalgar* (once Nelson's ship), and long since anchored for life at Portsmouth.

Trailing coat (*Irish — spread to England in 19 cent.*). Defiance. In Irish village fights the man trailed his coat by way of challenge — he who took up the cartel trod on it, and the fight began.

Irishmen in the postal service may say that in introducing his 'blacklegs' Mr Raikes was 'trailing his coat'.—*D. N.*, 10th July 1890.

Train too fine (*Soc. and Sport*, 1890 on). Push things too oppressively —from sporting life, where men with too much training overdo the training.

There is undoubted ground for the belief that our bishops as a body are beginning to 'train too fine'.—*D. T.*, 10th June 1898.

Tram-fare (*London Streets'*, 1882). Twopence. Until the toll over Waterloo Bridge (London)—one halfpenny—was abolished, the lower women of the streets used to ask for coin to go over the bridge.

Transfer (*Society*). To steal.

Translate the truth (*Soc.*, 1899). Lie evasively. In general use during this year.

The resources of the French language for putting a polish of politeness on ugly facts are infinite. When M. Delcassé's mendacity in connection with the Muscat incident was exposed, a leading Paris paper extenuated his offence by the ingenious excuse that, after all, he merely 'translated the truth'.—*People*, 19th March 1899.

Translated (*Soc.*, 80's). Emphatically — intoxicated. Probably a reminiscence of Shakespeare — 'Bless thee, Bottom, thou art translated' (*Midsummer Night's Dream*).

Trap (*Australian*, 1870). Mounted trooper.

Travelling tinkers (*Inter - regimental*). 30th Regiment—Lancashire regiment.

Treacle-man (*Thieves'*). Beautiful male decoy who is the pretended young man of the housemaid and the real forerunner of the burglar. (*See* Leaveyer-homer.)

Often used to designate the commercial traveller who has to make sales of type-writers, sewing machines, etc. to young girls and old women. Sometimes bitterly applied by drapers' assistants to any one of their number who makes the smartest sales.

Treason - mongers (*Polit.*, 1885). Contemptuous name found for dynamiters as their great schemes for the destruction of London faded into nothingness.

None but treason-mongers will dispute the applicability of the inscription on the pedestal, which, in the familiar words from *Henry VIII.*, represents him as having fallen a martyr for his country.— *Globe*, 1st July 1885.

Trelawny (*West Cornwall*). War-cry of the Cornish men; derived from one of the three leading septs of Cornwall—

By Tre, Pol, and Pen
Ye shall know the Cornish men.

Used as a defiance.

Trifa (*Jewish*). Unclean — clean things may become trifa; others, such as pork and shell-fish, are always trifa. Applied widely in E. London.

Tripha, ritually unclean.—I. Zangwill, *Children of the Ghetto*.

The slaughterer must be a man of high moral character. In opening the animal, he must make a thorough inspection of it, and if he finds it in any way diseased, he pronounces 'trefa'—that it is unfit for the food of Jews.

(*See* Kosher.)

Trilby (*Soc.*, 1894). Woman's exquisite foot. American - English. From Du Maurier's book (1894) *Trilby*—the name of the book, and of the heroine, whose beautifully rare foot is insisted on.

Having exhausted palmistry an American paper has spent its energy of psychological investigation on the foot (I beg pardon, the trilby), but a rival comes out with a page of illustrated description of the mouth.—*People*, 7th July 1895.

Trimming (*Polit.*, 18 *cent.* on). Not sailing straight.

'He's a trimmer of trimmers, and he lies by heredity.'

Trimming was the name which the 18th century politician gave to what we now call opportunism.—Ouida, *An Altruist* (1896).

Trimmings (*Trade*, 1897). Masked alcohol. When, by the contrivance of Mr Gladstone, it was attempted to modify the attraction of the public-house by giving licenses to sell alcoholic drinks to various tradesmen, some linen-drapers and silk-mercers who gave credit, opened liberal refreshment rooms at their establishments, and put down their lady-customers' wine-lunches as 'trimmings' in the bills sent to the husbands. Hence the word became synonymous with secret drinking by women.

The *Drapers' World* declares 'alcoholic trimmings' to be fiction.—*D. T.*, 18th January 1897.

Trinity kiss (*Soc.*, about 1870). A triple kiss — generally given by daughters and very young sons, when going to bed, to father and mother.

Tripe (*Journalistic*). Rubbish, 'rot'.

Yet she puts in six or seven pages of her own tripe, and limits me to three columns. — T. Le Breton, *The Modern Christian* (1902), ch. 8.

Tripe, Blooming six foot o' (*Street*, 1880). A giant policeman. 'Yer blooming six foot o' tripe, how's yer fat old head?'—attack upon a tall policeman.

Triper (*Streets'*, *E. London*). Trifa (?) — this being the Jewish for unclean.

Tripos pup (*Cambridge Univ.*) Undergrad cantabs.

Every year the coaches exact more and more work out of their 'Tripos pups'.—*D. N.*, 14th June 1887.

Triumphant toast (*Soc.*, 18 *cent.*). Toast in excelsis.

Miss Chudleigh next was the triumphant toast: a lively, sweet-tempered, gay, self-admired, and not altogether without reason, generally-admired lady—she moved not, without crowds after her. She smiled at every one.—Richardson, *Lettters from Tunbridge Wells*, 1748.

Trot (*Com. Lond.*, 1875). A walk—probably suggested by the ordinary quick movement of most young Englishmen.

Trot the udyju Pope o' Rome (*Street*). This is very enigmatic English, composed of rhyming and transposition styles, and is generally used by one man to another when he wants the wife, or other feminine person, out of the way. Udyju is judy (wife) transposed — judy being very common word for wife or mistress equally. Pope o' Rome is rhyming for home.

Trots (*Common London*). Feet — derived from 'trotting'.

Trots (*Peoples'*, 1846). Policemen. Refers to these officers being always on the go—or beat.

Trotter-cases (*Com. London*, 1860). Boots.

Trotting away from the pole (*American*). In error — wandering from subject. From horse-trotting sport; the pole being the winning post.

Trouble (*American*, 1870). Distinct American for 'anxiety'.

Troubled with the slows (*Aquatics*). Observed of the losing boat or swimmer.

Trouting (*Piscatorial*). Catching trout.

April and May are the best months for trouting on the Thames.—*People*, 3rd April 1898.

Trowser (*E. London*, 1895 on). Jack of all trades and master of none.

Sir Reginald Hanson: What is a 'trowser'. Sweeting: Vy, a man as does any hod jobs. Anythin'.—*D. T.*, 4th November 1897.

True bill, judgment, execution (*Anglo-American*). Medical analysis of the course of paralysis.

True inwardness (*Literary*, 1890 on). Reality. One of the principal shapes of literary jargon produced in the '90's. Probably the only serious survival of the æsthetic craze of the '80's.

250

Trying it on the dog (*Theatrical*). Abbreviation of 'the matinée dog'. Derived from the amiable habit, in the good old times of testing a present of eatables by giving a portion to the dog. In the present relation it is a contemptuous reference to the lower judging capacities of afternoon theatrical audiences. Testing the value of a new piece by an afternoon audience is trying it on the matinée dog—who is below consideration, but may be useful.

If any enterprising person desires to make money from a play or a composition of music he does not boldly attempt the experiment upon the public. His shrewd suspicion that they would avenge the torture induces him to adopt the preliminary precaution of 'trying it on the dog.—*D. T.*, 4th February 1897.

Tub practice (*Boating*). Unskilled efforts in broad-bottomed boats.

During the intervals of racing in the eight they should have been taken out for 'tub' practice in convenient gig pairs.—*D. T.*, 17th June 1897.

Tubbichon (*Peoples'*, '60's). Corruption of *tire - buchon* (corkscrew) which was the Paris argot in the '60's for the long solitary ringlet of a portion of the back hair worn in front of the left shoulder, a fashion created by the Empress Eugenie, and accepted in London by the middle - classes immediately after that lady visited London (1855), when for a time everything French was very popular.

Miss Spong's fair hair is all pushed into a gold net, save for one long *tire-bouchon* hanging over the left shoulder.—*D. T.*, 21st January 1898.

Tug of war (*Peoples'*). Contest final and settling. Now applied to two sets of boys or men pulling from the two ends of rope—the tug being to get one side a mere inch over the dividing chalk line.

Tumbling down to grass (*Peoples'*, 1884). Equivalent to going to the bad. Breaking up, failing. From the fact of land going out of cultivation 1875-85.

Tunnels (*Theat.*, 1885). Opera Comique Theatre (swept away by Strand improvements) — Strand. From the several subterranean passages leading to this underground theatre.

These same 'coarse bullies' have often enough been Mr W. S. Gilbert's staunchest supporters at the Savoy, and at the Royalty and the Tunnels.—*Ref.*, 10th January 1886.

(Mr Gilbert had been complaining of the angry reception, by the gallery, of a play by him.)

Tup (*Streets' — especially in Woolwich*). Arrested. It is derived from 'locked up', the 't' of locked being prefixed to up.

Tuppenny 'apenny ones (*Street*). Very poor and common sort.

Tupper (*Soc.*, 1850 on). A commonplace honest bore who talks or writes A B C. Takes its rise from Mr Martin Tupper who wrote a phenomenally successful book called *Proverbial Philosophy*—composed entirely of self-evident propositions.

Turf (*Street*, 19 cent.). Prostitution. From loose women being on parade. Thence came turfer.

Turn down your cup (*Soc.*, 19 cent., 1785-1890). Die—from the once existing provincial habit of reversing one's cup in one's saucer when no more tea or coffee was required. Finish—hence the figure of speech.

This last word put Mr Palmer half his breakfast; on hearing it he turned down his cup with a profound sigh.—Miss M. Edgeworth, *Manœuvring*.

Turn over (*Press*, 1860 on). Last column on the right of the front page of a newspaper, especially an evening one. So called from the social article which fills that column turning a few lines, for the sake of effect, over on to top of first column on second page.

Turn paper collars (*American*). Figurative for poverty. (*See* Out o' collar.)

Turn round pudding (*Peoples'*). Any slop pudding or porridge made by turning round the ingredients with a spoon, in a saucepan. (*See* Stir about, Hasty pudding.)

Turn the best side to London (*Peoples'*). Shrewd way of recommending the hearer to make the best of everything.

Turn the tap on (*Common London*). To be ready with tears.

'You noticed, perhaps', said my companion, 'that when she had finished her song she fell a crying? That's what she's strong in. She can turn the taps on at a moment's notice, and that in a way you'd never think was any other than natural.'—*D. T.*, 8th February 1883.

Turn turtle (*Naval*). Tumble down drunk—from the over-turning of a vessel—which is to turn turtle.

Turn up (*Universal*). Appear unexpectedly.

Turn up friendly lead (*Coster*, 1870). Final jovial co-operation. A public-house sing-song to pay the burial expenses of a dead friend, or a pal who has turned up life.

Turnover (*Cornish mining*). Capital. Alas — it is generally the shareholders in these toils who are turned over.

Turn-over (*Lit.*, 1880). A work to dip into rather than read.

The book has as a 'turn over' much of the character of a good volume of *Punch*, and it has the merits (both rare in French comic drawing) of bringing no blush on the cheek of the young person, and of having its work finished and not merely indicated in outline.—*Sat. Rev.*, 26th December 1885.

Turn-up (*Thieves'*). Acquittal—the prosecution being turned up, or abandoned. 'This will be only a turn up.' Also used socially. 'Ginger May's turned me up', does not mean that this yellow-haired Circe has committed an assault upon the speaker, but has abandoned him.

Dear Parnell,—For heaven's sake stop the boycotting and the Moonlighting and the outrages. I have promised you Home Rule, and you shall have it; but if you let your lads play old gooseberry with law and order as they are doing now, I shall have to turn it up.— Salisbury, *Ref.*, 18th October 1885.

Turnups (*Lower Peoples'*). Rejection of a suitor. She dismisses him—or turns him up—said to be from hospital practice of turning up the ordinary joint bedstead when a patient left it for the grave. Corrupted into an idea of turnips — generally pronounced turnups by the vulgar.

Turkey-buyer (*Leadenhall market*). Swell, toff, dude, person of consequence, banker. Because it requires more than two-pence to buy gobblers.

Turkey merchant (*City*). Extensive financier in scrip — a city plunger. supposed to have some reference to the gaming traffic in Turkish bonds which continued until 1878. More probably a name-word, a corruption of 'T. K.' — the initials of some past away speculator, whose only legacy to the world was this phrase.

Turtle soup (*Workmen's*). Sheep's head broth. (*See* Clare market duck, City sherry.)

Tweedle-dum sirs (*Soc.*). Baronets or knights who gain their titles by way of music. Started when Sir Michael Costa obtained his title. Almost forgotten when Sir Arthur Sullivan was knighted. (*See* Gally-pot baronet.)

Twelve o'clock (*Artizans*'). Action —time to be moving. Derived from the fact that this is (or rather was), the dinner hour, and that the diners move rapidly towards home.

Twelve pound actor (*Theatrical*). A well-weighted newly-born baby—a child born in 'the profession' of course.

Mrs James O'Neill has added a twelve-pound actor to Jimmy's board account.

20 in the pounder (*Peoples'*). Gentleman who, owing a sovereign, does not make a composition, but pays his 240 pence in full.

Twicers (*Lower Class*, 19 *cent.*). Twins.

Twisting the lion's tail. (*See* Tail-twisting.)

Twixter (*L. London*). Either a lady-like young man, or a man-like young woman—as the case may be.

Two 'arts in a pond (*Lower Class*). Two hearts (*bullocks'*), in a pond-dish, this receptacle being a baking dish divided in two parts by a transverse wall — hence the ponds. Used on Sunday morning at the bake-houses to describe dinner baked there — and called for.

Two brothers alive, and one married (*Music Hall*, 1897). The one married being as bad as dead.

Two buckle horses (*Stables'*). Tuberculosis.

Two ends and the middle of a bad lot (*Middle-class*). Evasive method of utter condemnation.

Two F's (*Mid.-class*, 1880). Fringe and followers—of lady servants.

As for the two F's—fringes (forehead hair) and followers—surely they should be permitted in moderation. The fringe need not become a fuzz, the followers need not degenerate into polyandry.— *D. N.*, 20th October 1886.

Two inches beyond upright (*Peoples'*). Hypocritical liar. Perversion of description of upright-standing man, who throws his back backwards beyond upright.

Two L.'s, The (*American - Eng.*, 1880). In England means certain destruction. In America — lead or liquor. Comes from the Wild West, and chiefly Arizona, where between taking eternal pulls at Bourbon whiskey, and for ever drawing lead at sight upon the next door neighbour, or being drawn upon—a man of thirty was a phenomenon of old age.

Two to one against you (*Peoples'*). Very much against you. Refers to the pawnbroker's golden sign 'the three balls'—two above one, implying that it is two to one that you will never get your pledge back.

Two upon ten (*Tradesmen's*). 'Two' eyes upon 'ten' fingers—warning that a thief is in the neighbourhood; generally given out by one shopman for the benefit of the others.

Two white, two red, and after you with the blacking brush—usually cut down—**two white, two red, and the brush** (*London Street*, 1860-70). This phrase is absolutely a legacy from the second French empire. Under Napoleon III., the use of colour cosmetics became very marked. Like most French fashions this came to London, and even penetrated for a short time into fairly respectable society, whence it rapidly reached the streets, with much exaggeration—hence the phrase which thus satirizes the vulgarity of the use of colours. It means 'two dabs of red, two of white, and the use of blacking brush to make up the eyebrows'. 'After you, miss, with the two two's and the two b's' (*i.e.*, blacking brush).

Two with you (*Tavern Life*). Suggesting a twopenny drink.

Arthur Roberts may be congratulated. At the finish his friends crowded around, and challenged him with a 'Two with you'.—*Ref.*, 12th June 1887.

Twopenny tube (*C. London*, 1900). The Central London Underground Electric Railway (opened in the first week in August 1900), gained this shortened designation within ten days. At once it became a phrase to stay. From the then one and only fare—twopence.

We have already, it is true, the omnibus, the hansom, the four-wheeler, the tramcar, the underground railway, and the 'two-penny tube'.—*D. T.* (Sir E. Arnold), 13th October 1900.

U

U.K. (*London*, 1870). Emphatic initials of United Kingdom.

Minnie Palmer is on all call nightly, and may be pronounced the finest antidyspeptic dose in the U.K.—U bet!—*Sunday Times*, 14th October 1883.

U.P. (*Lower Social*). 'Up' spelt, to make the word more forcible. Usually used with all — as 'It's all U.P. with him', which may mean that he is about to die, or fail in business, or his winnings, or his power of work of any kind.

Still the box did not come down, and I thought certainly it was 'U.P.' with all of us. By this time some of the men who felt better had climbed up, but most of us were not strong enough to do so.—*D. T.*, 17th May 1897.

See N.G. and G.T.T.

Ud's my life (*Peoples'*, 18 *cent.*). One of the evasive forms of religious swearing, 'God's my life'. (*See* Zounds, etc.)

Ugger, The (*Oxford*). The Union.

Marvels have been done with the most unpromising material. For example, one would have thought that 'the Union' defied corruption. But not so. Some ingenious wit had an inspiration and called it 'the Ugger', and his friends bowed low before him. — *D. T.*, 14th August 1899.

Ugly (*Common Coffee - house*, 19 *cent.*). Thick. (*See* Ungryome.)

Ugly (*Soc.*, 50's). Bonnet shade. 'Ugly'. The passing name bestowed by common consent upon the hideous shades worn upon the front of the bonnet, and made of silk drawn in gathers upon wires.

Ugly rush (*Parliamentary*). Speed to prevent enquiry — forcing a bill. (*See* Hard and fast line.)

Uhlan (*Parliamentary*, 1883). Free lance — or perhaps free-booter. Lord Randolph Churchill. The Uhlans were first familiarly known in England during the Franco-German War (1870-71)—but only by report. They were the *avant - courriers* of the German advance into France, their appearance presaging the arrival of a numerous body. The word soon came to represent a daring, headstrong skirmisher. Lord Randolph in politics answering this description, ultimately acquired this title.

Such an idea had long been in the mind of Lord Randolph Churchill, the Uhlan of the Conservative army.—*D. N.*, 17th February 1883.

Ulster (*Anglo - Amer.*). Skin of anything. Jocosely suggested by the long ulster coat covering the whole body.

Ultra-crepidation (*Soc.*, 19 *cent.*). Plunging, vaulting ambition. From *Ne sutor ultra crepidam.*

But be that as it may, the man whom proverbial wisdom exhorts to 'stick to his last' is the very man who most often sets that advice at nought. He has been 'ultra-crepidating', to use a word of Coleridgian coinage, throughout all history.—*D. T.*, 14th May 1895.

Ululation (*Press*, about 1875). First night condemnation by all the gallery and the back of the pit. (*See* Damned, Hornpipe.)

Umble-cum-stumble (*Low. Class*). Thoroughly understood.

Unattached (*Parliamentary*, 1850, on). A member of the legislation whose vote is never quite to be counted upon by any party.

Unavoidable circumstances (*American Satirical*). Court kneebreeches.

Unbounded assortment of gratuitous untruths (*Polit.*, 1885). Extensive systematic lying. From speech (11th November 1885) of Mr Gladstone's at Edinburgh, wherein may be found:—

It has become the fashion with a portion of the Tory party to circulate in reference to myself personally and individually an unbounded assortment of the most gratuitous untruths.

Unconscious self (*Soc.*, 1885). Genius—the quality of exceptional and inexplicable production of intellectual work.

Dore's very best drawings look like the work of an inspired 'unconscious self', to borrow the latest terminology of psychical research.—*D. N.*, 25th June 1885.

Uncrowned king (*Political*, 1881). Satirical name for C. S. Parnell, M.P. for Cork, the leader of the Irish movement. The crown referred to that of Ireland, from one of whose kings, like most Irish leaders, C. S. Parnell was descended.

Under or over (*American-English*, 1860 on). Contraction of under the grass or over the grass—this phrase being a metaphor of death (under the grass) and of life (over the grass). Applied to widows—meaning either a husband who is dead, or a husband in divorce, who of course is over and above the grass.

This widow of 'Under the grass' and 'Over the grass', the dead husband and the divorced one, is very fascinating, very brilliant, and certainly cynical.—*D. T.*, 9th August 1899.

Under the rose v. Sub rosa.

Underdone (*Colloquial*). Pale complexion. Took the place of doughy.

Underground Russia (*Socialistic*). Nihilistic Russia.

André Frangoli has himself played an important part in the Russian revolutionary movement; nobody is better acquainted than he with 'Underground Russia', and his name is not unknown in England. I give the story, word for word, as he gave it to me.—*D. N.*, 15th September 1883.

Understudy (*Theatrical*). Presumed inferior actor or actress, who learns a part played by a presumedly superior actor or actress, and who only gets a chance of appearing as the result of illness or other indisposition on the part of the superior being.

In the theatrical profession it is always understood to be a perfectly legitimate proceeding, and occasionally in the interests of art, for an 'understudy' to pray for the collapse of a principal.—*D. T.*, 20th May 1897.

Undigested Ananias (*Peoples'*, 1895). Triumphant liar.

'Just listen to him!' exclaimed Mrs Quick; 'look at his impudence. Hear how he cheeks the Court. Why, it's as bad as when he once called my husband an "undigested Ananias"'. — *D. T.*, 24th June 1896.

Unfair done by (*Peoples'*, *Hist.*). Ill-treated.

Ungryome (*Common Coffee-house*, 1880). Unaspirated and collided condition of the two words, 'hungry' and 'home'. (*See* Ugly.)

Unhitched (*Liverpool — spreading*). Let go, released, separated.

When all the arrangements were made and the pair stood up the 'Squire gazed at them over his spectacles and unhitched on them in the most solemn and impressive tones.—*N. Y. Mercury*, April 1886.

Unicorn carman (*L. Streets*', 19 *cent.*). Driver of three horses harnessed tandem.

Unkinned (*Soc.*, 1884). Satirical pronunciation of 'unkind'—the result of the production (1884) of *Hamlet* at the Princess's Theatre, where Mr Wilson Barrett in the title-rôle, acting under advice, used kin instead of kind in the great soliloquy.

Unrelieved holocaust (*Society*, 1883). In 1882 the destruction of the Ring Theatre (Vienna), and of a circus at Berdîtscheff (Russia), both accompanied by terrible loss of life, led a writer in the *Times* to use the above odd phrase in reference to these catastrophes—whereupon the satirical spirits of society adopted it to ridicule the most absurd incidents.

Up (*Sporting*). In the saddle. 'Archer up'—favourite cry meaning success—in 1880-83.

That most enterprising of picture publishers, Mr George Rees, of Russell Street, Covent Garden, has issued a splendidly got up coloured lithograph of St Blaise (a horse), 'with Charlie Wood up'.

Up (*Theatrical*). Up—the stage. Under this condition as a rule the up'd one has only to look on. (*See* Come down.)

Up a tree for tenpence (*Peoples*', 1850 on). Moneyless, stone-broke.

Up fields (*Westminster School*). Enclosure of Vincent Square, Westminster, practically the private property of St Peter's. It is historically the field where the Westminsters played, and play—especially football.

Up my sleeve (*Ancient English*). This phrase is very obscure, but it is certainly used in the sense of being intoxicated.

It was six pots up my sleeve when we reached port; and Sarah asked me to her next Sunday tea fight.

Up or down (*Peoples*'). Heaven or Hades.

Up School (*Westminster School*). Short for 'Upper School'—the great school-room.

Up the pole (*Peoples*', 1896 on). Drunk.

Plaintiff: I did not; but your little girl was frequently saying that you were 'up the poll'.

The Judge: Up the what?—Up the poll, sir.

What is that?—You know, sir. Up the poll.

The Judge: I don't know.

The High Bailiff explained that the term was a slang one for being intoxicated.—*D. T.*, 11th December 1897.

The approach to drunkenness is 'getting on the pole'.

Up to date (*Soc. and Peoples*', 1873 on). Total modernity.

The two principals were made up like Corbett and Fitzsimmons, and the entertainment was a triumph of 'the up-to-date'.—*Peoples*', 4th April 1897.

Up to the scratch (*Peoples*', 19 *cent.*). Fit, sufficient, allowable. Said to be from the lady committee of Almacks approving of names submitted to them by scratching some cabalistic mark intimating that the owner of the name might be allowed to enter Almacks. 'Not up to the scratch' referred to the fact that all who applied for entrance were not found worthy. Said to have been started by Beau Brummel.

The picture-destroyer pays his polite attentions to Mr Herbert as well as to Mr Alma Tadema. Who can say after this that Mr Herbert's pictures are not up to the scratch?—*Entr'acte*, 30th May 1885.

Up-end (*Street*, 1880 on). Fling down heavily, so that the heels fly up. Used figuratively for amazement — as 'I was fair-upended!'

Up-keep (*Soc.*, 1897). Maintenance, keeping up, keeping as a going concern. First noticed in print in this year.

The Council has now resolved to relieve local authorities of the cost of the up-keep of those places which they at present defray.—*D. T.*, 1st December 1897.

Upper and downer (*Lower People*). Wrestling struggle, in which combatants upset, but rarely if ever strike, each other. Generally for a bet.

Upper ten set (*Servants*'). Ladies and gentlemen employed by the upper ten thousand. Phrase found by themselves for themselves.

Uppertendom (*New York*). Word coined from upper ten.

Use (*High Church*, 1890 on). Function.

On Palm Sunday the benediction of palms carried in procession was more than ever the 'use', not merely in very advanced Anglican churches, and in more than one case a bishop was the chief officiator.—*World*, April 1897.

Usher of the hall (*Soc.*, 1883). Odd kitchen man—male. Equivalent of char or chore woman.

Mr M'Coan asked as to 'the sentence upon George Gardiner, described as a tutor, charged with stealing a jug of beer and sentenced to six weeks' imprisonment. Sir W. Harcourt, amid much laughter, explained that owing to the custom in large establishments of the odd man being called 'the Usher of the Hall', a position held by Gardiner, the writer of the newspaper paragraph had converted him into a tutor.—*House of Commons*, 19th April 1883.

Util (*Theatrical*). Utility. The util actor in a company. He is the odd man — ready to do anything. Generally a clever man who has missed his mark.

V

V.C. (*London*, about 1882). Plucky. The initials of Victoria Cross.

V.C. (*American - Eng.*, 19 *cent.*). Abbreviation of Vigilance Committee. A body of American neighbours bound together to punish an evil - doer, murderer, highwayman, horse-stealer, or unscrupulous sensualist who contrives to evade the law. Chiefly operates in out - lying and southern districts. 'Take care, or you'll be V.C.'d' (veeceed). (*See* Burke, Wainwright).

V.R. (*Peoples'*). Evasive reference to the prison van, which, in the reign of Victoria, bore these initials on each side. (*See* Black Maria, Virtue rewarded, Vagabonds removed, Sardine box).

V.R., V.R., V.R. (*Jubilee*, 1897). Ve are, ve are, ve are=we are, we are, we are. One of the jocular readings of 'V.R.' during the Diamond Jubilee. Applied to a placard in Kensington when the Queen visited that suburb (28th June 1897).

Vagabonds removed (*Peoples'*). Droll application of the initials V.R. —the letters standing, of course, for Victoria Regina, which appeared on the outside of the prison van to the end of the reign of Victoria.

Vales (*Soc.*, 18 *cent.*). Presents to servants. Still used in old houses.

Valse (*Anglo - Amer.*). Synonym for airy walking, especially in quitting a room. (*See* Balley, Polka, Skip).

Vanderbilt (*American*). The U.S.A. synonym for Rothschild (*q.v.*). To describe a very rich man—the Vanderbilts of New York being historical millionaires.—1884.

Vapourage (*American*). Medical vapour bathing.

Vardy the carsey (*Criminal*). Italian. Look at the house. One of the Italian organ-men's expressions—passed on. From ' vedere ' and ' casa '.

Variant (*Lit.*, '90's). Variation, divergency.

He piloted *Florodora* into the harbour of safety by his diverting variant of John Wellington Wells.—*D. T.*, 13th November 1899.

Variety stage (*Music Hall*, 1880). As distinct from the dramatic. Outgrowth of the prosperity of music halls.

Varnish (*Soc.*, 19 *cent.*). Bad champagne.

Vary means (*Polit.*, 18 *cent.*). Contradict, turn - coat, prevaricate. Introduced by Burke. Held its ground until 1840.

The contradiction between his methods is due, he pleads, to the identity of the object at which he aimed then, and at which he aims now. He varies his means, as Burke expressed it, to secure the essential unity of his end.—W. E. Gladstone (Edinburgh, 11th November 1885).

Venture girl (*Anglo-Indian*). Early Victorian. Poor young lady sent out to India to obtain a husband.

Verandah (*S. London*). The gallery of the old Victoria theatre.

Very famillionaire (*Soc.*, 1870). Referring to the shape of patronage displayed by rich men. Derived from the satirist Heine.

Very froncey (*Soc.*, 19 *cent.*). Too pronounced. Shape of Très Français. Supposed to be an elegant evasion of saying a given thing is vulgar.

Very well (*Soc.*, 1860 on). Second degree of approval—Not Bad being the first.

Vestrify (*Parliamentary*, 1884). To minimise; to reduce in dignity.

Mr Chaplin has enriched the English dictionary with the verb 'vestrify', which is perhaps destined to a longer life than the somewhat uncouth verb 'boycott'.— *D. N.*, 31st December 1884.

Vic (*Theatrical*). When the first theatre was built in the New Cut (Lambeth) it was called the Brunswick, in honour of the Princess Charlotte. It was burnt down before it was opened, and by the time it was rebuilt the poor Princess Charlotte was dead, and the eyes of the nation turned to the Princess Victoria. The new theatre was baptized the Royal Victoria, cut down by the New Cut warriors to Vic, before the first dramatic week was out. Strangely enough, the Princess Royal came to be called by this prompt diminutive. She is often thus named in the Queen's Diary. (*See* Bird, Brit., 'Delphi, Eff, Lane).

Viewy (*Political*, 1860-70). Mistrustedly theoretical, *dilletante*, lacking breadth. Invented in opposition to the philosophy of J. S. Mill. Remained as a condemnatory adjective.

Village blacksmith (*Music Hall—passing to theatres*). An artiste who never has a longer engagement than a week. Euphemism for a failure. Figuratively derived from a verse in Longfellow's poem:

'*Week in, week out*, from noon till night
You can hear his bellows roar.'

Vintage (*Anglo-American*). Year of birth.

'I want to sue a man for breach of promise,' said a maiden of the vintage of 1842, coming into a lawyer's office.— *N.Y. Mercury*, 1883.

Virgins' bus (*Peoples'*, 1870). The last bus from Piccadilly Corner westward. So named satirically in reference to the character of the chief patronesses at that late hour. No longer runs—the tubes bowled over this vehicle. (*See* Covered brougham).

Virtue rewarded (*Peoples'*). Prison van—ironical reference to the moral nature of its occupants, and based upon the initials V.R., which used to be seen on each side.

Vogue (*Soc.*, 1897). Fashion. This word was markedly used only early in 1897.

A remarkable instance of the commercial value of 'vogue' in art occurred at Christie's on Saturday.— *D. T.*, 8th March 1897.

Voice, To (*Soc.*, 1897 on). Assert, declare loudly. This use of a noun as a verb is very significant of public life.

London yesterday voiced the very spirit of the country.—*D. T.*, 17th October 1899.

Volunteer knee drill. Abject adulation. Outcome of volunteer movement.

Vote khaki, To (*Peoples'*, 1900). Opting for the Conservatives, plumping for the Liberal Unionist. First heard in the May of 1900.

One would give something to hear Mr Hosea Biglow's opinion upon 'voting khaki'.—*M. Leader*, W. Archer, 27th October 1900.

Voulez-vous squatty-vous? (*Theatre gods'*). Will you sit down? One of the half French nonsense phrases which began with the frequency of French *emigrés* and prisoners in England. Started by Grimaldi.

W

W. 2. (*Peoples'*, 1896). Double-u Two — satirical description of the Emperor William II., following on his telegram to President Kruger on New Year's Day 1896. Said of any military-looking man stalking town.

W.P.B. (*Press*). Waste paper basket. Ominous initials—generally referring to communications.

If the criticism or remark is nice, I read and enjoy it; if it is nasty, it is thrown into the W.P.B., and it troubles me not'—*Ref.*, 2nd March 1884.

I should say the printer's devil picked up the pieces from the editor's W.P.B., and handed them in for copy.

Wabbler (*Sporting*). Pedestrian.

Mr Edward Payson Weston, the well-known long-distance pedestrian, illustrated 'endurance without alcohol' by walking 50 miles in ten hours, or rather in nine hours fifty minutes, for the 'wabbler' saved ten minutes of his advertised time.

Wad (*Navy*). Gunner—interesting as a survival from the days of muzzle-loading cannon.

Wade in (*American*). To begin a fight. This expression was begun during the Civil War, and was probably started by some farmer recruits who obtained the figure of speech from the memory of the courage with which ducklings take to the water almost as soon as born.

Waggernery, O (*Lower Soc.*, '80's). New shape of 'O agony', based upon the ignorant contempt for the great German, Wagner, through this decade.

Waistcoat piece (*Tailors'*). Breast and neck of mutton—from its resemblance to the shape of half the front of a waistcoat not made up. (*See* Hyde Park railings.)

Waistrel (*Lancashire and the North generally—old*). A wretched, half-starved wanderer.

Wait (*Theatrical*). Time between the acts; the time between the appearances of an actor in the same piece.

Wait till the clouds roll by (*Peoples'*, 1884). Catch line used to induce hopefulness—from an American ballad, in which this phrase formed the chief feature of the chorus.

Wherever I have been lately and found the people festively inclined I have gathered that they intend to 'wait till the crowds roll by'.—*Ref.*, August 1884.

Wait a quarter of a sec! (*Society*). Intensification of 'Half a sec!' Protest against being over-hurried.

Wake snakes (*American - Eng.*). Provoke to the uttermost.

Walk out (*American - Eng., Theatrical*, 1890 on). Failure — from the American habit of condemning a bad play before it is over by going home. Reached England by way of Liverpool.

I am delighted to find, on the assurance of the author, that though New York 'walked out', Washington 'walked in' and received it warmly, and the Boston audience gave it a most enthusiastic reception also. — *D. T.*, 24th February 1897.

Walk out with the bat (*Soc.*, 1880). Victory—from the last cricketer in an innings taking his bat out, the last player but one having 'gone out'.

Walk turkey (*American - Eng.*). Promenade with constrained effort, like the movement of the turkey.

Walking round (*Peoples'* — *old*). Preparing for assault. From dogs walking round each other to look for the safest attack.

Walled (*Artists'*, 1882). Picture accepted—took the place of hung.

Wallop down (*Com. Lond.*). To fall with a crash.

Waltzing off on the ear (*American*). A person who acts upon the first word to which he happens to listen.

Wander (*Street*, 19 *cent.*). Satirical expression and meaning 'Be off'.

Want of proportion (*Criticism*, 1883). Term providing a new shape of attack upon the inductive process. Attributed to Mr Theodore Watts Dunton.

Want to score (*Peoples'*). Desire to succeed. From scoring, or marking in all athletic and many other exercises.

He was engaged in the most difficult scenes of a risky play. And he helped it, not because he 'wanted to score', but because he is a thorough artist, and knows the responsibility of his business. —*D. T.*, 6th January 1896.

Wants a apron (*Workman's*). Out of work—the apron off.

Wants salt (*American - English*, 1880 on). Wants grit.

Oh, thunder, you want salt on you. A super is an adjunct to the stage.—*Bad Boy's Diary*, 1883.

War Cry (*Salvation Army*, 1882-83). The 'huzza' of this body and of religious, and a title to their peculiar newspaper.

That's a very pretty dona, though, I came across in Regent Street the other evening who sold me a *War Cry*.—1883.

War - cry (*Public - house*, 1882). Mixture of stout and mild—ale understood. Applied satirically by 'topers' because the Salvation Army spoke stoutly and ever used mild terms. (*See* Brighton bitter, Cold four, Baby and nurse.)

War - paint (*Soc.*, 1875). Court, state, and evening dress in general—jewels, white gloves, etc., etc. Derived from North American Indians who always painted themselves when going into battle. (*See* Full fig.)

Wardour Street woods (*Cabinet-makers'*). Imitation old furniture, knocked together yesterday. Name obtained from Wardour Street (Soho,

London), because that place is or was supposed to be the headquarters of this business. (*See* Worm-eater.)

Warm as they make them (*Street*). Immoral.

Warm bit (*Com. London*, 1880). Vigorous woman.

Warm corner (*Soc., Sporting*). A nook where birds are found in plenty.

Warm with (*London Taverns*). Refers to orders for spirits and water, the 'with' refers to sugar.

Warrocks (*American — passing to Eng.*). Beware! This seems to be a corruption of war - hawks — meaning tomahawks. Certainly it is menacing and comes originally from the vocabulary of the North American Indians.

Warwick weed (*Warwickshire*). Warwick *elm*. Disguised self-glorification of the splendour of the county elms.

Passing through the ridge and furrow country where the elm, the 'Warwickshire weed', rises straight out of the corn, etc.—*D. N.*, August 1885.

Warwickshire Will. Name given to Shakespeare in his county.

Washer-dona (*Com. Lond.*, 19 *cent.*). Washer-woman.

Watch him like a hawk (*Hist.*). Watch to the very death.

Hawks were tamed by watching. Shakespeare has several allusions to this. Desdemona in assuring Cassio how she will urge his suit with Othello, says:

'I'll watch him tame, and talk him out of patience.'

Selden, in his *Table Talk*, says: 'Lecturers get a great deal of money, because they preach the people tame, as a man watches a hawk.'

Watchers (*Election*). Euphemism for spies on the look out for bribery.

Water - bottle (*Street*). Total abstainer. (*See* Rum - bottle, Milk-bottle, Ink-bottle, etc., etc.)

Water down (*Political*). Weaken —minimise results.

It is no use increasing the number of voters if you water down and minimise the political influence which the vote confers.—Mr J. Chamberlain, 13th June 1883.

Water dona (*Lower Class*). Washer-woman—a lady who disports herself in water, together with soap and suds.

Waterloo (*Streets*, 19 *cent.* to about 1870). Half-penny—as thus. There was a half-penny toll over Waterloo Bridge, on the Surrey side of which lived most of the poorer common women who harassed the Strand. As midnight arrived, these moneyless women who hung about Wellington Street at the Strand end of the bridge begged for a 'Waterloo' to pay their toll over the bridge.

Wauns (*Peoples', provincial*). Wounds — God's wounds. Another shape of zounds.

Wauns — so sound that they never wake? I wish my wife lay there.— Farquhar, *The Recruiting Officer*.

Way of all flesh (*Peoples'*). Dead —probably from Puritanic phrase.

Weak in the arm (*Public-house*). Caustic euphemism for a short pull of beer, as compared with the long pull. Chiefly refers to half-pint drawn in a pint pot.

Weaken (*Amer.*, 1880). Soften.

Wears a revolver-pocket (*Doubtful Soc.*, 1880 on). Evasive statement to the effect that the speaker carries a revolver.

The hateful and barbarous custom of carrying these deadly weapons has risen to an incredible height; it has long been known to the Home Office, who need only to have asked the tailors how many revolver pockets they now make. — Mitchell Henry, *Times*, 23rd January 1885.

Wears the broad arrow (*Thieves'*). Elegant evasion of a reference to convict life. (*See* Taken stripes.)

Wears the head large (*Low. Mid.-class*). Recovering from alcoholic excess.

It was half-past six before all was over, and during the day heads were worn large.—*Ref.*, 15th August 1886.

Wears the leek (*Popular*). Is a Welshman. It seems likely that the wearing of the leek actually came into usage when Henry VII. conquered at Bosworth by the aid of his Welsh followers under the Tudor colours, white and green, suggestive of the leek itself. To this view a Harleian MS., written by a Welshman, in the time of James I., gives some grounds.

Weasel (*East Anglia*). Bribe—probably from this animal slimly introducing himself into pocket-like rabbit holes.

Weases (*Amer.*). People of S. Carolina.

Weather peeper (*Nautical*). Best eye.

Web-foots (*Provincial*). People of Lincolnshire, probably bestowed upon them by their higher county neighbours, who did not live in the wretched fens of Lincolnshire. Also called yellow-bellies. Taken together suggestive of fen-game, such as wild ducks and geese, widgeon, all common to the fens. In the States, most of the state nicknames are derived from the flora, fauna, or prevailing geology of the district.

Why English people give each other comical names is a question fitter for a learned essay than a descriptive sketch: but the fact remains that we have besides Yorkshire 'tykes', Norfolk 'dumplings', Cheshire 'cats', Essex 'calves', and Suffolk 'punches', as well as Lincolnshire folk, who are web-foots.—*D. N.*, August 1884.

This term web-foot is applied to the people of Oregon—but as an alternative to web-foot they are often called hard-cases.

Wedge (*Thieves'*). Jew. A wedge fixes objects or breaks them up. So a Jew-fence, in relation with thieves, or a Jew ordinary, in his everyday business, is supposed to 'wedge' the other.

Wee - wees (*Peoples'* — *Hogarth period*). Frenchmen—from the habit of Frenchmen, common to this day, of repeating the ordinary affirmative *oui*.

This looks very much as if the English race were dwindling into a people of town-loafers, afraid to risk themselves in new enterprises in rude lands, and as incapable of being genuine colonists as the despised 'men of Wee Wee'—the French.—*D. N.*, 20th October 1886.

Weed out (*Polit.*, 1870). Change politics.

The Chairman had said that he had no hesitation in saying that if Mr Goschen did not weed himself out of the Liberal party, the Liberal party would not attempt to weed him out.—Mr J. Morley, Nottingham, October 1885.

Weeper (*Soc.*, 1884). Long sweeping moustache. Probably adapted from the long ends of crape worn at funerals until burial reform (1866-67) swept them away.

Weg (*Polit.*, 1885). Initials of William Ewart Gladstone. Given in memory of Mr Wegg (*Our Mutual Friend*), who was a great sayer of words.

It seems that in 1857 a speech was delivered by a Mr James Hall who called Weg a great political coward. This speech is now reprinted in the *Globe* nearly thirty years afterwards.—*Ref.*, 17th May 1885.

(*See* G.O.M.)

Welcher or welsher (*Racing*). A cheat. When a book-maker does not pay his debts after a race he is often fallen upon with cries of 'welcher', and his clothes almost as often are torn off his back. It is said the word takes its rise from the name of a man who, after repeated warnings, was the first to suffer from this adaptation of Lynch law.

Weigh in (*American-Eng.*). Assert oneself — from weighing, in horse-racing.

The journal 'weighs in' with a prismatic Christmas number.—*D. N.*, November 1885.

Weigh out (*L. London*). Give one his fair share. Fine idea of the distribution of stolen plate melted down to avoid identification.

'I made Criss weigh out my share!'—*Peoples'*, 6th January 1895.

Weighing the thumb (*L. Class*, 19 *cent.*). Cheating in weight by sticking down the scale with the thumb, so as to give the idea of full weight, and then seizing the scale before the rebound occurs.

For practising the old trick of 'weighing his thumb' to the disadvantage of the customer, a City coster, named James Martin, who said he thought it 'a light affair', was directed to pay a fine of 20s. and costs.—*D. T.*, 25th August 1896.

Well (*Soc.*, 1860). Capital, very good, satisfactory. Used as an adjective instead of an adverb.

Well certainly (*American Soc.*). This phrase is very common in U.S.A. —now and again used in England.

Well-groomed (*Peoples'*, 1881). Perfectly dressed. From the stables, when the highest praise is to speak of a horse as well-groomed.

Well-sinking (*Anglo-Indian*, 18 *cent.* on). Digging for treasure. Generally—making money.

Questioned as to why he had no pension for his wounds, Fraser stated that after the relief of Lucknow he bought his discharge; he had then upwards of £200. He got the money by 'well-sinking', i.e., the discovery of buried treasure.—*People*, 22nd September 1895.

Well shod (*Anglo-American*). Well off. Specimen of figurative slang—a horse only going prosperously when well shod.

Well sot up (*Provincial American*). Well-dowried. Only said of middle-class brides, chiefly agriculturally.

Wellingtons (*Mid.-class*, 1812 on). Plural of Wellington, and referring to boots named after the Iron Duke. 'Where are my Wellingtons?' (*See* Von Blucher).

Wen, The (*Middle-class*). London —from its shape, and figuratively from its absorbing quality.

Cobbett called the London of his day ' The Wen '. The movement of the rural population townwards was only then beginning.—*D. N.*, 26th June 1885.

Wet a line (*Anglers'*). Go fishing. Year by year the communications with the lovely Thames Valley have been increased until there is no difficulty in the way of the Thames angler 'wetting a line'.

Wet-bobs (*Eaton*). Bobs means boys—the phrase designates boating Etonians, as distinct from dry-bobs, or cricketers.

Wet canteen (*Military*). Where liquors are sold. Antithesis of dry canteen — which is the stores-centre of the barracks, where all things but beer may be obtained—on payment.

Wet ship (*Nautical*). Ship in which captain and company drink deeply.

Wet 'uns (*Low. Class*, 19 *cent.*). Wet ones—meaning tears.

Whack up (*American, from Irish*). To subscribe.

Whales (*American—passing to England*). Desperately devoted.

'The Red Lamp' belongs to the Princess Claudia Morakoff, who is whales on Nihilist-hunting.—*Ref.*, 24th April 1887.

What a bean feast! (*Peoples'*). Satirical exclamation in reference to a riot, quarrel, or wretched meal; or other entertainment. (*See* Bean feast.)

What a Collins! (*Exeter*, 19 *cent.*). Greedy person—evidently from name of a gourmand who has long since been forgotten.

What a tale our cat's got (*Peoples' proverbial—old*). Figure of speech to describe a woman or girl flaunting in a new dress, and swinging the hind part of the skirt from side to side with a haughty motion of the hips.

What do you think? (*Mid.-class*, 1882). What is your general opinion of things? Introduced in this year by a comic singer, who interpolated the enquiry at various strong points in his song; accent on '*you*'.

What ho! she bumps! (*London*, 1899). Satirical cry upon any display of vigour—especially feminine. Said to be derived from a report of a boating adventure, where this term was used as 'she' fetched land. A popular song made this term more popular.

To see Willie Edouin dance a hornpipe is a liberal education, and his official proclamation, 'I trade in bumps. Oblige me by not saying, "What ho!"' almost tempted an Ibsenite to smile.— *D. T.*, 13th November 1899.

What next, and next? (*Peoples'*, 19 *cent.*). Exclamation signifying contempt for audacious assertion. A favourite phrase of William Cobbett's.

The Tories must be hard up for a stick to bang Gladstone with when the *Globe* actually has to reprint an attack upon him from the *Oswestry Observer* of 1857. Ye gods! what next, and next?—*Ref.*, 17th May 1885.

What Paddy gave the drum (*Irish Military*, 1845). Elegant euphemism for a sound thrashing, as ' I'll give you what Paddy gave the drum'.

What the Connaught man shot at (*Irish*). Roundabout for 'nothing at all'.

'What the Connaught man shot at' has been of late far from 'nothing'.— *D. N.*, 1883.

(*See* Footless stocking without a leg.)

What the hell! (*Peoples'*). Exclamation of anger. Is it one of the Catholic corruptions? 'What the hail!'—from 'Hail, Mary'?

What will you liq.? (*Middle-class*). What will you drink?

What would Mrs Boston say? (*American-Eng.*, 1850 on). Equivalent to—What would Mrs Grundy say? Sometimes heard in England. The people of Boston hold Boston to be the most superior city in the U.S.A.

Whatchir! (*Sailors'*). Shape of 'What cheer?'

What-er, A (*Street*). Shape of 'what' — thus formed in answer to some reply as to what the speaker is. He may say I'm a chimbler (chimney-sweep)—to which the reply, always in response to a noun ending in 'er'—'A what-er?'

What's the dynamite now? (*Soc.*, 1890 on). Protest against a burst of ill-temper, as suggestive of blowing people up.

What's the hullaballoo? (*Peoples'*, 18 *cent.* and 19 *cent.*). Riot, noise, contention. Is this one of the Catholic corruptions—is it 'What's the holy belly'—'Ventre Saint Gris'—the nickname of Henri IV. of Navarre—and referring to the dead, therefore grey, body of Christ. On the other hand, 'Hurliberlieu' is a French term.

What's the lyddite? (*Boer War*, 1899-1900). Latest shape of 'What's the row?'

What's the mat? (*Public-school*, 1880). Abbreviation of 'matter'.

What's yer fighting weight? (*Street*, 1883). 'At what weight do you fight, and are you fit? I'm your man!'

What's yer Gladstone weight? (*Street*, 1885). Satirical shape of 'What's your fighting weight?' Means that the speaker doubts if you will fight if invited. From the disrepute into which Mr Gladstone passed with the Jingoes, or war party, for his alleged unwillingness to carry on the war in the Soudan with eagerness.

What's your poll to-day? (*Printers'*, 19 *cent.*). Amount of piece wages— from numbers on a statement of votes.

Whaty?, A (*Peoples'*, 18 *cent.*). An enquiry made when any strange statement is made: *e.g.*, 'He's a jimjack' —'A whaty?'—'A jimjack.' This diminutive is probably of court descent; for all the familiar memoirs of George III. give an anecdote of his defiance to some peeress to fog him with Scotch, and his immediate defeat, when he cried 'A whaty, my lady—a whaty?' The popular interchange of 'v' and 'w', which has now utterly passed away, was a singular evidence of even the lowest of the people accepting and adopting the early royal Georgian modes of pronouncing English. Sam Weller made this mode classic. Old puns reek with it. 'Oh—it's a wherry is it?—werry good, etc., etc.'

Wheel-house, Abaft the (*Amer.*). Below the small of the back.

The next instant a huge bull charged out of the door, and, catching the hero of Valley Forge abaft the wheelhouse, incontinently slammed him into a big apple tree.—*Newsp. Cutting.*

Wheeled (*Low Life*). Moved upon wheels, as distinct from wheel, which is 'barrered' (*q.v.*). Instance of expressed awe in the contemplation of unaccustomed luxury. That is wheeled —in a cab.

Wheeze (*Theatr.*). Gag, *i.e.*, lines (usually comic) interpolated in the text by the player.

Wheezer (*Music Hall*, 1897). Phonograph.

Whelps (*American*). People of Tennessee.

When at Rome do as Rome does (*Proverbial*). Recommendation to fall in with the arrangements of those about you. Counsel to be not too conscientious.

Where are you a-going to—can't yer! (*Low. London*, 1880). Really meaning, Take care who you're shoving against.

Where did you get the Rossa? (*Peoples'*, 1885). Enquiry as to borrowed plumes. Arose from the trial of a Mrs Dudley (New York, July 1885) for shooting at O'Donovan Rossa.

When Rossa said his name was Jeremiah O'Donovan Rossa, Mrs Dudley asked, 'Where did you get the Rossa?' —*D. N.*, 1st July 1885.

It was supposed that the Rossa was a flight of fancy. This phrase commenced in New York, thence went to Liverpool and over all England.

Where do I come in? (*Peoples'*, '90's). Personal protest. From a police-court case in which a shrew put this question until she was turned out.

'Where', to use a phrase which Mr Labouchere has made Parliamentary, 'do we come in?' Unfortunately, we do not come in at all.—*D. T.*, 5th August 1899.

Where the flies won't get it (*American*). To swallow 'it' — generally drink.

Where's the war? (*Peoples'*, 1900). Applied to some scattered and divided street wrangle. From the Boer War after June 1900 — when both sides seemed to be distributed over creation, and never appeared to get really face to face.

Whig (*Mid-class*, 1860-99). Irresolute person — even a turncoat. From the Whig, in parliament, being generally a temporiser.

Whipped out of one's boots (*American*). Completely conquered.

Whirl (*Anglo-American*). A stormy turn, a general challenge.

Whisht (*Provincial*). Dangerous— to be avoided. Probably an onomatope from the catching of the breath in fear.

Companionship offered to such beings (Protestant nuns) in a remote rural neighbourhood in England was not all kindly. They were 'whisht' women, even witches, to the rustics.—*D. N.*, 29th December 1884.

Whiskbroom 'with' (*American - Eng.*, 1897). Cry describing drunkenness. This phrase came from U.S.A. on 8th of July 1897.

Prohibition (U.S.A.) has always been followed by a remarkable display of ingenuity in evasion, but, according to Miss Kate Field, no State ever evaded the prohibitory law so neatly as Kansas. Desiring to purchase a whiskbroom when on a lecture tour out there, Miss Field went into a druggist's where they were displayed in the window. 'Will you have one with or without?' asked the man behind the counter. 'I do not understand your meaning,' she replied. Holding up two whiskbrooms apparently exactly alike, he parted the wisps of one, disclosing a small flask, and with a little whirl of his thumb and finger the top of the broom came off, like the cork out of a bottle. Miss Field bought the two whiskbrooms, one for ordinary use, the other to exhibit to audiences as an argument in her lecture, 'Does Prohibition Prohibit?'—*D. T.*, 8th July 1897.

The whiskbroom is a small coir brush about a foot long.

Whisker-fake (*Theatrical*). Cosmetic for facial hair.

Whiskeries (*London*, 1888). Irish Exhibition in London.

Early on Monday morning I arose and donned my caubeen, my brogues and other things, and lighting my dhudeen, and selecting my finest shillelagh, went off to Olympia to assist at the opening of the Whiskyries, otherwise the Irish Exhibition.—*Ref.*, 10th June 1888.

Whisky-bottle (*Scotch*). A Scotch drunkard.

Whisky stalls (*Press*, 1883). End stalls, or near the end, so that an occupier can adjourn to the refreshment bar without much inconvenience to himself, or a long line of neighbours.

Whisky straight (*American Saloon*). Whisky—with no water about it.

Whispering gallery (*Theatrical*, 1883). The then Gaiety Bar — long since razed, and its site aiding in the formation of the front of Aldwych. Derived from the Whispering Gallery of St Paul's Cathedral. Said in satire of the poorer actors 'out of a ship', who frequented that hostelry, and whispered to any one of their more fortunate brethren — as, 'Could you lend me half a dollar?' (*See* Pros' Avenue.)

Whist drive (*Soc.* 1895). Whist— where the players are shifted, at the end of a rubber, to other tables and other players.

Whistle for wind (*Peoples'*, 19 *cent.*). Description of a fool.

The reef-points clatter upon your fair white mainsail and the helmsman whistles softly for the wind which will not come. —Sir E. Arnold, *D. T.*, 31st March 1897.

Whistler (*E. London*). Chance labourer at docks — from the poor fellow whistling for work.

Only fifty men were wanted beyond the 'royals', or regular hands. So a hundred and fifty needy 'whistlers'— the dock term for chance labourers—had to turn with heavy hearts away.—*Ref.*, 29th March 1885.

Whistler (*Soc.*, 1880). Misty, dreamy, milky, softly opalescent atmosphere — from many peculiarly exceptional pictures painted by the artist of this name. Came to be applied to ethics, æsthetics, and even conversation, where the doctrines enunciated were foggy.

The river, too, never looks better than on one of these 'Whistler' evenings. Symphonies in silver and gold and blue and purple and cold grey are to be found on the embankments, notably on the south of the river, for the trouble of going there. — *D. N.*, 11th November 1884.

Whistlers (*Scotland*). Bag-pipers. In their native wilds, the people of Fife are known as 'whistlers', not on account of their musical proclivities, but because their country take its name from a very highly-pitched musical instrument, between which and a 'whistle' the Caledonian ear distinguishes little difference. —*D. T.*, 4th March 1898.

White Army, The (*Street*, 1883). A band of men who formed themselves together to combat social evil.

Another 'army' has been formed. This time it is a band of youths and men who are to wear a white cross, and battle against the social evil. The White Army may be very earnest, but if it is to parade the streets like the other armies it will be just what it is formed to put down.—*Ref.*, 18th February 1883.

White Brahmins (*Anglo-Indian*, 19 *cent.*). Excessively exclusive persons. Invented by Hindoo satire to describe the Brahminic-like exclusiveness of those of the English in India, who wished to prevent the native Indian from obtaining any power.

When Indians mean to be sarcastic, they denominate the English in India White Brahmins.—*D. N.*, 9th December 1884.

White elephant (*Soc.*, 18 *cent.* and on). An article (generally large and expensive), for which you have no use. Again, a present which entails more expense than advantage, one generally bestowed by a donor who wishes to relieve himself of a burden. Derived from a habit of the remoter Kings of Siam, who, when they wished to ruin a courtier, made him a present of a white elephant, whose sacred nature made his keep and that of his attendants so expensive that the owner was necessarily reduced to beggary.

White horse (*Irish*). Cowardice. Derived from the tradition that James II. fled from the battle of the Boyne on a white horse.

White light (*Railway—now spread to Peoples'*). All right, correct, safe. From a white light throughout the railway world representing safety, and freedom from danger. (*See* All over red, Be green.)

White magic (*Soc.*, 19 *cent.*). In general, innocent legerdemain, but figuratively applied to very beautiful fair women. Also applied by Protestant writers to the Roman Catholic ritual.

White nigger (*Negro*). Term of contempt and offence used by blacks against white folk.

The emancipated blacks of Sierra Leone not only address each other as 'niggers', but salute as 'white niggers' all Europeans with whom they are not on friendly terms.—*D. N.*, 20th June 1883.

White soup (*Thieves'*). Melted silver—run down from stolen plate, to avoid identification.

One or two colleges at Oxford have a crozier or so of the fourteenth century, or a platter of the time of Edward IV. But most of the college plate made 'white soup' at the time of the Civil War, and went unavailingly to buy horses and feed men for the King.— *D. N.*, 5th May 1887.

Whitechapel (*Peoples'*, 1888). Woman murder. In and about 1888 a number of women of the town in the East of London were murdered and mutilated. Before the year was out a woman murder came to be called a Whitechapel.

When charged prisoner said he knew nothing about the murder; he was very drunk. A witness who worked with him said he had heard Nicholson say, 'I shall do a Whitechapel on my wife yet'.

Whitechapel oner (*Local London*). A leader of light and youth in the Aldgate district—chiefly in the high coster interests. (*See* Roader.)

Whitechapel warriors (*E. London*). Militia of the Aldgate district.

Whitechokery (*Peoples'*, 1870). Figure of speech for the general scheme of life maintained by the various classes who wear white neckties habitually— or only in the evening.

Whitehall (*Military*, 19 *cent.*). Metaphor of cheerfulness. When a soldier has leave of absence to London, his sergeant probably says to him, 'Don't go near Whitehall, or we shan't see you to time'. This refers to the fact that a soldier can generally get an extension of leave of absence if he makes personal application for it at the Horse Guards, which is the very heart of Whitehall. It is popularly supposed in the army that if a soldier on leave goes near Whitehall he cannot resist the temptation to apply for extra leave. Hence when a soldier looks particularly cheerful, it is said of him, 'He's been to Whitehall'.

White-washed (*Builders'*). Compounded with creditors or passed through the bankruptcy court.

Whittington Priory (*Debtors'*). Holloway prison for debt—from its propinquity to Highgate, and the associations of Highgate with Whittington.

Whittling (*Polit.*). Niggling and reducing things by fragments. From the ancient and past away habit of agricultural Americans, shaving away a stick with a clasp-knife, while talking. Is now used for petty, wasteful action, as distinct from sheer evident work.

Lord Salisbury put forward with great ingenuity and ability what he called the Tory programme at Newport. He has since been engaged in whittling it away until what was little before has become small by degrees and beautifully less; until there is hardly any of it left for your consideration. — Mr Chamberlain (Birmingham), 3rd November 1885.

Who are yer? (*Street*, 1883). Enquiry in an offensive tone, made in the street, and which, when answered, usually receives the counter-enquiry, 'who are *you*?'

Who did you say? (*L. Streets'*, '90's). Satire levelled at a passing person of evident, or self-asserting importance, and uttered by one friend to another, without any preliminary statement on any side.

Who pawned her sister's ship? (*Local London, Clare Market, Strand*). The meaning of the term is quite obscure, but during the last year of this historical ramshackle and labyrinthine spot, this sentence would always create a burst of laughter amongst the intimates of that doubtful locality. May have been an evasion of 'shift'.

Who shot the dog? (*L. C.*, '60's). Term of contempt levelled at volunteers, who were not at their initiation popular with the masses, who had not got over the revulsion of feeling in favour of the real soldier. The phrase arose from the rash shooting of a dog in the streets by a Surrey Volunteer.

'Who shot the dog?' was a very ill-natured cry prevalent in London streets in the early days of the Volunteer movement, and was supposed to refer to a misadventure of some rifleman who had inadvertently shot a dog.—*D. T.* (G. A. Sala), 28th July 1894.

Who stole the goose? (*Peoples'*—*provincial*). Interjection of contempt, which appears to have some hidden meaning, probably of an erotic nature.

Who sups with the devil must have a long spoon (*Historical*). Brought into fashion again by Mr J. Chamberlain (1898), meaning of course, that in dealings with rascals one must keep one's eye open—said in reference to Russia's action in China.

Who took it out of you? (*Street*). Meaning wholly unknown to people not absolutely of lower class.

Who? who? (*Soc.*, 1852). Doubtful, to be mistrusted. From a parliamentary episode.

The 'Who? who? Government'. The story went that the Duke of Wellington, asking Lord Derby one evening in the House of Commons for the names of the new Ministers, and knowing nothing of many of them, had to call out 'Who? who?' so often in tones audible to the whole House, that the attention of friends and enemies was alike attracted, and the humour of the day found a title for the Ministry out of the Duke's astonished and repeated enquiry. — *D. N.*, 10th December 1884.

Whoa, bust me (*Low. London*). Protest. A very common expression through the 19th century.

Whoa, carry me out (*Common London*, 19 cent.). Here we have the protecting 'Whoa' preceding a droll affectation of being shocked to death, which involves being effectually carried out.

Whoa, Emma! (*Street*, '80's). Entreaty to be modified—addressed to women with marked appearance or behaviour in the streets. It came from an inquest on a woman who had died under astounding circumstances. She was suffering from inflammation; she induced her husband to allay her pain by the use of a small Dutch clock weight. Finding relief from the contact of the cold iron, she urged the husband to continue the operation—whereupon she died. At the inquest the husband had to defend himself. He urged that he said to his wife 'Whoa Emma!' over and over again, but she would not listen to him. For years this phrase lasted as a street protest, too often shot at drunken women. (*See* Outside Eliza, Now we're busy.)

Whoa, Jameson! (*Peoples'*, 1896). An admiring warning against plucky rashness. When Dr Jameson invaded the Transvaal, with a handful of men, and lost, the people recognised his equal pluck and rashness.

Whole hog (*Anglo - American*). Thorough bare-faced lie—derived in the first place from a recommendation to a man of Connecticut (where pork affords the chief menu) to go the whole hog—the man having made a statement as to a quantity of pork he had eaten. As usual with popular phrases, it passed into a song—'The whole Hog or None.'

Whole souled time (*American*, 1882). Perfect delight.

It was a whole-souled time, as the Americans call it — now unknown. — *Graphic*, 17th March 1883.

Whole team (*American*, 1878). Perfect, absolute — from the agricultural states, where the 'whole team' does the work.

It is an Americanism. We cannot tell who invented it, but it means that a man is in possession of uncommon powers of mind. That he is a whole team when he is smart; when he is very smart he is a whole team and a horse to spare, and when the smartest, a whole team and a horse to spare and a pair of coach dogs under the waggon.—*N. Y. Mercury*, 2nd March 1878.

Whole team and a little dog under the waggon (*American*). Distinguished, liberal, proper—said of anything.

Wholeskin brigade (*Transvaal War*). Cautious cowards in its general application, but in actual war meaning a regiment, battalion or brigade which has not been in action. Does not necessarily mean that the brigade in question has shirked action.

. . . the 'wholeskin brigade', to borrow a phrase from the pungent vocabulary of the British private in South Africa, etc. —*D. T.*, 31st October 1901.

Whoop up (*American*). To tune a musical instrument.

Whooperups (*Theatrical and Entertainment generally*). Inferior, noisy singers.

Whoy-oi! (*Street*). Cry used by coster - class upon sight of a gaily-dressed girl passing near them. Also the cry of welcome amongst London costermongers.

Whyms (*Club*, 1882). Consolidation into a word of the initials 'Y.M.C.A.' (*q.v.*).

Widow, The (*Army*, 1863 on). Affectionate name for Queen Victoria. In no way disparaging.

Widow, The (*Soc.*, 1850 on). Clicquot champagne — brand of *la Veuve Cliquot*, hence the term. (*See* Squat, Dutchman, etc.)

Wielder of the willow (*Sporting*). Cricketer—from the bats being made of this wood.

Wife out of Westminster (*Old English*). Doubtful spouse — sometimes still heard in the East of London.

Wig-faker (*Low. London*, 18 cent. on). Hair-dresser.

Wigs on the green (*Irish*, 18 cent.). Fighting. The Irish Parliament House (1782-1800) was on the Green, Dublin, in days when wigs were worn. The Green was the constant scene of riots, and as constantly wigs would strew the roadway. Still used figuratively all over Ireland.

In taking leave of Bayreuth and the 'Ring', I can only counsel a continuance of that policy of peace which seems happily to have been adopted both by ardent Wagnerites and by those who choose to cleave to the older ways of music. Twenty years ago, if the chroniclers tell us truth, it was almost a case of 'wigs on the green' at Festival time, to such heights did party feeling run.—*D. T.*, 25th August 1896.

Wild - goose (*American mining*). Promise of fortune. A thin vein of ore, generally referring to silver, which presages the discovery of valuable veins.

Wilhelm II. much (*Soc.*, 1898). Wilhelm Too much. Obvious chaff suggesting the extremely busy activity of the Emperor of Germany.

Will you short? (*Australian Tavern*). Pay for a small dose of spirits.

Willie — we have missed you (*Peoples'*, 1899). Welcome. In the 'fifties a ballad with this title was very popular. Finally it became a march which is played to this day. On 20th November the Emperor of Germany arrived at Portsmouth, and this march was the first music to welcome him when he came on shore.

While the inspection was in progress the band of the Royal Marine Light Infantry played 'Willie, we have missed you', a playful attention which pleased the Emperor, who heartily shook the bandmaster, Lieutenant Miller, by the hand as he passed. — *D. T.*, 21st November 1899.

Willie—Willie—wicked, wicked! (*Street*). Satiric street reproach addressed to a middle-aged woman talking to a youth. From a county court case in which a middle-aged landlady sued for a week's rent from a young man lodger whose defence was that he left the house because the plaintiff would not only come into his room, but would proceed to sit on his bed.

Windfall (*Hist.*). Unexpected fortune.

Window (*Street*, 1860). Eye-glass —invented to meet the requirements of the round, rimless, stringless eye-glass which so many young men still carry, as by a miracle, in the right eye.

Wine ('*Varsities*, 19 *cent.*). Abbreviation of wine-party.

His first 'wine', given in his own room, was an awful ordeal. — *D. N.*, 6th March 1885.

(*See* Tea-pot.)

Wing (*Theatrical*). Perform with much help from the prompter—who stands at the wing.

Let us take the slang verb 'to wing'. It indicates the capacity to play a rôle without knowing the text, and the word itself came into use from the fact that the artiste frequently received the assistance of a special prompter, who often stood upon the stage, but screened from the audience by a piece of the scenery or a wing.—*Stage*, 31st August 1885.

Wingers — sometimes called **Flanges** (*Colloquial* — about 1865). After the Crimean beard, which meant all the hair growable on the face, had lasted in fashion about ten or twelve years, the chin came to be once more shown, and the whiskers were thrown back, or pulled away from the cheeks, and allowed to grow as long as nature decided. The name was obtained from their streaming and waving character.

Winifred, O (*Peoples'*, '90's). Exclamation importing disbelief — from St Winifred's Well, in Wales.

St Winifred's Well, in Flintshire, whose miraculous cures are the envy of Lourdes and the wonder of the North of England, is not to be turned into a soda-water manufactory without a struggle.—*D. T.*, 15th December 1898.

Wink (*American Saloon*). Dumb mode of ordering liquor.

Winter campaign (*Peoples'*, 1884). Riot, shrewishness, drunken disturbance—from the name given by the dynamiters to their operations in the winter months, when general darkness threw but little light upon their proceedings.

After the explosion of 30th May there was a lull, and then there commenced what, on the other side of the Atlantic, they were pleased to call the 'winter campaign'. There was an attempt to blow up London Bridge, then there was the explosion in the railway tunnel near King's Cross, and afterwards the explosions at Westminster and the Tower. *D. N.*, 3rd March 1885.

Wipe off your chin (*American*, 1860). To drink a liqour—probably suggested by the habit of a bearded man wiping the moustache and beard about the chin, with the hand, after a drink. Also used as a recommendation to be silent—from chin being used to mean speech.

Wiping feet (*Hoppers'—Kent*). Asking for beer-money. Mode of asking for money from visitors to hopfields. The boots are brushed with hop-bines, and the money is waited for.

Wire in and get your name up (*Peoples'*, 1862). Recommendation to struggle for success, but originally very erotic.

By-and-bye, when the white heat of excitement is over, no one will be able to say that anybody connected with this maladorous squabble missed a chance of 'wiring in and getting his name up'.— *Ref.*, 21st October 1888.

Without any (*L. Class*, 1890 on). Abstinence from any shape of alcohol. One of the elegant evasions.

The old lady made a curtsey to the Bench as she entered the dock, and repeated her obeisance when asked what she had to say. She said she had gone for years 'without any', and was afraid she had taken too much.—*D. T.*, 17th December 1897.

Without authorial expenses (*Literary*). Cheating, piracy, theft.

From this phrase being used against the U.S.A. to explain that the original English author has been paid nothing for the reprinted work.

Witness-stand (*American*). Witness-box in court of law. Rather a misnomer, as the witnesses are seated. In the English witness-box no witness is allowed a seat while he can keep his feet.

Talk of volubility, why, a darkey lady on the witness-stand is irrepressible. They are all ladies, and I observed that each of them referred to the other as a lady, even when she was an opponent.—*D. T.*, 2nd April 1897.

Woffle (*Music Hall and Music generally*). To mask, evade, manipulate a note or even difficult passage.

Wollies (*E. London*). Well known term for olives, of which the great mass brought to London are consumed by the Jews and other East Londoners. Probably an abbreviation of the call, 'O! olives!' by the street vendors of these delicacies.

Wolverines (*American*). People of Michigan—probably from the territory being over-run with wolves.

Won't run to it, It (*Sporting Peoples'*). Too poor. Figure of speech from a horse not reaching the post; in other words—a horse with no stay. Very common expression.

Won't take off his coat (*Street*). Equal to a coward.

Won't wash (*Peoples'*). No permanent value—derived from the printed calico trade.

Wood-spoiler (*Navy*). Merely average ship's carpenter.

Woodbine (*L. London*). Name of the maker of a penny packet of five cigarettes.

Wooden nutmegs (*American*). People of Connecticut. Given in consequence of these traders having been the first to discover this spice, which, it has been said, they once palmed off upon the unwary.

Wooden spoon (*Soc.*, 19 *cent.*) Thick-head; idiot. From Cambridge University — a wooden spoon being until recently given as the lowest possible mathematical honour—but at least an honour—at the Tripos Examinations. (Now no longer given, Tripos being abolished.)

He will never do any good—he is too quite a wooden spoon.

This year a student from Caius College and another from St Catharine's were bracketed equal for the honour of the 'wooden spoon' in the Mathematical Tripos, and to each was presented a huge trophy in the form of a malt shovel, gaily adorned with his college arms and colours.—*D. T.*, 19th June 1894.

Wooden Ulster (*Street*). Coffin.

Word-mongering (*Press*, 1878). Redundancy of description. Used in critical scorn.

Work (*Theatrical and Music Hall*). Perform. Natural affected outcome of calling the theatre 'shop' (*q.v.*).

Work the steam off (*Soc.*, 1870 on). Get rid of superabundant energy.

Work up (*Peoples'*). To aggravate.

Worker (*Polit.*, *American*). A civil service placeman who politically works to bring in his candidate, so that this voter may not go out of office at the next presidential election.

Workus (*Church of England*). Methodist chapel — from its plain, white-washed appearance.

Worm-eater (*Trade—Cabinet makers'*). A deft artisan who drills very diminutive holes in imitation old furniture, to give the effect of wormholes to the wood. (*See* Wardour Street Woods.)

Worrab (*Costers' transposed word*). Barrow.

Worrocks (*Peoples'*). Beware. Probably a corruption of ''Ware hawks'—ware being short for beware. The phrase implies—look after your pockets; there are thieves about—a threat presaging attack.

Worry down (*American*). To swallow greedily, like a dog.

Worry the dog (*Peoples'*). Bully —said of a man who upsets even the welcome of the house-dog, which retreats at his approach.

Worth (*Soc.*, 1860-85). Most fashionable costume. From name of a man-milliner of the second French empire.

Wotchero! (*Peoples'*). Agglomeration of 'What cheer oh!'

Wotchero! another one.—*E. T.*, 11th April 1885.

Wreckers, First-night (*Theatr.*). In 1882 a small band of men, chiefly very young, but led by a man of fifty, who combined to wreck pieces on their first night, became very troublesome. They numbered about ten or a dozen, were chiefly superior journeymen, and combined only in relation to their behaviour in the theatres, rarely even drinking together. Injudicious approval of one or two of their remarks, published in one or two cheap Sunday papers, touched their vanity, and they proceeded from objection to objection until nothing pleased them. They received their first check at the Vaudeville on the first night of *The Guv'nor*, when they were 'rushed' from pit and gallery. But their great shock was experienced on the first appearance of Miss Lotta at the Opera Comique (1883), where they were attacked by friends of the management, in which it was said the son of a military duke took victorious part as against the wreckers. So powerful did these people become in the '80's, that managers, even including Irving, changed their first nights from Saturday to some other day in the week, in the belief that the wreckers were generally patrons who could only, as a rule, frequent the theatres on the last night of the week.

Happily there are good reasons for believing that the managerial belief in 'first-night wreckers', as they are called, is greatly exaggerated. — *D. N.*, 25th September 1884.

Wrecking (*Financial*, 1880). Destroying without mercy—and obviously adopted from the old Cornish custom of attracting vessels by false lights, and then destroying all who came ashore. About 1880, the immense height of consols encouraged speculation, and for some three years a vast number of limited liability companies were started, of which nine out of ten came to complete grief. A class of financial solicitors then sprang into existence, who gained doubtful incomes by 'wrecking' companies and grabbing what they could.

Wriggle off (*Lond.*, 1860). Take one's departure.

Wriggling in for a commish (*American*). Sneaking for the payment of a commission.

Writ-pushers (*Legal — vulgar*). Lawyers' clerks.

Write one's name across another's (*Sporting*). To strike in the face.

Mr John Coleman, having been accused of being the author of a certain book, writes to the papers demanding to know the originator of the 'slander'. Mr Coleman is anxious 'to write my signature across his'. This picturesque phrase will be a useful addition to the vocabulary of the ring. — *Globe*, 5th October 1885.

Wrong scent (*Hunting*, 19 *cent.*). Mistaken enquiry. From the phrase 'on a wrong scent'. Good parallel is Barking up a wrong tree (*q.v.*).

Wrong side of the hedge (*Coaching times*). A figurative way of describing a fling from a coach-top.

Wroth of reses (*Theatrical*, 1882). He wore a wrothe of reses—letter inversion of 'wreath of roses'. This treatment was started by Mr F. C. Burnaud (*Punch*, about 1877), who began with 'she smole a smile', etc., etc. Said of a male singer who vocalises too sentimentally.

Wrux (*Modern Public-school*, 1875). A rotter; a humbug.

X

X. S. (*Peoples'*, 1860, etc.). Abbreviation of expenses.

X. X. (*Tavern*). Double X—abbreviation of 'double excellent'.

X. X. X. (*Tavern*). Treble X—Treble excellent.

X's hall (*Thieves'*). Sessions House, Clerkenwell. X's is a corruption of Hicks — Hicks being a dreaded judge who sat for many years on the bench. In the time of imprisonment for debt, every county jail was called by its Governor's name with hotel added —as Chelmsford Jail was called MacGorrorey's Hotel. (*See* Slaughter house.)

Y

Y. M. C. A. (*Anglo-Amer.*). Goody-goody, pure in excelsis. Initials of 'Young Men's Christian Association'.

Yaller-bellies (*Lincoln*). People of Lincolnshire — from the quantity of geese which came from the county of Lincoln. The belly feathers of the goose are yellowish in the shade.

Yaller dog (*American*). Yellow is the tint of most dogs in America— hence it is the most searching term of ordinary contempt.

Yankee main tack (*Navy*). Direct line; is generally associated with a threat to knock a man down. 'I'll lay you along like a Yankee main tack.'

Yankee paradise (*England*). Paris. In the time of the Second Empire, it was said, 'All good Americans go to Paris when they die'. As, however, the century wore on, the excessive extortions of the Parisians drove the touring Americans to London, where they remain in peace and comparative economy.

Yankeeries (*London*, 1887). American and American-Indian display at Earl's Court Gardens.

Bill West's Wild Buffalo — I mean West Buffalo's Wild Bill—at any rate, you know what I *do* mean, though I can't get it quite right—has been the Jubilee boom up to the present. Her gracious Majesty has been to the Yankeeries.—*Ref.*, 15th May 1887.

Yard of satin (*Women's*). Glass of gin. Specimen of grim satire, comparing the colour and smoothness of the spirit with a material generally far distant from the fashions of the patronesses of gin.

Yardnarb (*Transposed word*, 1880). This is confused back-phrasing, being 'brandy'. Here the 'y' for ease in pronunciation is converted into 'yar' to collide with the 'd'.

Ye gods and little fishes! (*Peoples'*). Exclamation of contempt, mocking the theatrical appeal to the gods by an added invocation to finny small fry.

Miss Hilton was engaged—O, ye gods and little fishes!—at a salary of £15 a week.—*Ref.*, 1st March 1885.

Probably means that the lady would be receiving quite enough.

Yell (*Yale College, U.S.A.*). Classical war-cry.

Yell-play (*Theatr.*). A farcical piece in several acts where the laughter is required to be unceasing.

Yellow journalism (*Political*). Extreme jingoistic and overwhelming views.

America remains true to her British friendship, and the stories of American Fenians invading Canada are officially characterised as 'the latest outbreak of yellow journalism'. — *D. T.*, 27th December 1899.

Yellow-backs (*Middle-class*). They were cheap two-shilling editions of novels, which were generally bound in a yellow, glazed paper, printed in colours.

Yellow-bellies. (*See* Web-foots.)

Yelp (*Music Hall*, 1870, etc.). To sing in chorus. In all music halls the audience join in the choruses.

Yere they come smoking their pipes (*Billingsgate*, '70's). Always said by buyers of fish at the auctions when the bids were awfully rapid and high—it meant probably independence and determination. (*See* Now we're busy.)

Yo Tommy (*Minor Theatr. and Peoples'*). Exclamation of condemnation by the small actor. Amongst the lower classes it is a declaration of admiration addressed to the softer sex by the sterner.

Yon kipper (*Yiddish*). The Day of Atonement—New Year's Day amidst the Hebrews. The phrase is yon kippur — this final word being a spondee.

Yorkshire (*Peoples'*). Fair and square payments.

You musn't squeal (*Peoples', Anglo-American*, 1898). Exhortation to be brave. Often satirically used. From the first speech by Mr Roosevelt, New York, to volunteers formed in May 1898, upon outbreak of war between U.S.A. and Spain.

You make me tired (*Anglo-American*, '90's). 'You bore me'— exact synonym. Sometimes now heard in London—supposed to be introduced by the Duchess of Marlborough (1898)—a then leader of fashion.

You'll get yourself disliked (*Street*, 1878). A satirical protest against any one who is behaving abominably.

Young person, The (*Soc.*, about 1880). Girl from fifteen to marriage.

To know 'Théo-Critt' is to like him. It is true that his morality is rather lax even for a cavalry officer, and that he cannot be recommended to the young person. But then there is such plenty of literature for the young person.—*Sat. Rev.*, 26th December 1885.

Young thing (*Masculine Women's Society*). A youth between seventeen and twenty-one.

You're off the grass (*Cricketing*). Without a chance.

Yurup (*American Street*). Europe—accent on the 'rup'.

Z

Zambo (*Merchant Marine*, 19 *cent.*). Probably a perversion of Sambo (*see*).

A term on the Spanish main for a race produced by the union of the negro and the Indian — it literally means bow-legged. — Smyth's *Sailors' Word-Book*.

Zarndrer (*Street*, 1863-70). The long single curl brought from the back hair over the left shoulder, and allowed to lie on the breast. From Alexandra, Princess of Wales, having brought over this fashion from Denmark.

Zeb (*Shortened inverted word*, 1882). Best.

The *zeb* way we know is to throw the crockery at her. If you owe rent, toss the landlord double or quits, and if you know anything of tossing you're bound to come off first zeb.

Zeb taoc (*Curtailed inverted word*). Best coat.

Zedding about (*Soc.*, 1883). Going zigzag, diverging.

Zoodikers (*Catholic Survival*). God's hooks — hook sometimes being hooker.—*Tom Jones*, bk. xviii., ch. 13.

Zooks (*Catholic Survival*). God's hooks—hooks being old English for nails; here meaning the nails used upon the cross.

'Zouks', said my father. — Sterne, *Tristram Shandy*.

Zounds (*Catholic Survival*). God's wounds—this word here rhyming with 'sounds'. This oath has survived even to our times. It was common in the time of Latimer.

Zounds and blood. May be found in *Tom Jones*, bk. xvi., ch. 4.

Zulu express (*Railway*). Name given to a Great Western afternoon express, at date of Zulu War.